LONELY PLANET PUBLICATIONS

TOM MASTERS
STEVE FALLON, VESNA MARIC

LONDON
CITY GUIDE

Millennium Bridge, with St Paul's Cathedral in the background

Sprawled endlessly along the magical banks of the Thames, London has been a beacon for people around the world for centuries, seamlessly absorbing their colourful influences while remaining quintessentially British.

It's a trick not every city can pull off and yet London has been excelling at the same game for almost a thousand years. Immigrants, the city's life blood, continue to pour in, providing London with a constantly self-renewing source of energy and dynamism, while the increasingly confident Mayor of London continues to give a much needed local focus to solving the city's problems, something he's been doing with not inconsiderable success.

As the British capital gears up for the Olympics being held here in 2012 there's everything to play for and the city has rarely felt so exciting and full of reasons to visit. Whether it's the history, art, fashion, music, food or nightlife that attracts you here (or a heady mixture of all the above), it's hard to imagine you'll come away feeling cheated.

Of course, London is so huge as to be almost overwhelming to the first-time visitor. The dazzling core sights alone can take a week to see, but with distractions in the form of all the great shopping, pubbing and clubbing to be had, you ideally need far more time than that. The good news is that whatever you do and wherever you stay, you'll not be bored for a second: London remains one of the world's great cities and it's high time you came to join the party.

LONDON LIFE

Even Londoners have been surprised by the changes the city has seen in recent years – from the rise of art from a minority interest to a mass national pastime (helped enormously by the superb Tate Modern, now London's most-visited sight) to the resurgence of London's music scene, with new talent from the capital bubbling over after a surprisingly long post-Britpop lull. The city became infinitely more progressive during the Blair years, which saw Cool Britannia, massive redevelopments of forgotten inner-city areas, a slew of millennial projects and of course the city's crowning glory, winning the Olympics.

The massive projects that are already under way in the Lea Valley in preparation for the games currently form the biggest construction site in Europe and an entire industrial wasteland is set to be utterly transformed in the coming years. Londoners have already become somewhat cynical about the Olympics though, worried as they are about the financial drain and local tax hikes the future games have caused, but they remain quietly proud that London will be the first triple Olympic city in history and will happily shrug off any doubts from outsiders.

This is all rather typical: Londoners love to gripe about their city, but if you join in with anything other than gentle fun-poking they're likely to get quite annoyed with you. After all, as they'll almost certainly remind you, this is the greatest city in the world…

Denied self-rule by the Conservatives for 14 years because of the loony-left tendencies of the leaders it invariably elected, London finally got its own mayor and Assembly in 2000 and has been addressing its myriad problems with admirable chutzpah ever since. Mayor Ken Livingstone has introduced a punishing but popular congestion charge on all cars entering the city centre, massively increased the provision of bike lanes and buses and is still trying to sort out the oldest, most dilapidated underground system in the world. Many of his critics disagree with his methods, but few can doubt that he is slowly getting results and may even have turned the corner with the tube.

In recent years London has replaced New York as the world's centre of international finance and the city skyline reflects this confidence in Brown's Britain today. Whether it be the already iconic London Eye and Gherkin or the newer Shard of Glass or Broadgate Tower, London is being transformed, with many more skyscrapers planned for the future.

Other bugbears have also been sorted: London has undergone a food revolution in the past decade and nowhere is this more obvious than at the organic farmers' markets and cutting-edge restaurants of the capital. Add to this newly liberalised drinking laws, a roundly welcomed smoking ban and a fantastic music scene and London makes for one of the best places for a night out on the planet. Take a deep breath, close your eyes and prepare to fall in love with the British capital.

Ceiling of the Gherkin, the ecofriendly skyscraper 30 St Mary Axe

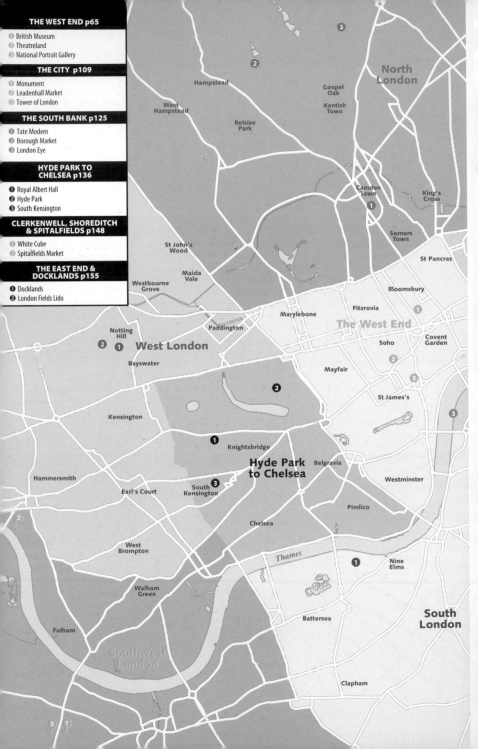

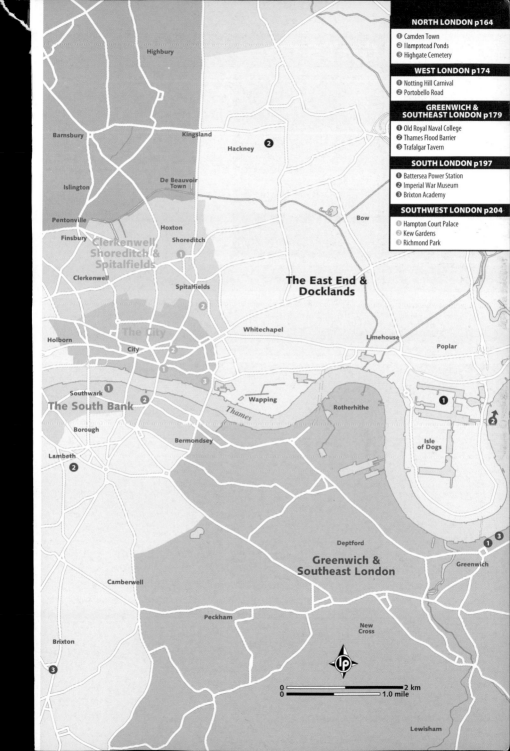

Highbury

Barnsbury

Kingsland

Hackney ❷

Islington

De Beauvoir Town

Clerkenwell, Shoreditch & Spitalfields

Pentonville

Hoxton

Finsbury

Shoreditch ❶

Clerkenwell

Spitalfields ❷

Bow

The East End & Docklands

The City

Holborn

City ❷

Whitechapel

Limehouse

Poplar

❶

❸

Southwark ❶

Wapping

The South Bank ❷

Thames

Rotherhithe

❶

❷

Borough

Bermondsey

Isle of Dogs

Lambeth ❷

Deptford

❶ ❸

Greenwich & Southeast London

Greenwich

Camberwell

Peckham

New Cross

Brixton ❸

0 — 2 km
0 — 1.0 mile

Lewisham

HIGHLIGHTS

1 **British Museum**
Discover the past in epic surroundings. (p89)

2 **Theatreland**
See a Hollywood star or home-grown talent tread the boards. (p35)

3 **National Portrait Gallery**
Look British history in the face at this gallery on Trafalgar Sq. (p76)

THE WEST END

At turns exciting, glitzy, busy and chaotic, the West End is London's beating heart, with far more than its fair share of the best shops, pubs, bars and restaurants in the capital.

THE CITY

The ancient centre of London, and home to London's financial world today, the City is jam packed full of fascinating historic sights and is a delight to explore, particularly at weekends when it's almost all yours.

❶ Monument
Climb to the top for a stunning view of the City's skyscrapers and the river. (p117)

❷ Leadenhall Market
Join the City workers for a pint at lunchtime in the pubs. (p118)

❸ Tower of London
Be king or queen for a day. (p119)

SOUTHBANK

Redevelopment and investment have turned this once rather desolate part of London into its cultural hub – you'll be hard pressed to visit without seeing art, drama and music being performed. From an international gallery to street performance, it's all here.

❶ Tate Modern
Drop in to the turbine hall to discover what exhibition Londoners are talking about this week. (p129)

❷ Borough Market
Pick up a gourmet picnic at the foodies' favourite. (p132)

❸ London Eye
Take in sweeping views of London from atop a London icon. (p125)

HYDE PARK TO CHELSEA

The Royal Borough, home to Her Majesty, really is fit for a king (or queen). With some of the most beautiful buildings, prestigious museums and superb outdoor spaces, this really is how the other half live.

❶ Royal Albert Hall
Enjoy a concert and make a beeline for the Proms. (p144)

❷ Hyde Park
Hold an impromptu picnic or laze the day away. (p145)

❸ South Kensington
Be amazed by the many museums. (p136)

CLERKENWELL, SPITALFIELDS & SHOREDITCH

The new life in London, these three ancient parishes now collectively house London's most creative talents, its best clubs and bars, and coolest shops. You'll most likely find your local friends suggesting going out in one of them time and time again.

❶ White Cube
See the latest Britart before exploring the bars of Hoxton Sq. (p149)

❷ Spitalfields Market
Browse the beautiful remaining sections of this market on a Sunday morning. (p152)

EAST END & DOCKLANDS

The East End is gearing up for massive change as the Olympics come to the Lea Valley in 2012. The Docklands is the future of London – a financial district to challenge the City itself, with plenty of interesting history to explore as well.

❶ Docklands
Take an Open House Architecture tour of the Docklands for a fascinating exploration of the area. (p81)

❷ London Fields Lido
Get into the swim at one of London's newest lidos. (p155)

NORTH LONDON

A glorious agglomeration of hilltop villages, leafy parks and charming high streets, each with its own long-standing identity, North London should be savoured and enjoyed at a slow pace.

❶ Hampstead Ponds
Take a dip in the ponds or the wonderful Parliament Hill Lido. (p325)

❷ Camden Town
Drink and dance the night away in this indie-rock nexus. (p288)

❸ Highgate Cemetery
Discover London's most wonderful place to be dead at this fantastic, Gothic cemetery. (170)

WEST LONDON

Old-money tradition meets multicultural fun-fest in the sprawling urban jungle of West London. The centre of gravity here is bustling Notting Hill, where great shopping, eating and drinking all combine to make any day out memorable.

❶ Notting Hill Carnival
Join the masses for Europe's biggest street festival. (p194)

❷ Portobello Road
Rummage through the great clothing and bric-a-brac market stalls. (p232)

GREENWICH & SOUTHEAST LONDON

With its fascinating naval, geographic and architectural heritage on display for all to enjoy, magical Greenwich is a must for any first-time visitor to the British capital. However, be sure to make time for some of the southeast's more off-beat sights as well.

❶ Old Royal Naval College
Wander around historic Greenwich and take in the best of English architecture. (p181)

❷ Thames Flood Barrier
Explore further afield and make a trip to see London's amazing flood barrier. (p184)

❸ Trafalgar Tavern
Quench your thirst with a well-earned pint at this historic tavern. (p293)

SOUTH LONDON

Residential, multicultural and always surprising – South London covers a vast swathe of the city, including rough-and-ready Brixton, suburban Clapham and often-overlooked Battersea.

❶ Battersea Power Station
Check out London's unique piece of architectural heritage. (p201)

❷ Imperial War Museum
Take a trip to Bedlam – better known today as the Imperial War Museum. (p197)

❸ Brixton Academy
Join the crowds heading to see the latest headline act. (p308)

SOUTHWEST LONDON

Wealthy Southwest London is home to some of London's most famous sights, at whose centre is Richmond, the posh London village famed as much for its antiques shopping and celebrity residents as it is for its rich history and royal connections.

❶ Hampton Court Palace
Explore the incredible complex that is London's superb Tudor palace – and be sure to get lost in the maze. (p211)

❷ Kew Gardens
Marvel at the vast collection of endlessly fascinating flora at the largest botanical gardens in the world. (p209)

❸ Richmond Park
See the red deer and enjoy the urban wilderness. (p207)

CONTENTS

Continued from previous page.

Tom Masters

Tom has lived all over London in the past 12 years, although Stoke Newington is now home again after an expensive three-year love affair with Clerkenwell. Tom's fascination with the Big Smoke began during his bucolic upbringing in nearby Buckinghamshire, when teenage Saturdays spent in awe wondering around the West End eventually translated into moving to Bloomsbury to study for a literature degree at University College London. Often to be found exploring the Lea Valley, wandering the City and cycling the backstreets of North London during the weekends, Tom's still as in awe of the capital as he ever was.

Tom was the coordinating author and wrote the Introducing London, Getting Started, London's Festivals & Events, Background and Gay & Lesbian London chapters. He also cowrote the Neighbourhoods chapter.

Steve Fallon

After more than four years of overly fresh air, monotonous greenery and the deafening tranquillity of rural Essex, Steve raced back to the pollution, concrete and general hubbub of London, one of the world's most vibrant and exciting cities. As always, he did everything the hard way: walking the walks, seeing the sights, taking (some) advice from friends, colleagues and the odd taxi driver, and digesting everything in sight – right down to that last pint. Says he: 'Thank God I'm a city boy (again).'

Steve wrote the Architecture, Eating and Sleeping chapters. He also cowrote the Neighbourhoods and Drinking chapters.

Vesna Maric

Vesna has lived in London for the past 10 years and swears it's the best city in the world and the only one she'd ever want to live in. She came to London from Hull (yes, it's dull) in 1997 and has gone from finding ways to have fun when totally broke as a student/refugee to being able to afford stuff when she started working. She can assure you that London's lovable whatever your budget. Though, obviously, it's more lovable with plenty of cash. She hopes Lonely Planet readers will enjoy this fantastic city as much as she does.

Vesna wrote the Shopping, Nightlife, The Arts, Sports & Activities, Excursions, Transport and Directory chapters. She also cowrote the Neighbourhoods and Drinking chapters.

London is a very straightforward destination and little forward planning is required, with the glaring exception of accommodation, which is always best booked in advance, and even then will take up way more of your budget than you'd ideally like. The city is a year-round destination where you'll always find more things to do than your time will ever allow.

WHEN TO GO

You might imagine that in a country with such a temperate and mild climate as England, the weather is not much of a topic for conversation, and yet, like their middle-England cousins, Londoners are relentless weather-watchers and every rise or fall of the mercury will provoke smiles or gloom respectively. It's good therefore that London is not a city where fun depends on the weather – do as Londoners do, expect overcast skies and rain (even in summer) and then be elated when the sun comes out.

While summer is a great time to visit (and recent years have seen some very Continental heatwaves), spring and autumn are also good times to come, when the crowds are far thinner and sights less crowded. Winter's all cold, wet and dark, although if you're after outdoor pleasures, you'll have them largely to yourself.

For a full list of events in and around London, look out for Visit London's bimonthly *Events in London* and its *Annual Events* pamphlet. You can also check the website at www .visitlondon.com.

COSTS & MONEY

London can be a wincingly expensive experience, but doesn't necessarily have to be. The main expense any visitor will have to bear is that of accommodation. To make your life easier, try hard to befriend a Londoner who has a spare room, otherwise you'll need to budget an absolute minimum of £25 per night for a hostel dorm, rising sharply to at least £60 for a room of your own almost anywhere, and further to £120 for a room you're actually likely to want to spend any time in. Booking in advance is always a good plan, and most hotels will offer reductions on the room prices if you're staying for more than a few days. Most hotels also do excellent web deals that dramatically undercut their rack rates, and websites such as www.lastminute.com filter out the very best of these.

Money is an issue in other aspects as well, with the general cost of living in London being far higher than anywhere else in Britain and, unless you're Norwegian or Japanese, probably higher than where you've arrived from.

Eating out can be done on a budget, with plenty of good cheap eats to be had in every neighbourhood (see p236). However, even at the cheapest of the cheap, it's no trifle – a decent sandwich will cost you around £3, and you're unlikely to get much change from a tenner for a sit-down meal. London's fashionable eating scene is a huge draw in itself, and it's not cheap. A good meal for two with wine is usually around the £80 to £100 mark, jumping rapidly to more than £150 for any of the city's leading establishments.

Getting around London can also be expensive. One obvious step to save cash is to get yourself an Oyster card immediately upon arrival (or even order one at home before you travel, see www.visitbritaindirect.com), as this will dramatically decrease the cost of using the public transport system (see p390).

Entertainment is likewise not cheap: cinema tickets in the West End have long since crossed the £10 threshold and many cinemas in further out areas are following, meaning seeing a film for under a tenner is becoming a bargain, although art-house and independent cinemas do still offer much more competitive prices. The big-name gigs are also fairly expensive, usually starting around £20 and going up to £150 for a superstar at Wembley or Earl's Court. Clubbing is a mixed bag: a Saturday night at Fabric (p300) will set you back £20 just for entry, while some of the best clubs in town are free or very cheap, it's just a question of research. Flyers with discounted entry rates are available all over the West End in music and fashion stores.

One surprising boon for such an expensive city is that all state-funded museums are free, meaning you can quite happily spend days in some of the world's best exhibition spaces and galleries for absolutely nothing, although it's always good to make a donation to each

ADVANCE PLANNING

The trick in London is either to book very early, or to try at the last minute and hope you get lucky.

Three to six months before you go For big-name restaurants, such as Gordon Ramsay in Chelsea (p251), you need to get organised six months ahead. Saturday-night performances of big West End shows (eg *Billy Elliot, Spamalot;* see p320) sell out three to six months ahead.

Two to three months before you go Check out sites such as www.ticketmaster.co.uk and www.seetickets.com, and think about bigger rock-music gigs. Also read www.guardian.co.uk/reviews, www.whatsonstage.com or www.time out.com before booking good Saturday-night tickets for serious theatre (eg Kevin Spacey performing at the Old Vic).

Two weeks before you go Sign up for an email newsletter, such as *Urban Junkies* at www.urbanjunkies.com, and double-check review sites. Two weeks is also usually ample time to get into trendy, interesting restaurants such as Les Trois Garçons (p256).

A few days before you go The latest blockbuster exhibition at the Royal Academy of Arts (p70), Tates Modern and Britain (p129 & p103) or the Victoria & Albert Museum (p139) can usually be booked a few days beforehand; actually, we've gained entry to the best with just a few hours' wait.

space to help keep them free (£3 is usually the standard suggested amount). Other sights are variably priced: some may balk at paying £16 for the Tower of London, but you can spend the most part of a day there and see one of the UK's top attractions, while a big commercial attraction such as Madame Tussauds is just plain overpriced at around £20 per person.

INTERNET RESOURCES

Unsurprisingly London is big on the web. Wi-fi covers much of the city now, although sadly you'll usually need to pay for it; some great exceptions are all along Upper St in Islington and on Leicester Sq. The whole of the City is covered by 'the Cloud', a service that is free for the first month you use it and then you have to pay, and wi-fi areas will hopefully continue to spread. The following websites are useful when wanting to learn more about London.

Flavorpill London (http://ldn.flavorpill.net/) A weekly email magazine profiling the best of London's cultural and entertainment possibilities.

Le Cool Magazine (www.lecool.com/london) A great free graphic email sent to subscribers detailing the better clubs, bars, music and other events in the capital.

London Underground Guide (www.goingunderground .net) Annie Mole's cultishly popular tube blog, a must for anyone fascinated by the world's oldest underground system.

Londonist (www.londonist.com) Our favourite London blog takes a wry look at the odder aspects of London

life, with a large pool of contributors writing about their various interests.

MayorWatch (www.mayorwatch.co.uk) A politically neutral site documenting the actions of the mayor of London and the London Assembly, with discussions and regular news updates.

Streetmap.co.uk (www.streetmap.co.uk) A website many Londoners use daily, Streetmap is simply a map of London upon which you can look up any street or postcode. Bizarrely vital.

Transport for London (www.tfl.gov.uk) An invaluable website from London Transport with a great journey planner to help you navigate your way across the city.

Visit London (www.visitlondon.com) The city's official tourism website is a great resource, with cheap hotel booking, listings of all sorts and links galore.

HOW MUCH?

Admission to a big-name club on a Friday £15
Adult football ticket £20 to £40
Bus ticket £2
Cinema ticket £10
DVD £15
Guardian newspaper 70p
Pint of lager £3
Three-course meal with wine/beer from £30
Tube ride within zone 1 £4
West End theatre ticket £50

HISTORY

London's history has been a long and turbulent two millennia in which many different settlements and long-established villages slowly grew together to form the immense city around the Roman core that still marks London's heart today.

LONDINIUM

The Romans are the real fathers of London, despite there being a settlement of some form or another along the Thames for several thousand of years before their arrival. Amazingly, the Roman wall built around the settlement of Londinium still more or less demarcates the City from neighbouring municipal authorities today.

The Romans first visited in the 1st century BC, traded with the Celts and had a browse around. In AD 43 they returned with an army led by Emperor Claudius and decided to stay, establishing the port of Londinium. They built a wooden bridge across the Thames (near the site of today's London Bridge) and used the settlement as a base from which to capture other tribal centres, which at the time provided much bigger prizes. The bridge became the focal point for a network of roads fanning out around the region, and for a few years the settlement prospered from trade.

This growth was nipped in the bud around AD 60 when an army led by Boudicca, queen of the Celtic Iceni tribe based in East Anglia, took violent retribution on the Roman soldiers, who had abused her family and seized their land. The Iceni overran Camulodunum (Colchester) – which had become capital of Roman Britannia – and then turned on Londinium, massacring its inhabitants and razing the settlement. Boudicca was eventually defeated (and according to legend is buried under platform 10 of King's Cross station), and the Romans rebuilt London around Cornhill.

A century later the Romans built the defensive wall around the city, fragments of which survive. The original gates – Aldgate, Ludgate, Newgate and Bishopsgate – are remembered as place names in contemporary London. Excavations in the City suggest that Londinium, a centre for business and trade although not a fully-fledged *colonia* (settlement), was an imposing metropolis whose massive buildings included a basilica, an amphitheatre, a forum and the governor's palace.

By the middle of the 3rd century AD Londinium was home to some 30,000 people of various ethnic groups, and there were temples dedicated to a large number of cults. When Emperor Constantine converted to Christianity in 312, this became the official religion of the entire empire, although the remains of the Temple of Mithras (see p116) survive in the City, a testament to London's pagan past.

Overstretched and worn down by ever-increasing barbarian invasions, the Roman Empire fell into decline, as did Londinium. When the embattled Emperor Honorius withdrew the last soldiers in 410, the remaining Romans scarpered and the settlement was reduced to a sparsely populated backwater.

TIMELINE

43	47–50	122
The Romans invade Britain, led by Emperor Claudius himself. Before this time the Britons paid tribute to Rome following an early incursion here by Julius Caesar in 55 and 54 BC.	The defensive fort at Londinium is built. The name Londinium is probably pre-Celtic and there is no evidence as to what it means, although 'settlement on the wide river' is one suggestion.	Emperor Hadrian pays a visit to Londinium and a large number of impressive municipal buildings are constructed. This is the height of Roman London and the settlement features temples, bathhouses, a fortress and a port.

LUNDENWIC

What happened to London after the Roman withdrawal is still the subject of much historical debate. While the Dark Ages have become considerably better illuminated in the past two decades with archaeological finds and improved technology, there remain several key unknowns including whether or not the Roman walled city was ever entirely abandoned. Most historians now think that some form of Romano-British continuity survived even as Saxon settlers established themselves throughout the southeast of England.

Lundenwic (or London marketplace) was established due west of Londinium (around Aldwych) as a Saxon trade settlement and by the early 7th century the Saxons were converted from paganism to Christianity. Rome designated Lundenwic as a diocese and the first St Paul's Cathedral was established at the top of Ludgate Hill.

Saxon settlement was predominantly outside the city walls to the west, towards what is now Aldwych and Charing Cross, but the settlement became the victim of its own success when it attracted the Vikings of Denmark, who raided the city in 842 and burned it to the ground 10 years later. Under the leadership of King Alfred the Great of Wessex, the Saxon population fought back, drove the Danes out in 886 and re-established what soon became Lundunburg as the major centre of trade.

Saxon London grew into a prosperous and well-organised town divided into 20 wards, each with its own alderman, and resident colonies of German merchants and French vintners. But the Danes wouldn't let it lie, and Viking raids finally broke the weakening Saxon leadership, which was forced to accept the Danish leader Canute as king of England in 1016.

With the death of Canute's son Harthacanute in 1042, the throne passed to the Saxon Edward the Confessor, who went on to found an abbey and palace at Westminster on what was then an island at the mouth of the River Tyburn (which now flows underground). When Edward moved his court to Westminster, he established divisions that would – geographically, at least – dominate the future of London. The port became the trading and mercantile centre (the area now known as the City), while Westminster became the seat of politics and administration.

THE NORMANS

The most famous date in English history, 1066 marks the real birth of England as a unified nation state. After the death of Edward the Confessor in 1066 a dispute over who would take the English throne spelled disaster for the Saxon kings. Harold Godwinson, Earl of Wessex, was anointed successor by Edward on his deathbed, but this enraged William, the duke of Normandy, who believed Edward had promised him the throne. William mounted a massive invasion of England from France and on 14 October defeated Harold at the Battle of Hastings, before marching on London to claim his prize. William the Conqueror was crowned king of England in Westminster Abbey on December 25 1066, ensuring the Norman conquest was complete. He subsequently found himself in control of what was by then the richest and largest city in the kingdom.

William distrusted 'the fierce populace' of London and built several strongholds, including the White Tower, the core of the Tower of London. Cleverly, he kept the prosperous merchants on side by confirming the City's independence in exchange for taxes. Sometime following the Norman conquest, London became the principal town of England, overtaking Winchester, the ancient capital of Wessex.

190–225	410	852
London Wall is constructed around Londinium to defend the settlement from outsiders, who had breached Hadrian's Wall. The wall encloses an area of just 132 hectares and is 5m high.	The Emperor Honorius decrees that the colony of Britannia should take care of its own defences, thus effectively ending the Roman presence in Londinium; while many Romans leave, many also stay.	Vikings settle in London, having attacked the city a decade previously. This is a period of great struggle between Wessex and Denmark for control of the Thames.

MEDIEVAL LONDON

Successive medieval kings were happy to let the City of London keep its independence as long as its merchants continued to finance their wars and building projects. When Richard I (known as 'the Lionheart') needed funds for his crusade to the Holy Lands, he recognised the City as a self-governing commune, and the appreciative merchants duly coughed up. The City's first mayor, Henry Fitz Aylwin, was elected sometime around 1190. A city built on money and commerce, London would always guard its independence furiously, as Richard's successor, King John, learned the hard way. In 1215 John was forced to cede to the powerful barons, and to curb his excessive demands for pay-offs from the City. Among those pressing him to seal the Magna Carta of 1215 (which effectively diluted royal power) was the by then powerful mayor of the City of London. The British Library holds two copies of the Magna Carta (see p167).

Trade and commerce boomed, and the noblemen, barons and bishops built lavish houses for themselves along the prime real estate of the Strand, which connected the City with the Palace of Westminster, the new seat of royal power. The first stone London Bridge was built in 1176, although it was frequently clogged, and most people crossed the river with waterboatmen (who plied their trade until the 18th century). Their touting shouts of 'Oars? Oars?' are said to have confused many a country visitor tempted by more carnal services.

Though fire was a constant threat in the cramped and narrow houses and lanes of 14th-century London, disease caused by unsanitary living conditions and impure drinking water from the Thames was the greatest threat to the burgeoning city. In 1348, rats on ships from Europe brought the Black Death, a bubonic plague that wiped out almost two-thirds of the population (of 100,000) over the following decades.

With their numbers subsequently down, there was growing unrest among labourers, for whom violence became a way of life, and rioting was commonplace. In 1381, miscalculating – or just disregarding – the mood of the nation, Richard II tried to impose a poll tax on everyone in the realm. Tens of thousands of peasants, led by the soldier Wat Tyler and the priest Jack Straw, marched in protest on London. The archbishop of Canterbury was dragged from the Tower and beheaded, several ministers were murdered and many buildings were razed before the Peasants' Revolt ran its course. Tyler died at the end of the mayor's blade, while Straw and the other ringleaders were executed at Smithfield. However, there was no more mention of poll tax (until Margaret Thatcher, not heeding the lessons of history, tried to introduce one in the 1980s – see p28).

London gained wealth and stature under the Houses of Lancaster and York in the 15th century, also the era of the charitable mayor Dick Whittington, immortalised for many children in the fairy tale of his rise to power from poverty. William Caxton set up the first printing press at Westminster in 1476.

The century's greatest episode of political intrigue occurred in 1483. The 12-year-old Edward V, of the House of York, reigned for only two months before vanishing with his younger brother into the Tower of London, never to be seen again. Whether or not their uncle Richard III – who became the next king – murdered the boys has been the subject of much conjecture over the centuries. (In 1674 workers found a chest containing the skeletons of two children near the White Tower, which were assumed to be the princes' remains and were reburied in Innocents' Corner in Westminster Abbey.) Richard III didn't have long to enjoy the hot seat, however, as he was deposed within a couple of years by Henry Tudor, the first monarch of the dynasty of that name.

886	1016	1066
King Alfred the Great, first King of England, reclaims London for the Saxons and founds a new settlement within the walls of the old Roman walls.	After more than a century of English rule, the Danes return to London and Canute is crowned king of England. Most famous in English folklore for failing to command the waves, Canute ushered in two decades of peace.	After his great victory over King Harold at the Battle of Hastings, William, Duke of Normandy, evermore known as William the Conqueror, is crowned in Westminster Abbey.

TUDOR LONDON

London became one of the largest and most important cities in Europe during the reign of the Tudors, which coincided with the discovery of the Americas and thriving world trade.

Henry's son and successor, Henry VIII, was the most ostentatious of the clan. Terribly fond of palaces, he had new ones built at Whitehall and St James's, and bullied his lord chancellor, Cardinal Thomas Wolsey, into gifting him Hampton Court.

His most significant contribution, however, was the split with the Catholic Church in 1534 after the Pope refused to annul his marriage to the nonheir-producing Catherine of Aragon. Thumbing his nose at Rome, he made himself the supreme head of the Church of England and married Anne Boleyn, the second of his six wives. He 'dissolved' London's monasteries and seized the church's vast wealth and property. The face of the medieval city was transformed; much of the land requisitioned for hunting later became Hyde, Regent's and Richmond Parks, while many of the religious houses disappeared, leaving only their names in particular areas, such as Whitefriars and Blackfriars (after the colour of the monks' habits).

Despite his penchant for settling differences with the axe (two of his six wives and Wolsey's replacement as lord chancellor, Thomas More, were beheaded) and his persecution of both Catholics and fellow Protestants that didn't toe the line, Henry VIII remained a popular monarch until his death in 1547.

The reign of Mary I, his daughter by Catherine of Aragon, saw a brief return to Catholicism, during which the queen sanctioned the burning to death of hundreds of Protestants at Smithfield and earned herself the nickname 'Bloody Mary'.

By the time Elizabeth I, Henry VIII's daughter by Anne Boleyn, took the throne, Catholicism was a waning force, and hundreds of people who dared to suggest otherwise were carted off to the gallows at Tyburn (p145).

ELIZABETHAN LONDON

The 45-year reign (1558–1603) of Elizabeth I is still looked upon as one of the most extraordinary periods in English history, and it was just as significant for London. During these four decades English literature reached new and still unbeaten heights; religious tolerance gradually became accepted doctrine, although Catholics and some Protestants still faced persecution. England became a naval superpower, having defeated the Spanish Armada in 1588; and the city established itself as the premier world trade market with the opening of the Royal Exchange in 1566.

London was blooming economically and physically; in the second half of the 16th century the population doubled to 200,000. The first recorded map of London was published in 1558, and John Stow produced A Survey of London, the first history of the city, in 1598.

This was also the golden era of English drama, and the works of William Shakespeare, Christopher Marlowe and Ben Jonson packed them in at new playhouses such as the Rose (built in 1587) and the Globe (1599). Both of these were built in Southwark, a notoriously 'naughty place' at the time, teeming with brothels, bawdy taverns and illicit sports such as bear baiting. Most importantly, they were outside the jurisdiction of the City, which frowned upon and even banned theatre as a waste of time.

When Elizabeth died without an heir in 1603, she was succeeded by her second cousin, who was crowned James I. Although the son of Catholic Mary, Queen of Scots, James was slow to improve conditions for England's Catholics and drew their wrath. He narrowly escaped death

1215	1397	1534
In a meadow in Runnymede, outside London, King John signs the Magna Carta (literally 'the great charter'), an agreement with England's barons forming the basis of constitutional law in England.	Richard Whittington is elected mayor of London, and instantly negotiates buying the city's liberties back from Richard II for £10,000. He goes on to be four times mayor of London and a much-loved character in London folklore.	After being denied a divorce from Catherine of Aragon by the Pope, Henry VIII splits with the Catholic Church, dissolves the monasteries and brings about the English Reformation.

when Guy Fawkes' plot to blow up the Houses of Parliament on 5 November 1605 was uncovered. The discovery of the audacious plan is commemorated on this date each year with bonfires, fireworks and the burning of Guy Fawkes effigies throughout England.

THE ENGLISH CIVIL WARS

When Charles I came to the throne in 1625 his intransigent personality and total belief in the 'divine right of kings' set the monarchy on a collision course with an increasingly confident Parliament at Westminster and a City of London tiring of extortionate taxes. The crunch came when Charles tried to arrest five antagonistic MPs who fled to the City, and in 1642 the country slid into civil war.

The Puritans, extremist Protestants and the City's expanding merchant class threw their support behind general Oliver Cromwell, leader of the Parliamentarians (the Roundheads), who battled against the Royalist troops (the Cavaliers). London was firmly with the Roundheads, and Charles I was defeated in 1646, although a Second Civil War (1648–49) and a Third Civil War (1649–51) continued to wreak havoc on what had been a stable and prosperous nation.

The outcome of the English Civil War was short-lived. Charles I was beheaded for treason outside Banqueting House (see p105) in Whitehall on 30 January 1649, famously wearing two shirts on the cold morning of his execution so as not to shiver and appear cowardly.

Cromwell ruled the country as a republic for the next 11 years, during which time Charles I's son, Charles II, continued fighting for the restoration of the monarchy. During the Commonwealth of England, as the English Republic was known, Cromwell banned theatre, dancing, Christmas and just about anything remotely fun.

THE RESTORATION: PLAGUE & FIRE

After Cromwell's death, Parliament decided that the royals weren't so bad after all and restored the exiled Charles II in 1660. Death was deemed too good for Cromwell, whose exhumed body was hung, drawn and quartered at Tyburn. His rotting head was displayed on a spike at Westminster Hall for two decades.

Despite the immense wealth that London experienced during the reign of the Tudors, the capital remained a crowded and filthy place where most of the population lived below the poverty line. A lack of basic sanitation (urine and faeces were routinely poured into the streets from the slop bucket), dirty water and overcrowding had all contributed to recurrent outbreaks of deadly illnesses and fevers. The city had suffered from outbreaks of bubonic plague since the 14th century, but all previous incidences were dwarfed by the Great Plague of 1665.

As the plague spread, the panicked population retreated behind closed doors, only venturing out for supplies and to dispose of their dead. Previously crowded streets were deserted, the churches and markets were closed, and an eerie silence descended on the city. To make matters worse, the mayor believed that dogs and cats were the spreaders of the plague and ordered them all killed, thus in one stroke ridding the disease-carrying rats of their natural predators. By the time the winter cold arrested the epidemic, 100,000 people had perished; the corpses were collected and thrown into vast 'plague pits', many of which stand empty of buildings to this day.

The plague finally began to wane in late 1665, leaving the city's population decimated and a general superstition that the deaths had been a punishment from God for London's moral

1558	1599	1605
The first detailed map of London is commissioned by a group of German merchants. In the same year the Elizabethan age begins when Queen Elizabeth takes the throne.	The Globe Theatre opens in Southwark alongside other London stages including the Rose, the Swan and the Hope. Most of Shakespeare's plays written after 1599 are staged here including *Macbeth*, *King Lear* and *Hamlet*.	A Catholic plot to blow up James I by hiding gunpowder in the cellars under the House of Commons is foiled. Guy Fawkes, just one of the plotters, is executed in 1606.

squalor. Just as Londoners breathed a sigh of relief, another disaster struck. The city had for centuries been prone to fire, as nearly all buildings were constructed from wood, but the mother of all blazes broke out on 2 September 1666 in a bakery in Pudding Lane in the City.

It didn't seem like much to begin with – the mayor himself dismissed it as 'something a woman might pisse out' before going back to bed – but the unusual September heat combined with rising winds created a tinderbox effect, and the fire raged out of control for days, razing some 80% of London. Only eight people died (officially at least), but most of London's medieval, Tudor and Jacobean architecture was destroyed. The fire was finally stopped at Fetter Lane, on the very edge of London, by blowing up all the buildings in the inferno's path. It is hard to overstate the scale of the destruction – 89 churches and more than 13,000 houses were razed, leaving tens of thousands of people homeless. Many Londoners left for the countryside, or to seek their fortunes in the New World.

OF RAKES & HARLOTS: HOGARTH'S WORLD

William Hogarth (1697–1764) was an artist and engraver who specialised in satire and what these days might be considered heavy-handed moralising on the wages of sin. His plates were so popular in his day that they were pirated, leading Parliament to pass the Hogarth Act of 1735 to protect copyright. They provide invaluable insights into the life – particularly the poor variety – of Georgian London. Hogarth's works can be seen in Sir John Soane's Museum (p87) in Holborn, Hogarth's House (p206) in Chiswick, the Tate Britain (p103) and the National Gallery (p75).

WREN'S LONDON

One positive aspect of the inferno was that it created a blank canvas upon which master architect Christopher Wren could build his magnificent churches. Wren's plan for rebuilding the entire city was unfortunately deemed too expensive, and the familiar pattern of streets that had grown up over the centuries since the time of the Romans quickly reappeared (by law, brick and stone designs replaced the old timber-framed, overhanging Tudor houses, to avoid a repeat of 1666; many roads were widened for the same reason). At this time, Charles II moved to St James's Palace, and the surrounding area was taken over by the gentry, who built the grand squares and town houses of modern-day Mayfair and St James's in order to be close to the court.

By way of memorialising the blaze – and symbolising the restoration and resurgence of the subsequent years – the Monument (p117), designed by Wren, was erected in 1677 near the site of the fire's outbreak. At the time it was by far the highest structure in the city, visible from everywhere in the capital.

In 1685 some 1500 Huguenot refugees arrived in London, fleeing persecution in Catholic France. Many turned their hands to the manufacture of luxury goods such as silks and silverware in and around Spitalfields and Clerkenwell, which were already populated with Irish, Jewish and Italian immigrants and artisans. London was fast becoming one of the world's most cosmopolitan places.

The Glorious (ie bloodless) Revolution in 1688 brought the Dutch king William of Orange to the English throne. He relocated from Whitehall Palace to a new palace in Kensington Gardens, and the surrounding area smartened itself up accordingly. In order to raise finances for his war

1665	1666	1707
The Great Plague ravishes London and wipes out a fifth of the capital's population. Although it had a far smaller effect than the Black Death of the 14th century, it is remembered as one of Europe's last outbreaks.	The Great Fire of London burns for five days, destroying the city Shakespeare had known and loved and changing London forever, leaving four-fifths of the metropolis in ruins.	The first ever sitting of the Parliament of the Kingdom of Great Britain occurs in London as the 1707 Acts of Union bring England and Scotland together under one parliament.

with France – and as a result of the City's transformation into a centre of finance rather than manufacturing – William III established the Bank of England in 1694.

London's growth continued unabated, and by 1700 it was Europe's largest city, with 600,000 people. The influx of foreign workers brought expansion to the east and south, while those who could afford it headed to the more salubrious environs of the north and west. London today is still, more or less, divided along these lines.

The crowning glory of the 'Great Rebuilding', Wren's St Paul's Cathedral (p109), was completed in 1710 – one of the largest cathedrals in Europe and one of the city's most prominent and visible landmarks to this day.

GEORGIAN LONDON

When Queen Anne died without an heir in 1714, the search began for a Protestant relative (the 1701 Act of Settlement forbade Roman Catholics to occupy the throne). Eventually George of Hanover, the great-grandson of James I, arrived from Germany and was crowned king of England, though he never even learned to speak English. Meanwhile, the increasingly literate population got their first newspapers, which began to cluster around Fleet St.

Robert Walpole's Whig Party controlled Parliament during much of George I's reign, and Walpole effectively became Britain's first prime minister. He was presented with 10 Downing St, which has been the official residence of nearly every prime minister since.

London grew at a phenomenal pace during this time, and measures were taken to make the city more accessible. When Westminster Bridge opened in 1750 it was only the second spanning of the Thames after London Bridge, first built by the Romans. The old crossing itself was cleared of many of its buildings, and the Roman wall surrounding the City torn down.

Georgian London saw a great creative surge in music, art and architecture. Court composer George Frederick Handel wrote his *Water Music* (1717) and *Messiah* (1741) while living here, and in 1755 Dr Johnson produced the first English dictionary. William Hogarth (see boxed text, p23), Thomas Gainsborough and Joshua Reynolds produced some of their finest engravings and paintings, and many of London's most elegant buildings, streets and squares were erected or laid out by the likes of John Soane and the incomparable John Nash (p80).

All the while, though, London was becoming ever more segregated and lawless. George II himself was relieved of 'purse, watch and buckles' during a stroll through Kensington Gardens. This was Hogarth's London, in which the wealthy built fine mansions in attractive squares and gathered in fashionable new coffee houses while the poor huddled together in appalling slums and drowned their sorrows with cheap gin.

To curb rising crime, two magistrates established the 'Bow Street Runners' in 1749, a voluntary group – effectively a forerunner to the Metropolitan Police Force (set up in 1829) – that challenged the official marshals (thief-takers) who were suspected (often correctly) of colluding with the criminals themselves.

In 1780 Parliament proposed to lift the law preventing Catholics from buying or inheriting property. One demented MP, Lord George Gordon, led a 'No Popery' demonstration that turned into the Gordon Riots. A mob of 30,000 went on a rampage, attacking Irish labourers, and burning prisons, 'Papishe dens' (chapels) and several law courts. At least 300 people died during the riots, including some who drank themselves to death after breaking into a Holborn distillery, and the army managed to restore order only after five days of rioting.

As the 18th century drew to a close, London's population had mushroomed to almost a million.

1749	1807	1838
The Bow Street Runners are established by the novelist and magistrate Henry Fielding to replace the previous 'thief-takers' who would arrest criminals for a small fee.	The Houses of Parliament finally abolish the slave trade, on which much Georgian wealth has been built, after a long and hard-fought campaign led by politician and philanthropist William Wilberforce.	The coronation of Queen Victoria at Westminster Abbey ushers in the greatest period in London's history, during which the British capital becomes the economic and political centre of the world.

INVASION OF THE BODY SNATCHERS

During the 18th and 19th centuries, as the understanding of anatomy and surgery advanced, there was a huge shortage of bodies on which doctors and students could experiment. Legally, only the corpses of executed criminals were fair game for the scalpel, but the demand for specimens far outstripped supply, leading to the rise of the notorious body snatchers, or resurrectionists. Gangs of men would surreptitiously remove recently interred bodies from their graves, replacing everything as they found it, so in many cases the relatives never found out. In fact, though horrific, the practice was not even illegal, as by law the human body was not a possession and thus taking it could not be deemed stealing. The area around St Bart's hospital was notorious for this practice, with entire gangs emptying local graveyards. However, the strongly held belief that the human body had to be intact to enter heaven meant that, when body snatchers were discovered, they were often on the receiving end of mob justice and torn to pieces on the streets. This macabre practice ended only after the Anatomy Act of 1832, which relaxed conditions for the medical uses of corpses.

VICTORIAN LONDON

While the growth and achievements of the previous century were impressive, they paled in comparison with the Victorian era, which began when the 19-year-old Victoria was crowned in 1838. During the Industrial Revolution, when small 'cottage' industries were suddenly overtaken by the advance of the great factories, spurring the creation of the first industrialised society on earth, London became the nerve centre of the largest and richest empire the world has ever known, one that covered a quarter of the earth's surface area and ruled more than 500 million people.

New docks in East London were built to facilitate the booming trade with the colonies, and railways began to fan out from the capital. The world's first underground railway opened between Paddington and Farringdon Rd in 1863 and was such a success that other lines quickly followed. Many of London's most famous buildings and landmarks were also built at this time: the Clock Tower (popularly known as 'Big Ben', 1859; see Houses of Parliament, p102), Royal Albert Hall (1871; p144) and the magnificent Tower Bridge (1894; p123).

The city, however, heaved under the burden of its vast size, and in 1858 London found itself in the grip of the 'Great Stink', when the population explosion so overtook the city's sanitation facilities that raw sewage seeped in through the floorboards of wealthy merchants' houses. Leading engineer Joseph Bazalgette tackled the problem by creating in the late 1850s an underground network of sewers, which would be copied around the world. London had truly become the first modern metropolis.

Though the Victorian age is chiefly seen as one of great imperial power founded on industry, trade and commerce, intellectual achievement in the arts and sciences was enormous. The greatest chronicler of the times was Charles Dickens, whose *Oliver Twist* (1837) and other works explored the themes of poverty, hopelessness and squalor among the working classes. In 1859 Charles Darwin published the immensely controversial *On the Origin of Species* here, in which he outlined his still-contentious theory of evolution.

This was also the era of some of Britain's most capable and progressive prime ministers, most notably William Gladstone (four terms between 1868 and 1894) and Benjamin Disraeli (who served in 1868 and again from 1874 to 1880).

BACKGROUND HISTORY

1884	1901	1908
Greenwich Mean Time is established, making Greenwich Observatory the centre of world time, against which all clocks around the globe are set.	Queen Victoria dies after a reign of more than 63 years – the longest (so far) in British history. As Victoria was averse to black funerals, London is instead festooned in purple and white.	London hosts its first Olympic Games, in the now demolished White City Stadium. A total of 22 teams take part and the entire budget is £15,000.

Waves of immigrants, from Chinese to Eastern European, arrived in London during the 19th century, when the population exploded from one million to six million people. This breakneck expansion was not beneficial to all – inner-city slums housed the poor in atrocious conditions of disease and overcrowding, while the affluent expanded out to leafy suburbs, where new and comfortable housing was built. The suburbs of London are still predominantly made up of Victorian terrace housing.

Queen Victoria lived to celebrate her Diamond Jubilee in 1897, but died four years later aged 81 and was laid to rest in Windsor. Her reign is seen as the climax of Britain's world supremacy, when London was the de facto capital of the world.

FROM EMPIRE TO WORLD WAR

Victoria's self-indulgent son Edward, the Prince of Wales, was already 60 by the time he was crowned Edward VII in 1901. London's *belle époque* was marked with the introduction of the first motorised buses, which replaced the horse-drawn versions that had plodded their trade since 1829, and a touch of glamour came in the form of luxury hotels such as the Ritz in 1906 and department stores such as Selfridges in 1909. The Olympics were held at White City in 1908.

What became known as the Great War (WWI) broke out in August 1914, and the first German bombs fell from zeppelins near the Guildhall a year later, killing 39 people. Planes were soon dropping bombs on the capital, killing in all some 650 Londoners (half the national total of civilian casualties).

While the young, moneyed set kicked up their heels after the relative hardships of the war, the 'roaring '20s' brought only more hardship for most Londoners, with an economic slump increasing the cost of living.

The population continued to rise, reaching nearly 7.5 million in 1921. The London County Council (LCC) busied itself clearing slums and building new housing estates, while the suburbs encroached ever deeper into the countryside.

Unemployment rose steadily as the world descended into recession. In May 1926 a wage dispute in the coal industry escalated into a nine-day general strike, in which so many workers downed tools that London virtually ground to a halt. The army was called in to maintain order and to keep the city functioning, but the stage was set for more than half a century of industrial strife.

Despite the economic woes, the era brought a wealth of intellectual success. The 1920s were the heyday of the Bloomsbury Group, which counted writer Virginia Woolf and economist John Maynard Keynes in its ranks. The spotlight shifted westwards to Fitzrovia in the following decade, when George Orwell and Dylan Thomas clinked glasses with contemporaries at the Fitzroy Tavern on Charlotte St.

Cinema, TV and radio arrived, and the British Broadcasting Corporation (BBC) aired its first radio broadcast from the roof of Marconi House on the Strand in 1922, and the first TV programme from Alexandra Palace 14 years later.

The royal family took a knock when Edward VIII abdicated in 1936 to marry a woman who was not only twice divorced but, heaven save us, an American. The same year Oswald Mosley attempted to lead the British Union of Fascists on an anti-Jewish march through the East End but was repelled by a mob of around half a million at the famous Battle of Cable St.

1936	1940–41	1953
George IV becomes king following the abdication of his brother, Edward VIII, who chooses to give up his throne for Wallis Simpson, an American divorcée who will never be acceptable to the British establishment.	London is devastated by the Blitz, although miraculously St Paul's Cathedral and the Tower of London escape the bombing unscathed.	Queen Elizabeth II's coronation is held at Westminster Abbey, the first major live event to be broadcast around the world on TV, and one for which many English families bought their first TV sets.

WWII & THE BLITZ

Prime Minister Neville Chamberlain's policy of appeasing Adolf Hitler during the 1930s eventually proved misguided as the Führer's lust for expansion could not ultimately be sated. When Germany invaded Poland on 1 September 1939, Britain declared war, having signed a mutual-assistance pact with the Poles a few days beforehand. WWII (1939–45), Europe's darkest hour, had begun.

The first year of the war was one of anxious waiting for London; although more than 600,000 women and children had been evacuated to the countryside, no bombs fell to disturb the blackout. On 7 September 1940 this 'phoney war' came to a swift and brutal end when the German Air Force, the Luftwaffe, dropped hundreds of bombs on the East End, killing 430 people.

The Blitz (from the German 'blitzkrieg' for 'lightning war') lasted for 57 nights, and then continued intermittently until May 1941. The Underground was turned into a giant bomb shelter, although one bomb rolled down the escalator at Bank station and exploded on the platform, killing more than 100 people. Londoners responded with legendary resilience and stoicism. The royal family – still immensely popular and enormously respected – were also to play their role, refusing to leave London during the bombing. Begged to allow her children to leave the capital, Queen Elizabeth (the present monarch's late mother) apparently replied, 'the children could not possibly go without me, I wouldn't leave without the King, and the King won't leave under any circumstances'. The king's younger brother, the Duke of Kent, was killed in active service in 1942, while Buckingham Palace took a direct hit during a bombing raid, famously prompting the Queen to announce that 'now we can look the East End in the face'. Winston Churchill, prime minister from 1940, orchestrated much of the nation's war strategy from the Cabinet War Rooms (see p104) deep below Whitehall, and it was from here that he made his stirring wartime speeches.

The city's spirit was tested again in January 1944, when Germany launched pilotless V-1 bombers (known as doodlebugs) over the city. By the time Nazi Germany capitulated in May 1945, up to a third of the East End and the City had been flattened, 32,000 Londoners had been killed and a further 50,000 had been seriously wounded. The scale of the destruction can only really be felt by taking a walk around the City – where postwar buildings (many of them monstrous) have been erected, this is where German bombs hit.

POSTWAR LONDON

Once the celebrations of Victory in Europe (VE) day had died down, the nation faced the huge toll that the war had taken. The years of austerity had begun, with much rationing of essential items and high-rise residences being built on bomb sites in Pimlico and the East End to solve the capital's chronic housing problem. Hosting the 1948 Olympics and the Festival of Britain in 1951 boosted morale. The festival recalled the Great Exhibition of a century earlier, with a new complex of arts buildings, the South Bank Centre (p313), built on the site of the festival.

The gloom returned, quite literally, on 6 December 1952 in the form of the Great Smog, the latest disaster to beset the city. A lethal combination of fog, smoke and pollution descended, and some 4000 people died of smog-related illnesses. This led to the 1956 Clean Air Act, which introduced zones to central London where only smokeless fuels could be burned.

Rationing of most goods ended in 1953, the year the current queen, Elizabeth II, was crowned following the death of her much-loved father King George VI the year before.

1956	1959	1966
Red Routemaster double-decker buses make their first appearance in London and instantly become an iconic symbol of the city. They are now only in use on two 'heritage routes' (the 15 and the 9).	The Notting Hill Carnival is started by Claudia Jones to promote good race relations in West London following the race riots of 1958 in which the local white and African Caribbean community clashed violently.	England beats Germany to win the World Cup at Wembley – possibly the greatest day in the history of British sport and one seared into the consciousness of every schoolboy.

Immigrants from around the world – particularly the former British colonies – flocked to postwar London, where a dwindling population had led to labour shortages. The city's character changed forever. However, as the Notting Hill race riots of 1958 attest, despite being officially encouraged to come, new immigrants weren't always welcomed on the streets.

Some economic prosperity returned in the late 1950s, and Prime Minister Harold Macmillan told Britons they'd 'never had it so good'. London was the place to be during the 1960s when the creative energy that had been bottled up in the postwar era was spectacularly uncorked. London became the epicentre of cool in fashion and music, and the streets were awash with colour and vitality. The introduction of the contraceptive pill, legalisation of homosexuality and the popularisation of drugs such as marijuana and lysergic acid diethylamide (LSD) through the hippy movement created an unprecedented permissive and liberal climate, outraging the conservative older generations and delighting the young. Two seminal events were the Beatles recording at Abbey Rd and the Rolling Stones performing free in front of half a million people in Hyde Park. Carnaby St was the most fashionable place on earth, and pop-culture figures from Twiggy and David Bailey to Marianne Faithfull and Christine Keeler became the icons of the new era.

PUNK LONDON

The party didn't last long, however, and London returned to the doldrums in the harsh economic climate of the 1970s, a decade marked by unemployment and Irish Republican Army (IRA) bombs. But, ever thriving on adversity, London ensured it was at the centre of the world's attention when in the mid-1970s a new aesthetic, punk, came vomiting and swearing into sight.

Despite the sexual liberation of the swinging '60s, London had remained a relatively conservative place, and the generation that had witnessed flower power as kids suddenly took things a step further, horrifying *Daily Mail* readers with strategically placed safety pins, dyed hair, mohawks and foul language. Punk was born – Vivienne Westwood shocked and awed the city with the wares from her clothing shop, Sex, on King's Rd, while the Sex Pistols' alternative national anthem, 'God Save the Queen', released during the national celebrations for Queen Elizabeth's Silver Jubilee in 1977, was more outrageous than anything the '60s had come up with.

While the music and fashion scene was in overdrive, torpor had set into Britain's body politic, as demonstrated by the brief and unremarkable Labour premiership of James Callaghan (1976–79). He was seen as weak and in thrall to the all-powerful trade unions, who crippled the UK with strikes in the late 1970s, most significantly during the 'Winter of Discontent' in 1978–79.

THE THATCHER & MAJOR YEARS

Recovery began – at least for the business community – under the iron fist of Margaret Thatcher, the leader of the Conservative Party, who was elected Britain's first female prime minister in 1979. Her monetarist policy created a canyon between rich and poor, while her determination to crush socialism and shut down huge swathes of Britain's outdated manufacturing industry sent unemployment skyrocketing. Her term was marked by rioting and unrest, most famously in Brixton in 1981 and Tottenham in 1985. Hugely popular abroad and largely reviled in her own country by anyone with a social conscience, Thatcher was nonetheless one of the most notable prime ministers of recent times.

1979	1981	1987
Margaret Thatcher is elected prime minister. Her radical policies will transform Britain beyond recognition – part much-needed modernisation, part cold-hearted social policy.	Brixton sees the worst race riots in London's history. Lord Scarman, delivering his report on the events, puts the blame squarely on 'racial disadvantage that is a fact of British life'.	A fire, probably started by a dropped match, at King's Cross underground station causes the death of 31 people. While smoking was banned on tube carriages and platforms in 1985, smokers still lit up on escalators.

The Greater London Council (GLC), under the leadership of 'Red' Ken Livingstone, proved to be a thorn in Thatcher's side and fought a spirited campaign to bring down the price of public transport. Thatcher responded in 1986 by abolishing the GLC, leaving London as the only European capital without a local government. The GLC wouldn't resurface for another 14 years, during which many of London's problems from transport to housing became entrenched.

While poorer Londoners suffered under Thatcher's assault on socialism, things had rarely looked better for the wealthy. Riding on a wave of confidence partly engendered by the deregulation of the Stock Exchange in 1986, London underwent explosive economic growth. New property developers proved to be only marginally more discriminating than the Luftwaffe, though some outstanding modern structures, including the Lloyd's of London building (p117), went up amid all the other rubbish.

Like previous booms, the one of the late 1980s proved unsustainable. As unemployment started to rise and people found themselves living in houses worth much less than what they had paid for them, Thatcher introduced a flat-rate poll tax. Protests around the country culminated in a 1990 march on Trafalgar Sq that ended in a fully-fledged riot. Thatcher's subsequent forced resignation brought to an end a divisive era in modern British history, and her roundly derided successor, her former Chancellor of the Exchequer, John Major, employed a far more collective form of government, something that was anathema to Thatcher.

In 1992, to the horror of most Londoners, the Conservatives were elected for a fourth successive term in government, even though the inspiring leadership of Thatcher was gone. The economy went into a tailspin shortly after, and Britain was forced to withdraw from the European Exchange Rate Mechanism (ERM), a humiliation from which it was impossible for the government to recover. To add to the government's troubles, the IRA detonated two huge bombs, one in the City in 1992 and another in the Docklands four years later, killing several people and damaging millions of pounds' worth of property.

top picks

HISTORICAL READS

- London: The Biography – Peter Ackroyd
- London at War – Philip Ziegler
- London in the Twentieth Century – Jerry White
- The Newgate Calender – Clive Emsley
- Restoration London, Elizabethan London and Dr Johnson's London – Liza Picard

BLAIR'S BRITAIN

Invigorated by its sheer desperation to return to power, the Labour Party, having elected the thoroughly telegenic Tony Blair to lead it, managed to ditch some of the more socialist-sounding clauses in its party credo and reinvent itself as New Labour, finally leading to a huge landslide win in the May 1997 general election. The Conservatives were atomised throughout the country, and the Blair era had begun.

Most importantly for London, Labour recognised the legitimate demand the city had for local government, and created the London Assembly and the post of mayor. Despite this laudable attempt to give Londoners back the much-needed representation stolen by Thatcher, Blair quickly discredited himself by attempting to rig the Labour mayoral selection process against New Labour's then *bête noire* Ken Livingstone, former leader of the GLC. Londoners

1990	1997	2000
Britain erupts in civil unrest, culminating in the poll tax riots in Trafalgar Sq. Thatcher's deeply unpopular poll tax is the iron lady's ultimate undoing and she is forced to resign in November.	Labour sweeps to victory after almost two decades of Tory power. Tony Blair's radical relaunch of the once left-wing Labour Party as centrist 'New Labour' gives him a huge landslide with a majority of 179.	Livingstone is elected Mayor of London, despite the government's attempts to shoehorn its own man into the job. Elected as an independent, Livingstone is soon welcomed back to the Labour Party.

THE WORLD IN ONE CITY

London is historically made up of immigrants – whether Roman, Viking, Anglo-Saxon, Norman, Huguenot or Jamaican, the city has always assimilated large numbers of ethnically diverse people. While Africans are well documented to have served in the Roman army, they first came to England in significant numbers as slaves in Elizabethan times. The first truly large influx of foreigners was in the late 17th century, when Huguenots, French Protestant refugees fleeing religious persecution at home, settled in Spitalfields and Soho. Wave upon wave followed. Jews have arrived throughout the past four centuries; their traditional areas have been the East End (particularly Spitalfields and Stamford Hill) and northwest London. The last large group of Jews arrived from India as late as the 1960s. During the potato famine in the mid-19th century there was massive migration from Ireland; Londoners with Irish ancestry remain concentrated in Kilburn today. WWII brought Poles, Ukrainians and other Eastern Europeans to London, and today the Poles are a long-established community in Hammersmith and Shepherd's Bush. The single biggest wave of immigration came in the 1950s, when, facing a labour shortage, the government allowed anyone born in a UK colony to have British citizenship. This brought a huge black population from the Caribbean and a large Asian diaspora from India, Bangladesh and Pakistan. The black population settled in West London and South London, while Asians were concentrated in the East End. Other less noticeable waves include Italians to Clerkenwell in the early 20th century, Vietnamese refugees to Hackney in the 1980s and the Iraqi diaspora that has grown in northwest London since the 1990s. Whoever you are, wherever you're from, you'll feel at home in London.

were incensed at Blair's attempts to parachute his close ally Frank Dobson into the position, and when Livingstone stood as an independent candidate he stormed the contest. However, Livingstone never became the thorn in Blair's side that many predicted. His hugely successful congestion charge has done wonders for the city's traffic flow, and following a quiet readmission to the Labour Party, is looked upon as one of the party's most significant weapons (see the boxed text, p49).

London became the focal point for popular scepticism about the invasion of Iraq in 2003. On 15 February 2003, it saw one of the largest demonstrations in its entire history when more than 750,000 people from all over the UK marched through the city to a mass rally in Hyde Park.

Two years later a far smaller crowd on Trafalgar Sq reacted jubilantly to the announcement on 6 July 2005 by the International Olympic Committee that London would be the first triple Olympic city in history, being awarded the 2012 games – which had been widely tipped to go to Paris. However, London's buoyant mood was shattered the very next morning when terrorists detonated a series of explosions on the city's public transport network killing 52 innocent people. Triumph turned to terror, followed quickly by anger and then defiance.

Despite at one time being the most popular leader in modern British history, by the end of Tony Blair's period in office he was deeply resented and mistrusted by Londoners. Still, Blair was able to choose his departure date from No 10 himself and there was never a serious rebellion against him in the Labour Party despite the mess of Iraq.

LONDON TODAY

Gordon Brown became Prime Minister on 27 June 2007, after a decade serving as Blair's chancellor of the exchequer. Having built up an enviable economic record getting Britain out of its Conservative-era boom and bust cycle, Brown positioned himself as being everything

2003	2005	2007
London's congestion charge is introduced by Livingstone, creating an outcry that soon disappears as London's streets begin to flow smoothly again.	Fifty two people are killed by Muslim extremist suicide bombers attacking the London transport network on 7 July. Two weeks later four more terrorists attempt a similar feat, and fail.	Gordon Brown becomes prime minister after a decade-long wait as Blair's chancellor. The feud between the two men, which has gripped and grid-locked Westminster for years, is finally over.

Blair wasn't – honest, plain speaking and unconcerned with spin. The following weekend two car bombs were found and defused in London, a sobering reminder of the terrorist threat the city still faces on a daily basis and the ongoing quagmire of Britain's involvement in the occupation of Iraq.

On a more prosaic level, public transport continues to be Londoners' most consistent complaint, with Ken's 'bendy buses' still far from loved, although most admit that bus and tube services have improved, prices (for Oyster Card users at least) have gone down, provision for cyclists has massively improved and the East London line extension will bring much-needed new tube stations to Hackney. London's successful bagging of the 2012 Olympic Games means that a vast building programme in East London has rolled into action. Most importantly for Londoners, the games will release money for much-promised new transport routes, including the Crossrail scheme that will see the construction of two brand-new underground train lines linking London's east to its west.

London remains a liberal, left-leaning boomtown. The perennial problems of the capital continue to dominate the local political agenda, but the day-to-day life of London continues to be that of creative maelstrom, financial buoyancy and developmental frenzy, something that it has been famous for since the arrival of its first colonisers.

ARTS

When a disused power station in a run-down part of London was transformed into the Tate Modern back at the turn of the century, few had any idea what a runaway success the gallery would be. Less than a decade later it's London's most visited sight and has inspired a city already laden with artistic merit to even greater heights of ambition. The Tate Modern is just another phase in the artistic and cultural renaissance that began in London during the 1990s with Britpop and the Young British Artists, an unleashing of cultural power into a post-Thatcher vacuum that flourished in Blair's Britain. Whether it be in art, literature, music, fashion, stage or screen, London has always been the artistic centre of the country and, in many ways, of Europe as a whole, particularly throughout the 20th century, when it led the way in music and fashion.

The arts make an important contribution to London's economic success, but it's the quality of life they contribute to that make them so significant – London's staggeringly rich cultural life brings many people here, while for others it's what keeps them in this city that's notoriously expensive and tough to get a break in.

Hollywood stars queue up to tread the boards of the capital's theatres, while London continues to be the heart of English literature, housing both the most innovative publishers in the country and some of writing's greatest stars. While the dust is still settling after the storm of Britart, a generation of less obviously shocking artists is emerging – not to mention a host of new galleries and museums that have opened in the past five years – ensuring that Londoners are still art crazy.

London's actors and actresses are known the world over, and the British film industry still throws out some notable productions, from Oscar-winning Helen Mirren's portrayal of good queen Bess in *The Queen* to the comic brilliance of *A Cock and Bull Story* and blockbusters such as the Harry Potter and James Bond series. Musically, the city is making a comeback from the post-Britpop torpor that set in around the turn of the millennium, while remaining one of the best places to see live bands anywhere on earth. London is also a capital of comedy, and its dance companies cut a splendid dash across the world stage.

LITERATURE
Old Literary London
In English literature, London has been portrayed in countless ways over six centuries, from Chaucer to Monica Ali, making a history of London writing a history of the city itself. London has been the inspiration for such timeless masters as Shakespeare, Defoe, Dickens, Thackeray, Wells, Orwell, Conrad, Greene and Woolf, to name but a few. It's hard to reconcile the bawdy

GRUB STREET

Grub St was the original name of a London street (now Milton St, located behind the Barbican) inhabited by impoverished writers and literary hacks. In the 18th century, any inferior book or work of literature was known as 'Grubstreet', but these days – and you shouldn't read anything into this – the term seems to be used for the whole London publishing industry. The London publishing world takes itself extremely seriously, and that's why publications such as *Private Eye* (see boxed text, p52) are so refreshing, always on the lookout for individuals or organisations that are getting too big for their boots.

portrayal of the city in the *Canterbury Tales* with Dickens' bleak hellhole in *Oliver Twist*, let alone Defoe's plague-ravaged metropolis with Zadie Smith's multiethnic romp in *White Teeth*. Ever changing, yet somehow eerily consistent – something brilliantly illustrated in Peter Ackroyd's *London: The Biography* – the capital has left its mark on some of the most influential writing in the English language. What follows is a small selection of seminal moments – you can get a detailed listing in *Waterstone's Guide to London Writing* (£3.99), available at Waterstone's bookshops everywhere.

The first literary reference to the city comes in Chaucer's *Canterbury Tales*, written between 1387 and 1400, where the pilgrims gather for their trip to Canterbury at the Tabard Inn in Southwark, although sadly the inn burned down in 1676. A blue plaque marks the site of the building today.

William Shakespeare spent most of his life as an actor and playwright in London around the turn of the 17th century, when book publishing was beginning to take off here. He trod the boards of several Southwark theatres and wrote his greatest tragedies – among them *Hamlet, Othello, Macbeth* and *King Lear* – for the original Globe theatre on South Bank. However, although London was his home for most of his life, Shakespeare was an ardent fantasist and set nearly all his plays in foreign or make-believe lands. Even his English historical plays are hardly ever set in the capital; only *Henry IV: Part II* includes a London setting: a tavern called the Boar's Head in Eastcheap.

Daniel Defoe was perhaps the first true London writer, both living in and writing about the city during the early 18th century. Most famous for *Robinson Crusoe* (1720) and *Moll Flanders* (1722), which he wrote while living in Church St in Stoke Newington, Defoe's *Journal of the Plague Year* is nonetheless his most interesting account of London life, documenting the horrors of the Great Plague in London during the summer and autumn of 1665, when the author was a child.

Two early-19th-century poets found inspiration here. John Keats wrote his *Ode to a Nightingale* while living near Hampstead Heath in 1819 and his *Ode on a Grecian Urn* after inspecting the Portland Vase in the British Museum. William Wordsworth visited in 1802 and was inspired to write the poem *On Westminster Bridge*.

Charles Dickens (1812–70) was the definitive London author. When his father and family were imprisoned for not paying their debts, the 12-year-old Charles was forced to fend for himself on the streets of Victorian London. Although his family were released three months later, those grim months were seared into the boy's memory and provided a font of experiences on which he would later draw. His novels most closely associated with the city are *Oliver Twist*, with its story of a gang of boy thieves organised by Fagin in Clerkenwell, and *Little Dorrit*, whose heroine was born in the Marshalsea – the same prison where his family were interned. His later *Our Mutual Friend* is a scathing criticism of contemporary London values – both monetary and social – and a spirited attack on the corruption, complacency and superficiality of 'respectable' London. The Old Curiosity Shop, made famous by the book of the same name, can still be seen standing just off Lincoln's Inn today.

Sir Arthur Conan Doyle (1858–1930) portrayed a very different London, and his pipe-smoking, cocaine-snorting sleuth, Sherlock Holmes, came to exemplify a cool and unflappable Englishness the world over. Letters to the mythical hero still arrive at 221b Baker St, where there's now a museum to everyone's favourite Victorian detective.

London at the end of the 19th century is described in a number of books. HG Wells' *The War of the Worlds* wonderfully captures the sense and mood of the times. W Somerset Maugham's first novel, *Liza of Lambeth*, was based on his experiences as an intern in the slums of South London, while *Of Human Bondage*, so English and of its time, provides an engaging portrait of late-Victorian London.

20th-Century Writing

Of the Americans writing about London at the end of the 19th century and start of the 20th century, Henry James, who settled and died here, stands supreme with *Daisy Miller* and *The Europeans*. *The People of the Abyss*, by American socialist writer Jack London, is a sensitive portrait of the poverty and despair of life in the East End. And we couldn't forget Mark Twain's *The Innocents Abroad*, in which the inimitable humorist skewers both the Old and the New Worlds. St Louis–born TS Eliot settled in London in 1915, where he published his poem *The Love Song of J Alfred Prufrock* almost immediately and moved on to his ground-breaking epic *The Waste Land*.

The End of the Affair, Graham Greene's novel chronicling a passionate and doomed romance, takes place in and around Clapham Common just after WWII, while *The Heat of the Day* is Elizabeth Bowen's sensitive, if melodramatic, account of living through the Blitz.

Between the wars, PG Wodehouse (1881–1975), the most quintessentially British writer of the early 20th century, depicted the London high life with his hilarious lampooning of the English upper classes in the Jeeves stories. Quentin Crisp, the self-proclaimed 'stately homo of England', provided the flipside, recounting what it was like to be openly gay in the sexually repressed London of the 1920s in his ribald and witty memoir, *The Naked Civil Servant*. George Orwell's experiences of living as a beggar in London's East End coloured his book *Down and Out in Paris and London* (1933), while sternly modernist Senate House on Malet St, Bloomsbury, was the inspiration for the Ministry of Truth in his classic dystopian 1949 novel *1984*.

Colin MacInnes described the bohemian, multicultural world of 1950s Notting Hill in *City of Spades* and *Absolute Beginners*, while Doris Lessing captured the political mood of 1960s London in *The Four-Gated City*, the last of her five-book *Children of Violence* series, and provides some of the funniest and most vicious portrayals of 1990s London in *London Observed*. Nick Hornby has found himself the voice of a generation, nostalgic about his days as a young football fan in *Fever Pitch* and obsessive about vinyl in *High Fidelity*.

Before it became fashionable, authors such as Hanif Kureishi explored London from the perspective of ethnic minorities, specifically young Pakistanis in his best-known novels *The Black Album* and *The Buddha of Suburbia* – he also wrote the screenplay for the ground-breaking film *My Beautiful Laundrette*. Author and playwright Caryl Phillips won plaudits for his description of the Caribbean immigrant's experience in *The Final Passage*, while Timothy Mo's *Sour Sweet* is a poignant and funny account of a Chinese family in the 1960s trying to adjust to English life.

The astronomical success of Helen Fielding's *Bridget Jones's Diary* effectively concluded the genre known as 'chick lit', a series of hugely successful books that were, depending on your perspective, about finding Mr Right or about independent, brassy young women finding their voice. Will Self – *enfant terrible* and incisive social commentator – has been the toast of London for the last decade. His *Grey Area* is a superb collection of short stories focusing on skewed and surreal aspects of the city, while his more recent *The Book of Dave* is the hilarious, surreal story of a bitter, present-day London cabbie (recognisable to anyone who's spent half an hour listening to a rant in transit) burying a book of his own observations only to have it discovered in the future and regarded as scripture by the people on the island of Ham (Britain is an archipelago now due to rising sea levels).

Peter Ackroyd is regarded as the quintessential London author and names the city as the love of his life. *London: The Biography* is his inexhaustible paean to the capital, while his most recent book, *The Clerkenwell Tales*, brings to life the 14th-century London of Chaucer.

PRIZE WRITERS

The Booker Prize is the most important literary-fiction prize in Britain. Since its foundation in 1969 it has only been open to Commonwealth and Irish authors, but new sponsors the Man Group insisted that it be opened to US writers by 2004, drawing uproar from sections of the British media. Despite fears that American competition would lead to no British writer ever winning the prize again, the 2004 Booker went to Londoner Alan Hollinghurst for his *The Line of Beauty*. Any well-read Londoner will have an opinion about the Booker Prize – some rubbish it as a self-promotional tool of publishing houses, while others slavishly read not only the winner but any book to make the short list. Either way, few are indifferent to the prize, and the winner is usually highly indicative of contemporary literary trends in Britain.

BACKGROUND ARTS

Finally, Iain Sinclair is the bard of Hackney, who, like Ackroyd, has spent his life obsessed with and fascinated by the capital. His acclaimed and ambitious *London Orbital*, a journey on foot around the M25, London's mammoth motorway bypass, is required London reading.

The Current Scene

London remains an exciting place for writers and readers alike and is the home of most of the UK's major publishers and its best bookshops. The frustrating predominance of several hugely powerful corporations within publishing, however, is very limiting and there's almost no will within the literary scene to throw off the hegemony of companies far more interested in turning a profit than pioneering good writing.

The frankly sad desperation with which agents and publishers are seeking 'the next big thing' is a total sign of the times. The shape of the industry is best exemplified by the 2000 runaway success *White Teeth*, a dazzling debut novel by Zadie Smith about multiethnic assimilation in North London. This novel propelled Smith, pretty much overnight, from obscurity to being the poster girl for young, hip literary London.

Smith arrived on the scene already represented by a ruthless literary agent who invited publishers to bid for the book on the strength of – not even a full manuscript – a sample of 100 pages. The feeding frenzy that followed has already passed into London legend. Smith fulfilled all the current criteria: as well as being a bloody good writer she was young, gorgeous and multicultural (ie eminently marketable). All the lights lit up and Grub St went into orbit. Penguin finally claimed victory when it paid the *unknown* author £250,000 for the *unknown* book.

As it turned out, Penguin's 'hunch' was spot on; *White Teeth* was fresh, original and generally fabulous, and the publisher made a handsome profit from it and from Smith's somewhat less impressive follow-up, *The Autograph Man*, in 2002. But it's the nature of the first book's publication that characterises London's literary scene right now. Publishers on a quest for the jackpot are shelling out bigger and bigger advances for new books by unknown authors in the hope that they'll uncover 'the next Zadie Smith'. In many cases of course, they don't, but large fees on a few gambles make it harder for other writers with less marketable qualities to get into print.

This sad state of affairs has, however, created an exciting literary fringe, which although tiny, is very active and passionate about good writing. London still has many small presses where quality and innovation are prized over public relations skills and box ticking, and events fizzle away at bookshops and in back rooms of pubs throughout the week.

Back in the mainstream, the big guns of the 1980s such as Martin Amis, Ian McEwan, Salman Rushdie and Julian Barnes are still going strong, although none has produced anything much to get excited about since the late 1990s. Even McEwan's Booker-winning *Saturday* was a fairly underwhelming affair. Rushdie was awarded a knighthood in 2007 for services to literature, which outraged many Muslims who consider his book *The Satanic Verses* to be blasphemous. The award was widely cheered in Britain as a mark of support for freedom of speech, notwithstanding the slight unease with what many in Britain perceive as Rushdie's distancing himself from the UK in recent years, despite being a British citizen and having enjoyed police protection for years at the cost of millions to the British taxpayer.

The current scene is most notable for the wealth of superb children's literature being produced. JK Rowling and Phillip Pulman have between them totally revolutionised the concept of what children's books can be and the reach they can have. The final Harry Potter book came out in summer 2007amid people queuing for copies for two days in a manner befitting the sale of a supergroups' world tour, and with Rowling famously richer than the Queen, it's safe to say that she won't be worrying about her pension.

That's not to say that new voices haven't broken through in the last decade – indeed, there have been some outstanding new London writers in recent years, from Monica Ali who brought the East End to life in *Brick Lane* to Jake Arnott and his intelligent Soho-based gangster yarn *The Long Firm* and Gautam Malkani's much-hyped *Londonstani*. Other authors worth exploring for a taste of the rising stars of the city's literary scene are Tony White, Martin Millar and Cathi Unsworth.

See the boxed text, p317, for details of readings and spoken-word events around the city.

RECOMMENDED READING

- *Absolute Beginners* (1959; Colin MacInnes) This brilliant novel is a must-read for anyone interested in the youth culture of London during the '50s, particularly the mod scene. It's infinitely more engaging than the film of the same name.
- *Brick Lane* (2003; Monica Ali) This debut novel tells the story of Nazneen, an Islamic Bangladeshi woman who comes to London after an arranged marriage and initially accepts her circumscribed life, before embarking on her own voyage of self-discovery. The author writes with wit and gentle irony.
- *The Buddha of Suburbia* (1991; Hanif Kureishi) This winner of the 1990 Whitbread prize is a raunchy, funny and insightful trawl of the hopes and fears of a group of Asian suburbanites in 1970s London, from the pre-eminent Anglo-Asian voice of his generation.
- *The End of the Affair* (1951; Graham Greene) Set in battle-scarred London at the end of WWII, this intensely emotional classic deals with a three-way collision between love of self, love of another and love of God (coloured by the tension felt by the author between his Roman Catholic faith and the compulsion of sexual passion).
- *Grey Area* (1994; Will Self) Piercing wit, narrative virtuosity and incisive social commentary characterise the writing of Self. In these nine short stories – or 'comic nightmares' – he lays into contemporary London and evokes the most disturbing failings of society.
- *Journal of the Plague Year* (1722; Daniel Defoe) Defoe's classic reconstruction of the Great Plague of 1665 scans the streets and alleyways of stricken London to record the extreme suffering of plague victims. At once grisly and movingly compassionate.
- *The Line of Beauty* (2003; Alan Hollinghurst) A surprise Booker Prize winner in 2004, this account of high society through the eyes of a young gay man in Thatcher's London paints a portrait of a divisive period in modern British history and brings West London society into sharp critical focus.
- *London Fields* (1989; Martin Amis) By using a constantly shifting narrative voice, Amis makes the reader work damn hard for the prize in this middle-class-fear-of-the-mob epic. Dark and postmodern, it is a gripping study of London lowlife.
- *London Observed* (1992; Doris Lessing) A collection of stories from the Iranian-born (and Rhodesian-raised) author, who observes London and its inhabitants with the shrewd and compassionate eye of an artist in 18 sketches of the city.
- *London Orbital* (2002; Iain Sinclair) Sinclair, Hackney's irrepressible voice of dissent, sets off to circumnavigate the capital on foot within the 'acoustic footprints' of the M25; hilarious and insightful.
- *London: The Biography* (2000; Peter Ackroyd) Regarded by some as the definitive history of London, this tome provides a fascinating tapestry of the capital, arranged by theme rather than chronologically.
- *The Long Firm* (2000; Jake Arnott) The first – and best – of a London trilogy set in the seedy world of 1960s Soho. Brutal but often hilarious reading that was made into a compelling British Broadcasting Corporation (BBC) drama series too.
- *Mother London* (2000; Michael Moorcock) This engaging, rambling novel follows three mentally disturbed characters who hear voices from the heart of London, providing for an episodic romp through the history of the capital from the Blitz to the end of the 2nd millennium. The city itself becomes a character, along with its outcasts and marginals, all treated with great compassion.
- *Mrs Dalloway* (1925; Virginia Woolf) Bloomsbury Group stalwart Woolf goes full throttle with her stream-of-consciousness style in this story, which follows a day in the life of various people trying to cope in 1923 London. It is beautifully crafted, and as brief as it is exhilarating.
- *The Naked Civil Servant* (1968; Quentin Crisp) This story of an openly gay man in London in the 1920s, a world of brutality and comedy, is told in Crisp's characteristically sarcastic, self-derogatory, bitchy and very funny way.
- *Oliver Twist* (1837; Charles Dickens) Although not necessarily Dickens' best, this moving story of an orphan who runs away to London and falls in with a gang of thieves is beautifully told, with unforgettable characters and a vivid portrayal of Victorian London.
- *White Teeth* (2000; Zadie Smith) Smith's hugely hyped novel is a funny, poignant, big-hearted and affectionate book about friendship and cultural differences, as seen through the eyes of three unassimilated families in North London.

THEATRE

London has more theatrical history than almost anywhere else in the world, and it's still being made nightly on the stages of the West End, the South Bank and the vast London fringe. No visit to the city is complete without taking in a show, and just a walk through 'theatreland' in the West End any evening of the week is an electrifying experience as thousands of people make their way to one of the many venerable dramatic institutions.

Dramatic History

Very little is known about London theatre before the Elizabethan period, when a series of 'playhouses', including the Globe, were built on the south bank of the Thames and in Shoreditch. Although the playwrights of the time – Shakespeare, Christopher Marlowe (Dr Faustus, Edward II) and Shakespeare's great rival, Ben Johnson (Volpone, The Alchemist) – are now considered timeless geniuses, theatre then was more about raucous popular entertainment, where the crowd drank and heckled the actors. As venues for such, the playhouses were promptly shut down by the Puritans after the Civil War in 1642.

Three years after the return of the monarchy in 1660, the first famous Drury Lane Theatre was built and the period of 'restoration theatre' began, under the patronage of the rakish Charles II. Borrowing influences from Italian and French theatre, restoration theatre incorporated drama, including John Dryden's 1677 All for Love, and comedy. It's the latter, known for its burlesque humour and sexual explicitness, that most holds the attention of today's audiences. During the restoration period the first female actors appeared on stage (in Elizabethan times men played female roles), and Charles II is recorded as having had an affair with at least one, Nell Gwyn.

Despite the success of John Gay's 1728 Beggar's Opera, Oliver Goldsmith's 1773 farce She Stoops to Conquer and Richard Sheridan's The Rivals and School for Scandal at Drury Lane, also in the 1770s, popular music halls replaced serious theatre during the Victorian era. Light comic operetta, as defined by Gilbert and Sullivan (HMS Pinafore, The Pirates of Penzance, The Mikado etc), was all the rage. A sea change was only brought about by the emergence at the end of the 19th century of such compelling playwrights as Oscar Wilde (An Ideal Husband, The Importance of Being Earnest) and George Bernard Shaw (Pygmalion).

Comic wits such as Noel Coward (Private Lives, Brief Encounter) and earnest dramatists such as Terence Ratigan (The Winslow Boy, The Browning Version) and JB Priestley (An Inspector Calls) followed. However, it wasn't until the 1950s and 1960s that English drama yet again experienced such a fertile period as the Elizabethan era.

Perfectly encapsulating the social upheaval of the period, John Osborne's Look Back in Anger at the Royal Court in 1956 has gone down as generation defining. In the following decade, a rash of new writing appeared, including Harold Pinter's Homecoming, Joe Orton's Loot, Tom Stoppard's Rosencrantz and Guildenstern are Dead and Alan Ayckbourn's How the Other Half Loves. During the same period many of today's leading theatre companies were formed, including the National Theatre under the directorship of Laurence Olivier in 1963.

Although somewhat eclipsed by the National Theatre in the cyclical world of London theatre, today's Royal Court retains a fine tradition of new writing. In the past decade it has nurtured such talented playwrights as Jez Butterworth (Mojo, The Night Heron), Ayub Khan-Din (East Is East), Conor McPherson (The Weir, Shining City) and Joe Penhall (Dumb Show).

For theatre listings, see p317.

The Current Scene

London remains a thrilling place to be for anyone who loves theatre. Nowhere else on earth, with the possible exception of New York, offers such a huge range of high-quality drama, excellent musical theatre and such a sizzling fringe. Whether it's to see Hollywood A-listers gracing tiny stages and earning Equity minimum for their efforts or lavish West End musicals that you'll remember for years afterwards, London remains an undisputed world leader and innovator in the field.

After several terrible years from late 2001, the mainstream West End has re-established its credentials putting on a series of extraordinary hits while the smarter end of the fringe continues to impress with risky, controversial productions that make sure theatre often makes the news. The hottest tickets in town remain those for the National Theatre, which under Nicholas Hytner has gone from strength to strength with productions such as History Boys, Jerry Springer – The Opera, Elmina's Kitchen and Coram Boy enjoying huge box-office success coupled with critical acclaim.

Other venues leading the way in innovation are off–West End venues such as the Arcola (the world's first carbon-neutral theatre and home to an alternative opera season called grimebourne), the Almeida, the Royal Court, the Soho Theatre and the Donmar Warehouse. At the latter Michael Grandage has recently celebrated five very successful years as artistic director by staging a new production of *Othello* featuring Ewan McGregor as Iago – just another example of the big names it's easy to see any night of the week on London's stage, whether it be Harry Potter star Daniel Radcliffe strutting around naked in *Equus* or the septuagenarian Dame Maggie Smith in side-splitting top form in *The Lady From Dubuque* at the Haymarket.

Perhaps the most significant trend of the past few years, with the Blair administration limping off stage left in 2007, has been the rediscovery of political satire and serious political content in many productions, equally in the West End and on the fringe. David Hare's *Stuff Happens,* about the run-up to the Iraq War, was staged at the National, as was a highly political new production of *Henry V* set in occupied Iraq. Elsewhere, the Tricycle Theatre put on *Called to Account* about the internal wrangling at Westminster in the lead-up to the war, and the whole British political and media establishment was sent up in *Who's the Daddy,* a play set amid the sex scandals at the *Spectator* magazine, the beating heart of the UK establishment. Other productions such as *A Weapons Inspector Calls* and *Guantanamo* prove that satire is firmly back on the capital's theatrical agenda.

Satire aside, there's something for all tastes in London's theatreland, and even the revivified West End juggles the serious with the frivolous. Recent productions attracting critical acclaim have included *Angels in America* at the Lyric Hammersmith, *Gaslight* at the Old Vic and the National's production of *Faust*. At the time of writing the musical causing the most excitement in town was *The Drowsy Chaperone* at the Novello Theatre, although a slew of superb musicals have raised the bar in recent years, from *Spamalot* and *Mary Poppins* to more left-field shows such as *Avenue Q* and *Wicked*.

Shakespeare's legacy is generously attended to on the city's stages, most notably by the Royal Shakespeare Company (RSC) and at the Globe Theatre. The RSC stages one or two of the bard's plays in London each year, although currently has no London home (its productions are based in Stratford-upon-Avon and usually transfer to the capital later on in the run), while the open-air Globe on the South Bank attempts to re-create the Elizabethan theatre experience. A faithful reconstruction of the original Globe, the building places audiences unusually close to the actors, and the management is quite happy to let them heckle each other. Since it opened in 1997 the Globe has enjoyed considerable success as a working theatre (as opposed to a mere curiosity). Artistic director Dominic Dromgoole, having taken over the reins at the start of 2006, plans to keep Shakespearean plays at the core of the theatre's programme and at the same time introduce a wider range of European and British classics.

Finally, if all this innovation and change is too much for you, drop by St Martin's Theatre where *The Mousetrap* has been running since 1952!

MUSIC

Modern music from the Kinks to Amy Winehouse is perhaps London's single greatest contribution to the world of arts, and after more than four decades at the top, it is still a creative hotbed and a magnet for bands and hopefuls from all over the world. Complementing the home-grown talent is the continuous influx of styles and cultures that keeps the music scene here so fresh.

For a list of venues, see p306.

The Swinging '60s

London's prolific output began with the Kinks and their North London songwriter Ray Davies, whose lyrics read like a guide to the city. 'You Really Got Me', 'All Day and All of the Night' and 'Dedicated Follower of Fashion' brilliantly capture the antiestablishment mood of the '60s, while 'Waterloo Sunset' is the ultimate feel-good London song.

Another London band, the Rolling Stones, got their first paying gig at the old Bull & Bush in Richmond in 1963. Originally an R&B outfit, they went on to define rock and roll, and success and teen mayhem quickly followed. Their second single 'I Wanna Be Your Man' came to them via a chance encounter on the street with John Lennon and Paul McCartney, two blokes down from Liverpool recording in Abbey Rd and on their way to making their band, the Beatles, the biggest the world has ever known. The Stones, no slouches in the fame stakes themselves, released 'Not Fade Away' in 1964, and they're doggedly sticking to their word after 40 years of swaggering, swilling and swearing. The Beatles themselves, while of course famously being from Liverpool, recorded most of their most famous songs in London and even performed their final concert on the roof of the Apple building in Mayfair.

Struggling to be heard above the din was inspirational mod band the Small Faces, formed in 1965 and remembered long afterwards. The Who, from West London, got attention by thrashing guitars on stage and chucking televisions out of hotel windows. The band is remembered also for rock operas and hanging around far too long flogging their back catalogue. Jimi Hendrix came to London and took guitar playing to levels not seen before or since, even tragically dying in a West London hotel under somewhat mysterious circumstances in 1970. In some ways, the swinging '60s ended in July 1969 when the Stones played a free concert in Hyde Park in front of more than a quarter of a million liberated fans.

top picks

A MUSICAL JOURNEY THROUGH LONDON

- Zebra crossing on Abbey Road, St John's Wood – the Beatles' most famous album cover
- Heddon Street, Soho – where the cover for *Ziggy Stardust* was photographed
- 23 Brook Street – former home to composers Handel and Hendrix
- St Martins College – first Sex Pistols gig
- Tree on Queen's Ride, Barnes – where Marc Bolan died in his Mini in 1977
- 3 Savile Row – site of the last Beatles performance on the roof of the Apple building in 1969

The '70s

A local band called Tyrannosaurus Rex had enjoyed moderate success. In 1970 they changed their name to T Rex, frontman Marc Bolan donned a bit of glitter and the world's first 'glam' band had arrived. Glam encouraged the youth of uptight Britain to come out of the closet and be whatever they wanted to be. Brixton boy and self-proclaimed 'chameleon of pop' David Bowie began to steal the limelight, sealing his international fame with *The Rise and Fall of Ziggy Stardust and the Spiders from Mars* in 1972, one of the best albums of the decade. Roxy Music, incorporating art rock and synth pop, sang 'Love Is the Drug' in 1975.

Meanwhile, a little band called Led Zeppelin formed in London in 1968 and created the roots of heavy metal. Seventeen-year-old Farok Bulsara came to London from India (via Zanzibar) in the '60s and, in 1970, changed his name to Freddie Mercury; the consummate showman formed Queen with a few local lads and went on to become one of the greatest rock-and-roll stars of all time. Fleetwood Mac stormed the US as much as Britain; their *Rumours* became the fifth-highest-selling album in history (one behind Cambridge boys Pink Floyd's *Dark Side of the Moon*). Bob Marley recorded his *Live* album at the Lyceum Theatre in 1975.

While glam and rock opened the door for British youth, punk came along and kicked the bloody thing down, and set about turning the whole British establishment on its head. The Sex Pistols were the most outrageous of a wave of bands, including the Clash and the Damned, which started playing around London in 1976. The Pistols' first single was, appropriately enough, 'Anarchy in the UK'. 'God Save the Queen' and 'Pretty Vacant' followed and were brilliant. The album *Never Mind the Bollocks Here's the Sex Pistols* was released a year later to critical acclaim.

Fortunately, fellow Londoners the Clash had harnessed the raw anger of the time and worked it into a collar-grabbing brand of political protest that would see them outlast all of their peers. They trod the fine line between being pissed-off punks and great songwriters. The Clash were protesters who raged against racism, social injustice, police brutality and disenfranchisement. The disillusioned generation finally had a plan and a leader; *London Calling* is a spirited call to arms.

The Sex Pistols' ranting and raving John Lydon (formerly Johnny Rotten) became an embarrassment to a generation weaned on punk, but the dismayed reaction to the death of Clash frontman Joe Strummer in late 2002 showed that there was still lots to be proud of.

In 1977 the Jam, punk pioneers *and* mod revivalists, went on tour opening for the Clash (what days!). Lead singer and bristling live performer Paul Weller followed up with a hugely successful solo career.

The '80s

Out of the ashes of punk came, God knows how, the New Wave and new romantics. Guitars were chucked away and replaced with keyboard synthesizers and drum machines. Fashion and image became as important as the music, and it's the seriousness with which the new romantics took themselves that gives the '80s such a bad rap. Overpriced, oversexed and way overdone, '80s London produced such unforgettables as Spandau Ballet, Culture Club, Bananarama, Wham! and Howard Jones' haircut. Wham!'s Georgios Panayiotou shaved his back, changed his name to George Michael and gained great success as a solo artist.

Depeche Mode broke new ground in neo-synth pop, while American London adoptee Chrissie Hynde formed the Pretenders and became the first bad-ass rock-and-roll chick; Northern-lads-turned-Londoners the Pet Shop Boys managed to avoid the '80s-pop path-to-oblivion, redeeming themselves with synth innovation and eventually symphonic spectacle as they performed their own score to Eisenstein's *Battleship Potemkin* on Trafalgar Sq alongside the Dresdner Sinfoniker in September 2004. Neneh Cherry started rapping, and Madness came up with a winning ska-pop combo and featured London in many of their hits and video clips.

But it was all to no avail, because blonde boy-band Bros emerged from South London to top the charts and confirm that the local music scene was really in deep shit. Relief was already coming from up north with the Smiths, and at the end of the decade the Stone Roses and the Happy Mondays broke through with a new sound that had grown out of the recent acid-house raves, with jangly guitars, psychedelic twists and a beat you just couldn't resist. Dance exploded onto the scene, with dilated pupils and Chupa Chups, in 1988's summer of love. A generation was gripped by dance music and a new lexicon had to be learned: techno, electronica, hip-hop, garage, House, trance and so on. Although the E generation that launched the rave/dance culture has grown up and the scene is, well, stagnant at best, London still ranks among the best club cities in the world (see p298).

(see p298)

Britpop

The early 1990s saw the explosion of yet another scene: Britpop, a genre broadly defined as back to (Beatles) basics, familiar old-fashioned three chords and all that jazz, with loads of slang and in-references which, frankly, made it so 'British'. There was a very public battle between two of the biggest bands, Blur from London and Oasis from Manchester, and the public loved the tit-for-tat between the cocky geezers from the capital and the swaggering, belligerent Mancs. When it came down to the line and both bands released a single on the same day, Blur overcame the northerners and got the number one slot; Blur bassist Alex James wore an Oasis T-shirt on *Top of the Pops* in a moment of utter brilliance to be remembered by a generation.

Also weighing in for the London side were the brilliant and erratic Suede (who finally disbanded in 2003) and Elastica (who disbanded in 2001), fronted by the punky, poppy Justine Frischmann, not to mention Sheffield defectors to the capital, Jarvis Cocker's Pulp.

Skirting around the edges, doing their own thing without the hullabaloo, were Radiohead (from Oxford, close enough to London), in our opinion one of the best groups of the era. As the Britpop bands and fans became more sophisticated, the genre died around 1997. Groups such as Coldplay enjoyed massive commercial and critical success, but the zeitgeist had well and truly disappeared around the start of the new millennium leaving London's music scene looking washed up and unexciting.

21st-Century Music

At the beginning of the 21st century multicultural London pushed things forward, to bend the words of Mike Skinner (aka the Streets), whose debut album, *Original Pirate Material,* took London by storm in 2002 and whose follow-up *A Grand Don't Come For Free* has seen equal success, with everyday tales from the life of a modern lad. It's a genre-straddling classic from a young white rapper originally from Birmingham and now living in Brixton, a cross-cultural gem that lights the way for London's music scene in the 21st century.

London's Asian community has also made a big splash in recent years, with Talvin Singh and Nitin Sawhney fusing dance with traditional Indian music to stunning effect, and Asian Dub Foundation bringing their unique brand of jungle techno and political comment to an ever-widening audience, despite being dropped by the major British record labels.

top picks

LONDON ALBUMS

- *Abbey Road* – The Beatles
- *Exile on Main Street* – The Rolling Stones
- *The Good The Bad and The Queen* – Damon Albarn et al
- *London Calling* – The Clash
- *Modern Life Is Rubbish* – Blur
- *Alright, Still* – Lily Allen
- *The Rise and Fall of Ziggy Stardust and the Spiders from Mars* – David Bowie
- *Silent Alarm* – Bloc Party
- *Something Else* – The Kinks
- *Sound Affects* – The Jam

Pete Doherty and Carl Barat single-handedly renewed interest in guitar music following its post-Britpop malaise. The Libertines, formed in a Stoke Newington flat, created a huge splash with their 2002 debut single *What a Waster*, which made it into the top 40 despite no mainstream radio play, and their first album went platinum. However, despite such huge success, the duo split up after Doherty broke into Barat's Marylebone flat to steal money for heroin. Kicked out, Doherty has gone on to form Babyshambles, who have also enjoyed some success, although they're arguably much better known for Doherty's never-dull private life and his problems with heroin addiction.

Other London talents that have come to the fore in the past few years include art rockers Bloc Party, South London maestroes Athlete and punkers the Paddingtons.

London Music Today

Parallel to the re-explosion of interest in punk rock has been London's exceptional electro scene, which continues to fulminate and produce amazing music today, despite many observers predicting it would be a flash in the pan. This has greatly influenced nu-wave, the best-known exponents of which are the Klaxons.

The London scene has fought its way back from being an overhyped late-'90s destination for those seeking cool by association and is again one of the major creative musical hubs on earth. Whether it's home-grown capital talent or refugees from the provinces seeking fame and fortune, London's music scene is throwing up plenty of exciting and ground-breaking music.

The toast of 2006 was Southgate's Amy Winehouse with her dazzling second album *Back to Black* charting at number 1 in the UK album charts and her antics on and off stage making her a cult figure almost overnight. West London's Lily Allen similarly broke through in the same year with her whimsical London songs – *Smile* and *LDN* became anthems in 2006 – and since then the two stars have been hyped side by side and pitted against each other for awards. Lesser known but equally exciting performers such as Jamie T and Just Jack both give a fantastically original slant on London life.

Grime and its successor dubstep, two real indigenous London musical forms born in the East End out of a fusion of hip-hop and Asian influences, are currently at the cutting edge of London music. Dizzee Rascal, Lady Sovereign, Lethal Bizzle and Roll Deep are perhaps the best-known singers and groups working in the genre – for a true East End night out track them down playing a local gig while you're in town.

VISUAL ARTS

London has attracted many of the greatest artists in the world from Monet to Van Gogh, even if Britain's contribution to the visual arts has historically not measured up to that of its European neighbours. Today, London is the art capital of Europe, with an exciting gallery scene and some of the world's best modern art collections.

Holbein to Turner

It wasn't until the rule of the Tudors that art took off in London at all. The German Hans Holbein the Younger (1497–1543) was court painter to Henry VIII, and one of his finest works, *The Ambassadors* (1533), hangs in the National Gallery (p75). A batch of great portrait artists worked at court during the 17th century. Best of them was Anthony Van Dyck (1599–1641), a Belgian who spent the last nine years of his life in London and painted some hauntingly beautiful portraits of Charles I, including *Charles I on Horseback* (1638), now in the National

Gallery. Charles I was a keen collector and it was during his reign that the Raphael Cartoons, now in the Victoria & Albert Museum (p139), came to London.

Local artists began to emerge in the 18th century. Thomas Gainsborough (1727–88) extended portraiture to include the gentry and is regarded as the first great British landscapist, even though most of his landscapes are actually backgrounds. William Hogarth (1697–1764), by contrast, is best known for his moralising serial prints of London lowlife (see the boxed text, p23).

England has a fine tradition of watercolourists, beginning with the poet and engraver William Blake (1757–1827), some of whose romantic paintings and illustrations (he illustrated Milton's *Paradise Lost,* for example) hang in the Tate Britain (p103). John Constable (1776–1837) was a much more skilful and important visual artist than Blake. He studied the clouds and skies above Hampstead Heath, sketching hundreds of scenes that he'd later match with subjects in his landscapes.

JMW Turner (1775–1851), equally at home with oils and watercolours, represented the pinnacle of 19th-century British art. Through innovative use of colour and gradations of light he created a new atmosphere that seemed to capture the wonder, sublimity and terror of nature. His later works – including *Snow Storm – Steam-boat off a Harbour's Mouth* (1842), *Peace – Burial at Sea* (1842) and *Rain, Steam, Speed* (1844), now in the Tate Britain and the National Gallery – were increasingly abstract, and although widely vilified at the time, later inspired the likes of Claude Monet.

The Pre-Raphaelites to Hockney

The Pre-Raphaelite Brotherhood (1848–54), founded in London, burst briefly onto the scene. Taking their inspiration from the works of the Romantic poets, they ditched the pastel-coloured rusticity of the day in favour of big, bright and bold depictions of medieval legends and female beauty.

Two of Britain's leading 20th-century painters emerged next. In 1945 the tortured, Irish-born painter Francis Bacon (1909–92) caused a stir when he exhibited his *Three Studies for Figures at the Base of a Crucifixion* – now on display at the Tate Britain – and afterwards carried on unsettling the world with his distorted, repulsive and fascinating forms. The chaos in Bacon's studio was almost as legendary as his Picasso-meets-Velázquez-meets-Van Gogh-meets-Scarfe paintings. He famously worked knee-deep in scraps of paper, paint rags, newspaper cuttings and other general litter. As he was largely homosexual, it was considered a rare find in the art world when a painting of one of his female lovers went on sale in 2001, and he was also in the news when a forgotten triptych of his was found in an Iranian gallery.

Australian art critic Robert Hughes has described Bacon's contemporary Lucian Freud (b 1922) as 'the greatest living realist painter', although Young British Artist Tracey Emin was less than impressed with his recent portrait of her friend, supermodel Kate Moss. From the 1950s the bohemian Freud has concentrated on pale, muted portraits – often nudes, and frequently of friends and family, although he has also painted the Queen. Twice married and rumoured to have up to 40 illegitimate children, Freud's recent self-portrait *The Painter Is Surprised by a Naked Admirer* fuelled a press frenzy, as journalists tried to guess the identity of the naked woman clinging to his leg.

After the initial shock of Bacon and Freud during the 1940s and '50s, pop art perfectly encapsulated the image of London in the swinging '60s. The brilliant David Hockney (b 1937) gained a reputation as one of the leading pop artists through his early use of magazine-style images (although he rejected the label). After a move to California, his work became increasingly naturalistic as he took inspiration from the sea, the sun, swimmers and swimming pools. Two of his most famous works, *Mr and Mrs Clark and Percy* (1971) and *A Bigger Splash* (1974), are displayed at the Tate Britain.

The Origins of Britart

Gilbert and George were the quintessential English conceptual artists of the 1960s. They, at the very least, paved the way for the shock and celebrity of Britart and were the art as much as the work itself. Despite their long careers, they are still at the heart of the British art world and represented Britain at the 2005 Venice Biennale, and had a very successful retrospective at the Tate Modern in 2007.

LOCAL VOICES: HILARY ROSEN *Interviewed by Steve Fallon*

Hilary Rosen (www.hilaryrosen.co.uk) is an award-winning water-colourist who resides in Muswell Hill N10 and has exhibited at the Royal Academy, the Barbican and, most recently, the National Theatre.

London gal born and bred? I was born within the sound of the Bow bells – well, sort of because they hadn't yet been repaired after the war. I grew up in Maida Vale and then moved to Muswell Hill, so I've gone from valley to hill.

Earliest memory? My grandmother lived in Cable St in the East End, where there was still a lot of war damage. I remember rubble with wallpaper stuck to it. They tell me we used to paddle in the Thames in those days. Certainly London is a major influence on my work.

You paint bridges a lot. Why's that? I started to get interested in architecture and that evolved into bridges. Bridges lead from one thing to another – they represent transition. If you think about it, bridges are a metaphor for moving from one part of life to another. Chelsea, Vauxhall, Battersea bridges... I love them all.

Does the great outdoors do it for you? Do you paint en plein–air in London? I *hate* open spaces. I'm terrified by empty space. London's parks have two edges for me – very green and very sinister with people lurking about.

Here for the duration? A friend from South Africa recently commented that London is a young city. I disagree. I'll enjoy living in London till I die.

Britart? What's your take? I follow what's going on and it's wonderful to see other work. It's all quite interesting but a bit like surrealism. They can do their thing and I'll do mine.

Producing, exhibiting, selling – which comes first? Exhibiting, for sure. It's really important for me to have something on show. It must be the theatrical side of me. My grandmother was a dancer at the interval in cinemas.

The general populace, art and culture... Is it getting better, worse or staying just the same? It's all so much better. Culture is much more accessible now and the audience is much more diverse. It's marvellous that museums are free. I detest a rarefied view of art.

On my perfect day, find me... Drawing and sketching by the Thames. Then I might walk up to Old Compton St in Soho and have a salad at Amato (p240). I might draw on the Soho streets but it attracts too much of an audience. I really can't work while being observed.

I'll always come back to London for... The Thames. Especially at night. And the tube. People think I'm mad but I adore it; it's very London. There's such a mix of people. I was incandescent when the bombs went off. I thought how *dare* these people do this to my city?

Despite its incredibly rich collections, Britain had never led, dominated or even really participated in a particular epoch or style. That all changed in the twilight of the 20th century, when Britart burst onto the scene with its sliced cows, elephant dung and piles of bricks. It's questionable whether the movement will leave a lasting impression, but one thing's for sure: during the 1990s London was the beating heart of the art world.

Britart sprang from a show called Freeze that was staged in a Docklands warehouse in 1988. It was organised by showman Damien Hirst and largely featured his fellow graduates from Goldsmiths College. Influenced by pop culture and punk, this loose movement was soon catapulted to notoriety by the advertising guru Charles Saatchi, who came to dominate the scene like a puppeteer. Indeed, you could almost say he created the genre with his free spending and commissioning. From 1992 Saatchi held a series of seven exhibitions entitled Young British Artists (YBAs), which burst onto the national stage with 1997's epoch-making Sensation exhibition at the Royal Academy.

The work was brash, decadent, ironic, easy to grasp and eminently marketable. To shock seemed the impulse, and the artists did just that. Hirst chipped in with a cow sliced into sections and preserved in formaldehyde; flies buzzed around another cow's head and were zapped in his early work, *A Thousand Years*. Chris Ofili provoked with the *Holy Virgin Mary*, a black Madonna made partly with elephant poo; the Chapman brothers produced mannequins of children with genitalia on their heads; and Marcus Harvey created a portrait of notorious child-killer Myra Hindley, made entirely with children's hand-prints.

The areas of Shoreditch, Hoxton and Whitechapel – where many artists lived, worked and hung out – became the epicentre of the movement and a rash of galleries moved in. Among these was White Cube, owned by one of the most important patrons of early Britart, Jay Jopling.

The exhibitions sent shockwaves around the world, as sections of society took turns to be outraged. Liberals were drawn into defending the works, the media went positively gaga promoting some of the artists like pop stars and Britart became the talk of the world. For the

10 years or so that it rode the wave of this publicity, its defining characteristics were celebrity and shock value. Damien Hirst and Tracey Emin became the inevitable celebrities – people the media knew they could sell to the mainstream.

One critic said the hugely hyped movement was the product of a 'cultural vacuum' and had become like the emperor's new clothes, which everyone was afraid to criticise for fear they'd look stupid. 'Cold, mechanical, conceptual bullshit', was how the culture minister described the nominations for the Turner Prize one year. Hirst finally admitted in 2005 that some of his own work irritated even him.

After Britart

Tracey Emin (b 1963) went on to become the most famous artist-behaving-badly. She was short-listed for the Turner Prize with an installation, *My Bed,* her unmade messy bed, strewn with blood-stained underwear and used condoms. For another installation, *Everyone I Have Ever Slept with 1963–1995,* she sewed the names of all the relevant people on a tent. She was perfect for Britart because she pandered to the public's darkest levels of voyeurism *and* their love of celebrity. When her cat went missing, people tore down the notices she put up and kept them as *objets d'art.*

But while the world was focusing on the stars, there were a lot of great artists hammering away on the fringes. A highlight of the era has to be Richard Wilson's iconic installation, *20:50* (1987). It's a room filled waist high with recycled oil, where you walk in and feel you've just been shot out into space. In his most famous work, *24 Hour Psycho,* Scottish video artist Douglas Gordon slowed Alfred Hitchcock's masterpiece down so much it was stripped of its narrative and viewed more like a moving sculpture, while Gary Hume quietly went about his work, the less-fashionable painting. Hume first came to prominence with his *Doors* series of full-size paintings of hospital doors, powerful allegorical descriptions of despair – or just perfect reproductions of doors.

Rachel Whiteread won the Turner Prize in 1993 for *House,* a concrete cast of an East End terrace dwelling that the council controversially knocked down shortly afterwards. In the same week she won £40,000 in the doubly lucrative prize for Worst British Artist of the year, an award set up by former disco funsters KLF, who out-shocked the Britartists by burning £1 million in cash in front of assembled journalists.

The biggest date on the current calendar is now the Turner Prize at the Tate Britain, won in recent years by Grayson Perry, a transvestite potter, and Jeremy Deller, a video artist who freely admits to not being able to draw.

The biggest-name British artists working today are Banksy, the anonymous street artist whose work has even made it to the Hollywood elite with his 2006 *Barely Legal* show in Los Angeles, and sculptor Anthony Gormley (who recently decorated the South Bank with his unmistakable 2.7m-high human sculptures based on himself) but who is best known for the 22m-high *Angel of the North,* beside the A1 trunk road near Gateshead in northern England.

Even Emin has gone from *enfant terrible* of the scene to pillar of the art establishment. In 2007 she was made a Royal Academician, admitting her to the true elite of British art and allowing her to exhibit six pieces at the annual Summer Exhibition. As if this wasn't enough to confirm her position, in the same year she also represented Britain at the Venice Biennale, only the second lone female ever to have done so.

CINEMA & TELEVISION

Television was born in London and is ageing well. Although locals complain about the constant dumbing down of the BBC and ever-falling standards as producers chase an ever lower common denominator, most countries would give their eye teeth to have television like that available here, from the extraordinary BBC natural history unit films to the cutting-edge comedy and drama across the channels. However, although the UK punches well above its weight in terms of presence on the international film scene, London is far from the centre of the film industry that it might be.

London on Film

Londoners are proud of their city, but few claim the city to be at the forefront of the film industry, with British film in general being massively hit and miss. Certainly, there have been some individual commercial triumphs, including recent Oscar-winner *The Queen* and the newly ripped and metrosexual James Bond sporting tight Speedos in *Casino Royale*, not to mention '90s smash hits such as *Four Weddings and a Funeral* and *Shakespeare in Love*. But there's an underlying frustration that the local film industry is not as strong as it should be, especially given the disproportionate influence of the Brits in Hollywood.

However, London is one of the most popular places to make films in the world. Recent converts have included that most die-hard of New Yorkers, Woody Allen, who has made *Match Point, Scoop* and *Cassandra's Dream* in the capital over the past few years. Other recent blockbusters shot here include *Basic Instinct 2, The Da Vinci Code* and *Batman Begins*.

Naturally, the eponymous West London neighbourhood pops up in 1999's *Notting Hill*, the Dickensian back streets of Borough feature in such polar opposites as chick-flick *Bridget Jones's Diary* and Guy Ritchie's gangster romp *Lock, Stock and Two Smoking Barrels*, while Smithfield is given a certain bleak glamour in *Closer*.

The city's combination of historic and ultramodern architecture certainly works to its advantage in this respect. Ang Lee's *Sense and Sensibility,* for example, could retreat to historic Greenwich for its wonderful parkland and neoclassical architecture. Inigo Jones' Queen's House, in particular, features in interior scenes. Merchant Ivory's costume drama *Howard's End* and the biopic *Chaplin* feature the neo-Gothic St Pancras Chambers, while the early 1980s film, *The Elephant Man,* took advantage of the moody atmosphere around the then-undeveloped Shad Thames (the site of today's Butler's Wharf).

There are some films that Londoners find heart-warming just because they feature ordinary shots of the contemporary city. *Sliding Doors* is quite fun to watch for the shots of the Underground, West London and Primrose Hill. Similarly, 2002's *28 Days Later* has amazing opening scenes of central London and Docklands lying abandoned after a monkey virus wipes out the population. Popcorn blockbuster *Mission: Impossible* features Liverpool St station, and John Landis' irrepressibly entertaining *An American Werewolf in London* finishes with a mad chase in Piccadilly Circus.

Fans often nostalgically refer back to the golden – but honestly rather brief – era of Ealing comedies, when the London-based Ealing Studios turned out a steady stream of hits. Between 1947 and 1955, when the studios were sold to the BBC, they produced enduring classics such as *Passport to Pimlico, Kind Hearts and Coronets, Whisky Galore, The Man in the White Suit, The Lavender Hill Mob* and *The Ladykillers*. This was also the time of legendary filmmakers Michael Powell and Emeric Pressburger, the men behind *The Life and Death of Colonel Blimp* and *The Red Shoes*.

Today, such halcyon days seem far distant, as the industry is stuck in a rut of romantic comedies (see Richard Curtis' horribly saccharine *Love Actually*), costume dramas (the usual adaptations of classic novels starring Helena Bonham Carter in a corset) and increasingly dire gangster pics. Producers, directors and actors complain about a lack of adventurousness in those who hold the purse strings, while film investors claim there are not enough scripts worth backing.

A system of public funding through the UK Film Council exists alongside private investment, and although in 2002 it only accounted for a minority of the £570 million spent on film in the UK, some critics object to the scheme. The *Evening Standard's* late, lamented former film critic Alexander Walker was one of those who suggested that it led to poor projects being made, simply because the money was there.

Meanwhile, well-known British actors such as Ewan McGregor, Ian McKellen, Ralph Fiennes, Jude Law, Liam Neeson, Hugh Grant, Rhys Ifans, Kristen Scott Thomas and Emily Watson spend time working abroad, as do many British directors, such as Tony Scott *(Top Gun, True Romance)*, Ridley Scott *(Bladerunner, Alien, Thelma & Louise, Gladiator)*, Anthony Minghella *(The English Patient, Cold Mountain)*, Michael Winterbottom *(The Claim)* and Sam Mendes *(American Beauty, The Road to Perdition)*.

Television

London is the home of TV; it was born and bred here, with John Logie Baird first demonstrating it in Soho to a select group of scientists, and then to the public a few years later. Perhaps more significantly, the world's first public broadcaster, the British Broadcasting Corporation (BBC), began here too and has originated some of the world's most recognised TV formats and personalities.

When it comes to televisual output, London plays with a somewhat stronger hand than in film: a huge amount of global TV content originates in Britain, from *Planet Earth* to *Who Wants to be a Millionaire*. There are five free-to-air national TV stations: BBC1, BBC2 (established 1964), ITV1 (1955), Channel 4 (1982) and Five (1997). Even though cable is now available and digital services were introduced in 1998, the BBC derives funding from a system of TV licences paid for by viewers. Ever since the BBC began broadcasts in 1932 (regularly from 1936), there's been a public service ethic driving British TV. John Reith, the first director-general of the BBC, took quite a paternalistic view of the audience, seeing the role of TV as to inform and educate as much as to entertain, and insisted on quality. There's still a hangover of all this today, although recent years have seen the BBC chase ratings to an extent that many thought was plainly embarrassing, supporting populist, prime-time rubbish over more Reithean pursuits such as documentaries, news and political debate.

A complete history of English TV is obviously not possible here, but anyone familiar with the subject will be aware of an enormously long roll call of classic series, from comedies such as *Fawlty Towers* and *Rising Damp* and cop shows such as *The Sweeney* and *The Professionals* to cult series such as *The Prisoner, The Avengers* and *Minder*; from 1970s comedies *(The Good Life)* to heritage offerings in the 1980s *(Brideshead Revisited)*; from thrillers *(Edge of Darkness)* to dramas *(The Singing Detective)* – the list could go on endlessly. However, undoubtedly, the two most famous TV serials associated with London itself are the long-running soap opera *EastEnders* and the police drama *The Bill*. Ironically, the first of these is actually filmed at the BBC studios in Elstree, Hertfordshire, although Albert Sq is said to be modelled on Fassett Sq in Dalston. *The Bill* is shot around the East End.

In recent years Britain, like elsewhere, has been in the grip of reality-TV fever. *Big Brother* and *Celebrity Big Brother* have made a huge splash, while wannabe pop stars were given the chance to be discovered and moulded in *Pop Idol*, spawning the now huge star Will Young and a few more forgettable sidekicks. Even more popular has been ITV's *I'm a Celebrity Get Me Out of Here!*, where D-list stars annually undergo humiliating and disgusting bush-tucker trials in order to win food in the Australian bush.

Comedy has always been something that Britain does particularly well, with Slough-set *The Office* and, um, Britain-set *Little Britain* now worldwide phenomena spawning US remakes. Two utter comic gems far more directly associated with London are *Nathan Barley,* the Chris Morris–penned much-needed comedic response to the Shoreditch scene and the wonderfully spot-on political satire *The Thick of It,* a fictional behind-the-scenes look at life in the Westminster village in the age of spin.

DANCE

Whether you're into contemporary, classical or crossover, London has the right moves for you. Recently in the throes of renewed *Billy Elliot* fever, thanks to the new musical, the city's up there with New York and Paris as one of the world's great dance capitals and has been the crucible of one of the most significant developments in modern choreographic history. Although it's been more than a decade since classical ballet was mixed with old-fashioned musical and contemporary dance in Matthew Bourne's all-male *Swan Lake,* that piece is seen as a watershed that catapulted dance from the back of the arts pages into the popular global mainstream.

Even today, Bourne's *Swan Lake* still tours the world, while the man himself produces newer pieces, from the Scottish-influenced *Highland Fling* to *The Car Man* (a *West Side Story*–style reworking of Bizet's *Carmen*). Having presented his own take on Tchaikovsky in *Nutcracker!,* Bourne crossed over into theatre in 2004, with his superlative *Play Without Words,* a two-part drama told solely through graceful movement. (He has also worked as a choreographer for the West End musical *Mary Poppins*.)

Other leading London-based talents have helped take the dance message to the wider world, with Rafael Bonachela scripting Kylie Minogue's Showgirl tour, and Wayne McGregor working on the latest Harry Potter film.

However, it's not just Bourne, Bonachela and McGregor in the vanguard. The Place (p313), in Euston, was where contemporary dance emerged in London in the 1960s, and it's recently been joined by Laban (p313) as a place to catch cutting-edge performances. Meanwhile, the revamped Sadler's Wells (p314) – the birthplace of English classical ballet in the 19th century – continues to stage an exciting programme of various styles from leading national ballets and international troupes, such as Pina Bausch, Twyla Tharp, Dance Theatre of Harlem and Alvin Ailey.

At Covent Garden's Royal Opera House (p316) principal ballerina Darcy Bussell bid goodbye to her adoring public in 2007 as she retired from the house's most prestigious position aged just 38. Going out at the height of her powers (her appearance in George Balanchine's *Apollo* the same year was considered by many to be her finest achievement to date) proved another canny move by the most famous English dancer since Margot Fonteyn; unlike Dame Margot, she will be remembered at her peak rather than for her long decline.

Despite a slight flirtation with newly commissioned pieces, including one with a Jimi Hendrix soundtrack, the capital's leading classical-dance troupe, the Royal Ballet, has largely been sticking to the traditional. Several back-to-back anniversaries have meant retrospectives devoted to choreographers Balanchine and Frederick Ashton, as well as to dancers Sergei Diaghilev and Dame Ninette de Valois (the latter was the ballet's founder). All the same, the Royal Ballet has made itself more accessible during this period by dropping some ticket prices to £10 (as at the National Theatre).

One troupe always worth keeping an eye out for is the innovative Rambert Dance Company. Another is that of former Royal Ballet dancers Michael Nunn and William Levitt. Having made their name, via a Channel 4 TV documentary, as the Ballet Boyz, and then the George Piper Dances, they have most recently teamed up with London-based French superstar Sylvie Guillem to perform works by acclaimed modern choreographer Russell Maliphant. Guillem, still a principal guest artist at the Royal Ballet, also reached out to London's strong South Asian dance tradition when she teamed up with contemporary choreographer and Kathak dance specialist Akram Khan.

The main London dance festival is Dance Umbrella (☎ 8741 5881; www.danceumbrella.co.uk). Running for six weeks from late September, it's one of the world's leading dance festivals of its kind. Otherwise, for the latest on what's on, check www.londondance.com. For more information on specific venues and companies, see p313.

ENVIRONMENT & PLANNING

THE LAND

Greater London comprises 1572 sq km enclosed by the M25 ring road. As well as being essential to the trade upon which London was built, the River Thames divides the city into north and south, a partition that had much more than geographical implications. The Romans designated the southern bank as a seedy London of gaming and debauchery, and for almost two millennia since, respectable and cultured folk settled on the northern side while the outcasts lived in the insalubrious south. The potential of the South Bank has only been realised in the last decade.

Although London grew from the area known as the City, it doesn't have a single focal point. Its expansion was never really planned; rather, the burgeoning city just consumed outlying settlements. Thus – as any reader of Dickens will appreciate – London today is more a patchwork of villages than a single city. Although the city can feel like a never-ending concrete jungle, there are actually huge swathes of green on its outskirts – take Richmond Park and Hampstead Heath, for example – and large parks such as Regent's and Hyde in the centre.

GREEN LONDON

The most serious environmental problem facing the centre of London, the pollution and chronic congestion caused by heavy traffic, has been partially alleviated since 2003 when the Mayor's Congestion Tax was introduced, whereby every car entering the centre had to pay £5 (now £8) for the privilege. Ken Livingstone has proven his commitment to helping the environment again and again, from introducing buses running on hydrogen fuel cells (admittedly only in their trial stages) and introducing a Lower Emissions Zone from February 2008 that sees additional charges being levied on heavy-polluting vehicles entering Greater London.

Local councils have also stepped up their efforts to be green, with Richmond council being the first to introduce higher parking fees for 'gas-guzzlers' and Hackney being the first council to introduce compulsory recycling in 2007. Recycling has been available in London for many years but mainly in the form of community bins rather than separate household ones, and the mainstream hasn't really been encouraged go green. Attitudes have changed recently and most people are doing their bit, but on the whole the UK has a pitiful record in this respect.

To look at the Thames' murky waters, you'd assume it was another pollution black spot, but below the surface, its health has improved dramatically in recent years and the river is playing an increasingly important role in recreation. By 1962 the combined impact of untreated sewage and industrial pollution had killed off virtually every sign of life in the river, but thanks to a massive clean-up it's now home to some 115 species of fish, including shad, sea lamprey and even salmon (for which special ladders have been built over the weirs). With them have come 10,000 herons, cormorants and other waterfowl that feed on the fish; even otters have been spotted on the river's upper reaches.

London boasts more parks and open spaces than any city of its size in the world – from the neatly manicured (Holland Park, St James's Park) to the semiwild (Richmond Park, Bushy Park). Between them they provide suitable habitats for a wide range of animals and birds.

The mammal you're most likely to spot on land is the grey squirrel, a North American import that has colonised every big park and decimated the indigenous red squirrel population. Hedgehogs also live here, though their numbers are dwindling, perhaps due to the increased use of slug pellets. Outside the very centre of town you're quite likely to see foxes if you go for a stroll after dark – their numbers are massively on the rise and most people either love or hate them. Richmond Park hosts badgers as well as herds of red and fallow deer. The oddest mammal yet was spotted in the capital in 2006 when a lost bottlenose whale swam up the Thames through central London. Sadly, the whale died after a long attempt to rescue her and release her back into the North Sea, and her skeleton can now be seen in the Natural History Museum (p141).

Bird-watchers, especially those keen on waterfowl, will love London. There are ducks, pelicans and the Queen's swans in St James's Park, and more ducks and beautiful, chestnut-headed great-crested grebes in Hyde Park's Serpentine. London canals are also happy hunting grounds for spotting waterfowl.

Garden birds, such as long-tailed and great tits, sparrows, robins and blackbirds, roost in all the parks, but some parks attract more interesting migrants. In Holland Park in spring you might glimpse flocks of tiny goldcrests. Kestrels nest around the Tower of London, as do the better-known ravens. The open stretches of the commons in Barnes and Wimbledon also harbour a rich assortment of birds and mammals.

Most unusual of all, brightly coloured parrots and parakeets can be seen living wild around Richmond, Kew and many other parts of Southwest London along the Thames – their origins are still debated, but they have been multiplying in recent years and seem to be able to survive in London thanks to global warming.

The London Wildlife Trust (LWT; ☎ 7261 0447; www.wildlondon.org.uk) maintains more than 50 nature reserves in the city, which offer the chance to see a range of birds and occasionally small mammals. Battersea Park Nature Reserve has several nature trails, while the Trent Country Park even boasts a Braille trail through the woodlands. Parts of Hampstead Heath have been designated a Site of Special Scientific Interest (SSSI) for their wealth of natural history.

Green fingers won't want to miss the exotic plants in the exceedingly lovely Kew Gardens (p209), while London's parks boast a variety of common or garden trees, shrubs and flowers. Many Londoners also take pride in their private gardens, which range from handkerchief-sized back yards to sprawling mini-estates, some of which open for a few days each summer through the National Gardens Scheme (NGS; ☎ 01483-211535; www.ngs.org.uk; Hatchlands Park, East Clandon, Guildford GU4 7RT). Admission usually costs £2, which goes to charity.

URBAN PLANNING & DEVELOPMENT

Central London has been considerably smartened up in recent years, and mayor Ken Livingstone is at the forefront of other bold and imaginative schemes to make the city a more pleasant place to live and visit. Olympic Games development in East London is currently seeing the concentration of efforts, and the communities living in pockets of the Lea River Valley have succumbed to the inevitable and been moved on (the area included several large Roma camps that have been there for decades).

The biggest challenge facing London is how to house its growing population without encroaching on the green belt surrounding the city. Previously run-down central areas such as Hoxton and Clerkenwell were dolled up in the 1990s with young populations moving in and converting warehouses. The repopulation of Docklands continues, but London is quickly running out of space. The mayor has taken measures to address the problem and in his London Plan he has also built in the protection of green space, although business interests are mobilising to scrap that protection and reduce the 'burden' on developers.

In what is perhaps a sign of things to come, the government is facing an inevitable conflict with environmentalists over the proposed regeneration of the Thames Gateway, the 60km on each side of the Thames from East London to the North Sea. The plan is to build 200,000 homes and provide 300,000 jobs but in an area that contains some of Britain's most valuable wildlife sites and a 25km stretch of shore that is designated as an EU high-priority special protection area.

GOVERNMENT & POLITICS

LOCAL GOVERNMENT

When 12th-century King Richard the Lionheart gave London the right to self-government in exchange for a little pocket money, supporters cheered 'Londoners shall have no king but their mayor'. That's still true for the City of London today, but Greater London, where the vast majority of the population lives and works, has had a trickier time of it.

Some form of the GLC was going about its business quietly for a few centuries, looking after local interests and acquiescently toeing the national government's line. That all changed when Labour man Ken Livingstone took over as boss of the council in the early 1980s, when Margaret Thatcher was prime minister. These two couldn't have been more different and a clash was inevitable. Livingstone campaigned for cheaper public transport in the capital and generally became a thorn in Thatcher's side. She got so fed up with him that in 1986 she abolished the GLC altogether, and London became the only major capital in the world without a self-governing authority. Fourteen years later the Labour government brought back a new version, the Greater London Assembly (GLA), and arranged elections for London's first-ever popularly elected mayor in 2000 (see boxed text, opposite).

The 25-member GLA has limited authority over transport, economic development, strategic planning, the environment, the police, fire brigades, civil defence and cultural matters. It is elected from GLA constituencies and by London as a whole. It is not a conventional opposition, but can reject the mayor's budget, form special investigation committees and hold the mayor to

---

DEATH AT HIGH TEA

London is no stranger to the grotesque – from the stabbing of Bulgarian dissident Georgi Markov on Waterloo Bridge in 1978 by a KGB agent using a poisoned umbrella to the 1982 hanging of the 'Pope's Banker' Roberto Calvi from underneath Blackfriars Bridge. However, in late 2006 the death of an almost unheard-of Russian dissident from radiation poisoning in London shocked the nation. Alexander Litvinenko was a mid-ranking officer in Russia's Federal Security Bureau (FSB) until having to flee the country in 2000 following a prison sentence for revealing the crimes of his FSB superiors. With close links to exiled Russian oligarch Boris Berezovsky, another Russian Londoner in exile, Litvinenko became a British citizen just weeks before his fateful meeting with FSB officers at the Millennium Hotel on Grosvenor Sq, Mayfair. Here, it's alleged, his tea was poisoned with a rare radioactive isotope, Polonium 210, which killed him within weeks.

Litvinenko's murder resulted in abnormally high radioactivity levels being detected throughout London and even on two British Airways planes flying the London–Moscow route. These were traced to Andrei Lugovoi, an FSB operative who now stands accused of killing Litvinenko. The British government formally requested the extradition of Andrei Lugavoi in 2007, and when it was rejected by the Russian government there followed a spate of tit-for-tat diplomacy not seen between the UK and Russia since the days of the Cold War.

RED KEN

London's first-ever popularly elected mayor is a colourful, charismatic character who has done much to improve London for tourists. As the leader of the Greater London Council (GLC) during the 1980s, 'Red Ken' – as the socialist was once popularly known – went head to head with that most conservative of prime ministers, Margaret Thatcher. He pushed a huge 'Fare's Fair' campaign to reduce the cost of public transport in London, and put a giant counter on the roof of County Hall, which gave updated unemployment figures and was clearly visible from the House of Commons. Thatcher became so infuriated with Livingstone that she scrapped the GLC altogether.

He entered Parliament as an MP and proposed many policies that seemed radical at the time, but which have since been adopted as government policy. His refusal to always toe the party line made him popular with Londoners but earned him the mistrust of the parliamentary Labour Party. He was a hate figure for the right-wing tabloids, and the *Sun* once called him 'the most odious man in Britain', and portrayed him as a freak for his love of newts (Ken's big hobby).

When Labour decided to reinstate the London council as the Greater London Assembly (GLA), popular Livingstone seemed a shoe-in for the job of mayor. However, Tony Blair was determined to halt Livingstone's election bandwagon and, shamelessly rigging the selection process against Livingstone, the Labour Party's nomination went to a Blair loyalist. Crash, bang, wallop…Livingstone resigned from the party and ran as an independent candidate, promising to lock horns with the central government whenever it came to London's best interest. He swept to victory on a tide of popular support in May 2000. Undermining Londoners' fierce independence was perhaps Tony Blair's single biggest mistake in his first term in power.

In eight years of power Ken has made transport his number-one priority, fighting tooth and nail against the government-proposed, part-privatisation of the Underground (and failing), improving bus services and introducing the bold, risky yet hugely successful congestion charge in 2003. His most important strategy is the £100 billion London Plan, a planning framework for the city over the next decade, which aims to overhaul London's use of resources and its relationship with the environment. One of its toughest and most contentious challenges is the provision of affordable housing and the mayor's plan to build 15 new skyscrapers by 2013 has been widely derided. Some say the plan will be the capital's biggest make-over since the aftermath of the Great Fire in 1666.

Despite a long-running feud with the influential right-wing London tabloid the *Evening Standard,* which has tried to smear him with charges ranging from corruption to anti-Semitism, Livingstone continues to enjoy a high level of popularity, which is rare for any elected leader in London. His readmission to a mercurial Labour Party (which quickly realised its mistake in ever taking him on as a rival) confirms that whatever take you have on London's mayor, he remains one of the most important and talented politicians of his time.

In 2008 London will go to the polls again, where Ken is likely to win a third term, meaning he'll control the capital until the Olympic year of 2012. The Conservative search for a big-name candidate to take him on has produced only Boris Johnson, an upper-class MP and media favourite. While popular for his buffoonish ways, it is hard to imagine him running City Hall. But time, as they say, will tell – and almost anything is possible in London.

public account. It currently comprises nine Conservatives, nine Labour Party members, five Liberal Democrats, two members of the Green Party and two members of the One London Group. It has its headquarters in the futuristic GLA building in Southwark, beside Tower Bridge.

The City of London has its own government in the form of the Corporation of London, headed by the Lord Mayor (note that only the City mayor gets to be Lord) and an assortment of oddly named and peculiarly dressed aldermen, beadles and sheriffs. It sits at the Guildhall. These men – and they usually *are* male – are elected by the City of London's freemen and liverymen. Though its government may appear obsolete in the 3rd millennium, the Corporation of London still owns roughly a third of the supremely wealthy 'Square Mile' and has a good record for patronage of the arts.

London is further divided into 33 widely differing boroughs (13 of which are in central London), run by democratically elected councils with significant autonomy. These deal with education and matters such as road sweeping and rubbish collection. The richest borough in terms of per capita income is Richmond in the west; the poorest is Barking in the east.

NATIONAL GOVERNMENT

London is, of course, the seat of the national government of Britain. Britain is a constitutional monarchy with no written constitution and operates under a combination of parliamentary statutes, common law (a body of legal principles based on precedents, often dating back centuries) and convention.

Parliament is made up of the monarch, the House of Commons (the lower house) and the House of Lords (the upper house). The monarch is essentially a figurehead with no real power, while the House of Commons is where the real power lies. It comprises a national assembly of 646 seats directly elected every four to five years. Each seat represents a constituency somewhere in the country. London is made up of 72 constituencies and thus has 72 representatives in the House of Commons.

The leader of the biggest party in the House of Commons is the prime minister, who appoints a cabinet of 20 or so ministers to run government departments. At the time of writing Prime Minister Gordon Brown's Labour Party held a comfortable majority of 66 MPs over the official opposition, David Cameron's Conservative Party. This majority he inherited from Tony Blair, who won the 2005 general election but then stood down as Prime Minister in June 2007. The next general election is likely to be held in 2009, although legally it could be held as late as 2010.

The Conservatives have been reinvigorated in the past few years after a decade of disarray. Their defenestration of Margaret Thatcher in 1991 tore the party to pieces and only since the arrival of Tony Blair–alike Cameron as leader in 2005 has the party regained any sense of unity. Cameron has liberalised the Tories, a political force that the British people often consider to be, in the words of one Tory grandee, 'the nasty party'. By embracing the environment, supporting single mothers and being progay, the Tories are in many ways unrecognisable compared with the 1980s collection of bigoted fat cats spearheaded by Thatcher. Critics point out, though, that despite the veneer of liberal ecofriendly fluff, the party remains utterly that of the establishment, with Cameron and much of his cabinet a product of Eton and Oxbridge.

The only other major political party in the UK is the Liberal Democrats, which currently holds just 63 seats. Despite a distinguished career and impeccable credentials, its leader Sir Ming Campbell is largely considered to have no hope of taking the party to victory due to his age (late 60s) and a perceived lack of charisma compared with the Lib Dems' previous leader, Charles Kennedy, who resigned the leadership in 2003 due to an alcohol problem.

The House of Lords has a little power but these days it's largely limited to delaying legislation – even then, it's only a question of time before it goes to the Queen to be rubber-stamped. For centuries the House of Lords consisted of some 900 'hereditary peers' (whose titles passed from one generation to the next), 25 Church of England bishops and 12 Law Lords (who also act as Britain's highest court). But Tony Blair targeted the Lords with the same zeal with which the mayor went for the Trafalgar Sq pigeons – the similarities possibly end there – and most of the hereditary peers were shuffled out in 1999. Ninety-two of them have been allowed to stay, for the time being. A new system of 'life peerage' was introduced which, critics say, allowed the prime minister to hand out plum jobs to loyal MPs who wouldn't have to go through the bother of getting elected in the future. In the second stage of Lords reform (for which there is no time frame), elected peers will enter the upper house for the first time and hereditary peers will be swept away altogether.

MEDIA

London is in the eye of the British media, an industry comprising some of the best and worst of the world's TV, radio and print media.

NEWSPAPERS

The main London newspaper is the fairly right-wing *Evening Standard,* a tabloid that comes out in early and late editions throughout the day. Foodies should check out the restaurant reviews of London's most influential critic, Fay Maschler, while style aficionados shouldn't miss Friday's *ES* magazine, a useful guide to the city's cutting edge. *Metro Life* is a useful listings supplement on Thursday.

Three free newspapers distributed at tube stations and on the streets wherever commuters can be stopped and a paper shoved in their face also vie for the attentions of Londoners – the *Evening Standard's* 'lite' version, *London Lite,* which is just a free, boiled-down version of the *Evening Standard*; another *Evening Standard* stable mate *Metro*; and the *London Paper,* a Murdoch-owned competitor. All three are lightweight, easy-to-digest reads with a firm focus on celebrity and can be found littering buses or tube carriages all over London.

National newspapers in England are almost always financially independent of any political party, although their political leanings are easily discerned. Rupert Murdoch is the most influential man in British media and his News Corp owns the *Sun,* the *News of the World,* the *Times* and the *Sunday Times.* The industry is self-regulating, having set up the Press Complaints Commission (PCC) in 1991 to handle public grievances, although many complain that the PCC is unable to really maintain any level of discipline among the unruly tabloids, being a 'toothless guard dog'.

There are many national daily newspapers, and competition for readers is incredibly stiff; although some papers are printed outside the capital, they are all pretty London-centric. There are two broad categories of newspapers, most commonly distinguished as broadsheets (or 'qualities') and tabloids, although the distinction is becoming more about content than physical size as most of the major broadsheets are now published in a smaller, easier to use tabloid size.

Readers of the broadsheets are extremely loyal to their paper and rarely switch from one to another. The right-wing *Daily Telegraph* is sometimes considered old-fogeyish, but nonetheless the writing and world coverage are very good. The *Times* is traditionally the newspaper of record and supports the government of the day; it's particularly good for sports. On the left side of the political spectrum, the *Guardian* features lively writing and an extremely progressive agenda, is very strong in its coverage of the arts and has some excellent supplements, particularly Monday's *Media Guardian,* a bible for anyone in the industry. It's also the best paper for white-collar job seeking. Politically correct, the *Independent* has single-issue front pages and rejoices in highlighting stories or issues that other papers have ignored. Its writing can be excellent and it's the paper of choice for nonpolitically aligned centrists and free thinkers.

The Sunday papers are as important as Sunday mornings in London. Most dailies have Sunday stable mates and predictably the tabloids have bumper editions of trashy gossip, star-struck adulation, fashion extras and mean-spirited diatribes directed at whomever they've decided to hunt for sport on that particular weekend. The qualities have so many sections and supplements that two hands are required to carry even one from the shop. The *Observer,* established in 1791, is the oldest Sunday paper and sister of the *Guardian;* there's a brilliant *Sports* supplement with the first issue of the month. Even people who normally only buy broadsheets sometimes slip a copy of the best-selling *News of the World* (sister paper to the *Sun*) under their arm for some Sunday light relief.

See p396 for a list of the major daily and Sunday newspapers.

MAGAZINES

There is an astonishing range of magazines published and consumed here, from celebrity gossip to political heavyweights. Lads' monthlies such as *FHM, Loaded* and *Maxim* powered the growth of consumer magazines in the 1990s, as new readers tucked into a regular diet of babes, irreverence and blokeishness.

London loves celebrities (especially when they are overweight, underweight or out of control) and *Heat, Closer* and *Grazia* are the most popular purveyors of the genre. US import *Glamour* is the queen of the women's glossies, having toppled traditional favourite *Cosmopolitan,* which is beginning to look a little wrinkled in comparison with its younger, funkier rival – maybe it's time for a nip and tuck. *Marie Claire, Elle* and *Vogue* are regarded as the thinking woman's glossies. A slew of style magazines are published here – *i-D, Dazed & Confused* and *Vice* – and all maintain a loyal following.

Political magazines are particularly strong in London. The satirical *Private Eye* (see the boxed text, p52) has no political bias and takes the Mickey out of everyone. You can keep in touch with what's happening internationally with the *Week,* an excellent round-up of the British and foreign press and the excellent *Economist* cannot be beaten for international political and business analysis.

Time Out is the listings guide *par excellence* and great for taking the city's pulse with strong arts coverage while the *Big Issue,* sold on the streets by the homeless, is not just an honourable project but a damned fine read. London is a publishing hub for magazines and produces hundreds of internationally renowned publications specialising in music, visual arts, literature, sport, architecture and so on.

See p396 for a list of the city's main magazines.

PRIVATE EYE LASHES ESTABLISHMENT

'Well at least you won your war' says a grumpy-looking Queen Elizabeth as she addresses Margaret Thatcher in a royal line up having just passed Tony Blair. This is a typical cover of London's best-known satirical magazine, *Private Eye,* a barometer of how well you know what's going on politically and culturally in the country.

It was founded in 1961 by a group of clever clogs that included the late comedian and writer Peter Cook and still retains the low-tech, cut-and-paste charm of the original. It specialises in gossip mongering about the misdeeds of public figures and in the giddy lampooning of anyone who takes themselves too seriously. There are lots of running jokes (the Queen is always referred to as Brenda, for example, Gordon Brown as Gordon Broon), wicked cartoons and regular features such as an editorial from Lord Gnome, a composite of media magnates. There's also a serious investigative side to the mag and its reports have contributed to the downfall of several high-fliers including Jeffrey Archer and Robert Maxwell.

But that it still exists at all is astonishing. It has regularly been sued by its targets and only remains afloat thanks to the charity of its readers. Its future is looking brighter these days with circulation above 600,000 and at its highest level in a decade. *Private Eye* is now far and away the most popular current affairs magazine in the land. Essential reading, even if you don't follow much more than the cartoons.

NEW MEDIA

There's a thriving alternative media scene catering to the many who feel marginalised by the mainstream media, much of which still covers global protests by describing the hairstyles of the 'ecowarriors'. Some sites worth checking out include the outstanding and original Urban 75 (www .urban75.com), the global network of alternative news at Indymedia (http://uk.indymedia.org), the weekly activists' newsletter from SchNews (www.schnews.org.uk), London-centric blog Londonist (www.londonist .com) and the video activists' Undercurrents (www.undercurrents.org).

Email magazines have taken off here in a big way, largely because they're so good. Fridaycities London (www.fridaytowers.com/tft) is a well-written and exceedingly cheeky weekly mag covering news, culture and current affairs. Online gossip sites have also gained notoriety in recent years by knocking spin on its arse and breaking some big stories about celebrities misbehaving. Check out Popbitch (www.popbitch.com) and the satirical technology newsletter Need to Know (www.ntk.net).

BROADCASTING

The BBC is one of the greatest broadcasting corporations in the world and one of the standard bearers of radio and TV journalism and programming (see p178). Its independence frequently irks the establishment and it incurred the very significant wrath of the British Government in 2003 because of its courageous probing of the events leading to the invasion of Iraq. When BBC journalist Andrew Gilligan alleged that Tony Blair's then press secretary Alistair Campbell had 'sexed up' a dossier of evidence against the Iraqi regime in order to generate public support for going to war, there was a huge outcry and mutual recriminations between Westminster and White City began. The country's chief weapons expert, Dr David Kelly, committed suicide after being named by the government as the source of the BBC's report, and when the government-appointed Hutton inquiry came down on the BBC as the wrongdoers, almost everybody in the media dismissed it as a whitewash. The BBC's Director General resigned the same day and, chastened, the BBC has since been taking a far less controversial line when it comes to reporting on the government. Just four years later and the corporation found itself in serious trouble again, when a fly-on-the-wall documentary about the Queen purported to show Her Maj storming out of a photoshoot with Annie Liebowitz after the veteran American photographer asked her to remove her tiara. However, it transpired that the footage of the queen 'storming out' was in fact her entrance to the photo shoot. With egg on its face, the BBC faced a devastating backlash from the public and the rest of the media, and despite an abject apology from Director General Mark Thompson, 2007 was definitely a new low for faith in the corporation.

New media ownership laws introduced in 2003 paved the way for major newspaper proprietors to own British terrestrial TV channels, namely Channel Five and ITV.

Britain still turns out some of the world's best TV programmes, padding out the decent home-grown output with American imports, Australian soaps, inept sitcoms and trashy chat and game shows of its own. There are five regular TV channels. BBC1 and BBC2 are publicly funded by a TV licensing system and, like BBC radio stations, don't carry advertising; ITV, Channel 4 and Channel Five are commercial channels and do. These regular channels are now competing with the satellite channels of Rupert Murdoch's BSkyB – which offers a variety of channels with less-than-inspiring programmes – and assorted cable channels.

Many listeners and viewers feel that the investment in new technology is damaging to the core channels and that the BBC is spreading itself too thinly, trying to chase ratings and compete with the commercial channels rather than concentrating on its public-service responsibilities. The entire country is gradually switching over to digital TV, and analogue broadcasting will end by 2012.

The BBC broadcasts several radio stations, including BBC 1, 2, 3, 4, 5, 6 and 7 catering to young, mature, classical, intellectual, talkback, mixed and comedy/drama audiences respectively. XFM is your best chance of hearing interesting music these days. In 2007 the government announced Channel 4 was to be awarded a licence to broadcast 10 more national digital radio channels, a huge shake-up for an industry in need of winning back loyal audiences.

FASHION

London has weathered a tough few years that saw its status as an international fashion centre drop, but the city is now back at the heart of the fashion universe boasting a new firmament of young stars who have caught the collective eye of the fashion pack.

Giles Deacon is the undisputed figurehead for the new London and with his witty designs and eclectic references the St Martins graduate has taken London by storm with his own label Giles. Alongside Deacon are other Brit stars with a buzz around them such as Jonathan Saunders, Christopher Kane and Greek-Austrian import Marios Schwab who shows in London and attended the hallowed St Martins as well. Nu-rave darling Gareth Pugh is also someone to look out for, another St Martins alumnus (can you see a pattern emerging? – see the boxed text, below) who has taken the underground club fashions of Shoreditch and transposed them to the shop floor, even having one Anna Wintour in the audience of his 2006 London show. Even New York golden boy Marc Jacobs showed his spring 2007 Marc by Marc Jacobs collection at London fashion week to celebrate the opening of his Mayfair boutique, bringing a much-needed injection of international glamour to the capital's famously edgy fashion week.

The influence of London's designers continues to spread well beyond the capital. The 'British Fashion Pack' still work at, or run, the major Continental fashion houses such as Chanel, Givenchy and Chloe. Meanwhile, regardless of whether they send models down the catwalks here, designers such as Alexander McQueen retain design studios in London, and erstwhile defectors to foreign catwalks such as Luella Bartley and Matthew Williamson have returned to London to show their collections.

London has always been about eccentricity when compared with the classic feel of the major Parisian and Milanese houses, or the cool street-cred of New York designers. Nobody summed up that spirit better than Isabella Blow, the legendary stylist who discovered – among many

ST MARTINS

Most of the stars of the British fashion industry have passed through the rather shabby doors of St Martins on Charing Cross Rd, the world's most famous fashion college. Founded in 1854, Central St Martins School of Art & Design – to give its rather cumbersome and correct title – began life as a place where cultured young people went to learn to draw and paint. In the 1940s a fashion course was created and within a few decades aspiring designers from around the world were scrambling to get in. Courses are more than 100 times oversubscribed these days and the college has faced some criticism for admitting names over talent (a famous Beatles' daughter, to name just one). St Martins graduate shows – for which Stella had friends Naomi Campbell and Kate Moss model – are one of the highlights of the fashion calendar and are *always* shocking, making huge statements, be they good, bad or ridiculous.

The less-conspicuous Royal College of Art only takes postgraduates and its fashion course is just as old and almost as successful as St Martins. Its alumni are said to provide the backbone of some of the world's most prestigious fashion houses.

others – Alexander McQueen, Stella Tennant and Sophie Dahl during her career at *Vogue* and *Tatler*. Blow sadly committed suicide in 2007 and although she wasn't widely known outside of the fashion world, her tragic loss was deeply felt in the fashion industry of the city she worked in. Never seen in public without an extraordinary Philip Treacy hat, Blow's sheer force of personality alone was a great generator of enthusiasm and excitement about London's changing fashion fates and the scene will be far less interesting without her.

An interesting trend that has come out of London over the past couple of years is the celebrity lines being sold in bargain chains. Karl Lagerfeld and Stella McCartney have designed lines for H&M, Kate Moss for Top Shop and Lily Allen for New Look, each one generating huge excitement and – in the case of Kate Moss's critically maligned collection – a virtual stampede from shoppers.

The British fashion industry has always been more on the edge of younger, directional stuff, and never really established that very polished 'Gucci Slick'; the London equivalent is the bespoke men's tailoring of Savile Row. London has no history of real couture like Paris or Milan, where tastes in styles and fabrics are much more classic and refined. The market also shapes British fashion to a large extent; customers here are more likely to spend £100 on a few different bargains – hence the boom in outlet malls – while their sisters in Paris and Italy will blow the lot on one piece, which they'll wear regularly and well.

So London fashion has always been about street wear and 'wow', with a few old reliables keeping the frame in place and mingling with hot new designers who are often unpolished through lack of experience, but bursting with talent and creativity. As a result London is definitely exciting on a global scale and nobody with an interest in street fashion will be disappointed by what they find here.

LANGUAGE

The English language is the country's greatest contribution to the modern world. It is an astonishingly rich language containing an estimated 600,000 uninflected words (compared with, for example, Indonesian's or Malay's 60,000). It's actually a magpie tongue – just as England plundered treasure for its museums, so too the English language dipped into the world's vocabulary, even when it already had several words of the same meaning. Dr Johnson, compiler of the first English dictionary, tried to have the language protected from foreign imports (possibly to reduce his own workload) but failed. As far as English goes, all foreigners are welcome.

English-speakers are spoilt for choice when they go looking for descriptive words such as nouns and adjectives, as you'll discover pretty quickly (fast, swiftly, speedily, rapidly, promptly) by looking in a thesaurus. Some 50 years ago linguists came up with Basic English, a stripped down version with a vocabulary of 850 words, which was all one needed to say just about anything. But where's the fun in that? Shakespeare himself is said to have contributed more than 2000 words, along with hundreds of common idioms such as poisoned chalice, one fell swoop, cold comfort and cruel to be kind.

Be grateful if English is your mother tongue because it's a bitch to learn, and has possibly the most illogical and eccentric approach to spelling and pronunciation of any language. Take the different pronunciation of rough, cough, through, though and bough. Attempts to rationalise English spelling are passionately resisted by people who see themselves as the guardians of proper English and rail against the American decision to drop the 'u' from words such as colour and glamour.

In terms of accent, Standard English or Received Pronunciation (RP) centres on London and, traditionally, was perceived to be that spoken by the upper classes and those educated at public schools. It is by no means the easiest form to understand; in fact, sometimes it's near impossible ('oh, eye nare' apparently means 'yes, I know'). Those 'what talk posh' despair at the perceived butchering of their

LONDON'S LANGUAGES

These days you'll encounter a veritable Babel of some 300 languages being spoken in London, and there are pockets of the capital where English is effectively the second language. Head to Southall if you want to see train station signs in Hindi, head to Gerrard St in Soho for telephone boxes with Chinese instructions, Golders Green or Stamford Hill for shop signs in Hebrew and Yiddish and Kingsland Rd for *everything* written in Turkish.

language by most ordinary Londoners, who speak what's come to be known as 'Estuary English', so called because it's a sort of subcockney that spread along the estuary in postwar London. And so a common language divides the city. Even the Queen, claim Australian linguistic researchers, has allowed elements of Estuary pronunciation to sully her clipped RP.

The BBC is considered the arbitrator on the issue, and by comparing the contrived – and frankly hilarious – tone of old newsreels from WWII with today's bulletins, it's obvious that Standard English has gone from posh to a more neutral middle register.

Some say that Estuary English – which can now be heard within a 100-mile radius of the capital – is quickly becoming the standard. Its chief features, according to Stephen Burgen in Lonely Planet's *British phrasebook,* are: rising inflection; constant use of 'innit'; a glottal 'T', rendering the double 'T' in butter almost silent and making 'alright' sound like 'orwhy'; and, in general, a slack-jawed, floppy-tongued way of speaking that knocks the corners off consonants and lets the vowels whine to themselves. The lack of speech rhythm that can result from blowing away your consonants is made good by the insertion of copious quantities of 'fucks' and 'fucking', whose consonants are always given the full nine yards. In London it's not rare to hear people whose speech is so dependent on the word 'fuck' they are virtually dumbstruck without it.

But like just about everything in London, the language is constantly changing, absorbing new influences, producing new slang and altering the meaning of words. The city's ethnic communities are only beginning to have an influence and many young Londoners these days are mimicking Caribbean expressions and what they perceive to be hip-hop speak from black urban America.

As England has absorbed wave after wave of immigrants, so too will the insatiable English language continue to take in all comers. Meanwhile, as class distinctions exist, the linguistic battle for London will rage on.

BACKGROUND LANGUAGE

BLUELIST[1] (blu,list) *v.*
to recommend a travel experience.
What's your recommendation? www.lonelyplanet.com/bluelist

NEIGHBOURHOODS

top picks

- **Tower of London** (p119)
  Historic fortress and home to the Crown Jewels.
- **St Paul's Cathedral** (p109)
  Wren's masterpiece soars with its incredible dome.
- **Westminster Abbey** (p99)
  Impressive and iconic, with a fascinating royal history.
- **Tate Modern** (p129)
  Join the crowds digesting this fantastic collection.
- **National Gallery** (p75)
  Superb national art collection that's one of Europe's best.
- **British Museum** (p89)
  A truly great (and controversial) museum collection.
- **Shakespeare's Globe** (p130)
  See the bard performed as the Elizabethans saw it.
- **Hampton Court Palace** (p211)
  The capital's greatest Tudor palace opens its doors daily.
- **British Airways London Eye** (p125)
  Take a 'flight' on the iconic Eye for unbeatable city views.
- **Hampstead Heath** (p170)
  Escape to hills with wonderful open spaces and great views.

NEIGHBOURHOODS

London is a tough city to divide, with its multitudinous villages, divergent councils, ancient parishes and haphazard postcodes, none of which take into account the borders of any of the others.

'much of London's charm rests in what you'll discover when you leave the beaten track and explore on your own'

The centre of the city is the commercial West End, with its kernel Soho and Covent Garden surrounded by academic Bloomsbury, bohemian Fitzrovia, chic Marylebone, superrich Mayfair, royal St James's and the political village of Westminster. Here you'll find much of the best shopping, eating and entertainment options in London, as well as most of the other visitors to the city.

The South Bank, facing the West End and the City across the Thames, serves up theatre, art, film and music, and features two of London's most iconic modern sights, Tate Modern and the London Eye, as well as the wonderful Borough Market.

The wealthy stretch of neighbourhoods from Hyde Park to Chelsea includes superexclusive Belgravia, shopping mecca Knightsbridge, the various guises of exceptionally posh Kensington and the large village of Chelsea, famed for the King's Rd. No visit to London is complete without checking out South Ken's museums, visiting Harrods and Harvey Nicks in Knightsbridge, or wandering the magnificent open spaces of Hyde Park.

To the east of the West End lie both the City (once the ancient Roman walled city, now the financial hub of London) and the once shabby neighbourhoods of Clerkenwell, Shoreditch and Spitalfields, now London's most creative and exciting districts. Here you'll find supercool Hoxton Sq with its clubs and bars, Spitalfields Market and fantastic Brick Lane, longtime curry hub of Banglatown and now one of the best clothes-shopping areas in London.

Further east lie the East End and Docklands: the East End is 'real' London, a multiethnic yet strangely traditional stretch of the city that's home of the famous cockney. The East End looks set to be transformed in the coming years as the London 2012 Olympics will be held in the valley of the River Lea in and around Stratford at the East End's furthest edge. Docklands is another, albeit government- and financial sector–driven, example of urban renewal – now seriously rivalling the City as the home of the capital's money men and London's tallest skyscrapers. The future belongs to the east due not only to the Olympics, but also to the Thames Gateway, a huge development of the Thames estuary.

North London is a hilly collection of charming villages, which often seem to exist as worlds within themselves, such as old money Hampstead and Highgate, celebrity-filled Primrose Hill, fashionable Islington, hippy Stoke Newington and well-healed Crouch End. In between are urban centres such as Finchley Rd, Camden Town, Holloway and Finsbury Park.

West London is grand, moneyed and home to some of London's most traditional must-sees including Buckingham Palace and the Houses of Parliament and gems such as Kensington Palace. West London, too, has its cooler side in Notting Hill and Portobello Rd, with its great street market, superb shopping and many of the city's better pubs and bars.

South of the river, Greenwich enchants with its huge historic importance as a centre of maritime activity, and, of course, time. Neighbouring Southeast London areas of Deptford, New Cross and Woolwich are showing signs of becoming South London's long-awaited answer to Shoreditch.

Vast, residential South London has multiple flavours, from the leafy Blackheath, Clapham, Putney and Richmond to the edgier, rougher likes of Brixton, Kennington and Vauxhall.

Southwest London includes such well-known urban villages as Putney, Barnes, Richmond, Wimbledon and Kew that between them attract huge visitor numbers for the wonderful botanical gardens, the tennis and the almost perfectly preserved tudor palace of Henry VIII at Hampton Court.

London takes years to get to know and even Londoners never entirely agree on what to call certain areas – so take things easily and always have a good map to hand – although much of London's charm rests in what you'll discover when you leave the beaten track and explore on your own.

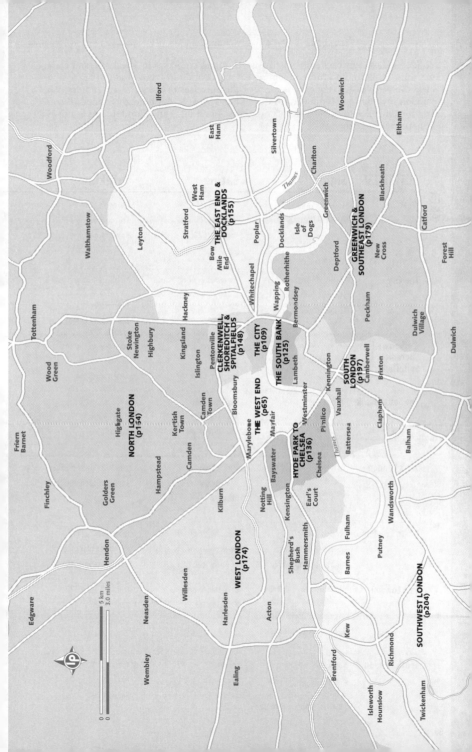

ITINERARY BUILDER

London is best approached in small, easy-to-digest chunks – its sheer size and variety of things to see and do (not to mention eat, drink and buy) may result in heart failure or at the very least severe exhaustion. For the purposes of our Itinerary Builder, West London includes our Hyde Park to Chelsea and West London neighbourhoods. South London includes the Greenwich & Southeast London, South London and Southwest London neighbourhoods.

ACTIVITIES	Sights	Eating	Drinking
West End	National Gallery (p75) National Portrait Gallery (p76) Sir John Soane's Museum (p87)	Gay Hussar (p239) Busaba Eathai (p245) Portrait (p240)	Gordon's Wine Bar (p280) French House (p278) Seven Stars (p280)
The City	Tower of London (p119) St Paul's Cathedral (p109) Temple Church (p113)	Paternoster Chop House (p248) Place Below (p249) Sweeting's (p248)	Ye Olde Cheshire Cheese (p282) Dickens Inn (p288) Jamaica Wine House (p282)
Clerkenwell, Shoreditch & Spitalfields	Geffrye Museum (p151) Dennis Severs' House (p152)	St John (p255) Moro (p255) Bacchus (p257)	Foundry (p285) George & Dragon (p286) Jerusalem Tavern (p285)
The South Bank	Tate Modern (p129) British Airways London Eye (p125) Southwark Cathedral (p131)	Skylon (p249) Anchor & Hope (p249) Blue Print Café (p250)	George Inn (p283) King's Arms (p283) Baltic (p282)
West London	Victoria & Albert Museum (p139) Kensington Place (p267) Leighton House (p176)	Tom Aikens (p252) Daquise (p253) Olivo (p254)	Windsor Castle (p292) Earl of Lonsdale (p292)
North London	London Zoo (p165) Hampstead Heath (p170) Highgate Cemetery (p170)	Manna (p262) Duke of Cambridge (p264) La Gaffe (p264)	Hollybush (p289) Elk in the Woods (p290) Edinboro Castle (p289)
East London	V&A Museum of Childhood (p158) Museum in Docklands (p161) Ragged School Museum (p159)	Café Spice Namaste (p260) Wapping Food (p261)	Bistrotheque (p287) Prospect of Whitby (p288) Grapes (p288)
South London	Royal Observatory (p181) Hampton Court Palace (p211) Imperial War Museum (p197)	Inside (p270) Glasshouse (p274) Lobster Pot (p272)	Trafalgar Tavern (p293) Barmy Arms (p296) So.uk (p294)

HOW TO USE THIS TABLE

The table below allows you to plan a day's worth of activities in any area of the city. Simply select which area you wish to explore, and then mix and match from the corresponding listings to build your day. The first item in each cell represents a well-known highlight of the area, while the other items are more off-the-beaten-track gems.

Shopping	Entertainment	Nightlife
Selfridges (p220)	Royal Opera House (p316)	End (p300)
Liberty (p220)	Curzon Soho (p315)	Madame Jo's (p301)
Habitat (p223)	Donmar Warehouse (p319)	Bar Rumba (p299)
Leadenhall Market (p233)	Barbican (p312)	
	Rhythm Factory (p309)	
Hoxton Boutique (p227)	Sadler's Wells (p314)	Fabric (p300)
Tatty Devine (p229)	93 Feet East (p298)	333 (p298)
Labour & Wait (p228)		
Konditioner & Cook (p226)	BFI Southbank (p314)	Ministry of Sound (p302)
Cockfighter of Bermondsey (p225)	National Theatre (p317)	
Black + Blum (p226)		
Harvey Nichols (p226)	Royal Albert Hall (p312)	Neighbourhood (p302)
Portobello Road market (p232)	Electric Cinema (p315)	Pacha (p302)
Fortnum & Mason (p219)	Notting Hill Coronet (p315)	Notting Hill Arts Club (p302)
Camden Market (p232)	Hampstead Heath Ponds (p325)	Cross (p300)
Housmans (p229)	Everyman Hampstead (p315)	Egg (p300)
Camden Passage (p233)	Almeida Theatre (p319)	Koko (p301)
Broadway Market (p229)	Arcola Theatre (p319)	Bethnal Green Working Men's Club (p299)
Fabrications (p229)	Whitechapel Art Gallery (p155)	Rhythm Factory (p309)
Burberry Factory Shop (p229)		Joiners Arms (p335)
Emporium (p234)	Ritzy (p316)	Fridge (p301)
Flying Duck Enterprises (p234)	Battersea Arts Centre (p319)	Carling Academy Brixton (p308)
Joy (p234)	Clapham Picture House (p314)	Dogstar (p300)

CENTRAL LONDON

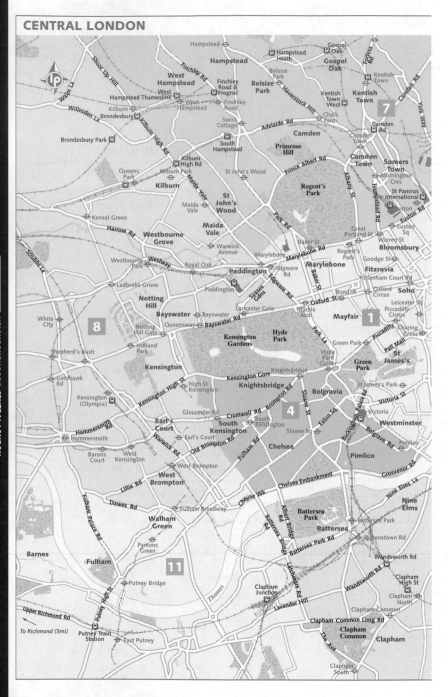

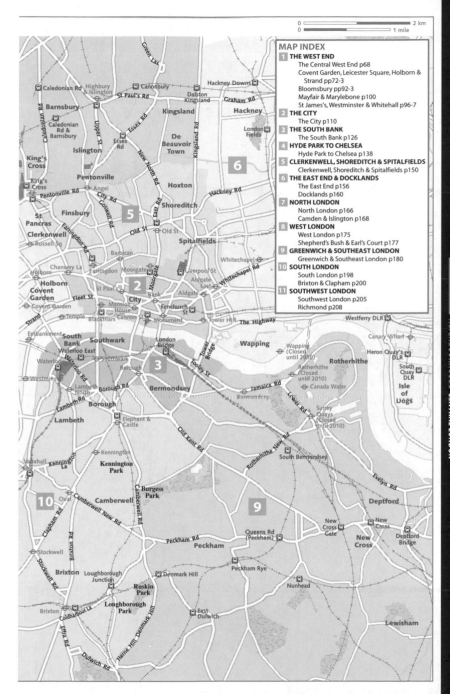

0 ————— 2 km
0 ————— 1 mile

NEIGHBOURHOODS CENTRAL LONDON

GREATER LONDON

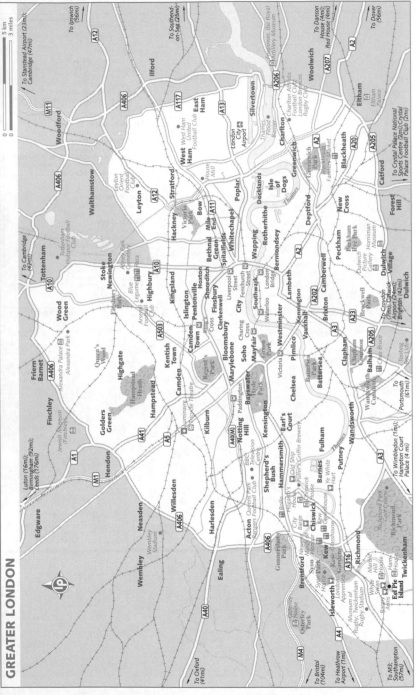

THE WEST END

Eating p237; Drinking p278; Shopping p216; Sleeping p342

London has always turned people on. Samuel Johnson raved about the city's 'wonderful immensity', and Henry James famously claimed that for him the British capital offered 'the most possible form of life'. Much of the complexity, chaos and vivacity that they found so enticing is centred on the West End, London's physical, cultural and social heart and where, whether you are a first-time visitor, regular or resident, you'll be gawping, rushing or strolling much of the time. The West End is a vague term (any Londoner you meet will give you their own take on which neighbourhoods it does and doesn't include), and its component areas are often startlingly unlike one another. Londoners may complain about the notorious crowds in the West End, but most find it irresistible. It's monumental and majestic, packed with sights and splattered with a gritty urbanity.

At its centre is Soho (below), famed for its history and loved for its rampant nightlife and excellent restaurants and bars. The nearby leafy area of Bloomsbury hides the British Museum (p89) and counters Soho's sauciness with its high-brow reputation – this is where university campuses abound and where Virginia Woolf and her posse lived and loved. Shoppers and tourists flock to Covent Garden (p71) for its street performers, boutiques and busy theatres. Aromatic Chinatown (p67) oozes authentic culture but its restaurants need careful choosing, while cinema-central and tourist-trap Leicester Sq (p86) clogs up with tourists, weekend inebriates and discount-ticket touts. Holborn & The Strand is where London's legal business gets sorted out and the city starts to dip its toes into the River Thames.

Piccadilly Circus (p67) flashes its illuminated adverts and even though it's busy with traffic, shoppers and tourists, most Londoners can't help but love it. Magnificent Trafalgar Sq (p74) is home to celebrations, protests and the city's best galleries, while Westminster (p99), Britain's political heart, is where many important decisions are made before breakfast, yet Westminster Abbey offers a calming influence. Soothing St James's Park (p95) leads to Buckingham Palace (p94), a place that needs no introduction, though it's safe to say that you won't find many Londoners gawping through its gates. If you fancy seeing an area of the West End that isn't heaving with human and vehicle traffic, stroll around the aristocratic neighbourhoods of Mayfair and St James's (p93), or try Marylebone (p105), a real London 'village' with a quaint High Street that's stacked with independent shops and small (but posh) eateries.

The best way to get to know the West End, and indeed the whole of London, is on foot. Most sights are within walking distance from one another, though if it gets too much, you're best resting your feet on a bus. While the tube will take you to most sights, sometimes the distances between two areas (eg Covent Garden and Leicester Sq or Piccadilly) are faster walked. Do arm yourself with an Oyster card (see p390) if you intend to use public transport at all, otherwise you may have to come up with a small fortune to cover the cost of a couple of tube rides.

top picks

THE WEST END

- British Museum (p89)
- National Gallery (p75)
- National Portrait Gallery (p76)
- Somerset House (p86)
- Trafalgar Square (p74)

SOHO & CHINATOWN

Even though Soho doesn't have a single 'proper' sight, it's still one of London's most popular hangouts thanks to the contagious energy it exudes. Soho's name is a hunting cry from Tudor times: the neighbourhood was the aristocratic hunting ground during the reign of Henry VIII. Its privileged status was knocked down considerably when the homeless victims of the Great Fire moved here, followed by many waves of immigrants, which gave Soho its infamous anarchic, bad-boy image that it still retains (though in a much diluted form). It's home to a 5000-strong community, the traditional heart of London's gay scene, numerous media companies, a red-light district, shops, restaurants, theatres, boozers, nightclubs and, of course, tourists, who can easily take part in the action.

THE WEST END OVERVIEW

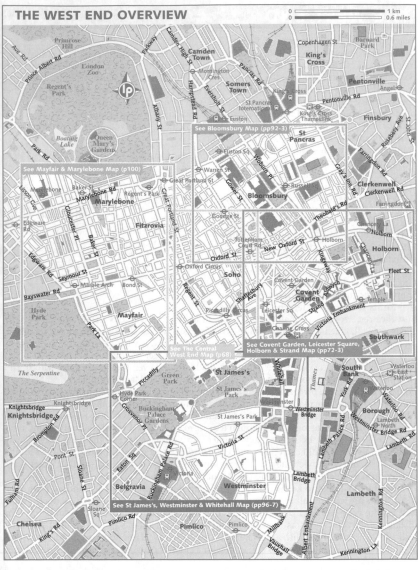

Soho is besieged by the four Circuses – Oxford, Piccadilly, Cambridge and St Giles's. Wardour St divides Soho neatly in two halves; high Soho to the east, and low or West Soho opposite. Old Compton St is the de facto main High Street and the gayest street in London. The West End's only fruit 'n' veg market is on atmospheric Berwick St. The epicentre of 1960s fashion, Carnaby and Newburgh Sts, have recovered from a decade of tourist tack

shops and are home to some of Soho's hippest shopping once again.

SOHO SQUARE & AROUND Map p68

At Soho's northern end, leafy Soho Sq is the area's back garden. This is where people come to laze in the sun on spring and summer days, and where office workers have their lunch or gather for a picnic. It was laid out in 1681, and originally named King's Sq, which is why the statue of Charles II stands in the northern part of the square. In the centre is a tiny mock-Tudor-style house – the gardener's shed – whose lift was a passage to underground shelters. Apart from being a relaxing green space, Soho Sq (along with the rest of Soho) is media central: 20th Century Fox and the British Board of Film Classification have their offices here.

Heading south of Soho Sq, down Dean Street, you'll come upon number 28, the place where Karl Marx and his family lived from 1851 to 1856. Marx, his wife Jenny and their four children lived in extreme poverty, without a toilet or running water, and three of their children died of pneumonia in this flat. While the father of communism spent his days researching *Das Kapital* in the British Museum, his main sources of income were money from writing articles for newspapers and financial help from his friend and colleague Friedrich Engels. The Marx family were eventually saved by a huge inheritance left to them by Mrs Marx' family, after which they upped sticks and moved to the more salubrious surroundings of Primrose Hill. Today it's a lively street lined with shops, bars and many other consumer outlets that no doubt would have given Marx indigestion.

Seducer and heart-breaker Casanova and opium-addicted writer Thomas de Quincey lived on Greek Street, whereas the parallel Frith Street (number 20) housed Mozart for a year from 1764.

CHINATOWN Map p68

Immediately north of Leicester Sq – but a world away in atmosphere – are Lisle and Gerrard Sts, the focal point for London's Chinese community. Although not as big as Chinatowns in many other cities – it's just two streets really – this is a lively quarter with fake oriental gates, Chinese street signs, red lanterns, many, many restaurants and great Asian supermarkets. London's original Chinatown was further east, near Limehouse, but it was moved here after heavy bombardments in WWII. To see it at its effervescent best, time your visit with Chinese New Year in late January/early February (see p191). Do be aware that the quality of food here varies enormously – it pays to get recommendations as many places are mediocre establishments aimed squarely at the tourist market. Try Jen Café (p243) or New World (p239).

PICCADILLY CIRCUS Map p68
⊖ Piccadilly Circus

Together with Big Ben and Trafalgar Sq, this is postcard London. And despite the stifling crowds and racing midday traffic, the flashing ads and buzzing liveliness of Piccadilly Circus always make it exciting to be in London. The circus looks its best at night, when the flashing advertisement panels really shine against the dark sky.

Designed by John Nash in the 1820s, the hub was named after the street Piccadilly, which earned its name in the 17th century from the stiff collars (picadils) that were the sartorial staple of the time (and were the making of a nearby tailor's fortune). At the centre of the circus is the famous lead statue, the Angel of Christian Charity, dedicated to the philanthropist and child-labour abolitionist Lord Shaftesbury, and derided when unveiled in 1893, sending the sculptor into early retirement. The sculpture was at first cast in gold, but it was later replaced by the present-day one. Down the years the angel has been mistaken for Eros, the God of Love, and the misnomer has stuck (you'll even see signs for 'Eros' from the Underground). It's a handy meeting place for tourists, though if you don't like the crowds, meet at the charging Horses of Helios statue at the edge of Piccadilly and Haymarket – apparently a much cooler place to convene.

John Nash had originally designed Regent St and Piccadilly to be the two most elegant streets in town (see Regent Street, p70), but curbed by city planners, Nash couldn't realise his dream to the full. In the many years since his noble plans, Piccadilly Circus has become swamped with tourists, with streets such as Coventry St flogging astronomically priced cheap tat at unsuspecting visitors. Coventry St leads to Leicester Sq, while Shaftesbury Ave takes you to the heart of the West End's theatre land. Piccadilly itself goes to the sanctuary of Green Park. On Haymarket, check out New Zealand House (built in 1959 on the site of the Carlton Hotel, bombed during the war), where the Vietnamese revolutionary leader Ho Chi Minh (1890–1969) worked as a waiter in 1913. Have a look down Lower Regent St for a glimpse of glorious Westminster.

Just east of the circus is London Trocadero (Map p68; ☎ 0906 888 1100; www.troc.co.uk; 1 Piccadilly Circus W1; admission free; ⌚ 10am-1am), a huge and soulless indoor amusement arcade

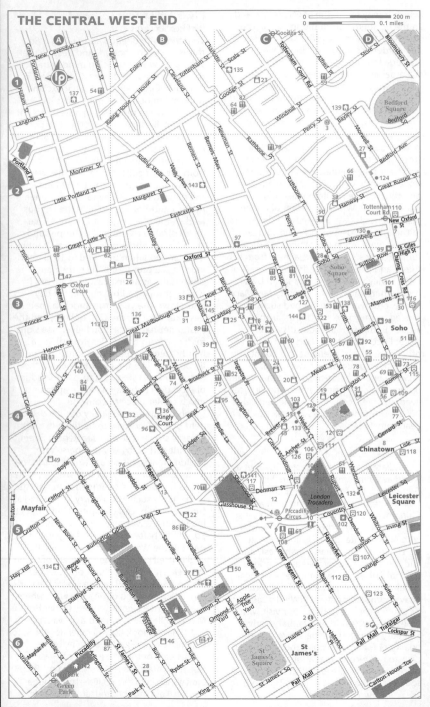

THE CENTRAL WEST END

0 ——————— 200 m
0 ——————— 0.1 miles

CENTRAL WEST END

that has six levels of hi-tech, high-cost fun for youngsters, along with cinemas, US-themed restaurants and bowling alleys. But the drabness of Trocadero has perked up a bit with the introduction of Amora – The Academy of Sex & Relationships (☎ 7734 2529; www .amoralondon.com; 13 Coventry St W1; ⏰ 11am-midnight; admission before 5pm £12, after 5pm £15). Amora calls itself an 'amusement park' and con-sists of several rooms that explore, well, sex

and relationships. The idea is that you take a tour around and come out enlightened and miles better at the stuff between the sheets, but it's had mixed reviews from Londoners, particularly from those who take their sex seriously. The silly themes, such as encouraging punters to 'find out how to kiss' (in the Sensorium) and a lesson aimed at improving foreplay skills (at the Sexplorium) don't help matters much.

SEX & DRUGS & ROCK'N'ROLL – THE HISTORY OF SOHO

Soho's character was formed by the many waves of immigration, and residential development started in the 17th century, after the Great Fire had levelled much of the city. An influx of Greek and Huguenot refugees and, later, the 18th-century influx of Italian, Chinese and other artisans and radicals into Soho replaced the bourgeois residents, who moved out of the area and into Mayfair. The following century saw Soho as no more than a slum, with cholera frequently attacking the impoverished residents. But despite its difficulties, the cosmopolitan vibe attracted writers and artists, and the overcrowded area became a centre for entertainment, with restaurants, taverns and coffee houses springing up.

The 20th century was even more raucous, when a fresh wave of European immigrants settled in, making Soho a bona fide bohemian enclave for two decades after WWII. Ronnie Scott's famous club, originally on Gerrard St, provided Soho's jazz soundtrack from the 1950s, while the likes of Jimi Hendrix, the Rolling Stones and Pink Floyd did their early gigs at the legendary Marquee club, which used to be on Wardour St. Soho had long been known for its seediness but when the hundreds of prostitutes who served the Square Mile were forced off the streets and into shop windows, it became the city's red-light district and a centre for porn, strip joints and bawdy drinking clubs. Gay liberation soon followed, and by the 1980s Soho was the hub of London's gay scene, as it remains today. The neighbourhood has a real sense of community, best absorbed on a weekend morning when Soho is at its most villagelike.

REGENT STREET Map p68

Regent St is the border separating the hoi polloi of Soho and the high-society residents of Mayfair. Designed by John Nash as a ceremonial route, it was meant to link the Prince Regent's long-demolished city dwelling with the 'wilds' of Regent's Park, and was conceived by the architect as a grand thoroughfare that would be the centrepiece of a new grid for this part of town. Alas, it was never to be – too many toes were being stepped on and Nash had to downscale his plan. There are some elegant shop fronts that look older than their 1920s origins (when the street was remodelled) but, as in the rest of London, the chain stores have almost completely taken over. Two distinguished retail outlets are Hamleys (p224), London's premier toy and game store, and the upmarket department store Liberty (p220).

ROYAL ACADEMY OF ARTS Map p68

☎ 7300 8000; www.royalacademy.org.uk; Burlington House, Piccadilly W1; admission varies; ☽ 10am-6pm, to 10pm Fri; ✆ Green Park; ♿
Britain's first art school was founded in 1768, though it only moved here in the following century. It's a great place to come for some free art, thanks to the John Madejski's Fine Rooms, where drawings ranging from Constable, Reynolds, Gainsborough and Turner to Hockney are displayed for nowt. The Academy's galleries have sprung back to life in recent years with mega-successful populist exhibitions such as the Art of the Aztecs and Turks, though the

famous Summer Exhibition (early June to mid-August), which has showcased art submitted by the general public for nearly 250 years, is the Academy's biggest event.

The Academy is enjoying its new Annenberg Courtyard, which features a dashing stone-paved piazza with choreographed lights and fountains flanking a statue of founder Joshua Reynolds, though he's often replaced or joined by various (and dubious) art pieces.

BURLINGTON ARCADE Map p68

51 Piccadilly W1; ✆ Green Park
Flanking Burlington House – home of the Royal Academy of Arts – on its western side is the curious Burlington Arcade, built in 1819 and evocative of a bygone era. Today it is a shopping precinct for the very wealthy and is most famous for the Burlington Berties, uniformed guards who patrol the area keeping an eye out for punishable offences such as running, chewing gum or whatever else might lower the arcade's tone. The fact that the arcade once served as a brothel isn't mentioned.

ST JAMES'S PICCADILLY Map p68

☎ 7734 4511; 197 Piccadilly W1; ☽ 8am-7pm; ✆ Green Park
The only church Christopher Wren built from scratch and on a new site (most of the others were replacements for ones razed in the Great Fire), this simple building is exceedingly easy on the eye and substitutes what some might call the pompous flourishes of his most famous

churches with a warm and elegant user-friendliness. The spire, although designed by Wren, was added only in 1968. This is a particularly sociable church: it houses a counselling service, stages lunchtime and evening concerts, provides shelter for an antiques market and an arts and crafts fair (from 10am to 6pm on Tuesday, and from Wednesday to Sunday, respectively), has a Caffé Nero attached on the side, as well as, what was the last thing…oh, yeah, teaching the word of God.

WHITE CUBE GALLERY Map p68
☎ 7930 5373; www.whitecube.com; 25-26 Mason's Yard SW1; admission free; ◷ 10am-6pm Tue-Sat; ⊖ Piccadilly

Opened in early summer 2007, this central sister to the Hoxton original (p149) has recently hosted two major high-profile exhibitions: an Andreas Gursky collection of photographs from North Korea; and the massively publicised Damien Hirst 'For the Love of God' exhibition –famed for its diamond skull – that brought back some of the media frenzy the Young British Artists (YBAs) were used to in the 1990s. Housed in Mason's Yard, a traditional courtyard with brick houses and an old pub, the White Cube looks like an ice block – white, straight-lined and angular. The two contrasting styles work well together and the courtyard often serves as a garden for the gallery on popular opening nights.

COVENT GARDEN & LEICESTER SQUARE

Covent Garden, though the throbbing heart of tourist London, is as beautiful and pleasant as tourist areas can get. Located east of Soho, the area is dominated by the piazza, which draws thousands of tourists into its elegant arched belly with boutiques, stalls, open-air cafés and pubs, and street entertainers who mostly perform outside St Paul's Church. Most Londoners avoid the human traffic jam of the area, but you should see it at least once. If you can, try to walk through the piazza after 11pm: it's calmer and almost totally empty, save for a busker or two, and you can appreciate its old-world beauty and Inigo Jones's design without the crowds. Additionally, there is an excellent antiques market on Monday that's worth a wander.

To the north of the piazza is the Royal Opera House, ruthlessly yet brilliantly rebuilt

in the late 1990s to make it one of the world's most superb singing venues. The wider area of Covent Garden is a honeypot for shoppers who revel in the High-Street outlets on Long Acre and independent boutiques along the little side streets. Neal St is no longer the grooviest strip, although the little roads cutting across it maintain its legendary style. Neal's Yard is a strange and charming little courtyard featuring overpriced vegetarian eateries. Floral St is where swanky designers such as Paul Smith have stores.

Covent Garden's history is quite different from its present-day character: it was a site of a convent (hence, 'covent') and its garden in the 13th century, owned by Westminster Abbey, which became the property of John Russell, the first Earl of Bedford, in 1552. The area developed thanks to his descendants, who employed Inigo Jones to convert a vegetable field into a piazza in the 17th century. He built the elegant Italian-style piazza, flanked by St Paul's Church to the west, and its tall terraced houses soon started to draw rich socialites who coveted the central living quarters. The bustling fruit and veg market – immortalised in *My Fair Lady* – dominated the piazza. London society, including writers such as Pepys, Fielding and Boswell, gathered here in the evenings looking for some action among the coffee houses, theatres, gambling dens and brothels. Lawlessness became commonplace, leading to the formation of a volunteer police force known as the Bow Street Runners (see Georgian London, p24). In 1897 Oscar Wilde was charged with gross indecency in the now-closed Bow St magistrate's court. A flower market designed by Charles Fowler was added at the spot where London's Transport Museum now stands.

During the 1970s, it became increasingly difficult to maintain the fruit and veg market amid the city traffic and the market was moved in 1974. Property developers loomed over the space and there was even talk of the market being demolished for a road, but thanks to the area's dedicated residential community who demonstrated and picketed for weeks, the piazza was saved and transformed into what you see today.

TRAFALGAR SQUARE Map pp72–3
In many ways this is the centre of London, where many great rallies and marches take place, where the New Year is ushered in by tens of thousands of revellers, and where locals congregate for anything from com-

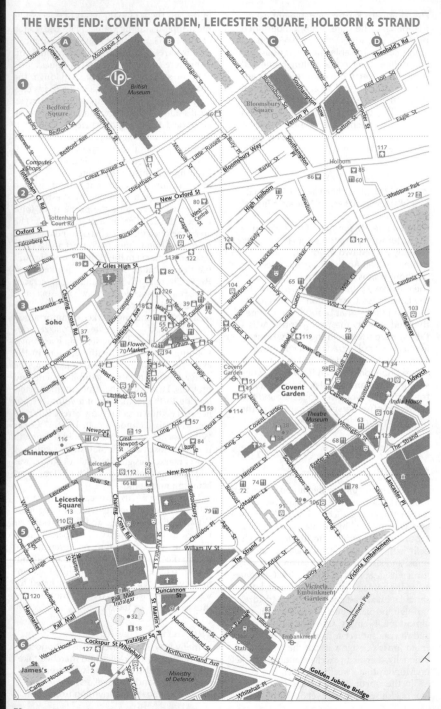

THE WEST END: COVENT GARDEN, LEICESTER SQUARE, HOLBORN & STRAND

British Museum

Bloomsbury Square

Bedford Square

Computer Shops

Tottenham Court Rd

Oxford St

Soho

Chinatown

Leicester Square

St James's

Covent Garden

Covent Garden

Theatre Museum

India House

Chinatown

Trafalgar

Duncannon St

Ministry of Defence

Victoria Embankment Gardens

Golden Jubilee Bridge

Embankment

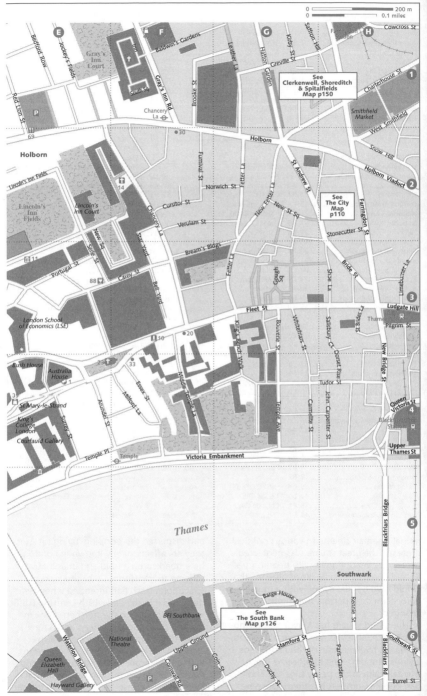

See
Clerkenwell, Shoreditch
& Spitalfields
Map p150

See
The City
Map
p110

See
The South Bank
Map p126

Thames

Southwark

Holborn

London School
of Economics (LSE)

73

THE WEST END: COVENT GARDEN, LEICESTER SQUARE, HOLBORN & STRAND

munal open-air cinema to various political protests. The great square was neglected over many years, ringed with gnarling traffic and given over to flocks of pigeons that would dive-bomb anyone with a morsel of food on their person. But things have changed.

The grand square has Mayor Ken Livingstone to thank for its new lease of life and, primarily, hygiene: one of the first things Livingstone did when he became mayor was take aim at the pesky pigeons and ban people from feeding them. Once he

had dispersed the pooping 'flying rats' (as they are affectionately known in London), he embarked on a bold and imaginative scheme to transform it into the kind of space John Nash had intended when he designed it in the early 19th century. Traffic was banished from the northern flank in front of the National Gallery, and a new pedestrian plaza built. The front of the National Gallery itself has been dolled up, with a new façade and entrance hall, and Ken has taken pains to organise cultural events to showcase the city's multiculturalism, with celebrations for Russian, Jewish and Chinese New Year, concerts of African music, or concerts celebrating Ken's friendship with Venezuela's left-wing president Hugo Chavez.

In 2005 Livingston, together with Wendy Woods (widow of the anti-apartheid journalist Donald Woods) and film director Lord Attenborough, applied to erect a 2.7m-tall statue of Nelson Mandela on the square's north terrace. The application was rejected by Westminster Council who suggested the statue be placed outside South Africa house. This, in turn, was rejected by the Mayor and Lord Attenborough, who claimed that the location would not allow the statue to be viewed properly. The debate continues.

The pedestrianisation has made it easier to appreciate not only the square but also the splendid buildings around it: the National Gallery, the National Portrait Gallery and the newly renovated church of St Martin-in-the-Fields. The ceremonial Pall Mall runs southwest from the top of the square. To the southwest stands Admiralty Arch (p85), with the Mall leading to Buckingham Palace beyond it. To the west is Canada House (1827), designed by Robert Smirke. The 52m-high Nelson's Column (upon which the admiral surveys his fleet of ships to the southwest) has stood in the centre of the square since 1843 and commemorates the admiral's victory over Napoleon off Cape Trafalgar in Spain in 1805. It was cleaned in 2006 and the admiral now shines with more confidence than ever.

NATIONAL GALLERY Map pp72–3
☎ 7747 2885; www.nationalgallery.org.uk; Trafalgar Sq WC2; admission free to permanent exhibits, prices vary for tem[...] ⏰ 10am-6pm Thu-Tue, to 9[...] Cross; ♿

With more than 2000 Wes[...] paintings on display, the N[...] is one of the largest galleri[...] But it's the quality of the w[...] the quantity, that impresses[...] most five million people visit each year, keen to see seminal paintings from every important epoch in the history of art, including works by Giotto, Leonardo da Vinci, Michelangelo, Titian, Velázquez, Van Gogh and Renoir, just to name a few. Although it can get ridiculously busy in here, the galleries are spacious, sometimes even sedate, and it's never so bad that you can't appreciate the works. That said, weekday mornings and Wednesday evenings (after 6pm) are the best times to visit, as the crowds are small. If you have the time to make multiple visits, focus on one section at a time to fully appreciate the astonishing collection.

The size and layout can be confusing, so make sure you pick up a free gallery plan at the entrance. To see the art in chronological order, start with the Sainsbury Wing on the gallery's western side, which houses paintings from 1260 to 1510. In these 16 rooms you can explore the Renaissance through paintings by Giotto, Leonardo da Vinci, Botticelli, Raphael and Titian, among others. This is where you'll also find the Micro gallery, a dozen computer terminals on which you can explore the pictorial database, find the location of your favourite works or create your own personalised tour.

The High Renaissance (1510–1600) is covered in the West Wing, where Michelangelo, Titian, Correggio, El Greco and Bronzino

THE FOURTH PLINTH

Three of the four plinths located at Trafalgar Sq's corners are occupied by notables, including King George IV on horseback, and military men General Charles Napier and Sir Henry Havelock. One, originally intended for a statue of William IV, has largely remained vacant for the past 150 years. The Royal Society of Arts conceived of the unimaginatively titled Fourth Plinth Project (www.fourthplinth.co.uk) in 1999, deciding to use the empty space for works by contemporary artists. The stunning Ecce Homo by Mark Wallinger (1999) was the first one, a life-size statue of Jesus which appeared tiny in contrast to the enormous plinth, commenting on the human illusions of grandeur; it was followed by Bill Woodrow's Regardless of History (2000) and Rachel Whiteread's Monument (2001), a resin copy of the plinth, turned upside down.

The Mayor's office has since taken over the Fourth Plinth Project, continuing with the contemporary-art theme, with Marc Quinn's Alison Lapper Pregnant (2005), a statue of the Thalidomide-affected artist (Alison Lapper) when expecting a child, being replaced by Tomas Schütte's Model for a Hotel 2007 (2007).

while Rubens, Rembrandt and
...gio can be found in the North Wing
...–1700). The most crowded part of the
...llery – and for good reason – is likely to
be the East Wing (1700–1900) and particularly the many works of the impressionists
and postimpressionists, including Van Gogh,
Gauguin, Cézanne, Monet, Degas and Renoir. Although it hardly stands out in such
exalted company, the impressive display
featuring 18th-century British landscape
artists Gainsborough, Constable and Turner
is also well worth checking out.

The gallery's collection cuts off at 1900
and therefore to see 20th-century art you
need to head to Tate Modern (p129) and, for
British art, Tate Britain (p103).

Temporary exhibitions – for which you
normally have to pay, and often book
in advance – go on show in the basement
of the Sainsbury Wing and are often
outstanding.

The highlights listed in the boxed text
(right) include many of the most important
works, but if you want to immerse yourself
in this pool of riches rather than just skim
across the surface, borrow a themed or
comprehensive audioguide (£4 donation
recommended) from the Central Hall. Free
one-hour introductory guided tours leave
from the information desk in the Sainsbury
Wing daily at 11.30am and 2.30pm, with an
extra tour at 6.30pm on Wednesday. There
are also special trails and activity sheets for
children.

The new National Dining Rooms (☎ 7747 2525;
www.thenationaldiningrooms.co.uk; ☼ 10am-5pm
Sun-Tue, to 8.30pm Wed), in the Sainbury Wing, is
a wonderful recent addition to the gallery.
Run by Oliver Peyton (the man behind Inn
the Park in St James's Park; see p245), this
is an excellent, well-lit space, with quality
British food in the restaurant, and pastries
and cakes in the bakery.

NATIONAL PORTRAIT GALLERY
Map pp72–3

☎ 7306 0055; www.npg.org.uk; St Martin's Pl
WC2; admission free, prices vary for temporary
exhibitions; ☼ 10am-6pm, to 9pm Thu & Fri;
⊖ Charing Cross or Leicester Sq; ⑤
Excellent for putting faces to names over
the last five centuries of British history, the
gallery houses a primary collection of some
10,000 works, which are regularly rotated,
among them the museum's first acquisition, the famous Chandos portrait of Shake-

NATIONAL GALLERY HIGHLIGHTS
- *Pentecost* – Giotto
- *Virgin and Child with St Anne and St John the Baptist* – Leonardo da Vinci
- *Arnolfini Wedding* – Van Eyck
- *Venus and Mars* – Botticelli
- *The Ansidei Madonna* – Raphael
- *The Madonna of the Pinks* – Raphael
- *Le Chapeau de Paille* – Rubens
- *Charles I* – Van Dyck
- *Bacchus and Ariadne* – Titian
- *The Entombment* – Michelangelo
- *Rokeby Venus* – Velásquez
- *The Supper at Emmaus* – Caravaggio
- *Bathers* – Cézanne
- *Sunflowers* – Van Gogh
- *The Water Lily Pond* – Monet
- *Miss La La* – Degas
- *The Hay-Wain* – Constable
- *The Fighting Temeraire* – Turner

speare. Despite the recent discovery that
the Royal Shakespeare Company's Flower
portrait of the Bard was a 19th-century
forgery, the National Portrait Gallery still
believes this one to have been painted during Shakespeare's lifetime.

To follow the paintings chronologically
you should take the huge escalator to the
top floor and work your way down. The 1st
floor is dedicated to the Royal family, but
the most fun is seeing one of the two portraits of the Queen made by Andy Warhol.
The ground floor is most interesting with
portraits of contemporary figures using a
variety of media, including sculpture and
photography. Among the most popular
of these is Sam Taylor-Wood's *David*, a
video-portrait of David Beckham asleep
after football training, which attracted a
lot of women to suddenly take interest in
this part of the gallery. There's an annual
Photographic Portrait Prize exhibition,
featuring some of the best contemporary
photographers.

Audioguides (a £3 donation is suggested) highlight some 200 portraits and
allow you to hear the voices of some of
the people portrayed. The Portrait Café
and bookshop are in the basement and
the Portrait restaurant (p240) is on the top
floor, offering some superb views towards
Westminster.

(Continued on page 85)

NEIGHBOURHOODS THE WEST END

ARCHITECTURE

Ornate choir stalls and quire of Wren's masterpiece, St Paul's Cathedral

LONDON ARCHITECTURE

Unlike some other great metropolises, London has never been methodically planned. Rather, it has developed in an organic (read: haphazard) fashion. There has traditionally been an aversion to the set piece here and, until relatively recently, buildings were rarely used as parts of a larger town or district plan.

LAYING THE FOUNDATIONS

London's roots lie in the walled Roman settlement of Londinium, established in AD 43 on the northern banks of the River Thames, roughly on the site of today's City. Few traces of it survive outside museums, but stretches of the Roman wall remain as foundations to a medieval wall outside Tower Hill tube station and in a few sections below Bastion Highwalk, next to the Museum of London.

The Saxons, who moved into the area after the decline of the Roman Empire, found Londinium too small and built their communities further up the Thames. Excavations carried out by archaeologists from the Museum of London during renovations at the Royal Opera House in the late 1990s uncovered extensive traces of the Saxon settlement of Lundenwic, including some wattle-and-daub housing. But the best place to see what the Saxons left behind *in situ* is the church of All Hallows-by-the-Tower (p123), northwest of the Tower of London, which boasts an important archway and the walls of a 7th-century Saxon church.

With the arrival of William the Conqueror in 1066, the country got its first example of Norman architecture in the shape of the White Tower (p121), the sturdy keep at the heart of the Tower of London. The church of St Bartholomew-the-Great (p114) at Smithfield also has Norman arches and columns marching down its nave. The west door and elaborately moulded porch at the Temple Church (p113) in Inner Temple are other outstanding details of Norman architecture.

Westminster Abbey, London's finest example of Early English Gothic architecture

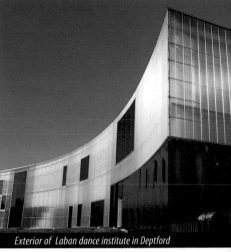

Night views of Tower Bridge and the River Thames *Exterior of Laban dance institute in Deptford*

MEDIEVAL LONDON

Westminster Abbey (p99), enlarged and refurbished between the 12th and 14th centuries, is a splendid reminder of what the master masons of the Middle Ages could produce, while Temple Church (p113) illustrates the transition from the round-arched, solid, Norman Romanesque style to the pointed-arched delicateness of Early English Gothic. Perhaps the finest surviving medieval church in the City is 13th-century Church of St Ethelburga-the-Virgin (Map p110; 78 Bishopsgate EC2) near Liverpool St station, which was restored after Irish Republican Army (IRA) bombings in 1993. The 15th-century Church of St Olave (Map p110; Hart St EC3), northwest of Tower Hill, is one of the City's few remaining Gothic parish churches, while the crypt at the largely restored church of St Ethelreda (Map p150; Ely Pl EC1), north of Holborn Circus, dates from about 1250.

Secular buildings are even scarcer, although the ragstone Jewel Tower (Map pp96–7; Abingdon St SW1) opposite the Houses of Parliament dates from 1365, and most of the Tower of London (p119) goes back to the Middle Ages. Staple Inn (Map pp72–3; High Holborn WC1) in Holborn dates from 1378, but the half-timbered shopfront façade (1589) is mostly Elizabethan and was heavily restored in the 1950s after wartime bombing.

AN AGE OF ARCHITECTS

The finest London architect of the first half of the 17th century was Inigo Jones (1573–1652), who spent a year and a half in Italy and became a convert to Palladian Renaissance architecture. His *chefs-d'œuvre* include Banqueting House (1622; p105) in Whitehall and Queen's House (1635; p182) in Greenwich. Often overlooked is the much plainer church of St Paul's (Map pp72–3) in Covent Garden, which he designed in the 1630s to go with the new piazza and described as 'the handsomest barn in England'.

The greatest architect ever to leave his mark on London was Sir Christopher Wren (1632–1723), responsible not just for his masterpiece and monument St Paul's Cathedral (1710; p109) but also for many of central London's finest churches. He oversaw the building of dozens of them, many replacing medieval churches lost in the Great Fire, as well as the Royal Hospital Chelsea (1692; p137) and the Old Royal Naval College (p181), begun in 1694 at Greenwich. His neoclassical buildings and churches are taller, lighter and generally more graceful than their medieval predecessors.

Nicholas Hawksmoor (1661–1736) was a pupil of Wren who worked with him on several churches before going on to design his own masterpieces. The restored Christ Church (1729; p152) in Spitalfields and the 1731 St George's Bloomsbury (Map pp92–3; Bloomsbury Way WC1), as well as St Anne's, Limehouse (1725; p161) and St George-in-the-East (1726; p163) at Wapping, are among his finest works.

Neo-Palladian mansion of Kenwood House, Hampstead

Another Wren protégé, James Gibb (1682–1754), was responsible for St Martin-in-the-Fields (1726; p85). The style of these two architects' buildings is usually defined as English baroque.

A few domestic buildings dating from before the 18th century still survive, among them the half-timbered 1611 Prince Henry's Room (Map pp72–3; 17 Fleet EC4) and several old pubs on Fleet St and along the Strand.

GEORGIAN MANNERS

The Georgian period saw the return of classicism (or neo-Palladianism). Among the greatest exponents of this revived style was Robert Adam (1728–92). Much of his work was demolished by the Victorians, but an excellent example that endures is Kenwood House (1773; p171), on Hampstead Heath.

Adam's fame has been eclipsed by that of John Nash (1752–1835), and rightly so: his contribution to London's architecture compares favourably to that of Wren. Nash was responsible for the layout of Regent's Park and its surrounding elegant crescents. To give London a 'spine', he created Regent Street (p70) as a straight north–south axis from St James's Park in the south to the new Regent's Park in the north. This grand scheme also involved the formation of Trafalgar Sq, and the development of the Mall and the western end of the Strand.

Nash's contemporary, John Soane (1753–1837), was the architect of the Bank of England (Map p110; Threadneedle St EC2), completed in 1833 (though much of his work was lost during the bank's rebuilding by Herbert Baker, 1925–39), as well as the Dulwich Picture Gallery (1814; p185). Robert Smirke (1780–1867) designed the British Museum (p89) in 1823, one of the finest expressions anywhere of the Greek Revivalist style.

A GOTHICK RETHINK

In the 19th century a reaction emerged in the form of the highly decorative neo-Gothic style, also known as Victorian High Gothic or 'Gothick'. Champions were George Gilbert Scott (1811–78),

Alfred Waterhouse (1830–1905), Augustus Pugin (1812–52) and Charles Barry (1795–1860). Scott was responsible for the elaborate Albert Memorial (1872; p144) in Kensington Gardens and St Pancras Chambers (1874; Map p168). Waterhouse designed the flamboyant Natural History Museum (1880; p141), while Pugin and Barry worked together from 1840 on the Houses of Parliament (p102), after the Palace of Westminster burned down in 1834. The last great neo-Gothic public building to go up in London was the Royal Courts of Justice (1882; p87), designed by George Edmund Street.

The emphasis on the artisanship and materials necessary to create these elaborate neo-Gothic buildings led to what has become known as the Arts and Crafts movement – 'British Art Nouveau', for lack of a better term – of which William Morris (1834–96) was a leading exponent. Morris' work can be best enjoyed in the Green Dining Room of the Victoria & Albert Museum (p139) and at his Bexleyheath residence, Red House (1860; p186). The 1902 Euston Fire Station (Map p168; 172 Euston Rd NW1) opposite St Pancras New Church is a wonderful example of Arts and Crafts architecture.

FLIRTING WITH MODERNISM

Not many public buildings of note were built during the first 15 years of the 20th century, apart from Admiralty Arch (1910; p85), in the Edwardian baroque style of Aston Webb (1849–1930), who also designed the Queen Victoria Memorial (1911) opposite Buckingham Palace and worked on the front façade of the palace itself. County Hall (p127), designed by Ralph Knott in 1909, was not completed until 1933.

In the period between the two world wars, English architecture was hardly more creative though Edwin Lutyens (1869–1944), whose work is sometimes classified as British Art Deco, designed the Cenotaph (1920; p105) on Whitehall as well as the impressive 1927 Britannic House (Map p150; Finsbury Sq EC2), now Triton Court, in Moorgate.

Europeans architects introduced the modernist style, but the monuments they left are generally on a small scale. Russian Berthold Lubetkin (1901–90) is perhaps the best remembered, principally because of his Penguin Pool at the London Zoo (p165), with its concrete spiral ramp. Built in 1934, it is considered to be London's earliest modernist structure.

POSTWAR RECONSTRUCTION

Hitler's bombs during WWII wrought the worst destruction on London since the Great Fire and the immediate postwar problem was a chronic housing shortage. Low-cost developments and

OPEN SESAME

If you want to stick your nose inside buildings you wouldn't normally be able to see, September is the time to visit. One weekend that month (usually the third one), the charity Open House arranges for owners of up to 600 private buildings to throw open their front doors and let in the public free of charge. Major buildings, some of them listed in this chapter (eg 30 St Mary Axe, City Hall, Lloyd's of London, St Pancras Chambers etc) have also participated.

For more details, contact Open House Architecture (☎ 0900 160 0061; www.londonopenhouse.org). The charity also runs three-hour, architect-led tours (☎ 7380 0412; adult/student £18.50/13) every Saturday at 10am departing from the Building Centre (see below) at 10am. There's a rolling program visiting the Square Mile, Bankside, the West End or Docklands. The tours, which include lively, well-informed commentary, are highly recommended. Best of all, you can ask questions to your heart's content.

Another annual event worth keeping an eye out for is Architecture Week (☎ 7973 5246; www.architectureweek .org.uk) in mid-June, which has an enticing mix of talks by leading architects, designers and well-known TV design critics, plus events involving actors and bands. It's run as a joint venture between the Royal Institute of British Architects (www.riba.org) and the Arts Council.

If you're interested in where architecture is headed in London visit the New London Architecture (www.new londonarchitecture.org) website or the Building Centre (Map pp92–3; ☎ 7692 4000; www.buildingcentre.co.uk; 26 Store St WC1E; admission free; 🕙 9.30am-6pm Mon-Fri, 10am-5pm Sat; ❹ Tottenham Court Rd or Goodge St). Along with changing exhibitions and an outstanding bookshop, it has a scale diorama model of London that is updated quarterly.

Heritage-listed BT Tower rises high above the West End

Classical and baroque merge in St Martin-in-the-Fields

ugly high-rise housing were thrown up on bomb sites and many of these blocks still contribute to London's urban blight today.

The Royal Festival Hall (p128), designed by Robert Matthew and J Leslie Martin for the 1951 Festival of Britain, attracted as many accolades as brickbats when it opened as London's first major public building in the modernist style. The former now far outweigh the latter after a two-year, £75 million refit. Hardly anyone seems to have a good word to say about Denys Lasdun's brutalist National Theatre (p128), however, begun in 1966 and finished a decade later.

The 1960s saw the ascendancy of the workaday glass-and-concrete high-rises exemplified by the mostly unloved 1967 Centre Point (Map p68; New Oxford St WC1) by Richard Seifert. But one person's muck is another's jewel; the once-vilified modernist tower has been listed by English Heritage, meaning that it represents a particular style, is of great value to the patrimony and largely cannot be altered outside (and in some cases inside as well). The 1964 BT Tower (Map pp92–3; 60 Cleveland St W1), formerly the Post Office Tower and designed by Eric Bedford, has also been given Heritage-listed status.

The 1970s saw very little building in London apart from roads, and the recession of the late 1980s and early 1990s brought much of the development and speculation in the Docklands and the City to a standstill. In 1990 the publication of *A Vision of Britain*, a reactionary tract by Prince Charles that argued for a synthetic 'English tradition', helped polarise traditionalists and modernists still further. For these and other reasons, the London skyline had little to compare with that of New York or Hong Kong.

POSTMODERNISM LANDS

London's contemporary architecture was born in the City and the Docklands in the mid-1980s. The former centrepiece was Lloyd's of London (1986; p117), Sir Richard Rogers' 'inside-out' masterpiece of ducts, pipes, glass and stainless steel. Taking pride of place in the Docklands was Cesar Pelli's 244m-high 1 Canada Square (1991), commonly known as Canary Wharf (see p161) and easily visible from central London.

REACHING FOR THE SKIES

Mayor Ken Livingstone has suggested that London needs another 10 to 15 skyscrapers within the next decade if it is to retain its pre-eminence as a financial capital. English Heritage initially contested some of the following proposed high-rises on the grounds that they might obstruct 'strategic' views of St Paul's Cathedral, but its fears have been assuaged. All five of the following received planning permission and are on their way up.

20 Fenchurch Street (Map p110; 20 Fenchurch St EC3) Rafael Vinoly; 177m. The idea behind the 'Walkie Talkie' shape is that bigger top floors can command more rent, making the tower more profitable than others.

Bishopsgate Tower (Map p110; 288m; 22-24 Bishopsgate EC2) Kohn Pedersen Fox Associates; 288m. Scaled down from more than 307m, the 'Helter Skelter' will still be the highest tower in the City when completed.

Heron Tower (Map p110; 202m; 110 Bishopsgate EC3) Kohn Pedersen Fox Associates; 202m. The four façades of this stepped skyscraper will each be different, reflecting the buildings they face.

Leadenhall Building (Map p110; 122 Leadenhall St EC3) Sir Richard Rogers; 224m. This 48-storey tower nicknamed the Cheese Grater faces the architect's own Lloyd's of London building.

London Bridge Tower (Map p126; 32 London Bridge St SE) Renzo Piano; 310m. Luxury Asian hotel group Shangri-La has already signed up as a tenant on 18 floors of this thin, tall glass spike.

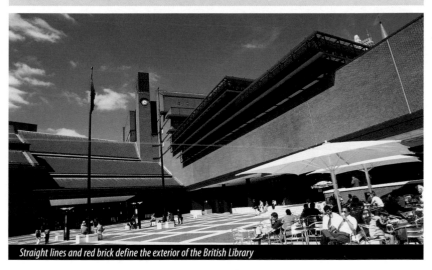

Straight lines and red brick define the exterior of the British Library

With a youthful New Labour in power at the end of the 1990s, Britain's economy on the up and the new millennium looming, attention turned to public buildings, including several landmarks that would define London in the early 21st century.

Tate Modern (Herzog & de Meuron, 1999; p129) was a success beyond even its architects' wildest dreams. From the disused Bankside Power Station (Sir Giles Gilbert Scott, 1963) they fashioned an art gallery that went straight to first place in the top 10 London tourist attractions, and then walked away with international architecture's most prestigious prize, the Pritzker. The stunning Millennium Bridge (Sir Norman Foster and Antony Caro, 2000; p130), the first bridge to be built over the Thames in central London since Tower Bridge (1894), had a case of the wobbles when it was first opened, but it is now much loved and much used. Even the Millennium Dome (Sir Richard Rogers; p181), the dunce of the class of 2000, probably through no fault of its tentlike exterior, has got a new lease of life as a sometime concert hall and sporting stadium called the 02.

The graceful British Library (Colin St John Wilson, 1998; p167), with its warm red-brick exterior, Asianesque touches and its wonderfully bright interior, met a very hostile reception. It has now become a popular and much loved London landmark.

Spiral staircase inside the glass-clad City Hall

TODAY & TOMORROW

The millennium icons and more recent structures such as the glass 'egg' of City Hall (2002; p133) and the ever-popular 30 St Mary Axe (2003; p116), or 'the Gherkin', have given the city the confidence to continue planning more heady buildings – especially of the tall variety.

By 2010 London will be home to Europe's tallest building: the needlelike London Bridge Tower (see boxed text, p83). And that will be accompanied by a host of other high-rises, from several new towers near the Lloyd's building in the 'City cluster' to further lofty constructions in the Docklands.

The current mayor of London, Ken Livingstone, favours 'clusters' of high-quality high-rises throughout the capital. The financial districts of the City and Canary Wharf, with the biggest concentration of existing skyscrapers, are obvious candidates for expansion though other neighbourhoods have been slated for redevelopment, including three distinct sections of Paddington to the west, Elephant & Castle to the south, Silvertown Quays at the Docklands in the east and the Greenwich Peninsula to the southeast.

London's most ambitious project of urban development this century is the 200-hectare Olympic Park (Map p64; www.london2012.com) in the Lea River Valley near Stratford, where most of the events of the 2012 Summer Olympiad will take place, but even in parts of London where you'd least expect it, there are innovative buildings to be seen – from the Laban (Herzog & de Meuron, 1999; p313) dance institute in Deptford and one-of-a-kind low-cost housing in Silvertown (Map p64; Evelyn Rd E16; Ash Sakula, 2004; Map p64; 60-66 Boxley St E16) – 2004 by Neal McLaughlin – and Southwark (Map p198; Wansey St SE17) – 2006 by De Rijke Marsh Morgan – to the award-winning Adjaye Associates 2006 Idea Store (Map p156; Whitechapel Rd E1), a library for the iPod generation, in Whitechapel. You'll make architectural discoveries at virtually every turn in this, the capital of Europe.

ST MARTIN-IN-THE-FIELDS Map pp72–3

☎ 7766 1100, for brass-rubbing 7930 9306, for concert box office 7839 8362; www.stmartin-in -the-fields.org; Trafalgar Sq WC2; admission free, pay for materials for brass-rubbing; ☿ 8am-6.30pm, brass-rubbing centre 10am-6pm Mon-Sat, noon-6pm Sun; ⊖ Charing Cross

The 'royal parish church' is a delightful fusion of classical and baroque styles that was completed by James Gibbs (1682–1754) in 1726. A £36 million refurbishment project, completed in October 2007, sees a new entrance pavilion and foyer, several new areas at the rear of the church, including spaces offering social care (many homeless and destitute people rely on the church's help), and a lovely 'contemplative space' accessible to the public. These are in addition to the main hall, where Mass and musical concerts are held, and the famous crypt café.

The refurbishment dig-up unearthed a 1.5-tonne limestone Roman sarcophagus containing a human skeleton in the churchyard; the yard also holds the graves of 18th-century artists Reynolds and Hogarth.

COVENT GARDEN PIAZZA Map pp72–3

London's first planned square is now the exclusive reserve of tourists who flock here to shop in the quaint old arcades, be entertained by buskers, pay through the nose for refreshments at outdoor cafés and bars, and watch men and women pretend to be statues.

On its western flank is St Paul's Church (☎ 7836 5221; www.actorschurch.org; Bedford St WC2; admission free; ☿ 8.30am-5.30pm Mon-Fri, 9am-1pm Sun). The Earl of Bedford, the man who had commissioned Inigo Jones to design the piazza, asked for the simplest possible church, basically no more than a barn. The architect responded by producing 'the handsomest barn in England'. It has long been regarded as the actors' church for its associations with the theatre, and contains memorials to the likes of Charlie Chaplin and Vivian Leigh. The first Punch and Judy show took place in front of it in 1662.

Check out the lovely courtyard in the back, perfect for a picnic.

LONDON TRANSPORT MUSEUM
Map pp72–3

☎ 7379 6344; www.ltmuseum.co.uk; Covent Garden Piazza WC2; adult/child/concession £5.95/2.50/4.50; ☿ 10am-6pm Sat-Thu, 11am-6pm Fri; ⊖ Covent Garden; ♿

This museum has had a massive renovation, with a revitalised existing collection (which consisted of buses from the horse age until today, plus taxis, trains and all other modes of transport) and more new collections, more display space and a 120-seat lecture theatre for educational purposes. You can get your Mind the Gap boxer shorts and knickers at the museum shop.

ADMIRALTY ARCH Map pp72–3
⊖ Charing Cross

From Trafalgar Sq, the Mall passes under this grand Edwardian monument, a triple-arched stone entrance designed by Aston Webb in honour of Queen Victoria in 1910. The large central gate is opened only for royal processions and state visits.

ROYAL OPERA HOUSE Map pp72–3

☎ 7304 4000; www.royaloperahouse.org; Bow St WC2; adult/concession £8/7; ☿ tours 10.30am, 12.30pm & 2.30pm Mon-Sat; ⊖ Covent Garden; ♿

On the northeastern flank of the Covent Garden piazza is the gleaming, redeveloped – and practically new – Royal Opera House. Unique 'behind the scenes' tours take you through the venue, and let you experience the planning, excitement and hissy fits that take place before a performance at one of the world's busiest opera houses. As it's a working theatre, plans can change so you'd best call ahead. Of course, the best way to enjoy it is by seeing a performance (see p316).

PHOTOGRAPHERS' GALLERY Map pp72–3

☎ 7831 1772; www.photonet.org.uk; 5 & 8 Great Newport St WC2; admission free; ☿ 11am-6pm Mon-Sat, noon-6pm Sun; ⊖ Leicester Sq, Covent Garden or Charing Cross; ♿

This tiny two-part gallery may be small in size, but it's certainly got a big reputation in the photography world. It won't even be that small come 2008, since plans are underway to relocate to 16-18 Ramillies St in Soho with the new premises designed by O'Donnell + Tuomey Architects. The prestigious Deutsche Börse Photography Competition (annually 9 February to 8

April) is of major importance for contemporary photographers; past winners include Richard Billingham, Luc Delahaye, Andreas Gursky, Boris Mikhailov and Juergen Teller. The gallery is always exhibiting excellent and thought-provoking photographers. The next-door café and exhibition space is a great place to sit in peace during weekdays, and the shop is good for photography books and quirky gifts.

LEICESTER SQUARE Map pp72–3
Enormous cinemas and nightclubs dominate this 'aesthetically challenged' square, which could really do with a makeover. It heaves with crowds on weekends and becomes the inebriates' playground at night. There was a serious pickpocketing problem here some years ago, until a heavy police presence improved matters, but still keep an eye on your bag/wallet, especially when the square is very crowded. Britain's glitzy film premiers take place here, as well as the majority of London Film Festival screenings. The major Odeon cinema boasts the biggest screen in the country, and definitely the highest ticket prices (a whopping £17!).

It's been on a major comedown since the 19th century, when the square was so fashionable that artists Joshua Reynolds and William Hogarth chose to hang their hats here. There's a small statue of Charlie Chaplin inside the little park, which is there mainly because of Leicester Sq's cinematic importance rather than any historical connection of the comedian to the area.

ST GILES-IN-THE-FIELDS Map pp72–3
☎ 7240 2532; 60 St Giles High St; ⏰ 9am-4pm Mon-Fri; ⊖ Tottenham Court Rd
Built in what used to be countryside between the City and Westminster, St Giles church isn't much to look at but has an interesting history, while the area around St Giles High St had perhaps the worst reputation of any London quarter. The current structure is the third to stand on the site of an original chapel built in the 12th century to serve the leprosy hospital. Until 1547, when the hospital closed, prisoners on their way to be executed at Tyburn stopped at the church gate and sipped a large cup of soporific ale – their last refreshment – from St Giles's Bowl. From 1650 the prisoners were buried in the church grounds. It was also within the boundaries of St Giles that the Great Plague

of 1665 took hold (this is cheerful, isn't it?). In Victorian times it was London's worst slum, oft namechecked by Dickens. Today the forbidding streets and drug-users who hang out around the area make you feel like things haven't changed much.

An interesting relic in the church is the pulpit that was used for 40 years by John Wesley, the founder of Methodism.

HOLBORN & THE STRAND
This area – compacted here for convenience's sake – comprises the rough square wedged between the City to the east, Covent Garden to the west, High Holborn to the north and the Thames to the south. Past glory and prominence are its key characteristics: The Strand, connecting Westminster with the City, used to be one of the most important streets in London and was lined with fabulous town houses built by local luminaries and aristocrats. This rich history is only vaguely evident today, but while much of this pocket is soulless and commercial, it is saved by some architectural gems, a few splendid galleries and the calm, green recesses of the charming Inns of Court, the cradle of English law. Behind the Strand runs the Victoria Embankment Gardens, a lovely place for a picnic, a stroll and splendid views across the Thames to the recharged South Bank.

Fleet St was the former home of British journalism. It was named after the River Fleet, which in the 17th and 18th centuries was a virtual sewer filled with entrails and other grisly bits from Smithfield Market (p115) upriver. Holborn was named after one of its tributaries. Both were filled in the late 18th century, with the River Fleet now running underground. The area was a notorious slum in Victorian times and although efforts were made to smarten it up in the early 20th century, it was probably no great loss when the Germans flattened much of it during WWII, after which the current business moved in.

SOMERSET HOUSE Map pp72–3
☎ 7845 4600; www.somerset-house.org.uk; the Strand WC2; ⏰ House 10am-6pm, Great Court 7.30am-11pm; ⊖ Temple or Covent Garden
Passing beneath the arch towards this splendid Palladian masterpiece, it's hard to believe that the magnificent courtyard in front of you, with its 55 dancing fountains, was a car park for tax collectors up until a spectacular refurbishment in 2000. William

Chambers designed the house in 1775 for royal societies and it now contains three fabulous museums. The courtyard is transformed into a popular ice rink in winter and used for concerts in summer, as well as an improvised fountain-bathing area for toddlers. Behind the house, there's a sunny terrace and café overlooking the embankment.

Immediately to your right as you enter the grounds of Somerset House from the Strand, you'll find the Courtauld Institute of Art (☎ 7848 2526; www.courtauld.ac.uk; adult/concession/UK student £5/4/free, free 10am-2pm Mon; ☺ 10am-6pm), a superb gallery connected to the Courtauld Institute of Arts, Britain's foremost academy of art history. Have an uncrowded stroll between the walls of this wonderful place, and see work by Rubens, Botticelli, Cranach, Cézanne, Degas, Renoir, Manet, Monet, Matisse, Gauguin, Van Gogh and Toulouse-Lautrec, to mention but a few. There are lunchtime talks on specific works or themes from the collection at 1.15pm every Monday and Friday. A little café and the plush Admiral 2 restaurant provide sustenance.

The vaults beneath the South Terrace have some of the finest Thames views and are home to the Gilbert Collection of Decorative Arts (Map pp72–3; ☎ 7420 9400; www.gilbert-collection.org.uk; adult/concession/UK student £5/4/free; ☺ 10am-6pm) In 1996 Anglo-American businessman Arthur Gilbert bequeathed to Britain his Italian mosaics, European silver, gold snuffboxes and portrait miniatures. The part-dazzling, part-gaudy display has been described as the most generous gift ever made to the nation. There are one-hour guided tours each Saturday at 3pm (free with admission ticket).

Finally, the Hermitage Rooms (☎ 7845 4630; www.hermitagerooms.com; adult/concession/UK student £5/4/free; ☺ 10am-6pm) are a charming outpost of the State Hermitage Museum in St Petersburg (which holds some three million pieces that make up one of the finest art collections in the world). Small but fascinating Russian-themed exhibits from the Hermitage collection revolve every six months. The galleries are modelled on those in the Imperial Winter Palace, and there's a live feed to St Petersburg and even a short video on the State Hermitage Museum itself.

You can get a pass for two collections (on the same day) for £8; see all three for £12.

ROYAL COURTS OF JUSTICE Map pp72–3
☎ 7936 6000; 460 The Strand; admission free; ☺ 9am-4.30pm Mon-Fri; ⊖ Temple

Where the Strand joins Fleet St, you'll see the entrance to this gargantuan melange of Gothic spires, pinnacles and burnished Portland stone, designed by aspiring cathedral builder GE Street in 1874. (It took so much out of the architect that he died of a stroke shortly before its completion.) Inside the Great Hall there's an exhibition of legal costumes, as well as a list of cases to be heard in court that day; if you're interested in 'the criminal mind' and decide to watch, leave your camera behind and expect airportlike security.

THE STRAND Map pp72–3
From the time it was built, at the end of the 12th century, the Strand (from the Old English and German word for beach) ran by the Thames. Its grandiose stone houses, built by the nobles, counted as some of the most prestigious places to live, sitting as they did on a street that connected the City and Westminster, the two centres of power; indeed, its appeal lasted for seven centuries, with the 19th-century prime minister Benjamin Disraeli pronouncing it 'the finest street in Europe'. It had the Savoy, the now-no-more Cecil Hotel, Simpson's, King's College and Somerset House.

But modern times haven't treated the Strand with the same sort of respect and awe: the street is now overrun by offices, cheap restaurants and odd souvenir shops, and despite the fact that the Savoy (which still does very glamorous cocktails), the building formerly Simpson's and the wonderful Somerset House still grace the street, it is hardly seen as the fine drag it once was. Still, there are some lovely things to see here, such as Twinings at No 216, a teashop opened by Thomas Twining in 1706 and believed to be the oldest company in the capital still trading on the same site and owned by the same family. It's also the centre of London philatelic life, with stamp- and coin-collector's mecca Stanley Gibbons at No 339.

SIR JOHN SOANE'S MUSEUM Map pp72–3
☎ 7405 2107; www.soane.org; 13 Lincoln's Inn Fields WC2; admission free, suggested donation £3; ☺ 10am-5pm Tue-Sat, plus 6-9pm 1st Tue of month; ⊖ Holborn

This little museum is one of the most atmospheric and fascinating sights in

INNS OF COURT

For all of the West End's urban mania, the area hides some unexpected pockets of Zenlike calm. Clustered around Holborn and Fleet St are the Inns of Court, with quiet alleys, open spaces and a serene atmosphere. All London barristers work from within one of the four inns, and a roll call of former members ranges from Oliver Cromwell and Charles Dickens to Mahatma Gandhi to Margaret Thatcher. It would take a lifetime working here to grasp the intricacies of the protocols of the inns – they're similar to the Freemasons, and both are 13th-century creations with centuries of tradition – and it's best to just soak in the dreamy atmosphere and relax.

Lincoln's Inn (Map pp72–3; ☎ 7405 1393; Lincoln's Inn Fields WC2; ⊗ grounds 9am-6pm Mon-Fri, chapel 12.30-2.30pm Mon-Fri; ⊖ Holborn) Lincoln's Inn is the most attractive of the four inns and has a chapel, pleasant square and picturesque gardens that invite a stroll, especially early or late in the day when the legal eagles aren't flapping about. The court itself, although closed to the public, is visible through the gates and is relatively intact, with original 15th-century buildings, including the Tudor Lincoln's Inn Gatehouse on Chancery Lane. Inigo Jones helped plan the well-preserved chapel which was built in 1623.

Gray's Inn (Map pp72–3; ☎ 7458 7800; Gray's Inn Rd WC1; ⊗ grounds 10am-4pm Mon-Fri, chapel 10am-6pm Mon-Fri; ⊖ Holborn/Chancery Lane) This inn – destroyed during WWII, rebuilt and expanded – is less interesting than Lincoln's Inn although the peaceful gardens are still something of a treat. The walls of the original hall absorbed the first ever performance of Shakespeare's *Comedy of Errors*.

Inner Temple (Map pp72–3; ☎ 7353 8559; King's Bench Walk EC4; ⊖ Temple or Blackfriars) Duck under the archway next to Prince Henry's Room and you'll find yourself in the Inner Temple, a sprawling complex of some of the finest buildings on the river. The church (see p113) was originally planned and built by the secretive Knights Templar between 1161 and 1185. At the weekend you'll usually have to enter from the Victoria Embankment.

Staple Inn (Map pp72–3; Holborn; ⊖ Chancery Lane) The 16th-century shop-front façade is the main interest at Staple Inn (1589), the last of eight Inns of Chancery whose functions were superseded by the Inns of Court in the 18th century. The buildings, mostly postwar reconstructions, are now occupied by the Institute of Actuaries and aren't actually open to the public, although nobody seems to mind a discreet and considerate look around. On the same side of Holborn but closer to Fetter Lane stood Barnard's Inn, redeveloped in 1991. Pip lived here with Herbert Pocket in Dickens' *Great Expectations*.

London. The building is the beautiful, bewitching home of architect Sir John Soane (1753–1837), which he left brimming with surprising effects and curiosities, and the museum represents his exquisite and eccentric taste.

Soane was a country bricklayer's son, most famous for designing the Bank of England. In his work and life, he drew on ideas picked up while on an 18th-century grand tour of Italy. He married a rich woman and used the wealth to build this house and the one next door, which has been bought by the museum and is planned to open as an exhibition and education space in late 2007.

The heritage-listed house is largely as it was when Sir John was carted out in a box, and is itself a main part of the attraction. It has a glass dome which brings light right down to the basement, a lantern room filled with statuary, rooms within rooms, and a picture gallery where paintings are stowed behind each other on folding wooden panes. You can see Soane's choice paintings, including Canalettos and

Turners, drawings by Christopher Wren and Robert Adam, and the original *Rake's Progress*, William Hogarth's set of cartoon caricatures of late-18th-century London lowlife. You'll have to ask a guard to open the panes so that you can view all the paintings. Among Soane's more unusual acquisitions are an Egyptian hieroglyphic sarcophagus, an imitation monk's parlour, and slave's chains.

Note that groups of seven or more need to book ahead and are not admitted on Saturday, which is by far the museum's busiest day. Evenings of the first Tuesday of each month are a choice time to visit as the house is lit by candles and the atmosphere is even more magical.

HUNTERIAN MUSEUM Map pp72–3
☎ 7869 6560; www.rcseng.ac.uk/museums; Royal College of Surgeons, 35-43 Lincoln's Inn Fields WC2; admission free; ⊗ 10am-5pm Tue-Sat; ⊖ Holborn
The collection of anatomical specimens of pioneering surgeon John Hunter (1728–93) inspired this fascinating, slightly morbid,

little-known, yet fantastic London museum. Among the more bizarre items on display are the skeleton of a 2.3m giant, half of mathematician Charles Babbage's brain, and, hilariously, Winston Churchill's dentures. Thanks to a massive refurbishment some years back, the atmosphere is less gory and allows decent viewing of things such as animal digestive systems, forensically documented in formaldehyde, and wonders such as the 'hearing organ' of a blue whale. Upstairs includes a display on plastic surgery techniques, which will impress and disgust in equal measure. There's a free guided tour every Wednesday at 1pm.

ST CLEMENT DANES Map pp72–3

☎ 7242 8282; The Strand WC2; ⏱ 8.30am-4.30pm Mon-Fri, 9am-3.30pm Sat, 9am-12.30pm Sun; ⊖ Temple

An 18th-centry English nursery rhyme that incorporates the names of London churches goes: 'Oranges and lemons, say the bells of St Clements', with the soothing final lines: 'Here comes a chopper to chop off your head, Chop chop chop chop the last man's dead!' Isn't that nice? Well, even though the bells of this church chime that nursery tune every day at 9am, noon and 3pm, this *isn't* the St Clements referred to in the first line the verse – that's St Clements Eastcheap, in the City. But we all know that historical fact needn't get in the way of a good story.

Sir Christopher Wren designed the original building in 1682 but only the walls and a steeple added by James Gibbs in 1719 survived the Luftwaffe, and the church was rebuilt after the war as a memorial to Allied airmen. Today it is the chapel of the Royal Air Force (RAF), and there are some 800 slate badges of different squadrons set into the pavement of the nave. The statue in front of the church quietly and contentiously commemorates the RAF's Sir Arthur 'Bomber' Harris, who led the bombing raids that obliterated Dresden and killed some 10,000 civilians during WWII.

BLOOMSBURY

Immediately north of Covent Garden – though worlds away in look and atmosphere – is Bloomsbury, a leafy quarter and the academic and intellectual heart of London. Here you will find the University of London and its many faculties and can the streets. And shade surrounded by Georgia houses that must b best museums: the Br beautiful squares were o 'Bloomsbury Group', a writers which included EM Forster, and the stories of their many intricate love affairs are as fascinating as their books. Charles Dickens, Charles Darwin, William Butler Yeats and George Bernard Shaw also lived here or hereabouts, as attested by the many blue plaques dotted around. Today Bloomsbury continues to teem with students, bookshops and cafés, while remaining relatively uncommercial. At its heart, London's largest green square, Russell Sq, is looking better than ever with an excellent refit and tidy up a few years ago. It remains a wonderful place for lunch and people-watching. Nearby is Brunswick Centre (www.brunswick .co.uk), a wonderful 1960s complex that consists of apartments, restaurants, shops and a cinema. A £24 million project saw it turned from a dreary, stern space to a lovely, cream-coloured airy square in 2006, and the centre is now packed with people seven days a week. The original architect, Partick Hodginson, worked on the renovations and claimed that the centre now looks like what he'd planned in the '60s, but that the design was stunted by the local council.

BRITISH MUSEUM Map pp92–3

☎ 7323 8000, tours 7323 8181; www.thebritish museum.ac.uk; Great Russell St WC1; admission free, £3 donation suggested; ⏱ galleries 10am-5.30pm Sat-Wed, to 8.30pm Thu & Fri, Great Court 9am-6pm Sun-Wed, to 11pm Thu-Sat; ⊖ Tottenham Court Rd or Russell Sq; ♿

One of London's most visited attractions, this museum draws an average of five million punters each year through its marvellous porticoed main gate on Great Russell St (a few go through the quieter Montague Pl entrance). One of the world's oldest and finest museums, the British Museum started in 1749 in the form of royal physician Hans Sloane's 'cabinet of curiosities' – which he later bequeathed to the country – and carried on expanding its collection (which now numbers some seven million items) through judicious acquisition and the controversial plundering of empire. It's an exhaustive and exhilarating stampede through world cultures, with galleries first and most impressive thing you'll see is the museum's Great Court, covered with a spectacular glass-and-steel roof designed by Norman Foster in 2000; it is the largest covered public square in Europe. In its centre is the world-famous Reading Room, formerly the British Library, which has been frequented by all the big brains of history: George Bernard Shaw, Mahatma Gandhi, Oscar Wilde, William Butler Yeats, Karl Marx, Vladimir Lenin, Charles Dickens and Thomas Hardy.

The northern end of the courtyard's lower level houses the terrific new Sainsbury African Galleries, a romp through the art and cultures of historic and contemporary African societies.

Check out the 1820 King's Library, the most stunning neoclassical space in London, which hosts a permanent exhibition 'Enlightenment: Discovering the World in the 18th Century'.

One of the museum's major stars is the Rosetta Stone (room 4), discovered in 1799. It is written in two forms of ancient Egyptian and Greek and was the key to deciphering Egyptian hieroglyphics. Another major star is the Parthenon Sculptures (aka Parthenon Marbles; room 18). The marbles once adorned the walls of the Parthenon on the Acropolis in Athens, and are thought to show the great procession to the temple that took place during the Panathenaic Festival, on the birthday of Athena, one of the grandest events in the Greek world. They are better known as the Elgin Marbles (after Lord Elgin, the British ambassador who shipped them to England in 1806), though this name is bound in controversy due to the British Museum's dispute with the Greek government, who want to see the pieces back in Athens. The battle continues, but you can read the museum's side of the story on a leaflet entitled 'Why are the Parthenon Sculptures always in the news?'

Prepare for a bit of gore in the Mexican Gallery (room 27), at the foot of the eastern staircase. The room features the 15th-century Aztec Mosaic Mask of Tezcatlipoca (The Skull of the Smoking Mirror), which has a turquoise mosaic laid over a human skull.

On a calmer note, rooms 33 and 34 host the Asian collections with the wonderful Amaravati Sculptures (room 33a), Indian goddesses, dancing Shivas and serene cross-legged Buddhas in copper and stone.

The story goes that bandits tried to steal the impressive Oxus Treasure (room 52), but the British rescued the collection of 7th- to 4th-century BC pieces of Persian gold which originated in the ancient Persian capital of Persepolis, and brought it to the museum.

The Lindow Man (room 50) is a 1st-century unfortunate who appears to have been smacked on the head with an axe and then garrotted. His remains were preserved in a peat bog until 1984 when a peat-cutting machine sliced him in half.

devoted to Egypt, Western Asia, Greece, the Orient, Africa, Italy, the Etruscans, the Romans, prehistoric and Roman Britain and medieval antiquities.

The museum is massive, so make a few focused visits if you have plenty of time, and consider the choice of tours. There are nine free 50-minute eyeOpener tours of individual galleries throughout the day, and 20-minute eyeOpener spotlight talks daily at 1.15pm focusing on different themes from the collection. Ninety-minute highlights tours (adult/concession £8/5) leave at 10.30am, 1pm and 3pm daily. If you want to go it alone there is a series of audioguide tours (£3.50) available at the information desk, including a family-oriented one narrated by comedian, writer and TV presenter Stephen Fry. One specific to the Parthenon Sculptures (aka the Parthenon Marbles or Elgin Marbles) is available in that gallery. You could also check out Compass, a multimedia public access system with 50 computer terminals

that lets you take a virtual tour of the museum, plan your own circuit or get information on specific exhibits.

DICKENS HOUSE MUSEUM Map pp92–3

☎ 7405 2127; www.dickensmuseum.com; 48 Doughty St WC1; adults/under 16yr/concession £5/3/4; ☻ 10am-5pm Mon-Sat, 11am-5pm Sun; ⊖ Russell Sq

The great Victorian novelist lived a nomadic life in the big city, moving around London so prolifically that he left behind him an unrivalled trail of blue plaques. This handsome four-storey house is his sole surviving residence before he upped and moved to Kent. Not that he stayed here for very long – he lasted a mere two-and-a-half years (1837–39) – but this is where his work really flourished: he dashed off *The Pickwick Papers*, *Nicholas Nickleby* and *Oliver Twist* despite worry over debts, deaths and his ever-growing family. The house was saved from demolition and the fasci-

NEIGHBOURHOODS WEST END

nating museum opened in 1925, showcasing the family drawing room (restored to its original condition) and 10 rooms chock-a-block with memorabilia. In the dressing room you can see texts Dickens had prepared for his reading tours, which include funny notes-to-self such as 'slapping the desk'. The said slapped desk is on display, a velvet-topped bureau purpose-made for his public readings.

NEW LONDON ARCHITECTURE
Map pp92–3

☎ 7636 4044; www.newlondonarchitecture .org; Building Centre, 26 Store St WC1; admission free; ☺ 9am-6pm Mon-Fri, 10am-5pm Sat, closed Sun; ⊖ Goodge St

An excellent way to see which way London's architectural development is going, this is a frequently changing exhibition that will capture the imagination and interest of anyone who loves London. A large model of the capital highlights the new building areas, showing the extent of the 2012 Olympics plans and various neighbourhood regeneration programmes. Photographs and details of individual buildings make it easy to locate each new structure, so that you can either go and see it in real life or spot it as you go along.

PERCIVAL DAVID FOUNDATION OF CHINESE ART Map pp92–3

☎ 7387 3909; www.pdfmuseum.org.uk; 53 Gordon Sq WC1; admission free; ☺ 10am-12.30pm & 1.30-5pm Mon-Fri; ⊖ Russell Sq

Although it feels like a fusty old institution, the friendly staff, lack of crowds and quirky collection here make for a rewarding visit. With some 1700 pieces, it's the largest collection of Chinese ceramics from the 10th to 18th centuries outside China. Sir Percival David donated it to the University of London in 1950 on the condition that every single piece be displayed at all times. Among the highlights are the David Vases (1351), the earliest dated and inscribed blue-and-white Chinese porcelain, named after Sir Percival himself.

PETRIE MUSEUM OF EGYPTIAN ARCHAEOLOGY Map pp92–3

☎ 7679 2884; www.petrie.ucl.ac.uk; University College London (UCL), Malet Pl WC1; admission free; ☺ 1-5pm Tue-Fri, 10am-1pm Sat; ⊖ Goodge St

If you've got any interest in things Egyptian, you'll love this quiet and oft-overlooked museum, where some 80,000 objects make up one of the most impressive collections of Egyptian and Sudanese archaeology in the world. Behind glass – and amid an atmosphere of academia – are exhibits ranging from fragments of pottery to the world's oldest dress (2800 BC). The museum is named after Professor William Flinders Petrie (1853–1942), who uncovered many of the exhibits during his excavations and donated the collection to the university in 1933. The entrance is through the University's Science Library.

POLLOCK'S TOY MUSEUM Map pp92–3

☎ 7639 3452; www.pollockstoymuseum.com; 1 Scala St W1; adult/child £3/1.50; ☺ 10am-5pm Mon-Sat; ⊖ Goodge St

Aimed at both kids and adults, this museum is simultaneously creepy and mesmerising. You walk in through the museum shop laden with excellent wooden toys and various games, and start your exploration by climbing up a rickety narrow staircase where displays begin with framed dolls from Latin America, Africa, India and Europe; upstairs is the museum's collection of toy theatres, many made by Benjamin Pollock himself, the leading Victorian manufacturer of the popular sets. Up another set of stairs and you see tin toys and weird-looking dolls in cotton nighties, and as you carry on the higgledy-piggledy trail of creaking stairs and floorboards, the dolls follow you with their glazed eyes. After you've climbed three flights of stairs, you'll descend four and, as if by magic, be led back to the shop.

THE SQUARES OF BLOOMSBURY
Map pp92–3

At the very heart of Bloomsbury is Russell Square. Originally laid out in 1800 by Humphrey Repton, it was dark and bushy until the striking face-lift that pruned the trees, tidied up the plants and gave it a 10m-tall fountain.

The centre of literary Bloomsbury was Gordon Square where, at various times, Bertrand Russell lived at No 57, Lytton Strachey at No 51 and Vanessa and Clive Bell, Maynard Keynes and the Woolf family at No 46. Strachey, Dora Carrington and Lydia Lopokova (the future wife of Maynard Keynes) all took

THE WEST END: BLOOMSBURY

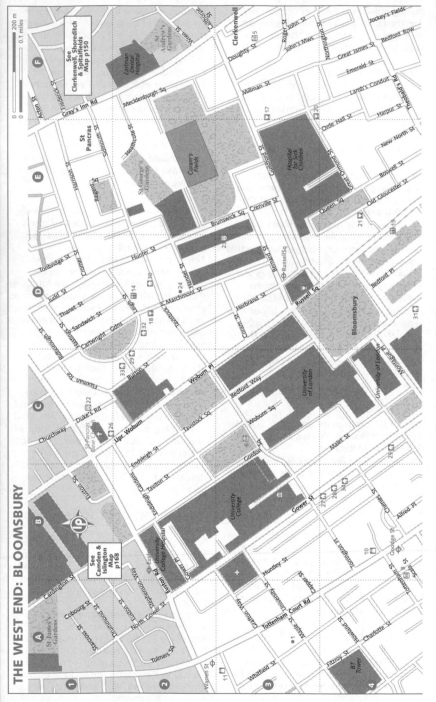

See Clerkenwell, Shoreditch & Spitalfields Map p150

See Camden & Islington Map p168

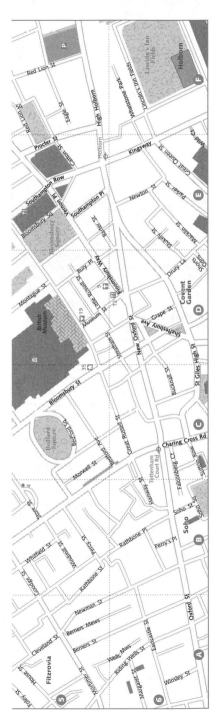

turns living at No 41. Not all the buildings, many of which now belong to the university, are marked with blue plaques.

Lovely Bedford Square, the only completely Georgian square still surviving in Bloomsbury, was home to many London publishing houses until the 1990s, when they were swallowed up by multinational conglomerates and relocated. They included Jonathan Cape, Chatto and the Bodley Head (set up by Woolf and her husband Leonard), and were largely responsible for perpetuating the legend of the Bloomsbury Group by churning out seemingly endless collections of associated letters, memoirs and biographies.

ST GEORGE'S BLOOMSBURY Map pp92–3
☎ 7405 3044; Bloomsbury Way WC1; ⊙ 9.30am-5.30pm Mon-Fri, 10.30am-12.30pm Sun; ⊖ Holborn or Tottenham Court Rd
Superbly restored in 2005, this Nicholas Hawksmoor church (1731) is distinguished by its classical portico of Corinthian capitals and a steeple that was inspired by the Mausoleum of Halicarnassus. It is topped with a statue of George I in Roman dress.

FITZROVIA
After the war, Fitzrovia – to the west of Bloomsbury – was a forerunner to Soho as a bohemian enclave populated by struggling artists and writers who frequented its many pubs, particularly the Fitzroy Tavern. It's home to hundreds of media offices, with tons of bars and restaurants along Charlotte St heaving after office hours. It's a bit of a tourist blind spot due to the fact that its one main sight, the 1960s BT Tower (once the highest structure in London), closed years ago as a result of terrorist threats.

ST JAMES'S
St James's is where the aristocrats are entertained in exclusive gentlemen's clubs (the Army and Navy sort as opposed to lap-dancing), and whose refined tastes are catered to in the many galleries, historic shops and elegant buildings. Despite much commercial development, its matter-of-fact elitism remains intact, and as you enter the seat of royal London along the grand, processional Mall that sweeps alongside the gorgeous St James's Park, up to Buckingham Palace and the Queen's driveway, you'll see why.

THE WEST END: BLOOMSBURY

The district took shape when Charles II moved his court to St James's Palace in the 17th century, and the toffs followed. The great Georgian squares – Berkeley, Hanover and Grosvenor – were built in the next century, by which time St James's was largely filled. By 1900 it was the most fashionable part of London, teeming with theatres, restaurants and boutiques. Savile Row is still where gentlemen go for tailoring, Bond Sts (old and new) are where ladies go for jewellery, and Cork St is where they go together for expensive art. Some residents couldn't keep up with the Joneses of St James's and moved out, to be replaced by businesses, offices and embassies. Grosvenor Sq is dominated by the US embassy.

BUCKINGHAM PALACE Map pp96–7

☎ 7766 7300, for disabled access 7766 7324; www .royalcollection.org.uk; Buckingham Palace Rd SW1; adult/child/concession/family £15/8.50/13.50/38.50; ⏱ 9.30am-4.30pm 28 Jul-25 Sep, timed ticket with admission every 15min; ⊖ St James's Park, Victoria or Green Park; ♿

Built in 1705 as Buckingham House for the duke of the same name, this palace has provided the royal family's London lodgings since 1837, when St James's Palace was judged too old-fashioned and insufficiently impressive. It is dominated by the 25m-high Queen Victoria Memorial at the end of the Mall. Tickets for the palace are on sale from a kiosk in Green Park.

After a series of crises and embarrassing revelations in the early 1990s, the royal spin doctors cranked things up a gear to try and rally public support behind the royals once again, and it was decided to swing open the royal doors of Buck House to the public for the first time. Well, to 19 of the 661 rooms, at least. And only during August and September, when HRH is holidaying in Scotland. And for a veritable king's ransom, but still, we mustn't quibble – no price is too great for an opportunity to see the Windsors' Polaroids plastered all over the fridge door.

The 'working rooms' are stripped down each summer for the arrival of the commoners, and the usual carpet is replaced with industrial-strength rugs, so the rooms don't look all that lavish. The tour starts in the Guard Room, too small for the Ceremonial Guard who are deployed in adjoining quarters; allows a peek inside the State Dining Room (all red damask and Regency furnishings); then moves on to the Blue Drawing Room, with a gorgeous fluted ceiling by John Nash; to the White Drawing Room, where foreign ambassadors are received; and to the Ballroom, where official receptions and state banquets are held. The Throne Room is pretty hilarious with kitschy his-and-hers pink chairs initialled 'ER' and 'P', sitting smugly under what looks like a theatre arch.

The most interesting part of the tour (for all but the royal sycophants) is the 76.5m-long Picture Gallery, featuring splendid works from the likes of Van Dyck, Rembrandt, Canaletto, Poussin, Canova and Vermeer, although the likes of these and much more are yours for free at the National Gallery. Wandering the gardens is another highlight here – it's bound to give you a real royal feeling.

Book in advance for disabled access.

CHANGING OF THE GUARD

☎ 7766 7300; Buckingham Palace, Buckingham Palace Rd SW1; ⏱ 11.30am daily Apr-Jul & alternate days, weather permitting Aug-Mar; ⊖ St James's Park or Victoria

This is a London 'must see' – if you actually get to see anything from the crowds. The old guard (Foot Guards of the Household Regiment) comes off duty to be replaced by the new guard on the forecourt of Buckingham Palace, and tourists get to gape – sometimes from behind as many as 10 people – at the bright red uniforms and bearskin hats of shouting and marching soldiers for just over half an hour. The official name for the ceremony is Guard Mounting, which, we dare say, sounds more interesting.

QUEEN'S GALLERY Map pp96–7

☎ 7766 7300; www.the-royal-collection.com; southern wing, Buckingham Palace, Buckingham Palace Rd SW1; adult/child/concession £8/4/7; ⏱ 10am-5.30pm; ⊖ St James's Park or Victoria; ♿

Paintings, sculpture, ceramics, furniture and jewellery are among the items displayed in the collection of art amassed by the royals over 500 years. The splendid gallery was originally designed by John Nash as a conservatory. It was converted into a chapel for Victoria in 1843, destroyed in a 1940 air raid and reopened as a gallery in 1962. A £20 million renovation for the Golden Jubilee in 2002 enlarged the entrance and added a Greek Doric portico, a multimedia centre and three times as much display space. Entrance to the gallery is through Buckingham Gate.

ROYAL MEWS Map pp96–7

☎ 7766 7302; www.the-royal-collection.com; Buckingham Palace Rd SW1; adult/child/concession £7/4.50/6; ⏱ 11am-4pm Mar-Jul, 10am-5pm Aug & Sep; ⊖ Victoria; ♿

South of the palace, the Royal Mews started life as a falconry but is now a working stable looking after the royals' immaculately groomed horses, along with the opulent vehicles the monarchy uses for getting from A to B. Highlights include the stunning gold coach of 1762, which has been used for every coronation since that of George III, and the Glass Coach of 1910, used for royal weddings. The Mews is closed in June during the four-day racing carnival of Royal Ascot, when the

royal heads try to win some horses.

ST JAMES'S PARK Map p

☎ 7930 1793; The Mall SW1; ⊖ St James's Park

This is one of the smallest but most gorgeous of London's parks. It has brilliant views of the London Eye, Westminster, St James's Palace, Carlton Terrace and Horse Guards Parade, and the view of Buckingham Palace from the footbridge spanning St James's Park Lake is the best you'll find (get those cameras out). The central lake is full of different types of ducks, geese, swans and general fowl, and its southern side's rocks serve as a rest stop for pelicans (fed at 3pm daily). Some of the technicolour flowerbeds were modelled on John Nash's original 'floriferous' beds of mixed shrubs, flowers and trees, and old-age squirrel feeders congregate under the trees daily, with bags of nuts and bread. Spring and summer days see Londoners and tourists alike sunbathing, picnicking and generally enjoying the sunshine, though sometimes in annoyingly large numbers. Nearby the popular café and restaurant Inn the Park (p245) stands the National Police Memorial, one column of marble and another of glass. Conceived by film director Michael (Death Wish) Winner and designed by architect Norman Foster and artist Per Arnoldi, it pays tribute to 1600 'bobbies' who have lost their lives in the line of duty.

ST JAMES'S PALACE Map pp96–7

Cleveland Row SW1; closed to the public; ⊖ Green Park

The striking Tudor gatehouse of St James's Palace, the only surviving part of a building initiated by the palace-mad Henry VIII in 1530, is best approached from St James's St to the north of the park. This was the official residence of kings and queens for more than three centuries and foreign ambassadors are still formally accredited to the Court of St James, although the tea and biscuits are actually served at Buckingham Palace. Princess Diana, who hated this place, lived here up until her divorce from Charles in 1996, when she moved to Kensington Palace. Prince Charles and his sons stayed on at St James's until 2004, before decamping next door to Clarence House, leaving St James's Palace to a brace of

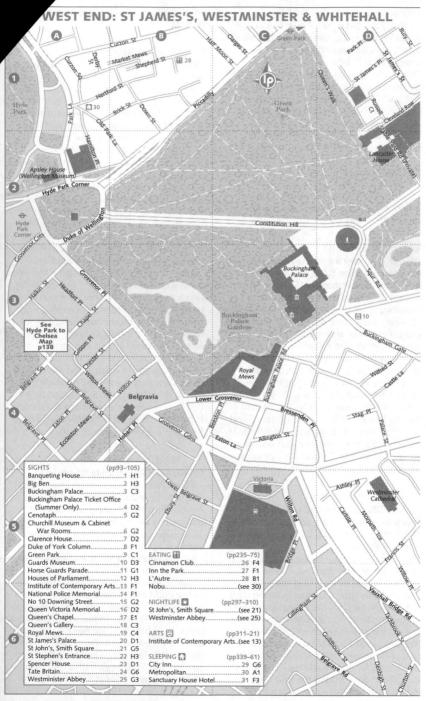

NEIGHBOURHOODS WEST END

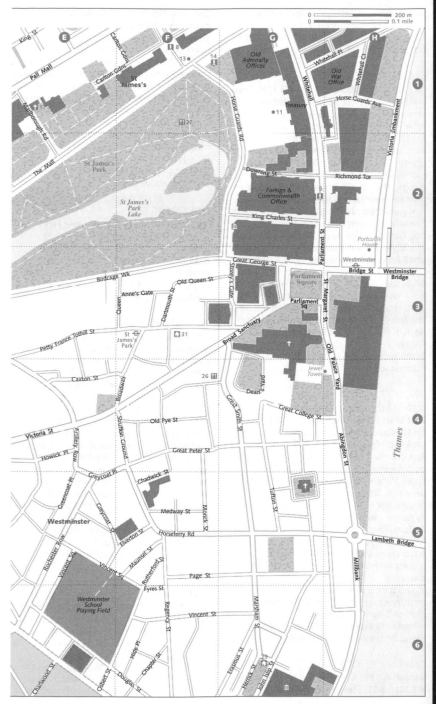

minor royals including Charles's famously tetchy sister, Princess Anne. Don't get too close in case she sends out a footman to tell you to naff off.

CLARENCE HOUSE Map pp96–7

☎ 7766 7303, for disabled access 7766 7324; Cleveland Row SW1; guided tour adult/concession £7/4; ⏰ 9.30am-5pm Aug-Oct; ⊖ Green Park; ♿

After his beloved granny the Queen Mum died in 2002, Prince Charles got the tradesmen into her former home of Clarence House and spent £4.6 million of taxpayers' money reshaping the house to his own design. The 'royal residences are held in trust for future generations', but the current generation has to pay to have a look at five official rooms when the Prince, his sons and Camilla are away on their summer hols. The highlight is the former Queen Mum's small art collection, including one painting by playwright Noël Coward and others by WS Sickert and Sir James Gunn. Admission is by tour only, which must be booked (far in advance); book also for disabled access. The house was originally designed by John Nash in the early 19th century, but – as Prince Charles wasn't the first royal to call in the redecorators – has been modified much since.

SPENCER HOUSE Map pp96–7

☎ 7499 8620; www.spencerhouse.co.uk; 27 St James's Pl SW1; adult/concession £9/7; ⏰ 10.30am-5.45pm Sun, last entry 4.45pm, closed Jan & Aug; ⊖ Green Park; ♿

Just outside the park, Spencer House was built for the first Earl Spencer, an ancestor of Princess Diana, in the Palladian style between 1756 and 1766. The Spencers moved out in 1927 and their grand family home was used as an office, until Lord Rothschild stepped in and returned it to its former glory in 1987 with an £18 million restoration. Visits to the eight lavishly furnished rooms of the house are by guided tour only.

The gardens, returned to their 18th-century design, are open only between 2pm and 5pm on a couple of Sundays in summer. Tickets cost £3.50 or £11 for combined house and garden entry.

QUEEN'S CHAPEL Map pp96–7

Marlborough Rd SW1; ⏰ only for Sunday services at 8.30am & 11.15am Apr-Jul; ⊖ St James's Park

The royal sights generally don't leave people breathless, but this one may touch your heartstrings: it's where all the contemporary royals from Princess Diana to the Queen Mother have lain in their coffins in the run-up to their funerals. The church was originally built by Inigo Jones in the Palladian style and was the first post-Reformation church in England built for Roman Catholic worship. It was once part of St James's Palace but was separated after a fire. The simple interior has exquisite 17th-century fittings and is atmospherically illuminated by light streaming in through the large windows above the altar.

GREEN PARK Map pp96–7

Piccadilly W1; ⏰ 5am-dusk; ⊖ Green Park

Less manicured than the adjoining St James's, this park has wonderful huge oaks and hilly meadows, and it's never as crowded as St James's. It was once a duelling ground and served as a vegetable garden during WWII.

GUARDS MUSEUM Map pp96–7

☎ 7976 0850; www.theguardsmuseum.com; Wellington Barracks, Birdcage Walk SW1; adult/child/concession £3/free/2; ⏰ 10am-4pm Feb-Dec, last entry 3.30pm; ⊖ St James's Park; ♿

If you found the crowds at the Changing of the Guards tiresome and didn't see a thing, get here for 10.50am on any day from April to August to see the guards entering formation outside the museum, for their march up to Buckingham Palace. In addition, check out the history of the five regiments of foot guards and their role in military campaigns from Waterloo on, in this little museum established in the 17th century during the reign of Charles II. There are uniforms, oil paintings, medals, curios and memorabilia that belonged to the soldiers. Perhaps the biggest draw here is the huge collection of toy soldiers in the shop.

INSTITUTE OF CONTEMPORARY ARTS Map pp96–7

ICA; ☎ 7930 3647; www.ica.org.uk; The Mall SW1; day membership adult/concession Mon-Fri £2/1.50, Sat, Sun & during exhibitions £3/2; ⏰ noon-10.30pm Mon, to 2am Tue-Sat, to 11pm Sun; ⊖ Charing Cross or Piccadilly Circus; ♿

Housed in a traditional building along the Mall, the ICA (as it's locally known) is as untraditional as you can possibly get. This was where Picasso and Henry Moore had their first UK shows, and ever since then the institute has sat comfortably on the cutting and controversial edge of the British arts world, with an excellent range of experimental/progressive/radical/obscure films, music and club nights, photography, art, theatre, lectures, multimedia works and book readings. Sure, you may see an exhibition here and come out none the wiser – we often do – and the place has been known to award a £26,000 prestigious sculpture prize for what was essentially a wonky shed, but the institute's programme is generally fantastic. Plus there's the licensed ICA Bar & Restaurant (to 2am most nights). The complex also includes an excellent bookshop, gallery, cinema and theatre.

The Duke of York Column, up the steps beside the ICA into Waterloo Pl, commemorates a son of George III. It was erected in 1834, but never quite caught the public imagination like Nelson's Column in Trafalgar Sq, although it's only 6m shorter.

MAYFAIR

London has many well-heeled neighbourhoods but none is so frightfully Jimmy Chooed up as this. Just wander up Old Bond St and you'll understand that this is a path walked by those with blue blood, old money and designer shoes. It's fascinating to witness the unabated flow of wealth and power stretching between Mayfair (the highest step on London's property ladder) and Chelsea.

Mayfair is west of Regent St and is where high society gives high-fives to one another; defining features are silver spoons and old-fashioned razzamatazz. But, in its southwestern corner, nudging Hyde Park, Shepherd Market is near the site of a rowdy and debauched fair that gave the area its name. The fair was banned in 1730, and today 'the old village centre of Mayfair' is a tiny enclave of pubs and bistros.

HANDEL HOUSE MUSEUM Map p100
7495 1685; www.handelhouse.org; 25 Brook St W1; adult/child/concession £5/2/4.50; 10am-6pm Tue-Sat, to 8pm Thu, noon-6pm Sun; Bond St;

George Frederick Handel lived in this 18th-century Mayfair building for 36 years until his death in 1759, and the house opened as a museum in late 2001. It has been restored to how it would have looked when the

great German-born comp[...]dence, complete with art[...] from several museums. E[...] early editions of Handel's [...] rios, although being in th[...] where he composed and [...] the likes of Water Music, M[...] Priest and Fireworks Music is ample attraction for any enthusiast. Entrance to the museum is on Lancashire Ct.

Funnily enough, the house at No 23 (now part of the museum) was home to a musician as different from Handel as could be imagined: American guitarist Jimi Hendrix (1942–69) lived there from 1968 until his death.

WESTMINSTER

WESTMINSTER ABBEY Map pp96–7
7222 5152; www.westminster-abbey.org; Dean's Yard SW1; adult/child/concession £10/free/6; 9.30am-3.45pm Mon-Fri, to 6pm Wed, to 1.45pm Sat, last entry 1hr before closing; Westminster;

Westminster Abbey is such an important commemoration site for both the British royalty and the nation's political and artistic idols, it's difficult to overstress its symbolic value or imagine its equivalent anywhere else in the world. With the exception of Edward V and Edward VIII, every sovereign has been crowned here since William the Conqueror in 1066, and most of the monarchs from Henry III (died 1272) to George II (died 1760) were also buried here.

There is an extraordinary amount to see here but, unless you enjoy feeling like part of a herd, come very early or very late.

The abbey is a magnificent sight. Though a mixture of architectural styles, it is considered the finest example of Early English Gothic (1180–1280). The original church was built in the 11th century by King (later St) Edward the Confessor, who is buried in the chapel behind the main altar. Henry III (r 1216–72) began work on the new building but didn't complete it; the French Gothic nave was finished in 1388. Henry VII's huge and magnificent chapel was added in 1519. Unlike St Paul's, Westminster Abbey has never been a cathedral – it is what is called a 'royal peculiar' and is administered directly by the Crown.

It is perhaps more impressive from outside than within. The interior is chock-a-block with small chapels, elaborate tombs

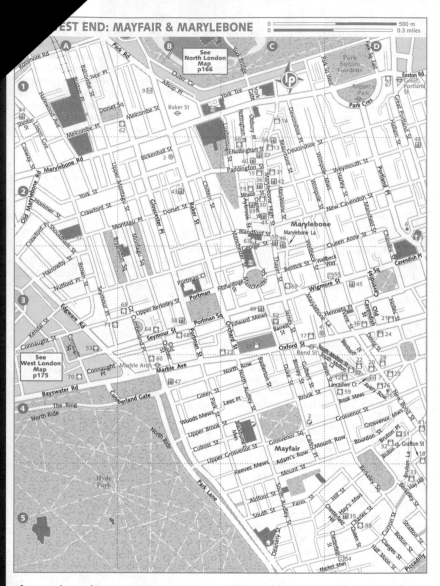

See
North London
Map
p166

See
West London
Map
p175

of monarchy, and monuments to various luminaries down through the ages. And, as you might expect for one of the most visited churches in Christendom, it can get intolerably busy.

Immediately past the barrier through the north door is what's known as Statesmen's Aisle, where politicians and eminent public figures are commemorated mostly by staggeringly large marble statues. The

Whig and Tory prime ministers who dominated late Victorian politics, Gladstone (who is buried here) and Disraeli (who is not), have their monuments uncomfortably close to one another. Nearby is a monument to Robert Peel, who, as home secretary in 1829, created the Metropolitan Police force. Robert's policemen became known as 'Bobby's boys' and later, simply, 'bobbies'.

THE WEST END: MAYFAIR & MARYLEBONE

At the eastern end of the sanctuary, opposite the entrance to the Henry VII Chapel, is the rather ordinary-looking Coronation Chair, upon which almost every monarch since the late 13th century is said to have been crowned. Up the steps in front of you and to your left is the narrow Queen Elizabeth Chapel, where Elizabeth I and her half-sister 'Bloody Mary' share an elaborate tomb.

The Henry VII Chapel, in the easternmost part of the abbey, has spectacular circular vaulting on the ceiling. Behind the chapel's altar is the elaborate sarcophagus of Henry VII and his queen, Elizabeth of York.

Beyond the chapel's altar is the Royal Air Force (RAF) Chapel, with a stained-glass window commemorating the force's finest hour, the Battle of Britain. Next to it, a plaque marks the spot where Oliver Cromwell's body lay for two years until the Restoration, when it was disinterred, hanged and beheaded. The bodies believed to be those of the two child princes (allegedly) murdered in the Tower of London in 1483 are buried here. The chapel's southern aisle contains the tomb of Mary Queen of Scots, beheaded on the orders of her cousin Elizabeth and with the acquiescence of her son, the future James I.

The Chapel of St Edward the Confessor, the most sacred spot in the abbey, lies just east of the sanctuary and behind the high altar; access may be restricted to protect the 13th-century floor. St Edward was the founder of the abbey and the original building was consecrated a few weeks before his death. His tomb was slightly altered after the original was destroyed during the Reformation.

The south transept contains Poets' Corner, where many of England's finest writers are buried and/or commemorated; a memorial here is the highest honour the Queen can bestow. Just north is the Lantern, the heart of the abbey, where coronations take place. If you face eastwards while standing in the centre, the sanctuary is in front of you. George Gilbert Scott designed the ornate high altar in 1897. Behind you, Edward Blore's chancel, dating from the mid-19th century, is a breathtaking structure of gold, blue and red Victorian Gothic. Where monks once worshipped, boys from the Choir School and lay vicars now sing the daily services.

The entrance to the Cloister is 13th century, while the cloister itself dates from the 14th. Eastwards down a passageway off the Cloister are three museums run by English Heritage. The octagonal Chapter House (🕑 9.30am-5pm Apr-Sep, 10am-5pm Oct, 10am-4pm Nov-Mar) has one of Europe's best-preserved medieval tile floors and retains traces of religious murals. It was used as a meeting place by the House of Commons in the second half of the 14th century. To the right of the entrance to Chapel House is what is claimed to be the oldest door in the UK – it's been there 950 years. The adjacent Pyx Chamber (10am-4.30pm) is one of the few remaining relics of the original abbey and contains the abbey's treasures and liturgical objects. The Abbey Museum (10.30am-4pm) exhibits the death masks of generations of royalty, wax effigies representing Charles II and William III (who is on a stool to make him as tall as his wife Mary), as well as armour and stained glass.

To reach the 900-year-old College Garden (10am-6pm Tue-Thu Apr-Sep, to 4pm Tue-Thu Oct-Mar), enter Dean's Yard and the Little Cloisters off Great College St.

On the western side of the cloister is Scientists' Corner, where you will find Sir Isaac Newton's tomb; a nearby section of the northern aisle of the nave is known as Musicians' Aisle.

The two towers above the west door are the ones through which you exit. These were designed by Nicholas Hawksmoor and completed in 1745. Just above the door, perched in 15th-century niches, are the latest sacred additions to the abbey: 10 stone statues of international 20th-century martyrs. These were unveiled in 1998 and they include the likes of Martin Luther King and the Polish priest St Maximilian Kolbe, who was murdered by the Nazis at Auschwitz.

To the right as you exit is a memorial to innocent victims of oppression, violence and war around the world. 'All you who pass by, is it nothing to you?' it asks poignantly.

There are 90-minute guided tours (7222 7110; £5) that leave several times during the day (Monday to Saturday) and limited audioguide tours (£4). One of the best ways to visit the abbey is to attend a service, particularly evensong (5pm weekdays, 3pm at weekends). Sunday Eucharist is at 11am.

HOUSES OF PARLIAMENT Map pp96–7

 7219 4272; www.parliament.uk; St Stephen's Entrance, St Margaret St SW1; admission free; during Parliamentary sessions 2.30-10.30pm Mon, 11.30am-7pm Tue & Wed, 11.30am-6.30pm Thu, 9.30am-3pm Fri; Westminster;
The House of Commons and House of Lords are housed here in the sumptuous Palace of Westminster. Charles Barry, assisted by interior designer Augustus Pugin,

built it between 1840 and 1860, when the extravagant neo-Gothic style was all the rage. The most famous feature outside the palace is the Clock Tower, commonly known as Big Ben. Ben is the bell hanging inside and is named after Benjamin Hall, the commissioner of works when the tower was completed in 1858. If you're very keen (and a UK resident) you can apply in writing for a free tour of the Clock Tower (see the website). Thirteen-tonne Ben has rung in the New Year since 1924, and the clock gets its hands and face washed by abseiling cleaners once every five years. The best view of the whole complex is from the eastern side of Lambeth Bridge. At the opposite end of the building is Victoria Tower, completed in 1860.

The House of Commons is where Members of Parliament (MPs) meet to propose and discuss new legislation, to grill the prime minister and other ministers, and to get their mugs on TV to show their constituents they are actually working. Watching a debate is not terribly exciting unless it's Prime Minister's Question Time, for which you will have to book advance tickets through your MP or local British embassy.

The layout of the Commons Chamber is based on that of St Stephen's Chapel in the original Palace of Westminster. The current chamber, designed by Giles Gilbert Scott, replaced the earlier one destroyed by a 1941 bomb. Although the Commons is a national assembly of 646 MPs, the chamber has seating for only 437. Government members sit to the right of the Speaker and Opposition members to the left. The Speaker presides over business from a chair given by Australia, while ministers speak from a despatch box donated by New Zealand.

When Parliament is in session, visitors are admitted to the House of Commons Visitors' Gallery via St Stephen's Entrance. Expect to queue for an hour or two if you haven't already organised a ticket. Parliamentary recesses (ie holidays) last for three months over the summer and a couple of weeks over Easter and Christmas, so it's best to ring in advance. To find out what's being debated on a particular day, check the notice board posted beside the entrance, or look in the Daily Telegraph or the freebie Metro newspaper under 'Today in Parliament', though it has to be said that the debates leave a lot to be desired both in terms of attendance and enthusiasm. Bags and cameras must be checked at a cloakroom before you enter the gallery and no large suitcases or backpacks are allowed through the airport-style security gate.

After campaign group 'Fathers 4 Justice' lobbed a condom full of purple powder at Tony Blair in May 2004 and prohunt campaigners broke into the Commons that September, security was further tightened, and a bulletproof screen now sits between members of the public and the debating chamber.

As you're waiting for your bags to go through the X-ray machines, look left at the stunning roof of Westminster Hall, originally built in 1099 and today the oldest surviving part of the Palace of Westminster, the seat of the English monarchy from the 11th to the early 16th centuries. Added between 1394 and 1401, it is the earliest known example of a hammer-beam roof and has been described as 'the greatest surviving achievement of medieval English carpentry'. Westminster Hall was used for coronation banquets in medieval times, and also served as a courthouse until the 19th century. The trials of William Wallace (1305), Thomas More (1535), Guy Fawkes (1606) and Charles I (1649) all took place here. In the 20th century, monarchs and Winston Churchill lay in state here.

The House of Lords Visitors' Gallery (☎ 7219 3107; admission free; ☿ 2.30-10pm Mon-Wed, 11am-1.30pm & 3-7.30pm Thu, 11am-3pm Fri) is also open for visits. Against a backdrop of peers' gentle snoring, you can view the intricate Gothic interior that led poor Pugin (1812–52) to an early death from overwork and nervous strain.

When Parliament is in recess, there are 75-minute guided summer tours (☎ 0870 906 3773; St Stephen's Entrance, St Margaret St; adult/child/concession £12/5/8) of both chambers and other historic buildings. Times change, so telephone or check www.parliament.uk for latest details.

TATE BRITAIN Map pp96–7

☎ 7887 8000, 7887 8888; www.tate.org.uk; Millbank SW1; admission free, prices vary for temporary exhibitions; ☿ 10am-5.50pm; ⊖ Pimlico; ☒

You'd think that Tate Britain may have suffered since its lavish, sexy sibling, Tate Modern (p129), took half its collection and all of the limelight up river when it opened in 2000,

but on the contrary, things have worked out perfectly for both galleries. The venerable Tate Britain, built in 1897, stretched out splendidly into all its increased space, filling it with its definitive collection of British art from the 16th to the late 20th centuries, while the Modern sister devoted its space to, well, modern art.

The permanent galleries are broadly chronological in order, and you can expect to see some of the most important works by artists such as Constable and Gainsborough – who have entire galleries devoted to them – and Hogarth, Reynolds, Stubbs, Blake and Moore, among others. Adjoining the main building is the Clore Gallery, which houses the superb JMW Turner, including the two recovered classics Shade and Darkness and Light and Colour which were nicked in 1994 and found nine years later.

Just before you thought that all the moderns and contemporaries were up at the Modern, Tate Britain's got work by Lucian Freud, Francis Bacon, David Hockney and Howard Hodgkin, as well as Anthony Gormley and bad-girl Tracey Emin. Tate Britain also hosts the prestigious and often controversial Turner Prize of contemporary art from October to early December every year.

There are several free one-hour thematic tours each day, mostly on the hour (last tour at 3pm), along with free 15-minute talks on paintings, painters and styles at 1.15pm Tuesday to Thursday in the Rotunda. Audioguide tours for the collection cost £3.50/3 (adult/concession). The best way to see both Tates and have a fabulous art day is to get the boat that connects the two galleries; see p387. A good time to visit the Tate is for its Late at Tate nights on the first Friday of every month, when the gallery stays open until 10pm.

HORSE GUARDS PARADE Map pp96–7

☎ 0906 866 3344; ☿ Changing of the Guard 11am Mon-Sat, 10am Sun; ⊖ Westminster

In a more accessible version of Buckingham Palace's Changing of the Guard, the mounted troopers of the Household Cavalry change guard here daily, at the official entrance to the royal palaces (opposite the Banqueting House). A lite-pomp version takes place at 4pm when the dismounted guards are changed. On the Queen's official birthday in June, the Trooping of the Colour is also staged here.

Fittingly, as the parade ground and its buildings were built in 1745 to house the Queen's so-called 'Life Guards', this will be the pitch for the beach volleyball during the London 2012 Olympics (see www .london2012.org). When this choice of venue was first announced, it had Tony Blair gloating about what a good view of the bikini-clad players he would have from his Downing St back window, though he may have to go around to Gordon Brown's now to get a glimpse (if Brown will let him in, that is).

ST JOHN'S, SMITH SQUARE Map pp96–7

☎ 7222 1061; www.sjss.org.uk; Smith Sq, Westminster SW1; ⊖ Westminster

In the heart of Westminster, this eye-catching church was built by Thomas Archer in 1728 under the Fifty New Churches Act (1711), which aimed to build 50 new churches for London's rapidly growing metropolitan area. Though they never did build all 50 churches, St John's, along with a dozen others, saw the light of day. Unfortunately, with its four corner towers and monumental façades, the structure was much maligned for the first century of its existence thanks to rumours that Queen Anne likened it to a footstool, though it's also said that she actually requested a church built in the shape of a footstool. Whatever the case, it's generally agreed now that the church is a masterpiece of English baroque, although it no longer serves as a church. After receiving a direct hit during WWII, it was rebuilt in the 1960s as a classical music venue (p309), and is renowned for its crisp acoustics.

The brick-vaulted restaurant in the crypt is called, predictably, the Footstool, and is open for lunch Monday to Friday, as well as for pre- and postconcert dinner.

WHITEHALL

Whitehall and its extension, Parliament St, is the wide avenue that links Trafalgar and Parliament Sqs, and it is lined with many government buildings, statues, monuments and other historical bits and pieces.

CHURCHILL MUSEUM & CABINET WAR ROOMS Map pp96–7

☎ 7930 6961; www.iwm.org.uk; Clive Steps, King Charles St SW1; adult/under 16yr/unemployed/senior & student £10/free/5/8; ⊗ 9.30am-6pm, last admission 5pm; ⊖ Charing Cross or Westminster; ♿

Down in the bunker where Prime Minister Winston Churchill, his cabinet and generals met during WWII, £6 million has been spent on a huge exhibition devoted to 'the greatest Briton'. This whizz-bang, multimedia Churchill Museum joins the highly evocative Cabinet War Rooms, where chiefs of staff slept, ate and plotted Hitler's downfall, blissfully believing they were protected from Luftwaffe bombs by the 3m slab of concrete overhead. (Turns out it would have crumpled like paper had the area taken a hit.) Together, these two sections make you forget the Churchill who was a maverick and lousy peacetime politician, and drive home how much the cigar-chewing, wartime PM was a case of right man, right time.

The Churchill Museum contains all sorts of posters, trivia and personal effects, from the man's cigars to a 'British bulldog' vase in his image, and from his formal Privy Council uniform to his shockingly tasteless red velvet 'romper' outfit. Even though the museum doesn't shy away from its hero's fallibilities, it does begin with his strongest suit – his stirring speeches, replayed for each goose-bumped visitor who steps in front of the matching screen. 'I have nothing to offer but blood, toil, tears and sweat', 'We will fight them on the beaches', 'Never in the course of human history has so much been owed by so many to so few'. Elsewhere, silver-tongued Winnie even gets credit for inspiring Orson Welles' famous rant about Switzerland and cuckoo clocks, with a speech he made to Parliament several years before The Third Man was filmed.

There's fantastically edited footage of Churchill's 1965 state funeral, making the April 2005 burial of Pope John Paul II look like a low-key family affair, and you can check on what the PM was doing nearly every day beforehand via the huge, table-top interactive lifeline. Touch the screen on a particular year, and it will open up into months and days for you to choose.

In stark contrast, the old Cabinet War Rooms have been left much as they were when the lights were turned off on VJ Day in August 1945 and everyone headed off for a well-earned drink. The room where the Cabinet held more than 100 meetings, the Telegraph Room with a hotline to Roosevelt, the cramped typing pool, the converted broom cupboard that was Churchill's office and scores of bedrooms have all been preserved.

You will pass the broadcast niche where Churchill made four of his rousing speeches to the nation, including one about Germany's fuelling 'a fire in British hearts' by launching the London Blitz. In the Chief of Staff's Conference Room, the walls are covered with huge, original maps that were only discovered in 2002. If you squint two-thirds of the way down the right wall, somebody (Churchill himself?) drew a little doodle depicting a cross-eyed and bandy-legged Hitler knocked on his arse.

The free audioguide is very informative and entertaining and features plenty of anecdotes, including some from people who worked here in the nerve centre of Britain's war effort – and weren't even allowed by their irritable boss to relieve the tension by whistling.

BANQUETING HOUSE Map pp96–7
☎ 0870 751 5178; www.hrp.org.uk; Whitehall SW1; adult/concession £4.50/3.50; ⊗ 10am-5pm Mon-Sat; ⊖ Westminster or Charing Cross; ⛫

This is the only surviving part of the Tudor Whitehall Palace, which once stretched most of the way down Whitehall and burned down in 1698. It was designed as England's first purely Renaissance building by Inigo Jones after he returned from Italy, and looked like no other structure in the country at the time. Apparently, the English hated it for more than a century.

A bust outside commemorates 30 January 1649 when Charles I, accused of treason by Cromwell after the Civil War, was executed on a scaffold built against a 1st-floor window here. When the royals were reinstated with Charles II, it inevitably became something of a royalist shrine. In a huge, virtually unfurnished hall on the 1st floor there are nine ceiling panels painted by Rubens in 1635. They were commissioned by Charles I and depict the 'divine right' of kings.

It is still occasionally used for state banquets and concerts, but fortunately you don't have to be on the royal A-list to visit, though if the house is rented for an event, it will be closed to the public, so phone in advance to check.

Book in advance for disabled access.

CENOTAPH Map pp96–7
Whitehall SW1; ⊖ Westminster or Charing Cross
The Cenotaph (Greek for 'empty tomb'), built in 1920 by Edwin Lutyens, is Britain's main memorial to the British and Commonwealth victims who were killed during the two world wars. The Queen and other public figures lay poppies at its base on the Sunday nearest 11 November.

NO 10 DOWNING STREET Map pp96–7
www.number10.gov.uk; 10 Downing St SW1; ⊖ Westminster or Charing Cross
As most people know, when it comes to property it's all 'location, location, location' and it's certain that British prime ministers have it pretty good postcode-wise. Number 10 has been the official office of British leaders since 1732, when George II presented No 10 to Robert Walpole, and since refurbishment in 1902 it's also been the PM's official London residence. As Margaret Thatcher, a grocer's daughter, famously put it, the PM 'lives above the shop' here.

For such a famous address, however, No 10 is a small-looking building on a plain-looking street, hardly warranting comparison to the White House, for example. A stoic bobby stands guard outside, but you can't get too close; the street was cordoned off with a rather large iron gate during Margaret Thatcher's times.

Breaking with tradition when he came to power, Tony Blair and his family swapped houses with the then-unmarried Chancellor, who traditionally occupied the rather larger flat at No 11. He also commandeered the offices at No 12, traditional base of the chief whip, claiming the need for more work space. We'll see what Brown does in his years in power.

MARYLEBONE

MADAME TUSSAUDS Map p100
☎ 0870 400 3000; www.madame-tussauds.com; Marylebone Rd NW1; adult/under 16yr £24/20; ⊗ 9.30am-5.30pm Mon-Fri, 9am-6pm Sat & Sun; ⊖ Baker St; ⛫

What can one say about Madame Tussauds? It's unbelievably kitsch and terribly overpriced, yet it draws more than 3 million people every year and sits high on the 'must-do' list of any visitor to London. Different strokes for different folks, as they say, but if you like the idea of wax celebrities, movie stars and fantastically lifelike figures of the Windsors, you're in for a treat.

Madame Tussauds dates back more than two centuries when the eponymous Swiss model-maker started making death masks of the people killed during the French Revolution. She came to London in 1803 and exhibited around 30 wax models in Baker St, on a site not far from this building, which has housed the waxworks since 1885. The waxworks were an enormous hit in Victorian times, when the models provided the only opportunity for visitors to glimpse the famous and infamous before photography was widespread and long before the advent of TV.

Madame Tussauds is very keen on public surveys telling it who the punters would like to see most, resulting in such highlights as a photo op with the Kate Moss figure (of a very poor similitude), an eco Prince Charles statue, the Blush Room where A-listers stand listlessly and where the J-Lo figure blushes if you whisper in her ear. Bollywood fans are treated with a smiling Shahrukh Khan and 'Big Bruvva' lovers can get into the Diary Room and take the video home. There are tons of temporary exhibits, such as the *Pirates of the Caribbean* chamber, potting holes with Tiger Woods, and so on.

Permanent photo opportunities include the political leaders in World Stage and the array of celebrities in Premiere Room. The famous Chamber of Horrors details the horrors of Jack the Ripper and is usually a huge hit with children. Finally you can take a ride in the Spirit of London 'time taxi', where you sit in a mock-up of a London black cab and are whipped through a five-minute historical summary of London, a mercifully short time to endure the god-awful scripts and hackneyed commentary. The old Planetarium is now the Stardome that screens an entertaining and educational animation by Nick Park, creator of *Wallace and Gromit* (it involves aliens and celebrities).

In case you were wondering what happens to the models of those people whose 15 minutes have passed, contrary to popular belief, they are never melted, but simply resting in storage.

If you want to avoid the queues (particularly in summer) book your tickets online and get a timed entry slot. They are cheaper this way too.

WALLACE COLLECTION Map p100

☎ 7563 9500; www.wallacecollection.org; Hertford House, Manchester Sq W1; admission free; ⏱ 10am-5pm; ⊖ Bond St; ♿

Arguably London's finest small gallery (relatively unknown even to Londoners), the Wallace Collection is an enthralling glimpse into 18th-century aristocratic life. The sumptuously restored Italianate mansion houses a treasure-trove of 17th- and 18th-century paintings, porcelain, artefacts and furniture collected by generations of the same family and bequeathed to the nation by the widow of Sir Richard Wallace (1818–90) on condition it should always be on display in the centre of London.

Among the many highlights here – besides the warm and friendly staff – are paintings by the likes of Rembrandt, Hals, Delacroix, Titian, Rubens, Poussin, Van Dyck, Velàzquez, Reynolds and Gainsborough in the stunning Great Gallery. There's a spectacular array of medieval and Renaissance armour (including some to try on), a Minton-tiled smoking room, stunning chandeliers and a sweeping staircase that is reckoned to be one of the best examples of French interior architecture in existence. There are also temporary exhibitions (admission payable) and very popular themed events involving Marie Antoinette and other French aristocrats, costumes and ballroom dancing (check the website for what's on when you're here).

Have lunch at the excellent glass-roofed restaurant, Café Bagatelle – which occupies the central courtyard and feels like something in southern Spain – and you'll have spent one of the most outstanding days in London.

SHERLOCK HOLMES MUSEUM Map p100

☎ 7935 8866; www.sherlock-holmes.co.uk; 221b Baker St; adult/child £6/4; ⏱ 9.30am-6pm; ⊖ Baker St

Though the museum gives its address as 221b Baker St, the actual fictional abode of Sherlock Holmes is the Abbey National building a bit further south. Fans of the books will enjoy examining the three floors of reconstructed Victoriana, deerstalkers, burning candles, flickering grates, but may balk at the dodgy waxworks of Professor Moriarty and 'the Man with the Twisted Lip'. The only disappointment is the lack of material and information on Arthur Conan Doyle.

BROADCASTING HOUSE Map p100
☎ 0870 603 0304; www.bbc.co.uk; Portland Pl; ✦ shop 9.30am-6pm Mon-Sat, 10am-5.30pm Sun; ✚ Oxford Circus

Broadcasting House is the iconic building from which the BBC began radio broadcasting in 1932, and where much of the BBC's radio output still comes from. There's a shop stocking any number of products relating to BBC programmes, even though the majority of the Beeb's output is produced in the corporation's glassy complex in Shepherd's Bush (hop on the website if you want to get tickets to a recording). Broadcasting House is currently having a vast extension built onto it, to where the World Service is scheduled to relocate when its lease on its current premises, Bush House on the Strand, expires in 2008.

ALL SOULS CHURCH Map p100
☎ 7580 3522; www.allsouls.org; Langham Pl W1; ✦ 9am-6pm, closed Sat; ✚ Oxford Circus

A Nash solution for the curving, northern sweep of Regent St was this delightful church, which features a circular columned porch and distinctive needlelike spire, reminiscent of an ancient Greek temple. Built from Bath stone, the church was very unpopular when completed in 1824 – a contemporary cartoon by George Cruikshank shows Nash rather painfully impaled on the spire through the bottom with the words 'Nashional Taste!!!' below it. It was bombed during the Blitz and renovated in 1951, and is now one of the most distinctive churches in central London.

THE WEST END WALK
Walking Tour
1 Covent Garden Piazza
Yes it's touristy, but it's worth seeing this wonderful Inigo Jones piazza (p85) and some of the street performers who make a living buffooning around in front of St Paul's Church.

2 Photographers Gallery
Small but with a hard artistic punch, this gallery (p85) is where top photographic exhibitions

take place. Check out the shop for great photography books.

3 Chinatown
Avoid Leicester Sq and walk down Lisle St under the ersatz Oriental gates of Chinatown (p67). Breathe in the aromatic spices, pick one of the restaurants – try Jen Café (p243) or New World (p239) for some delicious Chinese food.

4 Shaftesbury Avenue
This is theatre land and Shaftesbury Ave is where some of West End's most prestigious theatres are. This is where Hollywood stars such as Juliette Lewis, Jessica Lange and Christian Slater have performed, along with London's own Daniel Radcliffe.

5 Piccadilly Circus
Hectic and traffic-choked, but still lovely, Piccadilly Circus (p67) is like London's Times Sq, full of flashing ads, tons of shops and tourists.

6 Piccadilly
An elegant stretch away from the Circus, Piccadilly gives a whiff of the nearby aristocratic St James's and Mayfair. Pop into St James's Piccadilly (p70), the only church Sir Christopher built from scratch, check out the market stalls selling crafts and antiques outside, and sit down for a coffee while the pigeons fight for the bread crumbs left behind. Or you could visit Minamoto Kitchoan (p222) Japanese sweet shop for a green tea and some sweeties.

Free art and pay-for exhibitions abound at the brilliant Royal Academy of Arts (p70), where the courtyard installations can often be quite bizarre.

7 Green Park
Walk past the Ritz and turn left into Green Park (p98), a quiet, green space with some stunning oak trees and olde-worlde street lamps.

8 Buckingham Palace
Admire the Queen's abode (p94), though if you're keen on seeing some of the rooms (public access summer only), you're better off buying a ticket in advance. Walk down the grandiose Mall, where processions often take place and the Queen's limousine is escorted by her guards.

9 St James's Park
One of London's smaller, but definitely one of its most beautiful, parks (p95), this place is wonderful in summer and winter. Feed the

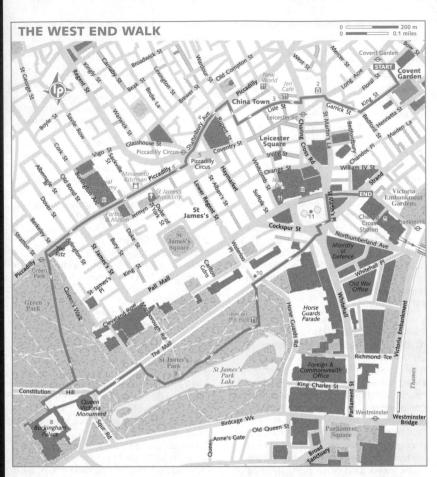

ducks, squirrels or swans, and take a look at the pelicans. Have a break in the stylish wooden Inn the Park (p246), where you can have some modern British food too. It's one of the more atmospheric places for dinner.

10 Institute of Contemporary Arts
Pop into the edgy ICA (p98) and have a look at whatever exhibition is taking place – you'll come out feeling something, good or bad.

11 Trafalgar Square
Another tourist magnet, but worth it all the way, Trafalgar Square (p74) is a magnificent beauty of a square. Check out the views of Big Ben from its southern side.

WALK FACTS
Start Covent Garden tube station
End Trafalgar Sq (Charing Cross tube station)
Distance 2.5 miles
Duration One hour 15 minutes
Fuel stops Jen Café (p243), New World (p239), Inn the Park (p245), National Gallery Dining Rooms (p76)

12 The National Gallery
Take a few hours to admire the artwork at the National Gallery (p75). Sit down for a well-deserved lunch or dinner in the new and stylish National Dining Rooms, where you can enjoy British cuisine in its finest form.

Eating p248; Drinking p282; Sleeping p349

The ancient, hallowed streets of the City are some of London's most fascinating. The Square Mile occupies pretty much exactly the same patch of land around which the Romans first constructed a defensive wall almost two millennia ago and probably contains more history than the rest of the city put together.

The tiny backstreets and ancient churches are today juxtaposed with skyscrapers and office blocks as this is the home of London's stock exchange, the Bank of England and countless other financial institutions. Very few people live in the City today, which was badly bombed during the Blitz, and so while it's very animated Monday to Friday, you can hear a pin drop at the weekend and even on a weeknight after 9pm once the commuters are all safely on their way home.

The centre of gravity for the City is Wren's masterpiece and London's great survivor, St Paul's Cathedral, still a must for all visitors to the capital. To the north of here is Smithfield, home to the notorious St Bartholomew's fair for centuries and a favoured spot for witch burnings and other gory public executions.

top picks

THE CITY

- St Paul's Cathedral (below)
- Tower of London (p119)
- Museum of London (p113)
- 30 St Mary Axe (p116)
- Temple Church (p113)

East of Smithfield is the Barbican, a vast arts complex and a visual statement that will either make your heart sing or your eyes ache depending what side of the architectural debate you bat for. Personally we love it, but there you go.

Further east still is Bank, the prosaically named district home to many of the major financial institutions of the country including the titular Bank of England. This is where the City can justly be called a bit sterile – pubs often only open Monday to Friday and eating choices split between Marks & Spencer sandwiches or five-course *haute cuisine* meals for those with expense accounts – yet beauties such as Lloyd's of London, the Gherkin and wonderful Leadenhall Market more than compensate for the lack of life at street level.

Further to the east still is Tower Hill, home to the world-famous Tower of London and iconic Tower Bridge. This is an area dominated by faceless office blocks, although pockets of colour do spill over from the neighbouring multicultural areas of Aldgate and Whitechapel and well-heeled Wapping. However, what the City lacks in great hangouts and community it more than makes up for with a wealth of historic sights and fascinating museums.

SMITHFIELD & ST PAUL'S

ST PAUL'S CATHEDRAL Map p110 & p112

☎ 7236 4128; www.stpauls.co.uk; St Paul's Churchyard EC4; adult/6-16yr/senior & student £9.50/3.50/8.50; ⏰ 8.30am-4pm (last entry) Mon-Sat; ⊖ St Paul's; ♿

Occupying a superb position atop Ludgate Hill, one of London's most recognisable buildings is Sir Christopher Wren's masterwork, completed in 1710 after the previous building was destroyed in the Great Fire of 1666. The proud bearer of the capital's largest church dome, St Paul's Cathedral has seen a lot in its 300-plus years, although Ludgate Hill has been a place of worship for almost 1400 years, the current incarnation being the fifth to stand on this site. St

Paul's almost didn't make it off the drawing board, as Wren's initial designs were rejected. However, since its first service in 1697, it's held funerals for Lord Nelson, the Duke of Wellington and Winston Churchill, and has played host to Martin Luther King as well as the ill-fated wedding of Charles and Diana. For Londoners the vast dome, which still manages to loom amid the far higher skyscrapers in the Square Mile, is a symbol of resilience and pride – miraculously surviving the Blitz unscathed. Today the cathedral is undergoing a huge restoration project to coincide with its 300th anniversary in 2010, so some parts may be under scaffold when you visit.

However, despite all the fascinating history and its impressive interior, people

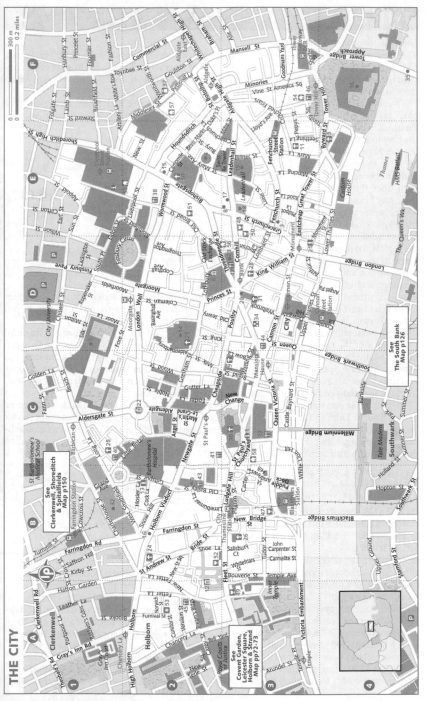

See
Clerkenwell, Shoreditch
& Spitalfields
Map p150

See
The South Bank
Map p126

See
Covent Garden,
Leicester Square,
Holborn & Strand
Map pp72–73

THE CITY

are usually most interested in climbing the dome for one of the best views of London imaginable. It's actually three domes, one inside the other, but it made the cathedral Wren's *tour de force* and only a handful of others throughout the world (mostly in Italy) outdo it in size. Exactly 530 stairs take you to the top, but it's a three-stage journey. The cathedral is built in the shape of a cross, with the dome at its intersection. So first find the circular paved area between the eight massive columns supporting the dome, then head to the door on the western side of the southern transept. Some 30m and precisely 259 steps above, you reach the interior walkway around the dome's base. This is the Whispering Gallery, so called because if you talk close to the wall it really does carry your words around to the opposite side, 32m away.

Climbing even more steps (another 119) you reach the Stone Gallery, which is an exterior viewing platform, with 360-degree views of London, all of which are rather obscured by pillars and other suicide-preventing measures.

The further 152 iron steps to the Golden Gallery are steeper and narrower than below but are really worth the effort as long as you don't suffer from claustrophobia. From here, 111m above London, the city opens up to you, your view unspoilt by superflu-

ous railings; you'll be hard pushed to see anything better.

Of course, back on the ground floor, St Paul's offers plenty of riches for those who like to keep their feet firmly on its black-and-white tiled floor – and the interior has been stunningly restored in recent years. Just beneath the dome, for starters, is a compass and an epitaph written for Wren by his son: *Lector, si monumentum requiris, circumspice* (Reader, if you seek his monument, look around you).

In the northern aisle you'll find the All Souls' Chapel and the Chapel of St Dunstan, dedicated to the 10th-century archbishop of Canterbury, and the grandiose Duke of Wellington Memorial (1875). In the north transept chapel is Holman Hunt's celebrated painting The Light of the World, which depicts Christ knocking at an overgrown door that, symbolically, can only be opened from the inside. Beyond, in the cathedral's heart, are the particularly spectacular quire (or chancel) – its ceilings and arches dazzling with green, blue, red and gold mosaics – and the high altar. The ornately carved choir stalls by Grinling Gibbons on either side of the quire are exquisite, as are the ornamental wrought-iron gates, separating the aisles from the altar, by Jean Tijou (both men also worked on Hampton Court Palace). Walk around the altar, with its massive gilded

ST PAUL'S CATHEDRAL

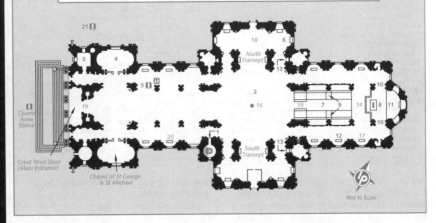

GROUND FLOOR

1 Entrance to Dome & Whispering Gallery
2 Dome & Wren's Epitaph
3 All Souls' Chapel
4 Chapel of St Dunstan
5 Duke of Wellington Memorial
6 The Light of the World
7 Quire
8 High Altar
9 Choir Stalls
10 Wrought-iron Gates
11 American Memorial Chapel
12 Effigy of John Donne
13 Crypt Entrances

CRYPT (keyed in italics)

14 OBE Chapel
15 Wellington's Tomb
16 Nelson's Tomb
17 Wren's Tomb
18 Treasury
19 Crypt Café
20 Shop
21 Monument to the People of London

oak canopy, to the American Memorial Chapel, a memorial to the 28,000 Americans based in Britain who lost their lives during WWII.

Around the southern side of the ambulatory is the effigy of John Donne (1573–1631). The one-time dean of St Paul's, Donne was also a metaphysical poet, most famous for the immortal lines 'No man is an island' and 'Ask not for whom the bell tolls, it tolls for thee' (both in the same poem!).

On the eastern side of both the north and south transepts are stairs leading down to the crypt, treasury and OBE Chapel, where weddings, funerals and other services are held for members of the Order of the British Empire. The crypt has memorials to up to 300 military demigods, including Florence Nightingale and Lord Kitchener, while both the Duke of Wellington and Admiral Nelson are actually buried here, Nelson having been placed in a black sarcophagus that is directly under the dome. On the surrounding walls are plaques in memory of those from the Commonwealth who died in various conflicts during the 20th century.

Wren's tomb is in the crypt, while architect Edwin Lutyens and poet William Blake are also remembered here. In a niche, there is

also an exhibit of Wren's controversial plans for St Paul's and his actual working model. St Paul's was one of the 50 commissions the great architect was given after the Great Fire of London wiped out most of the City.

The treasury displays some of the cathedral's plate, along with some spectacular needlework, including Beryl Dean's jubilee cope (bishop's cloak) of 1977, showing spires of 73 London churches, and its matching mitre. There is a Crypt Café (9am-5pm Mon-Sat, 10.30am-5pm Sun) and the restaurant Refectory (9am-5.30pm Mon-Sat, 10.30am-5.30pm Sun), in addition to a shop (9am-5pm Mon-Sat, 10.30am-5pm Sun).

Just outside the north transept, there's a simple monument to the people of London, honouring the 32,000 civilians killed (and another 50,000 seriously injured) in the defence of the city and the cathedral during WWII. Also to the left as you face the entrance stairway is Temple Bar, one of the original gateways to the City of London. This medieval stone archway once straddled Fleet St at a sight marked by a griffin (Map pp72–3) but was removed to Middlesex in 1878. Temple Bar was restored and made a triumphal return to London (albeit in a totally new place) alongside the redevelopment of Paternoster Sq in 2003.

Audioguide tours in multiple languages lasting 45 minutes cost £3.50 for adults, or £3 for seniors and students; guided tours lasting 1½ to two hours (adult/senior and student/child aged six to 16 years £3/2.50/1) leave the tour desk at 11am, 11.30am, 1.30pm and 2pm. There are free organ recitals at St Paul's at 5pm most Sundays, as well as celebrity recitals (adult/concession £8/5.50) at 6.30pm on the first Thursday of the month between May and October. Evensong takes place at 5pm Monday to Saturday and at 3.15pm on Sunday.

There is limited disabled access. Call ahead for further information.

MUSEUM OF LONDON Map p110

☎ 0870 444 3852, 7600 0807; www.museumo flondon.org.uk; London Wall EC2; admission free; ☺ 10am-5.50pm Mon-Sat, noon-5.50pm Sun; ⊖ Barbican; ♿

The Museum of London is one of the capital's best museums but remains largely off the radar for most visitors. That's not surprising when you consider that it's encased in concrete and located above a roundabout in the Barbican. Despite this, once you're inside it's a fascinating walk through the various incarnations of the capital from Anglo-Saxon village to global financial centre.

The newest gallery, called London Before London, outlines the development of the Thames Valley from 450 million years ago. Harnessing computer technology to enliven its exhibits and presenting impressive fossils and stone axe heads in shiny new cases, it somehow feels less warm and colourful than the more-established displays. In these you begin with the city's Roman era and move anticlockwise through the Saxon, medieval, Tudor and Stuart periods. Continuing down a ramp and past the ornate Lord Mayor's state coach, this history continues progressively until 1914, although at the time of writing the galleries were being expanded and improved to take visitors up to the present day. The finished galleries are due to open in late 2009.

Aside from the magnificently over-the-top state coach, highlights include the 4th-century lead coffin, skeleton and reconstructed face of a well-to-do young Roman woman whose remains were discovered in Spitalfields in 1999; the Cheapside Hoard, an amazing find of 16th- and 17th-century jewellery; the lo-fi but heartfelt Great Fire

of London diorama, na[...] renowned diary of San[...] timeline of London's c[...] during the 18th and 19[...] are two mock-ups of cit[...] resents Roman London,[...] Victorian Walk and hark[...] century (although Leader[...] creates a slightly less authentic, but more lively Victorian feeling).

You can pause for a breather in the pleasant garden in the building's central courtyard or head for the adjoining Museum Café, which serves light meals from 10am to 5.30pm (from 11.30am on Sunday). Alternatively, on a sunny day, pack some sandwiches and lunch in the next-door Barber Surgeon's Herb Garden.

When arriving, look for the Barbican's gate seven; before leaving, don't forget to have a browse through the well-stocked bookshop and check what the temporary exhibits are as these tend to be some of London's more interesting.

TEMPLE CHURCH Map p110

☎ 7353 3470; www.templechurch.com; Temple EC4; admission free; ☺ usually approx 2-4pm Wed-Sun, but call or email ahead to check as these change frequently; ⊖ Temple or Chancery Lane

This magnificent church lies within the walls of the Temple, built by the legendary Knights Templar, an order of crusading monks founded in the 12th century to protect pilgrims travelling to and from Jerusalem. The order moved here around 1160, abandoning its older headquarters in Holborn. Today the sprawling oasis of fine buildings and pleasant traffic-free green space is home to two Inns of Court (housing the chambers of lawyers practising in the City), the Middle and the Lesser Temple.

The Temple Church has a distinctive design: the Round (consecrated in 1185 and designed to recall the Church of the Holy Sepulchre in Jerusalem) adjoins the Chancel (built in 1240), which is the heart of the modern church. Both parts were severely damaged by a bomb in 1941 and have been lovingly reconstructed. Its most obvious points of interest are the life-size stone effigies of nine knights that lie on the floor of the Round. These include the Earl of Pembroke, who acted as the go-between for King John and the rebel barons, eventually leading to the signing of the Magna Carta in 1215. In recent years the church has become readers of *The Da Vinci Code*, key scene was set here.

g the week, the easiest access to hurch is via Inner Temple Lane, off et St. At the weekends, you'll need to enter from the Victoria Embankment.

CENTRAL CRIMINAL COURT (OLD BAILEY) Map p110

☎ 7248 3277; cnr Newgate & Old Bailey Sts; admission free; ⊙ approx 10am-1pm & 2-5pm Mon-Fri; ⊖ St Paul's

Just as fact is often better than fiction, taking in a trial in the Old Bailey leaves watching a TV courtroom drama for dust. Of course, it's too late to see author Jeffrey Archer being found guilty of perjury here, watch the Guildford Four's convictions being quashed after their wrongful imprisonment for IRA terrorist attacks or view the Yorkshire Ripper Peter Sutcliffe being sent down. However, 'the Old Bailey' is a byword for crime and notoriety. So even if you sit in on a fairly run-of-the-mill trial, simply being in the court where such people as the Kray twins and Oscar Wilde (in an earlier building on this site) once appeared is memorable in itself.

Choose from 18 courts, of which the oldest – courts one, two and three – usually have the most interesting cases. As cameras, video equipment, mobile phones, large bags and food and drink are all forbidden inside, and there are no cloakrooms or lockers, it's important not to take these with you. Take a cardigan or something to cushion the hard seats though, and if you're interested in a high-profile trial, get there early.

The Central Criminal Court gets its nickname from the street on which it stands: *baillie* was Norman French for 'enclosed courtyard'. The current building opened in 1907 on the combined site of a previous Old Bailey and Newgate Prison. Intriguingly, the figure of justice holding a sword and scales in her hands above the building's copper dome is *not* blindfolded (against undue influence, as is traditionally the case). That's a situation that has sparked many a sarcastic comment from those being charged here.

DR JOHNSON'S HOUSE Map p110

☎ 7353 3745; www.drjohnsonshouse.org; 17 Gough Sq EC4; adult/child/concession/family £4.50/1.50/3.50/10; ⊙ 11am-5.30pm Mon-Sat May-Sep, to 5pm Mon-Sat Oct-Apr; ⊖ Chancery Lane or Blackfriars

This wonderful house, which was built in 1700, is a rare surviving example of a Georgian city mansion. All around it today huge office blocks loom and tiny Gough Sq can be quite hard to find as a result. The house has been preserved, of course, as it was the home of the great Georgian wit Samuel Johnson, the author of the first serious dictionary of the English language (transcribed by a team of six clerks in the attic) and the man who proclaimed 'When a man is tired of London, he is tired of life'.

The museum doesn't exactly crackle with Dr Johnson's immortal wit, yet it's still an atmospheric and fascinating place to visit with its antique furniture and artefacts from Johnson's life (his brick from the Great Wall of China must surely be the oddest of these). The numerous paintings of Dr Johnson and his associates, including his black manservant Francis Barber and his clerk and biographer James Boswell are sadly not particularly revealing of the great minds who would have considered the building home from home. A more revealing object is a chair from Johnson's local pub, the Old Cock Tavern on Fleet St.

There's a rather ponderous video, plus leaflets telling how the lexicographer and six clerks (Boswell wasn't among them, yet) developed the first English dictionary in the house's attic during the period he lived here from 1748 to 1759. Children will love the Georgian dressing-up clothes on the top floor, and the temporary exhibits in the attic look at other aspects of 18th-century life.

Across Gough Sq is a statue of Johnson's cat, Hodge, sitting above the full quote explaining why when a man is tired of London, he is tired of life: 'For there is in London all that life can afford.'

ST BARTHOLOMEW-THE-GREAT
Map p110

☎ 7606 5171; www.greatstbarts.com; West Smithfield EC1; adult/concession £4/3; ⊙ 8.30am-5pm Mon-Fri, to 4pm mid-Nov–mid-Feb, plus 10.30am-4pm Sat & 8.30am-8pm Sun year-round; ⊖ Farringdon or Barbican

This spectacular Norman church dates from 1123, originally a part of the monastery of Augustinian Canons, but becoming the parish church of Smithfield in 1539 when King Henry VIII dissolved the monasteries. The authentic Norman arches, the weathered and blackened stone, the dark wood carvings and the low lighting lend this space an ancient calm – especially as you'll often be the only visitor. There are historical associations with William Hogarth, who was baptised here, and with politician Benjamin Franklin, who worked on site as an apprentice printer. The church sits on the corner of the grounds of St Bart's Hospital, on the side closest to Smithfield Market. Another selling point for modern audiences is that scenes from *Shakespeare in Love* (and parts of *Four Weddings and a Funeral*) were filmed here. The location managers for those movies knew what they were doing: St Bartholomew-the-Great is indeed one of the capital's most atmospheric places of worship.

ST BRIDE'S, FLEET STREET Map p110
☎ 7427 0133; www.stbrides.com; St Bride's Lane EC4; ⊗ 8am-6pm Mon-Fri, 11am-3pm Sat, 10am-1pm & 5-7.30pm Sun; ⊖ St Paul's or Blackfriars
Rupert Murdoch might have frogmarched the newspaper industry out to Wapping in the 1980s, but this small church off Fleet St remains 'the journalists' church'. Candles were kept burning here for reporters John McCarthy and Terry Anderson during their years as hostages in Lebanon during the 1990s, and a memorial plaque here keeps tab of the growing number of journalists killed in Iraq.

There's a brief, well-presented history of the printing industry in the crypt, dating from 1500 when William Caxton's first printing press was relocated next to the church after Caxton's death. St Bride's is also of architectural interest. Designed by Sir Christopher Wren in 1671, its add-on spire (1703) reputedly inspired the first tiered wedding cake.

ST ANDREW HOLBORN Map p110
☎ 7353 3544; Holborn Viaduct EC4; ⊗ 9am-4.30pm Mon-Fri; ⊖ Chancery Lane
This church on the southeastern corner of Holborn Circus, first mentioned in the 10th century, was rebuilt by Wren in 1686 and was the largest of his parish churches. Even though the interior was bombed to smithereens during WWII, much of what you see inside today is original 17th century as it was brought from other churches.

THE GOLDEN BOY OF PYE CORNER
Map p110
This small statue of a corpulent boy opposite St Bartholomew's Hospital, at the corner of Cock Lane and Giltspur St, has a somewhat odd dedication: 'In memory put up for the fire of London occasioned by the sin of gluttony 1666'. All becomes clear, however, when you realise the Great Fire was started in a busy bakery on Pudding Lane and that the fire finally burned itself out in what was once called Pye (Pie) Corner, where the statue now stands. This was interpreted by many as a sign that the fire was an act of God as punishment for the gluttony of Londoners.

SMITHFIELD MARKET Map p110
☎ 7248 3151; West Smithfield EC1; ⊖ Farringdon
Smithfield is central London's last surviving meat market. Its name derives from it being a smooth field where animals could be grazed, although its history is far from pastoral. Built on the site of the notorious St Bartholomew's fair, where witches were traditionally burned at the stake, this is where Scottish Independence leader William Wallace was executed in 1305 (there's a large plaque on the wall of St Bart's Hospital south of the market) as well as the place where the leader of the Peasants' Revolt Wat Tyler met his fate in 1381. Described in terms of pure horror by Dickens in *Oliver Twist*, this was once the armpit of London, where animal excrement and entrails created a sea of filth. Today it's an increasingly smart area full of bars, and the market itself is a wonderful building, although one constantly under threat of destruction and redevelopment into office blocks.

HOLBORN VIADUCT Map p110
⊖ St Paul's or Farringdon
This fine iron bridge was built in 1869 in an effort to smarten up the area, as well as to link Holborn and Newgate St above what had been a valley created by the River Fleet. The four bronze statues represent Commerce and Agriculture (on the northern side) and Science and Fine Arts (on the south).

BANK
By its very nature, much of the work of the City goes on behind closed doors. However, a short exploration of the streets around Bank tube station will take you to the door of many financial, as well as political and religious,

landmarks. Here, at the tube station's main exit, seven bank-filled streets converge. Take Princes St northwestwards to get to the Guildhall or head northeastwards along Threadneedle St for the Bank of England Museum. (All the following sights are on the City map, p110.)

The Royal Exchange (founded by Thomas Gresham) is the imposing, colonnaded building you see at the juncture of Threadneedle St and Cornhill to the east. It's the third building on a site originally chosen in 1564 by Gresham. It has not had a role as a financial institution since the 1980s and now houses a very upmarket (and much needed) shopping centre.

In the angle between Lombard St and King William St further south you'll see the twin towers of Hawksmoor's St Mary Woolnoth (☎ 7626 9701; ⏰ 8am-5pm Mon-Fri), built in 1717. The architect's only City church, its interior Corinthian columns are a foretaste of his Christ Church in Spitalfields.

Between King William St and Walbrook stands the grand, porticoed Mansion House (☎ 7626 2500; www.cityoflondon.gov.uk), the official residence of the Lord Mayor of London, which was built in the mid-18th century by George Dance the Elder. It's not open to the public, though group tours are sometimes available when booked in advance.

Along Walbrook, past the City of London Magistrates Court, is St Stephen Walbrook (☎ 7283 4444; 39 Walbrook EC3; ⏰ 10am-4pm Mon-Thu, to 3pm Fri), built in 1679. Widely considered to be the finest of Wren's City churches and a forerunner to St Paul's Cathedral, this light and airy building is indisputably impressive. Some 16 pillars with Corinthian capitals rise up to support its dome and ceiling, while a large cream-coloured boulder lies at the heart of its roomy central space. There is an altar by sculptor Henry Moore, cheekily dubbed 'the Camembert' by critics.

Queen Victoria St runs southwestwards from Bank. A short way along it on the left, in front of Temple Court at No 11, you'll find the remains of the 3rd-century AD Temple of Mithras. Truth be told, however, there's little to see here. If you're interested in this Persian God and the religion worshipping him, you're better off checking out the Museum of London (p113), where sculptures and silver incense boxes found in the temple are on display.

Due west of Bank is Poultry. The modern building at the corner, with striped layers of blond and rose stone, is by Stirling Wilford (the Wilford in question is also

behind the much-acclaimed Lowry centre in Salford Quays near Manchester). Behind this, Poultry runs into Cheapside, site of a great medieval market. On the left you'll see another of Wren's great churches, St Mary-le-Bow (☎ 7248 5139; Cheapside EC2; ⏰ 6.30am-6pm Mon-Thu, to 4pm Fri), built in 1673. It's famous as the church whose bells dictate who is – and who isn't – a cockney; it's said that a true cockney has to have been born within earshot of Bow Bells, although before the advent of motor traffic this would have been a far greater area than it is today. The church's delicate steeple is one of Wren's finest works and the modern stained glass is striking.

30 ST MARY AXE Map p110

☎ 7071 5008; www.30stmaryaxe.com; St Mary Axe EC3; ⊖ Aldgate or Bank

Known to one and all as 'the Gherkin' for obvious reasons when you see its incredible shape, 30 St Mary Axe – as it is officially and far more prosaically named – remains London's most distinctive skyscraper, dominating the city despite actually being slightly smaller than the neighbouring NatWest Tower. The phallic Gherkin's futuristic, sci-fi exterior has become as emblem of modern London as recognisable as Big Ben or the London Eye.

Built in 2002–03 to a multi-awardwinning design from Norman Foster, this is London's first ecofriendly skyscraper: Foster laid out the offices so they spiral around internal 'sky gardens'. The windows (one of which popped out of its frame in 2005) can be opened and the gardens are used to reprocess stale air, so air-conditioning is kept to a minimum. Its primary fuel source is gas, low-energy lighting is used throughout the building and the design heightens the amount of natural light let into the building, meaning that less electricity is used.

Its 41 floors mainly house the reinsurance giant Swiss Re's London offices, and tours are not currently possible. The gorgeous top-floor restaurant is usually open only to staff and their guests, but it's possible to gain access by booking one of the private dining rooms, although this will need to be done well in advance. In some years mere mortals are granted access during the superb Open House Weekend (www.open house.org.uk), an annual September event. When included as a venue, the Gherkin is always one of the most popular openings.

MONUMENT Map p110

☎ 7626 2717; Monument St EC3; adult/5-15yr £2/1; ⏱ 9.30am-5pm; ⊖ Monument

The vast column of Monument is definitely one of the best vantage points over London due to its centrality as much as to its height: the river, St Paul's and the City are all around you and you truly feel at London's bustling heart. The column itself is a memorial to the Great Fire of London in 1666, which, in terms of the physical devastation and horrifying psychological impact it wreaked on the city, must have been the 9/11 of its day. Fortunately, this event lies further back in history and few people died, so it's possible to simply enjoy Sir Christopher Wren's 1677 tower and its panoramic views of London. Slightly southeast of King William St, near London Bridge, the Monument is exactly 60.6m from the bakery in Pudding Lane where the fire started and exactly 60.6m high. To reach the viewing platform, just below a gilded bronze urn of flames that some call a big gold pincushion, you will need to climb 311 steps on the impressive circular staircase. On descent, you're given a certificate to say you did it, and if you did go all the way to the top, you'll feel it's justly deserved.

BARBICAN Map p110

☎ information 7638 8891, switchboard 7638 4141; www.barbican.org.uk; Silk St EC2; ⏱ 9am-11pm Mon-Sat, noon-11pm Sun; ⊖ Barbican or Moorgate

Londoners remain fairly divided about the architectural legacy of this vast housing and cultural complex in the heart of the City. While the Barbican is named after a Roman fortification protecting ancient Londinium that may once have stood here, what you see here today is very much a product of the 1960s and '70s. Built on a huge bombsite abandoned since WWII and opened progressively between 1969 and 1982, it's fair to say that its brutalist concrete isn't everyone's cup of tea. Yet despite topping several recent polls as London's most ugly building, many Londoners see something very beautiful about its cohesion and ambition – incorporating Shakespeare's local church St Giles Cripplegate into its brave-new-world design and embellishing its public areas with lakes and ponds. With a £7 million refit in 2005, the Barbican is much better loved than London's other modernist colossus, the South Bank Centre. Trendy urban architects are racing to get hold of the back-in-fashion apartments and the residences in the three high-rise towers that ring the cultural centre are some of the city's most sought after living spaces.

Home of the London Symphony Orchestra and one of the best places to see dance in capital, the Barbican is still London's pre-eminent cultural centre, boasting three cinemas that show a combination of commercial and independent films, two theatres which feature touring drama as well as dance performances and the highly regarded Barbican Gallery (adult/senior, student & 12-17yr £8/6; ⏱ 11am-8pm, to 6pm Tue & Thu), which stages excellent temporary exhibits.

See The Arts chapter for details of the theatres (p317), cinemas (p314) and concert halls (p312).

LLOYD'S OF LONDON Map p110

☎ 7623 1000; 1 Lime St EC3; ⊖ Aldgate or Bank

While the world's leading insurance brokers are inside underwriting everything from trains, planes and ships to cosmonauts' lives and film stars' legs, people outside still stop to gawp at the stainless steel external ducting and staircases of the Lloyd's of London building. French free climber, or 'spiderman', Alain Robert even felt moved to scale the exterior with his bare hands in 2003.

Lloyd's is the work of Richard Rogers, one of the architects of the Pompidou Centre in Paris, and although it was a watershed for London when it was built in 1986, it's since been overtaken by plenty of other stunning architecture throughout the capital. However, its brave-new-world postmodernism still strikes a particular contrast with the olde-worlde Leadenhall Market next door.

While you can watch people whizzing up and down the outside of the building in its all-glass lifts, sadly you can't experience it yourself. Access to the elevators and the rest of the interior is restricted to employees or professional groups, who must book in advance. Some years the Lloyd's building takes part in Open House Weekend, which gives the public very rare access to the inside of the building.

LEADENHALL MARKET Map p110
www.leadenhallmarket.co.uk; Whittington Ave EC1; 7am-5pm Mon-Fri; Bank

Like stepping into a small slice of Victorian London, a visit to this dimly lit, covered mall off Gracechurch St is a minor time-travelling experience. There's been a market on this site since the Roman era, but the architecture that survives is all cobblestones and late-19th-century ironwork; even modern restaurants and chain stores decorate their façades in period style here. The market also appears as Diagon Alley in *Harry Potter and the Philosopher's Stone*. For details of what's on sale, see p233.

BANK OF ENGLAND MUSEUM Map p110
7601 5545; www.bankofengland.co.uk; Bartholomew Lane EC2; admission free, audioguides £1; 10am-5pm Mon-Fri; Bank

When James II declared war against France in the 17th century, he looked over his shoulder and soon realised he didn't have the funds to finance his armed forces. A Scottish merchant by the name of William Paterson came up with the idea of forming a joint-stock bank that could lend the government money and, in 1694, so began the Bank of England and the notion of national debt. The bank rapidly expanded in size and stature and moved to this site in 1734. During a financial crisis at the end of the 18th century, a cartoon appeared depicting the bank as a haggard old woman, and this is probably the origin of its nickname 'the Old Lady of Threadneedle St', which has stuck ever since. The institution is now in charge of maintaining the integrity of the sterling and the British financial system and even sets interest rates since Gordon Brown empowered it to as Chancellor of the Exchequer in 1997. The gifted Sir John Soane built the original structure, although the governors saw fit to demolish most of his splendid bank in the early 20th century and replace it with a utilitarian, no-frills model that they would soon regret.

The centrepiece of the museum – which explores the evolution of money and the history of this venerable institution, and which is not *nearly* as dull as it sounds – is a postwar reconstruction of Soane's original stock office complete with mannequins in period dress behind original mahogany counters. A series of rooms leading off the office are packed with

exhibits ranging from photographs and coins to a gold bar you can lift up (it's amazingly heavy) and the muskets once used to defend the bank.

GUILDHALL Map p110
7606 3030; www.cityoflondon.gov.uk; Gresham St EC2; admission free; always call ahead; Bank;

Bang in the centre of the Square Mile, the Guildhall has been the City's seat of government for nearly 800 years. The present building dates from the early 15th century, making it the only secular stone structure to have survived the Great Fire of 1666, although it was severely damaged both then and during the Blitz of 1940.

Most visitors' first port of call is the impressive Great Hall, where you can see the banners and shields of London's 12 guilds (principal livery companies), which used to wield absolute power throughout the City. The lord mayor and sheriffs are still elected annually in the vast open hall, with its chunky chandeliers and its church-style monuments. It is often closed for various other formal functions, so it's best to ring ahead. Meetings of the Common Council are held here every third Thursday of each month (except August) at 1pm, and the Guildhall hosts the awards dinner for the Man Booker Prize, the leading British literary award.

Among the monuments to look out for if the hall is open are statues of Winston Churchill, Admiral Nelson, the Duke of Wellington and the two prime ministers Pitt the Elder and Younger. In the minstrels' gallery at the western end are statues of the biblical giants Gog and Magog, traditionally considered to be guardians of the City; today's figures replaced similar 18th-century statues destroyed in the Blitz. The Guildhall's stained glass was also blown out during the Blitz but a modern window in the southwestern corner depicts the city's history; look out for a picture of London's first lord mayor, Richard 'Dick' Whittington, and his famous cat.

Beneath the Great Hall is London's largest medieval crypt, with 19 stained-glass windows showing the livery companies' coats of arms. The crypt can be seen only as part of a free guided tour (7606 3030, ext 1463).

The buildings to the west house Corporation of London offices and the Guildhall

Library (☎ 7606 3030; Aldermanbury EC2; ☯ 9.30am-4.45pm Mon-Sat), founded in about 1420 under the terms of Dick Whittington's will. It is divided into three sections for research: printed books; manuscripts; and prints, maps and drawings. Also here is the Clockmakers' Company Museum (☎ 7332 1868; Guildhall Library, Aldermanbury EC2; admission free; ☯ 9.30am-4.45pm Mon-Fri), which has a collection of more than 700 clocks and watches dating back some 500 years. The clock museum sometimes closes for an hour or two on Monday to wind the clocks.

GUILDHALL ART GALLERY & ROMAN LONDON AMPHITHEATRE Map p110

☎ 7332 3700; www.guildhall-art-gallery.org.uk; Guildhall Yard EC2; adult/senior & student £2.50/1, all day Fri & daily after 3.30pm free; ☯ 10am-5pm Mon-Sat, noon-4pm Sun; ⊖ Bank

The gallery of the City of London provides a fascinating look at the politics of the Square Mile over the past few centuries, with a great collection of paintings of London in the 18th and 19th centuries, as well as the vast frieze entitled *The Defeat of the Floating Batteries* (1791), depicting the British victory at the Siege of Gibraltar in 1782. This huge painting was removed to safety just a month before the gallery was hit by a German bomb in 1941 – it spent 50 years rolled up before a spectacular restoration in 1999.

An even more recent arrival is a sculpture of former prime minister Margaret Thatcher, which has to be housed in a protective glass case as the iron lady was decapitated here by an angry punter with a cricket bat soon after its installation in 2002. Today, following some tricky neck surgery, the Maggie has finally rejoined the gallery's collection, but her contentious legacy lives on.

The real highlight of the museum is deep in the darkened basement, where the archaeological remains of Roman London's amphitheatre, or coliseum, lie. Discovered only in 1988 when work finally began on a new gallery following the original's destruction in the Blitz, they were immediately declared an Ancient Monument, and the new gallery built around them. While only a few remnants of the stone walls lining the eastern entrance still stand, they're imaginatively fleshed out with a black-and-fluorescent-green trompe l'oeil of the

missing seating, and comput outlines of spectators and gl roar of the crowd goes up a the end of the entrance tur central stage, giving a real Roman London might have felt. on the square outside the Guildhall mark out the original extent of the amphitheatre, allowing people to imagine the scale of the original building.

ST LAWRENCE JEWRY Map p110

☎ 7600 9478; Gresham St EC2; admission free; ☯ 7.30am-2.15pm; ⊖ Bank; ♿

To look at the Corporation of London's extremely well-preserved official church, you'd barely realise that it was almost completely destroyed during WWII. Instead, it does Sir Christopher Wren, who built it in 1678, and its subsequent restorers proud, with its immaculate alabaster walls and gilt trimmings. The arms of the City of London adorn the organ above the door at the western end. The Commonwealth Chapel is bedecked with the flags of member nations. Free piano recitals are held each Monday at 1pm; organ recitals at the same time on Tuesday.

As the church name suggests, this was once part of the Jewish quarter – the centre being Old Jewry, the street to the southeast. The district was sadly not with out its pogroms. After some 500 Jews were killed in 1262 in mob 'retaliation' against a Jewish moneylender, Edward I expelled the entire community from London to Flanders in 1290. They did not return until the late 17th century.

TOWER HILL

TOWER OF LONDON Map p120

☎ 7709 0765; www.hrp.org.uk; Tower Hill EC3; adult/5-15yr/senior & student/family £16/9.50/13/45; ☯ 9am-6pm Tue-Sat, 10am-6pm Sun & Mon Mar-Oct, 9am-5pm Tue-Sat, 10am-5pm Sun & Mon Nov-Feb, last admission on all days 1hr before closing time; ⊖ Tower Hill; ♿

The absolute kernel of London with a history as bleak and bloody as it is fascinating, the Tower of London should be first on anyone's list of London's sights. Despite ever-growing ticket prices and the hoards of tourists that descend here in the summer months, this is one of those rare pleasures: somewhere worth the hype. Throughout

NEIGHBOURHOODS THE CITY

es, murder and political skulduggery
reigned as much as kings and queens,
tales of imprisonment and executions
will pepper your trail.

The Tower is in fact a castle, and not
towerlike at all (although in the Middle
Ages it's easy to imagine how the White
Tower would have dwarfed the huts of the
peasantry surrounding the castle walls)
and has been the property (and sometime
London residence) of the monarch since it
was begun during the reign of William the
Conqueror (1066–87). By far the best preserved medieval castle in London, it's one
of the capital's four Unesco World Heritage
sites (the others are Westminster Abbey,
Kew Gardens and Maritime Greenwich), and
will fascinate anyone with any interest at all
in history, the monarchy and warfare.

With more than two million visitors a
year, crowds are quite serious in the high
season and it's best to buy a ticket in
advance as well as to visit later in the day.
You can buy Tower tickets online, or at
any tube station up to a week beforehand,
which can save you a long time when you
arrive. Also, after 3pm the groups have usually left and the place is a lot more pleasant
to stroll around. During the winter months
it's far less crowded, so there's no need to
do either of the preceding.

Your best bet is to start with a free
hour-long tour given by the Yeoman
Warders, which are a great way to bring
the various parts of the tower to life. The
Yeoman Warders have been guarding the
tower since 1485, and have all served a
minimum of 22 years in the British Armed

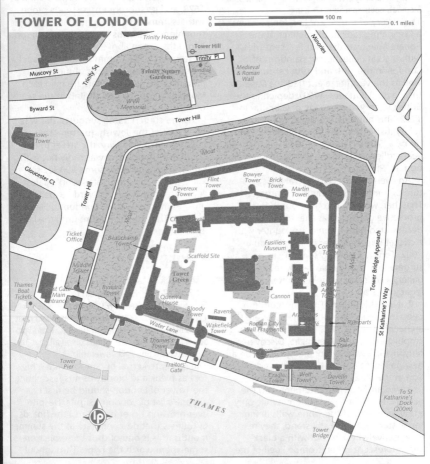

TOWER OF LONDON

Forces. Known affectionately as 'beefeaters' by the public (due to the large rations of beef given to them in the past), there are 35 Yeoman Warders today, including Moira Cameron, the first ever female beefeater, who began serving in 2007. While officially they guard the tower and Crown Jewels at night, their role is as tour guides (and to pose for photographs with curious foreigners). These tours leave from the Middle Tower every 30 minutes from 9.30am (10am on Sunday) to 3.30pm (2.30pm in winter) daily. The warders also conduct about eight different short talks (35 minutes) and tours (45 minutes) on specific themes. The first is at 9.30am Monday to Saturday (10.15am on Sunday in summer, 11.30am in winter), the last at 5.15pm (3pm in winter). Less theatrical are the self-paced audioguides available in five languages for £3 from the information point on Water Lane.

You enter the tower via the West Gate and proceed across the walkway over the dry moat between the Middle Tower and Byward Tower. The original moat was finally drained of centuries of festering sewage in the 19th century, necessitated by persistent cholera outbreaks, and a superbly manicured lawn now surrounds the Tower. Before you stands the Bell Tower, housing the tower's curfew bells and one-time home to Thomas More. The politician and author of Utopia was imprisoned here in 1534 before his execution for refusing to recognise King Henry VIII as the new head of the Church of England in place of the Pope. To your left are the casements of the former Royal Mint, which was moved from this site to new buildings northeast of the castle in 1812.

Continuing past the Bell Tower along Water Lane between the walls you come to the famous Traitors' Gate, the gateway through which prisoners being brought by river entered the tower. Above the gate, rooms inside St Thomas's Tower show what the hall and bedchamber of Edward I (1272–1307) might once have looked like. Here also archaeologists have peeled back the layers of newer buildings to find what went before. Opposite St Thomas's Tower is Wakefield Tower, built by Henry III between 1220 and 1240. Its upper floor is actually entered via St Thomas's Tower and has been even more enticingly furnished with a replica throne and huge candelabra to give an impression of how, as an anteroom

in a medieval palace, it might have looked In Edward I's day. During the 15th-century War of the Roses between the Houses of Lancaster and York, Henry VI was almost certainly murdered in this tower.

Below, in the basement of Wakefield Tower, there's a Torture at the Tower exhibition. However, torture wasn't practised as much in England as it was on the Continent apparently, and the display is pretty perfunctory, limiting itself to a rack, a pair of manacles and an instrument for keeping prisoners doubled up called a Scavenger's Daughter. Frankly, you'd see scarier gear at any London S&M club (or, the London Dungeon across the river in London Bridge, see p132). To get to this exhibition and the basement level of Wakefield Tower, you enter the tower courtyard through the arch opposite Traitors' Gate.

As you do so, you'll also see at the centre of the courtyard the Norman White Tower with a turret on each of its four corners and a golden weather vane spinning atop each. This tower has a couple of remnants of Norman architecture, including a fireplace and garderobe (lavatory). However, most of its interior is given over to a collection of cannons, guns and suits of armour for men and horses, which come from the Royal Armouries in Leeds. Among the most remarkable exhibits are the 2m suit of armour made for John of Gaunt (to see that coming towards you on a battlefield must have been terrifying) and alongside it a tiny child's suit of armour designed for James I's young son Henry. Another unmissable suit is that of Henry VIII, almost square-shaped to match the monarch's body by his 40s, and featuring what must have been the most impressive posing pouch in the kingdom.

The stretch of green between the Wakefield and White Towers is where the Tower's famous ravens are found. Opposite Wakefield Tower and the White Tower is the Bloody Tower, with an exhibition on Elizabethan adventurer Sir Walter Raleigh, who was imprisoned here three times by the capricious Elizabeth I, most significantly from 1605 to 1616.

The Bloody Tower acquired its nickname from the story that the 'princes in the tower', Edward V and his younger brother, were murdered here to annul their claims to the throne. The blame is usually laid at the door of their uncle Richard III, although

Henry VII might also have been responsible for the crime.

Beside the Bloody Tower sits a collection of black-and-white half-timbered Tudor houses that are home to Tower of London staff. The Queen's House, where Anne Boleyn lived out her final days in 1536, now houses the resident governor and is closed to the public.

North of the Queen's House, across Tower Green, is the scaffold site, where seven people were executed by beheading in Tudor times: two of Henry VIII's six wives, the alleged adulterers Anne Boleyn and Catherine Howard; the latter's lady-in-waiting, Jane Rochford; Margaret Pole, countess of Salisbury, descended from the House of York; 16-year-old Lady Jane Grey, who fell foul of Henry's daughter Mary I by being her rival for the throne; William, Lord Hastings; and Robert Devereux, Earl of Essex, once a favourite of Elizabeth I.

These people were executed within the tower precincts largely to spare the monarch the embarrassment of the usual public execution on Tower Hill, an event that was usually attended by thousands of spectators. In the case of Robert Devereux, the authorities perhaps also feared a popular uprising in his support.

Behind the scaffold site is the Beauchamp Tower, where high-ranking prisoners including Anne Boleyn and Lady Jane Grey were jailed and where unhappy inscriptions from the condemned are on display today.

Behind the scaffold site lies the Chapel Royal of St Peter ad Vincula (St Peter in Chains), a rare example of ecclesiastical Tudor architecture and the burial place of those beheaded on the scaffold outside or at nearby Tower Hill. Unfortunately, it can only be visited on a group tour or after 4.30pm, so if you aren't already part of a group hang around until one shows up and then tag along. Alternatively, attend a service, which takes place at 9am on Sunday.

To the east of the chapel and north of the White Tower is the building that visitors most want to see: Waterloo Barracks, the home of the Crown Jewels. You file past footage of Queen Elizabeth II's coronation backed by stirring patriotic music before you reach the vault itself (check out the doors as you go in – they look like they'd survive a nuclear attack). Once inside you'll be confronted with ornate sceptres, plates, orbs and, naturally, crowns. A very slow-moving travelator takes

you past the dozen or so crowns that are the centrepiece, including the £27.5 million Imperial State Crown, set with diamonds (2868 of them to be exact), sapphires, emeralds, rubies and pearls, and the platinum crown of the late Queen Mother, Elizabeth, which is famously set with the 105-carat Koh-i-Noor (Mountain of Light) diamond. Surrounded by myth and legend, the 14th-century diamond has been claimed by both India and Afghanistan. It reputedly confers enormous power on its owner, but male owners are destined to die a tormented death.

Behind the Waterloo Barracks is the newly opened Bowyer Tower, where George, Duke of Clarence, brother and rival of Edward IV, was imprisoned and, according to a long-standing legend that has never been proved, was drowned in a barrel of Malmsey (sweet Madeira wine).

The Fusiliers Museum to the east of Waterloo Barracks is run by the Royal Regiment of Fusiliers, who charge a separate nominal entrance fee. This museum covers the history of the Royal Fusiliers dating back to 1685, and has models of several battles. A 10-minute video gives details of the modern regiment.

The redbrick New Armouries in the southeastern corner of the inner courtyard houses the New Armouries Café where you can grab a pricey sandwich or soup lunch.

There are plenty of other attractions, as well as churches, shops and toilets within the tower complex, but before you leave you should also walk along the inner ramparts. This Wall Walk begins with the 13th-century Salt Tower, probably used to store saltpetre for gunpowder, and takes in Broad Arrow Tower, which houses an exhibit about the gunpowder plotters imprisoned here, many of their original inscriptions having been discovered on the walls. The walk ends at the Martin Tower, which houses an exhibition about the original coronation regalia. Here you can see some of the older crowns, which have had their jewels removed. The oldest surviving crown is that of George I, which is topped with the ball and cross from James II's crown. It was from the Martin Tower that Colonel Thomas Blood attempted to steal the Crown Jewels in 1671, disguised as a clergyman.

Finally for those interested in the obscure ritual and ceremony of the British monarchy, the Key Ceremony takes place every evening at 9.30pm. This elaborate locking of the main gates makes the changing of the guard at Buckingham Palace look like a recently invented tourist trick – the guards have been performing the ceremony every day unbroken for more than 600 years. Even when a bomb hit the Tower of London during the Blitz, the ceremony was delayed by just 30 minutes, which as everyone agrees is the essence of the famed stiff upper lip. Entry to the ceremony is free, but in a suitably antiquated style you have to apply for tickets by post as demand is so high. See the website for details.

There is limited disabled access to the tower. Call ahead for more information.

AROUND THE TOWER OF LONDON
Map p120

Despite the Tower's World Heritage Site status, the area immediately to the north is fairly disappointing, especially as in recent years much of it has been a construction site. Just outside Tower Hill tube station, a giant bronze sundial depicts the history of London from AD 43 to 1982. It stands on a platform offering a view of the neighbouring Trinity Square Gardens, once the site of the Tower Hill scaffold and now home to Edwin Lutyens' memorial to the marines and merchant sailors who lost their lives during WWI. A grassy area, off the steps leading to a subway under the main road, lets you inspect a stretch of the medieval wall built on Roman foundations, with a modern statue of Emperor Trajan (r AD 98–117) standing in front of it. At the other end of the tunnel is a postern (gate) dating from the 13th century.

TOWER BRIDGE Map p110
 Tower Hill

Perhaps second only to Big Ben as London's most recognisable symbol, Tower Bridge doesn't disappoint up close. There's something about its neo-Gothic towers and blue suspension struts that that make it quite enthralling to look at. Built in 1894 as a much-needed crossing point in the east, it was equipped with a then revolutionary bascule (seesaw) mechanism that could clear the way for oncoming ships in three minutes. Although London's days as a thriving port are long over, the bridge still does its stuff, lifting around 1000 times per year and as many as 10 times per day in summer. (For information on the next lifting ring 7940 3984 or check the following website.)

The Tower Bridge Exhibition (7940 3985; www .towerbridge.org.uk; adult/under 5yr/5-15yr/senior & student/family £6/free/3/4.50/14; 10am-6.30pm Apr-Oct, 9.30am-6pm Nov-Mar, last admission 1hr before closing) explains the nuts and bolts of it all. If you're not particularly technically minded, however, it's still interesting to get inside the bridge and look out its windows along the Thames.

ALL HALLOWS-BY-THE-TOWER Map p110
 7481 2928; Byward St EC3; admission free; 9am-5.45pm Mon-Fri, 10am-5pm Sat & Sun; Tower Hill

All Hallows is the parish where famous diarist Samuel Pepys recorded his observations of the nearby Great Fire of London in 1666. Above ground it's a pleasant enough church, rebuilt after WWII. There's a copper spire added in 1957 to make the church stand out more, a pulpit from a Wren church in Cannon St destroyed in the war, a beautiful 17th-century font cover by the master woodcarver Grinling Gibbons and some interesting modern banners.

However, a church by the name All Hallows (meaning 'All Saints') has stood on this site since AD 675, and the best bit of the building today is undoubtedly its atmospheric Saxon undercroft, or crypt (admission £3; 10am-4pm Mon-Sat, 1-4pm Sun). There you'll find a pavement of reused Roman tiles and walls of the 7th-century Saxon church, as well as coins and bits of local history.

William Penn, founder of Pennsylvania, was baptised here in 1644 and there's a memorial to him in the undercroft. John Quincy Adams, sixth president of the USA, was also married at All Hallows in 1797.

THE CITY WALK
Walking Tour
1 Dr Johnson's House

Find your way to this miraculously well-preserved Georgian mansion (p114) in the heart of the City and explore the story of Dr Johnson's amazing life and wit within, perhaps even dropping by to his local, Ye Olde Cheshire Cheese on Fleet St (see p282).

2 St Paul's Cathedral

Wren's masterpiece, this cathedral (p109) is an unlikely survivor of the Blitz and one of the London skyline's best-loved features. Join the crowds to see the dazzling

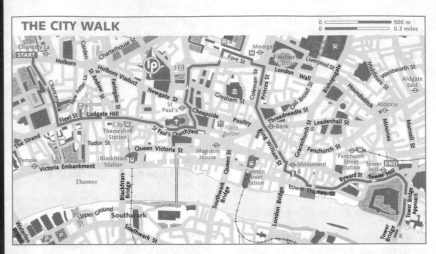

THE CITY WALK

WALK FACTS

Start **Chancery Lane tube station**
End **Tower Bridge (Tower Hill tube station)**
Distance **1.5 miles**
Duration **Two hours**
Fuel stop **Place Below (p249)**

interior, the fascinating crypt, the whispering gallery and the breathtaking views over the capital from the cupola.

3 Museum of London

This wonderful museum (p113) may not look like much from the outside, but it's one of the city's best, totally devoted to documenting the multifaceted history of the capital through its many stages of development from Saxon Village to three-time Olympic city.

4 Barbican

Built on the site of an old Roman watch-tower whence its name, the modern Barbican (p117) is the City's fabulous arts centre and an architectural wonder all of its own – love it or hate it, it's worth a visit; check out the greenhouse, the lakes and Shakespeare's parish Church, St Giles' Cripplegate.

5 Guildhall

Once the very heart of the City, seat of power and influence, the Guildhall (p118) is today still the home to the Corporation of London,

which runs not only the City but many of the capital's biggest parks. Here delve into the bizarre ritual of the guilds, see the excellent art gallery and go back in time two millennia to see the remains of London's Roman amphitheatre.

6 Monument

This column (p117) marks the Great Fire of London, and – while not for the vertiginous – is a superb way to see the City up close. Despite the number of high rises all around, the Monument still feels extremely high, giving you an idea of how massive it would have looked in the 17th century!

7 Tower of London

The sheer amount of history within the massive stone walls of the Tower of London (p119) is hard to fathom. The White Tower, the Crown Jewels, the Yeoman Warders, the Scaffold Site and Traitor's Gate all have fascinating stories associated with them and the Tower of London deserves at least a half day's visit at the end of the walk.

8 Tower Bridge

A wonderful icon of Victorian engineering, Tower Bridge (p123) has been a symbol of London since the day it was built when it was the largest bascule bridge in the world. A walk across it (and visit to the interesting exhibition from which the views are spectacular) is a must to appreciate old Father Thames at its widest and most spectacular.

THE SOUTH BANK

Eating p249; Drinking p282; Shopping p224; Sleeping p350

The transformation of this neighbourhood, which was until relatively recently considered to be the 'wrong' side of the Thames, has been nothing short of astonishing. This is where new London faces off old London, and both come out winners. Indeed, two of the city's major new landmarks have come to be located here, and they stare a pair of its oldest icons straight in the face. The British Airways London Eye 'wheel of good fortune' has been raised across the water from the neo-Gothic Parliament at Westminster, while the disused Bankside Power Station has morphed into Tate Modern, London's most visited sight, opposite St Paul's Cathedral.

top picks

THE SOUTH BANK

- BFI Southbank (p128)
- Borough Market (p132)
- British Airways London Eye (below)
- Shakespeare's Globe (p130)
- Tate Modern (p129)

The South Bank is made up of five contiguous areas, which tend to blend into one another without much warning. From west to east they are: the area around Waterloo railway station and the renovated Southbank Centre complex of theatres and concert halls; Bankside and, to the south, Southwark, with the stunning Millennium Bridge pushing off from between Tate Modern and Shakespeare's Globe; and Borough, with London's most popular (and trendy) food market, and Bermondsey, boasting a slew of popular museums, including the London Dungeon and the Design Museum.

The best way to see this neighbourhood is on foot. And if you follow the Silver Jubilee Walkway and the South Bank section of the Thames Path (see p206) along the southern riverbank – one of the most pleasant strolls in town – you're in pole position to see it. Images of the industrial age such as the Art Deco Oxo Tower have been given new life, while shiny space-age confections such as City Hall have also sprung up. And always in sight is Father Thames himself.

WATERLOO

In 1951 the British government attempted to raise the spirits of a nation still digging through rubble and on restricted rations six years after the end of WWII by holding a national celebration called the Festival of Britain. Its permanent legacy in London was the brutalist Royal Festival Hall, a building that helped shape the face of the river-facing South Bank for the next two decades.

A cluster of concrete buildings known as the Southbank Centre still stands but has undergone a remarkable makeover over the past decade. Though it will never compete with the impressive County Hall or iconic London Eye in a beauty or popularity contest, the remodelled centre will at least be easier on the eye and continue to be the capital's most important cultural complex.

Waterloo, named after a field in Belgium where the Duke of Wellington stopped Napoleon's advance through Europe once and for all, was nearly all marshland until the 18th century, as the name of one of the area's main streets, Lower Marsh, suggests. Bridges from the northern bank of the Thames at Westminster and Waterloo changed all that and massive Waterloo train station opened in 1848.

BRITISH AIRWAYS LONDON EYE
Map p126

☎ 0870 500 0600; www.londoneye.com; Jubilee Gardens SE1; adult/5-15yr/senior £14.50/7.25/11; ☯ 10am-8pm, to 9pm Jun-Sep, closed 1 week in Jan; ⊖ Waterloo; ♿

It's difficult to remember what London looked like before the landmark London Eye began twirling at the southwestern end of Jubilee Gardens during the millennium year. Not only has it fundamentally altered the skyline of the South Bank but, standing 135m tall in a fairly flat city, it is visible from many surprising parts of the city (eg Kennington and Mayfair). A ride – or 'flight', as sponsors British Airways (BA) like to call it – in one of the wheel's 32 glass-enclosed gondolas holding up to 25 people is something you really can't miss if you want to say you've 'done' London. It takes a gracefully slow 30 minutes and, weather permitting, you can see 25 miles in every direction from the top of what is the world's tallest Ferris

THE SOUTH BANK

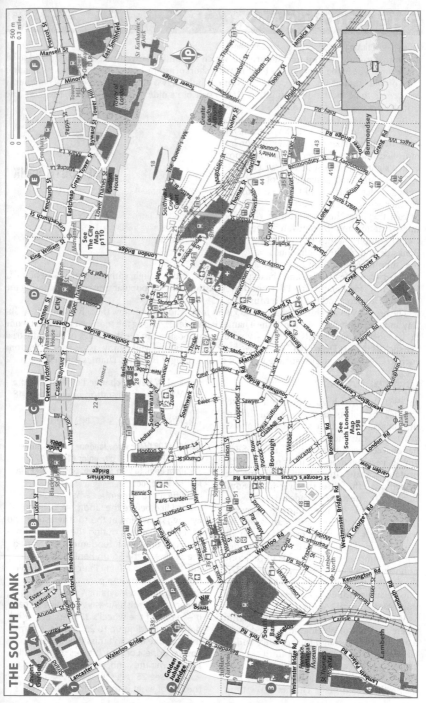

THE SOUTH BANK

wheel. To the west lies Windsor, while to the east the sea. In between, you have the chance to pick out familiar landmarks.

You can save 10% on standard flight prices and avoid the queues to buy tickets by booking online (minimum two hours before your chosen time). Be sure to arrive 30 minutes in advance.

COUNTY HALL Map p126
Westminster Bridge Rd SE1; ⊖ **Westminster or Waterloo;** &

Begun in 1909, County Hall took more than five decades to complete. Today it contains an art museum and gallery, vast aquarium and two hotels.

It seems that no major European city is complete these days without a museum devoted to the work of Salvador Dalí, and Dalí Universe (☎ 0870 744 7485; www.daliuniverse .com; adult/4-7yr/8-16yr/senior & student/family £12/5/8/10/30; ☺ 10am-6.30pm) is the world's largest, with 500 of the prolific surrealist

artist's twisted paintings, etchings, sculptures and other works on display in a series of low-lit galleries arranged according to theme: Sensuality and Femininity, Religion and Mythology, and Dreams and Fantasy. Keep an eye out for Dalí's famous melting pocket watch (Persistence of Memory), Mae West Lips Sofa and the backdrop he painted for Hitchcock's film Spellbound. Temporary exhibitions, which have in the past focused on such artists as Picasso or Warhol, are located in the adjacent County Hall Gallery (☺ 10am-6.30pm); entry is included in the general admission price.

The London Aquarium (☎ 7967 8000; www.lon donaquarium.co.uk; adult/3-14yr/senior & student/family £13.25/9.75/11.25/44; ☺ 10am-6pm, to 7pm late Jul-Aug; ⊖ Westminster or Waterloo; &) is one of the largest in Europe and, as room after room of fish tanks go, this is a pretty good one. Fish are grouped in some 14 zones according to their geographic origin, from the Pacific to the Atlantic Oceans and from temperate waters to tropical seas. The coral-reef (zone 10) and mangrove (zone 13) displays are particularly impressive, and there's a 'touch pool' with manta rays for the kids.

SOUTHBANK CENTRE Map p126

☎ 0871 663 2509; www.southbankcentre.co.uk; Belvedere Rd SE1; ⊖ waterloo; ♿

The flagship venue of the Southbank Centre, the collection of concrete buildings and walkways wedged between Hungerford and Waterloo Bridges, is the Royal Festival Hall. It is the oldest building of the centre that is still standing, having been erected to cheer up a glum postwar populace as part of the 1951 Festival of Britain. Its slightly curved façade of glass and Portland stone always won it more public approbation than its 1970s neighbours, but a two-year refit costing £75 million has added new pedestrian walkways, food outlets, bookshops and music stores below it and a fabulous new restaurant called Sklylon (p249).

Just north, Queen Elizabeth Hall is the second-largest concert venue in the centre and hosts chamber orchestras, quartets, choirs, dance performances and even opera. It also contains the smaller Purcell Room. Underneath its elevated floor, you'll find a real skateboarders' hang-out, suitably decorated with master-class graffiti tagging.

The Hayward Gallery (☎ 0870 380 0400; www.hayward.org.uk; admission from £5; ⏰ 10am-6pm, to 10pm Fri & Sat) is one of London's premier exhibition spaces for major international art shows. The grey fortresslike building dating from 1968 it makes an excellent hanging space for the blockbuster exhibitions it puts on. Admission prices depend on what's on.

BFI SOUTHBANK Map p126

☎ 7255 1444, bookings 7928 3232; www.bfi.org.uk; Theatre Ave SE1; ⏰ 11am-11pm; ⊖ waterloo; ♿

Tucked almost out of sight under the arches of Waterloo Bridge, and until recently called the National Film Theatre, is the revamped British Film Institute Southbank containing four cinemas that screen some 2000 films a year, a gallery and the new Mediatheque (☎ 7928 3535; admission free; ⏰ 11am-8pm), where you watch film and TV highlights from the BFI National Archive. The BFI is largely a repertory or art-house theatre, runs regular retrospectives and is the major venue for the London Film Festival in late October.

The Riverside Walk Market (⏰ 10am-7pm Sat & Sun), with prints and second-hand books, takes place immediately in front of the BFI Southbank under the arches of the bridge.

BFI IMAX CINEMA Map p126

☎ 0870 787 2525; www.bfi.org.uk/imax; 1 Charlie Chaplin Walk SE1; adult/4-14yr/senior & student from £8.50/5/6.25; ⏰ 7 screenings 11am-8pm, additional screening at 11.15pm Sat; ⊖ Waterloo; ♿

The renamed British Film Institute IMAX Cinema in the centre of a busy roundabout screens the predictable mix of 2-D and IMAX 3-D documentaries about travel, space and wildlife, lasting from 40 minutes to 1½ hours, as well as recently released blockbusters. The drum-shaped building sits on 'springs' to reduce vibrations and traffic noise from the traffic circle and subways below, and the exterior changes colour at night. And size does matter here: the 477-seat cinema is the largest in Europe, with a screen measuring 20m high and 26m wide.

NATIONAL THEATRE Map p126

☎ 7452 3400; www.nationaltheatre.org.uk; South Bank SE1; ⊖ Waterloo; ♿

This is the nation's flagship theatre complex, comprising three auditoriums: the Olivier, Lyttelton and Cottesloe. Opened in 1976 – one of your humble authors (no prize for guessing which one) worked in the staff canteen that spring and watched Albert Finney rehearse in Peter Hall's *Tamburlaine the Great* by Christopher Marlowe – and modernised to the tune of £42 million in the late 1990s, it's been undergoing an artistic renaissance under the directorship of Nicholas Hytner. Backstage tours (adult/concession/family £5/4/13; ⏰ tours 6 times Mon-Fri, 2 times Sat) lasting 1¼ hours are also offered. There are sometimes art exhibitions in the lobby and other public areas.

BANKSIDE & SOUTHWARK

Outside the jurisdiction of the City and notorious for its brothels, bear-baiting and prisons, Bankside was London's very own Sodom and Gomorrah during Elizabethan times. And it was for this reason that Shakespeare's Globe Theatre and the nearby Rose Theatre were built here. A full five centuries on, the area's entertainments are somewhat more highbrow. The Globe has gone respectable and a disused power station has become the world's leading modern art gallery (and, importantly, London's most visited sight).

TATE MODERN Map p126

☎ general enquiries 7887 8000, tickets 7887 8888, recorded information 7887 8008; www.tate.org.uk /modern; Queen's Walk SE1; admission free, special exhibitions £6-10; ⏱ 10am-6pm Sun-Thu, to 10pm Fri & Sat; ⊖ St Paul's, Southwark or London Bridge; ♿

The public's love affair with this phenomenally successful modern art gallery shows no sign of waning. Serious art critics have occasionally swiped at its populism (eg Carl Höller's funfairlike slides, Olafur Eliasson's participatory *The Weather Project,* both in the vast Turbine Hall) and poked holes in its collection. But five million visitors appear to disagree, making it the world's most popular contemporary art gallery and – almost unbelievably – the most visited sight in London, just ahead of the British Museum.

The critics are right in one sense, though: this 'Tate Modern effect' is really more about the building and its location than about the mostly 20th-century art inside. Leading Swiss architects Herzog & de Meuron won the Pritzker, architecture's most prestigious prize, for their transformation of the empty Bankside Power Station, which was built between 1947 and 1963 and decommissioned 23 years later. Leaving the building's single central chimney, adding a two-storey glass box onto the roof and using the vast Turbine Hall as a dramatic entrance space were three strokes of genius. Then, of course, there are the wonderful views of the Thames and St Paul's, particularly from the restaurant-bar on the 7th level and coffee bar on the 4th. There's also a café on the 2nd level, plus places to relax overlooking the Turbine Hall. An 11-storey glass tower extension to the southwest corner in the form of a ziggurat – a spiralling stepped pyramid – by the same architects is now under way and will be completed in 2012.

Tate Modern's permanent collection on levels 3 and 5 is now arranged by both theme and chronology. States of Flux is devoted to early-20th-century avant-garde movements, including cubism and futurism. Poetry and Dream examines surrealism through various themes and techniques. Material Gestures features European and American painting and sculpture of the 1940s and '50s. Idea and Object looks at minimalism and conceptual art from the 1960s onward.

More than 60,000 works are on constant rotation here, and the curators have at their disposal paintings by Georges Braque, Henri Matisse, Piet Mondrian and Andy Warhol, as well as pieces by Joseph Beuys, Marcel Duchamp, Damien Hirst, Rebecca Horn, Claes Oldenburg and Auguste Rodin. Mark Rothko's famous Seagram murals have been given their own space on level 3; other familiar favourites include Roy Lichtenstein's *Whaam!* (level 5), Jackson Pollock's *Summertime: No 9A* (level 3) and Andy Warhol's *Marilyn Diptych* (level 5).

Special exhibitions (level 4) in the past have included retrospectives on Edward Hopper, Frida Kahlo, August Strindberg, Nazism and 'Degenerate' Art and local 'bad boys' Gilbert & George. Audioguides, with four different tours, are available for £2. Free guided highlights tours depart at 11am, noon, 2pm and 3pm daily.

The Tate Boat, painted by Damien Hirst, operates between the Bankside Pier at Tate Modern and the Millbank Pier at sistermuseum Tate Britain (p103), stopping en route at the London Eye. Services from Tate Modern depart from 10am to 4.40pm daily, at 40-minute intervals (see p387).

PICK OF THE STYX: LONDON'S UNDERGROUND RIVERS

The Thames is not London's only river: many have been culverted over the centuries and now course unseen underground. Some survive only in place names: Hole Bourne, Wells, Tyburn, Walbrook and Westbourne, which was dammed up in 1730 to form the Serpentine in Hyde Park. The most famous of these Rivers Styx is the Fleet, which rises in Hampstead and Kenwood ponds and flows south through Camden Town, King's Cross, Farringdon Rd and New Bridge St, where it empties into the Thames at Blackfriars Bridge. It had been used as an open sewer and as a dumping area for entrails by butchers for centuries; the Elizabethan playwright Ben Jonson describes a voyage on the Fleet on a hot summer's night in which every stroke of the oars 'belch'd forth an ayre as hot as the muster of all your night-tubs discharging their merd-urinous load'. After the Great Fire Christopher Wren oversaw the deepening and widening of a section of the Fleet into a canal, but this was covered over in 1733 as was the rest of the river three decades later.

MILLENNIUM BRIDGE Map p126

Arguably the most useful of all the so-called millennium projects to open in 2000, the Millennium Bridge pushes off from the south bank of the Thames in front of Tate Modern and berths on the north bank at the steps of Peter's Hill below St Paul's Cathedral. The low-slung frame designed by Sir Norman Foster and Antony Caro looks pretty spectacular, particularly lit up at night with fibre optics, and the view of St Paul's from the South Bank has swiftly become one of London's iconic images. The bridge got off on the wrong, err, footing when it had to be closed just three days after opening in June 2000 because of the alarming way it swayed under the weight of pedestrians. An 18-month refit costing £5 million eventually saw it right.

SHAKESPEARE'S GLOBE Map p126

☎ 7902 1500; www.shakespeares-globe.org; 21 New Globe Walk SE1; exhibition entrance incl guided tour of theatre adult/5-15yr/senior & student/family £9/6.50/7.50/20; ⏲ 9am-noon & 12.30-5pm Mon-Sat, 9am-11.30am & noon-5pm Sun mid-Apr–mid-Oct, 10am-5pm mid-Oct–mid-Apr, tours every 15-30min; ⊖ London Bridge; &
Shakespeare's Globe consists of the reconstructed Globe Theatre and, beneath it, an exhibition hall, entry to which includes a tour of the Globe Theatre except when matinées are being staged. Then the tour shifts to the nearby Rose Theatre (right). The exhibition focuses on Elizabethan London and stagecraft and the struggle to get the theatre rebuilt in the 20th century. The exhibits devoted to Elizabethan special effects and costumes are especially interesting as are the recordings of some of the greatest Shakespearean performances ever.

The original Globe – known as the 'Wooden O' after its circular shape and roofless centre – was erected in 1599 with timber taken from the demolished Theatre (1576) on Curtain Rd in Shoreditch. The Globe was closed in 1642 after the English Civil War was won by the Puritans, who regarded the theatre as the devil's workshop, and it was dismantled two years later. Despite the worldwide popularity of Shakespeare over the centuries, the Globe was barely a distant memory when American actor (and later film director) Sam Wanamaker came searching for it in 1949. Undeterred by the fact that the foundations of the theatre had vanished beneath a row of listed Georgian houses, Wanamaker set up the Globe Playhouse Trust in 1970 and began fundraising for a memorial theatre. Work started only 200m from the original Globe site in 1987, but Wanamaker died four years before it opened in 1997.

The new Globe was painstakingly constructed with 600 oak pegs (there's not a nail or a screw in the house), specially fired Tudor bricks and thatching reeds from Norfolk that – for some odd reason – pigeons don't like; even the plaster contains goat hair, lime and sand as it did in Shakespeare's time. Unlike other venues for Shakespearean plays, this theatre has been designed to resemble the original as closely as possible – even if that means leaving the arena open to the skies and roar of passing aircraft, expecting the 500 'groundlings' to stand even in the rain, and obstructing much of the view from the seats closest to the stage with two enormous 'original' Corinthian pillars. The Globe Café on the Piazza level and the Globe Restaurant on the 1st floor are open for lunch and dinner till 10pm or 11pm.

The season runs from May to early October. For ticket details see p318. Attempts to raise funds to complete the indoor Inigo Jones Theatre, a replica of a Jacobean playhouse connected to the Globe for winter performances, have not been successful.

ROSE THEATRE Map p126

☎ 7902 1500; www.rosetheatre.org.uk; 56 Park St SE1; adult/5-15yr/senior & student £6.50/3.50/5.50; ⏲ 1-5pm Tue-Sun May-Oct; ⊖ London Bridge; &
The Rose, for which Christopher Marlowe and Ben Jonson wrote their greatest plays and in which Shakespeare learned his craft, is unique in that its original 16th-century foundations have been unearthed. They were discovered in 1989 beneath an office building at Southwark Bridge and given a protective concrete cover. Administered by the nearby Globe Theatre, the Rose is open to the public only when matinées are being performed at the Globe Theatre.

GOLDEN HINDE Map p126

☎ 0870 011 8700; www.goldenhinde.org; St Mary Overie Dock, Cathedral St SE1; adult/child, senior & student/family £6/4.50/18; ⏲ 9am-5.30pm; ⊖ London Bridge
Okay, it looks like a dinky theme-park ride and kids do love it, but stepping aboard this replica of Sir Francis Drake's famous Tudor ship will inspire genuine admiration for

the admiral and his rather short – average height: 1.6m – crew. This tiny five-deck galleon was home to Drake and his crew from 1577 to 1580 as they became the first sailors to circumnavigate the globe. Adult visitors wandering around stooped must also marvel at how the taller, modern-day crew managed to spend 20 years at sea on this 37m-long replica, after it was launched in 1973.

Tickets are available from the Golden Hinde Shop (☎ 7403 0123; Pickfords Wharf, 1 Clink St SE1) just opposite the ruins of Winchester Palace. You can also spend the night aboard for £39.50 per person, including a supper of stew and bread and a breakfast of bread and cheese.

CLINK PRISON MUSEUM Map p126
☎ 7403 0900; www.clink.co.uk; 1 Clink St SE1; adult/senior, student & child/family £5/3.50/12; ⏱ 10am-6pm, to 9pm Jul-Sep; ⊖ London Bridge
This erstwhile private jail in the park of Winchester Palace (below), a 28-hectare area known as the Liberty of the Clink and under the jurisdiction of the bishops of Winchester and not the City, was used to detain debtors, whores, thieves and even actors. This was the notorious address that gave us the expression 'in the clink' (in jail). The poky, rather hokey museum inside reveals the wretched life of the prisoners who were forced to pay for their own food and accommodation. There's a nice little collection of instruments of torture, too.

WINCHESTER PALACE Map p126
Clink St SE1; ⊖ London Bridge
All that remains of a huge palace complex, built by the powerful and corrupt bishops of Winchester in the early 12th century, is a 14th-century rose window carved in a wall from the Great Hall, and parts of the flooring, both visible from the street. The palace was built in 1109 and remained the bishops' home for more than 500 years, before being converted into a prison for royalists under the puritanical Oliver Cromwell in 1642. The rose window was discovered in a Clink St warehouse in 1814.

VINOPOLIS Map p126
☎ 0870 241 4040; www.vinopolis.co.uk; 1 Bank End SE1; tours £16-31; ⏱ noon-10pm Mon, Thu & Fri, 11am-9pm Sat, noon-6pm Sun; ⊖ London Bridge; ♿
Vinopolis, spread over a hectare of Victorian railway vaults in Bankside, cashes in

on Londoners' love affair with things red, white and rosé. Vinopolis provides a pretty cheesy tour of the world of wine and it's very popular with hen parties; need we say more? However, those with time and patience who want to know a little more about wine production and regional varieties from France to South Africa and Chile to Australia will find it interesting enough. Be advised, though, that you need to follow the audioguide to make sense of the exhibits, which introduce visitors to the history of wine-making, vineyards and grape varietals, regional characteristics and which wine goes with which food. All tours, including the Original Tour (£16), end in the Grand Tasting Halls, where you sample five different wines from around the world. The Discovery (£21), Vintage (£26) and Champagne (£31) Tours include additional wine tastings as well as other alcoholic libations.

BANKSIDE GALLERY Map p126
☎ 7928 7521; www.banksidegallery.com; 48 Hopton St SE1; admission free; ⏱ 11am-6pm; ⊖ St Paul's, Southwark or London Bridge; ♿
Bankside Gallery is home to the Royal Watercolour Society and the Royal Society of Painter-Printmakers. There's no permanent collection at this friendly upbeat place, but there are frequently changing exhibitions of watercolours, prints and engravings. Call ahead for the occasional Artists' Perspectives, where artists talk about their work, and other events.

BOROUGH & BERMONDSEY
Although parts of these two are still pretty rundown, the area is very much on the up and up and trend-followers like to bill it as 'the new Hoxton'. Indeed, all the prerequisites are already in place here: a trendy market, a community of creative types living in loft buildings such as the former Hartley jam factory, and a growing cluster of gastropubs, restaurants and hip cafés in and around popular Bermondsey St. The HMS *Belfast*, the London Dungeon and the neighbourhood's several museums are all worth exploring.

SOUTHWARK CATHEDRAL Map p126
☎ 7367 6700; www.southwark.anglican.org/cathedral; Montague Close SE1; admission free, requested donation £4; ⏱ 8am-6pm; ⊖ London Bridge; ♿
The earliest surviving part of this relatively small cathedral is the atmospheric retrochoir,

which was part of the 13th-century Priory of St Mary Overie (from 'St Mary over the Water'). However, most of the building, including the nave, is Victorian.

You enter via the southwest door and immediately to the left is the Marchioness memorial to the 51 people who died when a pleasure cruiser on the Thames hit a dredger and sank near Southwark Bridge in 1989. In the north transept, you'll see a memorial tablet to Lionel Lockyer (a quack doctor celebrated for his pills) and its humorous epitaph. On the eastern side of the north transept is the Harvard Chapel, originally the chapel of St John the Evangelist but now named after John Harvard, founder of Harvard University in Cambridge, Massachusetts, who was baptised here in 1607.

A few steps to the east is the 16th-century Great Screen separating the choir from the retrochoir. The screen was a gift of the bishop of Winchester in 1520. On the choir floor is a tablet marking the tomb of Edmond Shakespeare, actor-brother of the Bard, who died in 1607.

In the south aisle of the nave is a green alabaster monument to William Shakespeare with depictions of the original Globe Theatre and Southwark Cathedral; the stained-glass window above shows characters from *A Midsummer Night's Dream*, *Hamlet* and *The Tempest*. Beside the monument is a plaque to Sam Wanamaker (1919–93), the American film director and actor who was the force behind the rebuilt Globe Theatre.

Audioguides (adult/child/senior & student £2.50/1.25/2) to the main cathedral, lasting about 40 minutes, are available from the gift shop. Evensong is at 5.30pm weekdays, 4pm Saturday and 3pm Sunday.

BOROUGH MARKET Map p126

☎ 7407 1002; www.boroughmarket.org.uk; cnr Southwark & Stoney Sts SE1; ⏱ 11am-5pm Thu, noon-6pm Fri, 9am-4pm Sat; ⊖ London Bridge
Here in some form or another since the 13th century, 'London's Larder' has enjoyed an enormous renaissance in recent years, overflowing with food-lovers, both experienced and wannabes, and has become quite a tourist destination. See also p242).

DESIGN MUSEUM Map p126

☎ 0870 833 9955; www.designmuseum.org; 28 Shad Thames SE1; adult/under 12/student & concession £7/free/4; ⏱ 10am-5.45pm; ⊖ Tower Hill or London Bridge; ♿

In recent years this museum, founded by Sir Terence Conran 20 years ago and housed in a 1930s-era warehouse, has abandoned its permanent collection of 20th- and 21st-century objects to make way for a revolving programme of special exhibitions. But although those shows are populist – a display of Manolo Blahnik shoes; Formula One racing cars; the evolution and use of what is our favourite material in the world, Velcro – they are also very popular. The informal White Café (⏱ 10am-5.30pm) is on the ground floor and the more formal Blue Print Café (p250) restaurant is upstairs.

A short distance to the south of the museum in the centre of Queen Elizabeth St is a bronze statue of Jacob, one of the many Courage Brewery dray horses stabled here in the 19th century. These workhorses delivered beer all over London from the brewery on Horselydown ('horse lie down') Lane, where the poor old things rested before crossing the bridge – again and again.

LONDON DUNGEON Map p126

☎ 7403 7221, recorded information 0900 160 0066; www.thedungeons.com; 28-34 Tooley St SE1; adult/5-15yr/16-18yr, student & senior £16.95/11.05/13.95; ⏱ 10am-5.30pm Apr-late Oct, to 5pm late Oct-Mar; ⊖ London Bridge
Under the arches of the Tooley St railway bridge, the London Dungeon was supposedly developed after somebody's kid didn't find Madame Tussauds Chamber of Horrors frightening enough. Well, they failed in that endeavour but the place continues to mint money.

It all starts with a stagger through a mirror maze (the Labyrinth of the Lost); followed by a waltz through the bubonic plague (c 1665); a push through a torture chamber; a run 'through' the Great Fire of London (where – to give you an idea of the production values – wafting fabric makes up the 'flames'); a close shave with Sweeney Todd, the demon barber of Fleet St; and an encounter with Jack the Ripper, where the Victorian serial killer is shown with the five prostitutes he sliced and diced, their entrails hanging out in full gory display. The best bits, though, are the vaudevillian delights of being sentenced by a mad, bewigged judge on trumped-up charges, the fairground-ride boat to Traitor's Gate and the new Extremis Drop Ride to Doom that has you 'plummeting' to your death by hanging from the gallows.

It's a good idea to buy tickets online (adult/five to 15 years/16 to 18 years, student and senior £19.50/16.95/18.25) for this camped-up 90-minute gore-fest to avoid the mammoth queues.

CITY HALL Map p126

☎ 7983 4100; www.london.gov.uk; The Queen's Walk SE1; admission free; ⊗ 8am-8pm Mon-Fri & 1st weekend of the month; ✚ Tower Hill or London Bridge; ⑤

Glass-clad City Hall, designed by Sir Norman Foster and Ken Shuttleworth, is transparent in both the figurative and literal senses. There's a visitors centre (☎ 9am-5.30pm) on the lower ground floor, which also includes the 'London Photomat', an aerial photo of 1000 sq metres of the city stuck to the floor and large enough for you to walk on and pick out individual buildings, and a café looking onto an outside amphitheatre. Some other areas, including the ramp, the meeting room on the 6th floor called 'London's Living Room' (available to any Londoner) and outside viewing gallery, are open on certain weekends. Check the website for details.

HMS BELFAST Map p126

☎ 7940 6300; www.hmsbelfast.org.uk; Morgan's Lane, Tooley St SE1; adult/under 16yr/senior & student £9.95/free/6.15; ⊗ 10am-6pm Mar-Oct, to 5pm Nov-Feb; ✚ London Bridge; ⑤

Moored in the Thames opposite the newly laid-out Potters Fields Park, HMS *Belfast* is a big toy that kids of all ages generally love. Of course, for most of its commissioned life this large, light cruiser had a rather more serious purpose than as a plaything. Launched in 1938 from the Belfast shipyard Harland & Wolff, it served in WWII, most noticeably in the Normandy landings, and during the Korean War.

It probably helps to be keen on things naval, but the HMS *Belfast* is surprisingly interesting for what it shows of the way of life on board a cruiser, laying out everything from its operations room – which has been reconstructed to show its role in the 1943 Battle of North Cape off Norway, which ended in the sinking of the German battleship *Scharnhorst* – and bridge (where you can sit in the admiral's chair) to its boiler room and living quarters. On

the open deck, there are 16 six-inch guns, whose sights you can peer through.

Your (free) audioguide will help you wend your way from one audio point to the next on five decks and four platforms.

There is some disabled access. Call ahead for more information.

BRITAIN AT WAR EXPERIENCE Map p126

☎ 7403 3171; www.britainatwar.co.uk; 64-66 Tooley St SE1; adult/under 16yr/concession/family £9.50/4.85/5.75/20; ⊗ 10am-5.30pm Apr-Sep, to 4.30pm Oct-Mar; ✚ London Bridge

Under another Tooley St railway arch, the Britain at War Experience aims to educate the younger generation about the effect WWII had on daily life while simultaneously playing on the nostalgia of the war generation who sit in the mock Anderson air-raid shelter listening to the simulated sounds of warning sirens and bombers flying overhead with extraordinary detachment. In general it's a tribute to ordinary people and comes off fairly well – though the rather musty displays make it feel like you're on a low-budget TV stage-set.

You descend by lift to a reproduction of an Underground station fitted with bunks, tea urns and even a lending library (as some of the stations really were) and then progress through rooms that display wartime newspaper front pages, posters and Ministry of Food ration books. The BBC Radio Studio allows you to hear broadcasts from everyone from Winston Churchill and Edward Murrow to Hitler and Lord Haw Haw; the Rainbow Corner is a mock-up of a club frequented by American GIs 'over here'. Finally, you emerge amid the wreckage of a shop hit by a bomb, with the smoke still eddying around and the injured – or dead – being carried from the rubble.

OLD OPERATING THEATRE MUSEUM & HERB GARRET Map p126

☎ 7188 2679; www.thegarret.org.uk; 9a St Thomas St SE1; adult/child/senior & student/family £5.25/3/4.25/12.95; ⊗ 10.30am-5pm; ✚ London Bridge

This unique museum, at the top of the narrow and rickety 32-step tower of St Thomas Church (1703), focuses on the nastiness of 19th-century hospital treatment. The garret was used by the apothecary of St Thomas's Hospital to store medicinal herbs and now houses an atmospheric medical museum delightfully hung with bunches of herbs that soften the impact of the horrible devices displayed in the glass cases.

Even more interesting is the 19th-century operating theatre attached to the garret. Here you'll see the sharp, vicious-looking instruments 19th-century doctors used, and you'll view the rough-and-ready conditions under which they operated – without antiseptic on a wooden table in what looks like a modern lecture hall. Placards explain how, without anaesthetic, surgeons had to perform quickly on patients; one minute to complete an amputation was reckoned about right. A box of sawdust was placed beneath the table to catch the blood and guts and contemporary accounts record the surgeons wearing frock coats 'stiff and stinking with pus and blood'. Don't eat lunch before visiting and you probably won't want it afterwards.

BRAMAH MUSEUM OF TEA & COFFEE
Map p126

☎ 7403 5650; www.bramahmuseum.co.uk; 40 Southwark St SE1; adult/child/senior & student/family £4/3/3.50/10; ⏱ 10am-6pm; ⊖ London Bridge; ♿

This is a pleasant, nostalgic place to while away half an hour – provided your visit does not coincide with the arrival of another tour group. Trace the route by which tea conquered the world, making its way to the sitting rooms of Holland and England and further afield from the eastern seaports of China; nearby Butler's Wharf once handled 6000 chests of tea in a single a day. Or simply enjoy the chintzy cornucopia of tea- and coffee-drinking equipment, from floral

teacups and silverware to Japanese canisters of tea. In the adjoining Tea Room (☎ 7.30am-6pm), your cuppa is served with an egg timer so you can get the infusion just right.

THE SOUTH BANK WALK
Walking Tour
1 County Hall
Across Westminster Bridge from the Houses of Parliament, this monumental building (p127) with its curved façade and colonnades was once home to the London County Council and then the renamed (1965) Greater London Council. It now houses museums and hotels.

2 BFI Southbank
The long-awaited new headquarters of the British Film Institute (p128) in South Bank is a mecca for film buffs and historians alike. It screens thousands of films in four theatres each year, and archived films are available for watching in the new Mediatheque.

3 Millennium Bridge
This pedestrian bridge (p130) linking the north and south banks of the Thames, a slender 'blade

WALK FACTS
Start **Waterloo tube station**
End **London Bridge tube station**
Distance **1.5 miles**
Duration **Two hours**
Fuel stop **Tas Pide (p275)**

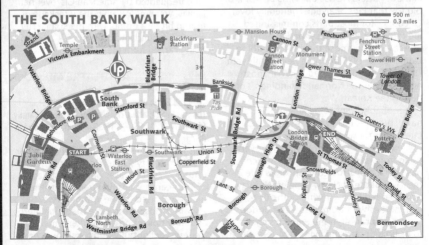

THE SOUTH BANK WALK

of light' designed by Sir Norman Foster, is everything contemporary architecture should be: modern, beautiful and useful. It carries up to 10,000 pedestrians each day.

4 Golden Hinde

Now that the *Cutty Sark* (p183) is on sick leave, the Golden Hinde (p130) is the only masted ship open to visitors in a city that was once the largest and richest port in the world. It's tiny but fascinating to visit.

5 Southwark Cathedral

Sometimes referred to as the 'Cinderella of English cathedrals', Southwark (p131) is often overlooked but well worth a visit, especially for its historical associations. A monument to Shakespeare, whose great works were originally written for the Bankside playhouses, takes pride of place here.

6 City Hall

Nicknamed 'the egg' (or, more cheekily, 'the testicle' because of its shape), this glass-clad building (p133) could also be likened to a spaceman wearing a helmet. It has an interior spiral ramp ascending above the assembly chamber to the building's roof, which has now been fitted with energy-saving solar panels.

Eating p251; Drinking p284; Shopping p226; Sleeping p351

The area stretching from Hyde Park – the largest of London's Royal Parks – to Chelsea is high-class territory. It's all groomed trust-fund babes, blond boys in convertibles, multimillion-pound property and glitzy shopping, and even though South Kensington encompasses a lot of the class, it isn't all about eye candy: thanks to Prince Albert and the 1851 Great Exhibition, the area is also home to the Natural History (p141), Science (p141) and Victoria & Albert (p139) Museums. This is also one of London's most sophisticated stretches, with sizable English, French, Italian and Far Eastern communities all snuggled happily under the umbrella of prosperity.

Chelsea has been one of London's most fashionable precincts ever since chancellor Thomas More moved here in the early 16th century. The 'village of palaces' became one of London's most desirable neighbourhoods, as it was close to the bustle of the City and Westminster yet still concealed behind a big bend in the river. Even when it was consumed by greater London in the 20th century, it retained its aristocratic angle and managed to mix it with a bohemian vibe, with the swinging '60s scene starting at its main artery, King's Rd. Chelsea didn't miss out on a big slice of punk cred in the following decade, either. These days its residents still have among the highest incomes of any London borough (shops and restaurants think that you do, too), and the community is as cosmopolitan as the local football team.

Belgravia has had a reputation for elitism

top picks

OBJECTS IN SOUTH KEN'S MUSEUMS

- Cast of Michelangelo's David (p139)
- Diplodocus dinosaur skeleton (p141)
- Fashion Room (p140)
- Ardabil Carpet (p140)
- SimEx Simulator Ride (p142)

ever since it was laid out by builder Thomas Cubitt in the 19th century, with its white stuccoed squares and charming, mainly residential streets and quaint cobbled mews. It's also home to numerous embassies and a few wonderful old-fashioned pubs.

Knightsbridge, once famous for highwaymen and raucous drinking, is now renowned for its swanky shopping and for being a playpen for moneyed and perpetually tanned middle-aged men and ditzy young rich girls (though they're not necessarily playing together).

Kensington High St, a lively blend of upmarket boutiques and chain stores, dominates the area of Kensington itself. North of here is Holland Park, a residential district of elegant town houses built around a wooded park.

The utterly splendid Hyde Park (p145) and Kensington Gardens – think of them as one big green entity – separate the glitz of Knightsbridge and Kensington from the noise and havoc of the West End, shooing the hoi polloi away with exclusive hotels and expensive shopping.

Finally, Victoria (p146). What can one say about this relatively drab neighbourhood which looks even less enticing after being grouped with the glam Kensington and Chelsea sisters? The one attraction worth pausing for in Victoria is the candy-striped Westminster Cathedral, a couple of hundred metres from the tube station. Apart from that, Victoria is best known as a transit area, via its huge train and coach stations. There's not all that much reason for staying unless you're a backpacker availing yourself of its cheap and predominantly cheerless accommodation. And while Victoria's unattractiveness has a smidgen of character, Pimlico, on the other hand, while being posh in appearance, is as flat as a pancake in terms of personality. Thomas Cubitt built most of it in the 19th century, but he had obviously put all his best ideas into creating swanky Belgravia and couldn't summon up much imagination for plain Pimlico. It does, however, have some excellent views across the river to the Battersea Power Station.

CHELSEA & BELGRAVIA

KING'S ROAD Map pp138–9

⊖ Sloane Sq or South Kensington

In the 17th century, Charles II set up a Chelsea love nest here for him and his mistress, an orange-seller turned actress at the Drury Lane Theatre by the name of Nell Gwyn. Heading back to Hampton Court Palace of an evening, Charles would make use of a farmer's track that inevitably came to be known as the King's Rd. The street was at the forefront of London, nay world, fashion during the technicolour '60s and anarchic '70s, and continues to be trendy now, albeit in a more self-conscious way. The street begins at Sloane Sq, to the north of which runs Sloane St, celebrated for its designer boutiques.

CHELSEA OLD CHURCH Map pp138-9
☎ 7795 1019; cnr Cheyne Walk & Old Church St SW3; ☉ 1.30-5.30pm Tue-Fri & Sun; ↔ Sloane Sq; ♿

This church is principally a monument to Thomas More (1477–1535), the former chancellor (and now Roman Catholic saint) who lost his head for refusing to go along with Henry VIII's plan to establish himself as supreme head of the Church of England. Original features include the More Chapel, and More's headless body is rumoured to be buried somewhere within the church. (His head, having been hung out on London Bridge according to the practice of the times, is now at rest a long way away in St Dunstan's Church, Canterbury.)

Outside is a gold statue of More, who lived in Chelsea with his family in a property expropriated by Henry VIII after the lord chancellor's execution.

CHELSEA PHYSIC GARDEN Map pp138-9
☎ 7352 5646; www.chelseaphysicgarden.co.uk; 66 Royal Hospital Rd SW3; adult/concession £7/4; ☉ noon-5pm Wed, 2-6pm Sun Apr-Oct, noon-5pm daily during the Chelsea Flower Show, 11am-3pm on Snowdrop Days (1st & 2nd Sun in Feb); ↔ Sloane Sq; ♿

Talk about discovering a secret garden in the midst of an urban jungle. Established by the Apothecaries' Society in 1673 for students working on medicinal plants and healing, this garden is one of the oldest of its kind in Europe. And what's more, Londoners are relatively ignorant of its existence, which means that the many rare trees, shrubs and plants are yours for quiet exploration. The fascinating pharmaceutical garden grows plants used in contemporary Western medicine; the world medicine garden has a selection of plants used by tribal peoples in Australia, China, India, New Zealand and North America, and there's a heady perfume and aromatherapy garden.

There is a statue of Sir Hans Sloane, the philanthropist who saved the garden from going under in the early 18th century. Opening hours are limited because the grounds are still used for research and education. Tours – informative and entertaining – can be organised by appointment.

ALBERT & BATTERSEA BRIDGES
Map pp138-9

One of London's most striking bridges, the Albert is a cross between a cantilever and a suspension bridge, buttressed to strengthen it as an alternative to closure in the 1960s. It was designed by Roland Mason Ordish in 1873, but later modified by the engineer Joseph Bazalgette, who then built the companion Battersea Bridge in 1890. Painted white and pink and with fairy lights adorning its cables, it looks stunning during the day and festive by night. The booths at either end survive from the days when tolls applied.

ROYAL HOSPITAL CHELSEA Map pp138-9
☎ 7881 5200; www.chelsea-pensioners.co.uk; Royal Hospital Rd SW3; admission free; ☉ 10am-noon & 2-4pm daily Apr-Sep, 10am-noon & 2-4pm Mon-Sat Oct-Mar; ↔ Sloane Sq; ♿

Designed by Christopher Wren, this superb structure was built in 1692 to provide shelter for ex-servicemen. Since the reign of Charles II, it has housed hundreds of war veterans, known as Chelsea Pensioners. They're fondly regarded as national treasures, and cut striking figures in the dark-blue greatcoats (in winter) or scarlet frock coats (in summer) that they wear on ceremonial occasions.

The building, however, needs refurbishing and at the time of writing the Chelsea Pensioners Appeal was trying to raise £35 million by 31 March 2008 in order to refurbish the Long Wards residential wing, as well as build a new Infirmary. If you're passionate about the cause, you can buy a brick on the website and support the pensioners, or like Jack and Meg White of the White Stripes, hold a gig and donate all the proceeds to the fund.

It's usually possible to visit the museum (which contains a huge collection of war medals bequeathed by former residents), as well as to look into the hospital's Great Hall, Octagon, Chapel and courtyards. Do note, however, that the hospital is off limits to visitors when it is hosting events.

The Chelsea Flower Show takes place here in May. For more on that, see www.rhs.org.uk.

Call ahead for disabled access information.

HYDE PARK TO CHELSEA

NATIONAL ARMY MUSEUM Map pp138–9

☎ 7881 2455, 7730 0717; www.national-army
-museum.ac.uk; Royal Hospital Rd SW3; admission
free but donations requested; ⏰ 10am-5.30pm;
⊖ Sloane Sq; ♿

Suitably located next door to the Royal
Hospital, this old-fashioned museum tells
the history of the British army from the perspective of the men and women who put
their lives on the line for king and country, conveying the horrors and perceived
glories of war with a refreshing lack of
meddling by modern technology. The best
pieces at the exhibition feature the life and
times of the 'Redcoat' (the term for the British soldier from the Battle of Agincourt in
1415 to the American Revolution), the tacti-
cal battle at Waterloo between Napoleon
and the Duke of Wellington and a display
of the skeleton of Napoleon's horse.

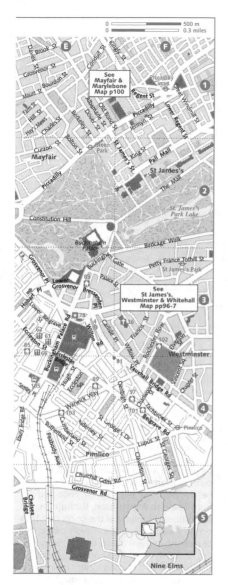

KNIGHTSBRIDGE, KENSINGTON & HYDE PARK

VICTORIA & ALBERT MUSEUM

Map pp138–9

☎ 7942 2000; www.vam.ac.uk; Cromwell Rd SW7; admission free; ⏰ 10am-5.45pm, to 10pm Wed & last Fri of month; ⊖ South Kensington; ♿

When you come to see the V&A, give yourself plenty of time, because we can guarantee that you'll sp[...] than planned in this br[...] Museum of Manufactu[...] originally known when [...] specialises in decorati[...] with four million obje[...] years from Britain and [...] It was part of Prince Albert's leg[...] nation in the aftermath of the successful Great Exhibition of 1851, and its original aims – which still hold today – were the 'improvement of public taste in Design' and 'applications of fine art to objects of utility'. It's done a fine job so far.

With so many things on display, it's wise to choose what you want to see and stick to it, otherwise it's easy to get overwhelmed. As you enter under the stunning Dale Chihuly Chandelier you can pick up a map of the museum at the information and ticket desk. (If the main entrance on Cromwell Rd is too busy, there's another around the corner on Exhibition Rd.) Consider one of the free introductory guided tours that leave the main reception area every hour from 10.30am to 4.30pm. There is also family activities information; ask at one of the desks.

Spread over nearly 150 galleries, the museum houses the world's greatest collection of decorative arts, including ancient Chinese ceramics, modernist architectural drawings, Korean bronze and Japanese swords, cartoons by Raphael, spellbinding Asian and Islamic art, Rodin sculptures, gowns from the Elizabethan era, dresses straight from this year's Paris fashion shows, ancient jewellery, a 1930s wireless set – and a lot more stuff hidden in storage.

Level 1 is mostly devoted to art and design from India, China, Japan and Korea, as well as European art. The museum has the best collection of Italian Renaissance sculpture outside Italy, as well as excellent French, German and Spanish sculpture. One of the museum's highlights are the Cast Courts in Rooms 46a and 46b, containing plaster casts collected in the Victorian era, such as Michelangelo's David, which was acquired in 1858. The fig leaf you can see around the back of the statue's plinth is said to have been used to protect Queen Victoria's sensibilities – the Queen was sufficiently shocked by the cast's nudity that the leaf was whipped out during royal visits and covered the offending anatomy by being hung on a pair of hooks. The museum's then director, Henry Cole, commissioned casts of Europe's finest works of art. The casts have not only been a great visitor attraction, but they were used by art students for many years.

Room 40, the museum's Fashion Room, is among the most popular, with displays ranging from Elizabethan costumes to Vivienne Westwood gowns, dodgy 1980s Armani outfits and designs from this year's catwalks. A fascinating display of women's undergarments shows the 'progress' from the stifling and life-endangering corsets from Victorian times to present-day Agent Provocateur's sexy corsets, now coveted and life-affirming luxury fashion pieces.

The Islamic Middle East in the Jameel Gallery opened in 2006 after years of renovations with more than 400 objects from the Muslim world, including ceramics, textiles, carpets, glass and woodwork from the 8th-century Islamic caliphate up to the years before WWI. The pieces were collected from Spain to Afghanistan, though the exhibition's highlight is the gorgeous 16th-century Ardabil Carpet, the world's oldest (and one of the largest) dated carpet, from Iran.

The newly replanted and landscaped Garden is a lovely shaded inner courtyard where you can collect your thoughts. The original Refreshment Rooms dating from the 1860s (Morris, Gamble and Poynter Rooms) were redesigned by McInnes Usher McKnight Architects (MUMA) in 2006 and are looking spectacular. MUMA is also renovating the V&A's Medieval and Renaissance galleries, and were behind the Royal Academy of Arts restaurant, all of which puts it at the forefront of London's new architecture and design.

The British Galleries, featuring every aspect of British design from 1500 to 1900, is on level 4. It includes *The Three Graces,* a famous marble statue by Antonio Canova, and Henry VIII's writing desk.

The Architecture gallery is also on level 4, with descriptions of architectural styles, videos, models and plans. The Photography collection is one of the country's best, with more than 500,000 images collected since 1852. Among the highlights are the 19th-century photographs of London by Lady Clementina Hawarden.

The V&A's temporary exhibitions – such as 2006/7's Kylie, 2007's Surreal Things, and New York Fashion – are compelling and bring lots of visitors (note admission fees apply), so find out what's on. It also has a brilliant programme of talks, events and club evenings, plus one of the best museum shops around.

NATURAL HISTORY MUSEUM Map pp138–9
☎ 7942 5725; www.nhm.ac.uk; Cromwell Rd SW7; admission free, half-hourly tours of 'wet' zoological exhibits in the Darwin Centre free, book in advance; ⏰ 10am-5.50pm Mon-Sat, 11am-5.50pm Sun; ⊖ South Kensington; ♿

The Natural History Museum is a mammoth institution dedicated to the Victorian pursuit of collecting and cataloguing, and walking into the Life Galleries, in the 1880 Gothic Revival building off Cromwell Rd, evokes the musty moth-eaten era of the Victorian gentleman scientist. The main museum building, with its blue and sand-coloured brick and terracotta, was designed by Alfred Waterhouse and is as impressive as the towering diplodocus dinosaur skeleton in the entrance hall. It's hard to match any of the exhibits with this initial sight, except for maybe the huge (but a bit tired-looking) blue whale.

Children, who are the main fans of this museum, are primed for more primeval wildlife by the dinosaur skeleton, and yank their parents to the Dinosaur gallery to see the roaring and tail-flicking animatronic T-rex dinosaur, the museum's star attraction (at least from the kiddies' point of view).

The Life Galleries are full of fossils and glass cases of taxidermied birds, and the antiquated atmosphere is mesmerising. There is also a stunning room on creepy crawlies, the Ecology Gallery's Quadrascope video wall and the vast Darwin Centre of zoological specimens. The first phase of the Darwin Centre

opened in 2002, and focuses on taxonomy (the study of the natural world), with some 450,000 jars of pickled specimens shown off during free guided tours every half-hour. The even-more-ambitious phase II of the Darwin Centre, estimated to cost more than £70 million, will showcase some 28 million insects and six million plants in 'a giant cocoon', due to open in 2009.

The second part of the museum, the Earth Galleries, is a thoroughly contemporary affair, exchanging the Victorian creakiness for a sleek, modern design. The entrance lies on Exhibition Rd and its main hall's black walls are lined with crystals, gems and precious rocks. Four life-size human statues herald the way to the escalator, which slithers up through a hollowed-out globe into displays about our planet's geological make-up.

Volcanoes, earthquakes and storms are all discussed on the upper floor, but the star attraction inside the Restless Surface gallery, the Kobe earthquake mock-up – a model of a small Japanese grocery shop that trembles in a manner meant to replicate the 1995 earthquake – is disappointingly lame. Better exhibitions on the lower floors focus on ecology, look at gems and other precious stones and explore how planets are formed.

The Wildlife Garden (open April to October, admission £1.50) displays a range of British lowland habitats.

To avoid crowds during school-term time, it's best to visit early morning or late afternoon, or early on weekend mornings year-round.

SCIENCE MUSEUM Map pp138–9
☎ 0870 870 4868; www.sciencemuseum.org.uk; Exhibition Rd SW7; admission free, adult/concession IMAX Cinema £7.50/6, SimEx Simulator Ride £4/3, Motionride simulator £2.50/1.50; ⏰ 10am-6pm; ⊖ South Kensington; ♿

This is one of the most progressive and accessible museums of its kind, and does a terrific job of bringing to lustrous life a subject that is often dull, dense and impenetrable for kids and adults alike. With five floors of interactive and educational exhibits, it's informative and entertaining and has something to snag the interest of every age group.

The revamped Energy Hall, on the ground floor as you enter, concentrates on 11 machines of the Industrial Revolution, showing how the first steam engines such as *Puffing*

Billy and *Stephenson's Rocket* helped Britain become 'the workshop of the world' in the early 19th century. Animations show how the machines worked and are accompanied by detailed overall explanations, including a section on the Luddites who opposed the march of technology.

Of course, it's impossible to miss the huge Energy Ring that now hangs over the open atrium from the gallery, Energy: Fuelling the Future, on the 2nd floor. Pop up here to enter your name and answers to several energy questions onto the electronic tickertape messages that run around the inside of the ring. On the same level you will also find a re-creation of Charles Babbage's mechanical calculator (1832), the famous forerunner to the computer.

The 3rd floor is a favourite place for children, with its gliders, hot-air balloon and varied aircraft, including the *Gipsy Moth*, in which Amy Johnson flew to Australia in 1930. This floor also features an adapted flight simulator that's been turned into a 'Motionride'. Level 1 contains displays on food and time, while the 4th and 5th floors contain exhibits on medical and veterinary history.

Nostalgic parents will delight in the old cars and the Apollo 10 command module. However, both they and their children will probably most enjoy the hi-tech Wellcome Wing, which is spread over several floors at the back of the building. The SimEx Simulator Ride and IMAX Cinema are found within this wing, with the usual crop of travelogues, space adventures and dinosaur attacks in stunning 3-D. There's a superlative exploration of identity on Level 1 entitled Who am I?, plus other hands-on displays for children.

There are no guided tours on offer, but you can pick up trail guides for children (lighter cover for younger kids, darker cover for older ones) or get a guidebook for £2. The Deep Blue Café on the ground floor of the Wellcome Wing opens from 10.30am to 5.30pm daily.

APSLEY HOUSE (WELLINGTON MUSEUM) Map pp138–9

☎ 7499 5676; www.english-heritage.org.uk; 149 Piccadilly W1; adult/child/concession incl audio tour £5.30/2.70/4; ✆ 10am–5pm Tue–Sun, last entry 4pm; ⊖ Hyde Park Corner

This stunning house was the first building one saw when entering the city from the west and is therefore known as 'No 1, Lon-

don'; what other place can boast such an address? Still one of London's finest, Apsley House was designed by Robert Adam for Baron Apsley in the late 18th century, but later sold to the first Duke of Wellington, who lived here for 35 years until his death in 1852. The duke cut Napoleon down to size in the Battle of Waterloo and is well known for lending his name to a practical, if none too flattering, style of rubber boot.

In 1947 the house was given to the nation, which must have come as a surprise to the duke's descendants who still live here; 10 of its rooms are open to the public today as the Wellington Museum. The house itself is magnificent and retains many of its original furnishings and collections. Wellington memorabilia, including his medals, some entertaining old cartoons and his death mask, fill the basement gallery, while there's an astonishing collection of china, including some of the Iron Duke's silverware, on the ground floor. The stairwell is dominated by Antonio Canova's staggering 3.4m-high statue of a naked Napoleon, adjudged by the subject as 'rather too athletic'. The 1st-floor rooms are decorated with paintings by Velàsquez, Rubens, Brueghel and Murillo, but the most interesting is Goya's portrait of the duke, which some years ago was discovered to have the face of Napoleon's brother, Joseph Bonaparte, beneath the duke's. Apparently, the artist had taken a punt on Napoleon winning the Battle of Waterloo and had to do a quick 'about face' when news of Wellington's victory arrived.

WELLINGTON ARCH Map pp138–9

☎ 7930 2726; www.english-heritage.org.uk; Hyde Park Corner W2; adult/student & child/senior £3.20/1.60/2.40; ✆ 10am–5pm Wed–Sun; ⊖ Hyde Park Corner

Opposite Apsley House in the little bit of green space being strangled by the Hyde Park Corner roundabout is England's answer to the Arc de Triomphe (except this one commemorates France's *defeat* – specifically, Napoleon's at the hands of Wellington). The neoclassical arch, erected in 1826, used to be topped by a disproportionately large equestrian statue of Wellington, but this was removed in 1882 and replaced some years later with the biggest bronze sculpture in Britain, *Peace Descending on the Quadriga of War*.

For years the monument served as the capital's smallest police station, but it was restored and opened up to the public as a three-level exhibition space focusing on London's arches. The balcony affords unforgettable views of Hyde Park, Buckingham Palace and the Houses of Parliament.

MICHELIN HOUSE Map pp138–9
81 Fulham Rd SW3; ⊖ South Kensington
Even if you're not up for dinner at Terence Conran's wonderful restaurant Bibendum (p253) in Michelin House, mosey past and have a look at the superb Art Nouveau architecture. It was built for Michelin between 1905 and 1911 by François Espinasse, and completely restored in 1985. The open-fronted ground floor provides space for upmarket fish and flower stalls, the famous roly-poly Michelin Man appears in the modern stained glass, while the lobby is decorated with tiles showing early-20th-century cars. The Conran Shop is also housed here.

KENSINGTON PALACE Map pp138–9
☎ 0870 751 5176; www.royalresidences.com; Kensington Gardens W8; adult/child/concession £12/6/10, park & gardens free; ☼ 10am-4.30pm; ⊖ Queensway, Notting Hill Gate or High St Kensington
Kensington Palace is welded in people's memory mostly as the residence of the late Diana, Princess of Wales. The palace's lawn was covered with a mountain of flowers following the death of the 'people's princess' in September 1997, an episode in history that showed the Brits significantly loosening the stiff upper lip and mourning the princess with an unprecedented sentimentality. A glimpse of Diana's fetching frocks in the Royal Ceremonial Dress Collection is always a highlight.

Of course, Kensington Palace already had a long history when Diana moved in after her divorce from Prince Charles in 1996. Built in 1605, it became the favourite royal residence under William and Mary of Orange in 1689, and remained so until George III became king and relocated to Buckingham Palace. Even afterwards the royals stayed occasionally, with Queen Victoria being born here in 1819.

In the 17th and 18th centuries, Kensington Palace was variously renovated by Sir Christopher Wren and William Kent, so you'll find yourself taking a self-guided audio tour through the surprisingly small,

wood-panelled State Apartments dating from William's time and then the grander apartments by Kent.

Most beautiful of all the quarters is the Cupola Room, where the ceremony of initiating men into the exclusive Order of the Garter took place and where Victoria was baptised; you can see the order's crest painted on the trompe l'oeil 'domed' ceiling, which is actually flat.

The King's Long Gallery displays some of the royal art collection, including the only known painting of a classical subject by Van Dyck. On the ceiling William Kent painted the story of Odysseus but slipped up by giving the Cyclops two eyes.

The King's Drawing Room is dominated by a monumentally ugly painting of Cupid and Venus by Giorgio Vasari (1511–74), an Italian mannerist painter who used to brag about the speed at which he worked and was better known for his historical record of the Renaissance. There are splendid views of the park and gardens from here; you can also see the Round Pond, once full of turtles for turtle soup but now popular for sailing model boats.

The King's Staircase is decorated with striking murals by William Kent, who painted himself in a turban on the fake dome.

The Sunken Garden near the palace is at its prettiest in summer; the nearby Orangery, designed by Vanbrugh and Hawksmoor as a free-standing conservatory in 1704, is a bright, if rather formal, place for tea.

1a Kensington Palace, formerly Princess Margaret's apartment, can only be visited by guided tour, which should run on the hour between 10.30am and 12.30pm and 2pm and 4pm. It features an exhibition of all the people who lived in the palace from the 18th to the 20th centuries. The space is to be used for other exhibitions, so check what's on before you go (though it's likely to be something to do with Diana).

KENSINGTON GARDENS Map pp138–9
☼ dawn-dusk; ⊖ Queensway, High St Kensington or Lancaster Gate
Immediately west of Hyde Park, across the Serpentine lake, these gardens are technically part of Kensington Palace. The Palace and the gardens have become something of a shrine to the memory of Princess Diana since her death. If you have kids, visit the Diana, Princess of Wales Memorial Playground, in the northwest corner of the gardens.

Art is also characteristic of these gardens: George Frampton's famous Peter Pan statue is close to the lake, south of which is an attractive area known as Flower Walk and also, near the main road that runs through the park, are sculptures by Henry Moore and Jacob Epstein.

SERPENTINE GALLERY Map pp138–9

☎ 7402 6075; www.serpentinegallery.org; Kensington Gardens W8; admission free; ⏰ 10am–6pm; ⬦ Knightsbridge; ♿

The Serpentine Gallery may be a gentle-looking 1930s tea pavilion in the midst of the leafy Kensington Gardens, but it's one of London's edgiest contemporary art galleries. Artists including Damien Hirst, Andreas Gursky, Louise Bourgeois, Gabriel Orozco and Tomoko Takahashi have all exhibited here, and the gallery's huge windows beam natural light onto the pieces, making the space perfect for sculpture and interactive displays.

Every year a leading architect (who has never built in the UK) is commissioned to build a new pavilion between May and September, which makes it the perfect time to visit. Past architects included Alvaro Siza, Oscar Niemeyer, Daniel Libeskind and Zaha Hadid. Reading, talks and open-air screenings take place here.

PRINCESS DIANA MEMORIAL FOUNTAIN Map pp138–9

Kensington Gardens W8; ⬦ Knightsbridge or South Kensington

The drama surrounding this memorial seems a predictably fraught postscript to a life that itself often hovered between the *Sun's* headlines, Greek tragedy and farce. Envisaged as a 'moat without a castle' (reflecting the Princess's supposed spiritual state?) draped 'like a necklace' (her elegance?) around Hyde Park near the Serpentine Bridge, this circular double stream had to be shut just a fortnight after it opened in 2004. The inclusive design by Kathryn Gustafson initially invited visitors, especially children, to wade in the fountain. But with fans flocking to the site in an unseasonably wet summer, the surrounding grass became muddy and slippery, leaves choked the drains causing an overflow and several people were injured when they slipped on the smooth granite basin.

A year later, the fountain was reopened with a gravel path encircling it to keep the Glastonbury-style mud bath to a minimum, and with park wardens patrolling the area to make sure visitors only delicately dip in their toes. Today there are no wardens around and visitors are managing by themselves; even if it's not quite what Gustafson imagined, people seem to love it, mesmerised as they are by the water's flow both left and right from the fountain's highest point, or sunning themselves around it.

ALBERT MEMORIAL Map pp138–9

☎ 7495 0916; 45min guided tours adult/concession £4.50/4; ⏰ tours 2pm & 3pm 1st Sun of the month; ⬦ Knightsbridge or South Kensington

On the southern edge of Hyde Park and facing Kensington Gore, this memorial is as over the top as the subject, Queen Victoria's German husband Albert (1819–61), was purportedly humble. Albert explicitly said he did not want a monument and 'if (as is very likely) it became an artistic monstrosity like most of our monuments, it would upset my equanimity to be permanently ridiculed and laughed at in effigy'. Ah, he didn't really mean it, they reckoned, and got George Gilbert Scott to build the 52.5m-high, gaudy Gothic monument in 1872, featuring the prince thumbing through a catalogue for his Great Exhibition, and surrounded by 178 figures representing the continents (Asia, Europe, Africa and America), as well as the arts, industry and science. The monument was unveiled again in 1998 after being renovated at huge expense. It's particularly eye-catching when lit up at night.

ROYAL ALBERT HALL Map pp138–9

☎ 7589 8212; www.royalalberthall.com; Kensington Gore SW7; ⬦ South Kensington; ♿

This huge, domed, redbrick amphitheatre adorned with a frieze of Minton tiles is Britain's most famous concert venue. The home of the BBC's Promenade Concerts (or 'Proms'; see p312) every summer, it was ironically never meant to be a concert venue. Instead, this 1871 memorial to Queen Victoria's husband was intended as a hall of arts and sciences, and consequently it spent the first 133 years of its existence tormenting concert performers and audiences with its terrible acoustics. It was said that a piece played here was assured of an immediate second hearing, so bad was the reverberation around the oval structure. A massive refurbishment was completed in 2004, however, installing air-conditioning, modernising the backstage areas, moving the entrance to the south of the building and fixing the acoustics. You can take a 45-minute guided tour (adult/concession £7.50/6.50; ⓨ tours hourly 10am-2.30pm Fri-Tue) of the hall.

If the classical Proms aren't your thing, there's pop, some rock and world music concerts here too, as well as a circus and book readings.

ROYAL GEOGRAPHICAL SOCIETY
Map pp138–9

☎ 7591 3000; www.rgs.org; 1 Kensington Gore SW7; admission free; ⓨ 10am-5pm Mon-Fri; ⊖ South Kensington; ⓺

A short distance to the east of the Royal Albert Hall is the headquarters of the Royal Geographical Society, housed in a Queen Anne–style redbrick edifice (1874) easily identified by the statues of explorers David Livingstone and Ernest Shackleton outside. The society holds a regular talks programme (many after hours) and photography exhibitions, while the Foyle Reading Room (☎ 7591 3040; adult/student per day £10/free) offers access to the society's collection of more than half a million maps, photographs, artefacts, books and manuscripts. The entrance to the society is on Exhibition Rd.

HYDE PARK Map pp138–9

ⓨ 5.30am-midnight; ⊖ Hyde Park Corner, Marble Arch, Knightsbridge or Lancaster Gate

London's legendary park spreads itself over a whopping 145 hectares of neatly manicured gardens and wild, deserted expanses of overgrown grass. Spring prompts the gorgeous Rose Gardens into vivacious bloom, and summers are full of sunbathers, picnickers, Frisbee-throwers and general London populace who drape themselves across the green. It's the largest of London's Royal Parks and a magnificent venue for open-air concerts, demonstrations and royal occasions. Gun salutes are fired here and soldiers ride through the park each morning on their way to Horse Guards Parade in Whitehall, while people on Rollerblades and bicycles impress passers-by with their tricks.

Hyde Park is separated from Kensington Gardens by the squiggly L-shaped Serpentine lake, which was created when the Westbourne River was dammed in the 1730s; it's a good spot for pleasure boating

in summer (around £5 per half-hour). Henry VIII expropriated the park from the Church in 1536, after which it became a hunting ground for kings and aristocrats; later it became a popular venue for duels, executions and horse racing. It became the first royal park to open to the public in the early 17th century, and famously hosted the Great Exhibition in 1851. During WWII it became an enormous potato bed.

You'll either love or hate the ornate Queen Elizabeth Gate (designed by Giuseppe Lund and David Wynne in 1993) leading on to Park Lane near Hyde Park Corner. The pale-green granite sweep of the new Australian War Memorial (Map pp138–9) nearby at Hyde Park Corner is a little more restrained.

SPEAKERS' CORNER Map pp138–9
⊖ Marble Arch

The northeastern corner of Hyde Park is traditionally the spot for oratorical acrobatics and soapbox ranting. It's the only place in Britain where demonstrators can assemble without police permission, a concession granted in 1872 as a response to serious riots when 150,000 people gathered to demonstrate against the Sunday Trading Bill before Parliament. If you've got something on your chest, you can get rid of it here on Sunday, although it'll be largely loonies and religious fanatics you'll have for company. Nobody else will take much notice.

MARBLE ARCH Map pp138–9
⊖ Marble Arch

John Nash designed this huge arch in 1827. It was moved here, to the northeastern corner of Hyde Park, from its original spot in front of Buckingham Palace in 1851, when it was adjudged too small and unimposing to be the entrance to the royal manor. There's a one-room flat inside, London's grandest bedsit. If you're feeling anarchic, walk through the central portal, a privilege reserved for the royal family by law.

TYBURN TREE Map pp138–9
⊖ Marble Arch

A plaque on the traffic island at Marble Arch indicates the spot where the infamous Tyburn Tree, a three-legged gallows, once stood. An estimated 50,000 people were executed here between 1300 and 1783, many having been dragged from the Tower of London.

TYBURN CONVENT Map pp138–9

☎ 7723 7262; www.tyburnconvent.org.uk; 8 Hyde Park Pl; admission free; ☷ tours of the crypt 10.30am, 3.30pm & 5.30pm, call beforehand; ✚ Marble Arch; ♿

One of the buildings of this sorrowful and silent place has the distinction of being the smallest house in London, measuring just over a metre in width. A convent was established here in 1903, close to the site of the Tyburn Tree gallows where many Catholics were executed because of their faith during the 16th century, and which later became a place of Catholic pilgrimage. The crypt contains the relics of some 105 martyrs, along with paintings commemorating their lives and recording their deaths. A closed order of Benedictine sisters lives here, as they have for more than a century.

BROMPTON ORATORY Map pp138–9

☎ 7808 0900; 215 Brompton Rd SW7; ☷ 6.30am-8pm; ✚ South Kensington

Also known as the London Oratory and the Oratory of St Philip Neri, this Roman Catholic church was built in the Italian baroque style in 1884. It has marble, candles and statues galore, and Tony Blair is a regular. There are six daily Masses on weekdays, one at 6pm on Saturday, and nine between 7am and 7pm on Sunday.

LINLEY SAMBOURNE HOUSE Map p177

☎ 7602 3316; www.rbkc.gov.uk/linleysambourne house; 18 Stafford Tce W8; adult/child/concession £6/1/4; ☷ tours at 11.15am, 1pm, 2.15pm, 3.30pm Sat & Sun; ✚ High St Kensington

Tucked away behind Kensington High St, this was the home of *Punch* political cartoonist and amateur photographer Linley Sambourne and his family from 1874 to 1910. It's one of those houses whose owners never redecorated or threw anything away. What you see is pretty much the typical home of a well-to-do Victorian family: dark wood, Turkish carpets and rich stained glass. Visits are by 90-minute guided tour only (with all but the first guide in period costume).

VICTORIA & PIMLICO

WESTMINSTER CATHEDRAL Map pp138–9

☎ 7798 9055; www.westminstercathedral.org .uk; Victoria St SW1; cathedral admission free, tower adult/concession £3/1.50, audioguides £2.50; ☷ cathedral 7am-7pm, tower 9am-5pm Apr-Nov, 9am-5pm Thu-Sun Dec-Mar; ✚ Victoria; ♿

John Francis Bentley's 19th-century cathedral is a superb example of neo-Byzantine architecture: its distinctive candy-striped redbrick and white-stone tower features prominently on the West London skyline. This is the headquarters of the Roman Catholic Church in Britain, and while work on it started in 1895, and worshippers began attending in 1903, the church ran out of money and the interior has never been completed. In some ways, it's London's version of Gaudí's La Sagrada Familia in Barcelona – a magnificent work in progress.

Remarkably few people think to look inside, but the interior is partly a stunning variety of 100 types of marble and mosaic and partly bare brick. The highly regarded stone carvings of the *14 Stations of the Cross* (1918) by Eric Gill and the marvellously sombre atmosphere make this a welcome haven from the traffic outside. The views from the 83m-tall Campanile Bell Tower are impressive, and the fact that it has a lift will have you thanking the heavens.

Seven Masses are said daily from Sunday to Friday and five on Saturday. There's a gift shop and a café here, open 10am to 4.30pm daily.

THE HYDE PARK WALK
Walking Tour
1 Hyde Park Corner

Climb the monumental Wellington Arch (p142) for great views and, in the same small square of green, you will find the rather tasteful wall of eucalypt green granite of the Australian War Memorial (p145). Nearby, the ornate – some say too ornate – Queen Elizabeth Gate (p145) was commissioned to honour the late Queen Mother. The aromatic, relaxing and beautifully colourful rose garden is one of the more magical places in London.

2 The Serpentine

Keep to the lake's northern side and interrupt your walk by renting a paddle boat from the Serpentine boathouse (☎ 7262 1330; adult/child per 30min £5/2,per 1hr £7/3; ☷ 10am-4pm Feb & Mar, 10am-6pm Apr-Jun, 10am-7pm Jul & Aug, 10am-5pm Sep & Oct, 10am-5pm Sat & Sun Nov). The Serpentine solar shuttle boat (ticket £3/£1.50; ☷ shuttles every half hr from noon-5pm), uses only solar power to get you from the boathouse to the Princess Diana Memorial

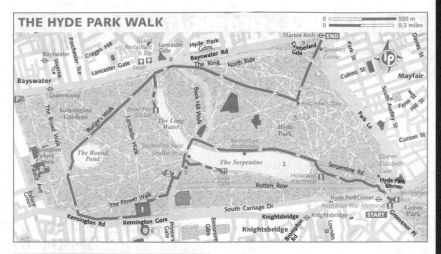

THE HYDE PARK WALK

0 — 500 m
0 — 0.3 miles

WALK FACTS

Start Hyde Park Corner tube station
End Marble Arch tube station
Distance 2.5 miles
Duration About 1½ hours
Fuel stops Coffee and cake at the Lido Café, end-of-walk drink at the Swan or the Island Restaurant & Bar

Fountain. Stop in at the Lido Café (🕑 9am-7.30pm Apr-Oct, 9am-4pm Nov-Mar).

3 Princess Diana Memorial Fountain

Despite early teething problems, this concrete 'necklace' of water (p144) sitting on perfectly manicured lawn is a popular chill-out spot today. Water flows from the highest point in both directions, into a small pool at the bottom. Bathing is forbidden, although you are allowed to dip your feet.

4 Serpentine Gallery

This former teahouse is now one of the city's best contemporary art galleries (p144), housing many interesting exhibitions and summer pavilions designed by world's leading architects. The space is small enough to get around before any kids accompanying you get bored.

5 Albert Memorial

Gilded and enormous, the grandness of the Albert Memorial (p144) is in stark contrast with the humble Prince Albert, Queen Victoria's much-loved husband.

6 Royal Albert Hall

Another memorial to Queen Victoria's beloved husband, this is Britain's most famous concert hall (p144) that's seen more big names in its time than any other, including the choral version of Blake's *Jerusalem* that was held to celebrate the granting of the vote to women.

7 Kensington Palace

Princes Diana's former home and a long-standing royal residence (p143), this is where you can stop off and take a look at the permanent and temporary exhibitions and the stunning interior, before surrendering to one of the park's many stretches of grass.

8 Lancaster Gate

There's plenty more to see in the park, if you have time, stamina and the strength of will to resist merely having a snooze on the grass or stopping in at the Swan (☎ 7262 5204; 66 Bayswater Rd W2; 🕑 10am-11pm) or the Island Restaurant & Bar (☎ 7551 6070; Lancaster Tce W2; 🕑 noon-11pm). Other well-known features include the Peter Pan Statue (p144).

9 Cumberland Gate

In the northeastern corner of the park, near Marble Arch tube station, there's also the Tyburn Tree (p145) and, of course, Speakers' Corner (p145).

CLERKENWELL, SHOREDITCH & SPITALFIELDS

This area of northeast London is the city's ground zero of cool, and its success at the expense of other nightlife areas such as Soho continues to astound pretty much everyone. It's made up of Clerkenwell, just north of the City; Shoreditch and its northern extension Hoxton, an area (roughly) between Old St tube station and just east of Shoreditch High St; and Spitalfields, centred around the market of that name and Brick Lane, Banglatown's main thoroughfare.

The Shoreditch/Hoxton phenomenon began in the late 1990s, when creative types chased out of the West End by prohibitive rents began buying warehouses in this then urban wasteland, abandoned after the collapse of the fabrics industry. Within a few years the area was seriously cool, boasting superslick bars, cutting-edge clubs, galleries and restaurants that catered to the new media-creative-freelance squad. The fact that it was in walking distance of the City and its high-spending, heavy-drinking denizens didn't hurt.

Yet despite the bursting of the dotcom bubble, and the general expectation that the Shoreditch scene would collapse under the weight of its own trucker hats, the regenerated area is flourishing stronger than ever. The entire neighbourhood remains rough enough around the edges to feel a bit of an adventure, but even the partial redevelopment of Spitalfields Market hasn't stopped it in it tracks, and it remains one of London's best nightlife scenes.

top picks

CLERKENWELL, SHOREDITCH & SPITALFIELDS

- Dennis Severs' House (p152)
- Geffrye Museum (p151)
- Spitalfields Market (opposite & p233)
- St John's Gate (opposite)
- White Cube Gallery (opposite)

Historic Clerkenwell lies in the valley of the River Fleet (from where the 'clerks' well' the neighbourhood is named after sprang), although the river itself has long been bricked over (see p129). Like Shoreditch, Clerkenwell has profited enormously from redevelopment since the late 1980s, and many once-empty warehouses have been converted into expensive flats and work spaces. Clerkenwell is still a great place to see historic landmarks from throughout London's history, including magnificent Smithfield Market, St John's Gate and St Bartholomew's Church.

CLERKENWELL

CHARTERHOUSE Map p150

☎ 7251 5002; Charterhouse Sq EC1; admission £10; ⏰ guided tours 2.15pm Wed Apr-Sep; ⊖ Barbican or Farringdon

You need to book nearly a year in advance to see inside this former Carthusian monastery, whose centrepiece is a Tudor hall with a restored hammer-beam roof. Its incredibly popular two-hour guided tours held six months a year begin at the 14th-century gatehouse on Charterhouse Sq, before going through to the Preachers' Court (with three original monks' cells in the western wall), the Master's Court, the Great Hall and the Great Chamber, where Queen Elizabeth I stayed on numerous occasions.

The monastery was founded in 1371 by the Carthusians, the strictest of all Roman Catholic monastic orders, who refrained from eating meat and took vows of silence, broken only for three hours on Sunday. During the Reformation, the monastery was oppressed, with at least three priors hanged at Tyburn and a dozen monks sent to Newgate, where they were chained upright and died of starvation. King Henry VIII confiscated the monastery in 1537, and it was purchased in 1611 by Thomas Sutton, known at the time as the 'richest commoner in England'. Sutton – of Sutton House (p158) fame – opened an almshouse for destitute gentlemen; some three dozen pensioners (known as 'brothers') live here today and lead the tours. To obtain tickets, send a stamped self-addressed envelope, a covering letter giving at least three dates when you would like to visit and a cheque made payable to 'Charterhouse' to Tour Bookings, Charterhouse, Charterhouse Sq, London EC1M 6AN.

ST JOHN'S GATE Map p150
⊖ Farringdon

What looks like a toy-town medieval gate cutting across St John's Lane turns out to be the real thing. It dates from the early 16th century but was heavily restored 300 years later. During the Crusades, the Knights of St John of Jerusalem were soldiers who took on a nursing role. In Clerkenwell they established a priory that originally covered around 4 hectares. The gate was built in 1504 as a grand entrance to their church, St John's Clerkenwell in St John's Sq.

Although most of the buildings were destroyed when Henry VIII dissolved every priory in the country between 1536 and 1540, the gate lived on. It had a varied afterlife, not least as a Latin-speaking coffee house run, without much success, by William Hogarth's father during Queen Anne's reign. The restoration dates from the period when it housed the Old Jerusalem Tavern in the 19th century. A pub of (almost) that name can now be found round the corner on Britton St (see p285).

Inside St John's Gate is the small Order of St John Museum (☎ 7324 40005; www.sja.org.uk/museum; St John's Lane EC1; admission free; ⏰ 10am-5pm Mon-Fri, to 4pm Sat; ⊖ Farringdon; ♿) which recounts in three galleries the history of the knights and their properties around the world, and of their successors, the modern British Order of St John and the St John Ambulance brigade. It also offers a potted history of Clerkenwell in photographs and documents.

Definitely try to time your visit for one of the guided tours (adult/senior £5/4; ⏰ tours 11am & 2.30pm Tue, Fri & Sat) of the gate and the restored church remains. This includes the fine Norman crypt with a sturdy alabaster monument commemorating a Castilian knight (1575); a battered monument portraying the last prior, William Weston, as a skeleton in a shroud; and stained-glass windows showing the main figures in the story. You'll also be shown the sumptuous Chapter Hall where the Chapter General of the Order meets every three months.

KARL MARX MEMORIAL LIBRARY
Map p150

☎ 7253 1485; www.marxlibrary.net; 37a Clerkenwell Green EC1; admission free; ⏰ 1-6pm Mon-Thu Feb-Dec; ⊖ Farringdon

Clerkenwell has quite a radical history. An area of Victorian-era slums (the so-called Rookery), it was settled by mainly Italian immigrants in the 19th century. Modern Italy's founding father Garibaldi dropped by in 1836, and during his European exile, Lenin edited 17 editions of the Russian-language Bolshevik newspaper *Iskra* (Spark) from here in 1902–03. Copies of the newspaper have been preserved in today's library, along with a host of other socialist literature. Non-members are free to look around between 1pm and 2pm, but you need to become a member (£10 per year, £6 day fee but usually valid for up to a week) to use the library or borrow any of its 150,000 books.

SHOREDITCH & HOXTON

WHITE CUBE GALLERY Map p150
☎ 7930 5373; www.whitecube.com; 48 Hoxton Sq N1; admission free; ⏰ 10am-6pm Tue-Sat; ⊖ Old St

Alongside Charles Saatchi, owner of the erstwhile Saatchi Gallery, the White Cube's Jay Jopling was the man responsible for bringing Britart to the public's attention in the 1990s. He worked with a young Damien Hirst before Saatchi came on the scene, showcased the works of sculptor Antony Gormley (responsible for Gateshead's huge *Angel of the North* sculpture and *Event Horizon,* in which 31 metal casts of the sculptor's naked body were perched on the edge of buildings surrounding the South Bank) and married artist Sam Taylor-Wood. White Cube is now firmly part of Britain's 'new establishment' but shows by Damien Hirst, Tracey Emin and other less well-known artists mean it's always worth coming just to have a look. There's another White Cube in St James's (see p71).

SPITALFIELDS

Across Commercial St from the church is the late-Victorian Spitalfields Market (p233). Until 1991 this was London's main fruit and vegetable market. Its proximity to Hoxton and Shoreditch means the Sunday market here is still the market of the moment, but with young clothes designers and producers of trendy furniture and ornaments selling their wares.

BRICK LANE Map p150
Immortalised in Monica Ali's award-winning eponymous novel, Brick Lane is the centre-

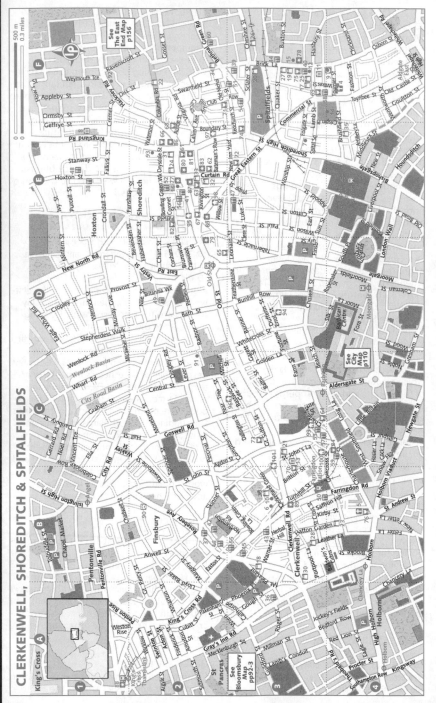

CLERKENWELL, SHOREDITCH & SPITALFIELDS

piece of a thriving Bengali community in an area nicknamed Banglatown. The lane itself is one long procession of curry and balti houses intermingled with sari and fabric shops, Indian cookery stores and outlets selling ethnic knick-knacks. Sadly, the once high standard of cooking in the curry houses is a distant memory, so you're probably better off trying subcontinental cuisine in Whitechapel (p259).

Just past Hanbury St is the converted Old Truman Brewery. This was once London's largest brewery and the Director's House on the left harks back to 1740, the old Vat House across the road with its hexagonal bell tower is early 19th century, and the Engineer's House next to it dates from

1830. The brewery stopped producing beer in 1989, and in the 1990s became home to a host of independent music businesses, small shops and hip clubs and bars.

GEFFRYE MUSEUM Map p150

☎ 7739 9893; www.geffrye-museum.org.uk; 136 Kingsland Rd E2; admission by donation; ⊙ 10am-5pm Tue-Sat, noon-5pm Sun; ⊖ Old St or Liverpool St; ⑤
Definitely Shoreditch's most accessible sight, this 18th-century ivy-clad series of almshouses with a herb garden draws you in immediately.

The museum is devoted to domestic interiors, with each recently renovated room of the main building furnished to show how the homes of the relatively affluent middle class would have looked from Elizabethan times right through to the end of the 19th century. A postmodernist extension completed in 1998 contains several 20th-century rooms (a flat from the 1930s, a room in the contemporary style of the 1950s, a 1990s converted warehouse complete with Ikea furniture) as well as a lovely herb garden, gallery for temporary exhibits, design centre with works from the local community, shop and restaurant.

Another development has been the exquisite restoration of a historic almshouse interior (adult/under 16yr £2/free). It's the absolute attention to detail that impresses, right down to the vintage newspaper left open on the breakfast table. The setting is so fragile, however, that this small almshouse is only open twice a month (usually on a Wednesday and Saturday).

DENNIS SEVERS' HOUSE Map p150
☎ 7247 4013; www.dennissevershouse.co.uk; 18 Folgate St E1; Sun/Mon/Mon evening £8/5/12; ◷ noon-4pm 1st & 3rd Sun of the month, noon-2pm Mon following 1st & 3rd Sun of the month, every Mon evening (times variable); ⊖ Liverpool St

This quirky hotchpotch of a cluttered house is named after the late American eccentric who restored and turned it into what he called a 'still-life drama'. Visitors find they have entered the home of a 'family' of Huguenot silk weavers common to the Spitalfields area in the 18th century. However, while they see the fabulous restored Georgian interiors with meals and drinks half-abandoned and rumpled sheets, and while they smell cooking and hear creaking floorboards, their 'hosts' always remain tantalisingly just out of reach. It's a unique and intriguing proposition by day, but the 'Silent Night' tours by candlelight every Monday evening (booking essential) are an even more memorable visit.

Dennis Severs' House is not the only fine Georgian house in Folgate St, north of Spitalfields market; the street is lined with them, and they too were once occupied by the Huguenots who fled religious persecution in France to settle here in the late 17th century. Bringing with them their skills as silk weavers, their presence is still recalled by such street names as Fleur-de-Lis St and Nantes Passage. There are yet more restored Georgian houses along Fournier St.

GREAT MOSQUE Map p150
Jamme Masjid; 59 Brick Lane E1; ⊖ Liverpool St

The best example of the changes in population that this area has experienced over the past several centuries is this house of worship on Brick Lane. Built in 1743 as the New French Church for the Huguenots, it served as a Methodist chapel for a time until it was transformed into the Great Synagogue for Jewish refugees from Russia and central Europe in 1899. In 1975 it changed faiths yet again, becoming the Great Mosque.

CHRIST CHURCH, SPITALFIELDS Map p150
☎ 7247 7202; www.christchurchspitalfields.org; Commercial St E1; ◷ 11am-4pm Tue, 1-4pm Sun; ⊖ Liverpool St

Diagonally opposite Spitalfields market on the corner of Commercial and Fournier Sts is this restored church, where many of the weavers worshipped. The magnificent English baroque structure, with a tall spire sitting on a portico of four great Tuscan columns, was designed by Nicholas Hawksmoor and completed in 1729. Restoration of the interior was completed in 2004.

MUSEUM OF IMMIGRATION & DIVERSITY Map p150
☎ 7375 1490; www.19princeletstreet.org.uk; 19 Princelet St E1; admission by donation; ⊖ Liverpool St

This unique Huguenot town house was built in 1719 and housed a prosperous family of weavers, before becoming home to waves of immigrants including Polish, Irish and Jewish families, the last of which built a synagogue in the back garden in 1869. In keeping with the house's multicultural past, it now houses a Museum of Immigration & Diversity, whose carefully considered exhibits are aimed at both adults and children. Unfortunately the house is in a terrible state of repair and as such opens only infrequently (usually no more than a dozen times a year). Check the website for dates.

SUNDAYS AT SPITALFIELDS & SHOREDITCH
Walking Tour
1 Spitalfields Market

This is London's best market (p233), and any Londoner's Sunday-morning joy. As you approach from Liverpool St, you'll see the new development, which, although trying to maintain an independent spirit and not hosting mega-chains, lacks the old market's rugged and spontaneous atmosphere. Enter the old market building and get lost among the many clothes, furniture and food stalls.

WALK FACTS

Best time Sunday mornings
Start Liverpool St tube station
End Old St tube station
Distance 2 miles
Duration One hour
Fuel Stops Food stalls at the back of Sunday Up Market, Brick Lane Beigel Bake (p258) drink at Hoxton Sq

2 Absolute Vintage

Check out the tons of vintage shoes in this excellent shop (p231). There are colours and sizes for all, with shoes ranging from designer vintage to something out of your grandma's storage. Clothes for men and women line the back of the shop.

3 Sunday Up Market

Having lost valuable stall space with the new development, the young designers moved their market (p233) inside the Old Truman Brewery. The new space is brilliant – not as crowded, with wonderful clothes, music and crafts, and the excellent food hall (on the Brick Lane end) has worldwide grub, from Ethiopian veggie dishes to Japanese delicacies.

SUNDAYS AT SPITALFIELDS & SHOREDITCH

4 Old Truman Brewery

This was the biggest brewery in London by the mid-18th century, and the Director's House on the left dates from 1740. Next to the 19th-century old Vat House is the 1830 Engineer's House and a row of former stables. The brewery shut down in 1989 and is now part of Sunday Up Market.

5 Brick Lane

In 1550 this was just a country road leading to brickyards, and by the 18th century it had been paved and lined with houses and cottages inhabited by the Spitalfields weavers. Today this vibrant street (p149) is taken up almost entirely by touristy curry houses. All the street names are in Bengali as well as English.

6 Brick Lane Market

Sundays at Brick Lane around the now defunct Shoreditch tube station are the best place to find good bargains for clothes, but the market (p233) is particularly good for furniture. Saunter down Cheshire St for little boutiques featuring new designers and vintage collections.

7 Brick Lane Beigel Bake

At the far end of Brick Lane, this excellent bagel business (p258) was started by some of the Jewish families who originally settled in the neighbourhood and still live here. It operates 24 hours a day and is always busy: with market shoppers on Sunday and Shoreditch clubbers by night.

8 Columbia Road Flower Market

Every Sunday from dawn market stalls sell freshly cut flowers, plants and orchids for Londoners' gardens and window sills. The earlier you arrive, the better the market (p233), though the best bargains are to be had later on (around noon). Make a beeline for the food stalls behind the main flower sellers for an exotic snack of fried king prawns and sweet chilli sauce.

9 Geffrye Museum

A small estate of Victorian houses, this fascinating museum (p151) is devoted to English furniture through the ages. End your walk in the lovely glass café in the back, and have a look at the museum's aromatic herb garden.

10 Hoxton Square

Walk back down Old St and pop into Hoxton Sq on the way. Check out the green and join the crowds having a drink outside if the weather is good.

11 White Cube Gallery

The first (of the two) creations of Britart pioneers Jay Jopling and his wife Sam Taylor-Wood, herself one of Britain's more prominent contemporary artists, this gallery (p149) always has something fun or controversial hanging on its pristine white walls.

THE EAST END & DOCKLANDS

Eating p258; Drinking p287; Shopping p229; Sleeping p355

The East End district of Whitechapel may lie within walking distance of the City, and neighbourhoods to the north and east such as Bethnal Green and Mile End be just one and two tube stops away respectively, but the change of pace and style is extraordinary. Traditionally this was working-class London, an area settled by wave upon wave of immigrants, giving it a curious mixture of French Huguenot, Irish, Jewish and Bangladeshi cultures, all of which can still be felt to varying degrees today. Rundown and neglected in the early 1980s, the East End is starting to look up in places. Signs of wealth have started to trickle into the areas around Whitechapel and Aldgate East. Property prices have risen enormously in Mile End, Bethnal Green and Bow, and there's even been a growing focus on ramshackle Hackney and Dalston, which will find itself with a station once the East London line extension is completed in 2010.

Anyone interested in modern, multicultural London should visit the East End. Alongside a couple of interesting museums you'll find some of London's best-value Asian cuisine in Whitechapel, as well as some of its most colourful markets. You may also want to pop into the trend-setting Whitechapel Art Gallery or take a dip in the beautifully renovated London Fields Lido.

Cobbled from the warehouses, docks and basins that made London so fabulously wealthy from the 18th century onward, the Docklands, the East End's southern extension, today is a world of contrasts. Eye-catching bridges across docks and futuristic buildings dominate the skyline; it really is today's view of London's future. But it is also an area rich in history, too, and the Museum in Docklands brings it all to life.

top picks

THE EAST END & DOCKLANDS

- Canary Wharf Tower (p161)
- Museum in Docklands (p161)
- Ragged School Museum (p159)
- Tower Hamlets Cemetery (p159)
- V&A Museum of Childhood (p158)

WHITECHAPEL

The East End's main thoroughfare, Whitechapel High St, hums with a cacophony of Asian and African languages, its busy shops selling everything from Indian snacks to Nigerian fabrics and Middle Eastern jewellery, as the East End's multitudinous ethnic groupings rub up against each other. It's still a chaotic and poor place, but it's one full of life and should not be missed.

WHITECHAPEL ART GALLERY Map p156

☎ 7522 7888; www.whitechapel.org; 80-82 Whitechapel High St E1; admission free; ☒ 11am-6pm Wed-Sun, to 9pm Thu; ⊖ Aldgate East; ☒

It's all change at the Whitechapel Art Gallery as it doubles its size by expanding into a disused library next door. During that time, one of the capital's more interesting contemporary art galleries becomes the Whitechapel Laboratory, with changing exhibitions, live music, poetry, talks and film. The new space will contain three new galleries, an Education and Research Tower and a street-facing café. The Whitechapel Art Gallery was founded in 1901 by Victorian philanthropist Samuel Barnett to bring art to the people of East London and it has made its name putting on exhibitions by both established and emerging artists, cartoonists and architects, including Gary Hume, Robert Crumb and Mies van der Rohe. Its ambitiously themed shows change every couple of months; check the programme online. Enter from Angel Alley.

WHITECHAPEL BELL FOUNDRY

Map p156

☎ 7247 2599; www.whitechapelbellfoundry.co .uk; 32-34 Whitechapel Rd E1; tours per person £8; ☒ tours 10am & 2pm Sat, shop 9.30am-4.15pm Mon-Fri; ⊖ Aldgate East

The Whitechapel Bell Foundry been standing on this site since 1738, although an earlier foundry nearby is known to have been in business in 1570. Both Big Ben (1858) and the Liberty Bell (1752) in Philadelphia were cast here, and the foundry also cast a

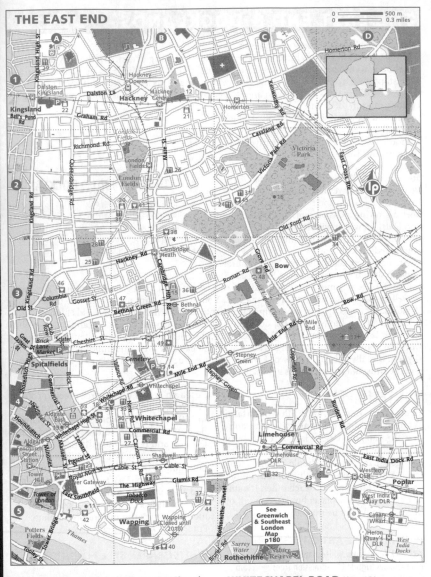

new bell for New York City's Trinity Church, damaged in the terrorist attacks of 11 September 2001. The 1½-hour guided tours on Saturday (children under 14 years not permitted) offer a revealing insight into a distinguished old trade, but bookings are essential. During weekday trading hours you can view a few small exhibits in the foyer or buy bell-related items from the shop.

WHITECHAPEL ROAD Map p156

Within a few minutes' walk of Whitechapel tube station you'll find the large East London Mosque (46-92 Whitechapel Rd E1) and behind it on Fieldgate St the Great Synagogue (1899).

Cable St, just south of Whitechapel Rd, towards Wapping, is where you'll find the former St George's Town Hall building (236 Cable St E1), now a library. On the east wall of the

THE EAST END

building facing Library Pl is a large mural commemorating the Cable St riots that took place here in October 1936. The British fascist Oswald Mosley led a bunch of his Blackshirt thugs into the area to intimidate the local Jewish population, but they were resoundingly repelled by local people – Jews and non-Jews alike.

You're now also deep in Jack the Ripper territory. In fact, the serial killer's first victim (of five), Mary Ann Nichols, was hacked to death on 31 August 1888 on what is now Durward St, north of (and just behind) Whitechapel tube station.

Along Whitechapel Rd itself, the criminal connections continue through the centuries. Just before the intersection with Cambridge Heath Rd sits the Blind Beggar Pub (☎ 7247 6195; 337 Whitechapel Rd), where the notorious gangster Ronnie Kray shot dead George Cornell in 1966, in a turf war over control of the East End's organised crime. He was jailed for life and died in 1995.

After the intersection with Cambridge Heath Rd, this traditionally poor area's history takes a more philanthropic turn, with a statue of William Booth, who established his Salvation Army Christian Mission here in 1865, and the Trinity Green Almshouses, poorhouses built for injured or retired sailors in 1695. The two rows of almshouses run at right angles away from the street, facing a village-type green and chapel.

WOMEN'S LIBRARY Map p156

☎ 7320 2222; www.thewomenslibrary.ac.uk; Old Castle St E1; admission free; ⏱ 9.30am-5pm Tue, Wed & Fri, to 8pm Thu, 10am-4pm Sat; ⊖ Aldgate East; ♿

Just round the corner from the Whitechapel Art Gallery, the Women's Library, part of the London Metropolitan University, is a unique repository for all manner of books and documents related to women's history. It contains a reading room open to the public, as well as archive and museum collections, and organises talks and special exhibitions (last seen – Prostitution: What's Going On?). The building is a modern take on the former Goulston Square Wash House, one of the oldest public baths in London.

BETHNAL GREEN & HACKNEY

Bethnal Green, the poorest district of London during Victorian times, and sprawling Hackney – whose Saxon name, from *haccan* (to kill with an axe or sword) and *ey* (river), indicates a place of battle – make up the 'proper' East End and can lay claim to being among the most ethnically diverse areas of the capital with sizable populations of Afro-Caribbeans, Turks, Kurds and Orthodox Jews. While neither district is on the tourist trail, both repay a visit amply.

COCKNEY RHYMING SLANG

Some visitors arrive in London expecting to find a city populated by people conversing in cockney à la Dick Van Dyke in Mary Poppins. Traditionally the cockneys were people born within earshot of the Bow Bells – the church bells of St Mary-le-Bow. Since few people live in the City, that means most cockneys are East Enders.

The term cockney is often used to describe anyone speaking what is also called estuarine English (in which 't' and 'h' are routinely dropped). In fact the true cockney language also uses something called rhyming slang, which may have developed among London's costermongers (street traders) as a code to avoid police attention. This code replaced common nouns and verbs with rhyming phrases. So 'going up the apples and pears' meant going up the stairs, the 'trouble and strife' was the wife, 'telling porky pies' was telling lies and 'would you Adam and Eve it?' was would you believe it? Over time the second of the two words tended to be dropped so the rhyme vanished. Few – if any – people still use pure cockney but many still understand it. You're more likely to come across it in residual phrases like 'use your loaf' ('loaf of bread' for head), 'ooh, me plates of meat' (feet) or "e's me best china' ('china plate' for mate). In 2007 a TV personality described a car he had test-driven as lacking power, being 'a bit ginger beer'. 'Beer' rhymes with 'queer' and he was upbraided for using language offensive to homosexuals.

V&A MUSEUM OF CHILDHOOD
Map p156

☎ 8983 5200, recorded information 8980 2415; www.vam.ac.uk/moc; cnr Cambridge Heath & Old Ford Rds E2; admission free; ☽ 10am-5.45pm; ⊖ Bethnal Green; ♿

Housed in a renovated Victorian-era building which has won a Royal Institute of British Architects (RIBA) award for outstanding design, this museum is aimed at both kids – with its activity rooms and corners of child-friendly, interactive exhibits, games and toys – and nostalgia-seeking grown-ups who come to admire the antique doll houses, model trains, teddy bears and other toys arranged thematically. In fact, the museum, part of the Victoria & Albert Museum in South Kensington and here since the 1860s, is home to one of the largest and oldest collections of toys in the world. From carved ivory figures (one – a 'paddle doll' dates back to 1300 BC) to stuffed animals, from Meccano to Lego and from peep shows to Viewmasters and video games, childhood artefacts from around the world are on display in this cheery museum.

SUTTON HOUSE Map p156

☎ 8986 2264; www.nationaltrust.org.uk; 2 & 4 Homerton High St E9; adult/child/family £2.70/60p/£6; ☽ 12.30-4.30pm Thu-Sun early Feb-late Dec; ☒ Hackney Central, ☒ 38, 106 or 394

It's difficult to imagine well-heeled Tudor noblemen such as Thomas Sutton, founder of the Charterhouse almshouse (p148), living in 'ackney, but as East London's oldest surviving house proves, they did, and in some style too. Abandoned and taken over by squatters in the 1980s (who have left

behind a large mural of an eye in the attic), what was originally known as Bryk Place when built in 1535 could have been tragically lost to history, but it's since been put under the care of the National Trust and magnificently restored.

The first historic room you enter, the Linenfold Parlour, is the absolute highlight, where the Tudor oak panelling on the walls has been carved to resemble draped cloth. Other notable rooms include the panelled Great Chamber, the Victorian study, the Georgian parlour and the intriguing mock-up of a Tudor kitchen. There's a shop and pleasant café on site.

MILE END & VICTORIA PARK

A busy junction where the Docklands meet Hackney and the inner city meets Bow and Stratford Marsh, Mile End and vicinity is an increasingly popular residential area with some decent bars and restaurants, a unique park that straddles the Mile End Rd and a more traditional one in the enormous and gorgeous expanse of Victoria Park, the East End's biggest and most attractive green lung. There's not a whole lot to attract the general traveller here, but anyone staying in the area or interested in East End history will find their time very profitably spent. Just east, over the busy A12 motorway, is Stratford and Olympic Park (www.london2012.org), where most of the events of the 2012 London Olympics will be held.

MILE END PARK Map p156
www.mileendpark.co.uk; ⊖ Mile End

The 32-hectare Mile End Park is a long, narrow green space wedged between Burdett and Grove Rds and the Grand Union Canal. Landscaped to great effect during the millennium year, it now incorporates a go-kart track, a children's centre for under-10s, areas for public art, an ecology area, an indoor climbing wall and a sports stadium. The centrepiece, though, is architect Piers Gough's 'green bridge' linking the northern and southern sections of the park over busy Mile End Rd. The bridge itself is actually yellow – the 'green' refers to the trees and shrubs that have been planted along its walkway.

RAGGED SCHOOL MUSEUM Map p156
☎ 8980 6405; www.raggedschoolmuseum.org.uk; 46-50 Copperfield Rd E3; admission by donation; 🕥 10am-5pm Wed & Thu, 2-5pm 1st Sun of month; ⊖ Mile End
Both adults and children are inevitably charmed by the Ragged School Museum, a combination of mock Victorian schoolroom – with hard wooden benches and desks, slates, chalk, inkwells and abacuses – on the 1st floor, and social history museum below. 'Ragged' was a Victorian term used to refer to pupils' usually torn, dirty and dishevelled clothes, and the museum celebrates the legacy of Dr Joseph Barnardo, who founded the first free school for destitute East End children in this building in the 1860s.

During term time, the museum runs a schools programme, where pupils are taught reading, writing and arithmetic by a strict school ma'am in full Victorian regalia called Miss Perkins; and if you're very good – no talking up the back, there – you can watch and listen to these lessons from the glassed-off gallery. On the first Sunday of the month, the Victorian lesson is offered to the general public at 2.15pm and 3.30pm. It's great fun.

TOWER HAMLETS CEMETERY PARK
Map p156
☎ 0790 418 6981; www.towerhamletscemetery.org; Southern Grove E3; admission free; 🕥 7am-dusk; ⊖ Mile End or Bow Rd
Opened in 1841, this 13-hectare cemetery was the last of the so-called Magnificent Seven, then-suburban cemeteries (including Highgate and Abney Park in Stoke Newington) created by an act of Parliament in response to London's rapid population growth and overcrowded burial grounds.

Some 270,000 souls were laid to rest here until the cemetery was closed for burials in 1966 and turned into a park and nature reserve. Today it is a quiet, restful site, its Victorian monuments slowly being consumed by creepers.

HOUSE MILL Map p64
☎ 8980 4626; www.housemill.org.uk; Three Mill Lane, Three Mills Island E3; adult/student & senior £3/1.50; 🕥 11am-4pm Sun May-Oct, 11am-4pm 1st Sun of Mar, Apr, Nov & Dec; ⊖ Bromley-by-Bow
The only remaining one of a trio of mills that once stood on this small island in the River Lea, the House Mill (1776) operated as a sluice tidal mill, grinding grain for a nearby distillery, until 1940. Tours, which run according to demand and last about 45 minutes, take visitors to all four floors of the mill and offer a fascinating look at traditional East End industry. There's a small café and shop on-site.

VICTORIA PARK Map p156
🕥 dawn-dusk; ⊖ Mile End
If you want a little more green than Mile End Park affords, head north from Mile End tube along Grove Rd, until you reach 87-hectare Victoria Park. This leafy expanse has lakes, fountains, a bowling green, tennis courts, a deer park and much more. It was the East End's first public park when it opened in 1845 and came about after a local MP presented Queen Victoria with a petition of 30,000 signatures. During WWII the park was largely closed to the public and was used as an anti-aircraft shelling site as well as an interment camp for Italian and then German prisoners of war (POWs).

DOCKLANDS
You'd probably never guess it while gazing up at the ultramodern skyscrapers that dominate the Isle of Dogs and Canary Wharf, but from the 16th century until the mid-20th century this area was the industrial heartland of the London docks. Here cargo from global trade was landed, bringing jobs to a tight-knit, working-class community. Even up to the start of WWII this community still thrived, but then the docks were badly firebombed during the war.

After the Blitz the docks were in no condition to cope with the postwar technological and political changes as the British Empire evaporated. At the same time, enormous new bulk carriers and container ships demanded deep-water ports and new loading and un-loading techniques. From the mid-1960s dock closures followed one another as fast as they had opened, and the number of dock workers dropped from as many as 50,000 in 1960 to about 3000 by 1980.

The financial metropolis that exists today was begun by the London Docklands Development Corporation (LDDC), a body established by the Thatcher government in the free-wheeling 1980s to take pressure for office space off the City. This rather artificial community had a shaky start. The low-rise toy-town buildings had trouble attracting tenants, the Docklands Light Railway – the main transport link – had teething troubles and the Canary Wharf Tower itself had to be res-cued from bankruptcy twice. Now, however, newspaper groups and financial behemoths have moved in – with Citigroup and HSBC boasting their own buildings – and, more than a quarter-century after it was begun, the Docklands is emerging as the mini-Manhattan it was envisaged as.

ISLE OF DOGS Map p160

Pundits can't even really agree on whether this is an island, let alone where it got its name. Strictly speaking it's a peninsula of land on the northern shore of the Thames, although without modern road and trans-port links it would *almost* be separated from the mainland at West India Docks. At the same time, etymologists are still out to lunch over the origin of the island's name. Some believe it's because the royal kennels

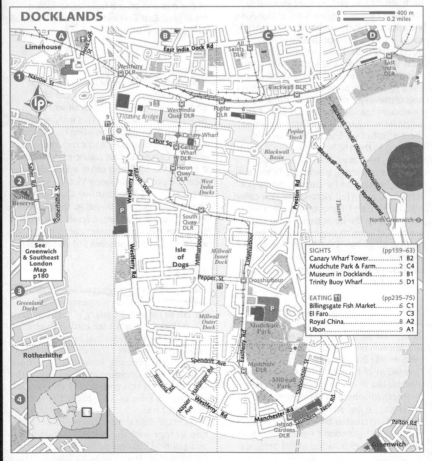

DOCKLANDS

SIGHTS	(pp159–63)
Canary Wharf Tower	1 B2
Mudchute Park & Farm	2 C4
Museum in Docklands	3 B1
Trinity Buoy Wharf	5 D1

EATING	(pp235–75)
Billingsgate Fish Market	6 C1
El Faro	7 C3
Royal China	8 A2
Ubon	9 A1

WAPPING & LIMEHOUSE

In his 16th-century *A Survey of London,* John Stow described Wapping High St as a 'filthy strait passage, with alleys of small tenements or cottages'. It's a far cry from that today; the converted warehouses and lofts that line the brick road now contain luxury flats that are among the most desirable in East London.

The area was traditionally home to sailors and dock workers. One of the most important historic sites is Execution Dock (Map p156) near the old river police station at Wapping New Stairs. This is where convicted pirates were hanged and their bodies chained to a post at low tide, to be left until three tides had washed over their heads.

There isn't much to Limehouse, although it became London's first Chinatown in the late 19th century when some 300 sailors from the South China coast settled, and was also mentioned in Oscar Wilde's *The Picture of Dorian Gray* (1891), when the protagonist passed by this way in search of opium. The most notable attraction is St Anne's, Limehouse (Map p160 ☎ 7987 1502; cnr Commercial Rd & Three Colt St). This was Nicholas Hawksmoor's earliest church and still boasts the highest church clock in the city. In fact, the 60m-high tower is still a 'Trinity House mark' for identifying shipping lanes on the Thames (thus the Royal Navy's White Ensign flag flying). Although the English baroque church was completed in 1725, it was not consecrated until 1730. There is a curious pyramid in the west churchyard that may be connected with the architect's supposed interest in the occult.

were located here during Henry VIII's reign. Others say it's a corruption of the Flemish *dijk* (dike), recalling the Flemish engineers who shored up the area's muddy banks.

It can be agreed, however, that the centrepiece of the Isle of Dogs is Canary Wharf. If you want to see how the isle once looked, check out Mudchute Park & Farm (☎ 7515 5901, 7531 4334; www.mudchute.org; Pier St E14; admission free; ☼ 9.30am-4.30pm; DLR Mudchute), an urban farm with livestock, an educational centre and events to the southeast.

CANARY WHARF Map p160

⊖ Canary Wharf

Cesar Pelli's 244m-high Canary Wharf Tower, built in 1991 at 1 Canada Sq and described as a 'square prism with a pyramidal top', presides over a toy-town, financial theme park, surrounded by more recent towers housing HSBC and Citigroup, and offices for Bank of America, Barclays, Lehmann Brothers, Morgan Stanley, Credit Suisse and more. It took a long time for the place to come this far, even. Canary Wharf Tower, still the tallest building in the UK and one of the largest property developments in Europe, had to be saved from bankruptcy twice before it reached today's levels of occupancy.

There's no public access to the tower, but on a sunny day you can head for the open-air cafés and bars of West India Quay. You can get here on the DLR but the grandeur of Sir Norman Foster's sleek Canary Wharf Underground station (Jubilee line) is a better introduction to this dynamic district.

MUSEUM IN DOCKLANDS Map p160

☎ 0870 444 3856, recorded information 0870 444 3857; www.museumindocklands.org.uk; Warehouse No 1, West India Quay E14; adult/student & under 16yr/senior £5/free/3; ☼ 10am-6pm, to 9pm 1st Thu of month; ⊖ Canary Wharf or DLR West India Quay; ♿

Housed in a converted 200-year-old warehouse once used to store sugar, rum and coffee, this museum offers a comprehensive overview of the entire history of the Thames from the arrival of the Romans in AD 43. But it's at its best when dealing with specifics close by such as the controversial transformation of the decrepit docks into Docklands in the 1980s and the social upheaval and dislocation that accompanied it.

Kids, however, usually adore the place, with its exhibits such as 'sailor town' (an excellent re-creation of the cobbled streets, bars and lodging houses of a 19th-century dock-side community and nearby Chinatown) and especially the hands-on Mudlarks gallery, where five- to 12-year-olds can explore the history of the Thames, tipping the clipper, trying on old-fashioned diving helmets, learning to use winches and even constructing a simple model of Canary Wharf.

The tour begins on the 3rd floor (take the lift to the top) with the Roman settlement of Londinium and works its way downwards through the ages. Keep an eye open for the scale mode of the old London Bridge and the *Rhinebeck Panorama* (1805–10), a huge mural of the upper Pool of London that has been likened to the view from the top of the London Eye (p125).

ST KATHARINE'S DOCK Map p156
www.skdocks.co.uk; ⊖ Tower Hill

With its cafés and restaurants, St Katharine's Dock makes an ideal spot to pause for a brief rest after a morning's sightseeing at Tower Bridge or the Tower of London. There's a row of twee shops and a popular pub called the Dickens Inn (p288) but it's more entertaining just admiring some of the opulent luxury yachts in the marina.

Sadly, the dock's history is rather less appealing than its appearance. Some 1250 'insanitary' houses and a brewery were razed and 11,300 people made homeless to make way for its creation in 1828. Its current incarnation, which happened after the docks closed, dates from the 1980s.

TRINITY BUOY WHARF Map p160
☎ 7515 7153; www.trinitybuoywharf.com; Orchard Pl E14; ⏱ 10am-6pm Sat & Sun; DLR East India

London's only lighthouse, built for Michael Faraday in 1863, is located at this brown field site about a mile northeast of Canary Wharf. Also here is the unusual Container City, a community of artists' studios made from brightly painted shipping containers, stacked side by side and one on top of the other. The web designers, architects and other creative tenants even have their own balconies. Also here is the much loved American-style Fat Boy's Diner (☎ 7987 4334; ⏱ 9.30am-4.30pm Mon-Sat), which was moved here from Spitalfields Market in 2001.

The wharf is open to the public daily and is clearly signposted from the East India

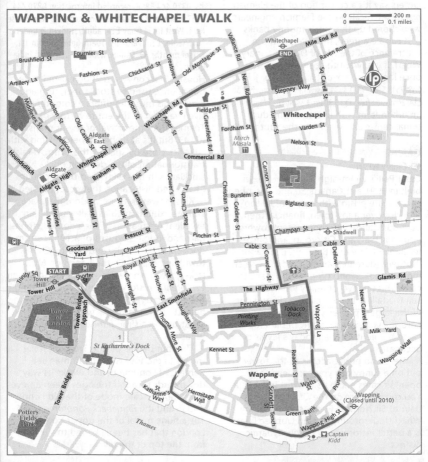

WAPPING & WHITECHAPEL WALK

DLR station; along the 20-minute walk you'll pass a bird sanctuary at East India Dock Basin.

WAPPING & WHITECHAPEL WALK
Walking Tour
1 St Katharine's Dock

If you pass under Tower Bridge from the Tower of London on foot you'll soon come to this symbolic 'entrance' to the Docklands. St Katharine's (opposite) was the first of the London docks to be renovated following its closure in 1968.

2 Execution Dock

Among the more famous people who died at this notorious site (p161) just off Wapping High St is one Captain William Kidd, hanged here in 1701 for piracy. A nearby landmark is the Captain Kidd pub (p288).

3 St George-in-the-East

All that remains of this church (Canon St Rd E1) erected by Nicholas Hawksmoor in 1726 and badly damaged in the Blitz of WWII is a shell enclosing a smaller modern core. It was closed for a time in the 1850s when the vicar introduced what was considered 'Romish' (Roman Catholic) liturgy.

WALK FACTS

Start Tower Hill tube station
End Whitechapel tube station
Distance 2.5 miles
Duration About two hours
Fuel stop Mirch Masala (p259)

4 Cable Street

This street (p156) where ropes were manufactured in the late 18th century – it was once as long as the standard English measure for cable (180m or 600ft) – was the site of the celebrated Cable St riots that evicted British fascists from the East End.

5 Tower House

This enormous building (41 Fieldgate St E1) recently redeveloped as an apartment block was once a hostel and then dosshouse whose residents included Lenin, Stalin and authors Jack London and George Orwell. The last describes it in detail in his *Down and Out in Paris and London* (1933).

6 Whitechapel Bell Foundry

In business for nigh on four and a half centuries, this foundry (p155) can lay claim to have produced some of the most recognisable bells in history, including Big Ben and the Liberty Bell in Philadelphia, Pennsylvania.

NORTH LONDON

Eating p261; Drinking p288; Shopping p229; Sleeping p355

North London is a vast place taking in a wealth of smaller neighbourhoods, most of which are ancient villages that have slowly been drawn into London's dark matter over the centuries as the agglomeration has expanded.

Starting north of the Euston Rd, this region of the capital includes King's Cross and Camden Town – two names both likely to elicit a response from Londoners. King's Cross has historically been one of the capitals nastiest urban blights, but a redevelopment of the tube station, the opening of the beautiful St Pancras International train terminal (p169) and the slow but thorough urban renewal going on elsewhere is making King's Cross more and more desirable, although it's fair to say it'll be a while before we're all meeting there for drinks. Camden is an even stranger beast – much reviled among Londoners for its touristy market and 'crusty' locals, outside of the Lock and away from Camden High St the area is actually a wonderful place full of great bars, restaurants and some architectural gems. It's a typical London phenomenon that two such different experiences can be had in one area.

Reactions are nearly always universally positive to the posh neighbourhoods of Primrose Hill, Belsize Park and Hampstead, in as much as very few of us can afford these lovely, leafy slices of urban village life, although many of us would like to. With their quiet, unpretentious gentility there's little surprise that these are the preferred neighbourhoods for the superstar classes. Luckily we can all visit Primrose Hill and Hampstead Heath (just don't try going for a walk in Belsize Park as there is no actual parkland there!).

Highgate, on the other side of massive Hampstead Heath, is London's highest point and possibly its most gorgeous urban village. Seriously posh, Highgate is a charming place where locals have developed freakishly large calf muscles from all that uphill walking. Nearby Crouch End and Muswell Hill are less expensive but retain a very well-off middle-class feel, while scruffier village Stoke Newington in Hackney is a wonderful blend of hippies, yuppies, gay and lesbian couples and pockets of Orthodox Jews and Turkish Muslims, all living in the most unlikely of harmonies.

North London covers a vast swathe of the city and is most easily reached from the centre of town, rather than by travelling between the separate areas. Hampstead and Highgate should be everyone's first choice for the sheer breadth of things to see and do. North London also includes one of the city's largest and most wonderful outdoor spaces, genteel Regent's Park, which features famous London Zoo and has the wonderful Regent's Canal running along its northern edge.

top picks

NORTH LONDON

- Hampstead Heath (p170)
- British Library (p167)
- Highgate Cemetery (p170)
- Camden Market (opposite)
- Kenwood House (p171)

REGENT'S PARK

REGENT'S PARK Map p166

☎ 7486 7905; ⏰ 5am-dusk; ⊖ Baker St or Regent's Park

The most elaborate and ordered of London's many parks, Regent's was created around 1820 by John Nash, who planned to use it as an estate upon which he could build palaces for the aristocracy. Although the plan never quite came off – like so many at the time – you can get some idea of what Nash might have achieved from the buildings along the Outer Circle, and in particular from the stuccoed Palladian mansions he built on Cumberland Tce.

Like many of the city's parks, this one was used as a royal hunting ground, and then as farmland, before it was used as a place for fun and leisure during the 18th century. These days it's a well-organised but relaxed, lively but serene, local but cosmopolitan haven in the heart of the city. Among its many attractions are the London Zoo, the Grand Union Canal along its northern side, an ornamental lake, an open-air theatre in Queen Mary's Gardens where Shakespeare is performed during the summer months, ponds and colourful flowerbeds, rose gardens that look spectacular in June, football pitches and summer games of softball.

On the western side of the park is the impressive London Central Islamic Centre & Mosque (☎ 7724 3363; www.iccuk.org; 146 Park Rd NW8; ⊖ Marylebone), a huge white edifice with a glistening dome. Provided you take your shoes off and dress modestly you're welcome to go inside, although its interior is fairly stark.

LONDON ZOO Map p168

☎ 7722 3333; www.zsl.org/london-zoo; Regent's Park NW1; adult/child/concession £14.55/11.40/13.20; ⊙ 10am-5.30pm mid-Mar–Oct, to 4pm Nov-Jan, to 4.30pm Feb–mid-Mar; ⊖ Baker St or Camden Town

Established in 1828, these zoological gardens are among the oldest in the world. This is where the word 'zoo' originated and after a patchy period in the 1990s, London Zoo has become one of the most progressive in the world. The zoo is in the middle of a long-term modernisation plan and the emphasis is now firmly placed on conservation, education and breeding, with fewer species and more spacious conditions.

The newest developments have brought Gorilla Kingdom, a £5.3 million project that involves a gorilla conservation programme in Gabon with the aim of providing habitat for Western gorillas and protecting them by providing the local communities and former poachers with work in the programme. The zoo now has three gorillas – Bobby, Zaire and Effie – who live on their own island, and their space measures 1600 sq metres. They are fascinating and gentle creatures, with very distinct (and strong) personalities that are fantastic to observe.

The Clore Rainforest Lookout and Nightzone is another excellent addition, with sloths, monkeys and other creatures wandering freely among the visitors inside the humid, tropical-climate room. The monkeys are especially happy to roam – they see it as their territory, so watch out!

The elegant and cheerful Penguin Pool, designed by Berthold Lubetkin in 1934, is one of London's foremost modernist structures, although the penguins didn't like it and are now bathing at a more ordinary

round pool. The most popular penguin, Roxy Rockhopper – who likes to be picked up and cuddled – has her own myspace page: www.myspace.com/roxyrockhopper.

Other highlights include Butterfly Paradise, Into Africa and Meet the Monkeys. The Victorian bird house was scheduled to open at Easter 2008, after extensive renovations, and the big cats' living area is up for renovations in 2009.

A great way to visit the zoo is by canal boat from Little Venice or Camden, but you can also reach it by walking along the canal towpath. There's a delightful children's zoo, which is built almost entirely from sustainable materials, and busy programmes of events and attractions (such as elephant bathing and penguin feeding) throughout the year.

CAMDEN

CAMDEN MARKET Map p168

cnr Camden High & Buck Sts NW1; ⊙ 9am-5.30pm Thu-Sun; ⊖ Camden Town or Chalk Farm

Although – or perhaps because – it stopped being cutting-edge several thousand cheap leather jackets ago, Camden market gets a whopping 10 million visitors each year and is one of London's most popular attractions. What started out as a collection of attractive craft stalls by Camden Lock on the Grand Union Canal now extends most of the way from Camden Town tube station to Chalk Farm tube station to the north. You'll find a bit of everything but in particular a lot of tourist-oriented tat (see p232 for more information). It's completely mobbed at the weekend, and something preferably avoided on those days.

JEWISH MUSEUM Map p168

☎ 7284 1997; www.jewishmuseum.org.uk; Raymond Burton House, 129-131 Albert St NW1; adult £3.50, student & child £1.50, senior £2.50, family £8; ⊙ 10am-4pm Mon-Thu, to 5pm Sun; ⊖ Camden Town; ♿

This branch of the Jewish Museum examines Judaism and Judaistic religious practices in the prestigious Ceremonial Art Gallery, and the story of the Jewish community in Britain from the time of the Normans to the present day through paintings, photographs and artefacts in the History Gallery. There's also a gallery for temporary exhibitions.

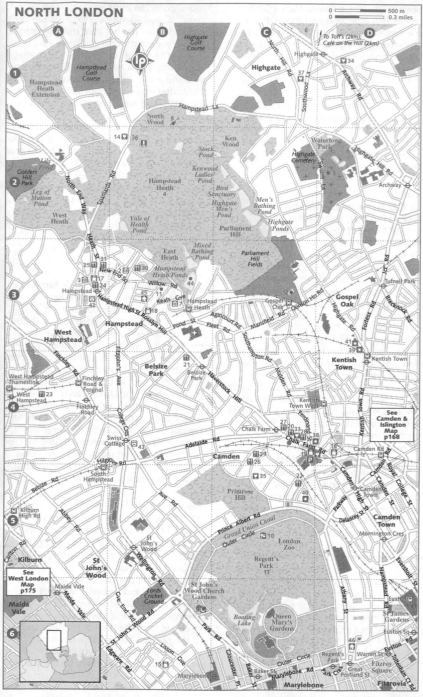

NORTH LONGON

0 _____ 500 m
0 _____ 0.3 miles

A **B** **C** **D**

Highgate
Golf
Course

Hampstead
Golf
Course

To Toff's (2km);
Café on the Hill (2km)

Highgate

Highgate

Hampstead Heath
Extension

Hampstead La

North
Wood

Ken
Wood

Waterlow
Park

Stock
Pond

Highgate
Cemetery

Lily
Pond

Golders
Hill
Park

Kenwood
Ladies'
Pond

Archway

Leg of
Mutton
Pond

Hampstead
Heath

Bird
Sanctuary

Men's
Bathing
Pond

West Heath

Vale of
Health
Pond

Highgate
Men's
Pond

Highgate
Ponds

Parliament
Hill

East
Heath

Mixed
Bathing
Pond

Parliament
Hill Fields

Tufnell Park

New End Rd

Hampstead
Heath Ponds

**Gospel
Oak**

Willow
Gdns

Keats Gve

Hampstead
Heath

Gospel
Oak

Hampstead

Roslyn Hill

Agincourt Rd

Mansfield Rd

**West
Hampstead**

Fleet Rd

Pond St

Southampton Rd

**Kentish
Town**

Kentish Town

West Hampstead
Thameslink

**Belsize
Park**

Haverstock Hill

Malden Rd

See
Camden &
Islington
Map
p168

West
Hampstead

Belsize
Park

Finchley
Road &
Frognal

Finchley
Road

Kentish
Town West

Swiss
Cottage

Adelaide Rd

Chalk Farm

Camden

Camden Rd

Hilgrove Rd

South
Hampstead

Camden
High St

**Camden
Town**

Primrose
Hill

Camden
Town

Kilburn

See
West London
Map
p175

**St
John's
Wood**

Prince Albert Rd

Mornington Cres

Grand Union Canal
Outer Circle

London
Zoo

Delancy St

**Maida
Vale**

St
John's
Wood

Regent's
Park

Lord's
Cricket
Ground

St John's
Wood Church
Gardens

Boating
Lake

Queen
Mary's
Gardens

Regent's
Park

Warren St

St James
Gardens

Euston

Euston Sq

Marylebone

Marylebone

Baker St

Great
Portland St

Warren St

Fitzroy
Square

Fitzrovia

lonelyplanet.com

NORTH LONDON

The Jewish Museum, Finchley (Map p64; ☎ 8349 1143; Sternberg Centre, 80 East End Rd N3; adult/child/concession £2/free/1; ⊙ 10.30am-5pm Mon-Thu, 10.30am-4.30pm Sun except Aug; ⊖ Finchley Central) houses the museum's social-history collections, including the oral-history and photographic archives, and hosts changing exhibitions. Its permanent collection includes reconstructions of the tailoring and cabinet-making workshops from the East End, as well as a Holocaust exhibition focusing on the experience of one Jewish Briton who survived Auschwitz.

KING'S CROSS & EUSTON

BRITISH LIBRARY Map p168

☎ switchboard 7444 1500, visitor services 7412 7332; www.bl.uk; 96 Euston Rd NW1; admission free; ⊙ 10am-6pm Mon & Wed-Fri, 9.30am-8pm Tue, 9.30am-5pm Sat, 11am-5pm Sun; ⊖ King's Cross; ♿
The British Library moved to these spanking-new premises between King's Cross and Euston Stations in 1998, and at a cost of £500 million it was Britain's most expensive building, and not one that is universally loved; Colin St John Wilson's exterior of straight lines of red brick, which Prince Charles reckoned was akin to a 'secret-police building', is certainly not to all tastes. But even people who don't like the building from the outside can't fault the spectacularly cool and spacious interior.

It is the nation's principal copyright library and stocks one copy of every British publication as well as historical manuscripts, books and maps from the British Museum. The library counts some 186 miles of shelving on four basement levels and will have some 12 million volumes when it reaches the limit of its storage capacity.

At the centre of the building is the wonderful King's Library, the 65,000-volume collection of the insane George III, which was given to the nation by his son, George IV, in 1823 and Is now housed in a six-storey, 17m-high glass-walled tower. To the left as you enter are the library's excellent bookshop and exhibition galleries.

Most of the complex is devoted to storage and scholarly research, but there are also several public displays including the John Ritblat Gallery: Treasures of the British Library, which spans almost three millennia and every continent. Among the most important documents here are the Magna Carta (1215); the Codex Sinaiticus, the first complete text of the New Testament, written in Greek in the 4th century; a Gutenberg Bible (1455), the first Western book printed using movable type; Shakespeare's First Folio (1623); manuscripts by some of Britain's best-known authors (eg Lewis Carroll, Jane Austen, George Eliot and Thomas Hardy); and even some of the Beatles' earliest hand-written lyrics.

You can hear historic recordings, such as the first one ever, made by Thomas Edison in 1877, James Joyce reading from *Ulysses* and Nelson Mandela's famous speech at the Rivonia trial in 1964, at the National Sound

NORTH LONDON: CAMDEN & ISLINGTON

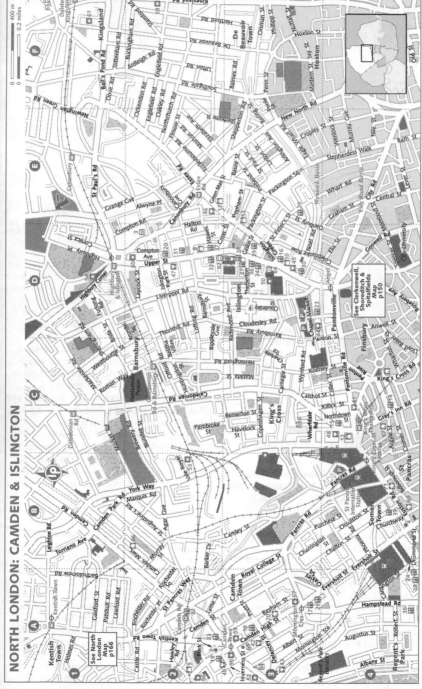

See North
London Map
p166

See Clerkenwell,
Shoreditch &
Spitalfields
Map p150

NORTH LONDON: CAMDEN & ISLINGTON

Archive Jukeboxes, where the selections are changed regularly. The Turning the Pages exhibit allows you a 'virtual browse' through several important texts including the *Sforza Book of Hours*, the *Diamond Sutra* and a Leonardo da Vinci notebook.

The Philatelic Exhibition, next to the John Ritblat Gallery, is based on collections established in 1891 with the bequest of the Tapling Collection, and now consists of more than 80,000 items, including postage and revenue stamps, postal stationery and first-day covers from almost every country and from all periods.

The Workshop of Words, Sounds & Images documents the development of writing and communicating through the written word by carefully examining the work of early scribes, printers and bookbinders. The sound section compares recordings on different media, from early-20th-century wax cylinders to modern CDs. The Pearson Gallery hosts some sensational special exhibitions, ranging from 'Oscar Wilde: A Life in Six Acts' to 'Chinese Printing Today'.

Access to the reading rooms is by reader's pass only. See the website for details of how to apply and the conditions that need to be met.

There are guided tours (adult/child £8/6.50) at 3pm Monday, Wednesday and Friday and at 10.30am and 3pm Saturday of the library's public areas, and another that includes a visit to one of the reading rooms at 11.30am and 3pm Sunday. Call the main number to make a booking.

ST PANCRAS INTERNATIONAL Map p168

☎ 7843 4250; www.stpancras.com; Euston Rd NW1; ⊖ King's Cross St Pancras

If you use the tube for any length of time, chances are you'll pass through King's Cross St Pancras station, in which case you should rise to the surface and check out this fabulously imposing Victorian Gothic masterpiece, which was built as a hotel by the renowned architect George Gilbert Scott in 1876. The train shed behind the façade has been converted into the stunning new St Pancras International, now departure point for HS1 (or Eurostar) high-speed services to Paris, Brussels and Lille.

LONDON CANAL MUSEUM Map p168

☎ 7713 0836; www.canalmuseum.org.uk; 12-13 New Wharf Rd N1; adult/child/student 3/1.50/2; ☽ 10am-4.30pm Tue-Sun & bank holidays; ⊖ King's Cross

This quirky but very worthwhile museum is housed in an old ice warehouse (with a deep well where the frozen commodity was stored) dating from the 1860s and traces the history of Regent's Canal, the ice business and the development of ice cream through models, photographs, exhibits and archive documentaries. The ice trade was huge in late Victorian London, and 35,000 tonnes of it were imported from Norway in 1899.

HAMPSTEAD & HIGHGATE

HAMPSTEAD HEATH Map p166

☎ 7485 4491; ❷ Hampstead, ℞ Gospel Oak or Hampstead Heath, ☒ 214 or C2 to Parliament Hill Fields

Sprawling Hampstead Heath, with its rolling woodlands and meadows, is a million miles away – well, approximately four – from the City of London. It covers 320 hectares, most of it woods, hills and meadows, and is home to about 100 bird species. It's a wonderful place for a ramble, especially to the top of Parliament Hill, which offers expansive views across the city and is one of the most popular places in London to fly a kite. Alternatively head up the hill in North Wood.

If walking is too pedestrian for you, another major attraction is the bathing ponds (separate beautiful ones for men and women and a slightly less pleasant mixed pond). Sections of the heath area are also laid out for football, cricket and tennis. Those of a more artistic bent should make a beeline to Kenwood House (opposite) but stop to admire the sculptures by Henry Moore and Barbara Hepworth on the way.

If you work up a thirst, there's no better place to quench it than at the atmospheric – and possibly haunted – Spaniard's Inn (p290), which has a fascinating history and a terrific beer garden.

By day and night the West Heath is a gay cruising ground that is so well established that the police often pitch up in the evenings to protect the men who spend their nights here. On South Green, opposite Hampstead Heath station, is one of Britain's oldest lavatories, which was built in 1897 and restored in 2000. This was gay playwright Joe Orton's lavatory of choice for 'cottaging' (cruising for gay sex). George Orwell worked in a bookshop opposite the toilets and doubtless used them now and then for their originally intended purpose.

HIGHGATE CEMETERY Map p166

☎ 8340 1834; www.highgate-cemetery.org; Swain's Lane N6; adults/under 16yr £2/free, plus £1 for a camera; ☯ 10am-5pm Mon-Fri, 11am-5pm Sat & Sun Apr-Oct, 10am-4pm Mon-Fri, 11am-4pm Sat & Sun Nov-Mar; ❷ Highgate

Most famous as the final resting place of Karl Marx and other notable mortals, Highgate Cemetery is set in 20 wonderfully wild and atmospheric hectares with dramatic and overdecorated Victorian graves and sombre tombs. It's divided into two parts. On the eastern side you can visit the grave of Marx. It's an amusing coincidence that buried opposite is the free-market economist Herbert Spencer – Marx and Spencer, does it ring a bell? This slightly overgrown and wild part of the cemetery is a very pleasant walk but it's merely the overflow area. It's the wonderfully atmospheric western section of this Victorian Valhalla that is the main draw. To visit it, you'll have to take a tour and deal directly with the brigade of sometimes stroppy silver-haired ladies who run the cemetery and act like they are the home guard defending it from the Germans (eyes straight, shoulders back, chest out, march!). It is a maze of winding paths leading to the Circle of Lebanon, rings of tombs flanking a circular path and topped with a majestic, centuries-old cedar tree. The guides are engaging and gladly point out the various symbols of the age and the eminent dead occupying the tombs, including the scientist Michael Faraday and the dog-show founder Charles Cruft. 'Dissenters' (non–Church of Englanders) were buried way off in the woods. Tours (£3, plus per camera £1) depart 2pm Monday to Friday (book ahead by phone) and every hour 11am to 4pm Saturday and Sunday (no bookings).

The cemetery still works – the most recent well-known addition was Russian dissident Alexander Litvinenko, who was done away with under most sinister circumstances in 2006 with the radioactive isotope Polonium 210 over tea in a Mayfair hotel (see p48) – and closes during burials, so you might want to call ahead just to be sure it will be open.

HIGHGATE WOOD Map p166

☯ dawn-dusk; ❷ Highgate

With more than 28 hectares of ancient woodland, this park is a wonderful spot for a walk any time of the year. It's also teeming with life, and some 70 different bird species have been recorded here, along with five types of bat, 12 of butterfly and 80 different kinds of spider. It also has a huge clearing in the centre for sports, a popular playground and nature trail for kids and a range of activities – from falconry to bat-watching – throughout the year.

KEATS HOUSE Map p166

☎ 7435 2062; www.keatshouse.org.uk; Wentworth Pl, Keats Grove NW3; adult/under 16yr/concession £3.50/free/1.75; ⏱ 1-5pm Tue-Sun; ⊖ Hampstead or ⓡ Hampstead Heath

Undergoing redevelopment at the time of writing and due to reopen in late 2008, this elegant Regency house was home to the golden boy of the Romantic poets from 1818 to 1820. Never short of generous mates, Keats was persuaded to take refuge here by Charles Armitage Brown, and it was here that he met his fiancée Fanny Brawne, who was literally the girl next door. Keats wrote his most celebrated poem, *Ode to a Nightingale*, while sitting under a plum tree in the garden (now replaced) in 1819. Original documents such as the poet's letters and the original *Bright Star* manuscript will be on display as part of the redevelopment. The house is dripping with atmosphere, thanks in part to the collection of Regency furniture amassed here in recent years. Rather than supplying pamphlets or audioguides, the staff here tell stories about Keats and the house as you wander around, perhaps examining the ring he gave Fanny (which she wore for the rest of her life) or the bust of Keats, which is set at the poet's exact height: barely 1.5m!

American visitors might like to know that the house was originally saved and opened to the public in 1925 largely due to the donations of Keats' devotees in the US.

KENWOOD HOUSE Map p166

☎ 8348 1286; www.english-heritage.org.uk; Hampstead Lane NW3; admission free; ⏱ house 11am-5pm Apr-Oct, to 4pm Nov-Mar, the Suffolk Collection (upstairs) 11am-4.30pm Thu-Sun; ⊖ Archway or Golders Green, then ⓑ 210; ♿

Hampstead's most impressive sight is this magnificent neoclassical mansion, which stands at the northern end of the heath in a glorious sweep of landscaped gardens leading down to a picturesque lake, around which classical concerts take place in summer (see p312). The house was remodelled by Robert Adam in the 18th century, and rescued from developers by Lord Iveagh Guinness, who donated it and the wonderful collection of art it contains to the nation in 1927. The Iveagh Bequest contains paint-ings by the likes of Gainsborough, Reynolds, Turner, Hals, Vermeer and Van Dyck and is one of the finest small collections in Britain.

Robert Adam's Great Stairs and the library, one of 14 rooms open to the public, are especially fine. The Suffolk Collection occupies the 1st floor. It includes Jacobean portraits by William Larkin and royal Stuart portraits by Van Dyck and Lely.

The Brew House Café has excellent grub, from light snacks to full meals (mains around £7), and plenty of room on the lovely garden terrace.

NO 2 WILLOW ROAD Map p166

☎ 7435 6166, 0149 475 5570; www.national trust.org.uk; 2 Willow Rd NW3; admission £4.90; ⏱ noon-5pm Thu-Sat Apr-Oct, noon-5pm Sat Mar & Nov, guided tours at noon, 1pm & 2pm; ⊖ Hampstead or ⓡ Hampstead Heath

Fans of modern architecture will want to swing past this property, the central house in a block of three, designed by the 'structural rationalist' Ernö Goldfinger in 1939 as his family home. Although the architect was following Georgian principles in creating it, many people think it looks uncannily like the sort of mundane 1950s architecture you see everywhere. They may look similar now, but 2 Willow Rd was in fact a forerunner; the others were mostly bad imitations. The interior, with its cleverly designed storage space and collection of artworks by Henry Moore, Max Ernst and Bridget Riley, is certainly interesting and accessible to all.

BURGH HOUSE Map p166

☎ 7431 0144; www.burghhouse.org.uk; New End Sq NW3; admission free; ⏱ noon-5pm Wed-Fri & Sun, 2-5pm bank holidays, by appointment Sat; ⊖ Hampstead

If you happen to be in the neighbourhood, this late-17th-century Queen Anne mansion houses the Hampstead Museum of local history, a small art gallery and the delightful Buttery Garden Café (⏱ 11am-5.30pm Wed-Sat), where you can get a decent and reasonably priced lunch (sandwiches £5).

FENTON HOUSE Map p166

☎ 7435 3471; www.nationaltrust.org.uk; Windmill Hill, Hampstead Grove NW3; adult/child £5.20/2.60; ⏱ 2-5pm Wed-Fri, 11am-5pm Sat & Sun Apr-Oct, 2-5pm Sat & Sun Mar; ⊖ Hampstead

One of the oldest houses in Hampstead, this late-17th-century merchant's residence has a charming walled garden with roses and an orchard, fine collections of porcelain and keyboard instruments – including a 1612 harpsichord played by Handel – as well as 17th-century needlework pictures and original Georgian furniture.

ISLINGTON

ESTORICK COLLECTION OF MODERN ITALIAN ART Map p168

☎ 7704 9522; www.estorickcollection.com; 39a Canonbury Sq N1; adult/concession £3.50/2.50; ⏱ 11am-6pm Wed-Sat, noon-5pm Sun; ⊖ Highbury & Islington

The only museum in Britain devoted to Italian art, and one of the leading collections of futurist painting in the world, the Estorick Collection is housed in a listed Georgian house and stuffed with works by such greats as Giacomo Balla, Umberto Boccioni, Gino Severini and Ardengo Soffici. The collection of paintings, drawings, etchings and sculpture, amassed by American writer and art dealer Eric Estorick and his wife Salome, also includes drawings and a painting by the even more famous Amedeo Modigliani. Well-conceived special exhibitions might concentrate on Italian divisionism or a collection of classic Italian film posters. The museum also encompasses an extensive library, café and shop. Highly recommended.

MUSWELL HILL & CROUCH END

ALEXANDRA PARK & PALACE Map p64

☎ 8365 2121; www.alexandrapalace.com; Alexandra Palace Way N22; ⓡ Alexandra Palace

Built in 1873 as North London's answer to Crystal Palace, Alexandra Palace suffered the ignoble fate of burning to the ground only 16 days after opening. Encouraged by attendance figures, investors decided to rebuild and it reopened just two years later. Although it boasted a theatre, museum, lecture hall, library and Great Hall with one of the world's largest organs, it was no match for Crystal Palace. It housed German POWs during WWI and in 1936 the world's first TV transmission – a variety show called *Here's Looking at You* – took place here. The palace burned down again in 1980 but was rebuilt for the third time and opened in 1988. Today 'Ally Pally' (as it is affectionately known, even though locals are paying increased council rates since it was rebuilt) is a multipurpose conference and exhibition centre with additional facilities, including an indoor ice-skating rink, the panoramic Phoenix Bar & Beer Garden and funfairs in summer.

The park in which it stands sprawls over some 196 hectares consisting of public gardens, a nature conservation area, a deer park and various sporting facilities including a boating lake, pitch-and-putt golf course and skate park, making it a great place for a family outing.

STOKE NEWINGTON

ABNEY PARK CEMETERY Map p64

☎ 7275 7557; Stoke Newington Church St N16; admission free; ⏱ 8am-dusk; ⓡ Stoke Newington, 🚌 73, 106 or 243

Unfairly dubbed 'the poor man's Highgate' by some, this magical place was bought up and developed by a private firm from 1840 to provide burial grounds for central London's overflow. It was the first cemetery for dissenters and many of the most influential London Presbyterians, Quakers and Baptists are buried here, including the founder of the Salvation Army, William Booth, whose grand tombstone greets you as you enter from Church St. Since the 1950s the cemetery has been left to fend for itself and, these days, is as much a bird and plant sanctuary as a delightfully overgrown ruin. The derelict chapel at the heart of the park could be straight out of a horror film, and the atmosphere of the whole place is nothing short of magical.

HAMPSTEAD & HIGHGATE WALK

Walking Tour
1 No 2 Willow Rd

Drop into this fascinating slice of modernism on your way to nearby Hampstead Heath. Here you'll find Ernö Goldfinger's pioneering international modernist apartment block (p171), run by the formidable dames of the National Trust. Just don't say that it looks like any other modern building – it really was the first.

2 Hampstead Heath

One of London's most lovely open spaces, the hills and woods of this gorgeous, rambling park (p170) are enough to inspire anyone to poetry (and of course Keats lived just nearby; see p171). Enjoy the view from Parliament Hill and cool off in the swimming ponds or in the fabulous Parliament Hill Lido (p325).

3 Kenwood House

On the northern edge of the heath, this grand mansion (p171) houses two superb collections of British art, features some gorgeous interiors and has lovely gardens to walk in, all for free.

HAMPSTEAD & HIGHGATE WALK

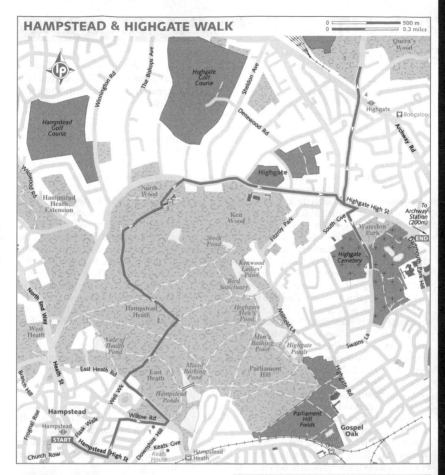

4 Highgate Village
Wandering up the hill to London's highest natural point, it's hard not to be seduced instantly by Highgate Village, with its charming shops, pubs and cafés.

5 Highgate Wood
Take a stroll in the thick foliage of this charming wood (p170), where you can combine a walk with plenty of other activities including bird-watching (although look out for the butterflies and even bats at dusk). Kids will especially love the nature trail, and the sports activities available at the heart of the wood are excellent.

6 Highgate Cemetery
Wandering down Highgate Hill – and you only ever want to walk down this hill, it was, after all the site of Europe's first cable car in

WALK FACTS
Start **Hampstead tube station**
End **Archway tube station**
Distance **5 miles**
Duration **Three hours**
Fuel stop **Boogaloo** (p289)

the late 19th century – you can walk down Swain's Lane to London's most famous burial ground (p170). Here lie Karl Marx, George Elliot, Christina Rossetti and recent arrival Alexander Litvinenko in some wonderful surroundings. Be sure to take the West Cemetery tour as while it's a pain to have to visit in a group, it's only here that you understand why Highgate is London's most desirable place to be dead.

WEST LONDON

Eating p266; Drinking p291; Shopping p230; Sleeping p356

The sprawl west of Hyde Park in all directions is one of the most vibrant areas of London and few parts of the capital can boast the area's sheer variety: its rampant multiculturalism (the Caribbean community in Notting Hill, the Poles in Hammersmith and the Australian home from home in Earl's Court), its exciting bars (check out Portobello Rd or Westbourne Grove) and its grand parks and mansions (wander the back streets of Holland Park to see how the rich and famous *really* live).

To the west of Primrose Hill are the very well-off, more urban-feeling areas of St John's Wood and Maida Vale – both sites of gorgeous mansions, charming canals and boutique shopping.

The status of the famous Notting Hill Carnival reflects the multicultural appeal of this part of West London, into which West Indian immigrants moved in the 1950s. After decades of exploitation, strife and the occasional race riot, the community took off in the 1980s and is now a thriving, vibrant corner of the city and an emblem for multicultural London. Although there's not a lot to see in Notting Hill – and it's nothing like its portrayal in the eponymous, saccharine Richard Curtis film – there's plenty to do, with lots of highly individual shops, restaurants and pubs. Narrow Portobello Rd is its heart and soul and most well known these days for hosting one of London's best markets (see p232). The neighbourhood also gives its name to the Notting Hill Carnival, a highlight of London's summer (see p194). Trendy Westbourne Grove, roughly in the northeastern corner, is lined with distinctive shops, pubs, artists' galleries and studios.

Despite the shabby, incoherent architecture of Shepherd's Bush Green and the general chaos that rules here, this West London hub is a decent place to hang out and eat, especially since a slew of gastropubs opened in the last few years. The name reputedly comes from the fact that shepherds would graze their flocks on the common here, en route for Smithfield Market in East London, back when Shepherd's Bush was another rural village outside the city. Synonymous for many with the sprawling BBC Television Centre in nearby White City that opened in 1960, the area had actually become famous 50 years earlier as the site of the 1908 London Olympics, as well as the Great Exhibition of the same year. During the '60s, Shepherd's Bush was used as the setting for The Who's film *Quadrophenia*, so mods on pilgrimage are not an uncommon sight. Today Shepherd's Bush is a multiethnic place full of quirky cafés, bars and character.

As West London fades from the old money of Kensington into the urban sprawl of Hammersmith, the two meet seamlessly in Earl's Court, a hard-to-define no-man's-land. Its '80s nickname 'Kangaroo Valley' attests to the area's popularity with backpackers from Down Under, which is still the case today. In the 1980s Earl's Court was the original gay village, later overtaken by Soho, but still not forgotten today. Freddie Mercury lived and died at 1 Garden Pl and remains the neighbourhood's most famous resident.

West Brompton is even quieter and less remarkable, but is home to one of London's most magnificent cemeteries and is pleasant for a stroll.

Hammersmith is a different story: it's a very urban neighbourhood dominated by a huge flyover and roundabout, with little to entice the visitor save some decent restaurants and the famously arty Riverside Studios (p316).

The Underground and buses are best for moving between the sights.

LORD'S CRICKET GROUND Map p175

☎ 7616 8595; www.lords.org; St John's Rd NW8; tours adult/child/concession/family £10/6/7/27; ☼ tours 10am, noon & 2pm Apr-Sep, noon & 2pm Oct-Mar when there's no play; ⊖ St John's Wood; ♿

The 'home of cricket' is a must for any devotee of this peculiarly English game: book early for the test matches here, but also take the absorbing and anecdotal 90-minute tour of the ground and facilities, which takes in the famous Long Room, where members watch the games surrounded by portraits of cricket's great and good, and a museum featuring evocative memorabilia that will appeal to fans old and new. Australian fans will be keen to pose next to the famous little urn containing the Ashes, which remain in English hands no matter how many times the Aussies beat them.

The ground itself is dominated by a striking media centre that looks like a clock radio, but you should also look out for

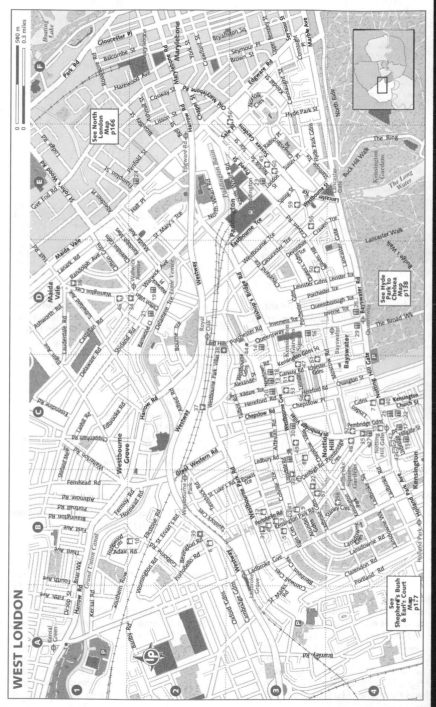

WEST LONGON

lonelyplanet.com

See North
London
Map
p166

See Hyde
Park to
Chelsea
Map
p138

See
Shepherd's Bush
& Earl's Court
Map p127

175

WEST LONDON

the famous weather vane in the shape of Father Time and the remarkable tentlike modern Mound Stand.

There's limited disabled access. Call ahead for details.

KENSAL GREEN CEMETERY Map p175

Harrow Rd, Kensal Green W10; tours £5; ⊗ tours 2pm Sun; ⊖ Kensal Green

Thackeray and Trollope are among the eminent dead folk at this huge and handsome Victorian cemetery, which made a name for itself in the 19th century as the place where the VIPs preferred to RIP. Supposedly based on the Cimetière du Père-Lachaise in Paris, the cemetery is distinguished by its Greek Revival architecture, arched entrances and the outrageously ornate tombs that bear testimony to 19th-century delusions of grandeur. Ambitious two-hour tours start from the Anglican chapel in the centre of the cemetery.

LEIGHTON HOUSE Map p177

☎ 7602 3316; www.rbkc.gov.uk; 12 Holland Park Rd W14; adult/concession £3/1; ⊗ 11am-5.30pm Wed-Mon; ⊖ High St Kensington

Leighton House sits on a quiet street near Holland Park, like a secret beauty that has to be sought out and appreciated. Designed in 1866 by George Aitchison, this was the home of Lord Leighton (1830–96),

a painter belonging to the Olympian movement. The ground floor is decorated in an Arabic style, with the exquisite Arab Hall added in 1879 and densely covered with blue and green tiles from Rhodes, Cairo, Damascus and Iznik (Turkey) and a fountain tinkling away in the centre. Even the wooden latticework of the windows and gallery was brought from Damascus. The house contains notable pre-Raphaelite paintings by Burne-Jones, Watts, Millais and Lord Leighton himself. Restoration of the back garden has returned it to its Victorian splendour – as has work on the stairwell and upstairs rooms.

BROMPTON CEMETERY Map p177

☎ 7352 1201; www.royalparks.gov.uk; Old Brompton Rd SW5; tours £3; ⊗ 8am-dusk, tours Sun; ⊖ West Brompton

As London's vast population exploded in the 19th century, seven new cemeteries opened, among them Brompton Cemetery, a long expanse running between Fulham Rd and Old Brompton Rd. There is a chapel and colonnades at one end, modelled after St Peter's in Rome. While the most famous resident is Emmeline Pankhurst, the pioneer of women's suffrage in Britain, the cemetery is most interesting as the inspiration for many of Beatrix Potter's characters. A local resident in her youth before she moved to the north, Potter seems to have taken many names

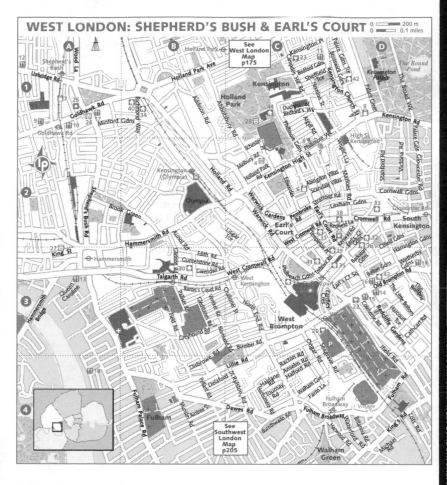

WEST LONDON: SHEPHERD'S BUSH & EARL'S COURT

from the deceased of Brompton Cemetery and immortalised them in her world-famous books. Names to be found include Mr Nutkin, Mr McGregor, Jeremiah Fisher, Tommy Brock – and even a Peter Rabbett.

Tours depart 2pm Sunday from the South Lodge, near the Fulham Rd entrance.

BBC TELEVISION CENTRE Map p64
☎ 0870 603 0304; Wood Lane W12; tour admission adult/student & child over 10yr £9.50/8.50; ⊖ White City; &

If you're interested in TV production, this is the perfect chance to visit the vast complex of studios and offices that bring the BBC's TV programmes to the world. TVC, as it's known to BBC staff, is a pretty monstrous 1960s concrete structure. Visit is by two-hour guided tour only and bookings of two days in advance are essential (no children under 10 years, nine tours daily). You'll see BBC News and Weather Centres as well as studios where shows are being made, and keep your eyes peeled all the while, because you're very likely to spot a celebrity wandering around the corridors – we saw Yoko Ono, Alice Cooper (!) and Jonathan Ross. You can also go and watch the recording of certain shows for free at one of the BBC's many London studios, though you'll have to book in advance. Log on to www.bbc.co.uk/whatson/tickets to see what's on during your stay. You'll also need to book for disabled access.

Eating p269; Drinking p292; Shopping p234; Sleeping p360

Southeast London by and large feels like a succession of small villages, and that's exactly what many of these suburbs were until as recently as the late 19th century. Although there's evidence of early prehistoric settlements in areas such as Forest Hill, Greenwich and Woolwich, for millennia this area was merely on the fringes of the big city.

Greenwich, right on the banks of the Thames, is something of an exception in this. Packed with splendid architecture, it has strong connections with the sea, science, sovereigns and – of course – time. Ever since it was decided to make Greenwich the prime meridian of longitude, Greenwich Mean Time has dictated how clocks and watches around the globe are set.

Now a Unesco World Heritage Site, Greenwich's leafy green expanses and white wedding-cake buildings give it an air of semi-rural gentility. This tranquil aura continues,

top picks

GREENWICH & SOUTHEAST LONDON

- Horniman Museum (p185)
- National Maritime Museum (below)
- Red House (p186)
- Royal Observatory (p181)
- Thames Flood Barrier (p184)

although to a lesser degree, as you venture further southeast, into a London that few out-of-towners see: places such as Blackheath, with its 110-hectare expanse of open common; Eltham, which boasts an Art Deco palace alongside one of a slightly more elite pedigree, dating back to the 14th century; and Dulwich, site of Britain's oldest public art gallery.

A lot edgier are the areas of Deptford and New Cross just west of Greenwich. Here you'll find a district in transition as was, say, Shoreditch a decade a go. Music studios are opening up in what used to be garages, galleries and art centres are squeezing between pie 'n' mash and kebab shops, and pubs are turning into bars.

GREENWICH

Greenwich (*gren*-itch) lies to the southeast of central London, where the Thames widens and deepens, and there's a sense of space that is rare elsewhere in the city. Quaint, villagelike and boasting the Royal Observatory and the fabulous National Maritime Museum, Greenwich has been on Unesco's list of World Heritage Sites (as Maritime Greenwich) since 1997. A trip there will be one of the highlights of any visit to London, and you should certainly allow a day to do it justice, particularly if you want to head down the river to the Thames Flood Barrier.

Greenwich is home to an extraordinary interrelated cluster of classical buildings; all the great architects of the Enlightenment made their mark here, largely due to royal patronage. In the early 17th century, Inigo Jones built one of England's first classical Renaissance homes, the Queen's House, which still stands today. Sir Christopher Wren built the Royal Observatory in 1675–76 and, with his acolyte Nicholas Hawksmoor, began work 20 years later on the Royal Hospital for Seamen, which became the Royal Naval College in

1873. Considerately, Wren altered his plans, splitting the college into two perfectly formed halves, to allow uninterrupted views of the Thames from the Queen's House.

Virtually everything in Greenwich can be easily reached from the Cutty Sark DLR station. A quicker way to get here from central London, however, is via one of the mainline trains from Charing Cross or London Bridge. An alternative from Docklands is to use the historic 390m-long foot tunnel running under the Thames, built in 1902. The lifts down to the tunnel are open from 7am to 7pm Monday to Saturday and from 10am to 5.30pm on Sunday. Otherwise you're facing between 88 and 100 steps down and – shudder – up (open 24 hours).

NATIONAL MARITIME MUSEUM
Map p180

☎ 8858 4422, recorded information 0870 781 5189; www.nmm.ac.uk; Romney Rd SE10; admission free; ⏰ 10am-5pm Sep-Jun, to 6pm Jul & Aug; 🚇 Greenwich or DLR Cutty Sark; ♿

Though it hardly sounds like a crowd-pleaser, this museum designed to tell the

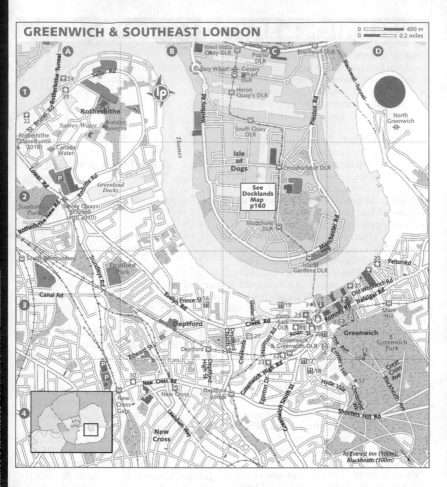

GREENWICH & SOUTHEAST LONDON

long and convoluted history of Britain as a seafaring nation is the most impressive sight in Greenwich. From the moment you step through the entrance to this magnificent neoclassical building you'll be won over. And it just gets better as you progress through the glass-roofed Neptune Court into the rest of this three-storey building.

The exhibits are arranged by theme, focusing on Explorers, Maritime London, Art and Sea and much more. Visual highlights include the golden state barge built in 1732 for Frederick, Prince of Wales, and the huge ship's propeller installed on level 1. The museum also owns the tunic that Britain's greatest sea-faring hero, Horatio Nelson, was wearing when he was fatally shot (including the actual bullet), plus a replica of the lifeboat *James Caird* used by explorer Ernest Shackleton and a handful of his men on their epic mission for help in Antarctica.

The environmentally minded are catered for with the Your Ocean exhibit on level 2, examining the science, history, health and future of the sea. Kids will love firing a cannon in the All Hands exhibit or manoeuvring a tanker into port by using the state-of-the-art bridge simulator on level 3. Even fashionistas will be wowed by Rank and Style (uniforms) and the Passengers exhibit (classic travel posters and the mock-up of the cocktail bar of a cruise ship).

ROYAL OBSERVATORY Map p180

☎ 8858 4422, recorded information 0870 781 5189; www.rog.nmm.ac.uk; Greenwich Park SE19; admission free; ☺ 10am-5pm Sep-Jun, to 6pm Jul & Aug; ☒ Greenwich or DLR Cutty Sark; ☒

In 1675 Charles II had the Royal Observatory built on a hill in the middle of Greenwich Park, intending that astronomy be used to establish longitude at sea (see p182). The Octagon Room, designed by Wren, and the nearby Sextant Room are where John Flamsteed (1646–1719), the first astronomer royal, made his observations and calculations.

The globe is divided between east and west at the Royal Observatory, and in the Meridian Courtyard you can place one foot either side of the meridian line and straddle the two hemispheres.

Every day at 1pm the red time ball at the top of the Royal Observatory continues to drop as has done since 1833. You can still get great views of Greenwich and spy on your fellow tourists at the same time by visiting the unique Camera Obscura. An ambitious £15 million project has added four new galleries exploring astronomy and time, including one on the search for longitude.

The 120-seat state-of-the-art Peter Harrison Planetarium (☎ 8312 8565; adult/child £6/4; ☺ hourly shows 1-4pm Mon-Fri, 11am-4pm Sat & Sun), which opened just south of the Royal Observatory in June 2007, has a £1 million digital laser projector that can show entire heavens on the inside of its bronze-clad roof and is the most advanced in Europe. Along with theme shows, there are galleries tracing the history of astronomy and interactive displays on such subjects the effects of gravity.

O2 (MILLENNIUM DOME) Map p180

wwp.millennium-dome.co.uk; Drawdock Rd SE10; ☒ North Greenwich

Since it closed at the end of 2000, having failed miserably in its bid to attract 12 million visitors, the huge circus tent–shaped O2 (renamed from the Millennium Dome in 2005) was, until recently, for the most part unemployed. It has now hosted Bon Jovi and Barbara Streisand concerts and a massive exhibition called Tutankhamun and the Golden Age of the Pharaohs, but that was little consolation (or cash) for developers Anschutz Entertainment Group, whose bid for it to house Britain's first regional supercasino had been rejected by the government that year. The future of the 380m-wide white elephant on Greenwich Peninsula that cost £750 million to build (and more than £5 million a year just to keep it erect) does look a lot brighter than it did, and it is now scheduled to host the 2009 World Gymnastics Championships and the artistic gymnastics and basketball events of the 2012 Olympic.

If you want to get a good view of what was the latest in tent technology at the turn of the millennium, you can see it from Docklands or Trinity Buoy Wharf (p162), or by taking a River Thames cruise to the Thames Flood Barrier (p184).

OLD ROYAL NAVAL COLLEGE Map p180

☎ 8269 4747; www.oldroyalnavalcollege.org; King William Walk SE10; admission free; ☺ 10am-5pm Mon-Sat, 12.30-5pm Sun; ☒ Greenwich or DLR Cutty Sark

There are two main rooms open to the public at the college – the Painted Hall and

THE LONG ROAD TO LONGITUDE

It was the challenge of the century. Establishing latitude – the imaginary lines that girdle the earth from north to south – was child's play; any sailor could do that by looking at the height of the sun or the Pole Star on the horizon. Finding longitude, however, was an entirely different matter and had stumped astronomers from the Greeks to Galileo.

As it takes 24 hours for the earth to complete one revolution of 360°, one hour is one twenty-fourth of a revolution – or 15°. By the 16th century astronomers knew that longitude could be found by comparing local time with the reading of a clock set at the time of home port or another place of known longitude. But that meant two *reliable* clocks, ones that would keep accurate time as the ship pitched and shook and the temperature rose or fell. Such technology was unavailable until the 18th century.

Reading longitude inaccurately lengthened sea voyages, cost shipping companies money and increased the number of sailors' deaths due to scurvy and accidents, as islands, rocks and reefs appeared almost out of nowhere. In 1714 Parliament offered a prize of £20,000 – a king's ransom in the 18th century – to anyone who could discover a method of finding longitude accurate to within 30 miles. It's a long story – one wonderfully (and briefly) told by Dava Sobel in her book *Longitude* – but Yorkshire clockmaker John Harrison was eventually awarded the prize for a marine chronometer tested from 1761 to 1762 by the Royal Observatory at Greenwich.

In 1884 the observatory's contribution in solving the longitude riddle was acknowledged when an international conference in Washington designated 'the meridian passing through the centre of the transit instrument at the Observatory of Greenwich as the initial meridian for longitude', or the prime meridian. Greenwich Mean Time (GMT) was then accepted worldwide as the universal measurement of standard time.

the chapel – which are accessed through the new visitors centre and adjoining Greenwich Tourist Information Centre in the Pepys Building. They're in separate buildings because when Christopher Wren was commissioned by William and Mary to build a naval hospital here in 1692, he designed it in two separate halves so as not to spoil the view of the river from the Queen's House (right), Inigo Jones' miniature masterpiece to the south.

Built on the site of the Old Palace of Placentia, where Henry VIII was born in 1491, the hospital was initially intended for those wounded in the victory over the French at La Hogue. In 1869 the building was converted to a Naval College. Now even the navy has left and the premises are home to the University of Greenwich and Trinity College of Music.

The Painted Hall is one of Europe's greatest banquet rooms. In the King William Building, it has been covered in decorative 'allegorical Baroque' murals by artist James Thornhill, who also painted the cupola of St Paul's Cathedral. The mural above the Lower Hall show William and Mary enthroned amid symbols of the Virtues. Beneath William's feet, you can see the defeated French king Louis XIV grovelling with a furled flag in hand. Up a few steps is the Upper Hall, where George I is depicted with his family on the western wall. In the bottom right-hand corner Thornhill drew himself into the picture, pointing towards his work.

Off the Upper Hall is the Nelson Room, originally designed by Nicholas Hawksmoor, then used as a smoking room and recently refurbished. For a week over Christmas 1805, this is where the brandy-soaked (for embalming purposes, of course) body of the great naval hero lay, before his state funeral at St Paul's. Today the room boasts a replica of the statue atop Nelson's column in Trafalgar Sq plus other memorabilia. If you want to view this room you must join one of the 90-minute guided tours (☎ 8269 4799; adult/under 16yr £4/free; ☯ tours 11.30am & 2pm) of the Jacobean undercroft of the former palace of Placentia leaving from the Painted Hall.

The chapel in the Queen Mary Building, opposite, is decorated in a lighter rococo style. The eastern end of the chapel is dominated by a painting by the 18th-century American artist Benjamin West showing *The Preservation of St Paul after Shipwreck at Malta*. It's certainly a beautiful room, but it's more famous for its organ and acoustics. If possible come on the first Sunday of the month, when there's a free 50-minute organ recital at 3pm, or time your visit for sung Eucharist, every Sunday at 11am.

QUEEN'S HOUSE Map p180
☎ 8858 4422, recorded information 0870 781 5189; www.nmm.ac.uk; Romney Rd SE10; admission free; ☯ 10am-5pm Sep-Jun, to 6pm Jul & Aug; ☉ Greenwich or DLR Cutty Sark

This building was first called the 'House of Dclight' and that's certainly still true. The first Palladian building by architect Inigo Jones after he returned from Italy, it's far more enticing than the art collection in it, even though that contains some Turners, Holbeins, Hogarths and Gainsboroughs. The house was begun in 1616 for Anne of Denmark, wife of James I. However, it wasn't completed until 1635, when it became the home of Charles I and his queen, Henrietta Maria. The Great Hall is the principal room – a lovely cube shape, with a helix-shaped Tulip Staircase and a gallery on level 3, where marine paintings and portraits from the National Maritime Museum's fine art collection are shown.

RANGER'S HOUSE Map p180

☎ 8853 0035; www.english-heritage.org.uk; Greenwich Park SE10; adult/under 5yr/5-15yr/senior & student £5.50/free/2.80/4.10; ◷ 10am-5pm Sun-Wed Apr-Sep; ☒ Greenwich or DLR Cutty Sark
This elegant Georgian villa in the southwest corner of Greenwich Park was built in 1723 and once housed the park's ranger. It now contains a collection of 650 works of art (medieval and Renaissance paintings, porcelain, silverware, tapestries etc) amassed by one Julius Wernher, a German-born railway engineer's son who struck it rich in the diamond fields of South Africa in the 19th century.

CUTTY SARK Map p180

☎ 8858 2698; www.cuttysark.org.uk; Cutty Sark Gardens SE10; ☒ Greenwich or DLR Cutty Sark
Rust and rot had been eating away at this Greenwich landmark, the last of the great clipper ships to sail between China and England in the 19th century, and she was undergoing £25 million repair work when disaster struck in May 2007. A fire, believed to have been deliberately set, damaged about 50% of the vessel. Luckily half of the ship's furnishings and equipment, including the mast, had been removed for conservation and were safe. The tragedy struck a chord among the citizens of the capital of this traditionally seagoing nation and contributions to bring the ship back to life began to pour in. We are assured that the *Cutty Sark* will rise, phoenixlike, from the ashes but it will take time and lots more money. All donations are gratefully accepted; see www.justgiving.com/cuttysark fire for details.

FAN MUSEUM Map p180

☎ 8305 1441; www.fan-museum.org; 12 Crooms Hill SE10; adult/7-16yr & senior £4/3; ◷ 11am-5pm Tue-Sat, noon-5pm Sun; ☒ Greenwich or DLR Cutty Sark; ♿
The world's only museum entirely devoted to fans has a wonderful collection of ivory, tortoiseshell, peacock-feather and folded-fabric examples alongside kitsch battery-powered versions and huge ornamental Welsh fans. The 18th-century Georgian town house in which the collection resides also has a Japanese-style garden with an Orangery (half-/full tea £3.50/4.50; ◷ 3-5pm Tue & Sun) serving afternoon tea.

GREENWICH PARK Map p180

☎ 8858 2608; www.royalparks.gov.uk; ◷ dawn-dusk; ☒ Greenwich or Maze Hill, DLR Cutty Sark
This is one of London's largest and loveliest parks, with a grand avenue, wide-open spaces, a rose garden, picturesque walks and impressive views across the River Thames to the Docklands from the top of the hill. Covering a full 74 hectares, it is the oldest enclosed royal park and is partly the work of Le Nôtre, who landscaped the palace gardens of Versailles for Louis XIV. It contains several historic sights, a teahouse, a café and a deer park called the Wilderness in the southeast corner.

DEPTFORD & NEW CROSS Map p180

Like most world-class cities where property is more valuable than bullion, London has a plethora of 'up-and-coming' areas and neighbourhoods, many of which simply end up going away. That doesn't seem to be the case with Deptford and its southern extension, New Cross, just over the Deptford Creek west of Greenwich. In recent years it's become something of a 'Shoreditch South' and nicknamed Rocklands due to its many music studios and shops, art galleries, the celebrated Laban (p313) dance institute and other cultural centres and creative outlets. But this neighbourhood's sights – most famously the Elizabethan playwright Christopher Marlow was stabbed to death here during a drunken brawl – are best seen on foot (see p186).

BLACKHEATH

☒ Blackheath
Though it might appear on the map as a southern extension of Greenwich Park, Blackheathand the 'village' of that name

to the southeast is very much a world of its own. Known locally as the 'Hampstead of the south', this 110-hectare expanse of open common has played a greater role in the history of London than its much bigger sister to the north. The Danes camped here in the early 11th century after having captured Alfege, the archbishop of Canterbury, as did Wat Tyler before marching on London with tens of thousands of Essex and Kentish men during the Peasants' Revolt in 1381. Henry VII fought off Cornish rebels here in 1497, and the heath was where Henry VIII met his fourth wife, Anne of Cleaves, in 1540 (he had agreed to marry her based on a portrait by Holbein, but disliked her immediately in the flesh and divorced her six months later). Later it became a highwaymen's haunt, and it was not until the area's development in the late 18th century – the lovely Paragon, a crescent of Georgian mansions on the southeastern edge of the heath, was built to entice 'the right sort of people' to move to the area – that Blackheath was considered safe. The name of the heath is derived from the colour of the soil, not from its alleged role as burial ground during the Black Death, the bubonic plague of the late 14th century.

Today the windswept heath is a pleasant place for a stroll, a spot of kite-flying or a drink at one of a pair of historic pubs to the south. The heath is also the starting point for the London Marathon in April.

To reach Blackheath from Greenwich Park, walk southward along Chesterfield Walk and past the Ranger's House (or southward on Blackheath Ave and through Blackheath Gate) and then cross Shooters Hill Rd.

CHARLTON & WOOLWICH

From early Iron Age hill forts to mammoth gates in the Thames designed to prevent flooding, humankind has been determined to leave a mark on these areas over the centuries. One of the most enduring landmarks has been the Royal Arsenal, which followed Henry VIII's royal dockyards out here in the 16th and 17th centuries. When it was finally closed in 1994, it made way for a museum.

THAMES FLOOD BARRIER Map p64

⊖ North Greenwich or ⓡ Charlton, then ⓑ 161, 177, 180 or 472

The sci-fi-looking Thames Flood Barrier is in place to protect London from flooding, and with global warming increasing the city's vulnerability to rising sea levels and surge tides, the barrier is likely to be of growing importance in coming years. Under construction for a decade and completed in 1982, the barrier consists of 10 movable gates anchored to nine concrete piers, each as tall as a five-storey building. The silver roofs on the piers house the operating machinery to raise and lower the gates against excess water. They make a surreal sight, straddling the river in the lee of a giant warehouse. Just opposite on the north bank of the Thames is the 7-hectare Thames Barrier Park.

The reason why London needs such a flood barrier is that the water level has been rising by as much as 60cm per century, while the river itself has been narrowing; in Roman times it was probably around 800m wide at the site of today's London Bridge while now it's barely 250m, with constant pressure to develop the foreshores. The Thames tide rises and falls quite harmlessly twice a day, and once a fortnight there's also a stronger 'spring' tide. The danger comes when the spring tide coincides with an unexpected surge, which pushes tons of extra water upriver. The barrier has been built to prevent that water pouring over the riverbanks and flooding nearby houses. Some 300 people were drowned on the east coast and the Thames Estuary in 1953 when the Thames burst its banks. Today environmentalists are already talking about a bigger, wider damming mechanism further towards the mouth of the river, before the current barrier comes to the expected end of its design life in 2030.

The barrier looks best when it's raised, and the only guaranteed time this happens is once a month, when the mechanisms are checked. For exact dates and times, ring or check the website of the Thames Barrier Information Centre (☎ 8305 4188; www.environment-agency.gov.uk; 1 Unity Way SE18; admission to barrier free, admission to downstairs information centre adult/child/senior £2/1/1; ⏰ 11am-3.30pm Oct-Mar, 10.30am-4.30pm Apr-Sep).

If you're coming from central London, take a train to Charlton from Charing Cross or London Bridge. Then walk along Woolwich Rd to Eastmoor St, which leads northward to the centre. If you're coming from Greenwich, you can pick up bus 177 or 180 along Romney Rd and get off at the Thames Barrier stop (near the Victoria Pub, 757 Woolwich Rd). The closest tube station is North Greenwich, from where you can pick up bus 472 or 161.

Boats also travel to and from the barrier, although they don't land. From Westminster it's a three-hour round trip; from Greenwich it takes just one hour. From April to October direct services run by Thames River Services (☎ 7930 4097; www.westminsterpier.co.uk; adult/child/senior/family one way £8.70/4.35/7/24, return £11/5.50/9/30.25) leave Westminster Pier on the hour from 10am to 3pm (leaving Greenwich from 11am to 4pm), passing the O2 (Millennium Dome) along the way. From November to March there's a reduced service from Westminster between 10.40am and 3.20pm. See the website for exact times.

FIREPOWER, THE ROYAL ARTILLERY MUSEUM Map p64
☎ 8855 7755; www.firepower.org.uk; Royal Arsenal, Woolwich SE18; adult/5-15yr/senior & student/family £5/2.50/4.50/12; ☉ 10.30am-5pm Wed-Sun Apr-Oct, 10.30am-5pm Fri-Sun Nov-Mar; ✪ North Greenwich then ☒ 161, 422 or 472, ☒ Woolwich Arsenal

Not a place for pacifists or those of a nervous disposition, Firepower is a shoot-'em-up display of how artillery has developed through the ages. The History Gallery traces the story of artillery from catapults to nuclear warheads, while a multimedia exhibit called Field of Fire tries to convey the experience of artillery gunners from WWI to Bosnia in a 15-minute extravaganza. There's a Gunnery Hall packed with weapons from the 20th century and a Medals Gallery with 7000 pieces. The Command Post at the end of the tour includes both a climbing wall and paintball range (£1.50 each, or £2.50 for both). The whole place is loud and reeking of adrenaline – and the kids just can't get enough of it. Reach the Royal Arsenal by rail from Charing Cross or London Bridge or on bus 161, 422 or 472 from the North Greenwich tube station.

DULWICH & FOREST HILL

Tucked away in the wide expanse of South London that the tube fails to reach, Dulwich (*dull*-itch) and Forest Hill are leafy, quiet suburbs with some fine architecture and an air of gentility. Both boast outstanding museums well worth a trip out here.

DULWICH PICTURE GALLERY Map p64
☎ 8693 5254; www.dulwichpicturegallery.org.uk; Gallery Rd SE21; adult/student & child/senior

£4.40/free/3.30; ☉ 10am-5pm Tue-Fri, 11am-5pm Sat & Sun; ☒ West Dulwich; ☒

The UK's oldest public art gallery, the Dulwich Picture Gallery was designed by the idiosyncratic architect Sir John Soane between 1811 and 1814 to house Dulwich College's collection of paintings by Raphael, Rembrandt, Rubens, Reynolds, Gainsborough, Poussin, Lely, Van Dyck and others. It's a wonderful, atmospheric place but with scarcely a dozen rooms to hang the artwork, wall space is limited and it is difficult to view some of the paintings properly. Unusually, the collectors, Noel Desenfans and painter Sir Peter Francis Bourgeois, chose to have their mausoleums, lit by a moody *lumière mystérieuse* (mysterious light) created with tinted glass, placed among the pictures. An annexe (additional £3) contains space for temporary exhibitions – last seen: Canaletto in England 1746–1755. Free guided tours of the museum are available at 3pm on Saturday and Sunday.

The museum is a 10-minute walk northwards along Gallery Rd, which starts almost opposite West Dulwich station. Bus P4 links the gallery with the Horniman Museum (below).

HORNIMAN MUSEUM Map p64
☎ 8699 1872, 8699 2339; www.horniman.ac.uk; 100 London Rd SE23; admission free; ☉ 10.30am-5.30pm Mon-Sat, 2-5.30pm Sun; ☒ Forest Hill; ☒

This museum is an extraordinary place, comprising the original collection of wealthy pack rat tea merchant Frederick John Horniman, who had the Art Nouveau building with clock tower and mosaics specially designed to house it in 1901. Today it encompasses everything from a dusty stuffed walrus and voodoo altars from Haiti and Benin to a mock-up of a Fijian reef and a wonderful collection of concertinas.

On the ground and 1st floors is the Natural History Gallery, the core of the Horniman collection with the usual animal skeletons and pickled specimens. In the basement you'll find African Worlds, the first permanent gallery of African and Afro-Caribbean art and culture in the UK. The Music Gallery next door has instruments from 3500-year-old Egyptian clappers and early English keyboards to Indonesian gamelan and Ghanaian drums, with touch screens so you can hear what they sound like and videos to see them being played *in situ*. The Centenary Gallery traces the history of the museum's first 100 years. The new aquarium is small but state of the art. The café, with seating in the stunning conservatory, is a delight as are the surrounding hillside gardens with views of London.

To get here from Forest Hill station, turn left out of the station along Devonshire Rd and then right along London Rd. The museum is about 500m on the right.

ELTHAM

Eltham was the favoured home of the Plantagenet kings. But after the Tudors switched the royal favours to Greenwich, the palace they built here lay neglected for more than five hundred years. Only when the wealthy Courtauld family arrived in the 1930s to build their fabulous home were the remains of the original Eltham Palace restored.

ELTHAM PALACE Map p64

☎ 8294 2548; www.english-heritage.org.uk; off Court Rd SE9; adult/under 5yr/5-15yr/concession £7.90/free/4/5.90; ☺ 10am-5pm Sun-Wed Apr-Oct, 11am-4pm Sun-Wed Nov, Dec, Feb & Mar, closed Jan; ☒ Eltham; ♿

No fan of Art Deco should miss a trip to Eltham Palace, not so much for the remnants of the palace building itself but for the fabulous Courtauld House on its grounds.

The house was built between 1933 and 1937 by the well-to-do textile merchant Stephen Courtauld and his wife Virginia; from the impressive entrance hall with its dome and huge circular carpet with geometric shapes to the black-marble dining room with silver-foil ceiling and burlwood-veneer fireplace it appears the couple had taste as well as money. They also, rather fashionably for the times, had a pet lemur, and the heated cage, complete with tropical murals and a bamboo ladder leading to the ground floor, for the spoiled (and vicious) 'Mah-jongg' is also on view.

Little remains of the 14th- to 16th-century palace where Edward IV entertained and Henry VIII spent his childhood before decamping for Greenwich, apart from the restored Great Medieval Hall. Its hammer-beam roof is generally rated the third best in the country, behind those at Westminster Hall and Hampton Court Palace.

BEXLEYHEATH

Formerly known as Bexley New Town and dominated by an expanse of open space, this attractive suburban development east of Eltham contains two important historic houses.

DANSON HOUSE Off Map p64

☎ 8303 6699; www.dansonhouse.com; Danson Park, Bexleyheath DA6; adult/senior & student £5/4.50; ☺ 11am-5pm Wed, Thu, Sun & Mon & bank holidays late Mar-Oct; ☒ Bexleyheath, then 20min walk southwest

This Palladian villa was built by one John Boyd, the son of a sugar trader and himself an East India Company director, in 1766. A 10-year restoration to bring the house back to its original Georgian style was completed in 2005, aided by the discovery of a series of fine watercolours of the interiors by the second owner's daughter in 1805. Highlights include the dining room's numerous reliefs and frescoes celebrating love and romance, the library and music room with its functioning organ, the dizzy-making spiral staircase accessing the upper floors and the Victorian kitchens (open occasionally). The English Garden is a delight, and on the large lake in Danson Park, which is flanked by some splendid Art Deco houses along Danson Rd to the east, you can rent rowing boats (☎ 8303 2228; 30/60min £5/7.50; ☺ 9.30am-5pm Sat & Sun Sep-Jun, daily Jul & Aug) and kayaks (15/30min £1.50/2.50).

RED HOUSE Off Map p64

☎ 8304 9878; www.nationaltrust.org.uk; 13 Red House Lane, Bexleyheath DA6; adult/5-15yr/family £6.40/3.20/16; ☺ 10.45am-4.15pm Wed-Sun Mar-Dec; ☒ Bexleyheath, then 20min walk south

From the outside, this redbrick house built by Victorian designer William Morris in 1860 conjures up a gingerbread house in stone. The nine rooms open to the public bear all the elements of the Arts and Crafts style to which Morris adhered – a bit of Gothic art here, some religious symbolism there. Furniture by Morris and the house's designer Philip Webb are in evidence, as are paintings and stained glass by Edward Burne-Jones. Entry is by guided tour only, which must be prebooked. The surrounding gardens were designed by Morris 'to clothe' the house. Don't miss the well with a conical roof inspired by the oast houses of Kent.

DEPTFORD & NEW CROSS WALK

Walking Tour

1 Creekside

This cobbled street running parallel to Deptford Creek is lined with galleries and artists' studios with regularly changing art exhibitions, including Art in Perpetuity (☎ 8694 8344; www.aptstudios.org; 6 Creekside SE8) and Creekside Artists (☎ 8297 2053; www.creeksideartists.co.uk; 8-12 Creekside SE8).

2 Laban

What is acknowledged as the largest and best equipped contemporary dance school (p313) in Europe is housed in an award-winning £23-million plastic-clad building (2003) at the northern end of Creekside designed by the same architects who did Tate Modern. Highly innovative are the turf-covered mounds of debris cleared from the site in the forecourt.

3 Statue of Peter the Great

This intriguing statue (end of Glaisher St SE8) commemorates the four-month stay of Tsar Peter I of Russia, who in 1698 came to Deptford to learn more about new developments in shipbuilding. The original party dude, Peter stayed with diarist John Evelyn and his drunken parties badly damaged the writer's house.

4 St Nicholas Church

This late-17th-century church (☎ 8691 3161; Deptford Green SE8) contains a memorial to playwright Christopher Marlowe, who was murdered in Deptford in a tavern brawl at the age of 29 in 1593. The fight supposedly broke out over

WALK FACTS

Start New Cross rail station
End Deptford rail station
Distance 1.5 miles
Duration Two hours

DEPTFORD & NEW CROSS WALK

who was to pay the bill but it is generally believed that Marlowe was in the employ of the Elizabethan intelligence service.

5 Albury Street

This delightful street is lined with Georgian buildings that once housed Deptford's naval officers, including (it is said) Lord Nelson and Lady Hamilton. Notice the exquisite wood carvings decorating may of the doorways. To the south is the baroque St Paul's Church (☎ 8692 7449; Mary Ann Gardens SE8), built in 1730.

6 Deptford Market

This colourful market (☎ 8691 8725; Deptford High St SE8; ☷ 8.30am-3pm Wed, Fri & Sat) is held in the centre of Deptford three days a week. Southwest is the Albany (☎ 8692 4446; www.thealbany.org.uk; Douglas Way SE8), a busy arts and community centre with comedy, music and theatre productions.

FESTIVALS & EVENTS

As you'd expect from one of the world's greatest and most multicultural cities, London has a year-long diary of festivals and events with something to suit all tastes and budgets. Thanks to the vagaries of the British climate, the livelier street parties are largely restricted to the summer months (and even then there's no guarantee that it won't rain), but the colder, darker days of winter offer some exciting spectacles too, ensuring that whatever time of year you visit, there'll be something of interest going on.

London's royal connections ensure a steady stream of pageantry and pomp throughout the months, and the mighty Thames is often the setting for races and firework displays that celebrate the city's traditions. But modern, ethnically diverse London also gets to show off to locals and visitors alike with a range of events, most famously the Notting Hill Carnival, and British eccentricity finds outlets in numerous, 'only in London' activities.

For some of the events following you need to book, often way in advance (see the relevant websites for more information), but for many it's just a case of showing up and joining in.

For a full list of everything going on in and around London, look out for Visit London's bimonthly *Events in London* and its *Annual Events* pamphlet. You can also check the website at www.visitlondon.com.

JANUARY–MARCH

1 New Year's Day
The mayor of Westminster leads 10,000 musicians and street performers through central London, from Parliament Sq to Berkeley Sq, in the lively London Parade.

2 International Boat Show
Excel, Docklands; www.londonboatshow .net
Early January sees this long-running display of all things aquatic held in one of London's main exhibition spaces.

3 London Art Fair
Business Design Centre, Islington; www.londonartfair.co.uk
In January more than 100 major galleries participate in this contemporary art fair, now one of the largest in Europe, with thematic exhibitions, special events and the best emerging artists.

4 Chinese New Year
Chinatown; www.chinatown-online.co.uk
In late January or early February, Chinatown fizzes, crackles and pops in this colourful street festival, which includes a Golden Dragon parade, and eating and partying aplenty.

5 Pancake Races
Spitalfields Market, Covent Garden & Lincoln's Inn Fields
On Shrove Tuesday, in late February/early March, you can catch pancake races and associated silliness at various venues around town.

6 Head of the River Race
Thames, from Mortlake to Putney; www.horr.co.uk
In March some 400 crews participate in this colourful annual boat race that's been going on for more than 80 years. There are many vantage points along the 7km course.

7 London Lesbian & Gay Film Festival
www.llgff.co.uk
One of the biggest gay and lesbian film festivals in the world, the LLGFF in late March/early April shows hundreds of independent films from around the globe at the National Film Theatre. Advance online booking is essential.

1 London Marathon
Greenwich Park to the Mall; www.london-marathon.co.uk
Some 35,000 masochists cross London in the world's biggest road race, held in April. Watch the thousands head off from Blackheath at the start, cheer them on around the course or clap them across the line on the Mall.

2 Clerkenwell Easter parade
Clerkenwell on Easter Sunday
Little Italy comes alive during this incredible parade from Exmouth Market to the Italian Cathedral on Clerkenwell Rd, during which the Virgin is transported through the streets of London.

3 Oxford & Cambridge Boat Race
From Putney to Mortlake; www.theboatrace.org
Big crowds line the banks of the Thames for this annual event, where the country's two most famous universities go oar-to-oar and hope they don't sink. Dates vary year to year so check the website.

4 Royal Windsor Horse Show
www.royal-windsor-horse-show.co.uk
This prestigious five-day equestrian event in May is attended by royalty, gentry and country folk and hosted in the Queen's private gardens at Windsor Castle – it's the only chance to visit them for most people.

5 Chelsea Flower Show
Royal Hospital Chelsea; www.rhs.org.uk
Every May, the world's most renowned horticultural show attracts gardeners from near and far and is one of the biggest social events of the season for the well heeled and green fingered.

6 Royal Academy Summer Exhibition
Royal Academy of Arts; www.royalacademy.org.uk
Beginning in June and running through August, this is an annual showcase of works submitted by artists from all over Britain, thankfully distilled to a thousand or so pieces.

7 Beating the Retreat
Horse Guards Parade, Whitehall
A warm-up for the Queen's birthday, this patriotic June evening full of royal pomp and circumstance involves military bands and much beating of drums.

8 Trooping the Colour
Horse Guards Parade, Whitehall
The Queen's official birthday (she was born in April but the weather's better in June) is celebrated with much flag-waving, parades, pageantry and noisy flyovers.

9 Architecture Week
www.architectureweek.org.uk
Late June is about exploring the city's architecture and urban landscapes through various events across town.

10 Wimbledon Lawn Tennis Championships
www.wimbledon.org
For two weeks in late June to early July, the normally quiet village of Wimbledon is the centre of the sporting universe as the greatest players on earth fight it out for the championship.

1 City of London Festival
www.colf.org
Two weeks of top-quality music, dance and theatre is held in some of the finest buildings, churches and squares in the capital's financial district from late June to early July.

2 Pride
www.pridelondon.org
The gay community in all its fabulous guises paints the town pink every June or July in this annual extravaganza, featuring a parade, a huge rally and a rather camp open-air concert featuring has-been gay favourites.

3 Greenwich & Docklands International Festival
www.festival.org
Every weekend in July you can catch (mostly) free outdoor dance, theatre and music performances on either side of the Thames, with the area's wonderful architecture often serving as a backdrop.

4 Soho Festival
www.thesohosociety.org.uk
London's liveliest neighbourhood enjoys all sorts of shenanigans at this July charity fundraiser, from a waiters' race to a spaghetti-eating contest, while the crowds can choose from lots of food stalls.

5 BBC Promenade Concerts (The Proms)
www.bbc.co.uk/proms
Lasting for two months from mid-July, these hugely popular and top-quality classical concerts at various prestigious venues are centred on the Royal Albert Hall in Kensington.

6 Rise: London United
www.risefestival.org
A free outdoor music and dance festival in July (at changing venues), paid for by the Mayor of London to promote antiracism and multiculturalism. The focus is on big-name headline acts, but there are lots of other activities to enjoy too.

7 Notting Hill Carnival
www.londoncarnival.co.uk
Two million people descend on Notting Hill over the August Bank Holiday Weekend for Europe's biggest street festival – a celebration of all things Caribbean that started nearly 50 years ago.

8 Great British Beer Festival
www.gbbf.org
The Campaign for Real Ale organises this superb early-August event where tens of thousands of beer lovers down a wonderful selection of local and international brews at Earl's Court Exhibition Centre.

9 The Mayor's Thames Festival
www.thamesfestival.org
Celebrating London's greatest natural asset, the Thames, this cosmopolitan September festival provides fun for all the family with fairs, street theatre, music, food stalls, fireworks, river races and a spectacular Lantern Procession.

10 Great River Race
From Ham House to the Isle of Dogs; www.greatriverrace.co.uk
Come September, barges, dragon boats and Viking longships race 35km down the Thames in what is definitely London's most enjoyable boat race. You can even take part if you have a boat handy.

11 London Open House
www.londonopenhouse.org
One of London's biggest treats. For one weekend in mid-September, the public can access more than 500 buildings that are normally off-limits. Londoners and visitors alike head to their favourite places in droves so get there early for the biggies.

12 Dance Umbrella
www.danceumbrella.co.uk
London's annual festival of contemporary dance features five weeks of performances by British and international dance companies at venues across London throughout October and into early November.

13 Trafalgar Day Parade
Trafalgar Sq
Commemorating Nelson's maritime victory over Napoleon in 1805, marching bands descend on Trafalgar Sq in October to lay a wreath at Nelson's Column.

14 London Film Festival
National Film Theatre & various venues; www.lff.org.uk
The city's premier film event attracts big names each October and is an opportunity to see more than 100 British and international films before their cinema release. Talks and Q&A sessions with world-famous moviemakers and actors are very popular too.

❶ London to Brighton Veteran Car Run
Serpentine Rd; www.vccofgb.co.uk /lontobri

In early November, pre-1905 vintage cars line up at dawn in Hyde Park before racing to Brighton.

❷ State Opening of Parliament
House of Lords, Westminster

The Queen visits Parliament by state coach amid gun salutes to summon MPs back from their long summer recess in late October or November. She also wears her ridiculously heavy crown while addressing parliament. A great day for any fan of pomp.

❸ Bonfire Night

One of Britain's favourite traditions, Bonfire Night celebrates Guy Fawkes' foiled attempt to blow up Parliament in 1605 with bonfires and fireworks on 5 November. Alexandra Palace, Clapham Common, Highbury Fields and Crystal Palace Park have some of the best pyrotechnic displays.

❹ Lord Mayor's Show
www.lordmayorsshow.org

In November, the Lord Mayor of the City of London travels in a state coach from Mansion House to the Royal Courts of Justice, to pledge allegiance to the Crown, with crowds cheering the accompanying floats and bands. Fireworks on the river round off the day's events.

❺ Remembrance Sunday
Cenotaph, Whitehall

A sombre ceremony on the Sunday nearest 11 November, wherein the Queen, prime minister and other notables lay wreaths at the Cenotaph to remember those who died in two world wars, while veterans look on.

❻ Lighting of the Christmas Tree & Lights

Come late November or December, a celebrity is chauffeured in to switch on the festive lights along Oxford, Regent and Bond Sts, while a huge Norwegian spruce is set up in Trafalgar Sq, an annual gift from Norway to Britain in thanks for WWII support.

❼ New Year's Eve

On 31 December, crowds gather in Trafalgar Sq and along the river to see in the New Year. River fireworks and free public transport add to the fun but the huge number of people can be frightening.

SOUTH LONDON

Eating p270; Drinking p293; Shopping p234

Londoners still talk as if the Thames was the huge barrier between north and south that it was in the Middle Ages. In fact, the psychological gulf between the two banks is as wide as ever; most people in North London (and that's most Londoners) refuse to believe there's anything of importance across the river. But it really isn't so grim down south. In recent years even former North Londoners have discovered there's something rather pleasant about the more affordable property prices and relaxed lifestyle of the river's former B-list side (referring, of course, to the number of place names beginning with that letter such as Battersea, Brixton, Balham and so on).

Anarchic and artistic Brixton is without a doubt the most interesting area. Besides coming here to go clubbing, to a attend a gig at the Carling Academy Brixton (p308) or to catch a film at the historic Ritzy (p316), probably the best way to taste the area's Afro-Caribbean flavour is to visit Brixton Market (p242).

Clapham has long been the flag-bearer for South London style, with upmarket restaurants and bars lining its High Street since the 1980s. Attention has started to focus more recently on Battersea, with its magnificent park and the announced conversion of the monolithic Battersea Power Station. Kennington has some lovely streets lined with Georgian terraced houses, so it can only be a matter of time before the gentrification of 'Little Portugal' – its southern extension of Stockwell – begins.

Lambeth can boast both the episcopal seat of the Church of England and one of London's finest museums.

top picks

SOUTH LONDON

- Battersea Park (p201)
- Battersea Power Station (p201)
- Carling Academy Brixton (p308)
- Imperial War Museum (below)
- Lambeth Palace (p198)

LAMBETH

The name Lambeth translates as 'muddy landing place', attesting to the fact that this, like nearby Waterloo, was largely marsh land and polder dams until the 18th century. Apparently, the only notables brave enough to live here earlier were archbishops of Canterbury, who began coming and going in barges from waterside Lambeth Palace in the 13th century. It was the arrival of bridges and the railways centuries later that finally connected Lambeth to London.

IMPERIAL WAR MUSEUM Map p198

☎ 7416 5320; www.iwm.org.uk; Lambeth Rd SE1; admission free; ☺ 10am-6pm; ⊖ Lambeth North; ☐

Despite the threatening pair of 15in naval guns outside the front entrance to what was once Bethlehem Royal Hospital, commonly known as Bedlam, this is for the most part a very sombre, thoughtful museum. Most of its exhibits are given over to exploring the human and social cost of conflict.

Although the museum's focus is officially on military action involving British or Commonwealth troops during the 20th century, it gives 'war' a wide interpretation. So it not only has serious discussion of the two world wars, Korea and Vietnam, but also covers the Cold War, 'secret' warfare (ie spying) and even the war on apartheid in South Africa.

The core of the six-floor museum is a chronological exhibition on the two world wars on the lower ground floor. In the Trench Experience you walk through the grim day-to-day reality of life on the Somme front line in WWI, and in the more hair-raising Blitz Experience you cower inside a mock bomb shelter during a WWII air raid and then emerge through ravaged East End streets.

On the upper floors you find the two most outstanding – and moving – sections: the extensive Holocaust Exhibition (not recommended for under 14s) on the 3rd floor, and a stark gallery called Crimes against Humanity devoted to genocide in Cambodia,

SOUTH LONDON

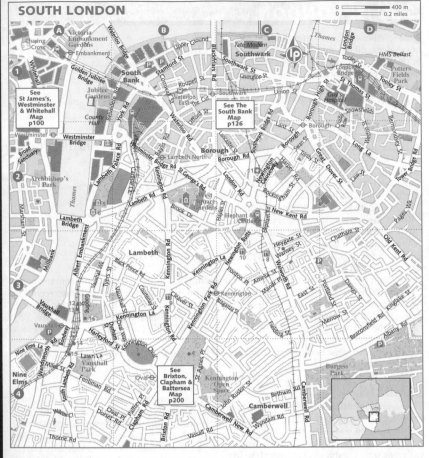

NEIGHBOURHOODS SOUTH LONDON

SOUTH LONDON

Yugoslavia and Rwanda (not recommended for under 16s). The 2nd floor features war paintings by the likes of Stanley Spencer and John Singer Sargent.

Audioguides to the permanent collection cost adult/concession £3.50/3. Temporary exhibits, which charge an admission fee, cover such topics as war reporting, camouflage and modern warfare and – our

favourite – the role of animals in conflicts from WWI to the present day.

LAMBETH PALACE Map p198

Lambeth Palace Rd SE1; ⊖ Lambeth North
The redbrick Tudor gatehouse beside the church of St Mary-at-Lambeth leads to Lambeth Palace, the London residence of the Archbishop of Canterbury. Although

the palace is not usually open to the public, the gardens occasionally are; check with a tourist office for details (see p400).

MUSEUM OF GARDEN HISTORY
Map p198

☎ 7401 8865; www.museumgardenhistory.org; St Mary-at-Lambeth, Lambeth Palace Rd SE1; admission free, requested donation £3; ☯ 10.30am-5pm Tue-Sun; ⊖ Lambeth North

In a city holding out the broad attractions of Kew Gardens, the modest Museum of Garden History housed in the church of St Mary-at-Lambeth is mainly for the seriously green-thumbed. Its trump card is the charming knot garden, a replica of a 17th-century formal garden, with topiary hedges clipped into an intricate, twirling design. Keen gardeners will enjoy the displays on the 17th-century Tradescant *père* and *fils* – a father-and-son team who were gardeners to Charles I and Charles II, globetrotters and enthusiastic collectors of exotic plants (they introduced the pineapple to London). Nongardeners might like to pay their respects to Captain William Bligh (of mutinous *Bounty* fame), who is buried here (he lived and died nearby at 100 Lambeth Rd). The excellent café has vegetarian food.

FLORENCE NIGHTINGALE MUSEUM
Map p198

☎ 7620 0374; www.florence-nightingale .co.uk; St Thomas's Hospital, 2 Lambeth Palace Rd SE1; adult/senior, student & child/family £5.80/4.80/16; ☯ 10am-5pm Mon-Fri, to 4.30pm Sat & Sun; ⊖ Westminster or Waterloo; ♿

Attached to St Thomas's Hospital, this small museum tells the story of feisty war heroine Florence Nightingale (1820–1910), who led a team of nurses to Turkey in 1854 during the Crimean War. There she worked to improve conditions for the soldiers before returning to London to set up a training school for nurses at St Thomas's in 1859. So popular did she become that baseball card–style photos of the gentle 'Lady of the Lamp' were sold during her lifetime. There is no shortage of revisionist detractors who dismiss her as a 'canny administrator' and 'publicity hound'; Nightingale was, in fact, one of the world's first modern celebrities. But the fact remains she improved conditions for thousands of soldiers in the field and saved quite a few lives in the process. We can hardly think of a more glorious achievement.

BRIXTON

'We gonna rock down to Electric Avenue,' sang Eddy Grant optimistically in 1983, about one of London's first shopping streets (1888) to be lit by electricity. (It's just to the left as you exit Brixton tube station.) But the Clash's 'Guns of Brixton' took a much darker tone when referring to community discontent with the police that provoked the riots of the 1980s. Historically, those are just two sides to this edgy, vibrant, multicultural potpourri of a neighbourhood.

There was a settlement on the site of today's Brixton as early as a year after the Norman invasion. But Brixton remained an isolated, far-flung village until the 19th century, when the new Vauxhall Bridge (1810) and the railways (1860) linked it with central London.

The years that most shaped contemporary Brixton, however, were the post-WWII 'Windrush' years, when immigrants arrived from the West Indies in reply to the British government's call for help in solving the labour shortage of the time. (*Windrush* was the name of one of the leading ships that brought these immigrants to the UK.) A generation later the honeymoon period was over, as economic decline and hostility between the police and particularly the black community (who accounted for only 29% of the population of Brixton at the time) led to the riots in 1981, 1985 and 1995. These centred on Railton Rd and Coldharbour Lane.

Since then the mood has been decidedly more upbeat. Soaring property prices have sent house-hunters foraging in these parts, and pockets of gentrification sit alongside the more run-down streets (see p202).

BATTERSEA & WANDSWORTH

Against the looming shell of the Battersea Power Station, this area southwest along the Thames was a site of industry until the 1970s. Now its abandoned factories and warehouses have been replaced by luxury flats. Even residents from well-heeled Chelsea are defecting across the Thames to what estate agents like to call 'Chelsea South'.

Wandsworth, the poorer working-class sibling of more affluent Battersea immediately downriver, has similarly gentrified in recent years. You'll hear the area repeatedly referred to as 'nappy valley'. Apparently Wandsworth has the highest birth rate of any borough in London.

SOUTH LONDON: BRIXTON, CLAPHAM & BATTERSEA

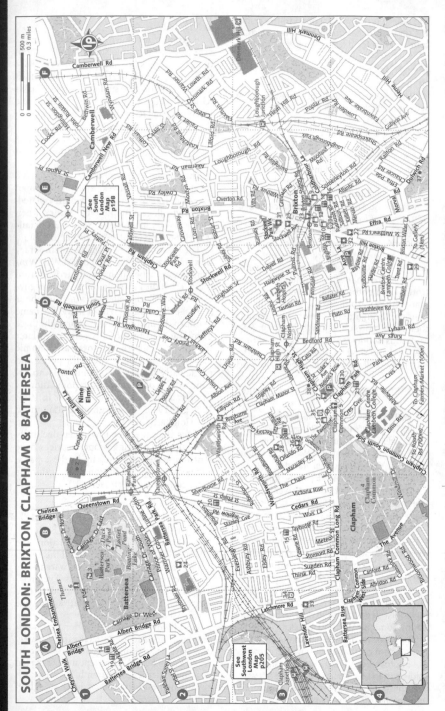

See South London Map p198

See Southwest London Map p205

SOUTH LONDON: BRIXTON, CLAPHAM & BATTERSEA

BATTERSEA POWER STATION Map p200

www.batterseapowerstation.com; 🚇 Battersea Park
Familiar to an entire generation from Pink Floyd's 1977 *Animals* album cover, with the four smokestacks that somewhat resemble a table turned upside down, Battersea Power Station is a building both loved and reviled. Built by Giles Gilbert Scott with two chimneys in 1933 (the other two were added in 1955), it ceased operations in 1983 and since then there have been innumerable proposals to give it a new life. In November 2006 it was sold to yet another group of developers; the previous ones, Parkview International, had owned it more than a dozen years from 1993 and had wanted to demolish the chimneys and turn the 'nave' of the structure into a 24-hour entertainment complex with restaurants, hotels, retail shops, cinemas etc. The power station's future seems as uncertain as ever as a new 'master plan' is redrawn, though one sensible proposal suggests that it house the government's new Energy Technologies Institute, established to research new technologies into combating climate change.

BATTERSEA PARK Map p200

🕿 8871 7530; www.batterseapark.org; 🕓 dawn-dusk; 🚇 Battersea Park
These 50 hectares of greenery stretch between Albert and Chelsea Bridges. With its Henry Moore sculptures and Peace Pagoda, erected in 1985 by a group of Japanese Buddhists to commemorate Hiroshima Day, its tranquil appearance belies a bloody past. It was once the site of an assassination attempt on King Charles II in 1671

and of a duel in 1829 between the Duke of Wellington and an opponent who accused him of treason.

A recent refurbishment has seen the 19th-century landscaping reinstated and the grand riverside terraces spruced up. At the same time, the Festival of Britain pleasure gardens, including the spectacular Vista Fountains, have been restored. There are lakes, plenty of sporting facilities, an art space called the Pump House Gallery (🕿 8871 7572; www.wandsworth.gov.uk/gallery; Battersea Park SW11; admission free; 🕓 11am-5pm Wed-Sun) and a small Children's Zoo (🕿 7924 5826; www.batterseaparkzoo.co.uk; adult/2-15yr/family £5.95/4.50/18.50; 🕓 10am-5pm Apr-Oct, to 4pm Nov-Mar).

WANDSWORTH COMMON Map p205

🚇 Wandsworth Common or Clapham Junction
Wilder and more overgrown than the nearby common in Clapham, Wandsworth Common is full of couples pushing prams on a sunny day. On the common's western side is a pleasant collection of streets known as the toast rack, because of their alignment. Baskerville, Dorlcote, Henderson, Nicosia, Patten and Routh Rds are lined with Georgian houses. There's a blue plaque at 3 Routh Rd, home to the former British prime minister David Lloyd George.

CLAPHAM

The so-called 'man on the Clapham omnibus' – English civil law's definition of the hypothetical reasonable person since the turn of the 20th century – has largely left this neighbourhood. Today Clapham is the home of well-heeled young professionals in their 20s and 30s, who eat in the area's many restaurants, drink in its many bars and generally drive up property prices. It was the railways that originally conferred on Clapham its status as a home for everyday commuters from the late 19th century. Clapham Junction is still the largest rail interchange in Britain, and in 1988 the tragic site of one of Britain's worst rail disasters.

Reaching further back in history, the area was first settled after the Great Fire of London in 1666, when noted diarist Samuel Pepys and later explorer Captain James Cook, among others, escaped the desecration of the City to build homes here. Its name dates back much further still; it's from Anglo-Saxon for 'Clappa's farm'.

CLAPHAM COMMON Map p200
Clapham Common

This large expanse of green is the heart of the Clapham neighbourhood. Mentioned both by Graham Greene in his novel *The End of the Affair* and Ian McEwan in his brilliant *Atonement,* it's now a venue for many outdoor summer events (see http://claphamhighstreet.co.uk). The main thoroughfare, Clapham High St, starts at the common's northeastern edge and is lined with many of the bars, restaurants and shops for which people principally come to Clapham. However, for a simple stroll it's much more pleasant to explore the more upmarket streets of Clapham Old Town, a short distance northwest of the tube station, and Clapham Common North Side at the common's northwesternmost edge.

On the corner of Clapham Park Rd and Clapham Common South Side you'll find the Holy Trinity Church (1776). This was home to the Clapham Sect, a group of wealthy evangelical Christians that included William Wilberforce, a leading antislavery campaigner, active between 1790 and 1830. The sect also campaigned against child labour and for prison reform.

KENNINGTON, OVAL & STOCKWELL

Only cricket-lovers and those who set up home here will really venture into this neck of the woods. It centres on Kennington Park, which isn't that much to look at but has an interesting

history. Off Kennington Lane, just west of its intersection with Kennington Rd, lies a lovely enclave of leafy streets – Cardigan St, Courtney St and Courtney Sq – with neo-Georgian houses. They're not really worth travelling to see, but make a nice diversion should rain interrupt play at the Oval just south.

KENNINGTON PARK Map p198
Oval

This unprepossessing space of green has a great rabble-rousing tradition. Originally a common, where all were permitted entry, it acted as a speakers' corner for South London. During the 18th century, Jacobite rebels trying to restore the Stuart monarchy were hanged, drawn and quartered here, and in the 18th and 19th centuries, preachers used to deliver hellfire-and-brimstone speeches to large audiences here; John Wesley, founder of Methodism and an antislavery advocate, is said to have attracted some 30,000 followers. After the great Chartist rally on 10 April 1848, where millions of working-class people turned out to demand the same voting rights as the middle classes, the royal family promptly fenced off and patrolled the common as a park.

BRIT OVAL Map p198
0871 246 1100; www.surreycricket.com; Surrey County Cricket Club SE11; test matches £45, last day £10, county fixtures £5-10; booking office 9.30am-12.30pm & 1.30-4pm Mon-Fri Apr-Sep; Oval

Home to the Surrey County Cricket Club, the Brit Oval is London's second cricketing venue after Lord's (p174). As well as Surrey matches, it also regularly hosts international test matches. The season runs from April to September.

BRIXTON WALK
Walking Tour
1 Brixton Market
At London's most exotic market (p242), you can drink in the heady mix of incense and the smells of the exotic fruits, vegetables, meat and fish on sale. It's also a good place to splash out on African fabrics and trinkets.

2 Ritzy
London's second-oldest movie house (after the Electric Cinema in Camden), the Ritzy (p316) opened as the Electric Pavilion in 1911. Next

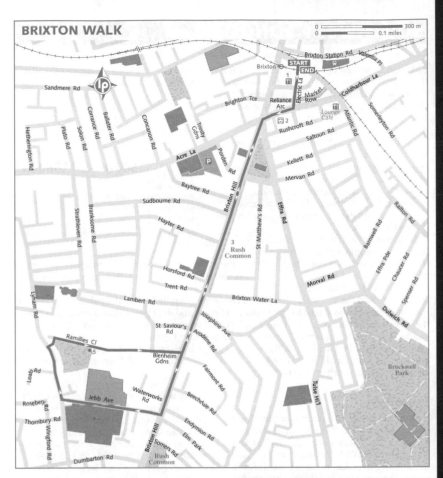

door is the Brixton Library (☎ 7926 1056; Brixton Oval SW2) built in 1892 by industrialist/philanthropist Sir Henry Tate, the man who gave London the Tate Gallery and the world the sugar cube.

3 Rush Common
An act of Parliament in 1806 declared a wide strip along the eastern side of Brixton Hill to be 'proscribed land' on which nothing could be built. Over the years, however, tracts of it were illegally walled off to create private front gardens. It is now being restored as common land (Brixton Hill SW2) but remains patchy in areas.

4 Brixton Prison
Serving a number of courts in South London, Brixton Prison (☎ 8588 6000; Jebb Ave SW2) started life as the Brixton House of Correction in 1819 and has done time as everything from a jail for

WALK FACTS
Start **Brixton tube station**
End **Brixton tube station**
Distance **2.75 miles**
Duration **2½ hours**
Fuel stop **Lounge Café** (p270)

women to a military prison. It now houses a mixture of remand and sentenced prisoners.

5 Brixton Windmill
Built for one John Ashby in 1816, this is the closest windmill (Blenheim Gardens SW2) to central London still in existence. It was later powered by gas and milled as recently as 1934. It's been refitted with sails and machinery for a wind-driven mill but is not open to the public at present.

203

SOUTHWEST LONDON

Eating p272; Drinking p294; Shopping p234; Sleeping p361

Although southwest London is a little far out if you're only in London for a long weekend, it's the perfect place to base yourself for a longer stay. Anyone wanting to get out of London for the day without too much trouble or expense should take a trip here, and for people who aren't big-city fans but need to be in London, it's a great place to stay.

During the day much of southwest London is a quiet residential area; you'll see lots of young mothers out pushing prams and doing their shopping. This is the best time to enjoy the area's many green spaces: walk along the Thames Path from Putney Bridge to Barnes, sup on a pint by Parson's Green or picnic on Barnes Common.

It's at night that the area comes alive. Fulham is a very popular place to go out in town, with a plethora of good pubs, bars and restaurants. Putney and Barnes like to think that they're a little more refined, though a trip to any of the pubs on the High Street on a Saturday night will put paid to that notion.

Further afield the well-to-do have been retreating from the city to the palaces and villas of London's riverside boroughs for more than 500 years, and its appeal to those wishing to escape the more frenetic pace of life in zones 1 and 2 is still very much apparent. Chiswick, Richmond and Kew in particular offer an expensive slice of village life far removed from the crowds of central London. Twickenham is the home of English rugby while Hampton boasts what is arguable the most ambitious palace in the country. Wimbledon and its enormous common is another place for an afternoon idyll.

top picks

SOUTHWEST LONDON

- Buddhapadipa Temple (p213)
- Hampton Court Palace (p211)
- Kew Gardens (p209)
- The Thames (p209)
- London Wetland Centre (opposite)

FULHAM

Fulham and Parson's Green merge neatly into one neighbourhood that sits comfortably in a curve of the Thames between Chelsea and Hammersmith. While the attractive Victorian terraces and riverside location have drawn a very well-to-do crowd, Fulham's blue-collar roots are still evident in the strong tradition of support for Fulham Football Club.

FULHAM PALACE Map p205

☎ 7736 8140; www.fulhampalace.org; Bishop's Ave SW6; admission free; ☉ palace & museum noon-4pm Mon & Tue, 11am-2pm Sat, 11.30am-3.30pm Sun, garden dawn-dusk daily; ⊖ Putney Bridge; ☖

Summer home of the bishops of London from 704 to 1973, Fulham Palace is an interesting mix of architectural styles set in beautiful gardens and, until 1924, enclosed by the longest moat in England. The oldest part to survive is the little redbrick Tudor gateway, but the main building you see today dates from the mid-17th century and was remodelled in the 19th century. There's

a pretty walled garden and, detached from the main house, a Tudor Revival chapel designed by Butterfield in 1866.

You can learn about the history of the palace and its inhabitants in the palace museum. Guided tours (☎ 7736 3233; tickets £5; ☉ tours 2pm 2nd & 4th Sun, 3rd Tue), which depart a couple of times a month on Sunday, usually take in the Great Hall, the Victorian chapel, Bishop Sherlock's Room and the museum and last about 1¼ hours. The palace has been undergoing extensive refurbishments in recent years so there may be some changes in the tour.

The surrounding land, once totalling almost 15 hectares but now reduced to just over five, forms Bishop's Park, and consists of a shady promenade along the river, a bowling green, tennis courts, a rose garden, a café and even a paddling pond with fountain for cooling off in on a hot day.

PUTNEY & BARNES

Putney is best known as the starting point of the annual Oxford and Cambridge Boat Race (p192), held each spring. There are references to the race in the pubs and restaurants in the area and along the Thames Path. Barnes is less well known and more villagey in feel. Its former residents include author Henry Fielding.

The best way to approach Putney is to follow the signs from Putney Bridge tube station for the footbridge (which runs parallel to the rail track), admiring the gorgeous riverside houses, with their gardens fronting the Thames, and thereby avoiding the tatty High Street until the last minute. Alternatively, catch the train from Vauxhall or Waterloo to Putney or Barnes stations.

LONDON WETLAND CENTRE Map p205

☎ 8409 4400; www.wwt.org.uk; Queen Elizabeth's Walk SW13; adult/4-16yr/senior & student/family £7.95/4.50/6/19.95; ⏰ 9.30am-6pm Mar-Oct, 9.30am-5pm Nov-Feb, to 8pm Thu Jun-late Sep; ↔ Hammersmith then ▣ 283 (Duck Bus), 33, 72 or 209, or ▣ Barnes; ♿

One of Europe's largest inland wetland projects, this 43-hectare centre run by the Wildfowl & Wetlands Trust was transformed from four Victorian reservoirs in 2000 and attracts some 140 species of birds as well as 300 types of moths and butterflies. From the Visitor Centre and glassed-in Observa-

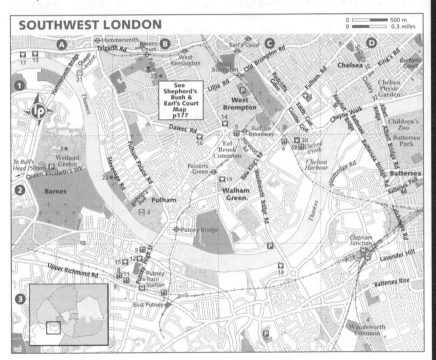

SOUTHWEST LONDON

tory overlooking the ponds, meandering paths and boardwalks lead visitors around the grounds, taking in the habitats of its many residents, including ducks, swans, geese and coots and the rarer bitterns, herons and kingfishers. There's even a large colony of parakeets, that may or may not be the descendants of caged pets. By no means miss the Peacock Tower, a three-storey hide on the main lake's eastern edge. Though there are half-a-dozen hides sprinkled elsewhere around the reserve, the tower is the mecca for the more serious birders, who will be happy to point out what they've spotted. Free daily tours, which are led by knowledgeable and enthusiastic staff members and are highly recommended, depart at 11am and 2pm daily.

CHISWICK

Notwithstanding the abomination of the A4 motorway, which cuts off the riverside roads from the centre, Chiswick (*chiz*-ick) is still a pleasant southwest London suburb that does not deserve the flak it gets for its well-heeled residents and unfeasibly grand mansions.

Chiswick High Rd itself is an upmarket yet uninspiring main drag, full of pubs and twee shops with the odd decent restaurant. There will be little to waylay you here, so best head straight over to the park and Chiswick House, up to Hogarth Lane and Hogarth House or down Church St to the riverfront.

CHISWICK HOUSE Map p64

☎ 8995 0508; www.english-heritage.org.uk; Chiswick Park, Burlington Lane W4; adult/child/senior & student £4.20/2.10/3.20; 10am-5pm Wed-Fri & Sun, to 2pm Sat Apr-Oct; Chiswick or Turnham Green;

This is a fine Palladian pavilion with an octagonal dome and colonnaded portico. It was designed by the third Earl of Burlington (1694–1753) when he returned from his grand tour of Italy, fired up with enthusiasm for all things Roman. Lord Burlington used it to entertain friends and to house his library and art collection.

Inside, some of the rooms are so grand as to be almost overpowering. The dome of the main salon has been left ungilded and the walls are decorated with eight enormous paintings. In the Blue Velvet Room look for the portrait of Inigo Jones, the architect much admired by Lord Burlington, over one of the doors. The ceiling paintings are by William Kent, who also decorated the Kensington Palace State Apartments.

Lord Burlington also planned the house's original gardens, now Chiswick Park surrounding the house, but they have been much altered since his time. The restored Cascade waterfall is bubbling again after being out of action for years.

The house is about a mile southwest of the Turnham Green tube station and 750m northeast of the Chiswick train station.

HOGARTH'S HOUSE Map p64

☎ 8994 6757; www.hounslow.info/hogarthshouse; Hogarth Lane W4; admission free; 1-5pm Tue-Fri, 1-6pm Sat & Sun Apr-Oct, 1-4pm Tue-Fri, 1-5pm Sat & Sun Nov, Dec, Feb & Mar; Turnham Green

Home between 1749 and 1764 to artist and social commentator William Hogarth, this house now showcases his caricatures and engravings, including such famous

THAMES PATH

The Thames Path National Trail is a long-distance trail stretching from the river's source at Thames Head near Kemble in the Cotswolds to the Thames Flood Barrier, a distance of some 184 miles. It's truly magnificent, particularly in its upper reaches, but tackling the entire course is for the truly ambitious (and indefatigable). The rest of us walk sections of it, such as the 16-mile section from Battersea to the barrier, which takes about takes about 6½ hours of waking). A much more manageable section for afternoon strollers, taking about 1½ hours, is the 4-mile one between Putney Bridge and Barnes Footbridge. The initial stretch along the Embankment that runs north from Putney Bridge on the southern bank of the river is always a hive of activity, with rowers setting off and returning to their boat clubs and punters from nearby pubs lazing by the water. The majority of the walk, though, is intensely rural – at times the only accompaniment is the call of songbirds and the gentle swish of old Father Thames (yes, we are still in London). From the footbridge Chiswick train station is about three quarters of a mile to the northwest.

Full details of these and other sections of the Thames Path can be found in Lonely Planet's *Walking in Britain* (3rd edition) or visit the National Trails (www.nationaltrail.co.uk/thamespath) website. Another useful source is the River Thames Alliance's Visit Thames (www.visitthames.co.uk) site.

OF RAKES & HARLOTS: HOGARTH'S WORLD

William Hogarth (1697–1764) was an artist and engraver who specialised in satire and what these days might be considered heavy-handed moralising on the wages of sin. His plates were so popular in his day that they were actually pirated, leading Parliament to pass the Hogarth Act of 1735 to protect copyright. They provide us with an invaluable look at life (particularly among the lowly) in Georgian London.

The *Marriage-à-la-Mode* series satirises the wantonness and marriage customs of the upper classes, while *Gin Lane* was produced as part of a campaign to have gin distillation made a crime (as it did under the Gin Act of 1751). It shows drunkards lolling about in the parish of St Giles in Soho, with the church of St George's Bloomsbury clearly visible in the background. His eight-plate series *A Harlot's Progress* traces the life of a simple woman from her arrival in London as country lass to convicted (and imprisoned) whore; some of the plates are set in Drury Lane. In *A Rake's Progress*, the debauched protagonist is seen at one stage being entertained in a Russell St tavern by a bevy of prostitutes, one of whom strokes his chest while the other relieves him of his pocket watch. The women's faces are covered with up to a half-dozen artificial beauty marks, which were all the rage at the time.

Hogarth's works can also be seen at Hogarth's House as well as the National Gallery, Tate Britain and in Sir John Soane's Museum in Holborn, which owns the original of *A Rake's Progress*.

works as the haunting *Gin Lane, Marriage-à-la-mode* and a copy of *A Rake's Progress* (see the boxed text, above). Here you'll also find the private engravings *Before* and *After* (1730), commissioned by the Duke of Montagu and bearing Aristotle's immortal aphorism *Omne Animal Post Coitum Triste* (Every creature is sad after intercourse). Although the house and grounds are attractive, very little original furniture remains so this is really a destination for ardent Hogarth fans.

FULLER'S GRIFFIN BREWERY Map p64
☎ 8996 2063; www.fullers.co.uk; Chiswick Lane South W4; adult/14-18yr (no tasting) £6/4.50; ⏱ tours 11am, noon, 1pm & 2pm Mon & Wed-Fri; ⊖ Turnham Green or ⓡ Chiswick
Of interest to anyone who enjoys bitter and/or wants to see it being made and/or would like to engage in a comprehensive tasting session, Fuller's is now the last working brewery extant in London. You can visit only on the 1½-hour guided tour, which must be booked in advance by phone.

RICHMOND

If anywhere in London could be described as a village, Richmond – with its delightful green and riverside vistas – is it. Centuries of history, some stunning Georgian architecture and the graceful curve of the Thames has made this one of London's swankiest locales, home to ageing rock stars and city high-flyers alike.

Richmond was originally named Sheen, but Henry VII, having fallen in love with the place, renamed the village after his Yorkshire earldom. This started centuries of royal association with the area; the most famous local, Henry VIII, acquired nearby Hampton Court Palace from Cardinal Wolsey after the latter's fall from grace in 1529, while his daughter Elizabeth I died here in 1603.

RICHMOND GREEN Map p208
A short walk west of the Quadrant where you'll emerge from the tube is the enormous open space of Richmond Green with its mansions and delightful pubs. Crossing the green diagonally will take you to what remains of Richmond Palace, just the main entrance and redbrick gatehouse, built in 1501. You can see Henry VII's arms above the main gate: he built the Tudor additions to the edifice, although the palace had been in use as a royal residence since 1125.

RICHMOND PARK Map p208
☎ 8948 3209; www.royalparks.gov.uk; admission free; ⏱ 7am-dusk Mar-Sep, from 7.30am Oct-Feb; ⊖ / ⓡ Richmond, then ⌷ 65 or 371
At just over 1000 hectares (the largest urban parkland in Europe), Richmond Park offers everything from formal gardens and ancient oaks to unsurpassed views of central London 12 miles away. It's easy enough to escape the several roads that cut up the rambling wilderness, making the park an excellent spot for a quiet walk or picnic, even in summer when Richmond's riverside can be heaving. Such is the magic of the place, it somehow comes as no surprise to happen upon herds of more than 600 red and fallow deer basking under the trees. Be advised that the creatures can be less

SOUTHWEST LONDON: RICHMOND

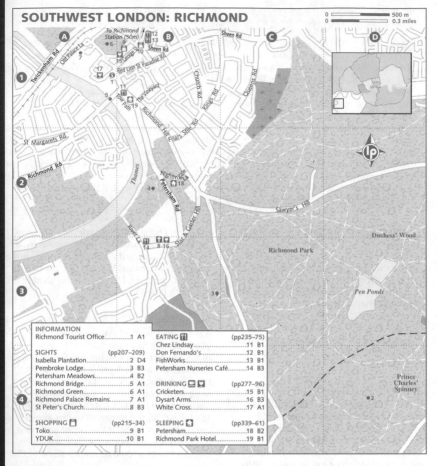

INFORMATION	
Richmond Tourist Office..............1 A1	

SIGHTS	(pp207–209)
Isabella Plantation.....................2 D4	
Pembroke Lodge.......................3 B3	
Petersham Meadows..................4 B2	
Richmond Bridge......................5 A1	
Richmond Green.......................6 A1	
Richmond Palace Remains.........7 A1	
St Peter's Church......................8 B3	

SHOPPING	(pp215–34)
Toko..9 B1	
YDUK.....................................10 B1	

EATING	(pp235–75)
Chez Lindsay...........................11 B1	
Don Fernando's........................12 B1	
FishWorks...............................13 B1	
Petersham Nurseries Café.........14 B3	

DRINKING	(pp277–96)
Cricketers................................15 B1	
Dysart Arms.............................16 B3	
White Cross.............................17 A1	

SLEEPING	(pp339–61)
Petersham..............................18 B2	
Richmond Park Hotel...............19 B1	

than docile in rutting season (May to July) and when the does bear young (September and October). It's a great place for bird-watchers too, with a wide range of habitats, from neat gardens to woodland and assorted ponds.

Coming from Richmond, it's easiest to enter via Richmond Gate or from Petersham Rd. Take a map with you and wander around the grounds; flower-lovers should make a special trip to Isabella Plantation, a stunning woodland garden created after WWII, in April and May when the rhododendrons and azaleas are in bloom.

Pembroke Lodge (10am-5.30pm summer, to 4.30pm winter), the childhood home of Bertrand Russell, is now a café set in a beautiful 13-hectare garden and affording great views of the city from the back terrace.

ST PETER'S CHURCH Map p208

☎ 8940 8435; Church Lane, Petersham TW10; admission free; 3-5pm Sun; / Richmond, then 65

This wonderful Norman church has been a place of worship for 1300 years and parts of the present structure date from 1266. It's a fascinating place, not least for its curious Georgian box pews, which local landowners would rent while the serving staff and labourers sat in the open seats in the south transept. Against the north wall of the chancel is the Cole Monument, which depicts barrister George Cole, his wife and child, all reclining in Elizabethan dress – an unusual design for an English church. Of interest to Canadians, St Peter's is the burial place of Captain George Vancouver, who was laid to rest here in 1798; his simple tomb is on the southern boundary wall of the cemetery.

THE THAMES

The stretch of the riverbank from Twickenham Bridge down to Petersham and Ham is one of the prettiest in London. The action is concentrated around Richmond Bridge, an original structure from 1777 and London's oldest surviving crossing, only widened for traffic in 1937. The lovely walk to Petersham is often overcrowded in nice weather; best to cut across Petersham Meadows and continue on to Richmond Park if it's peace and quiet you seek. There are several companies near Richmond Bridge, including Richmond Boat Hire (☎ 8948 8270), that offer skiff hire (adult/child £4/2 per hour, £12/6 per day).

HAM HOUSE Map p64
☎ 8940 1950; www.nationaltrust.org.uk; Ham St, Ham TW10; adult/5-15yr/family £9/5/22, gardens only £3/2/7; ✆ house 1-5pm Mon-Wed, Sat & Sun late Mar-Oct, gardens 11am-6pm Mon-Wed, Sat & Sun; ⊖ / ⊠ Richmond, then ⊟ 371; ⧖
Known as 'Hampton Court in miniature', Ham House was built in 1610 and became home to the first Earl of Dysart, an unlucky individual who had been employed as 'whipping boy' to Charles I, taking the punishment for all the king's wrongdoings. Inside it's furnished with all the grandeur you might expect; the Great Staircase is a magnificent example of Stuart woodworking. Look out for ceiling paintings by Antonio Verrio, who also worked at Hampton Court Palace, and for a miniature of Elizabeth I by Nicholas Hilliard. Other notable paintings are by Constable and Reynolds. The grounds of Ham House slope down to the Thames, but there are also pleasant 17th-century formal gardens. Just opposite the Thames and accessible by small ferry is Marble Hill Park and its splendid mansion. There is partial disabled access. Call for more information.

KEW & BRENTFORD

Kew will be forever associated with World Heritage–listed Botanic Gardens, headquarters of the Royal Botanical Society and boasting one of the world's finest plant collections. A day at Kew Gardens will appeal even to those with no knowledge of plants and flowers. This smart Southwest London suburb is also a pleasant place for an idle wander; watch out for cricket matches played on central Kew Green in summer.

Across a mighty bend in the Thames is Brentford, essentially nondescript except for sprawling Syon Park and its magnificent house.

KEW GARDENS Map p64
☎ 8332 5655; www.kew.org; Kew Rd TW9; adult/under 17yr/senior & student £12.25/free/10.25; ✆ gardens 9.30am-6.30pm Mon-Fri, to 7.30pm Sat & Sun Apr-Aug, 9.30am-6pm Sep & Oct, 9.30am-4.15pm Nov-Feb, glasshouses 9.30am-5.30pm April-Oct, 9.30am-3.45pm Nov-Feb; ⊖ / ⊠ Kew Gardens; ⧖
Royal Botanic Gardens at Kew is one of the most popular visitors' attractions in London, which means it can get very crowded during summer, especially at weekends. Spring is probably the best time to visit, but at any time of year this 120-hectare expanse of lawns, formal gardens and greenhouses has delights to offer. As well as being a public garden, Kew is an important research centre, and it maintains its reputation as the most exhaustive botanical collection in the world.

Its wonderful plants and trees aside, Kew has several specific sights within its borders. Assuming you come by tube and enter via Victoria Gate, you'll come almost immediately to a large pond overlooked by the enormous Palm House, a hothouse of metal and curved sheets of glass dating from 1848 and housing all sorts of exotic tropical greenery; the aerial walkway offers a birds'-eye view of the lush vegetation. Just northwest of the Palm House is the tiny but irresistible Water Lily House (✆ Mar-Dec), dating from 1852 and the hottest glasshouse at Kew.

Further north is the stunning Princess of Wales Conservatory, opened in 1987 and housing plants in 10 different computer-controlled climatic zones – everything from a desert to a mangrove swamp. In the tropical zone you'll find the most famous of Kew's 38,000-odd plant species, the 3m-tall *titan arum*, or 'corpse flower', which is overpoweringly obnoxious-smelling when it blooms in April. Just beyond the conservatory is Kew Gardens Gallery bordering Kew Green, which houses exhibitions of paintings and photos mostly of a horticultural theme.

Heading westwards from the gallery you'll arrive at the redbrick Kew Palace (adult/under 17yr/senior & student £5/2.50/4; 10am-5.30pm late Mar-late Oct), a former royal residence once known as Dutch House and built in 1631. It was the favourite home of George III and his family; his wife, Queen Charlotte, died here in 1818. The palace underwent extensive renovations for almost a decade and reopened in 2006; don't miss the Georgian rooms restored to how they would look in 1804 and Princess Elizabeth's wonderful doll's house.

Other highlights include the Temperate House, the world's largest ornamental glasshouse, and nearby Evolution House, tracing plant evolution over 3500 million years; the idyllic Queen Charlotte's Cottage (10am-4pm Sat & Sun Jul & Aug) was another place popular with 'mad' George III and his wife. Don't forget to see the Japanese Gateway and the celebrated 10-storey Pagoda (1761), designed by William Chambers.

Just north is the Marianne North Gallery featuring paintings on a botanical theme. Marianne North was one of those indomitable Victorian female travellers who roamed the continents from 1871 to 1885, painting plants and trees along the way. The results of her labour now cover the walls of this small purpose-built gallery. The Orangery near Kew Palace contains a restaurant, café and shop.

If you want a good overview of the gardens, jump aboard the Kew Explorer minitrain (adult/under 17yr £3.50/1), which allows you to hop on and off at stops along the way. The full circuit takes about 40 minutes.

You can get to Kew Gardens by tube or train. Come out of the station and walk straight (west) along Station Ave, cross Kew Gardens Rd and then continue straight along Lichfield Rd. This will bring you to Victoria Gate. Alternatively, from April to October, boats run by the Westminster Passenger Services Association (7930 2062; www .wpsa.co.uk) sail from Westminster Pier to Kew Gardens up to four times a day (see p387).

SYON HOUSE Map p64

 8560 0881; www.syonpark.co.uk; Syon Park, Brentford TW7; adult/5-16yr/student & senior/family £8/4/7/18, gardens only adult/concession/family £4/2.50/9; 11am-5pm Wed, Thu & Sun late Mar-Oct, gardens 10.30am-4pm or 5pm; Gunnersbury or Gunnersbury, then 237 or 267

Just across the Thames from Kew Gardens, Syon House started life as a medieval abbey named after Mt Zion, but in 1542 Henry VIII dissolved the order of Bridgettine nuns who were peacefully established here and had the abbey rebuilt into a handsome residence. (In 1547, they say, God got his revenge when Henry's coffin was brought to Syon en route to Windsor for burial and burst open during the night, leaving the king's body to be set upon by the estate's hungry dogs.)

The house from where Lady Jane Grey ascended the throne for her nine-day reign in 1553 was remodelled in the neoclassical style by Robert Adam in the 18th century and has plenty of Adam furniture and oak panelling. The interior was designed along gender-specific lines, with pastel pinks and purples for the ladies' gallery, and mock Roman sculptures for the men's dining room. The estate's 16-hectare gardens, including a lake and the landmark Great Conservatory (1820), were landscaped by Capability Brown. Syon Park is filled with all kinds of attractions for children, including an adventure playground, aquatic park and trout fishery.

TWICKENHAM

As Wimbledon is to tennis, so Twickenham is to rugby, and you'll find one of the few museums in the world devoted to the sport here. Otherwise there's not much to detain you in this quiet and pretty Middlesex suburb aside from the delights of fine Marble Hill House overlooking the Thames.

MUSEUM OF RUGBY Map p64

 0870 405 2001; www.rfu.com/microsites/museum/index.cfm; Twickenham Stadium, Rugby Rd TW1; stadium guided tour & museum adult/child/family £10/7/34, museum only on match days (match ticket holders only) £3; 10am-5pm Tue-Sat, 11am-5pm Sun; Hounslow East, then 281, or Twickenham;

This museum, which will clearly appeal only to rugby-lovers, is tucked behind the eastern stand of the stadium. Relive highlights of old matches in the video theatre, take a tour of the grounds and visit the museum collection. Tours depart at 10.30am, noon, 1.30pm and 3pm Tuesday to Saturday and at 1pm and 3pm on Sunday. NB: there are no tours on match days. The museum itself is very rich, exhibiting or storing some 10,000 items related to the sport.

MARBLE HILL HOUSE Map p64

☎ 8892 5115; www.english-heritage.org.uk; Richmond Rd TW1; adult/under 15yr/senior & student £4.20/2.10/3.20; ⌚ 10am-2pm Sat, to 5pm Sun, guided tours noon & 3pm Tue & Wed Apr-Oct; ⍙ St Margaret's, Richmond; ♿

This is an 18th-century Palladian love nest, originally built for George II's mistress Henrietta Howard and later occupied by Mrs Fitzherbert, the secret wife of George IV. The poet Alexander Pope had a hand in designing the park, which stretches down to the Thames. Inside you'll find an exhibition about the life and times of Henrietta, and a collection of early-Georgian furniture.

To get there from St Margaret's station, turn right along St Margaret's Rd. Then take the right fork along Crown Rd and turn left along Richmond Rd. Turn right along Beaufort Rd and walk across Marble Hill Park to the house. It is also easily accessible by pedestrian ferry from Ham House (p209). It's a 25-minute walk from Richmond station.

There is partial disabled access. Call for more information.

HAMPTON

Out in London's southwestern outskirts, the wonderful Hampton Court Palace is pressed up against 445-hectare Bushy Park (www.royalparks .gov.uk), a semiwild expanse with herds of red and fallow deer.

HAMPTON COURT PALACE

☎ 0870 751 5175; www.hrp.org.uk/Hampton CourtPalace; Hampton Court Rd, East Molesey KT8; all-inclusive ticket adult/5-15yr/senior & student/ family £13/6.50/10.50/36; ⌚ 10am-6pm late March-Oct, to 4.30pm Nov-late Mar; ⍙ Hampton Court; ♿

London's most spectacular Tudor palace is the 16th-century Hampton Court Palace, located in the city's suburbs and easily reached by train from Waterloo Station. Here history is palpable, from the kitchens where you can see food being prepared and the grand living quarters of Henry VIII to the spectacular gardens complete with a 300-year-old maze. This is one of the best days out London has to offer and should not be missed by anyone with any interest in British history. Set aside plenty of time

to do it justice, bearing in mind that if you come by boat from central London the trip will have already eaten up half the day.

Like so many royal residences, Hampton Court Palace was not built for the monarchy at all. In 1515 Cardinal Thomas Wolsey, Lord Chancellor of England, built himself a palace in keeping with his sense of self-importance. Unfortunately, even Wolsey couldn't persuade the pope to grant Henry VIII a divorce from Catherine of Aragon and relations between king and chancellor soured. Against that background, you only need to take one look at the palace to understand why Wolsey felt obliged to present it to Henry, a monarch not too fond of anyone trying to muscle in on his mastery, some 15 years later. The hapless Wolsey was charged with high treason but died before he could come to trial in 1530.

As soon as he acquired the palace, Henry set to work expanding it, adding the Great Hall, the exquisite Chapel Royal and the sprawling kitchens. By 1540 this was one of the grandest and most sophisticated palaces in Europe, but Henry only spent an average three weeks a year here. In the late 17th century, William and Mary employed Sir Christopher Wren to build extensions. The result is a beautiful blend of Tudor and 'restrained baroque' architecture.

Tickets are on sale in the shop to the left as you walk up the path towards the main Trophy Gate. Be sure to pick up a leaflet listing the daily program, which will help you plan your visit. This is important as some of the free guided tours require advance booking.

Passing through the main gate you arrive first in the Base Court and then the Clock Court, named after the fine 16th-century astronomical clock that still shows the sun revolving round the earth. The second court is your starting point; from here you can follow any or all of the six separate sets of rooms in the complex. Here behind the colonnade you'll also find the useful Introductory Exhibition, explaining what's where and how the compound functions.

The stairs inside Anne Boleyn's Gateway lead up to Henry VIII's State Apartments, including the Great Hall, the largest single room in the palace, decorated with tapestries and what is considered the country's best hammer-beam roof. The Horn Room, hung with impressive antlers, leads to the Great Watching Chamber where guards controlled access to the king. Leading off from the chamber is the smaller Pages' Chamber and the Haunted Gallery. Arrested for adultery and detained in the palace in 1542, Henry's fifth wife Catherine Howard managed to evade her guards and ran screaming down the corridor in search of the king. Her woeful ghost is said to do the same thing to this day.

Further along the corridor you'll come to the beautiful Chapel Royal, built in just nine months and still a place of worship after 450 years. The blue-and-gold vaulted ceiling was originally intended for Christ Church, Oxford, but was installed here instead, while the 18th-century reredos was carved by Grinling Gibbons.

Also dating from Henry's day are the delightful Tudor kitchens, again accessible from Anne Boleyn's Gateway and originally able to rustle up meals for a royal household of some 1200 people. The kitchens have been fitted out to look as they might have done in Tudor days and palace 'servants' turn the spits, stuff the peacocks and frost the marzipan with real gold leaf. Don't miss the Great Wine Cellar, which handled the 300 barrels each of ale and wine consumed here annually in the mid-16th century.

To the west of the colonnade in the Clock Court is the entrance up to the Wolsey Rooms and the Young Henry VIII Exhibition. To the east of the colonnade you'll find the stairs up the King's Apartments, completed by Wren for William III in 1702. A tour of the apartments takes you up the grand King's Staircase, painted by Antonio Verrio in about 1700 and flattering the king by comparing him to Alexander the Great. Highlights here include the King's Presence Chamber, which is dominated by a throne backed with scarlet hangings. The King's Great Bedchamber, with a bed topped with ostrich plumes and the King's Closet (where His Majesty's toilet has a velvet seat) should also not be missed.

William's wife, Mary II, had her own separate Queen's State Apartments, which are accessible up the Queen's Staircase, decorated by William Kent. When Mary died in 1694, work on these rooms was incomplete; they were finished during the reign of George II. The rooms are shown as they might have been when Queen Caroline used them for entertaining between 1716 and 1737. In comparison with the King's Apartments, those for the queen seem rather austere, although the Queen's Audience Chamber has a throne as imposing as that of the king.

Also worth seeing are the Georgian Rooms used by George II and Queen Caroline on the court's last visit to the palace in 1737. The first rooms you come to were designed to accommodate George's second son, the Duke of Cumberland, whose bed is woefully tiny for its grand surroundings. In the Cartoon Gallery, the real Raphael Cartoons (now in the Victoria & Albert Museum; p139) used to hang; nowadays you have to make do with late-17th-century copies.

Beyond the Cartoon Gallery are the Queen's Private Apartments: her drawing room and bedchamber, where she and the king would sleep if they wanted to be alone. Particularly interesting are the Queen's Bathroom, with its tub set on a floor cloth to soak up any spillage, and the Oratory, an attractive room with its exquisite 16th-century Persian carpet.

Once you're finished with the palace interior there are still the wonderful gardens to appreciate. Carriage rides for up to five people around the gardens are available; they cost £10 and last 20 minutes. Look out for the Real Tennis Court, dating from the 1620s and designed for real tennis, a rather different version of the game from that played today. In the restored 24-hectare Riverside Gardens, you'll find the Great Vine. Planted in 1768, it's still producing just under 320kg of grapes per year; it's an old vine, no doubt about it, but not the world's oldest, as they say it is here (that one is in Slovenia). The Lower Orangery in the gardens houses Andrea Mantegna's nine *Triumphs of Caesar* paintings, bought by Charles I in 1629; the Banqueting House was designed for William III and painted by Antonio Verrio. Look out, too, for the iron screens designed by Jean Tijou.

No-one should leave Hampton Court without losing themselves in the famous (and recently renovated) 800m-long maze, which is made up of hornbeam and yew and planted in 1690. The average visitor takes 20 minutes to reach the centre. The maze is included in entry, although those not visiting the palace can enter the maze for £3.50 (£2/10 for children/families). Last admission is at 5.15pm in summer and 3.45pm in winter.

There are trains every half-hour from Waterloo direct to Hampton Court station (30 minutes), from where it's a three-minute walk to the palace entrance. The palace can also be reached from Westminster Pier in central London twice daily on riverboats operated by Westminster Passenger Services Association (☎ 7930 2062; www.wpsa.co.uk) from April to October. This is a great trip if the weather is good, but be aware that it takes three hours. For details see p387.

WIMBLEDON

For a few weeks each June the sporting world's attention is fixed on the quiet southern suburb of Wimbledon, as it has been since 1877 (see p328). Then the circus leaves town and Wimbledon returns to unremarkable normality. That said, it's a pleasant little place, and the Wimbledon Lawn Tennis Museum will excite any tennis fan, even in darkest December.

WIMBLEDON COMMON

www.wpcc.org.uk; ⊖ Wimbledon, then ☐ 93
Running on into Putney Heath, Wimbledon Common covers 460 hectares of South London and is a wonderful expanse of open space for walking, nature trailing and picnicking. There are a few specific sights on Wimbledon Common, however, including Wimbledon Windmill (☎ 8947 2825; www.wimbledon windmillmuseum.org.uk; Windmill Rd SW19; adult/child £1/50p; ☒ 2 5pm Sat, 11am 5pm Sun late Mar-Oct; ⊖ Wimbledon), a fine smock mill (ie octagonal-shaped with sloping weatherboarded sides) dating from 1817 which now contains a museum with working models on the history of windmills and milling. It was during a stay in the mill in 1908 that Robert Baden-Powell was inspired to write parts of his *Scouting for Boys*.

On the southern side of the common, the misnamed Caesar's Camp is what's left of a roughly circular earthen fort built in the 5th century BC, which proves that Wimbledon was settled before Roman times.

WIMBLEDON LAWN TENNIS MUSEUM

☎ 8946 6131; www.wimbledon.org; Gate 3, Church Rd SW19; adult/child/concession £8.50/4.75/7.50, museum & tour £14.50/11/13; ☒ 10.30am-5pm, spectators only during championships; ⊖ Wimbledon, then ☐ 93
This museum is of specialist interest, dwelling as it does on the minutiae of the history of tennis playing, traced back here to the invention of the all-important lawnmower

in 1830 and of the India-rubber ball in the 1850s. It's a state-of-the-art presentation, with plenty of video clips to let fans of the game relive their favourite moments. The museum houses a tearoom and a shop selling all kinds of tennis memorabilia.

BUDDHAPADIPA TEMPLE

☎ 8946 1357; www.buddhapadipa.org; 14 Calonne Rd SW19; admission free; ☒ temple 1-6pm Sat, 8.30-10.30am & 12.30-6pm Sun, grounds 8am-9.30pm summer, to 6pm winter; ⊖ Wimbledon, then ☐ 93
A surprising sight in a residential neighbourhood half a mile from Wimbledon Village, this is as authentic a Thai temple as ever graced this side of Bangkok. The Buddhapadipa Temple was built by an association of young Buddhists in Britain and opened in 1982. The *wat* (temple compound) boasts a *bot* (consecrated chapel) decorated with traditional scenes by two leading Thai artists. Remember to take your shoes off before entering.

To get to the temple take the tube or train to Wimbledon and then bus 93 up to Wimbledon Parkside. Calonne Rd leads off it on the right.

RICHMOND WALK
Walking Tour
1 Richmond Green

With its lovely houses and crowds of families playing ball games, it's easy to imagine this beautiful stretch of grass as the site of jousting contests during the Middle Ages. The path across the green (p207) takes you to the meagre remains of Richmond Palace, where Queen Elizabeth I spent her final years.

2 Richmond Bridge

London's oldest river crossing still in use and dating back to 1777, this five-span masonry bridge (p209) gracefully curves over the Thames towards Twickenham. Just before it, along one of the loveliest stretches of the Thames, is tiny Corporation Island, which has been colonised by flocks of feral parakeets (see London Wetland Centre, p205).

3 Petersham Meadows

These meadows fronting the Thames and at the foot of Richmond Hill are still grazed by cows. At the southern end is St Peter's Church (p208), a Saxon place of worship since the 8th

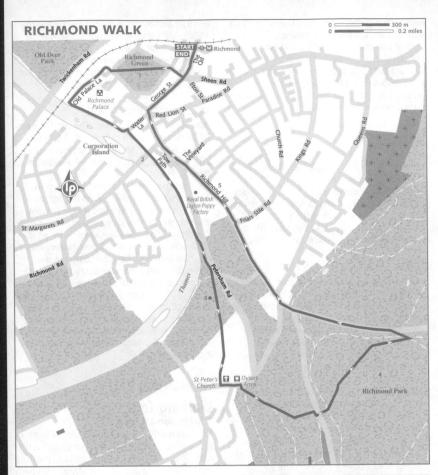

RICHMOND WALK

century, which contains an unusually laid out Georgian interior.

4 Richmond Park

Petersham Gate leads to London's most sumptuous green space. Established by Edward I in the 13th century, this royal park (p207) has changed little since that time. There are unbroken views to the centre of London.

5 Richmond Hill

The view from the top of Richmond Hill has inspired painters and poets for centuries and still beguiles. It is the only view – which includes St Paul's Cathedral about 10 miles way – in the country to be protected by an act of Parliament.

WALK FACTS

Start Richmond tube station
End Richmond tube station
Distance 2.5 miles
Duration About two hours
Fuel stop Dysart Arms (p296)

6 Royal British Legion Poppy Factory

This rather unusual factory (☎ 8940 3305; www .britishlegion.org.uk; 20 Petersham Rd TW10; admission free; ⏰ tours 10am Mon-Fri, 1.30pm Mon-Thu) turns out 34 million poppies and 107,000 wreaths and sprays that are worn and displayed on Remembrance Day (11 November) each year. Guided tours (only) take about two hours.

BLUELIST[1] (blu͵list) *v.*
to recommend a travel experience.
What's your recommendation? www.lonelyplanet.com/bluelist

SHOPPING

top picks

- Apple Store (p218)
- Minamoto Kitchoan (p222)
- Aram (p222)
- Harrods (p226)
- Labour & Wait (p228)
- Rosslyn Delicatessen (p229)
- Vivienne Westwood (p221)
- Selfridges (p220)
- Tatty Devine (p229)
- Urban Outfitters (p221)

SHOPPING

Shopping is a major part of many Londoners' lives. The city has around 30,000 shops, both chain and independent, and a massive variety – from the clever High-Street fashion of Topshop (p221) to the luxurious delights of Harrods (p226), and the cutting-edge clothes from young designers at Spitalfields Market (p227) to the antiques of Portobello (p232). In fact, shopping has become such a preoccupation that there are frequent news stories of shoppers queuing at 4am for a certain product, camping outside department stores for Christmas sales (a long-standing London tradition), beating each other to get to a pair of cheap pants, or trampling shop-assistants on their way to the latest designer-endorsed clothes lines on the High Street. So, you may ask, what's the fuss about?

London's main attractions are sheer variety and shopping opportunities. The big-name emporiums, such as Selfridges, Harvey Nichols, Hamleys, Fortnum & Mason and Liberty, are both sightseeing attractions in their own right and temples to shopping devotees; the side-street boutiques – the capital's true delights – also sell just about anything, from clothes to old-style British homeware. Despite the fact that High-Street chains are progressively taking over more and more of the city, funky street-wear outlets in places such as Hoxton, Brick Lane and Spitalfields continue to thrive, and there are signs that after years of the rule of cheap High-Street fashion, Londoners are increasingly returning to the charm of individual design and décor.

If you're in the market for something a little more exclusive and expensive, New Bond St and around are laden with designer shops, and a whole host of hot young British designers, such as Stella McCartney and Matthew Williamson, maintain lavish outlets where admiring the setting is an integral part of the experience. You'll probably be familiar with classic British brands such as Burberry, Mulberry and Pringle, which have radically reinvented themselves and become part of high fashion.

But perhaps fashion is not your obsession? Worry not, the British capital has just about anything on sale, from handmade umbrellas to technology or exotic foodstuffs. Check out the comprehensive retail catalogue *Time Out Shopping Guide* (£9.99).

The strong pound and the high cost of living might keep London from ever being a bargain, but its sheer array is irresistible. In short, no trip to the English capital would be complete without a shopping interlude. Bring your credit card.

OPENING HOURS

The good news is that you can go shopping every day of the week. The bad news is that this is not universally true throughout the city.

Generally, shops open from 9am or 10am to about 6pm or 6.30pm Monday to Saturday, at least. Shops in the West End (Oxford St, Soho and Covent Garden) open late (to 9pm) on Thursday; those in Chelsea, Knightsbridge and Kensington open late on Wednesday.

In the West End and in Chelsea, Knightsbridge and Kensington, many shops are also open on Sunday, typically from noon to 6pm but sometimes 10am to 4pm. Sunday trading is also common in Greenwich and Hampstead and along Edgware and Tottenham Court Rds.

Because the Square Mile, or the City of London, does most of its business during the week, most shops in this area open only Monday to Friday. Additionally, smaller designer stores tend to keep hours to suit their owners,

opening later in the morning and often closing on a Monday or Tuesday to stay open on weekends. It's a good idea to ring ahead, as these places often have last-minute changes.

If there's a major market on a certain day – say, Columbia Road Flower Market on a Sunday morning – it's a good bet that neighbouring stores will fling open their doors.

THE WEST END

We're not sure the West End's shopping needs introducing. This is the very area where you can spend your salary on a pair of shoes or a handbag, and the tills turn over the GDP of a small country. Oxford St is heaven or hell, depending on your shopping stamina: it is *the* quintessential High Street and brimming with an ocean of people most of the day. It can be a nightmare to tackle, so if you want to shop here, focus on what you want – you might find that strolling is more stressful than is warranted. Covent Garden is better thanks to its smaller-size High-Street outlets and little side-street boutiques. It throbs with shoppers on weekends, but is less hectic than Oxford St. Carnaby St and Newburgh Sts, and the independent boutique-laden Kingly Ct, are excellent for fashion – vintage and designer. Soho is superb for music stores (see the boxed text, p225), and Charing Cross Rd for books. You'll find excellent electronics and computer shops along Tottenham Court Rd (Map p68).

Just minutes from Oxford St is Marylebone 'village', whose High Street is a miraculously calm and stylish strip. A weekly farmers' market (Map p100; 10am-2pm Sun) is held in the nearby Cramer St car park, behind Waitrose.

BBC WORLD SERVICE SHOP
Map pp72–3   Books
☎ 7557 2576; www.bbcshop.com; Bush House, Strand WC2; ⊖ Holborn or Temple
All the wonderful episodes of *Planet Earth* or gross hilarity of *Little Britain* are available here, as well as British film and TV classics.

CLOTHING SIZES

Women's clothing

Aus/UK	8	10	12	14	16	18
Europe	36	38	40	42	44	46
Japan	5	7	9	11	13	15
USA	6	8	10	12	14	16

Women's shoes

Aus/USA	5	6	7	8	9	10
Europe	35	36	37	38	39	40
France only	35	36	38	39	40	42
Japan	22	23	24	25	26	27
UK	3½	4½	5½	6½	7½	8½

Men's clothing

Aus	92	96	100	104	108	112
Europe	46	48	50	52	54	56
Japan	S		M	M		L
UK/USA	35	36	37	38	39	40

Men's shirts (collar sizes)

Aus/Japan	38	39	40	41	42	43
Europe	38	39	40	41	42	43
UK/USA	15	15½	16	16½	17	17½

Men's shoes

Aus/UK	7	8	9	10	11	12
Europe	41	42	43	44½	46	47
Japan	26	27	27½	28	29	30
USA	7½	8½	9½	10½	11½	12½

Measurements approximate only, try before you buy

BLACKWELL'S Map pp72–3   Books
☎ 7292 5100; www.bookshop.blackwell.co.uk; 100 Charing Cross Rd WC2; ⊖ Tottenham Court Rd
Once a specialist in academic titles, this has now branched out into travel and other general-interest books. It is still, however, the favourite haunt for those hunting for academic textbooks and it's perfect for anyone starting a new course.

BORDERS Map p68   Books
☎ 7292 1600; www.borders.co.uk; 203 Oxford St; ⊖ Oxford Circus
This is one of London's bigger bookshop chains, with five floors of books, magazines and newspapers from around the world, plus CDs, tapes and DVDs.

DAUNT BOOKS Map p100   Books
☎ 7224 2295; www.dauntbooks.co.uk; 83-84 Marylebone High St W1; ⊖ Baker St
An original Edwardian bookshop, with oak panels and gorgeous skylights, Daunt is one of London's loveliest travel bookstores. It has two floors and the ground level is stacked with fiction and nonfiction titles; the lower ground is where to head if you're travel focused.

FORBIDDEN PLANET MEGASTORE
Map pp72–3   Books
☎ 7836 4179; www.forbiddenplanet.com; 179 Shaftesbury Ave WC1; ⊖ Leicester Sq or Tottenham Court Rd
A massive trove of comics, sci-fi, horror and fantasy literature, this is an absolute dream for anyone into Manga comics or off-beat genre titles.

FOYLE'S Map p68   Books
☎ 7437 5660; www.foyles.co.uk; 113-119 Charing Cross Rd WC2; ⊖ Tottenham Court Rd
London's best and most legendary book-shop, where you can bet on finding even the most obscure of titles. Music store and lovely café at Ray's Jazz Shop (see the boxed text, p225) are on the 1st floor.

GOSH! Map pp72–3   Books
☎ 7636 1011; www.goshlondon.com; 39 Great Russell St WC1; ⊖ Tottenham Court Rd
Draw up here for graphic novels, manga, newspaper-strip collections and children's books such as the Tin Tin and Asterix series.

TAXES & REFUNDS

In certain circumstances visitors from non-EU countries are entitled to claim back the 17.5% value-added tax (VAT) they have paid on purchased goods. The rebate only applies to items purchased in stores displaying a 'tax free' sign (there are plenty of these along Bond St). To claim it, visitors must be staying in the UK for less than six months.

The procedure to follow is relatively simple: don't forget to pick up the relevant form in the shop at the time of sale, and then hand it in at the airport when you leave. For details on getting your tax back, see p392.

It's also perfect for finding presents for children and teenagers.

GRANT & CUTLER Map p68 — Books
☎ 7734 2012; www.grantandcutler.com; 55-57 Great Marlborough St W1; ⊖ Oxford Circus
This is London's best-stocked foreign-language bookshop, running the gamut from Arabic to Zulu. However, sometimes staff aren't as knowledgeable as you'd hope in recommending specific books.

LONDON REVIEW BOOKSHOP
Map pp72–3 — Books
☎ 7269 9030; www.lrb.co.uk; 14 Bury Pl WC1; ⊖ Russell Sq
The bookshop of *London Review of Books* lit magazine doesn't believe in piles of books, taking the clever approach of stocking wide-ranging titles in one or two copies only. It often hosts high-profile author talks.

MURDER ONE Map pp72–3 — Books
☎ 7734 3485; www.murderone.co.uk; 76-78 Charing Cross Rd WC2; ⊖ Leicester Sq
Crime fiction from the likes of Harlan Coben, Carl Hiaasen, Elmore Leonard and Alexander McCall Smith join true crime, Sherlock Holmes and romances (including Mills & Boons), with a (freaky) Sherlock mannequin greeting you from the shop window.

STANFORD'S Map pp72–3 — Books
☎ 7836 1321; www.stanfords.co.uk; 12-14 Long Acre WC2; ⊖ Leicester Sq or Covent Garden
As a 150-year-old seller of maps, guides and literature, the granddaddy of travel

bookstores is a destination in its own right. Ernest Shackleton, David Livingstone, Michael Palin and even Brad Pitt have all popped in here.

WATERSTONE'S Map p68 — Books
☎ 7851 2400; www.waterstones.co.uk; 203-206 Piccadilly W1; ⊖ Piccadilly Circus
The chain's megastore is the biggest bookshop in Europe, boasting knowledgeable staff and regular author readings. This is London's biggest Waterstone's, with four floors of titles, a café in the basement and a nice rooftop bar.

APPLE STORE Map p68 — Computers
☎ 7153 9000; www.apple.com/uk/retail/regent street; 235 Regent St W1; ☉ 10am-9pm Mon-Sat, noon-6pm Sun; ⊖ Oxford Circus
Mac geeks of the world unite! Here's your temple, your winter fireplace, so come and warm your faces on the soft glow emanating from MacBooks and iPods, laptops and desktops, inside this white and airy two-storey emporium. Weekly workshops and talks help you get to know your computer, and the banks of iMacs are a free-for-all internet surfing base – a practice that's approved by Apple staffers. Come and worship.

DR HARRIS Map p68 — Cosmetics
☎ 7930 3915; www.drharris.co.uk; 29 St James's St SW1; ☉ 8.30am-6pm Mon-Fri, 9.30am-5pm Sat; ⊖ Green Park
Operating as chemist and perfumer since 1790, come here for your moustache wax and pick up a bottle of DR Harris Crystal Eye Drops to combat the red eyes after a late night and combine it with Dr Harris' own hangover cure: a bitter herbal concoction called DR Harris Pick-Me-Up.

MOLTON BROWN Map pp72–3 — Cosmetics
☎ 7240 8383; www.moltonbrown.co.uk; 18 Russell St WC2; ☉ 10am-7pm Mon-Fri, 10am-6pm Sat, noon-6pm Sun; ⊖ Covent Garden
A fabulously fragrant British natural beauty range, Molton Brown is *the* choice for boutique hotel and posh restaurant bathrooms. Its skin-care products offer plenty of pampering for men and women. In this store you can also have a facial, and buy make-up or even home accessories. There are branches across the city.

SPACE NK Map pp72–3 Cosmetics

☎ 7379 7030; www.spacenk.co.uk; Thomas Neal Centre, 37 Earlham St WC2; ⊗ 10am-7pm Mon-Sat, to 7.30pm Thu, noon-5pm Sun; ⊖ Covent Garden

It's always a bit intimidating to face the glowing skin of SPACE NK's shop assistants/skin-care experts, but it's what gives so many people the confidence in the products – the shop stocks Dr Hauschka, Eve Lom, Chantecaille, Kiehl's or Phyto, and anti-ageing ranges such as 24/7 and Dr Sebagh. Men's products range from Anthony to Kiehl's for men. There are Space NK branches across the city.

TAYLOR OF OLD BOND STREET

Map p68 Cosmetics

☎ 7930 5321; www.tayloroldbondst.co.uk; 74 Jermyn St SW1; ⊗ 9am-6pm Mon-Fri, 8.30am-6pm Sat; ⊖ Green Park

This shop has been plying its trade since the mid-19th century and has much contributed to the expression 'well-groomed gentleman'. It stocks every sort of razor, shaving brush and flavour of shaving soap imaginable.

FORTNUM & MASON

Map p68 Department Stores

☎ 7734 8040; www.fortnumandmason.co.uk; 181 Piccadilly W1; ⊗ 10am-6.30pm Mon-Sat, noon-6pm Sun; ⊖ Piccadilly Circus

London's oldest department store celebrated its 300th birthday in 2007 by not yielding to modern times (its staff are still dressed in old-fashioned tail-coats) and keeping its glam food hall supplied by the famed food hampers, cut marmalade, speciality teas and so on. Downstairs is an elegant wine bar designed by the man

---

SHOPPING STRIPS

London Mayor Ken Livingstone has talked about making Oxford St a traffic-free paradise, with breezy trams going up and down, but until that becomes even a remote reality, the street's ocean of consumers and stagnant traffic is likely to feel simultaneously overwhelming (in terms of its crowds) and underwhelming (regarding its offerings). This is where, however, you'll find the chain 'headquarters' with massive H&Ms, Zaras, Urban Outfitters and large department stores such as John Lewis, Debenhams and Selfridges.

Camden Market at weekends is just as likely to make you want to flee rather than spree, so try to visit during the week, unless you enjoy crowds. Better central areas to head to are listed below. (Apart from the chains listed under High St Kensington, where no address details are given for a particular store it is reviewed more fully in the relevant section of this chapter.)

Clerkenwell, Shoreditch & Spitalfields (see p227) This is London's trendiest shopping area, home to fabulous Sunday's Spitalfields Market where young cutting-edge designers display their creations; Brick Lane, Dray Walk and Cheshire St are full of quirky shops, vintage dens and cool household havens. Come here if you want to see London at its hippest and search out small boutiques for something unique.

Covent Garden (see p216) Visit, but don't shop at the touristy old market hall. Instead branch out into the little side streets for a whole lot of cool fashion and hit Long Acre and Neil St for less hectic High Street chains. The Thomas Neal Centre on Earlham St is packed with urban/skate/surf fashions from the likes of High Jinks.

High Street Kensington (see p226) The less crowded, more salubrious alternative to Oxford St, this has all the High Street chains, plus trendy stores, such as Miss Sixty (No 63) and Urban Outfitters (No 36). Snap up antiques along Church St.

King's Road (see p226) A far cry from its 1960s mod heyday, well-heeled King's Rd is now strong on household goods, with the Designer's Guild (No 269), Habitat (No 206) and Heal's (No 234). Children are well catered for too, with Daisy & Tom (p226) and Trotters (No 34).

Knightsbridge (see p226) Harrods (p226) is a national institution, so go and witness the exuberant food halls and dramatic Egyptian Hall of gifts at least once. Harvey Nichols (p226) is within easy reach, and there are many nearby stores for cashed-up fashionistas.

Marylebone High Street (see p216 & p222) You'll feel like you're in a small town of its own along this quaint and elegant street, where homeware stores such as Cath Kidston (p223), Conran Shop (No 55) and Skandium (No 86) are aplenty. But food is the neighbourhood speciality, with London's best butcher Ginger Pig (Map p100; 8-10 Moxon St).

behind the Wolseley (p246). Clothes, gifts and perfumes occupy the other six floors.

JOHN LEWIS Map p100 — Department Stores
☎ 7629 7711; www.johnlewis.co.uk; 278-306 Oxford St W1; 🕒 9.30am-7pm Mon-Sat, to 8pm Thu; ⊖ Oxford Circus
'Never knowingly undersold' is the motto of this store, whose range of household goods, fashion and luggage is better described as reliable rather than cutting-edge. Strong points include its fabrics department.

LIBERTY Map p68 — Department Stores
☎ 7734 1234; www.liberty.co.uk; 210-220 Regent St W1; 🕒 10am-7pm Mon-Sat, to 8pm Thu, noon-6pm Sun; ⊖ Oxford Circus
An irresistible blend of contemporary styles in an old-fashioned mock-Tudor atmosphere, Liberty has a huge cosmetics department and an accessories floor, along with a breathtaking lingerie section on the 1st floor. A classic London souvenir is a Liberty (fabric) print.

SELFRIDGES Map p100 — Department Stores
☎ 7629 1234; www.selfridges.com; 400 Oxford St W1; 🕒 10am-8pm Mon-Fri, 9.30am-8pm Sat, noon-6pm Sun; ⊖ Bond St
Selfridges is so confident in its consumer appeal that its 2006 winter sale advertising featured the subversive anticonsumer-ist slogan 'I Shop Therefore I Am' by New York artist Barbara Kruger, as if to poke fun at its shoppers and turn rebellion on its head. Selfridges loves innovation – it's famed for its inventive window displays by international artists, gala shows promoting countries/products, and above all an amazing range of products. It's the funkiest and most vital of London's one-stop shops, with labels such as Boudicca, Luella Bartley, Emma Cook, Chloé and Missoni; an unparalleled food hall; and Europe's largest cosmetics department.

AQUASCUTUM Map p68 — Fashion & Designer
☎ 7675 8200; www.aquascutum.co.uk; 100 Regent St W1; 🕒 10am-6.30pm Mon-Sat, to 7pm Thu, 11am-5pm Sun; ⊖ Piccadilly Circus
Despite the store's modern look, Aquascutum's mackintoshes, scarves, bags and hats remain traditional. For men, this means classic gabardine; for women, the look is straight lines, classic fashion and natural beauty, as worn by the super-rich.

BURBERRY Map p100 — Fashion & Designer
☎ 7839 5222; www.burberry.com; 21-23 New Bond St SW1; 🕒 10am-7pm Mon-Sat, noon-6pm Sun; ⊖ Bond St
The first traditional British brand to reach the heights of fashion, you'll know you've reached Burberry when you see hordes of giggling Japanese girls standing outside. It's known for its innovative take on classic pieces (bright-coloured trench coats, khaki pants with large and unusual pockets), its brand check pattern, and a tailored, groomed look. You'll see a lot of its catwalk pieces ripped-off by High Street shops such as H&M.

DUFFER OF ST GEORGE
Map pp72–3 — Fashion & Designer
☎ 7836 3722; www.thedufferofstgeorge.com; 29 Shorts Gardens WC2; 🕒 10.30am-7pm Mon-Fri, to 6.30pm Sat, 1-5pm Sun; ⊖ Covent Garden
The first to bring Evisu jeans to London and a good place for Oeuf T-shirts, Duffer remains the master of London menswear despite growing competition. 'Shield' formal wear such as shirts and classic Italian handmade suits, as well as more urban sweats, bags and accessories are all on sale.

KOH SAMUI Map pp72–3 — Fashion & Designer
☎ 7240 4280; www.kohsamui.co.uk; 65-67 Monmouth St WC2; 🕒 10.30am-6.30pm Mon-Sat, to 7pm Thu, 11.30am-6pm Sun; ⊖ Covent Garden
It's high-end fashion galore at this little boutique that prides itself on finding new designer talent and specialises in floaty pieces from Brit designers such as Chloé, Marc Jacobs, Clements Ribeiro and Julien MacDonald. You'll drool over the handsome Chloé bags.

MULBERRY Map p100 — Fashion & Designer
☎ 7491 3900; www.mulberry.com; 41-42 New Bond St W1; 🕒 10am-6pm Mon-Sat, to 7pm Thu; ⊖ Bond St
Is there a woman in the world who doesn't covet a Mulberry bag? They are voluptuous, soft and a massive style statement. The brand followed in the footsteps of its other British design brethren, Burberry and Pringle, and modernised itself in recent years.

PAUL SMITH Map pp72–3   Fashion & Designer
☎ 7379 7133; www.paulsmith.co.uk; 40-44 Floral St WC2; 🕐 10am-6.30pm Mon-Sat, to 7pm Thu, noon-5pm Sun; ✆ Covent Garden
Paul Smith represents the best of British classic with innovative twists. Super-stylish menswear, suits and tailored shirts are all laid out on open shelves in this walk-in closet of a shop. Smith also does womenswear. There's also a sale shop (Map p100; ☎ 7493 1287; 23 Avery Row W1; 🕐 10am-6pm Mon-Sat, to 7pm Thu, 1-5pm Sun; ✆ Bond St).

PRINGLE Map p100   Fashion & Designer
☎ 0800 360 200, 7297 4580; www.pringleofscot land.com; 112 New Bond St W1; 🕐 10am-6.30pm Mon-Sat, to 7.30pm Thu; ✆ Bond St
Fabulously classy and somehow sexy at the same time (we're talking golfers' V-necks and knitted cardies), this trad-Brit brand turned slightly hip when London rekindled its passion for knitwear. An item will set you back at least £150, however.

SHOON Map p100   Fashion & Designer
☎ 7487 3001; www.shoon.com; 94 Marylebone High St W1; 🕐 10am-6pm Mon-Fri; ✆ Baker St
With its eclectic, upmarket mix of active sportswear, African knick-knacks, travel books and shoes, this spacious store has broad appeal.

STELLA MCCARTNEY
Map p100   Fashion & Designer
☎ 7518 3100; www.stellamccartney.co.uk; 30 Bruton St W1; 🕐 10am-6pm Mon-Sat, to 7pm Thu; ✆ Bond St or Green Park
Does Stella McCartney need introducing? Her floaty designs send many-a-girl's heart aflutter (as do her prices), Kate Moss makes her jeans the most covetable in the UK, and her 'ethical' approach to fashion is very of the moment. This three-storey terraced Victorian home is a temple to all things Stella – a ritzy glasshouse garden, an olde-worlde 'apothecary' selling perfume, vegetarian shoes and not-leather bags, plus bespoke tailoring. Depending on your devotion and wallet, you'll feel right at ease or like an intruder.

TOPSHOP & TOPMAN
Map p68   Fashion & Designer
☎ 7636 7700; www.topshop.co.uk; 36-38 Great Castle St W1; 🕐 9am-8pm Mon-Sat, to 9pm Thu, noon-6pm Sun; ✆ Oxford Circus

Topshop is the it-store when it comes to High-Street shopping. Encapsulating London's supreme skill at bringing catwalk fashion to the youth market affordably and quickly, it constantly innovates by working with young designers and celebrities. Owner Philip Green famously (and controversially) paid Kate Moss around £3 million for a signature clothing line in 2007, a venture which proved so popular the crowds were queuing outside the Oxford Circus store at dawn on the day of the launch.

URBAN OUTFITTERS
Map p68   Fashion & Designer
☎ 7759 6390; www.urbanoutfitters.com; 200 Oxford St W1; 🕐 10am-8pm Mon-Sat, to 9pm Thu, noon-6pm Sun; ✆ Oxford Circus
Probably the trendiest of all chains, this cool American store serves both men and women and has the best young designer T-shirts, an excellent designer area (stocking Paul & Joe Sister, Hussain Chalayan, See by Chloé, among others), 'renewed' secondhand pieces, saucy underwear, silly homewares and quirky gadgets. There are also a Covent Garden branch (Map pp72–3; Seven Dials House, 42-56 Earlham St; ✆ Covent Garden) and a Kensington branch (Map p177; 36-38 Kensington High St; ✆ High St Kensington).

VIVIENNE WESTWOOD
Map p68   Fashion & Designer
☎ 7439 1109; www.viviennewestwood.com; 44 Conduit St W1; 🕐 10am-6pm Mon-Sat, to 7pm Thu; ✆ Bond St or Oxford Circus
The ex-punk who dressed the punks and created the punk look now says that 'fashion is boring' and that she disagrees with everything she used to say. Always a controversial character with a reputation for being a bit barmy (she flashed her privates to the paparazzi after receiving her OBE), Ms Westwood is, thankfully, still designing clothes as bold, innovative and provocative as ever, featuring 19th-century-inspired bustiers, wedge shoes and loads of tartan.

ALGERIAN COFFEE STORES
Map p68   Food, Drink & Confectionery
☎ 7437 2480; www.algocoffee.co.uk; 52 Old Compton St W1; 🕐 9am-7pm Mon-Sat; ✆ Leicester Sq
Stop and have a shot of espresso made in-store, while you select your fresh-ground

coffee beans. Choose among dozens of varieties of coffees and teas.

MINAMOTO KITCHOAN
Map p68   Food, Drink & Confectionery
☎ 7437 3135; www.kitchoan.com; 44 Piccadilly W1; ⏰ 10am-7pm Sun-Fri, to 8pm Sat; ➡ Piccadilly Circus
Walking into this Japanese sweet shop is a mind-blowing experience. *Wagashi* – Japanese sweets – are made out of all sorts of beans and rice and shaped into glazed red cherries, green-bean bunches or spiky kidney bean rolls. Order a couple, sit down and enjoy with a complimentary green tea, or buy a box for a sure-hit souvenir.

NEAL'S YARD DAIRY
Map pp72–3   Food, Drink & Confectionery
☎ 7240 5700; 17 Shorts Gardens WC2; ⏰ 9am-7pm Mon-Sat; ➡ Covent Garden
A fabulous, smelly-cheese house that would fit in rural England, this place is proof that the British can do just as well as the French

when it comes to big rolls of ripe cheese. There are more than 70 varieties that the shopkeepers will let you taste, including independent farmhouse brands. Condiments, pickles, jams and chutneys are also available.

VINTAGE HOUSE
Map p68   Food, Drink & Confectionery
☎ 7437 2592; 42 Old Compton St W1; ⏰ 9am-11pm Mon-Fri, 9.30am-11pm Sat, noon-10pm Sun; ➡ Leicester Sq
A whisky connoisseur's paradise, this shop stocks more than 1000 single-malt Scotches, from smooth Macallan to peaty Lagavulin.

ARAM Map pp72–3   Household
☎ 7557 7557; www.aram.co.uk; 110 Drury Lane WC2; ⏰ 10am-6pm Mon-Sat, to 7pm Thu, closed Sun; ➡ Covent Garden or Holborn
Despite the fact that most of the furniture stocked by Aram is unaffordable to ordinary mortals, admiring the designer pieces

ON THE HIGH STREET

Overseas retailers, such as Diesel, Gap, H&M, Mango, Muji and Zara, abound. The UK also has many home-grown clothing and shoe chains, some of which are listed following. Most stores are from 10am to 8pm Monday to Wednesday, from 10am until 9pm from Thursday to Saturday and from noon until 7pm on Sunday.

French Connection UK (Map p100; ☎ 7629 7766; 396 Oxford St W1; ➡ Bond St) This chain's clothes are more sober than the FCUK sobriquet suggests, though their advertising's always risqué.

Jigsaw (Map p100; ☎ 7491 4484; 126-127 New Bond St W1; ➡ Bond St) Classic women's clothes, with an emphasis on tweeds and knits, plus some chiffon and glitter.

Joseph (Map pp138–9; ☎ 7823 9500; 77 Fulham Rd SW3; ➡ South Kensington) Show them who wears the trousers, with classically smart pants and pants suits, plus a whole range of other fashion.

Karen Millen (Map pp72–3; ☎ 7836 5355; 32-33 James St WC2; ➡ Covent Garden) An upmarket womenswear store, with glam suit-trousers, voluptuous knits, shiny trench coats and evening frocks.

Marks & Spencer (Map p100; ☎ 7935 7954; www.marksandspencer.co.uk; 458 Oxford St W1; ➡ Bond St) Rising from the years of being synonymous with 'quality knickers' M&S has pulled its socks up with some fabulous fashion lines.

Miss Selfridge (Map p100; ☎ 7927 0188; 325 Oxford St W1; ➡ Oxford Circus or Bond St) Fun, throwaway fashion (but is it ethical?) for female teens.

Oasis (Map pp72–3; ☎ 7240 7445; 13 James St WC2; ➡ Covent Garden) Good catwalk rip-offs that are sure to keep you in fashion.

Office (Map pp72–3; ☎ 7379 1896; 57 Neal St WC2; ➡ Covent Garden) Shoes that go the distance from work to after-hours drinks.

Reiss (Map p68; ☎ 7637 9111; www.reiss.co.uk; 14-17 Market Pl W1; ➡ Oxford Circus) Its sales are constantly rising, as are its prices, and Reiss is becoming synonymous with quality on the High Street. Men's and women's street fashion is given a mature edge with quality materials and precise tailoring.

Warehouse (Map pp72–3; ☎ 7240 8242; 24 Long Acre WC2; ➡ Covent Garden or Leicester Sq) Somewhere between Topshop and Oasis in the fashion stakes.

in this fantastic shop is an experience to be cherished. Originally opened by Zeev Aram on King's Rd in 1964, the shop was a key player in the Conran-led furniture design revolution that saw the end of a chintz-laden Britain. The shop grew and eventually moved to this four-floor, free-standing luminous building, where the furniture is given the space it deserves, as if in a museum. Among the many accomplished designers, Aram stocks pieces by Alvar Aalto, Eileen Grey, Eames, Le Corbusier and Arne Jacobsen. The top floor is an exhibition space, where you can see new talent in fine or applied art and design.

CATH KIDSTON Map p100 — Household
☎ 7935 6555; www.cathkidston.co.uk; 51 Marylebone High St W1; ⊙ 10am-7pm Mon-Sat, 11am-5pm Sun; ⊖ Baker St
Cath Kidston has single-handedly made floral patterns and pastel colours fashionable again. She splashes her homewares and handbags with funky floral designs, and is famous for her polka-dot picnic tableware and 1950s-style watering cans.

HABITAT Map pp92–3 — Household
☎ 7631 3880; www.habitat.net; 196 Tottenham Court Rd W1; ⊙ 10am-6.30pm Mon-Sat, to 8pm Thu, noon-6pm Sun; ⊖ Goodge St
Started by the visionary designer and restaurateur Terence Conran in the 1950s, Habitat still does what it originally set out to do – brighten up your home with inventive and inspiring furniture and decorations. Artists, actors, musicians and fashion designers are often employed to design something of their own. The chain is found across London.

HEAL'S Map pp92–3 — Household
☎ 7636 1666; www.heals.co.uk; 196 Tottenham Court Rd W1; ⊙ 10am-6pm Mon-Wed, 10am-8pm Thu, 10am-6.30pm Fri & Sat, noon-6pm Sun; ⊖ Goodge St
Heal's is more serious, classical and expensive than Habitat, servinng a more conservative, yet practical clientele. It's a long-established furniture and homewares store. Check out the great kitchenware section.

BUTLER & WILSON
Map p100 — Jewellery & Accessories
☎ 7409 2955; www.butlerandwilson.co.uk; 20 South Molton St SW1; ⊙ 10am-6pm Mon-Sat, to 7pm Thu, noon-6pm Sun; ⊖ Bond St

There's a sybaritic 1920s Shanghai vibe to Butler & Wilson's central branch, where costume jewellery, handbags, T-shirts and knick-knacks are sold beneath red Chinese lanterns, watched by Chinese shop dummies. The Chelsea store (Map pp138–9; ☎ 7352 3045; 189 Fulham Rd SW3) has a large collection of retro dresses, too.

GARRARD Map p100 — Jewellery & Accessories
☎ 7758 8520; www.garrard.com; 24 Albemarle St W1; ⊙ 10am-5.30pm Mon-Sat; ⊖ Bond St or Green Park
Creative director Jade Jagger helped turn Britain's old-fashioned crown jeweller into somewhere funky enough for Missy Elliot to advertise its bling. Jewel-encrusted clothing and gifts are sold upstairs.

JAMES SMITH & SONS
Map pp72–3 — Jewellery & Accessories
☎ 7836 4731; www.james-smith.co.uk; 53 New Oxford St WC1; ⊙ 9.30am-5.30pm Mon-Fri, 10am-5.30pm Sat; ⊖ Tottenham Court Rd
'Outside every silver lining is a big black cloud', claim the cheerful owners of this quintessential English shop. Nobody makes and stocks such elegant umbrellas, walking sticks and canes as this traditional place, and thanks to bad English weather, they'll hopefully do great business for years to come.

JESS JAMES Map p68 — Jewellery & Accessories
☎ 7437 0199; www.jessjames.com; 3 Newburgh St; ⊙ 11am-6.30pm Mon-Fri, to 7pm Thu, 11am-6pm Sat; ⊖ Oxford Circus
Special-occasion jewellery, from Jess James and other designers, is artistically arranged around an aquarium at this shop. Customers worried about the provenance of their diamonds can opt for the ethically sourced range.

WRIGHT & TEAGUE
Map p100 — Jewellery & Accessories
☎ 7629 2777; www.wrightandteague.com; 1a Grafton St W1; ⊙ 10am-6pm Mon-Fri, to 7pm Thu, 10am-5pm Sat; ⊖ Green Park
The Wright & Teague gold charm bracelets are absolutely ravishing, as are its elegant silver and gold bangles, long necklaces and rings for men and women. What's more, many are very affordable. The couple met while studying at St Martins School of Art

more than 20 years ago and have been together ever since.

AGENT PROVOCATEUR Map p68   Lingerie
☎ 7439 0229; www.agentprovocateur.com; 6 Broadwick St W1; ☺ 11am-7pm Mon-Sat, to 8pm Thu, noon-5pm Sun; ⊖ Oxford Circus

For women's lingerie that is to be worn and seen, and certainly *not* hidden, pull up to Joseph (son of Vivienne Westwood) Corre's wonderful Agent Provocateur. Its sexy and saucy corsets, bras and nighties for all shapes and sizes exude confident and positive sexuality.

ANN SUMMERS Map p68   Lingerie
☎ 7434 2475; www.annsummers.co.uk; 79 Wardour St W1; ☺ 10am-6pm Mon-Sat, to 8pm Thu, noon-6pm Sun; ⊖ Piccadilly Circus

This is one of Britain's most successful stores – so who says the Brits are a reserved lot? Just look at the racy lingerie (usually in flaming reds and fluffy lace), accompanied with furry handcuffs, breast enhancers, G-strings, leather whips, nurse uniforms and other playful accessories.

RIGBY & PELLER Map p68   Lingerie
☎ 7491 2200; 22a Conduit St W1; ☺ 9.30am-6pm Mon-Sat, to 7pm Thu; ⊖ Oxford Circus

This old-fashioned place makes the Queen's bras, but Rigby & Peller's fitting and alteration service – open to us plebs – is equally legendary. Get yourself measured – many a customer has been surprised to discover they've been wearing the wrong size for years. Off-the-peg underwear and swimwear is also available. There's also a Knightsbridge branch (Map pp138–9; 3 Hans Rd; ⊖ Knightsbridge).

KURT GEIGER Map p100   Shoes
☎ 7758 8020; www.kurtgeiger.com; 65 South Molton St W1; ☺ 10am-7pm Mon-Sat, to 8pm Thu, noon-6pm Sun; ⊖ Bond St

Fashion, quality and affordability all come together at this superlative men's and women's shoe store, where footwear from the likes of Birkenstock, Chloé, Hugo Boss, Marc Jacobs, Paul Smith and United Nude adorns the shelves.

POSTE Map p100   Shoes
☎ 7499 8002; 10 South Molton St; ☺ 10am-7pm Mon-Sat, noon-6pm Sun; ⊖ Bond St

Sitting on one of London's most fashionable streets, this very cool shop is aimed at boys who like good shoes, and stocks everything from vintage street labels to razor-sharp Italian imports.

POSTE MISTRESS Map pp72–3   Shoes
☎ 7379 4040; 61-63 Monmouth St WC2; ☺ 10am-7pm Mon-Sat, noon-6pm Sun; ⊖ Leicester Sq

This is where all shoe fetishists should head for the wonderful collection of women's shoes from Emma Hope, Vivienne Westwood, Miu Miu and Dries Van Noten. Money should be no object.

BENJAMIN POLLOCK'S TOYSHOP
Map pp72–3   Toys
☎ 7379 7866; www.pollocks-coventgarden.co.uk; 1st fl, 44 Covent Garden Market WC2; ☺ 10am-6.30pm Mon-Sat, 11am-4pm Sun; ⊖ Covent Garden

Here's a traditional toy shop that's loved by kids of all ages. There are Victorian paper theatres, wooden marionettes and finger puppets, plus antique teddy bears that might be too fragile to play with.

HAMLEYS Map p68   Toys
☎ 0870 333 2455, 7494 2000; www.hamleys.com; 188-196 Regent St W1; ☺ 10am-8pm Mon-Sat, noon-6pm Sun; ⊖ Oxford Circus

Reportedly the largest toy store in the world and certainly the most famous, Hamleys is like a layer cake of playthings. Computer games are in the basement, with the latest playground trends at ground level. Science kits are on the 1st floor, preschool toys on the 2nd, girls' playthings on the 3rd, model cars on the 4th, while the whole confection is topped off with Lego world and its café on the 5th floor.

THE SOUTH BANK

The fabulous South Bank has become one of London's most popular promenades. It's been improving rapidly since Tate Modern, the Millennium Bridge, the Globe Theatre and the London Eye have been drawing locals and tourists over to the riverbank, and, naturally, business has followed. Borough Market (see the boxed text, p242), London's best food market, has benefited from the surge in visitors and shouldn't be missed, and if you

INDEPENDENT MUSIC STORES

It is sad that independent music shops find it difficult to keep going, especially in central London. That said, Britons buy more music per head than any other nation on earth (much of it in London), so here's to hoping that little fish don't get munched by big nasty chains. Most are open 10am until 6pm Monday to Saturday and noon until 5pm on Sunday. Here's a selection of the city's best:

BM Soho (Map p68; ☎ 7437 0478; www.bm-soho.com; 25 D'Arblay St W1; ✛ Oxford Circus) Formerly Black Market Records, this is where club DJs flock for the latest international dance music.

Haggle Vinyl (Map p168; ☎ 7354 4666; www.haggle.freeserve.co.uk; 114 Essex Rd N1; ☺ 9am-7pm Mon-Sat, 10am-5.30pm Sun; ✛ Angel) Vinyl records from as little as £2.50 for the stuff that has spilled over into the boxes on the floor. From 1950s crooners to early hip-hop.

Harold Moore's (Map p68; ☎ 7437 1576; www.hmrecords.co.uk; 2 Great Marlborough St W1; ✛ Oxford Circus) London's finest classical-music store stocks an extensive range of vinyl, CDs and videos, plus jazz in the basement.

Honest Jon's (Map p175; ☎ 8969 9822; 276-278 Portobello Rd W10; ✛ Ladbroke Grove) Two adjoining shops with jazz, soul and reggae.

Music & Video Exchange (Map p175; ☎ 7243 8573; 38 Notting Hill Gate W11; ✛ Notting Hill Gate) Secondhand store *par excellence*. One of countless London branches of 'Exchange' shops. Get a leaflet and check them all out.

On the Beat (Map p68; ☎ 7637 8934; 22 Hanway St W1; ✛ Tottenham Court Rd) Mostly '60s and '70s retro, and helpful staff.

Phonica (Map p68; ☎ 7025 6070; www.phonicarecords.co.uk; 51 Poland St W1; ✛ Tottenham Court Rd) A cool and relaxed Poland St store that stocks a lot of House, electro and hip-hop, but you can find just about anything from reggae to dub, jazz and rock.

Ray's Jazz Shop (Map p68; ☎ 7440 3205; www.foyles.co.uk; 1st fl, Foyle's, 113-119 Charing Cross Rd WC2; ✛ Tottenham Court Rd) Quiet and serene with friendly and helpful staff, this is one of the best jazz shops in London, with a fab independent café in tow.

Revival (Map p68; ☎ 7437 4271; 30 Berwick St W1; ✛ Oxford Circus) The old Reckless Records store was replaced by Revival, though the outfit hasn't changed much. It's still new and secondhand records/CDs, from punk, soul, dance and independent to mainstream.

Rough Trade (Map p175; ☎ 7229 8541; 130 Talbot Rd W11; ✛ Ladbroke Grove) With its underground, alternative and vintage rarities, this home of the eponymous punk-music label remains a haven for vinyl junkies who get misty-eyed about the days before CDs (also on sale) and MP3 players. Check out the Covent Garden branch (Map pp72–3) in Neil's Yard.

Sister Ray (Map p68; ☎ 7734 3297; www.sisterray.co.uk; 34-35 Berwick St W1; ✛ Oxford Circus) If you were a fan of the late, great John Peel on the BBC/BBC World Service, this specialist in innovative, experimental and indie music is just right for you.

Sounds of the Universe (Map p68; ☎ 7734 3430; www.soundsoftheuniverse.com; 7 Broadwick St W1; ✛ Oxford Circus) Outlet of Soul Jazz Records label responsible for so many great soul, reggae, funk and dub albums, this place stocks CDs and vinyl plus some original 45s.

Sterns Music (Map pp92–3; ☎ 7387 5550; www.sternsmusic.com; 74-75 Warren St W1; ✛ Warren St) A world-music oldie, Sterns has been around since the 1980s, lording it over London's world-music scene. Excellent website where you can listen to albums in the shop's charts.

like household and fashion design, head for Oxo Tower, home to two dozen small design studios with clothes, jewellery and quirky homeware. Gabriel's Wharf has some sweet boutiques and curious fashionistas might appreciate a quick scout in and around Bermondsey St.

COCKFIGHTER OF BERMONDSEY
Map p126   Fashion & Designer
☎ 7357 6482; www.cockfighter.co.uk; 96 Bermondsey St SE1; ☺ 11am-6pm Tue & Wed, to 7pm Thu & Fri, to 6pm Sat, to 4pm Sun; ✛ London Bridge
T-shirts with attitude, and other clothing and accessories, are found in this small

boutique and worn across the pages of celebrity magazines by DJs and pop stars.

KONDITOR & COOK
Map p126   Food, Drink & Confectionery

☎ 7407 5100; 10 Stoney St SE1; ⏱ 7.30am-6pm Mon-Fri, 8am-2.30pm Sat; ⊖ London Bridge
This elegant cake shop and bakery produces wonderful cakes – lavender and orange, lemon and almond, massive raspberry meringues – and loaves of warm bread with olives, nuts and spices. K&C's shops can be also found at 22 Cornwall Rd, SE1 (Map p126); 46 Gray's Inn Rd WC1 (Map pp72–3) and at Curzon Soho cinema (p315).

BLACK + BLUM Map p126   Household

☎ 7633 0022; www.black-blum.com; Unit 2.07, 2nd fl, Oxo Tower Wharf, Barge House St SE1; ⏱ 9am-5pm Mon-Fri, 11am-4pm Sat & Sun; ⊖ Southwark
You might see 'James the doorman' (a human-shaped doorstop) and 'Mr and Mrs Hang-up' (anthropomorphic coat hangers that can indicate your mood) in numerous museum and/or design shops across town, but this Anglo-Swiss partnership produces more wonderful stuff in its shop, such as the intricate wire candelabras or the brilliant 'loo read' (a combined toilet-roll holder and magazine rack).

HYDE PARK TO CHELSEA
This well-heeled section of London is all about high fashion, fabulously glam shops and groomed shoppers, home to Chelsea's famously chic King's Rd. Knightsbridge draws the hordes with typically English department stores and glamorous boutiques. Among the glitz, venerable and atmospheric stores sur-

vive thanks to centuries of catering to the whims and vanities of the rich and refined folk who live here. High St Kensington has a good mix of chains and boutiques.

DAISY & TOM Map pp138–9   Children's

☎ 7352 5000; www.daisyandtom.com; 181 King's Rd SW3; ⏱ 9.30am-6pm Mon-Sat, to 7pm Thu & Sat, 11am-5pm Sun; ⊖ Sloane Sq
This superb children's department store has a marionette show, carousel rides, rocking horses, play areas, traditional and modern toys, and a big book room where kids can loll about while flicking through the latest Harry Potter. Upstairs there are fashion labels fit for (your) little princes and princesses.

HARRODS Map pp138–9   Department Stores

☎ 7730 1234; www.harrods.com; 87 Brompton Rd SW1; ⏱ 10am-7pm Mon-Sat; ⊖ Knightsbridge
It's garish and stylish at the same time, and sure to leave you reeling with a consumer-rush after you've spent a few hours within its walls. It's an obligatory stop for many of London's tourists, always crowded and with more rules than an army boot camp. And despite the tacky elements such as the wax figure of proprietor Mohammad Al Fayed and weird memorial fountain to Dodi and Di, you're bound to swoon over the spectacular food hall and impeccable 5th-floor perfumery. Harrods 102, across the street, is a luxury food shop that also does alternative remedies and dry cleaning.

HARVEY NICHOLS
Map pp138–9   Department Stores

☎ 7235 5000; www.harveynichols.com; 109-125 Knightsbridge SW1; ⏱ 10am-8pm Mon-Fri, 10am-7pm Sat, noon-6pm Sun; ⊖ Knightsbridge
This is London's temple of high fashion, where you'll find Chloé and Balenciaga bags, London's best denim range, a massive make-up hall with exclusive lines, great jewellery, and the fantastic restaurant, Fifth Floor.

PETER JONES Map pp138–9   Department Stores

☎ 7730 3434; www.peterjones.co.uk; Sloane Sq SW1; ⏱ 9.30am-7pm Mon-Sat; ⊖ Sloane Sq
The slightly more upmarket brother of John Lewis, Peter Jones' makeover has made it competitive with Selfridges and Harvey Nicks. Upmarket china, furnishings and gifts

top picks

BOOKSTORES

- Foyle's (p217)
- London Review Bookshop (p218)
- Daunt Books (p217)
- Stanford's (p218)
- Books for Cooks (p230)

are its forte, though it stocks accessories and cosmetics too. There's a top-floor café.

LULU GUINNESS
Map pp138–9   Fashion & Designer

☎ 7823 4828; www.luluguiness.com; 3 Ellis St SW1; ⊗ 10am-6pm Mon-Fri, 11am-6pm Sat; ⊖ Sloane Sq
Female silhouettes, dice, board games and various other playful insignia grace her range of coin purses, cosmetic bags, handbags and totes, while some of her collectable evening bags come in striking shapes, such as fans. As Lulu inscribes her bags, it's 'handbags at dawn' girls.

ROCOCO Map pp138–9   Food, Drink & Confectionery

☎ 7352 5857; www.rococochocolates.com; 321 King's Rd SW3; ⊗ 9am-7pm Mon-Sat, noon-6pm Sun; ⊖ Sloane Sq
Rococo is synonymous with real chocolate that comes in glorious moulds and flavours. There are truffles, Swiss chocolates, organic bars, surprising vegan varieties and bags of assorted 'broken chocolate' so you can taste different varieties.

CLERKENWELL, SHOREDITCH & SPITALFIELDS

This is the area for exploring for little shops or wandering market stalls for vintage clothes and up-and-coming designers – head to Spitalfields Market (www.visitspitalfields.com) on Sunday (see p233). There are tonnes of shops off Brick Lane, especially the burgeoning Cheshire St, Hanwell St and the Old Truman Brewery on Dray Walk.

Each June and November there's a major showcase of the latest products, clothes, jewellery and art at Shoreditch Town Hall; see www.eastlondondesignshow.co.uk.

Nearby Clerkenwell is mostly known for its jewellery. For classic settings and unmounted stones, visit London's traditional jewellery and diamond trade area, Hatton Garden (Map p150; www.hatton-garden.net; ⊖ Chancery Lane). The Clerkenwell Green Association (Map p150; www.cga.org.uk; cnr Clerkenwell Green & Clerkenwell Rd) is an excellent starting point for searching out crafts and design items.

MAGMA Map p150   Books

☎ 7242 9503; www.magmabooks.com; 117-119 Clerkenwell Rd EC1; ⊖ Farringdon

Books, magazines and more on cool, cutting-edge design. There's a smaller branch in Covent Garden (Map pp72–3; ☎ 7240 8498; 8 Earlham St, ⊖ Covent Garden) which now includes a small design sale shop that is the perfect place for present shopping.

ANTONI & ALISON
Map p150   Fashion & Designer

☎ 7833 2002; www.antoniandalison.co.uk; 34 Rosebery Ave EC1; ⊗ 10.30am-6.30pm Mon-Fri, noon-4pm Sat; ⊖ Farringdon
Quirky tees, mad floral skirts, gorgeous leather purses and funky cashmere knits are Antoni & Alison's trademark products, and you can find sweet key rings and brooches too. Look out for its brilliant sales.

HOXTON BOUTIQUE
Map p150   Fashion & Designer

☎ 7684 2083; www.hoxtonboutique.co.uk; 2 Hoxton St; ⊗ 10am-6pm Mon-Fri, 11am-5pm Sat, noon-5pm Sun; ⊖ Old St
If you want to look like a true Hoxtonite, come here for your (women's) street wear – there's Isabel Marant, Hussein Chalayan, Repetto shoes, and the shop's own brand, +HOBO+. The boutique is meant to resemble Studio 54, with a mirror ball, white walls and neon lights.

JUNKY STYLING Map p150   Fashion & Designer

☎ 7247 1883; www.junkystyling.co.uk; 12 Dray Walk, Old Truman Brewery, 91 Brick Lane E1; ⊗ 11am-5.30pm Mon-Fri, 10.30am-6pm Sat & Sun; ⊖ Liverpool St or Aldgate East
On retail-friendly Dray Walk, Junky 'recycles' traditional suits into sleek, eye-catching fashion pieces. A man's jacket might become a woman's halterneck top, for example, or tiny shorts with heart-shaped hot-water bottles for back pockets. Menswear includes short-sleeved half-shirts/half-T-shirts, and jackets with sweatsuit-material sleeves and suit-material hoods. Bring your own clothes to be transformed.

LADEN SHOWROOMS
Map p150   Fashion & Designer

☎ 7247 2431; www.laden.co.uk; 103 Brick Lane E1; ⊗ noon-6pm Mon-Sat, 10.30am-6pm Sun; ⊖ Liverpool St or Aldgate East
The unofficial flagship for the latest Hoxton street wear, Laden was once 'London's

best-kept secret'…probably until the thrifty Victoria Beckham declared it as such and it was revealed that Pete Doherty shops here. Unlike many spartan *über*-cool boutiques, it's stuffed to the gills with a wide variety and large quantity of women's and men's clobber, making it a perfect one-stop shop.

NO-ONE Map p150   Fashion & Designer
☎ 7613 5314; www.no-one.co.uk; 1 Kingsland Rd E2; ⊙ 11am-8pm Mon-Sat, noon-6pm Sun; ⊖ Old St or Liverpool St
Sitting inside the Old Shoreditch station bar, No-one stocks Eley Kishimoto, Peter Jensen and new labels for women and men. It's all ultrahip, with fashion magazines, quirky accessories and shoes.

START Map p150   Fashion & Designer
☎ 7739 3636; 42-44 Rivington St; ⊙ 10.30am-6.30pm Mon-Fri, 11am-6pm Sat, 1-5pm Sun; ⊖ Liverpool St or Old St
Punk rock and fashion meet in a boutique by Brix Smith, a cult rocker who loves girly clothes. (Smith is former guitarist with the Fall, one-time paramour of wild-child violinist Nigel Kennedy and now part of Start's husband-and-wife management.) Designer labels such as Miu Miu and Helmut Lang dominate and Smith prides herself on her selection of flattering jeans. A menswear store (Map p150; 59 Rivington St) is over the road.

VERDE'S Map p150   Food & Drink
☎ 7247 1924; www.jeanettewinterson.com; 40 Brushfield St, Old Spitalfields Market E1; ⊙ 8am-8pm; ⊖ Liverpool St
It's all about slow food and quality ingredients these days, and novelist Jeanette Winterson joined the ranks some years ago with this stylish, olde-worlde deli on the ground floor of her listed London home. The atmosphere is rustic and broody and the food delicious. Don't expect to find her serving behind the counter, though.

LABOUR & WAIT Map p150   Household
☎ 7359 0796; www.labourandwait.co.uk; 18 Cheshire St E2; ⊙ 1-5pm Sat, 10am-5pm Sun, by appointment Fri; ⊖ Liverpool St or Aldgate East
Dedicated to simple and functional yet scrumptiously stylish traditional British homeware, Labour & Wait specialises in items by independent manufacturers who make their products the old-fashioned way. There are school tumblers, enamel coffee pots, luxurious lambswool blankets, elegant ostrich-feather dusters and gardening tools. Note the limited opening hours.

LESLEY CRAZE GALLERY
Map p150   Jewellery & Accessories
☎ 7608 0393; www.lesleycrazegallery.co.uk; 33-35a Clerkenwell Green EC1; ⊙ 10am-5.30pm Mon-Sat; ⊖ Farringdon
Considered one of Europe's leading centres for arty, contemporary jewellery, this has exquisitely understated, and sometimes

SENDING OUT AN SOS

London's size and appeal seem only to be growing from year to year, but while the economy booms, small and independent local businesses are paying the price. With ever-increasing interest from big businesses in many parts of the city's central areas, local councils are selling off council property to large companies, making it difficult for local shops to keep paying rising rents. This is particularly the case with businesses that don't generate much turnover, such as antique shops, or those that suffer from direct competition with large chains (think small coffee shop versus Starbucks, or local record shops versus Virgin Megastores).

Areas traditionally rich in local businesses are: Old Conduit St (near Holborn tube station), Amwell St (near Angel), Brick Lane and Spitalfields, Chiswick and some of Richmond, Soho, Endell St (near Covent Garden), Camden Passage (Angel tube), Farringdon, Clerkenwell and Marylebone High St.

Do seek out independent shops on your visit to London, and you're guaranteed to find original products and a personal atmosphere, meet some of London's funny characters and get under the skin of the city better than in any other way.

If you're spending some time in London or are moving here, consider purchasing a **Wedge Card** (£10; www.wedgecard.co.uk), an affinity card that encourages people to shop locally by giving them a discount in shops that have signed up to be part of the Wedge initiative. The brilliant project was started by John Bird, founder and editor-in-chief of *The Big Issue*. We're hoping that London's local and independent stores will serve their communities for decades to come.

pricey, metal designs. There's also a smaller selection of mixed-media bangles, brooches, rings and the like (to the right of the main door), where prices start from about £20.

TATTY DEVINE Map p150 Jewellery & Accessories
☎ 7739 9009; www.tattydevine.com; 236 Brick Lane E1; ⏰ 10am-6pm Mon-Fri, 11am-5pm Sat & Sun; ⊖ Liverpool St

Duo Harriet Vine and Rosie Wolfenden make hip and witty jewellery that's become the favourite of many young Londoners. Their original designs feature record earrings and plectrum bracelets (that High-Street stores have ripped off since), pea necklaces, knitted stilettos, and key rings that look like crinkle-cut crisps. Perspex name necklaces (made to order; £25) are also a treat. There's a Soho shop (Map p68; 57b Brewer St W1).

THE EAST END & DOCKLANDS

Even though there isn't much shopping to be done in this area, the Burberry connection ensures a steady flow, while Broadway Market (Map p156; www.broadwaymarket.co.uk; ⓡ London Fields, 🚍 26, 48, 55, 106 or 253) in Hackney is one of London's up-and-coming retail scenes. There are massive underground shopping malls beneath the skyscrapers around Canary Wharf with upmarket shops, bars and restaurants.

BURBERRY FACTORY SHOP
Map p156   Fashion & Designer
☎ 8985 3344, 8328 4320; 29-53 Chatham Pl E9; ⏰ 11am-6pm Mon-Fri, 10am-5pm Sat, 11am-5pm Sun; ⊖ Bethnal Green then 🚍 106 or 256 to Hackney Town Hall, ⓡ Hackney Central

This warehouse stocks seconds and samples from reborn-as-trendy Brit brand's current collection or stuff from last season. Prices can be up to 50% to 70% lower than those in the West End, with the best deals on accessories.

FABRICATIONS Map p156   Household
☎ 7275 8043; www.fabrications1.co.uk; 7 Broadway Market E8; ⏰ noon-5pm Tue-Sat; ⓡ London Fields, 🚍 26, 48, 55, 106 or 253

Fabrications is the best-known and most eye-catching store along Broadway Market. The shop's owner, Barley Massey, does a lot for the recycling cause, making clothes and soft furnishings from unexpected material, from bicycle tyre tubes to used ribbon. Bespoke tailoring is also available.

NORTH LONDON

The wealth of some of North London's inhabitants means that often, like in Hampstead, upmarket outlets frequently just mean upmarket chains and you'd better have your credit card well-oiled. But the best of Hampstead are its independent food shops. Muswell Hill has a good selection of independent stores, while Crouch End has some good charity shops.

Shopping in Camden is more about cheap, disposable fashion and made-for-tourist trinkets at the huge market (see the boxed text, p232), although you might be tempted to occasionally pop into one of the many clothes boutiques lining the High Street.

Islington is another good area for independent shops, particularly around Camden Passage, where you can find some wonderful vintage clothes shops (see the boxed text, p231). Camden Passage is fighting to keep its businesses running (see the boxed text, opposite).

King's Cross is being regenerated and Starbucks appearing, but independent shops, such as Housmans, are standing their ground.

HOUSMANS Map p168   Books
☎ 7837 4473; www.housmans.com; 5 Caledonian Rd N1; ⊖ King's Cross/St Pancras

Great radical store, which stocks books you won't find anywhere else. Also has a good stationery section. It's worth chatting to the owner here for some unadulterated insights into the area's past and present.

LOUIS PATISSERIE
Map p166   Food & Confectionery
☎ 7435 9908; 32 Heath St NW3; ⏰ 9am-6pm; ⊖ Hampstead or Belsize Park

One of London's oldest coffee and cake shops, Louis Patisserie was started by Hungarian immigrant Louis Permayer in 1963 and it hasn't changed a bit since. Eclairs, almond pretzels, marzipan cookies, cream slices and macaroons wink from the window, and they're packed in a pretty striped box for you to take away. You can also sit down in the little tearoom, best on Sunday when Hampstead's Eastern European ladies and gentlemen come here for coffee and cake.

ROSSLYN DELICATESSEN
Map p166   Food & Confectionery
☎ 7794 9210; www.delirosslyn.co.uk; 56 Rosslyn Hill NW3; ⏰ 10am-6pm Mon-Fri; ⊖ Hampstead or Belsize Park

This enchanting store has been voted the best local delicatessen in London by radio station LBC and the *Independent* newspaper, and we wholeheartedly agree with the verdict. There is a fantastic meat counter, with the most aromatic pancetta you'll ever try; the jarred chutneys, terrines and marinated vegetables are a wonder; and you'll find unusual flavours such as caramelised onions, damson jam and mulberry salad dressing. The cakes, chocolates and Union Roasters coffee are delicious, too.

ARIA Map p168 Household

☎ 7704 1999; www.aria-shop.co.uk; 295-297 Upper St N1; ⏰ 10am-7pm Mon-Fri, 10am-6.30pm Sat, noon-5pm Sun; ⊖ Angel or Highbury & Islington
The mugs, toasters, kitchen equipment and furniture crowd inside the store and in the window display, inviting all lovers of a good browsing session to get lost among the many lovely objects.

PAST CARING Map p168 Household

76 Essex Rd N1; ⏰ noon-6pm Mon-Sat; ⊖ Angel
Stuffed full of secondhand retro bric-a-brac from ashtrays to curtain material, this shop is so removed from the modern world that it doesn't even have a phone number.

WEST LONDON

Portobello Rd has to be a priority for any market lover, with its wall-to-wall antique stores, funky fashion stores, knick-knack shops and weekend market (see p232). Moneyed Notting Hill and Westbourne Grove have the best (and priciest) boutiques and designer shops.

Otherwise, shopping in the west is definitely not wild. Try Shepherd's Bush Market (Map p177; ⏰ 9.30am-5pm Mon-Wed, Fri & Sat, 9.30am-1pm Thu), stretching underneath the Hammersmith & City line between Goldhawk Rd and Shepherd's Bush tube stations, and the superb Troubadour Delicatessen (Map p177; ☎ 7341 6341; 267 Old Brompton Rd SW5; ⊖ Earl's Court), next to the café-bar-eatery of the same name.

BLENHEIM BOOKS Map p175 Books

☎ 7792 0777; www.blenheimbooks.co.uk; 11 Blenheim Cres W11; ⊖ Ladbroke Grove
Formerly a gardeners' bookstore, Blenheim now specialises in design, architecture and photography, though its garden section is still extensive.

BOOKS FOR COOKS Map p175 Books

☎ 7221 1992; www.booksforcooks.com; 4 Blenheim Cres W11; ⊖ Ladbroke Grove
All the recipe books from celeb and non-celeb chefs. Perfect for some of the more adventurous cooks among you, or those looking for 'exotic' cookbooks. The café has a test kitchen where you can sample recipes.

TRAVEL BOOKSHOP Map p175 Books

☎ 7229 5260; www.travelbookshop.co.uk; 13 Blenheim Cres W11; ⊖ Ladbroke Grove
Still known as the bookshop on which Hugh Grant's was modelled in the movie *Notting Hill,* this is crammed with guidebooks, travel literature and antiquarian gems.

COCO RIBBON Map p175 Fashion & Designer

☎ 7229 4904; www.cocoribbon.com; 21 Kensington Park Rd W11; ⏰ 10am-6pm Mon-Sat, 12.30-5.30pm Sun; ⊖ Ladbroke Grove
Coco Ribbon is so girly, even Barbie might feel a tad butch when walking into this award-winning boutique. There are chiffon dresses and faux-fur gilets, Calypso Rose's customisable Clippy Kit handbags, light-hearted words of wisdom for newlyweds or new parents and, for your broken-hearted gal pals, 'boyfriend replacement' kits (sugar pills and chocolate, of course).

PAUL & JOE Map p175 Fashion & Designer

☎ 7243 5510; 39-41 Ledbury Rd W11; ⏰ 10.30am-6pm Mon-Fri, 10.30am-7pm Sat, 1-6pm Sun; ⊖ Notting Hill Gate
Paul & Joe has such scrumptious clothes that it may be difficult to wrist-slap yourself and not spend hundreds of pounds on the frocks and cry until your next pay cheque (while looking fabulous, of course). The store itself is sexy and stylish and it feels like you've stumbled into someone's boudoir, with vintage dressing tables and glass cabinets. Its menswear is also sleek and stylish, so your beau won't feel bored.

CERAMICA BLUE Map p175 Household

☎ 7727 0288; www.ceramicablue.co.uk; 10 Blenheim Cres W11; ⏰ 11am-5pm Mon, 10am-6.30pm Tue-Sat; ⊖ Ladbroke Grove
A wonderful place for original and beautiful crockery, stemming from more than a dozen countries: there's Japanese crackle-glaze tea-cups, serving plates with tribal South African designs, and much in between.

LONDON LOVES VINTAGE

Gripped as it is by looking good and a permanent shopping fever, London's latest (and seemingly lasting) love affair is with vintage apparel. Vintage designer pieces from Chanel, Dior, Miu Miu, Vivienne Westwood, you name it – and odd bits and pieces from the 1920s to the 1980s (the latter being the focus of the latest retro-frenzy) are all busting the rails in shops that are often as extravagant as the clothes they stock.

The rise of burlesque and cabaret club nights (see the boxed text, p303) has meant that 1920s to 1950s costume dresses and jewellery have become much coveted, and it's fascinating to see the mastery and effort that goes into dressing up for such events. Some vintage shops can be quite expensive, with designer and rare pieces costing up to £300, but you can find cheaper things (between £10 and £50) if you dig deep; if you don't feel like buying it's fantastic to simply browse around and see what your grandma's generation used to wear (or remember your own '80s excesses). If you, however, discover the vintage king or queen inside you, check out the cabaret nights, dress up and join in!

The best areas for vintage shops are: Camden Passage at Islington; Kingly Ct, off Carnaby St; Spitalfields Market, Cheshire St and on and around Brick Lane; Portobello Rd and Notting Hill. Try charity shops in areas such as Chelsea, Notting Hill and Kensington – they usually have cheap designer wear (the general rule is, the richer the area, the better the secondhand shops).

Vintage Shops

The following typically trade from 10am to 7pm Monday to Saturday and from noon until 6pm on Sunday.

Absolute Vintage (Map p150; ☎ 7247 3883; 15 Hanbury St E1; ✚ Liverpool St) If you don't mind shoes that have been worn by other feet, enter this huge barn full of stilettos, peep-toes, ankle-/knee-high boots and glittery vintage Manolos. Men's shoes are stocked too, and there are frocks and suits at the back. It's handily close to Spitalfields Market.

Alfie's Antiques Market (Map p166; ☎ 7723 6066; www.alfiesantiques.com; 13-25 Church St NW8; ✚ Marylebone) Alfie's Market is an entire ex–department store, Art Deco building, dedicated to fab 20th-century furniture and rare 1920s to 1950s pieces. An absolute delight.

Annie's Vintage Costumes & Textiles (Map p168; ☎ 7359 0796; 12 Camden Passage N1; ✚ Angel) One of the most enchanting vintage shops, Annie's has costumes to make you look like Greta Garbo.

Bang Bang Exchange (Map p68; ☎ 7631 4191; www.myspace.com/bangbangexchange; 21 Goodge St W1; ✚ Goodge St) Got some designer pieces you're tired of? Bang Bang exchanges, buys and sells vintage pieces, proving the saying 'One girl's faded Prada dress is another girl's top new wardrobe piece'.

Marshmallow Mountain (Map p68; ☎ 7434 8498; www.marshmellowmountain.com; Kingly Ct, 49 Carnaby St W1; ✚ Oxford Circus) One of our favourites, with eccentric, cherry-picked dresses and wonderful shoes.

Orsini (Map p177; ☎ 7937 2903; www.orsini-vintage.co.uk; 76 Earl's Court Rd W8; ✚ Earl's Court) One of the best vintage designer collections in town, Orsini is small, beautiful and friendly. Alterations are available in store.

Radio Days (Map p126; ☎ 7928 0800; 87 Lower Marsh Rd SE1; ✚ Waterloo) Radio Days loves 1920s and '30s clothes and jewellery, with vintage electrics, hats, phones and magazines.

Rellik (Map p175; ☎ 8962 0089; 8 Golborne Rd W10; ✚ Westbourne Park) Its owners were among the top 100 influences on British fashion, so it's no wonder this is the fashionistas' favourite London retro store. It stocks the likes of Ossie Clark, Zandra Rhodes and Vivienne Westwood.

Retro Woman (Map p175; ☎ 7221 2055; 20 Pembridge Rd W11; ✚ Notting Hill Gate) Contains an excellent collection of secondhand designer shoes. More stock is in the unmarked sister store at No 16, while Retro Man is at No 34.

Steinberg & Tolkien (Map pp138–9; ☎ 7376 3660; 193 King's Rd SW3; ✚ South Kensington) London's oldest and most bizarre vintage shop, S&T has had its frocks featured in *Vogue*, among other magazines; shoppers are always taken aback by its dark and eccentric atmosphere.

MARKET FORCES

Shopping at London's markets isn't just about picking up bargains and rummaging through tonnes of knick-knacks, clothes and all sorts of mystical ephemera and earthly accoutrements – although they give you plenty of opportunity to do that. It's also about taking in the character of this vibrant city, in all its many facets and moods.

For information on farmers' markets, see p251.

Borough

Here in some form since the 13th century, Borough Market (Map p126; ☎ 7407 1002; www.boroughmarket .org.uk; cnr Borough High & Stoney Sts SE1; ⏰ 11am-5pm Thu, noon-6pm Fri, 9am-4pm Sat; ⊖ London Bridge) is testament to the British public's increasing interest in good food. Helped by celebrity shopper Jamie Oliver, 'London's Larder' has enjoyed an enormous renaissance in recent years, overflowing with food lovers. As well as a section devoted to quality fresh fruit, exotic vegetables and organic meat, there's a fine-foods retail market, with products such as home-grown honey and homemade bread. Throughout, takeaway stalls allow you to sample a sizzling gourmet sausage or tuck into a quality burger. Shoppers queue at the excellent Monmouth Coffee Company, Neal's Yard Dairy, the Spanish deli Brindisa or Ginger Pig butcher. Plans for a new railway link threaten to cut the market in two, but the market's trustees claim 'it won't affect the market' (which seems hard to believe). Check the website for updates.

Brixton

This market (Map p200; Reliance Arcade, Market Row, Electric Lane & Electric Ave SW9; ⏰ 8am-6pm Mon-Sat, 8am-3pm Wed; ⊖ Brixton) is a heady, cosmopolitan mix, ranging from silks, wigs, knock-off fashion, Halal butchers and the occasional Christian preacher on Electric Ave to the foodstuffs in the covered Brixton Village (formerly Granville Arcade). Tilapia fish, pig's trotters, yams, mangoes, okra, plantains and Jamaican *bullah* cakes (gingerbread) are just some of the exotic products on sale.

Camden

Although this market (Map p168; www.camdenlock.net/markets; ⊖ Camden Town) remains a top attraction, its heyday is a distant memory. Commercial tat has long taken over from the truly inventive, although you might find some good retro pieces. The place is busiest at weekends, especially Sunday, when the crowds elbow each other all the way north from Camden Town tube station to Chalk Farm Rd. It's composed of several separate markets, which tend to merge.

Camden Canal Market (Map p166; cnr Chalk Farm & Castlehaven Rds NW1; ⏰ 10am-6pm Sat & Sun; ⊖ Chalk Farm) Further north and just over the canal bridge, Camden Canal Market has bric-a-brac from around the world. If you're pushed for time, this is the bit to skip.

Camden Lock Market (Map p168; Camden Lock Pl NW1; ⏰ 10am-6pm Sat & Sun, indoor stalls 10am-6pm daily) Right next to the canal lock, with diverse food, ceramics, furniture, oriental rugs, musical instruments and designer clothes.

Camden Market (Map p168; cnr Camden High & Buck Sts NW1; ⏰ 9am-5.30pm Thu-Sun) This covered market houses stalls for fashion, clothing, jewellery and tourist tat.

Stable (Map p166; Chalk Farm Rd NW1; ⏰ 8am-6pm Sat & Sun; ⊖ Chalk Farm) Just beyond the railway arches, opposite Hartland Rd, the Stables is the best part of the market, with antiques, Asian artefacts, rugs and carpets, pine furniture, and '50s and '60s clothing.

Portobello Road

Perhaps because it's less crowded and littered than Camden, Londoners generally prefer this market (Map p175; Portobello Rd W10; ⏰ 8am-6pm Mon-Wed, 9am-1pm Thu, 7am-7pm Fri & Sat, 9am-4pm Sun; ⊖ Notting Hill Gate or Ladbroke Grove). Though shops and stalls open daily, the busiest days are Friday, Saturday and Sunday. There's an antiques market on Saturday, and a flea market on Portobello Green on Sunday morning. Fruit and veg are sold all week at the Ladbroke Grove end, with an organic market on Thursday. Antiques, jewellery, paintings and ethnic stuff are concentrated at the Notting Hill Gate end of Portobello Rd. Stalls move downmarket as you move north. Beneath the Westway a vast tent covers more stalls selling cheap clothes, shoes and CDs, while the Portobello Green Arcade is home to some cutting-edge clothing and jewellery designers.

Spitalfields

This market (Map p150; www.visitspitalfields.com; Commercial St, btwn Brushfield & Lamb Sts E1; ☉ 9.30am-5.30pm Sun; ⊖ Liverpool St) was originally the place to snaffle the latest street wear at good prices, with young clothes designers joined by jewellers, furniture makers and a variety of fresh-produce stalls. Unfortunately, with big businesses wanting a piece of the action, part of the old market was converted into a new restaurant and shopping complex in 2006. The old market still stands, thankfully, and much of the young designer stalls have moved up the road to the Old Truman Brewery's Sunday UpMarket (Map p150; www.sundayupmarket.co.uk), basically a Spitalfields extension. The space is a car park during the week, but on Sunday it's filled with excellent clothes, delicious international cuisine, jewellery and music stands.

Other Markets

Bermondsey (Map p126; Bermondsey Sq; ☉ 5am-1pm Fri; ⊖ Borough or Bermondsey) Reputedly, it's legal to sell stolen goods here before dawn, but late risers will find this market altogether upright and sedate, with cutlery and other old-fashioned silverware, antique porcelain, paintings and some costume jewellery.

Berwick Street (Map p68; Berwick St W1; ☉ 8am-6pm Mon-Sat; ⊖ Piccadilly Circus or Oxford Circus) South of Oxford St and running parallel to Wardour St, this fruit-and-vegetable market is a great place to put together a picnic or shop for a prepared meal.

Brick Lane (Map p150; Brick Lane E2; ☉ 8am-1pm Sun; ⊖ Aldgate East) Goods on sale range from clothes, fruit and vegetables to household goods, paintings and bric-a-brac.

Camden Passage (Map p168; Camden Passage N1; ☉ 7am-2pm Wed, 8am-4pm Sat; ⊖ Angel) Not to be confused with Camden Market, this is a series of four arcades selling antiques and curios, located in Islington, at the junction of Upper St and Essex Rd. Stallholders know their stuff, so bargains are rare. Wednesday is busiest, but it's worth visiting on Sunday for the Islington Farmers' Market between 10am and 2pm.

Columbia Road Flower Market (Map p150; Columbia Rd E2; ☉ 7am-1pm Sun; ⊖ Bethnal Green, ⊛ Cambridge Heath, ⊟ 26, 48 or 55) London's most fragrant market shouldn't be missed. Between Gosset St and the Royal Oak pub merchants lay out their blooms, from everyday geraniums to rare pelargoniums.

Covent Garden (Map pp72–3; ⊖ Covent Garden) The shops in the touristy piazza are open daily, while handicrafts and curios are sold in the North Hall. Don't miss the antiques market in the Jubilee Hall on Monday before 3pm; quality crafts are sold on Saturday and Sunday inside Jubilee Hall.

Greenwich (Map p180; College Approach SE10; ☉ 9am-5pm Thu, 9.30am-5.30pm Sat & Sun; DLR Cutty Sark) Greenwich Market is ideally suited for a relaxed few hours' rummaging through its secondhand household objects, glass, rugs, prints and wooden toys. In between, you can snack on speciality foods in the food court. Thursday is the day for antiques, while the general market is open on weekends. Stores around the market open daily, but weekends are best.

Leadenhall Market (Map p110; Whittington Ave EC1; ☉ 7am-4pm Mon-Fri; ⊖ Bank) As well as being a small attraction in its own right (see p118), this market, off Gracechurch St, has clothes stores and curio shops, a fishmonger, a butcher and a cheesemonger. As it serves a City clientele, prices tend to be high.

Leather Lane (Map p150; Leather Lane EC1; ☉ 10.30am-2pm Mon-Fri; ⊖ Chancery Lane or Farringdon) South of Clerkenwell Rd and parallel to Hatton Garden, Leather Lane attracts local office workers with its suspiciously cheap DVDs, tapes and CDs, household goods and clothing sold by archetypal cockney stallholders.

Petticoat Lane (Map p110; Middlesex & Wentworth Sts E1; ☉ 8am-2pm Sun, Wentworth St only 9am-2pm Mon-Fri; ⊖ Aldgate, Aldgate East or Liverpool St) The famous lane itself has been renamed Middlesex St. The market, however, soldiers on, selling cheap consumer items and clothes.

Ridley Road (Map p156; Ridley Rd E8; ☉ 8.30am-6pm Mon-Sat; ⊛ Dalston Kingsland) Massively enjoyed by the Afro-Caribbean community it serves, this market is best for its exotic fruit and vegetables, as well as specialist cuts of meat.

Riverside Walk (Map p126; Riverside Walk SE1; ☉ 10am-5pm Sat & Sun; ⊖ Waterloo or Embankment) Great for cheap secondhand books long out of print, this is held in all weather outside the National Film Theatre, under the arches of Waterloo Bridge. In summer it helps the South Bank vaguely resemble Paris' Left Bank. Occasionally, individual dealers set up during the week.

Smithfield (Map p110; West Smithfield EC1; ☉ 4am-noon Mon-Fri; ⊖ Farringdon) London's last surviving meat market is still clinging on, despite nearly getting the chop for an office development in 2005. While cattle were slaughtered here once, today this is the most modern of its kind in Europe. Note, this is a wholesale market only.

GREENWICH & SOUTHEAST LONDON

This is a heaven for lovers of retro clothes stores and secondhand bookshops, the latter of which you'll come upon every few steps. The vintage clothes shops are cheaper than those in the West End, and if you roll up your (vintage) sleeves, you can find some pretty good stuff. Alternatively, get stuck into some retro household shops and general 'present-shopping' stores around DLR Cutty Sark.

EMPORIUM Map p180 Fashion
☎ 8305 1670; 332 Creek Rd SE10; ⏰ 10.30am-6pm Wed-Sun; DLR Cutty Sark
Each piece is individual at this lovely vintage shop (unisex), where glass cabinets are adorned with paste jewellery, old perfume bottles (under the Shell advertising lamp) and straw caps, and gorgeous jackets and blazers snuggle on the coat hangers.

COMPENDIA Map p180 Gifts
☎ 8293 6616; www.compendia.co.uk; Shop 10, Greenwich Market; ⏰ 11am-5.30pm Mon-Fri, 10.30am-5.30pm Sat & Sun; DLR Cutty Sark
Compendia's owners are madly enthusiastic about games – board or any other kind – and they'll look for the rarest of things if you ask them to. The shop is brilliant for gifts you can enjoy with your mates – backgammon, chess, Scrabble, solitaire and rarities such as Mexican Train Domino.

FLYING DUCK ENTERPRISES
Map p180 Household
☎ 8858 1964; www.flying-duck.com; 320-322 Creek Rd SE10; ⏰ 11am-6pm Tue-Fri, 10.30am-6pm Sat & Sun; DLR Cutty Sark
Taking kitsch to new heights, this little shop has two small rooms mainly lit by retro lamps jam-packed with everything from snow domes and Bakelite telephones, to Tretchikoff paintings of exotic women and '70s cocktail kits.

SOUTH LONDON

Brixton Market (see the boxed text, p232) is the best place for shopping in South London, though the area has some interesting

shops such as Joy (Map p200; ☎ 7787 9616; 432 Coldharbour Lane SW11; ⏰ 10am-7.30pm Mon-Sat, 11am-7pm Sun; ⊖ Brixton), where you can pick up quirky accessories.

In Clapham there are several worthwhile stores near the common, including gift shop Oliver Bonas (Map p200; ☎ 7720 8272; www.oliverbonas.com; 23 The Pavement SW4; ⊖ Clapham Common) and shoe store Bullfrogs (Map p200; ☎ 7627 4123; 9 The Pavement SW4; ⊖ Clapham Common).

Northcote Rd in Wandsworth offers some quality food shopping.

SOUTHWEST LONDON

Fulham and Parson's Green are pretty uninspiring when it comes to shopping, but you can find a few designer furniture and fabric shops, one of the best being Mufti (☎ 7610 9123; 789 Fulham Rd SW6; ⊖ Parson's Green); for antiques head to the northern end of Munster Rd. North End Road Market (⏰ 9am-5pm Mon-Sat) is great for fresh fruit and veg, cheap clothing and household goods.

Overgentrified Putney is full of grim chains. Instead, head to Church Rd and High St in Barnes, both of which are lined with interesting shops such as Blue Door (☎ 8748 9785; www.bluedoorbarnes.co.uk; 74 Church Rd; ⊠ Barnes), with gorgeous Swedish and French home furnishings. Anyone wishing to indulge their ankle-biters could try children's toy shops Farmyard (☎ 8878 7338; www.thefarmyard.co.uk; 63 Barnes High St; ⏰ 9.30am-5.30pm Mon-Sat; ⊠ Barnes), and Bug Circus (☎ 8741 4244; 153 Church Rd; ⏰ 9.30am-5.30pm Mon-Sat; ⊠ Barnes).

Richmond High St is full of chains, but there are some independent stores around. There's YDUK (Map p208; ☎ 8940 0060; 4 The Square TW9; ⊖ Richmond) for street wear. In an enclave of cobbled streets you'll find jewellery stores such as Toko (Map p208; ☎ 8332 6620; 18 Brewers Lane TW9; ⊖ Richmond).

In Chiswick don't miss the fantastic Mortimer & Bennett (☎ 8995 4145; www.mortimerandbennett.co.uk; 33 Turnham Green Tce W4; ⏰ 8.30am-6pm Mon-Fri, 8.30am-5.30pm Sat; ⊖ Turnham Green) deli, or Sunday's Chiswick Farmers & Fine Foods Market (Masonian Bowls Hall, Duke's Meadow W4; ⏰ 10am-2pm Sun; ⊖ Turnham Green). Antiques are also a local speciality; try Strand Antiques (☎ 8994 1912; 46 Devonshire Rd W4; ⊖ Turnham Green) or the Old Cinema (☎ 8995 4166; 160 Chiswick High Rd W4; ⊖ Turnham Green).

BLUELIST[1] (blu list) *v.*
to recommend a travel experience.
What's your recommendation? www.lonelyplanet.com/bluelist

EATING

top picks

- **New Tayyab** (p259)
- **Nyonya** (p267)
- **Snazz.Sichuan** (p263)
- **Asadal** (p243)
- **Lucio** (p253)
- **Café Spice Namaste** (p260)
- **El Faro** (p261)
- **Anchor & Hope** (p249)
- **Roussillon** (p254)
- **Capital** (p252)

London's victories in the culinary arena over the past dozen or so years have been nothing short of phenomenal. Some wags might suggest that there was only one way but up from cafs serving greasy breakfasts and chips deep-fried in rancid-smelling oil, but don't pay them any mind. London has caught up with and, in some respects, overtaken its European cousins.

So what exactly happened? At some point the purveyors of stodge were lined up against the wall, stripped of their aprons and replaced by a savvy new generation of young chefs including the likes of Gordon Ramsay, Gary Rhodes, Heston Blumenthal, Jamie Oliver and Tom Aikens. As trailblazing restaurants progressively raised the bar, the competition followed. Markets selling fresh, free-range, organic produce sprang up, staff were drilled into professional service and the designers were brought in to create some of the world's coolest and most aesthetically pleasing eating spaces. As a result, food in all its guises became the new sex, and everyone wanted a piece of the action. Another change is that since July 2007 there has been a total ban on smoking in all enclosed spaces in England including, of course, restaurants.

Eating out in London can be as diverse, stylish and satisfying as anywhere else on the planet, and it's by no means an exaggeration to call London a food destination. Designer eating is all the rage, with restaurant openings attracting as much glitz and glamour as fashion parades, and every week there seems to be a hot new place where half of London is trying to get a reservation.

That's not to say you can't still get greasy fries, overcooked vegetables and traditional British stodge (particularly in pubs, although this is changing too with the inevitable arrival of a gastropub to a High Street near you), but with chefs absorbing the influences of this most cosmopolitan of cultures, you're more likely to get the world on your plate.

Just don't count on value for money. We can't count the number of times we've dropped over over £40 a head for refined Italian food or the ubiquitous Modern European that tasted like it had been microwaved (ding!), and wondered why we'd bothered. On the other hand we've had Pakistani food in Whitechapel, Turkish in Dalston and Malaysian in Notting Hill that has made our hearts sing, our tastebuds zing and our wallets only slightly lighter.

Eating out in London can be a real hit-or-miss affair. What we've done in this chapter is separate the wheat from the chaff. The restaurants and other eateries appearing below range from pretty good (convenient location, cheap price, unusual cuisine) to fantabulous (worth a big splurge or a lengthy journey). Hopefully this list will lead you in the right direction and you won't walk out wondering why *you* bothered. *Bon appétit!*

HISTORY & SPECIALITIES

English food will never win any awards on the world culinary stage, but when well prepared – be it a Sunday lunch of roast beef and Yorkshire pudding (light batter baked until fluffy and eaten with gravy) or a cornet of fish and chips eaten on the hoof – it can have its moments.

Pubs generally serve low-cost traditional dishes of varying quality such as pies – pork pies, Cornish pasties and steak and kidney pie. (Shepherd's pie, on the other hand, has no crust but is a baked dish of minced lamb and onions topped with mashed potatoes.) On a pub menu you'll also usually find bangers and mash (sausages served with mashed potatoes and gravy), sausage rolls and the ploughman's lunch (thick slices of bread served with Cheddar or Cheshire cheese, chutney and pickled onions). The catalogue of calorific desserts includes bread and butter pudding, steamed pudding (a cake that contains beef suet, a key ingredient) served with treacle (molasses) or jam, and the frighteningly named spotted dick, a steamed suet pudding with currants and raisins that has now been rechristened 'spotted Richard' by the supermarket giant Tesco for reasons, it says, of propriety.

The most English of dishes, though, is fish and chips: cod, plaice or haddock dipped in batter, deep-fried and served with chips (French fries) doused in vinegar and sprinkled with salt. With the arrival of American-style fast-food joints, authentic 'chippies' are becoming rarer, but we still like the Rock & Sole Plaice (p241) in Covent Garden, the North Sea Fish Restaurant (p244) in Bloomsbury, Seashell of Lisson Grove (p247) and upmarket Geales (p267) in Notting Hill.

From the middle of the 19th century until just after WWII the staple lunch for many Londoners was a pie filled with spiced eel (then abundant in the Thames) and served with mashed potatoes and liquor, a parsley sauce. Nowadays the pies are usually meat-filled and the eel served smoked or jellied as a side dish. The best places to try this are the pie 'n' mash shops listed in the boxed text, p260.

VEGETARIANS & VEGANS

London has been one of the best places for vegetarians to dine out since the 1970s. That's mostly due to its many Indian restaurants, which always cater for people who don't eat meat for religious reasons, though several health scares over British beef may have pushed some into the meatless camp. For dedicated vegetarian eateries, try Blah Blah Blah (p269), Blue Légume (p266), Eat & Two Veg (p248), Food for Thought (p243), Gate (p269), Manna (p262), Mildred's (p240), Place Below (p249), Rasa (p266), Red Veg (p240) and Woodlands (p264).

PRACTICALITIES

Opening Hours

In contrast to people in Continental European cities, Londoners tend to eat their evening meal early, generally between 7pm and 9.30pm. Most places serve lunch between noon and 2.30pm or 3pm and dinner from 6pm or 7pm to 10pm; many midrange restaurants stay open throughout the day. Hours can change from one neighbourhood to the next – for example, many restaurants in Soho close on Sunday, and those in the City close for the whole weekend; we've noted which venues stray from the standard.

How Much?

Eating out in London is outlandishly expensive compared with the USA, most of the rest of Europe and Australia. And if you don't earn

PRICE GUIDE

The symbols below indicate the cost per main course at the restaurant in question.

£££	more than £20
£££	£10-20
£	less than £10

sterling, chances are that you'll rarely get what you consider value for money. Go to a top restaurant, order three courses à la carte and wash it down with a decent European red, and two of you will be lucky to get much change out of £200. Then again, you can have an excellent meal for half that at the same place if you arrive at times when you can opt for a set meal. If you choose carefully it is possible to have a meal that you both remember fondly for £40 per person. In this guide the range of prices for main courses is included after the establishment's address.

Booking Tables

Making reservations has become just about compulsory for all central restaurants in London from Thursday to Saturday, and for the hippest places at any time. A good internet booking service is www.toptable.co.uk, which is reliable and often offers substantial discounts. Many of the top-end restaurants run the annoying system of multiple sittings, where you have the option of an early or late slot, for example 7pm to 9pm or 9pm to 11pm. It's always best to go for the latter and not be rushed.

Tipping

Most restaurants now automatically tack a 'recommended' or 'discretionary' 12.5% service charge onto the bill and this should be clearly advertised (you don't have to pay it if you feel service wasn't good enough). If they still leave space for a tip on the credit-card slip, just ignore it.

Self-Catering

Along with Londoners' new-found passion for dining out comes a greater appreciation for food in general, and if you're keen to self-cater you'll find lots of great food and farmers' markets (see the boxed text, p242), Continental delis, and ethnic and organic stores sprinkled all over town. You can find mini versions of the big supermarkets all across the city for basic shopping requirements.

THE WEST END

With neighbourhoods as diverse as Soho, Mayfair, Bloomsbury and Marylebone, the West End is a difficult area to encapsulate, but it's true: many of the city's most eclectic, fashionable and, quite simply, best restaurants are

top picks

TABLES WITH A VIEW

- Blue Print Café (p250)
- Oxo Tower Restaurant & Brasserie (p249)
- Portrait (p240)
- Skylon (p249)
- Ubon (p261)

dotted around this area. As with most things in London, it pays to be in the know: while there's a huge concentration of mediocre places to eat along the main tourist drags, the best eating experiences are frequently tucked away on backstreets and not at all obvious. You'll find everything here, from Hungarian to Korean and from *haute cuisine* to vegetarian cafés. Chinatown, as you might guess, is a great spot for inexpensive Chinese and other Asian food.

SOHO & CHINATOWN

CRITERION GRILL Map p68   French ££-£££
☎ 7930 0488; www.whitestarline.org.uk; 224 Piccadilly W1; mains £15.50-28.50; ⊖ Piccadilly Circus
This beautiful Marco Pierre White restaurant is all chandeliers, mirrors, marble and sparkling mosaics – one breathless wag has compared it to the inside of a Fabergé egg – but its most spectacular feature is the classic French food, which ranges from the delicate tian of Devon crab to roast suckling pig mussel. The daily lunch specials (usually British favourites such as shepherd's pie and fish and chips) are a snip at £12.50.

BAR SHU Map p68   Chinese £-£££
7287 8822; www.bar-shu.co.uk; 28 Frith St W1; mains £7.90-28; ⊖ Leicester Sq
The story goes that a visiting businessman from Chengdu, capital of Sichuan Province in China, found London's Chinese food offerings so inauthentic that he decided to open up his own restaurant with five chefs from home. Well, it's authentic all right, with dishes redolent of smoked chillies and the all-important Sichuan peppercorn. We love the spicy *gung bao* chicken with peanuts, the *dan dan* noodles and the *mapo doufu* (bean curd braised with minced pork and chilli).

RED FORT Map p68   Indian ££-£££
☎ 7437 2525; www.redfort.co.uk; 77 Dean St W1; mains £14.50-22; ⊗ closed lunch Sat & Sun; ⊖ Tottenham Court Rd
The Red Fort has always been a trailblazer; as far back as the 1980s it was one of the very few places in London offering genuine Indian cuisine. It still retains its edge with glamorous décor and such dishes as *nizami kaliya* (kingfish in a spicy sauce with curry leaves) and *mahi tikka* (smoked dorade with fresh mint, garlic and green chilli).

LA TROUVAILLE Map p68   French ££-£££
☎ 7287 8488; www.latrouvaille.co.uk; 12a Newburgh St W1; 2-/3-course set lunch £15/18.50, dinner £27.50/33; ⊗ closed Sun; ⊖ Oxford Circus
Just what its name suggests it is, the 'Find' is perfect for a romantic dinner. Here you'll find a gorgeous, warm space perfect for candlelit canoodling and an excellent menu of rich traditional French cuisine – quail and foie gras terrine, guinea fowl hotpot – on a quiet backstreet.

KETTNERS Map p68   Italian £-££
☎ 7734 6112; www.kettners.com; 29 Romilly St W1; mains £9.30-19.90; ⊖ Leicester Sq
This Soho institution founded in 1867 has three dining rooms serving all manner of Modern European food but most people come here for the fabulous pizzas (£9.15 to £12.15), enjoyed with a glass of champagne and in a wonderful atmosphere of gently fading grandeur and a piano tinkling softly in the background.

VEERASWAMY Map p68   Indian £-££
☎ 7734 1401; www.veeraswamy.com; 1st fl, 99 Regent St (enter from Swallow St) W1; mains £9.50-19; ⊖ Piccadilly Circus
Having opened in 1926, this upmarket curry house can lay claim to being the oldest Indian restaurant in Britain. It's now owned by the same people who run Masala Zone (p265) and the standards are as high as ever, with the kitchen producing such crowd-pleasers as slow-cooked Hyderabad lamb biryani and Keralan-style sea bass.

ARBUTUS Map p68   Modern European ££
☎ 7734 4545; www.arbutusrestaurant.co.uk; 63-64 Frith St W1; mains £13.95-18.95; ⊖ Tottenham Court Rd
No-one seems to have a bad thing to say about this Michelin-starred brainchild of

Anthony Demetre. Is it the inventive dishes (squid and mackerel 'burger', slow-cooked lamb, sweetbreads and artichokes) or the non-Soho affordable prices (£17.50 for a three-course lunch)? One thing is for certain: it is not the take-no-risks décor.

GAY HUSSAR Map p68   Hungarian £-££
☎ 7437 0973; www.gayhussar.co.uk; 2 Greek St W1; mains £9.50-16.50; ⊗ closed Sun; ⊖ Tottenham Court Rd
This is the Soho of the 1950s, when dining was still done in the grand style in wood-panelled rooms with brocade and sepia prints on the walls. And it serves portions only the Hungarians do: try the roast duck leg with all the trimmings (£16.50) or the 'Gypsy quick dish' of pork medallions, onions and green peppers (£14.25). A two-/three-course lunch is £16.50/18.50.

ANDREW EDMUNDS
Map p68   Modern European £-££
☎ 7437 5708; 46 Lexington St W1; mains £9.60-16; ⊖ Piccadilly
This cosy little place is exactly the sort of restaurant you wish you could find everywhere in Soho. Two floors of wood-panelled bohemia with a mouth-watering

YAUATCHA Map p68   Dim Sum £-££
☎ 7494 8888; 15 Broadwick St W1; mains £3.80-15.90; ⊖ Oxford Circus
This most glamorous of dim sum restaurants housed in the award-winning Ingeni building is divided into two parts. The upstairs tearoom offers an exquisite blue-bathed oasis of calm from the chaos of Berwick St Market as well as some of the most arrestingly beautiful cakes we've ever seen. The downstairs dining room has a smarter, more atmospheric feel with constellations of 'star' lights and an original offering of the three main categories of dim sum (steamed, fried and *cheung fun* – long, flat rice-flour rolls stuffed with meat, seafood or vegetables) all day.

NEW WORLD Map p68   Chinese £
7734 0677; 1 Gerrard Pl W1; mains £6.50-9.90; ⊖ Leicester Sq
Chinatown doesn't have much to recommend itself in the way of food these days but if you hanker after dim sum, the

SOHO CAFÉS

Soho presents the nearest thing London has to a sophisticated café culture to match that of its Continental neighbours. The area has been synonymous with sipping and schmoozing since Victorian times but its heyday came with the mod hangouts of the '60s.

Bar Italia (Map p68; ☎ 7437 4520; 22 Frith St W1; sandwiches £4.50-6.50; ⊗ 24hr; ⊖ Leicester Sq or Tottenham Court Rd) Pop into this Soho favourite at any time of day or night and you'll see slumming celebrities lapping up reviving juices and chunky sandwiches amid retro '50s décor.

Maison Bertaux (Map p68; ☎ 7437 6007; 28 Greek St W1; cakes £3-3.50; ⊗ 8.30am-10.30pm Mon-Sat, to 8pm Sun; ⊖ Tottenham Court Rd) Bertaux has exquisite confections, unhurried service, a French bohemian vibe and 130 years of history on this spot. Seating is limited to a half-dozen tables.

Monmouth Coffee Company (Map pp72–3; ☎ 7836 5272, 7379 3516; www.monmouthcoffee.co.uk; 27 Monmouth St WC2; cakes from £2.50; ⊗ 8am-6.30pm Mon-Sat; ⊖ Tottenham Court Rd or Leicester Sq) Essentially a shop selling beans from just about every coffee-growing country in the world, Monmouth has a few wooden alcoves at the back where you can squeeze in and savour blends from around the world.

Pâtisserie Valerie (Map p68; ☎ 7437 3466; www.patisserie-valerie.co.uk; 44 Old Compton St W1; sandwiches £4.75-6.95, cakes from £2; ⊗ 7.30am-8pm Mon & Tue, 7.30am-11pm Wed-Sat, 9.30am-8pm Sun; ⊖ Tottenham Court Rd or Leicester Sq) This sweet institution was established in 1926 and is growing fast: at last count there were 10 outlets in London. All have delicious, delicate pastries, stylish sandwiches and filled croissants.

Star Café (Map p68; ☎ 7437 8778; www.thestarcafe.co.uk; 22 Great Chapel St W1; mains £6.25-8.50; ⊗ 7am-4pm Mon-Fri; ⊖ Tottenham Court Rd) So Soho, this wonderfully atmospheric café has vintage advertising and Continental décor that makes it feel like not much has changed since it opened in 1933. It's best known for its breakfast, particularly the curiously named Tim Mellor Special of smoked salmon and scrambled eggs.

three-storey New World can oblige. All the old favourites – from *ha gau* (prawn dumpling) to *pai gwat* (steamed pork spare rib) – are available from steaming carts wheeled around the dining room daily 11am to 6pm.

BARRAFINA Map p68   Spanish £
7813 8016; www.barrafina.co.uk; 54 Frith St W1; tapas £4.20-9.50; ⊖ Tottenham Court Rd
This tiny tapas bar has caught Soho by the tastebuds and doesn't look like letting go for quite a while. Along with *gambas al ajillo* (prawns in garlic), there are more unusual things such as tuna tartare and grilled quails with aioli. If you can't get enough, try one of the large platters of cold Spanish meats (£9.50 to £12.50).

MILDRED'S Map p68   Vegetarian £
☎ 7494 1634; www.mildreds.co.uk; 45 Lexington St W1; mains £6.95-8.25; ⊗ closed Sun; ⊖ Oxford Circus
Central London's most inventive veggie restaurant, Mildred's heaves at lunchtime so don't be shy about sharing a table in the skylit dining room. Expect the likes of roasted fennel and chickpea terrine and Puy lentil casserole as well as more standard (and hugely portioned) salads and stir-fries. Drinks include juices, coffees, beers and organic wines.

C&R CAFÉ Map p68   Malaysian, Indonesian £
☎ 7434 1128; 4-5 Rupert Court W1; mains £5-7.50; ⊖ Leicester Sq
When we're in the mood for a bit of Asian, we know of no better place than this hole-in-the-wall serving fairly authentic Singapore noodles, *laksa* (soup noodles with seafood) and *gado-gado* (salad with peanut sauce). For those who answer to a higher authority, it's halal. There's a larger Westbourne Grove branch (Map p175; ☎ 7221 7979; 52 Westbourne Grove W2; ⊖ Bayswater).

LEON Map p68   Modern European £
☎ 7437 5280; www.leonrestaurants.co.uk; 35 Great Marlborough St W1; mains £2.80-5.50; ⊗ 8am-10.30pm Mon-Fri, 9.30am-10.30pm Sat, 10.30am-6.30pm Sun; ⊖ Oxford Circus
A definite stand-out among Soho's budget eateries, Leon is delightful – cheap, friendly and perfectly located. Serving such delicious treats as chicken with herb oil and lemon, Moroccan meatballs and sweet potato

falafel, Leon puts labels on everything so you know just what you're getting. What's more, it's licensed. There are five other outlets including a Spitalfields branch (☎ 7247 4369; 3 Crispin Pl E1; ⊖ Liverpool St).

Also recommended:

Amato (Map p68; ☎ 7734 573373; www.amato.co.uk; 14 Old Compton St W1; mains £3.95-8.50; ⊗ 8am-10pm Mon-Sat, to 8pm Sun; ⊖ Piccadilly Circus) Long-term Italian fixture; does pastas and salads along with legendary cakes and pastries.

Red Veg (Map p68; ☎ 7437 3109; www.redveg.com; 95 Dean St W1; mains £2.95-4.35; ⊗ noon-9.30pm Mon-Sat, to 6.30pm Sun; ⊖ Tottenham Court Rd) Delicious vegetarian vegan fast food (burgers, falafels, wraps).

Kulu Kulu (Map p68; ☎ 7734 7316; 76 Brewer St W1; sushi £1.50-3.60; ⊖ Piccadilly Circus) This simple, bustling place just off Piccadilly Circus has the best inexpensive conveyor-belt sushi in London.

COVENT GARDEN & LEICESTER SQUARE

J SHEEKEY Map pp72–3   Fish ££-£££
☎ 7240 2565; www.j-sheekey.co.uk; 28-32 St Martin's Ct WC2; mains £11.75-37.50; ⊖ Leicester Sq
A jewel of the local scene, this incredibly smart restaurant whose pedigree stretches back to 1896 has four elegant, discreet and spacious wood-panelled rooms in which to savour the riches of the sea, cooked simply and exquisitely. The fish pie (£11.75) is justifiably legendary though the Cornish fish stew is just as good. Three-course weekday lunch is £24.75.

CHRISTOPHER'S Map pp72–3   American ££-£££
☎ 7240 4222; www.christophersgrill.com; 18 Wellington St WC2; mains £14-32; ⊖ Covent Garden
This sleek American bar and grill is housed in a vast Georgian mansion just off the Strand. Its interior is suitably grand, with a busy downstairs bar and a stylish upstairs dining room, where classic but clever dishes such as blackened salmon with jambalaya risotto are served up next to a wonderful array of gargantuan USDA steaks and surf-and-turf combinations. Brunch (11.30am to 3.30pm) at the weekend pulls in the crowds.

PORTRAIT Map pp72–3   British ££-£££
☎ 7312 2490; www.npg.org.uk/live/portrest .asp; 3rd fl, St Martin's Pl WC2; mains £13.95-28.95;

🍴 restaurant 11.30am-3pm Sat-Wed, 11.30am-3pm & 5.30-8.30pm Thu & Fri, lounge & bar 10am-5pm Sat-Wed, 10am-10pm (last orders food 8.30pm) Thu & Fri; ⊖ Charing Cross

This stunningly located restaurant above the excellent National Portrait Gallery – with views over Trafalgar Sq and Westminster! – and just past the Tudors is a place for a decent meal after the gallery; why not pop in for brunch when the two-/three-course menu is £19.95/24.95? Unfortunately, Portrait is restricted in its opening times by the gallery, so it only serves (early-ish) dinner on Thursday and Friday.

RULES Map pp72–3   Traditional British ££-£££

☎ 7836 5314; www.rules.co.uk; 35 Maiden Lane WC2; mains £16.95-21; ⊖ Covent Garden
Established in 1798, this very posh and very British establishment is London's oldest restaurant. The menu is inevitably meat-oriented – Rules specialises in classic game cookery, serving up tens of thousands of birds between mid-August and January from its own estate – but fish dishes are also available. Puddings are traditional: trifles, treacles and lashings of custard.

JOE ALLEN Map pp72–3   American £-££

☎ 7836 0651; www.joeallen.co.uk; 13 Exeter St WC2; mains £9-18; ⊖ Covent Garden
This long-established late-night (open till 1am most nights) restaurant is always packed with West End actors and crew members and remains a star-spotters' paradise. There's a real buzz here and it gets crowded, so book ahead. Starters and main dishes (lamb chops, grilled halibut etc) are varied, but you won't find its legendary burgers on the menu; just ask. Come here too for breakfast (from 8am weekdays) or weekend brunch (from 11.30am).

SARASTRO Map pp72–3   Mediterranean £-££

☎ 7836 0101; www.sarastro-restaurant.com; 126 Drury Lane WC2; mains £8.50-17.50; ⊖ Covent Garden
Any place that bills itself as 'The Show after the Show' has got to be more concerned with entertainment than food. Come to Sarastro, behind the Theatre Royal and round the corner from the Royal Opera House, for opera music (piped and impromptu) and faux baroque décor that is camper than a bunch of Boy Scouts (think kitsch frescoes and fake 'opera boxes'

adorning three sides of the restaurant). It's all quirky good fun and certainly a night you won't forget.

MELA Map pp72–3   Indian £-££

☎ 7836 8635; www.melarestaurant.co.uk; 152-156 Shaftesbury Ave; mains £5.95-15.95; ⊖ Leicester Sq
Despite its location in the heart of theatre-land, this bustling Shaftesbury Ave eatery serves some pretty authentic dishes from across India (with an emphasis on tandoor) and there is magnificent choice for vegetarians. We love the décor too, with colourful papier-mâché Ferris wheels and naive paintings of carnivals and fairs (Mela means 'festival' in Hindi).

ROCK & SOLE PLAICE
Map pp72–3   Fish & Chips £-££

☎ 7836 3785; 47 Endell St WC2; mains £4.50-14; ⊖ Covent Garden
Its cutesy name notwithstanding, the approach at this no-nonsense fish-and-chips shop dating back to Victorian times is simplicity: basic wooden tables and décor and delicious cod, haddock or skate in batter served with a generous portion of chips. Another plus: it's now licensed.

PORTERS Map pp72–3   Traditional British £-££

☎ 7836 6466; www.porters-restaurant.com; 17 Henrietta St WC2; mains £9.95-12.95; ⊖ Covent Garden
Porters specialises in pies, long a staple of English cooking but not regularly found on menus nowadays. There are unusual ones such as lamb and apricot or chicken and broccoli as well as the more commonplace steak, Guinness and mushroom pie. It also does a mean a mean fish and chips and roast beef with Yorkshire pudding.

ASSA Map pp72–3   Korean £

☎ 7240 8256; 53 St Giles High St WC2; mains £5.50-9; 🕐 closed lunch Sun; ⊖ Tottenham Court Rd
The best of a trio of Korean restaurants behind the unsightly (and listed) Centre Point building, Assa attracts a rough and very ready crowd of friendly young Asians who come for the cut-price soup noodles, *bibimbab* (rice served in a sizzling pot topped with thinly sliced beef, preserved vegetables and chilli-laced soy bean paste) and potent *soju* (Korean saki).

TO MARKET, TO MARKET

At first glance, London's food markets may seem to have changed beyond recognition in recent years. Borough Market on the South Bank, equal to or even better than anything you'll find on the Continent, is now a top tourist attraction and Broadway Market caters to the capital's Gordon Ramsay and Nigella Lawson wannabes. But for those who still want to experience a traditional London market, where the oranges and lemons come from who knows where and the barrow boys and girls speak with Cockney accents straight out of Central Casting, there's more than ample opportunity.

For information on farmers' markets, which tend to sell much more local, organic and – inevitably – expensive produce, see the boxed text, p251.

Berwick Street Market (Map p68; Berwick St W1; ⊙ 8am-6pm Mon-Sat; ✚ Piccadilly Circus or Oxford Circus) South of Oxford St and running parallel to Wardour St, this fruit-and-vegetable market has managed to hang onto its prime location since 1830. It's a great place to put together a picnic or shop for a prepared meal.

Billingsgate Fish Market (Map p160; Trafalgar Way E14; ⊙ 5-8.30am Tue-Sat; DLR West India Quay) This whole-sale fish market is open to the public, but you'll have to be up at the crack of dawn. People will tell you that you have to buy in bulk here, but most of the wise-crackin' vendors are prepared to do a deal.

Borough Market (Map p126; see also p132) Set up in 1998, this must-see is testament to the British public's increased interest in good food over the past decade. As well as a section devoted to quality fresh fruit, exotic vegetables and organic meat, there's a fine-foods retail market, with the likes of home-grown honey and homemade bread. Throughout, takeaway stalls allow you to sample a sizzling gourmet sausage or tuck into a quality burger. Shoppers queue at the excellent Monmouth Coffee Company, Neal's Yard Dairy, the Spanish deli Brindisa or butcher Ginger Pig, and generally bleed the local cash machines dry on Saturday.

Brixton Market (Map p200; Electric Ave SW9; ⊙ 8am-6pm Mon, Tue & Thu-Sat, 8am-3pm Wed; ✚ Brixton) This market is a heady, cosmopolitan mix with everything from halal butchers and fishmongers touting tilapia to yams, mangoes, okra, plantains and other produce on sale in the covered Brixton Village (formerly Granville Arcade). Try the Jamaican *bullah* cakes (gingerbread).

Broadway Market (Map p156; ⊙ 9am-5pm Sat; ✚ Bethnal Green, 🚃 Cambridge Heath) Offering some serious competition to overextended Borough, this much more manageable market with almost a village feel, south of London Fields E8, has the choicest produce, dairy products and baked goods on offer.

Chapel Market (Map p168; Chapel Market N1; ⊙ 9am-3.30pm Tue, Wed, Fri & Sat, 9am-1pm Thu & Sun; ✚ Angel) This rough-and-ready all-day market sells mostly fruit and vegetables along an Islington street called Chapel Market just off Liverpool Rd.

Exmouth Market (Map p150; www.exmouthmarket.co.uk; Exmouth Market EC1; ⊙ 11am-6pm Fri, 9am-4pm Sat; ✚ Farringdon or Angel) The latest arrival on the market scene, this small but varied producers' market sells quality produce, meat, fish and cheese.

Leadenhall Market (Map p110; Whittington Ave EC1; ⊙ 7am-4pm Mon-Fri; ✚ Bank) This market serves food and drink to City folk and has a fishmonger, a butcher and a cheesemonger. The selection is excellent for an urban market, and the Victorian glass-and-iron market hall, designed by Horace Jones in 1881, is an architectural delight. It's off Gracechurch St. See also p118.

Ridley Road Market (Map p156; Ridley Rd E8; ⊙ 8.30am-6pm Mon-Sat; 🚃 Dalston) In many ways this African Caribbean and Turkish market in the East End is more colourful than the one in Brixton, and it's certainly less touristed. You'll find more types of Turkish delight and Caribbean tubers than you'll know what to do with.

Roman Road Market (Map p156; Roman Rd E3; ⊙ 8am-4pm Tue, Thu & Sat; ✚ Mile End, 🚌 8 or 277) This market along Roman Rd between St Stephen's and Parnell Rds has pretty standard fare on offer, though some people rave about the low prices.

Smithfield Market (Map p110; see also p115) London's last surviving meat market is still clinging on, despite nearly getting the chop for an office development in 2005. While cattle were slaughtered here once, today this is the most modern of its kind in Europe and almost bloodless (though it would still be a vision of hell itself for vegetarians).

JEN CAFÉ Map pp72–3 Chinese £

☎ 7287 9708; 7-8 Newport Pl WC2; mains £5-7.95; ⏱ 11am-8.30pm Mon-Wed, to 9.30pm Thu-Sun; ⊖ Leicester Sq

This is the best place to come for home-made wonton soup and dumplings – bar none. And you can be assured of their freshness by looking through the plate glass window where they're in the process of being made.

FOOD FOR THOUGHT

Map pp72–3 Vegetarian £

☎ 7836 9072; 31 Neal St WC2; mains £3.10-6.90; ⏱ noon-8.30pm Mon-Sat, to 5pm Sun; ⊖ Covent Garden

This tiny vegetarian café is big on sociability and flavour, and small on price and space. Food ranges from soups and salads to stews and stir-fries with brown rice. Dishes might be vegan, organic and/or gluten-free. Food for Thought is earthy, unpretentious and deservedly packed.

Also recommended:

Canela (Map pp72–3; ☎ 7240 6926; www.canelacafe .com; 33 Earlham St WC2; mains £7.50-8.90; ⊖ Covent Garden) Tiny café serving tasty Portuguese and Brazilian dishes.

Wahaca (Map pp72–3; ☎ 7240 1883; www.wahaca .com; 66 Chandos Pl WC2; mains £3.50-6.50; ⏱ noon-3.30pm & 5.30-11pm Mon-Sat, noon-3.30pm & 5.30-10.30pm Sun; ⊖ Covent Garden) This delightful cantina styles itself as a 'Mexican market eating' experience and the food is as authentic as you'll find in central London. The misspelling of Oaxaca, the central Mexican city famous for its cuisine, is deliberate.

Scoop (Map pp72–3; ☎ 7240 7086; www.scoopgelato .com; 40 Shots Gardens, WC2; ice creams £2-5; ⏱ 8am-11pm; ⊖ Covent Garden) This is the only true *gelateria* in London and, boy, does it set a precedent. Storms of ice cream swell in the fridge, all the ingredients are natural and the taste is just divine.

HOLBORN & THE STRAND

MATSURI Map pp72–3 Japanese £££

☎ 7430 1970; www.matsuri-restaurant.com; Mid City Place, 71 High Holborn; set menus £22-45; ⏱ closed Sun; ⊖ Holborn

This high-quality and very authentic Japanese restaurant on the fringe of the City can sometimes feel a little sterile, although the quality of the food is extremely high. With a sushi counter and stylish dining

room on the ground floor and a large *teppanyaki* (hotplate) room in the basement where the meals are prepared in all seriousness by celebrated chef Hiroshi Sudo, there's plenty of choice.

SHANGHAI BLUES Map pp72–3 Chinese £-£££

☎ 7404 1668; www.shanghaiblues.co.uk; 193-197 High Holborn WC1; mains £9.50-42; ⊖ Holborn

What was once the St Giles Library now houses one of London's most stylish Chinese restaurants. The dark and atmospheric interior – think black and blue tables and chairs punctuated by bright red screens – recalls imperial Shanghai with a modern twist, and the menu is just as disarming, particularly the 'new style' dim sum served as appetisers, the *pipa* duck and the twice-cooked pork belly. There's a vast selection of teas, some of them quite rare. There's a three-course weekday lunch for £15 and live jazz on Friday and Saturday nights.

SIMPSON'S-IN-THE-STRAND

Map pp72–3 Traditional British ££-£££

☎ 7836 9112; 100 Strand WC2; mains £16.95-28.95; ⊖ Covent Garden

For traditional English roasts and joints (as in meat) from the trolley, Simpson's is hard to beat. It's been dishing up fleshy fare in a fine panelled dining room since 1848 (when it was called Simpson's Divan & Tavern). It's a gorgeous place, although something of a museum piece these days. Breakfast is available from 7.15am weekdays.

ASADAL Map pp72–3 Korean £-££

☎ 7430 9006; www.asadal.co.uk; 227 High Holborn WC1; mains £6.50-11.50; ⏱ closed lunch Sun; ⊖ Holborn

If you fancy Korean but want a bit more style thrown into the act than what you'll find at Assa (p241), head for this spacious basement restaurant next to the Holborn tube station. The *kimchi* (pickled Chinese cabbage with chillies) is searing, the barbecues (£7 to £11.50) are *à table* and the *bibimbab* – rice served in a sizzling pot topped with thinly sliced beef, preserved vegetables and chilli-laced soybean paste – the best in town.

Also recommended:

Hummus Bros (Map pp92–3; ☎ 7404 7079; www.hbros .co.uk; Victoria House, 37-63 Southampton Row WC1; mains £2.50-6; ⊖ Holborn) The deal at this new mini chain is a bowl of filling hummus with your choice of topping (beef, chicken, chickpeas etc) eaten with warm pita bread.

BLOOMSBURY

NORTH SEA FISH RESTAURANT
Map pp92–3   Fish £-££

☎ 7387 5892; 7-8 Leigh St WC1; mains £8.45-17.95; ⊗ closed Sun; ⊖ Russell Sq

The North Sea sets out to cook fresh fish and potatoes, a simple ambition in which it succeeds admirably. Look forward to jumbo-sized plaice or halibut steaks, deep-fried or grilled, and a huge serving of chips. There's takeaway next door if you can't handle the soulless dining room.

SHIOK Map pp92–3   Singaporean £-££

☎ 7436 9706; 75 Southampton Row WC1; mains £7-15.95; ⊗ closed Sun; ⊖ Holborn

Any place whose name means 'fantastic' in Malay slang gets our vote, especially when it serves chilli crab (£14.95), Singapore curry and *char kway teow* (fried flat noodles) as authentic as this. The surrounds are comfortable in a 'minimalist canteen-style' kind of way. Come here for lunch or a midafternoon fix of rice or noodles.

ABENO Map pp92–3   Japanese £-££

☎ 7405 3211; 47 Museum St WC1; mains £6.50-12.80; ⊖ Tottenham Court Rd

This understated little Japanese restaurant specialises in *okonomiyaki,* a kind of savoury pancake from Osaka of cabbage, egg and flour that is combined with the ingredients of your choice (there are more than two dozen varieties, including anything from sliced meats and vegetables to egg, noodles and cheese) and cooked on the hotplate at your table. There is quite a range of set lunches (£7.80 to £12.80).

FITZROVIA

HAKKASAN Map p68   Chinese £-£££

☎ 7907 1888, 7927 7000; 8 Hanway Pl W1; mains £9.50-42; ⊖ Tottenham Court Rd

This basement restaurant – hidden down a most unlikely back alleyway – combines celebrity status, stunning design, persuasive cocktails and surprisingly sophisticated Chinese food – it was the first Chinese restaurant to receive a Michelin star – to great success. The low, nightclub-style lighting (lots of red) makes it a good spot for dating, while the long, glitzy bar is a great place for truly inventive cocktails. For dinner in the formal main dining room you'll have to book far in advance and no doubt be allocated a two-hour slot. Do what savvy Londoners do and have lunch in the more informal Ling Ling lounge.

VILLANDRY Map p100   Modern European ££-£££

☎ 7631 3131; www.villandry.com; 170 Great Portland St W1; mains £11.50-22.50; ⊗ closed dinner Sun; ⊖ Great Portland St

This excellent Modern European restaurant with a strong Gallic slant has an attractive market-delicatessen attached (not to mention a bar) so freshness and quality of ingredients is guaranteed. Try the cassoulet (£17) or one of the several daily fish dishes.

BACK TO BASICS Map p68   Fish ££-£££

☎ 7436 2181; www.backtobasics.uk.com; 21a Foley St W1; mains £13.75-21.75; ⊗ closed Sun; ⊖ Oxford Circus

There are two or three other options on the menu (see 'Fish not Your Dish'), but seafood is the focus at this superb corner restaurant run by a bevy of affable young Poles in what's become know as Titchfield Village. A dozen varieties of exceedingly fresh fish, and a dozen original, mouth-watering ways to cook them, are chalked up on a blackboard every day. Two-course set lunch is £10. There's outside seating in summer.

ROKA Map p68   Japanese £-££

☎ 7580 6464; www.rokarestaurant.com; 37 Charlotte St W1; mains £9.60-18.60; ⊖ Goodge St or Tottenham Court Rd

This stunner of a Japanese restaurant combines casual dining (wooden benches) with savoury titbits delivered from the *robatayaki* (grill) kitchen in the centre. It has modern décor, with the dominating materials grey steel and glass. Sushi is £4.90 to £7.90, set lunch is £35.

FINO Map p68   Spanish £-££

☎ 7813 8010; www.finorestaurant.com; 33 Charlotte St (enter from Rathbone St) W1; tapas £1.80-16.50; ⊖ Goodge St or Tottenham Court Rd

Critically acclaimed (and it's easy to see why), Fino represents the resurgence of Spanish cuisine in a London all too dominated by dreary and uninventive tapas bars. Set in a glamorous basement on one of the city's premier eating strips, Fino is a tapas restaurant with a difference. Try the Jerusalem artichoke cooked with mint, the prawn tortilla with wild garlic or the foie gras with chilli jam for a feast of innovative and delightful Spanish cooking.

RASA SAMUDRA Map p68 — Indian ££-££

☎ 7637 0222; www.rasarestaurants.com; 5 Charlotte St W1; mains £6.25-12.95; ⊗ closed lunch Sun; ⊖ Goodge St or Tottenham Court Rd
This bubblegum-pink eatery just up from Oxford St showcases the seafood cuisine of Kerala state on India's southwest coast, supported by a host – eight out of 14 main courses – of more familiar vegetarian dishes. The fish soups are outstanding, the breads superb and the various curries heavenly spiced. The same group runs the South Indian vegetarian restaurant Rasa (p266) in Stoke Newington.

BUSABA EATHAI Map p68 — Thai £

☎ 7299 7900; 22 Store St WC1; mains £6.40-8.90; ⊖ Goodge St
We prefer the slightly less hectic Store St premises of this West End favourite, but there are also a couple more locations, including a Wardour St branch (Map p68; ☎ 7255 8686; 106-110 Wardour St; ⊖ Tottenham Court Rd). Here the sumptuous Thai menu greets you via an electronic screen outside and the über-styled interior is softened by communal wooden tables. This isn't the place to come for a long and intimate dinner, but it's a superb option for an excellent and (usually) speedy meal of stir-fries and noodles.

ST JAMES'S

NOBU Map pp96–7 — Japanese £-£££

☎ 7447 4747; www.noburestaurants.com; 1st fl, Metropolitan Hotel, 19 Old Park Lane W1; mains £5-29.50, set lunches/dinners from £50/70; ⊖ Hyde Park Corner
A London designer's idea of a Japanese restaurant with some of the best Asian food in town, Nobu is minimalist in décor, anonymously efficient in service, and out of this world when it comes to exquisitely prepared and presented sushi and sashimi. The black cod with miso and salmon kelp roll are divine.

L'AUTRE Map pp96–7 — Polish, Mexican ££

☎ 7499 4680; 5b Shepherd St W1; mains £10.60-13.60; ⊗ closed lunch Mon-Fri; ⊖ Green Park
How this small restaurant in Shepherd's Market came to serve dishes as incongruous as borscht and burritos is a tale too complex to tell here, but the food and the atmosphere (mock Tudor décor with Georgian elements) work well together. Overall, though, we'd head east for dishes such as golambki (stuffed cabbage) and Polish roast pork (£13.50) rather than south of the border.

INN THE PARK Map pp96–7 — British ££

☎ 7451 9999; St James's Park; mains £15; ⊗ 8am-11pm Sun-Thu, 9am-11pm Fri & Sat; ⊖ Trafalgar Sq
This stunning wooden café and restaurant has cakes and tea, as well as substantial and quality British food. It gets quite busy in the summer, but if you're up for a special dining experience, come here for dinner, when the park is quiet and slightly illuminated.

MAYFAIR

GORDON RAMSAY AT CLARIDGE'S

Map p100 — Modern British £££
☎ 7499 0099, 7592 1373; www.gordonramsay.com; 55 Brook St W1; 3-course set lunch/dinner £30/65; ⊖ Bond St
This match made in heaven – London's most celebrated chef in arguably its grandest hotel – will make you weak at the knees. A meal in the gorgeous Art Deco dining room is a special occasion indeed; the Ramsay flavours will have you reeling, from the pressed foie gras marinated in white port and the cannon of salt marsh lamb with crystallised walnuts and cumin all the way to the cheese trolley, whether you choose the one with French, British or Irish number plates. Consider the six-course tasting menu (£75).

GREENHOUSE Map p100 — Modern European £££

☎ 7499 3331; 27a Hay's Mews W1; 2-/3-course set lunch £28/32, 3-course set dinner £60; ⊗ lunch Mon-Fri, dinner Mon-Sat; ⊖ Green Park
Located in an incongruously uninspiring building in a mews at the end of a wonderful sculpted 'garden', Greenhouse offers some of the best food in Mayfair served with none of the attitude commonly found in restaurants of this class.

Try the veal sweetbreads with hazelnuts and the hare with black truffles. The tasting menu (£75) is only for the intrepid and truly hungry. Greenhouse doles out so many freebies – from *amuses-gueule* (literally 'throat amusers'; snacks or appetisers) and inter-course sorbets to petits fours at the finale – you'll never get up.

TAMAN GANG Map p100   Asian Fusion ££-£££

☎ 7518 3160; www.tamangang.com; 141 Park Lane W1; mains £16-52.50; ☾ dinner Mon-Sat; ⊖ Marble Arch

This basement restaurant just metres from the traffic chaos of Marble Arch is an oasis of tranquillity, suffused with incense and buzzing with a smart yet surprisingly informal Park Lane crowd. The interesting menu fuses Indonesian and Malaysian with Chinese and Japanese classics. On our last visit, the crispy aromatic duck roll was superb, while honey-glazed lamb cutlets with crispy lotus was of a similarly high standard but low size.

SKETCH Map p68   Modern European ££-£££

☎ 0870 777 4488; www.sketch.uk.com; 9 Conduit St W1; Gallery mains £19-28, Lecture Room & Library mains £39-48; ☾ closed Sun; ⊖ Oxford Circus

The stunning collection of bars and restaurants at what was once the Christian Dior headquarters in Mayfair remains a draw for fashionistas, the curious and the downright loaded. The Gallery restaurant downstairs buzzes informally in shimmering white and features video art projections. The Glade on the ground floor is the place for affordable lunch (two/three courses for £19.50/24) and the stunning Parlour patisserie to the right of the main entrance is great for tea and cakes. The ultimate attraction is the more formal Lecture Room & Library upstairs, where the high prices and *haute cuisine* in sumptuous surroundings from three-starred Michelin chef Pierre Gagnaire attract an exclusive crowd (tasting menus £65 to £90). Upstairs you'll also find the East Bar, with a dozen of London's most unusual individual loos.

WOLSELEY Map p68   Modern European £-£££

☎ 7499 6996; www.thewolseley.com; 160 Piccadilly W1; mains £9.50-34; ☾ 7am-midnight Mon-Fri, 8am-midnight Sat, 8am-11pm Sun; ⊖ Green Park

This erstwhile Bentley car showroom has been transformed into an opulent

top picks

DINING WITH KIDS

- Blue Kangaroo (p272)
- Frankie's Italian Bar & Grill (p253)
- Frizzante@City Farm (p260)
- Marine Ices (p262)
- Nando's (p274)

Viennese-style brasserie, with golden chandeliers and stunning black-and-white tiled floors, and it remains a great place for spotting celebrities. That said, the Wolseley tends to work better for breakfast, brunch or tea, rather than lunch or dinner, when the dishes (choucroute à l'Alsacienne, Wiener schnitzel) are somewhat stodgy and the black-attired staff more than a bit frayed. Daily specials are £15.75.

MOMO Map p68   North African ££-£££

☎ 7434 4040; www.momoresto.com; 25 Heddon St W1; mains £15-22.50, 2-/3-course set lunches £14/18; ⊖ Piccadilly Circus

Sister of the celebrated 404 in Paris' Marais district, this wonderfully atmospheric North African restaurant is stuffed with cushions and lamps, and staffed by all-dancing, tambourine-playing waiters. It's a funny old place that manages to be all things to all diners, who range from romantic couples to raucous office-party ravers. Service is very friendly and the dishes are as exciting as you dare to be, so after the meze (£4 to £6.50) eschew the traditional and ordinary *tajine* (stew cooked in a traditional clay pot) and tuck into the splendid Moroccan speciality *pastilla*, a scrumptious nutmeg and pigeon pie. There's outside seating in this quiet backstreet in the warmer months.

SAKURA Map p68   Japanese £

☎ 7629 2961; 9 Hanover St W1; mains £6.50-9.50; ⊖ Regent St

This very authentic Japanese restaurant has something for everyone throughout the day – from sushi and sashimi (£2 to £5) to tempura, sukiyaki and a host of sets (£9 to £24). Just opposite is a small Japanese shopping centre with grocery store, café-restaurant and pub.

KERALA Map p68   Indian £

☎ 7580 2125; 15 Great Castle St W1; mains £4.95-8.95; ⊖ Oxford Circus

Oxford Circus may seem an odd place to go for Indian food, but this little gem gets consistent thumbs-ups for its South Indian dishes. Try one of its distinctive biryanis or the prawns cooked in masala sauce.

WESTMINSTER

CINNAMON CLUB Map pp96-7   Indian ££-£££

☎ 7222 2555; www.cinnamonclub.com; Old Westminster Library, 30 Great Smith St SW1; mains £11-32; ⊘ closed lunch Sat & all day Sun; ⊖ St James's Park

Domed skylights, high ceilings, parquet flooring and a book-lined mezzanine – this just had to be a library in a former life – and the hushed, efficient staff only add to the illusion. The atmosphere is colonial club and the food modern – or perhaps palace – Indian. Set lunches of two/three courses are £19/22.

MARYLEBONE

LOCANDA LOCATELLI Map p100   Italian £££

☎ 7935 9088; www.locandalocatelli.com; 8 Seymour St W1; mains £20-29.50; ⊖ Marble Arch

Cofounder celebrity-chef Giorgio Locatelli has brought some of the best Italian cooking to London in the past decade and the menu here continues to show his inventiveness and attention to detail. It's still hard to get a table here without booking way in advance, but it's worth the effort, especially for the sublime pasta dishes (£8 to £12.50).

PROVIDORES & TAPA ROOM
Map p100   Spanish ££-£££

☎ 7935 6175; www.theprovidores.co.uk; 109 Marylebone High St W1; mains £18-24.50; ⊖ Baker St or Bond St

This place is split over two levels, with tempting tapas (£2.80 to £13.40) grazers on the ground floor and full meals along the same innovative lines – Spanish and just about everything else – in the elegant and understated dining room above. It's popular enough to be frenetic at busiest times; don't come for quiet conversation over your plate of chorizo and chillies.

SIX 13 Map p100   Jewish, Kosher ££-£££

☎ 7629 6133; www.six13.com; 19 Wigmore St W1; mains £15.50-23.50; ⊘ lunch Mon-Fri, dinner Mon-Thu; ⊖ Bond St

Central London's poshest kosher restaurant, Six 13 (the name comes from the 613 *mitzvots*, or commandments, that are binding on religious Jews) is certified glatt by the Sephardic Kashrut Authority of the UK. Dishes are relatively inventive but authentic; a three-course set meal is £42.50 but they'll also pack you a selection of five slim sandwiches for £17.50.

REUBENS Map p100   Jewish, Kosher £-£££

☎ 7486 0035; 79 Baker St W1; mains £9.95-22; ⊘ closed after lunch Fri, all day Sat; ⊖ Baker St

This central café-restaurant has all the Ashkenazi favourites: gefilte fish, *latkes* (potato pancakes) and sandwiches as well as more complicated (and filling) main courses. It's pricey for what you get but if you answer to a higher authority, it's money well spent.

SEASHELL OF LISSON GROVE
Map p100   Fish £-££

☎ 7224 9000; www.seashellrestaurant.co.uk; 49-51 Lisson Grove NW1; mains £9.50-18.95; ⊘ closed Sun; ⊖ Marylebone

This stylish place around the corner from Marylebone station is mostly about fish and chips (mostly the former) and must be doing something right. It's been in the business for more than 40 years. It does a brisk lunch and takeaway business as well.

WALLACE Map p100   French ££

☎ 7563 9505; www.wallacecollection.org; Hertford House, Manchester Sq W1; mains £12.50-18; ⊘ 10am-5pm Sun-Thu, 10am-11pm Fri & Sat; ⊖ Bond St; &

There are few more idyllically placed restaurants than this French brasserie in the courtyard of the Wallace Collection, London's finest small gallery and virtually unknown to most Londoners. Michelin-starred chef Thierry Laborde's seasonal menus are a veritable *tour de France* and cost £32 to £36 for three courses.

LA FROMAGERIE Map p100   French £-££

☎ 7935 0341; 2-4 Moxon St W1; mains £7.95-13.40; ⊘ 10.30am-7.30pm Mon, 8am-7.30pm Tue-Fri, 9am-7pm Sat, 10am-6pm Sun; ⊖ Baker St

This branch of a celebrated French cheese shop in Highbury has a small café attached that turns out exquisite French-inspired dishes at lunch. You can also enjoy breakfast from opening time and afternoon tea daily from 3.30pm.

GOLDEN HIND Map p100 — Fish & Chips £-££

☎ 7486 3644; 73 Marylebone Lane W1; mains £6.90-10.60; ⊗ closed lunch Sat & all day Sun; ⊖ Bond St

This 90-year-old chippie has a classic interior, chunky wooden tables and builders sitting alongside suits. And from the vintage fryer comes some of the best cod and chips available in London.

EAT & TWO VEG Map p100 — Vegetarian £

☎ 7258 8595; www.eatandtwoveg.com; 50 Marylebone High St W1; mains £8.50-9.95; ⊖ Baker St

One of the best vegetarian experiences in London, Eat & Two Veg is bright and breezy with charming, friendly staff and a smart 21st-century American-diner look. The menu is international eclectic – Thai green curry, Lankawi hotpot – and the mock meat dishes ('sausage' and mash, cheeseburger and fries) would fool even carnivores. There's plenty on offer for vegans too.

STARA POLSKA Map p100 — Polish £

☎ 7486 1333; 69 Marylebone Lane W1; mains £6.95-9.95; ⊗ closed dinner Sun; ⊖ Bond St

As authentic a *restauracja polska* as you'll find west of Warsaw, 'Old Poland' serves up simple but well-made favourites to veteran and newly arrived Polish London residents alike. Surely this is just the start of a trend towards 'mom and pop' Polish eateries across London.

Also recommended:

Ping Pong (Map p100; ☎ 7009 9600; www.pingpongdimsum.com; 10 Paddington St W1; dim sum £2.99, set lunches £9.90-11.90; ⊖ Baker St) Marylebone branch of a trendy six-outlet chain that is trying to make dim sum the new sushi (and making some waves).

Le Pain Quotidien (Map p100; ☎ 7486 6154; www.lepainquotidien.com; 72-75 Marylebone High St W1; mains £6.25-10.50; ⊖ Baker St) Simple, stripped-down French-style café serves salads, soups and *tartines* (open-face sandwiches; £6.25 to £8.50).

Quiet Revolution (Map p100; ☎ 7487 5683; 28 Marylebone High St W1; mains £5.75-9.95; ⊗ 9am-6pm Mon-Sat, 11am-5pm Sun; ⊖ Baker St) The omelettes, quiches and salads at this bright café are not 100% vegetarian (there are a couple of meat and fish dishes lurking about) but they're all organic. Excellent (and vigorous) juice combos too.

THE CITY

In the not-so-distant past, the City – that 'Square Mile' of brokers and bankers – could be an irritating place to find a decent and affordable restaurant that was patronised (or, indeed, stayed open) after the stock market closed. But with more people working later hours and living in and around the area (eg Barbican and Hoxton), you can now choose among cutting-edge Modern British, Italian and even Indian restaurants that all keep the welcome mat out at dinnertime. By and large though, the City caters mostly to a well-heeled weekday clientele.

SWEETING'S Map p110 — Seafood ££-£££

☎ 7248 3062; 39 Queen Victoria St EC4; mains £12.50-27.50; ⊗ lunch Mon-Fri; ⊖ Mansion House

Sweeting's is a City institution, having been around since 1830. It hasn't changed much, with its small sit-down restaurant area, mosaic floor and narrow counters, behind which stand waiters in white aprons. Dishes include wild smoked salmon, oysters (in season from September to April), potted shrimps, eels and Sweeting's famous fish pie (£12.50).

CITY MIYAMA Map p110 — Japanese £-£££

☎ 7489 1937; 17 Godliman St EC4; mains £9-25; ⊗ closed dinner Sat & all day Sun; ⊖ St Paul's

This rather soulless Japanese basement restaurant serves some of the finest sushi in the City, which comes in both 'traditional' and 'new' styles. Set lunches, representing the best deals, are £13 to £25.

WHITE SWAN PUB & DINING ROOM

Map p110 — Gastropub £-£££

☎ 7242 9696; www.thewhiteswanlondon.com; 108 New Fetter Lane EC4; pub mains £8.95-14; ⊗ closed Sat & Sun; ⊖ Chancery Lane

A gastropub that everyone wishes were in their neighbourhood (and kept weekend hours), the White Swan has a convivial bar downstairs, with everything from fish and chips to lamb burgers (and a stuffed swan in a glass case) and an upstairs dining room with a more ambitious menu (two-/three-course meal £24/29).

PATERNOSTER CHOP HOUSE

Map p110 — British ££-£££

☎ 7029 9400; www.danddlondon.com; Warwick Ct, Paternoster Sq EC4; mains £16.50-20; ⊗ closed all day Sat & dinner Sun; ⊖ St Paul's

At this Conran City restaurant next to St Paul's Cathedral delightfully British fare is on offer – from the 'beast of the day' (£21) to a huge shellfish and grill selection and faves such as bubble and squeak (left over veggies from a roast dinner), and haggis. Sunday brunch (noon to 4pm) features a carvery.

ROYAL EXCHANGE GRAND CAFÉ & BAR Map p110
Modern European ££

☎ 7618 2480; www.danddlondon.com; Royal Exchange Bank, Threadneedle St EC3; mains £12-17.50; ☯ 8am-11pm Mon-Fri; ⊖ Bank

This café sits in the middle of the covered courtyard of the beautiful Royal Exchange Bank building. The food runs the gamut from sandwiches to oysters (from £10.75 a half-dozen), fisherman's pie (£18.50) and seafood platters (from £26.50). It's the perfect place for an informal business meeting.

WINE LIBRARY Map p110
Modern European ££

☎ 7481 0415; www.winelibrary.co.uk; 43 Trinity Sq EC3; set meals £14.95; ☯ 10am-6pm Mon, 10am-8pm Tue-Fri; ⊖ Tower Hill

This is a great place for a light but boozy lunch in the City. Buy a bottle of wine at retail price (no mark-up; £4.50 corkage fee) from the large selection on offer at this vaulted-cellar restaurant and then snack on pâtés, cheeses and salads for £14.95.

Also recommended:

Ciro's Pizza Pomodoro (Map p110; ☎ 7920 9207; www .pomodoro.co.uk; 7-8 Bishopsgate Churchyard EC2; mains £5.50-10.50; ☯ closed Sat & Sun; ⊖ Liverpool St) Passable pasta and pizza in a sublimely tiled *hammam* (Turkish-style bath) off Old Broad St and dating from 1894.

Place Below (Map p110; ☎ 7329 0789; St Mary-le-Bow Church, Cheapside EC2; dishes about £7.25; ☯ 7.30am-3pm Mon-Fri; ⊖ Mansion House) Old-school (pasta, bakes, salads) vegetarian restaurant is in a church crypt.

Salade (Map p110; ☎ 7248 6612; 3 Old Bailey St EC4; salads £4-6; ☯ 7am-5pm Mon-Fri; ⊖ St Paul's, 🚇 City Thameslink) This 'compose your own salad' place offers some of the freshest and most interesting ingredients around – from sprouts and Puy lentils to crayfish.

THE SOUTH BANK

The revitalised South Bank, with the Tate Modern, the replicated Globe Theatre and the splendid Millennium Bridge its drawing cards, offers an array of restaurants unimaginable just a few short years ago. Many, including the Oxo Tower and Blue Print Café, take full advantage of their riverine locations, offering a titbit of romance as a prelude to the main course. Borough and Bermondsey, historically important but run-down and almost forgotten in modern times, are no longer just the provinces of smoked and jellied eel; you're just as likely to find yourself sitting in a Victorian market pavilion and enjoying fresh oysters or a perfectly grilled steak.

WATERLOO

OXO TOWER RESTAURANT & BRASSERIE Map p126
Modern International ££-£££

☎ 7803 3888; www.harveynichols.com; 8th fl, Barge House St SE1; brasserie mains £16.50-18.25, 2-/3-course set lunch £17.50/21.50, restaurant mains £19.50, 3-course set lunches £31.50; ⊖ Waterloo

The Oxo Tower is about event dining, with the emphasis generally more on the event than the food. In the stunning glassed-in terrace you have a front-row seat to probably the best view in London here, and you're paying for this (not the fusion food) handsomely in the brasserie and stratospherically in the restaurant. Fish dishes – smoked haddock soufflé, Japanese-style scallops, Thai red curry sea bass – make up half the menu.

SKYLON Map p126
Modern International £-£££

☎ 7654 7800; www.skylonrestaurant.co.uk; 3rd fl, Royal Festival Hall, South Bank Centre, Belvedere Rd SE1; restaurant 2-/3-course meals £29.50/34.50, grillroom mains £8-18.50; ☯ bar 11am-1am, grillroom noon-11.45pm, restaurant lunch & dinner to 10.45pm; ⊖ Waterloo

This cavernous restaurant on the top of the refurbished Royal Festival Hall is divided into grill and fine-dining sections with a large bar in the centre of the room separating the two. Floor-to-ceiling windows offer stunning views of the Thames and the City, and the décor of muted colours and period chairs harkens back to the 1951 Festival of Britain when the hall opened. Try the stuffed baby squids with preserved lemon and the smoked halibut with spring artichokes. Weekday lunch is £19.51/24.50 for two/three courses.

ANCHOR & HOPE Map p126
Gastropub ££

☎ 7928 9898; 36 The Cut SE1; mains £11.50-14.80; ☯ closed lunch Mon & dinner Sun; ⊖ Southwark or Waterloo

The hope is that you'll get a table without waiting hours, because unfortunately you can't book at this quintessential gastropub. The anchor is the gutsy, unashamedly carnivorous British food. The critics love this place but with dishes such as duck hearts, pink lamb's neck and deep-fried pig's head, it's decidedly not for vegetarians. A second restaurant, Great Queen Street (Map pp72–3; ☎ 7242 0622; 32 Great Queen St WC2; ◉ Garden or Holborn) in Covent Garden, is smaller, does not have a pub and – joy of joys – takes reservations.

BOROUGH & BERMONDSEY

ROAST Map p126   Modern British ££-£££
☎ 7940 1300; www.roast-restaurant.com; 1st fl, Floral Hall, Borough Market, Stoney St SE1; mains £13.50-28; ☽ closed dinner Sun; ◉ London Bridge
Iqbal Wahhab of Cinnamon Club (p247) fame has perched this unique restaurant directly above Borough Market, so he won't have to go far for his raw materials. The focal point here is the glassed-in kitchen with an open spit, where ribs of beef, suckling pigs, birds and game are roasted. The emphasis is on roasted meats and seasonal vegetables, though there are lighter dishes from salads through to grilled fish.

CHAMPOR-CHAMPOR
Map p126   Asian Fusion £££
☎ 7403 4600; www.champor-champor.com; 62-64 Weston St SE1; 2/3 courses £23.50/27.90; ☽ lunch Mon-Sat; ◉ London Bridge
Not surprisingly, a restaurant whose name means 'mix and match' serves up some unusual creations. East–west cuisine include herbed ostrich sausages in Sichuan pepper and Japanese miso, veal cutlets crusted with coriander seeds, peppercorn-crusted lamb cutlets with peanut sauce, and several vegetarian options that the waiter will probably have to explain ('baked silk tofu with black vinegar', anyone?). Some dishes work, others don't. The eclectic décor – some Asian, a bit of African – is a delight.

BLUE PRINT CAFÉ
Map p126   Modern International ££
☎ 7378 7031; www.danddlondon.com; 1st fl, Design Museum, Butler's Wharf SE1; mains £12.50-18; ☽ closed dinner Sun; ◉ Tower Hill
Behind glass on the 1st floor of the Design Museum and aided by opera glasses at each table, customers have stunning views

of Tower Bridge and the so-called Gherkin at 30 St Mary Axe. Food is simple but tasty, with the most straightforward dishes usually working best. Look for Jerusalem artichoke soup, beetroot salad and fish dishes such as bream with seakale, cabbage, clams and bacon.

DELFINA Map p126   Modern International ££
☎ 7357 0244, 7564 2400; www.delfina.org.uk; 50 Bermondsey St SE1; mains £10.95-16.95; ☽ lunch Mon-Fri, dinner Fri; ◉ London Bridge
It's a crying shame that this upmarket artists' canteen with a woman chef at the helm serves just weekday lunches and one dinner a week as it really does offer some fine modern international cuisine (emphasis on poultry, fish and vegetables). The space is wonderful – large and light-filled – and the menu changes fortnightly. Coffee and cakes are served at the Studio Café from 8am to noon and 3pm to 5pm Monday to Friday.

BERMONDSEY KITCHEN
Map p126   Modern European £-££
☎ 7407 5719; www.bermondseykitchen.co.uk; 194 Bermondsey St SE1; mains £9.50-16; ☽ closed dinner Sun; ◉ London Bridge
As it's a great place to curl up on the sofas with the Sunday newspapers or enjoy brunch, it's hardly surprising that many locals seem to have made this their second living room. The Modern European food (with a nod towards the Mediterranean) that comes from the open grill is as homy and unpretentious as the rough-hewn tables, and the refreshingly brief menu (five starters and as many mains) changes daily.

WRIGHT BROTHERS Map p126   Fish £-££
☎ 7403 9554; www.wrightbros.eu.com; 11 Stoney St SE1; mains £8.50-15.50; ☽ closed Sun; ◉ London Bridge
Should you be tempted by the offerings of the fishmongers of Borough Market and must have a fix of iodine right then and there, head for this excellent oyster bar and porter house. You'll find up to a dozen different types of the bivalve (£7 to £16.25 for six) available at any given time, along with more substantial main courses.

GARRISON Map p126   Gastropub £-££
☎ 7089 9355; www.thegarrison.co.uk; 99 Bermondsey St SE1; mains £6.80-14; ☽ breakfast,

FARMERS' MARKETS

For fresh fruit, vegetables, dairy products, meat and fish, bread and other foodstuffs that taste the way they did when you were a kid, head to one of the growing number of weekend farmers' markets that have been springing up around London in the past decade. Here producers sell their own wares, the atmosphere is sociable and the produce is guaranteed fresh. The following are some of the best and most central; for a complete listing see www.lfm.org.uk.

Blackheath (Map p64; Blackheath train station car park SE10; 🕑 10am-2pm Sun; 🚇 Blackheath)

Clapham (Bonneville Primary School, Bonneville Gardens SW4; 🕑 10am-2pm Sun; 🚇 Clapham South)

Finchley (Map p166; 02 Centre car park, near Homebase, Finchley Rd NW3; 🕑 10am-3pm Wed; 🚇 West Hampstead or Finchley Rd)

Islington (Map p168; William Tyndale School, behind Islington Town Hall, Upper St N1; 🕑 10am-2pm Sun; 🚇 Highbury & Islington or Angel) London's original farmers' market, this one sells organic produce and other foodstuffs grown or reared within a 50-mile radius of the capital.

Marylebone (Map p100; Cramer St car park, off Marylebone High St W1; 🕑 10am-2pm Sun; 🚇 Baker St or Bond St) The largest farmers' market in town, with 40 producers coming from within a 100-mile radius of the M25.

Notting Hill (Map p175; car park behind Waterstone's, Kensington Pl W8; 🕑 9am-1pm Sat; 🚇 Notting Hill Gate)

Pimlico Road (Map pp138–9; Orange Sq, cnr Pimlico Rd & Ebury St; 🕑 9am-1pm Sat; 🚇 Sloane Sq)

Wimbledon (off Map p64; Wimbledon Park First School, Havana Rd SW19; 🕑 9am-1pm Sat; 🚇 Wimbledon Park)

---

lunch & dinner daily, brunch Sat & Sun; 🚇 London Bridge

The Garrison's traditional green-tiled exterior and minimalist (distressed, rather) beach-shack interior are both appealing and it boasts an actual cinema in its basement, but it's the comfort food (shepherd's pie, kedgeree, lentil and pumpkin vegetarian loaf) that brings the punters to this evergreen gastropub. If you don't fancy nearly bashing your neighbour's elbow every time you lift your fork, though, come for breakfast (8am to 11.30am weekdays) or weekend brunch (9am to 11.15am).

Also recommended:

Masters Super Fish (Map p126; ☎ 7928 6924; 191 Waterloo Rd SE1; mains £7-16.50; 🕑 closed Sun; 🚇 Waterloo) Superlative fish (brought in fresh daily from Billingsgate Market and grilled rather than fried if desired) at this rather humble-looking institution.

Hartley (Map p126; ☎ 7394 7023; www.thehartley.com; 64 Tower Bridge Rd SE1; mains £8-13; 🕑 closed dinner Sun; 🚇 London Bridge) Fence-sitter of a pub/gastropub does steak and kidney and lime-mousse brûlée with equal aplomb.

Coffee@Bermondsey (Map p126; ☎ 7403 7638; 163-167 Bermondsey St SE1; dishes £2.95-3.50; 🕑 7am-8pm daily; 🚇 London Bridge) Natural nosh (some organic, some vegan) at this very relaxed café with internet access and bulletin boards. There's a Spitalfields branch, Coffee@Brick Lane (Map p150; ☎ 7247 6735; 154 Brick Lane E1; 🚇 Liverpool St).

HYDE PARK TO CHELSEA

In the early 18th century, the influx of foreign migrants to London, already Europe's largest city, led to the expansion of the working-class areas to the east and the south while the more affluent high-tailed it for the north and, to an even greater extent, the west. Naturally, quality gravitates to where the money is, and you'll find some of London's finest establishments in the swanky hotels and ritzy mews of Chelsea, Belgravia and Knightsbridge. The king of them all, Gordon Ramsay, has three Michelin stars in its crown and resides in Chelsea. Chic and cosmopolitan South Kensington has always been reliable for pan-European options.

CHELSEA & BELGRAVIA

GORDON RAMSAY

Map pp138–9   Modern European £££

☎ 7352 4441; www.gordonramsay.com; 68 Royal Hospital Rd SW3; 3-course lunches/dinners £40/85; 🕑 lunch & dinner Mon-Fri; 🚇 Sloane Sq

One of Britain's finest restaurants and still the only one in the capital with three

Michelin stars, this is hallowed turf for those who worship at the altar of the stove. It's true that it is a treat right from the taster to the truffles but you won't get much time to savour it all. Bookings are made in specific eat-it-and-beat-it slots and you dare not linger. The blow-out tasting Menu Prestige (£110) is seven courses of absolute perfection.

CHEYNE WALK BRASSERIE & SALON
Map pp138–9   French ££–£££

☎ 7376 8787; www.cheynewalkbrasserie.com; 50 Cheyne Walk SW3; mains £13.50-29.50, 2-/3-course set lunches £16.95/19.95, Sun brunches £20/25; ⏰ lunch Tue-Sun, dinner Mon-Sat, brunch Sun; ⊖ Sloane Sq

With a reputation for especially tender steaks, the focus of the food preparation at this brasserie is the large open grill in the centre of the ground-floor dining room. However, you might prefer prawns flambéed in pastis sardine with a delightful salad of green beans, pistachio and mint. The *belle époque* decoration is just this side of kitsch, with turquoise banquettes, red leather chairs, chandeliers and crystal lamps topped with pink shades. From the very red star-dotted upstairs cocktail salon are great views of the Thames.

AMAYA Map pp138–9   Indian £–££
☎ 7823 1166; www.amaya.biz; Halkin Arcade, 19 Motcomb St SW1; mains £7.50-20; ⊖ Knightsbridge

Hidden down a little arcade behind Starbucks lies a swish, stylish restaurant, with low-lit interior, colourful jewelled inlays in the wood, hanging crystal strings and chandeliers. But what will really hold your attention are the chefs at work in the open kitchen, as they slave over an iron skillet *(tawa)*, charcoal grill *(sigri)* or clay oven *(tandoor)*. Varied set menus (eg a vegetarian tasting one at £22, an express lunch at £19.50) put the emphasis on sharing dishes with your dining companions.

TUGGA
Map pp138–9   Portuguese, Mediterranean £–££

☎ 7351 0101; www.tugga.com; 312-314 King's Rd SW3; mains £9-15.80; ⏰ lunch Sat & Sun, dinner daily; ⊖ Sloane Sq, then ⊒ 11, 19, 22, 49 or 319

The psychedelically floral wallpaper and cerise and purple cushions in this King's Rd restaurant make it a favourite with the Chelsea set, who come to enjoy the Portuguese cuisine (which is sold as modern but is actually more classic). The long menu of *pestiscos* (starters; £4.50 to £7) allows you to sample such classics as roasted chorizo, *caldo verde* (Portuguese green cabbage soup) and *bacalhau à Brás* (dried cod with potatoes, egg and onion).

OGNISKO Map pp138–9   Polish £–££
☎ 7589 4635; www.ognisko.com; 55 Exhibition Rd SW7; mains £9.90-14.40; ⊖ South Kensington

This is Polish of another world and time: a baroque dining room complete with portraits of military heroes (that would be the White Army) and chandeliers and mirrors; it overlooks a verdant square. But stick with the basics at 'The Hearth': *barszcz czwerwony* (beetroot soup) and *pierogi* (dumplings stuffed with meat or cheese and potatoes). Outside seating in the warmer months.

KNIGHTSBRIDGE, KENSINGTON & HYDE PARK

TOM AIKENS Map pp138–9   Modern European £££
☎ 7584 2003; www.tomaikens.co.uk; 43 Elystan St SW3; 3-course set lunches/dinners £29/65; ⏰ lunch & dinner Mon-Fri; ⊖ South Kensington

The Tom of the title made his name by picking up two Michelin stars at Pied à Terre by the time he was only 26. He returned with this handsome restaurant in 2003 and, three years later, the even more relaxed Tom's Kitchen (see p254) nearby. The food here is excellent, with phenomenal starters such as braised scallops with pork belly and partridge with truffled mash. The tasting menu is £80 (or £140 with accompanying wines).

CAPITAL Map pp138–9   Modern European £££
☎ 7589 5171; www.capitalhotel.co.uk; Capital Hotel, 22-23 Basil St SW3; 3-course set lunches/dinners £29.50/55; ⊖ Knightsbridge

Of the five restaurants in London to have won two Michelin stars, the Capital behind Harrods department store is probably the least known – and so much the better. The modern yet warmth-inducing décor, welcoming and accommodating staff and chef Eric Chavot's award-winning dishes – a large, glass plate like an artist's palate of duck preparations called *assiette Landaise*, pan-roasted lobster with crab ravioli, roasted fillet of venison served with pan-fried foie gras – all remain our secrets. And now yours. The tasting menu is £70 (add £47 for accompanying wines).

BIBENDUM
Map pp138–9 Modern European ££–£££
☎ 7581 5817, 7589 1480; www.bibendum.co.uk; Michelin House, 81 Fulham Rd SW3; mains £16.50-28, 2-/3-course set lunches £24/28.50; ⊖ South Kensington
Housed in the listed Art Nouveau Michelin House (1911), Bibendum offers upstairs dining in a spacious and light room with stained-glass windows, where you can savour fabulous and creative food, and what, it must be said, is fairly ordinary service. The Bibendum Oyster Bar offers a front-row seat of the building's architectural finery while lapping up terrific native and rock oysters.

BOXWOOD CAFÉ
Map pp138–9 Modern European ££–£££
☎ 7235 1010; www.gordonramsay.com; Berkeley Hotel, Wilton Pl (enter from Knightsbridge) SW1; mains £16-28, set lunches £25; ⊖ Knightsbridge
Gordon Ramsay's New York–style (almost) café is the kind of place you can come for a single course or a glass of wine, and while the décor is a little bland – way too dark in the depths of the main restaurant – the food is generally first rate. Simple starters such as fried West Mersea oysters with fennel and lemon, salmon ceviche and glazed pea and leek tart are generally tastier than the fussier main courses. Run-the-gamut tasting menus are £46 and £55.

NAHM
Map pp138–9 Thai ££–£££
☎ 7333 1234; www.halkin.co.uk; Halkin Hotel, Halkin St SW1; mains £19.50-21.50, set lunch/dinner £20/26; ⓨ lunch Mon-Fri, dinner daily; ⊖ Hyde Park Corner
Australian chef David Thompson is the man behind the excellent tucker at this hotel restaurant, the only Thai eatery in Europe to have a Michelin star. On offer are Thai classics such as tom yam gai (hot and sour chicken coconut soup) as well as more exotic fare such as minced trout curry with basil and stir-fried pigeon with bamboo. The surrounds may be somewhat sterile but the leafy views are worth a booking alone. Go for lunch.

AWANA
Map pp138–9 Malaysian ££–£££
☎ 7584 8880; www.awana.co.uk; 85 Sloane Ave SW3; mains £12.50-21, 2-/3-course set lunch £12.50/15; ⊖ South Kensington
London's (and perhaps the northern hemisphere's) first fine-dining Malay restaurant,

Awana has all our favourite dishes (beef rendang, Hainan-style chicken, butterfish wrapped in banana leaves with herbs and char-grilled) in a dining room done up to look like a relaxed kampong (village) house. (The uninitiated may want to consider the Malaysian Journey sampling menu at £36.) The Satay Bar serves delicious skewers of chicken, beef, lamb and prawns accompanied by the restaurant's own spicy peanut sauce. We'll be back.

LUCIO
Map pp138–9 Italian ££–£££
☎ 7823 3007; www.luciorestaurant.com; 257-259 Fulham Rd SW3; mains £16.50-20.50, 2-/3-course set lunch £15.50/19; ⊖ South Kensington
One of our favourite Italian eateries in London, Lucio is decidedly top-end but not overly so. Try the exquisitely cooked pasta with clams, the crab ravioli or, when in season, the deep-fried courgette. The surrounds are understatedly stylish, the clientele subdued and the service seamless.

RACINE
Map pp138–9 French ££
☎ 7584 4477; 239 Brompton Rd SW3; mains £13.25-19.50, 2-/3-course set lunch £16.50/18.50; ⊖ Knightsbridge
Regional French cooking is the vehicle here and all-round, dedicated service to the customer the destination. Expect the likes of tête de veau (the classic French veal dish), grilled rabbit with mustard and smoked duck. Being French and very classic, dishes might feel heavy to some, but the sauces and the desserts are all spot on.

FRANKIE'S ITALIAN BAR & GRILL
Map pp138–9 Italian ££
☎ 7590 9999; www.frankiesitalianbarandgrill .com; 3 Yeoman's Row SW3; mains £10.50-13.50; ⊖ Knightsbridge
Brain child of jockey Frankie Dettori and seminal chef Marco Pierre White, Frankie's has resuscitated that age-old formula for success in the catering trade: good, solid, old-fashioned food (in this case Italian) – and lots of it. The menu, popular with families, is top heavy with steaks and fish though burgers (£6.95) and pastas (£8.50) also figure.

DAQUISE
Map pp138–9 Polish £–££
☎ 7589 6117; 20 Thurloe St SW7; mains £5.50-13.50; ⊖ South Kensington
This place is a real dinosaur – but a loveable little tyrannosaurus indeed – and very

close to the museums of South Kensington. It's a rather dowdy Polish café-cum-diner, with a good range of vodkas and extremely reasonably priced dishes, including the oft-seen *bigosz*, a 'hunter's stew' of cabbage and pork, and ravioli-like *pierogi*.

JAKOB'S Map pp138–9   Armenian £

☎ 7581 9292; 20 Gloucester Rd SW7; mains £6.50-9.50; ✚ Gloucester Rd

This charismatic Armenian-owned restaurant serves delicious and wholesome (and sometimes organic) salads, vegetarian lasagne, filo pie, falafel and kebabs that you choose at the counter after having laid claim to a table in the back. A plate of three/four choices is £6.50/9.50. Desserts are very good.

Also recommended:

Tom's Kitchen (Map pp138–9; ☎ 7349 0202; www .tomskitchen.co.uk; 27 Cale St SW3; mains £10.50-21.50; ✚ South Kensington) Tom Aikens roughing it round the corner in Chelsea, with less fussy interpretations of 'beef, birds and pork' served at chunky butcher-block tables.

Pizza Organic (Map pp138–9; ☎ 7589 9613; www .pizzaorganic.co.uk; 20 Old Brompton Rd SW7; pizzas £5.90-13.95; ✚ South Kensington) Excellent pizza and pasta at this family-friendly place on a busy corner of South Kensington.

VICTORIA & PIMLICO

ROUSSILLON Map pp138–9   French £££

☎ 7730 5550; www.roussillon.co.uk; 16 St Barnabas St SW1; 3-course set lunches £35, 3-/4-course set dinners £48/60; ◷ closed lunch Sat & all day Sun; ✚ Sloane Sq

On a quiet side street off Pimlico Rd, Roussillon offers such fine service, lovely muted décor and settings, and fresh English ingredients dexterously cooked *à la française* that we're almost hesitant to show off this sparkling gem to the world. There's no à la carte; choose from among eight starters and main courses at lunch or dinner, or there's a more extravagant tasting menu (£70) of eight courses. The Menu Légumes (£60) puts vegetarian cooking in the Michelin league.

KEN LO'S MEMORIES OF CHINA
Map pp138–9   Chinese ££-£££

☎ 7730 7734; www.memories-of-china.co.uk; 65-69 Ebury St SW1; mains £11.75-34; ◷ closed Sun; ✚ Victoria

The late Kenneth Lo brought Chinese food to new levels in London, and the service and décor of the place reflect that position. The interior is elegant, oriental minimalism and the noise levels are agreeably low. There are several set menus (£18.50 to £21.50) – including a vegetarian one and an unforgettable 'Gastronomic Tour of China' (£30 per person) – and all the well-proportioned dishes feature a splendidly light touch and wonderful contrasts of flavours and textures.

LA POULE AU POT Map pp138–9 French ££-£££

☎ 7730 7763; 231 Ebury St SW1; mains £15.50-21, 2-/3-course set lunches £16.75/18.75; ✚ Sloane Sq

Lit by candlelight even at lunch, the 'Chicken in the Pot' is a long-established country-style French restaurant that is long on romance and cosiness and somewhat shorter on what it serves. Still, the alfresco front terrace is a lovely spot in the warmer months.

OLIVO Map pp138–9   Italian ££

☎ 7730 2505; 21 Eccleston St SW1; mains £12.50-17.50; ◷ lunch & dinner Mon-Sat; ✚ Victoria or Sloane Sq

This colourful restaurant specialises in the food and wine of Sardinia and Sicily, and has a dedicated clientele of sophisticates who, quite frankly, would rather keep it to themselves. Not surprising, really, because this place near Victoria station is a true gem. As a general rule, drink Sicilian and eat Sardinian. Excellent pasta dishes (£10.50 to £13.75).

Also recommended:

Jenny Lo's Tea House (Map pp138–9; ☎ 7259 0399; 14 Eccleston St SW1; mains £6.50-8.75; ◷ closed lunch Sat & all day Sun; ✚ Victoria) Good-value place in Victoria for rice and noodles set up by the daughter of the late Chinese food supremo Kenneth Lo.

CLERKENWELL, SHOREDITCH & SPITALFIELDS

A decade ago culinary boundaries between the City, with its mostly expense-account diners, and the hip Hoxton scene were clearly drawn. Now, the lines between 'establishment' and 'stylish' have started to blur, with Spitalfields and Shoreditch accommodating plenty of cool places where even stockbrokers want to be seen. Less scruffy Clerkenwell is another place where City prices are married with Shoreditch levels of cool. Brick Lane, the centre of what has become known as Banglatown, is lined with Indian and Bangladeshi restaurants. Not all of them are very good – choose carefully.

CLERKENWELL

LE CAFÉ DU MARCHÉ Map p150   French £££
☎ 7608 1609; 22 Charterhouse Sq, Charterhouse Mews EC1; 3-course set menus £29.95; ⊗ closed Sat & Sun; ⊖ Barbican
Tradition is a watchword at this quaint French bistro housed in an exposed-brick warehouse down a tiny alleyway near Smithfield Market. The food is mostly gutsy French fare – hearty steaks with garlic and rosemary flavours, fish soup with aioli – and there's piano playing and jazz upstairs. Meals are set-menu only.

SMITHS OF SMITHFIELD
Map p150   Modern British ££-£££
☎ 7251 7950, 7236 6666; www.smithsofsmithfield.co.uk; 67-77 Charterhouse St EC1; mains £11.50-28.50; ⊗ breakfast, lunch & dinner, depending on fl; ⊖ Farringdon
After the hubbub of the cavernous bar and café on the ground floor, where you can grab breakfast (all day from £4.50) and lunch, there are three quieter places to dine: the wine rooms on the 1st floor (small plates and sandwiches), the brasserie (mains all £11.50 and £12.50) on the 2nd floor and the rooftop dining room (£16.50 to £28.50) above that, which has great views of Smithfield Market and St Paul's Cathedral. The linking factor is a focus on top-quality British meat and organic produce.

FLÂNEUR Map p150   French/Mediterranean ££-£££
☎ 7404 4422; www.flaneur.com; 41 Farringdon Rd EC1; 2-/3-course set meals £19.50/24.50; ⊖ Farringdon
Dining while shoppers browse in the delicatessen-greengrocers around you may not sound appealing, but it's just part of the charm of this gourmet deli and unsurprisingly excellent restaurant. Beautifully attired in woods with high shelves stocked with all manner of rare and wonderful delicacies, tables are scattered around the shop, and diners keep the place busy for both lunch and dinner.

ST JOHN Map p150   British ££-£££
☎ 7251 0848; www.stjohnrestaurant.co.uk; 26 St John St EC1; mains £14.50-22; ⊗ closed lunch Sat & all day Sun; ⊖ Farringdon
Clerkenwell's most famous restaurant and its famous carve-'im-up pig logo has spawned its own book (Nose to Tail Eating, by chef Fergus Henderson), and indeed this much-acclaimed, enduringly hip place really is for adventurous carnivores who want to sample old-style English cuisine. The signature dish is roast bone-marrow salad with parsley, and the changing daily menu includes such specialities as chitterlings and chips, calf's brain terrine and smoked eel with beetroot. There are more familiar choices, including the odd vegetarian dish, but St John, with its minimalist white dining room and patient staff, remains a Rabelaisian experience.

CLUB GASCON Map p110   French £-££
☎ 7796 0600; www.clubgascon.com; 57 West Smithfield EC1; tapas £8.50-19; ⊗ closed lunch Sat & all day Sun; ⊖ Farringdon or Barbican
One of Clerkenwell's leading restaurants since it was awarded a Michelin star in 2002, Club Gascon takes a different approach to fine dining, with a selection of tapas-style portions (that would, naturally, leave an ordinary tapas restaurant for dust). They're arranged in five categories, one of which is entirely devoted to foie gras; order from about four per person. A set menu called Le Marché is £42 (or £65 with wine).

MORO Map p150   North African, Spanish ££
☎ 7833 8336; www.moro.co.uk; 34-36 Exmouth Market N1; mains £14.50-17.50; ⊖ Farringdon or Angel
As its name implies, this landmark restaurant run by husband and wife Sam and Sam Clark serves 'Moorish' cuisine, a fusion of Spanish, Portuguese and North African flavours. Some diners love it, while others complain about odd seasonings and small portions; we're in the former camp and have been since we attended launch night in… well, a long time ago. The constantly changing menu might include such dishes as wood-roasted bream with moros y christianos (black beans and rice) and fennel cooked in anise and chicken cooked in Pedro Ximénez sherry.

QUALITY CHOP HOUSE
Map p150   British £-££
☎ 7837 5093; www.qualitychophouse.co.uk; 92-94 Farringdon Rd EC1; mains £6.95-16.95; ☟ closed lunch Sat; ⊖ Farringdon

Subtitled 'For people who love food' (as opposed to those who have stapled their mouths shut?) this chop house is a bit faux-retro for our tastes, but the food is good and harkens back to its past life as a workmen's caf with white-and-black tiled floor and wooden benches. But now the old-fashioned British staples such as eel, sausage with bubble and squeak and salmon fish cakes (£11.95) are set before a middle-class media crowd. There's a two-course set lunch weekdays for £9.95.

MEDCALF Map p150   British ££
☎ 7833 3533; www.medcalfbar.co.uk; 40 Exmouth Market EC1; mains £10.50-16; ☟ closed dinner Fri & Sun; ⊖ Farringdon or Angel

Despite its erratic kitchen hours (the bar itself is open all day), Medcalf is one of the best-value hangouts in Exmouth Market. Housed in a beautifully converted butcher shop dating back to 1912, Medcalf serves up innovative yet relatively affordable British fare. Highlights on our visit were whelks and winkles with parsley and white wine, scrumptious devilled kidneys and goose with black pudding that was cooked to perfection.

EAGLE Map p150   Gastropub £-££
☎ 7837 1353; 159 Farringdon Rd EC1; mains £9-14; ☟ closed dinner Sun; ⊖ Farringdon

London's first gastropub is still going strong after all these years. Even though the original owners and many chefs have left, the customers still come, at lunch or after work, for dishes that tend to nod in the direction of the Mediterranean. The atmosphere is nicely relaxed and chatty.

COACH & HORSES Map p150   Gastropub ££
☎ 7278 8990; www.thecoachandhorses.com; 26-28 Ray St EC1; mains £10-13; ⊖ Farringdon

Just around the corner from London's original gastropub, the Eagle, this upstart is giving the competition a run for its money. Despite this, it's still easy to get a seat within its traditional walls and absorb the menu, which will include such things as a salad of duck hearts, beetroot and orange, and braised ox cheek.

AKI Map p150   Japanese £-££
☎ 7837 9281; www.akidemae.com; 182 Gray's Inn Rd WC1; mains £4.85-11.30; ☟ closed Sat lunch & all day Sun; ⊖ Chancery Lane

This charmingly shabby *izakaya* ('sake bar with food' or Japanese-style bistro) is an excellent and very authentic place for noodles (£4.80), sushi (£1.60 to £2.80) or one of the dozen sets, including tempura (£22) at dinner.

Also recommended:

Ambassador (Map p150; ☎ 7837 0009; www.theambassadorcafe.co.uk; 55 Exmouth Market EC1; mains £9.50-14.75; ⊖ Farringdon) Super find with inventive bistro cuisine and a killer set lunch at £12.50/16 for two/three courses.

SHOREDITCH & HOXTON

LES TROIS GARÇONS Map p150   French ££-£££
☎ 7613 1924; www.lestroisgarcons.com; 1 Club Row E1; mains £17.50-33; ☟ dinner Mon-Sat; ⊖ Liverpool St

Walk through the door of this enormous erstwhile pub and your jaw will surely drop: giraffe heads stick out from the wall at a right angle, stuffed swans wear tiaras, alligators are crowned and the mirrors are listed. The food – classic French with the likes of duck confit, *riz de veau* (sweetbreads) and plates of pork *charcuterie* (sausage) on offer – is good if not excellent and at least one of the eponymous 'three boys' is usually on hand to meet and greet. Service can sometimes be so attentive as to be almost overbearing.

EYRE BROTHERS
Map p150   Spanish, Portuguese ££-£££
☎ 7613 5346; www.eyrebrothers.co.uk; 70 Leonard St EC2; mains £14-25; ☟ closed lunch Sat & all day Sun; ⊖ Old St

Geographically located in Shoreditch, but stylistically with one foot in the City, this dark-panelled, low-ceilinged den with lots of photos on the walls excels with an interesting range of fare inspired by the food of Spain and Portugal. Diners tuck into a largely vegetarian-unfriendly menu, including scallops with *jamón* (ham) *Serrano*, grilled Mozambique prawns *piri-piri* (chilli) and Catalan-style rabbit stew. The Eyre brothers were behind London's first gastropub, the Eagle (left). They still know what they're doing.

FIFTEEN Map p150   Italian £-£££

☎ 0871 330 1515, 7251 3909; www.fifteenrestau
rant.com; 15 Westland Pl N1; mains £9.50-23.50;
⊖ Old St

Now an international minichain with branches in Melbourne, Amsterdam and even far-flung Cornwall, this is celeb chef Jamie Oliver's gaff, where he trains and employs 15 young chefs and the profits go to charity. It's difficult to get a reservation, but one-third of the seating in the downstairs trattoria, where breakfast is available from 7.30am on weekdays and from 9am at the weekend, is kept for walk-ins. We've had mixed reviews about the food and bad ones about the high prices (£8 for a fry-up?) but it's for a good cause. Expect a decent selection of fish and vegetarian dishes.

BACCHUS Map p150   Modern European ££

7613 0477; www.bacchus-restaurant.co.uk; 177
Hoxton St N1; mains £12-19; ⏰ lunch Mon-Fri,
dinner Mon-Sat; ⊖ Old St

The speciality of chef Nuno Mendes (see boxed text, p259) – sous-vide cooking in which ingredients are slow-cooked in a vacuum for hours and hours – is put to the test at this smart erstwhile pub and succeeds. The rabbit mousse is just this side of absolute perfection but you must try the langoustines with Catalan mix to experience one of Mendes' signature foams (in this case a hot garlic one). For mains, expect the likes of warm cod wrapped in chicken skin and sesame-crusted squab with foie gras.

HOXTON APPRENTICE

Map p150   Modern European £-££

☎ 7749 2828; www.hoxtonapprentice.com; 16
Hoxton Sq N1; mains £8.50-16.95; ⊖ Old St

The poor man's Fifteen (above) – in celebrity-pulling power, it must be stressed, and not in style or affordability – this is another training restaurant where worthy applicants do their time at the stove. It's pricey for what it is and serves, but we enjoyed a perfect saddle of rabbit with apple and black pudding on a recent visit. Weekday lunches of two/three courses are £9.99/12.99 and, at the weekend, brunches are long (11am to 6pm). Have a look at the 'hall of mirrors' on the mezzanine level.

CAY TRE Map p150   Vietnamese £

☎ 7729 8662; www.vietnamesekitchen.co.uk; 301
Old St EC1; mains £4.50-7; ⊖ Old St

As much as we'd like to, we can't recommend any of the Vietnamese cafés or restaurants in Little Hanoi on Kingsland Rd north of here. Trust us; they smell more of faux than pho (noodle soup). Instead stay in Hoxton and head to the 'Vietnamese Kitchen' for classic Vietnamese beef noodle soup, banh xeo (a kind of pancake with prawns, chicken and vegetables) and wonderful pan-fried basa fish with lemongrass and shallots.

SPITALFIELDS

ST JOHN BREAD & WINE

Map p150   British ££-£££

☎ 7251 0848; www.stjohnbreadandwine.com;
94-96 Commercial St; mains £10.20-29; ⏰ closed
dinner Sun; ⊖ Liverpool St

Little sister to St John (p255), this place is cheaper and more relaxed but offers similar 'nose to tail' traditional fare (duck hearts on toast, jellied ham, salt lamb and turnips) in an austere (though airy) space popular with Spitalfields creative types. There's also excellent British cheese and puddings.

MESÓN LOS BARRILES Map p150 Spanish ££

☎ 7375 3136; 8a Lamb St E1; mains £10.50-17.50;
⏰ closed Sat, dinner Sun; ⊖ Liverpool St

This restaurant inside Spitalfields Market serves up some very fresh fish main courses but hardly anyone comes here for those. The draw at the 'Barrels House' is the excellent selection of tapas (£3 to £7.95). Sawdust on the floor and air-dried hams overhead add to the rustic market feel of the place.

ARKANSAS CAFÉ

Map p150   North American £-££

☎ 7377 6999; Unit 12, Spitalfields Market, 107b
Commercial St E1; mains £5.50-16; ⏰ lunch Sun-
Fri; ⊖ Liverpool St

Good ole down-home Arkansas barbecue is what is served up in this unprepossessing unit on the edges of Spitalfields Market. Whether it's platters of pork ribs, corn-fed chicken or steak, you can rest assured they'll be of truly excellent quality, with lots of potatoes, coleslaw and other stuff on the side.

GREEN & RED Map p150   Mexican £-££

7749 9670; www.greenred.uk.co; 51 Bethnal
Green Rd E1; mains £9.50-14.50; ⏰ dinner daily;
⊖ Liverpool St

Mexican food is enjoying something of a renaissance in London and this bar and

LOCAL VOICES: JOE COOKE *Interviewed by Steve Fallon*

A resident of Chingford, Joe Cooke owns F Cooke (see the boxed text, p260), a pie and mash shop that's been on the same Hoxton street for more than a century. Just opposite is Bacchus (see the boxed text, opposite), serving a distinctly different cuisine.

Nice name in your trade. Local boy? It's got an 'e' at the end. Yeah, born in Clapton – that's with a 'p' – not Clacton with a 'c' – and I live in Chingford. My family has had a pie shop on this street since 1902 and the business has been in the family since 1862.

Don't people prefer pizza and fried chicken nowadays? Whither goest pie and mash? It's got nothing to do with preferring one over the other. Years ago a High Street had three places to eat in: a caf, a fish and chips place and pie and mash shop. Our portion of the take was one-third. Now every conceivable kind of food is available.

Like molecular gastronomy at Bacchus, across the way. Been there? For every weird food there'll be a weird customer. Nah, I only wish them lots of luck. And I thought the *Evening Standard* was overly harsh on them. Barely gave them a chance to show off how it all works.

Who comes in? There's not a lot of passing trade, but we get all sorts: young and old, locals and tourists. You name it. Yanks, Afghans, Hindus (who are not always necessarily adhering to their dietary laws) and Japanese (who love to take pictures).

And what goes in? The same exact ingredients as when we first opened. Everything is done on the premises. We make all of our own dough, bone all the meat, grind all the parsley for the liquor and jelly the eels. The only big change in recent years is we now sell vegetables pies. Frankly lots of proper pie shops have disappeared because they're a lot of work.

Proper pie shops? If they serve gravy with their pies it's not a real pie and mash shop.

Where do the ingredients come from? The meat's from Smithfield Market, the potatoes are Maris Pipers at the moment and the parsley is English. Eels are local until the season ends in late autumn. Then we get farmed ones from Holland. We tried to import them. Irish ones are the best but the New Zealand ones: ugh, they've got a skin on them like a donkey's foreskin. We've never changed any of the recipes.

Simple as that? Look, if you start off with cream ingredients you'll still have something good even if you balls it all up. Crap ingredients make crap dishes.

When I'm not behind the stove… I'm behind a pot of tea and a rum baba at Maison Bertaux (see the boxed text, p239).

cantina is a welcome addition to Bangla-town. The shacklike décor sets the mood for such authentic dishes as slow-cooked pork belly with chillies and orange salt and roasted vegetable in chilli salsa. In the bar downstairs choose your poison from among the more than 100 tequilas on offer.

CANTEEN   Map p150   British £-££

☎ 0845 686 1122; www.canteen.co.uk; 2 Crispin Pl, off Brushfield St E1; mains £7-11.50; ❤ 8am-11pm Mon-Fri, 9am-11pm Sat & Sun; ✚ Liverpool St

Voted the *Observer Food Monthly*'s Best UK Restaurant in 2007, this very stylish yet affordable eatery just west of Spitalfields Market has an all-day menu that will please almost every taste – from macaroni and cheese and shop-made pies to smoked haddock. The management and waiting staff are young and very keen.

Also recommended:

Tas Firin (Map p150; ☎ 729 6446; 160 Bethnal Green E2; mains £7.50-13.50; ✚ Liverpool St) The 'Stone Oven' is just about as authentic a Turkish grill restaurant as you'll find in this neighbourhood.

Café 1001 (Map p150; ☎ 7247 9679; www.cafe1001 .co.uk; 91 Brick Lane E1; mains £2.50-3.50; ❤ 6am-midnight; ✚ Liverpool St) Popular and huge café with grills and cakes, lounge seating upstairs and live music.

Brick Lane Beigel Bake (Map p150; ☎ 7729 0616; 159 Brick Lane E2; filled bagels 70p-£2.90; ❤ 24hr; ✚ Liverpool St) You won't find fresher (or cheaper) bagels anywhere in London than at this bakery and delicatessen; just ask any taxi driver (it's their favourite nosherie).

THE EAST END & DOCKLANDS

The changes that have occurred in the East End dining scene over the past decade have been nothing short of phenomenal. Who would have imagined that a five-star gastropub would land in Hackney just north of Victoria Park? And while the Docklands pretty much remains the land of expense accounts and quick lunches, you can now find some excellent Asian food there. In fact the East End's multiculturalism means its ethnic cuisine stretches pretty far, with everything from Vietnamese, vegetarian Thai and even Georgian available. But the best – by far – is its Indian and Pakistani offerings. If you fancy the real McCoy, head for the bare-bones subcontinental eateries of Whitechapel – most of them BYO alcohol and all of them halal.

WHITECHAPEL

NEW TAYYAB Map p156   Indian, Pakistani £–££
☎ 7247 9543; www.tayyabs.co.uk; 83-89 Fieldgate St E1; mains £4-11; ⊖ Whitechapel, 🚍 25
From the enticing aroma on entering, it's clear this buzzing Punjabi restaurant is in another league to its Brick Lane equivalents. *Seekh* kebabs, *masala* fish and other starters served on sizzling hot plates are delicious, as are accompaniments such as dhal, naan and raita. With New Tayyab now appearing regularly in guidebooks and the huge London Royal Hospital round the corner, you should expect to wait for a table (and there will always be a doctor in the house).

LAHORE KEBAB HOUSE
Map p156   Indian, Pakistani £
☎ 7481 9737, 7488 2551; 2 Umberston St E1; mains £5-10; ⊖ Whitechapel, 🚍 25
This restaurant with a large kitchen viewable through glass is not an aesthetic experience, and ever since City workers discovered it the standard of cooking seems to have slipped. Still, it remains popular with the local community and has some excellent meat and chicken biryanis.

MIRCH MASALA Map p156   Indian, Pakistani £
☎ 7377 0155; 111-113 Commercial Rd E1; mains £3.50-10; ⊖ Whitechapel, 🚍 25
The new(ish) kid on the block and thus even more eager to please, 'Chilli and Spice' is a less hectic alternative to New Tayyab and the Lahore Kebab House, and the food is every bit as good. Order the prawn tikka as a 'warmer' followed by the *masala karella*, a curry-like dish made from bitter gourd, and a *karahi* meat dish.

LOCAL VOICES: NUNO MENDES *Interviewed by Steve Fallon*

Lisbon-born Nuno Mendes lives in Bethnal Green E2 and is the chef and owner of Bacchus (p257), a temple of 'molecular gastronomy' just across the street from F Cooke's pie and mash shop (see the boxed text, opposite).

From El Bulli in Barcelona via Jean Georges in New York to a made-over pub in Hoxton. How does that work? After 14 years in the States I wanted to come back to Europe and there's a lot happening on the London food scene right now. I like what Heston (Blumenthal of Fat Duck fame; see p379) is doing. But it's not just about mimicking. I'm trying to present some of his techniques in a laid-back place.

OK, tick, trendy Hoxton. But why the wrong – northern – end of trendy Hoxton? I wanted to open in East London. This area reminds me of the West Village in New York. I like the 24-hour feeling that this place has.

Sous-vide. What's that all about again? Sous-vide is cooking 'under vacuum'. Food is cooked very slowly in a plastic bag at a constant temperature, allowing ingredients to retain their weight, structure and nutrients. It only came about because of advances in cooking science and technology, with things like circulators which keep the cooking temperature to within 1%.

Right. But foam? Isn't that the stuff you skim off soups and jams and tip into the bin? To me, foam is the best way to express the flavour of an ingredient as clearly as possible. No texture. It is nothing but pure taste.

Pork jowl with cinnamon oil and langoustine with rosewater purée. Now that's a lot of tastes on a plate. I start with two ingredients, focusing on two flavours – say lamb and goat's cheese – that work together. I then add ingredients that work with each of them and begin to form a network of flavours.

Have people been receptive to this 'molecular gastronomy'? By and large yes. People like to experiment with food and this is an area of London in which to do it. Hoxton draws lots of creative people; it's an area known for new ideas. A couple of critics didn't like it though.

Will this type of cooking carry on or is it just, err, a flash in the pan? Like everything, cooking will evolve. My cooking is a reflection of new technology and as that changes it will push forward.

When you're not cooking, where are you eating? My cooking and tastes reflect all the places I've worked in. I like a place called Yauatcha (p239) which does excellent dim sum. I'm very close to Green & Red (p257).

Have you developed a taste for traditional English? I like St John Bread & Wine (p257) and I go to the pie and mash place opposite. They don't come here, but I go there.

PIE 'N' MASH SHOPS

Those curious about how Londoners used to eat before everything went trendy, modern and nouvelle should sample a pie made from minced beef and 'mash' (fake mashed potatoes made from powder) available at any of the following establishments for £1.75 to £2.50. Jellied eels, mushy peas and 'liquor' (a green sauce made from parsley and vinegar) are optional extras. A slightly more modern take on this traditional staple is available at the Square Pie Company (Map p150; ☎ 7377 1114; Spitalfields Market E1; pies £6.50; ☼ 10.30am-3pm Mon-Fri, 10am-6pm Sun).

Castle's (Map p168; ☎ 7485 2196; 229 Royal College St NW1; ☼ 10.30am-3.30pm Tue-Sat; ✆ Camden Town, ▣ Camden Rd)

Clark's (Map p150; ☎ 7837 1974; 46 Exmouth Market EC1; ☼ 10.30am-4pm Mon-Thu, to 5.30pm Fri & Sat; ✆ Farringdon)

F Cooke (Map p150; ☎ 7729 7718; 150 Hoxton St N1; ☼ 10am-7pm Mon-Thu, 9.30am-8pm Fri & Sat; ✆ Old St or Liverpool St)

Manze's (Map p126; ☎ 7407 2985; 87 Tower Bridge Rd SE1; ☼ 10.30am-2pm Tue-Sat; ✆ London Bridge)

BETHNAL GREEN & HACKNEY

LITTLE GEORGIA Map p156   Georgian ££
☎ 7739 8154; 87 Goldsmith's Row E2; mains £10-11; ☼ closed dinner Tue & Wed; ✆ Bethnal Green, ▣ Cambridge Heath
A charming slice of the Caucasus in East London, LG is an excellent introduction to the cuisine of Georgia (as in Tbilisi, not Atlanta or midnight trains). Here the menu includes dishes such as *nigziani* (red pepper or aubergine stuffed with walnuts, herbs and roast vegetables), chicken *satsivi* in walnut sauce and the Georgian classic staple *khachapuri* (cheese bread). The café is a good place for breakfast and does takeaway lunch (£4 to £5.50).

GREEN PAPAYA Map p156   Vietnamese £
☎ 8985 5486; www.greenpapaya.co.uk; 191 Mare St E8; mains £5.50-8; ☼ dinner Tue-Sun; ▣ Hackney Central, ▣ D6, 253 or 277
This oasis just south of the landmark Hackney Empire music hall serves Vietnamese food of very high quality and tends to put a 'modern' spin on many of the dishes. Try the *banh tom* (lightly fried strips of sweet potato and king prawns), the banana flower salad and the 'Mama's Pork', slow-cooked with mushrooms and vegetables. The staff are enthusiastic and helpful.

Also recommended:

Thai Garden (Map p156; ☎ 8981 5748; www.thethaigar den.co.uk; 249 Globe Rd E2; mains £4.50-11; ☼ lunch Mon-Fri, dinner Mon-Sat; ✆ Bethnal Green, then ▣ 8) This is a rare bird indeed – a mostly vegetarian (with some seafood dishes) Thai restaurant in Bethnal Green – and well worth the trip.

Frizzante@City Farm (Map p156; ☎ 7739 2266; www .frizzanteltd.co.uk; Hackney City Farm, 1a Goldsmith's Row E2; mains £4.80-8.75; ☼ 10am-4.30pm or 5.30pm Tue-Sun; ✆ Bethnal Green, ▣ Cambridge Heath) Award-winning family restaurant serving good Italian food next door to one of London's half-dozen city farms for children.

MILE END & VICTORIA PARK

EMPRESS OF INDIA Map p156   Gastropub £-££
☎ 8533 5123; www.theempressofindia.com; 130 Lauriston Rd E9; mains £9.50-16.50; ✆ Mile End, ▣ 277
This exquisite, much welcomed pub conversion on the western edge of Victoria Park belts out excellent modern British cuisine, with such fine dishes as sorrel soup with Cheddar scone, saddle of venison and roast suckling pig. We love the elegant bar, the Raj-era murals on the wall, the chandeliers made of mussel shells and the seamless service. Breakfast is available daily from 8.30am.

CAFÉ SPICE NAMASTE Map p156   Indian ££
☎ 7488 9242; www.cafespice.co.uk; 16 Prescot St E1; mains £12.25-15.75; ☼ closed lunch Sat & all day Sun; ✆ Tower Hill
Chef Cyrus Todiwala has taken an old magistrates' court just a 10-minute walk from Tower Hill and decorated it in 'carnival' colours; the service and atmosphere are as bright as the walls. The Parsee and Goan menu is famous for its superlative *dhansaak* (lamb stew with rice and lentils) but just as good are the spicy chicken

EATING THE EAST END & DOCKLANDS

frango piri-piri and the Goan king prawn curry. They make their own chutneys here. Another bonus is the little Ginger Garden behind the dining room that's open in the warmer months.

NAMO Map p156 — Vietnamese £

☎ 8533 0639; 178 Victoria Park Rd E9; mains £4.50-9; ⌚ lunch Thu-Sun, dinner Tue-Sun; ⊖ Mile End, ▣ 277

This very bohemian place takes the Vietnamese dishes so characteristic of nearby Dalston and pulls them into the 21st century; expect things such as chilli jam with your slow-cooked pork and a new take on *bo bun hue* (£7), the signature beef noodle soup. Seating is a bit cramped, but the array of plants and flowers brings nearby Victoria Park even closer.

DOCKLANDS

UBON Map p160 — Japanese £-£££

☎ 7719 7800; www.noburestaurants.com; 4th fl, Holmes Pl, 34 Westferry Circus E14; mains £9.75-29.50; ⌚ lunch Mon-Fri, dinner Mon-Sat; ⊖ /DLR Canary Wharf

Ubon gets as many rave reviews as its big sister, Nobu (p245), which is of course its name spelt backward. While customers argue over whether you really get value for money here (set lunch is a snip at £21 to £31), the selling point has to be the breathtaking Thames views from every corner, including the fabulous sushi bar. The restaurant has its own dedicated entrance next to the Four Seasons hotel and its own lift.

ROYAL CHINA Map p160 — Chinese £-£££

☎ 7719 0888; www.royalchinagroup.co.uk; 30 Westferry Circus E14; mains £7.50-22.50; ⊖ /DLR Canary Wharf

Though admittedly just one of four outlets of a chain, including the Bayswater branch (Map p175; ⊖ 7221 2535; 13 Queensway W2; Bayswater), this is London's best Cantonese restaurant and excels in both standard and unusual dim sum, available daily from 11am to 5pm. This branch has impressive Thames views, especially in the warmer months when tables are set out at the water's edge.

WAPPING FOOD Map p156 — Modern European ££

☎ 7680 2080; www.thewappingproject.com; Wapping Hydraulic Power Station, Wapping Wall E1; mains £12.50-19.75; ⌚ closed dinner Sun; ⊖ Wapping

We've all seen converted factories masquerading as restaurants but nothing compares with this erstwhile power station (and now restaurant-gallery-performance space), which has chosen to let all of its hydraulic equipment hang out. The food is modern European bending towards the Mediterranean, the wine list all-Australian and the staff pleasant.

EL FARO Map p160 — Spanish ££

☎ 7987 5511; www.el-faro.co.uk; 3 Turnberry Quay, Pepper St E14; mains £13.95-19.50; ⌚ closed dinner Sun; DLR Crossharbour

An E14 address rarely signifies a destination restaurant but hop on the DLR (a picturesque and worthwhile ride) and travel to the 'Lighthouse' for what are acclaimed as the best tapas (£4.25 to £8.50) and Spanish dishes in town. The location on a basin in the Docklands is quite restful and yet within easy walking distance of Canary Wharf.

NARROW Map p156 — British £-££

☎ 592 7950; www.gordonramsay.com/thenarrow; 44 Narrow S E14; mains £9-12.50; DLR Limehouse

This gastropub with commanding views of the Thames may or may not be Mr Ramsay's idea of slumming it – or at least be Gordon without the glam. Housed in what was once the Limehouse Basin dockmaster's residence, the place comes with a lot of history and tradition and the food reflects that. Expect such old favourites as London Particular (pea and ham soup), braised Gloucester pig cheeks with bashed neeps and Huntingdon fidget pie made with bacon, onion and apple.

NORTH LONDON

Whoever said that London was a 'collection of villages' must have had the northern boroughs in mind; nowhere is that old chestnut more applicable to neighbourhoods as disparate as Islington, Camden, Stoke Newington and Hampstead. Once the capital's foodie hub, Islington has definitely lost its '90s cachet as a home of innovation. That said, it's still got more than its fair share of great restaurants, especially along busy Upper St. Multiethnic Camden is another kettle of fish, with a pride of Greek restaurants as well as tasty offerings of Caribbean, Russian and even Afghani cuisine. Here's where you'll also find a gourmet vegetarian restaurant.

CAMDEN

ENGINEER Map p166   Gastropub ££
☎ 7722 0950; www.the-engineer.com; 65 Gloucester Ave NW1; mains £12.95-15.50; ⊖ Chalk Farm
One of London's original gastropubs, the Engineer serves up consistently good international cuisine – from Moroccan roast lamb chump and *coq au vin* to miso-marinated cod – and is hugely popular with impeccably hip North Londoners. The splendid walled garden is the highlight.

LEMONIA Map p166   Greek £-££
☎ 7586 7454, 89 Regent's Park Rd NW1; mains £9.75-14.75; ☽ closed lunch Sat & dinner Sun; ⊖ Chalk Farm
Some people's favourite Greek restaurant in London, this attractive and very popular *taverna* offers good-value food and a lively atmosphere. A selection of meze costs £14 per person and the vegetarian moussaka is excellent. There's a two-course set weekday lunch for £7.75.

MARINE ICES Map p166   Italian £-££
☎ 7482 9003; 8 Haverstock Hill NW3; mains £6-14.50; ⊖ Chalk Farm
As its name suggests, this Chalk Farm institution started out as an ice-cream parlour (in fact, a Sicilian *gelateria*) but these days it does some savoury dishes as well, including pizzas and hearty pasta dishes. Be sure to try some of the excellent ice cream, which has its own menu.

BAR GANSA Map p168   Spanish ££
☎ 7267 8909; 2 Inverness St NW1; mains £13.50; ⊖ Camden Town
Bar Gansa is a focal point of the Camden scene, has a late licence and is howlingly popular. The menus – mostly tapas (£1.85 to £4.60) – are good value, especially the weekday lunch menu, when three tapas with olives and bread are £6.50. There's live flamenco on Monday evening.

MANGO ROOM Map p168   Caribbean ££
☎ 7482 5065; www.mangoroom.co.uk; 10 Kentish Town Rd NW1; mains £10-13.50; ⊖ Camden Town
With delightful pastel décor and genteel service, Mango Room is a kind of decaf Caribbean experience, although there's no holding back with the food: cod fritters with apple chutney, salt fish with ackee (a yellow-skinned Jamaican fruit that has an uncanny resemblance to scrambled eggs), and curried goat with hot pepper and spices. The early-ska/Jamaican-jazz soundtrack is wicked.

MANNA Map p166   Vegetarian £-££
☎ 7722 8082; www.manna-veg.com; 4 Erskine Rd NW1; mains £9.50-13; ☽ lunch Sun, dinner daily; ⊖ Chalk Farm
Tucked away on a side street in Primrose Hill, London's most glamorous inner-city village, this little place does a brisk trade in inventive vegetarian cooking. The menu features such mouth-watering dishes as Kashmiri curry, aubergine tempura and organic fennel schnitzel (though some reports suggest that not all dishes are a howling success).

CAFÉ CORFU Map p168   Greek £-££
☎ 7269 8088; www.cafecorfu.com; 7-9 Pratt St NW1; mains £8.95-12.50; ☽ closed Mon; ⊖ Camden Town
Corfu is the best of a host of Greek restaurants in the neighbourhood. Décor is sleek and stylish, the delicious food feels light (modern Greek?) but fills, and there's more than retsina to slake your thirst. A belly dancer and DJ aid the digestion on Friday and Saturday nights and there's live Greek music on Sunday.

TROJKA Map p166   Russian, Eastern European £-££
☎ 7483 3765; www.trojka.co.uk; 101 Regent's Park Rd NW1; mains £7.50-10.50; ⊖ Chalk Farm
This café-restaurant serves good-value and pretty authentic Russian and Eastern European, with a wide variety of *zakuski* (Russian tapaslike starters) from £2.50 to £7.95 and mains such as Russian *pierog* (a pie of sauerkraut and vegetables), *bigos* (a cabbage 'stew' with mixed meats) and salt beef, in an attractive skylit restaurant frequented by local bohos. Avoid the house wine by bringing your own (£3 corkage). There's live Russian music at the weekend.

EL PARADOR Map p168   Spanish £
☎ 7387 2789; www.elparadorlondon.com; 245 Eversholt St NW1; tapas £3.90-6.50; ☽ closed lunch Sat & Sun; ⊖ Mornington Cres
This laid-back Spanish place has a generous selection of tapas – try the *empanadillas*

de espinacas y queso (spinach and cheese dish) from all over Spain. There's a walled garden for when the sun's out and you're feeling moderately Mediterranean; the reasonably priced rioja (from £16.90) should help.

Also recommended:

Belgo Noord (Map p166; ☎ 7267 0718; www.belgo-restaurants.com; 72 Chalk Farm Rd NW1; mains £8.95-17.95; ⊖ Chalk Farm) Branch of a Belgian restaurant chain; one of the few places in town that still serves *moules frites* (mussels and chips/French fries; £12.25).

Asakusa (Map p168; ☎ 7388 8533; 265 Eversholt St NW1; mains £5.50-12; 🕑 dinner Mon-Sat; ⊖ Mornington Cres) This somewhat scruffy but clean place has cheap sushi for £1.10 to £1.30 per piece, along with more elaborate set menus (£5.80 to £9.90).

KING'S CROSS & EUSTON

MESTIZO Map p168   Mexican £-££
☎ 7387 4064; www.mestizomx.com; 103 Hampstead Rd NW1; mains £9.50-18.50; ⊖ Warren St
If your idea of Mexican food is tacos and gluggy refried beans, think again. At this large and very attractive restaurant and tequila bar just down from the Latin Quarter guitar shop you'll find everything from *quesadillas* (cheese-filled pasties) to filled corn enchiladas. But go for the specials: *pozole*, a thick fresh corn soup with meat, and several different preparations of *mole*, chicken or pork cooked in a rich sauce containing everything but the proverbial sink (including chocolate).

ACORN HOUSE Map p168   Modern European ££
☎ 7812 1842; www.acornhouserestaurant.com; 69 Swinton St WC1; mains £12-17; ⊖ King's Cross St Pancras
London's first totally ecofriendly restaurant with 10 trainees as fresh as the seasonal ingredients they're working with, an open kitchen and monthly changing menus. The dining room is a bit narrow for our taste but it accommodates a well-stocked and very long bar.

SNAZZ.SICHUAN Map p168   Chinese £-££
☎ 7388 0808; www.newchinaclub.co.uk; 37 Chalton St NW1; mains £9.80-15.80; ⊖ Euston
As one London-based hack who knows a thing or two about Chinese food put it, 'Snazz is almost *too* authentic'. And we

know what he means; tongue in hot oil, pig ear with ginger and special cooked pig blood in casserole just don't cut the mustard even with old China hands like us. But other Sichuan favourites – twice-cooked pork, *gong bo* chicken with chillies and peanuts, a noodle dish with mince called 'ants climbing trees' – are also available at this very authentic restaurant catering almost exclusively to Chinese people. Look for the rickshaw out front.

ADDIS Map p168   Ethiopian £
☎ 7278 0679; www.addisrestaurant.co.uk; 40-42 Caledonian Rd N1; mains £6.95-8.50; ⊖ King's Cross St Pancras
Cheery Addis serves pungent Ethiopian dishes such as *ye beg tibs,* chunks of tender lamb cooked with onions and spices, and *doro wat,* chicken cooked with hot pepper and spices, which are eaten on a platter-sized piece of soft but slightly elastic *injera* bread. It's normally full of Ethiopian and Sudanese punters, which is always a good sign. The Addis Special Platter (£15.99) lets you sample all the highlights.

DIWANA BHEL POORI HOUSE
Map p168   Indian, Vegetarian, £
☎ 7387 5556; www.diwanarestaurant.com; 121-123 Drummond St; mains £5-6.95; ⊖ Euston or Euston Sq
The first of its kind – and still the best on this busy street, in our humble opinion – Diwana specialises in Bombay-style *bhel poori* (a sweet and sour, soft and crunchy 'party mix' snack) and *dosa*s (filled pancakes made from rice flour). Thalis offering a selection of tasty treats are £6.75 to £8.50 and the all-you-can-eat lunchtime buffet (£6.50) is legendary.

Also recommended:

Ravi Shankar (Map p168; ☎ 7388 6458; 133-135 Drummond St NW1; mains £3.50-6.95; ⊖ Euston or Euston Sq) Not our favourite *bhel poori* house on Drummond St – that would be Diwana (above) – but this place with the memorable name is a close(ish) second choice.

HAMPSTEAD & HIGHGATE
BLACK & BLUE Map p166   Steakhouse £-£££
☎ 7443 7744; 205-207 Haverstock Hill NW3; mains £8-23; ⊖ Belsize Park
This new, very stylish steakhouse with a branch at Borough Market (Map p126; ☎ 7357

9922; 1-2 Rochester Walk SE1; ☻ London Bridge) is easily identifiable by the bright red life-size plaster cow standing outside. In addition to a panoply of steaks (£13 to £23) there are also gourmet burgers (£8 to £12) with everything.

LA GAFFE Map p166   Italian ££
☎ 7794 7526; 107-111 Heath St NW3; mains £11.95-19.95; ☽ lunch Thu-Sun, dinner daily; ☻ Hampstead
This comfortable, family-run restaurant in an 18th-century cottage that is now a hotel is a Hampstead landmark and serves reliably good Italian dishes. The choice of fresh pasta dishes (£6.25 to £9.95) is especially good. There's a three-course set lunch (£12.50) available weekdays.

WOODLANDS Map p166   Vegetarian, Indian £-££
☎ 7794 3080; www.woodlandsrestaurant.co.uk; 102 Heath St NW3; mains £5.95-17.95; ☽ lunch Fri & Sat, dinner Mon-Sat; ☻ Hampstead
This South Indian vegetarian restaurant, whose rallying cry is 'Let Vegetation Feed the Nation', sets out to prove that South Indian vegetarian food can be as inventive as any meat-based cuisine and does a pretty convincing job of it. Superb thalis (£15.75 to £17.95) and *dosa*s (Indian-style pancakes; £5.95 to £6.95) are highlights. There's also a Marylebone branch (Map p100; ☎ 7486 3862; 77 Marylebone Lane W1; ☻ Bond St).

WELLS TAVERN Map p166   Gastropub £-££
☎ 7794 3785; www.thewellshampstead.co.uk; 30 Well Walk NW3; mains £9.95-15; ☻ Hampstead
The Wells was once a raucous venue for 'clandestine or unpremeditated marriages' at Hampstead Spa. Now it's a popular gastropub, with comfortable sofas and couches, dark walls and big flower arrangements. The modern European food is well above average and, particularly at lunch, offers pretty good value – for Hampstead.

JIN KICHI Map p166   Japanese £-££
☎ 7794 6158; www.jinkichi.com; 73 Heath St NW3; dishes £3.60-12.90; ☽ lunch Sat & Sun, dinner Tue-Sun; ☻ Hampstead
A disproportionate number of London's Japanese residents live in Hampstead, and a disproportionate number of them eat at this slightly shabby and cramped little place. It's a particularly good bet for *sumi-*

yaki (char-grilled meats) with sets at £8.70 and £10.90, though it does standard stuff such as sushi, sashimi and tempura. Be sure to book.

ISLINGTON

METROGUSTO Map p168   Italian ££
☎ 7226 9400; www.metrogusto.co.uk; 13 Theberton St N1; mains £13.50-17.50; ☽ closed lunch Mon-Thu & all day Sun; ☻ Angel
This laid-back place with delightful modern art on the walls serves progressive, modern (if somewhat pricey) Italian cuisine. Choose something like pizza or pasta (£11.50 to £12.50) or more substantial mains such as the *carne del giorno* (meat of the day) and *pesce di mercato* (fish of the market) from £16.50. Two-/three-course set dinners are £24.50/27.50. Seating is a bit cramped.

CANTINA ITALIA Map p168   Italian ££
☎ 7220 9791; 19 Canonbury Lane N1; mains £12.90-17.50; ☻ Highbury & Islington
Though this funky little trattoria with modern art on the walls and a Sardinian connection does more ambitious *secondi* (mains) such as the stewlike *stinco di maiale* (£13.50), most people come here for the fine pizzas (£4.30 to £8.90) and pasta (£7.90 to £11.90). Don't miss the linguine tossed with *bottarga* (cured mullet roe), oil, garlic, parsley and red pepper flakes.

CASALE FRANCO Map p168   Italian £-££
☎ 7226 8994; 134-137 Upper St N1; mains £8.50-17.50; ☽ lunch Sat & Sun, dinner Tue-Sun; ☻ Angel or Highbury & Islington
Still our favourite cheap and cheerful Italian on Upper St, Casale Franco offers the usual Italian comfort food (the pizza is excellent) in warm surroundings. Avoid sitting on the 1st floor (nowheresville) and kill for a outside table in the warm weather. Service is friendly and attentive.

DUKE OF CAMBRIDGE
Map p168   Gastropub £-££
☎ 7359 9066; www.dukeorganic.co.uk; 30 St Peter's St N1; mains £9.50-15; ☻ Angel
It may feel like a typical London gastropub, with bare wooden boards, tables and sofas, but the Duke can lay claim to being the only certified organic pub in London and the first – wait for it – in the world when it opened in 1998. Indeed, everything, right

down to the lager is produced without chemicals or pesticides (though the cider is better). The Italian-/French-/Spanish-influenced menu is reliable enough and the idea of eating healthily a bonus.

GLAS Map p168 — Swedish £-££
☎ 7359 1932; www.glasrestaurant.co.uk; 1st fl, The Mall, 359 Upper St N1; mains small £4-7.50, large £11-13.50; ⊗ closed dinner Sun; ⊖ Angel
A favourite when it was in Borough Market, Glas remains a mecca in its new location perched above Upper St in Islington. It's still the best Swedish restaurant in town and its 'grazing' portions (£4 to £7.50) allow you to try a number of specialities, including the phenomenal herring three ways and salmon pudding with horseradish sauce. Two-/three-course set lunch is £12.50/15. The welcome here is always warm and the service friendly.

MASALA ZONE Map p168 — Indian £-££
☎ 7359 3399; 80 Upper St N1; mains £7.75-11.95; ⊖ Angel
This spacious place with outside seating set back from Upper St in Islington is one of the best Indian budget options in London. Thoroughly modern in design, it serves up meals centred on its famous thalis, as well as *tandoor* and grilled dishes. There's also a Soho branch (Map p68; ☎ 7287 9966; 9 Marshall St W1; ⊖ Oxford Circus) serving equally authentic fare.

OTTOLENGHI Map p168 — Italian £
☎ 7288 1454; www.ottolenghi.co.uk; 287 Upper St N1; mains £7-9.50; ⊗ 8am-10pm Mon-Sat, 9am-7pm Sun; ⊖ Highbury & Islington/Angel
The busiest of what is now a three-outlet operation, including the Notting Hill branch (Map p175; ☎ 7727 1121; 63 Ledbury Rd W11; ⊗ 8am-8pm Mon-Fri, to 7pm Sat, to 6pm Sun; ⊖ Notting Hill Gate), this very sleek, very minimalist bakery-cum-restaurant looks as good as its food tastes, and that's saying something. The set menus (£8.50 to £13.50) are great value for food of this quality, although the desserts are the real highlight. The electric cables hanging over the table are actually for toasters at breakfast (£5.20 to £8.50).

BREAKFAST CLUB Map p168 — Breakfast £
☎ 7226 5454; www.thebreakfastclubangel.com; 31 Camden Passage N1; dishes £3-9; ⊗ 8am-5pm

Mon-Thu, 8am-midnight Fri, 9.30am-midnight Sat, 10am-11pm Sun; ⊖ Angel
Still our favourite place for something to wake up to, especially after a tough Saturday night on the tiles, this bright and flowery oasis in Islington's Camden Passage follows in the footsteps of the Breakfast Club Soho (Map p68; ☎ 7434 2571; 33 D'Arbly St; ⊖ Oxford Circus). But, despite the name, breakfast (£3 to £7) is not the only game here and it also does sandwiches, salads and decent pies (£8 to £9).

GALLIPOLI Map p168 — Turkish £
☎ 7359 0630; www.gallipolicafe.com; 102 Upper St N1; mains £6.25-7.75; ⊖ Angel or Highbury & Islington
A popular, cheek-by-jowl restaurant with fusty Turkish decorations and acceptable food (for its location), including everything from meze to spicy vegetarian moussaka. There's an overspill restaurant, Gallipoli Again (Map p168; ☎ 7359 0630; 120 Upper St N1; ⊗ closed lunch Mon-Thu & all day Sun) nearby.

AFGHAN KITCHEN Map p168 — Afghani £
☎ 7359 8019; 35 Islington Green N1; mains £5.50-6.50; ⊗ lunch & dinner Tue-Sat; ⊖ Angel
This tiny gem with seating on the 1st floor serves up some of Islington's best-value and most interesting cuisine: traditional Afghan dishes such as *qurma suhzi gosht* (lamb cooked with spinach) and *qurma e mahi* (fish stew) alongside a large vegetarian selection including *borani kado* (pumpkin with yogurt) and *moong dall* (lentil dhal).

Also recommended:

Le Mercury (Map p168; ☎ 7354 4088; 140a Upper St N1; mains £6.45-9.45; ⊖ Angel or Highbury & Islington) Budget French, with silverware, white linen and good-quality food that has withstood the test of time.

MUSWELL HILL & CROUCH END
TOFF'S — Fish & Chips £-££
☎ 8883 8656; 38 Muswell Hill Broadway N10; mains £8.95-17.50; ⊗ closed Sun; ⊖ Highgate then 🚌 134
This one-time British chipper of the year is renowned for providing large quantities of fresh fish, beautifully battered and flawlessly fried. It's a friendly place and it does takeaway as well.

CAFÉ ON THE HILL · Café £-££

☎ 8444 4957; 46 Fortis Green Rd N10; mains
£7.95-14.95; ⊖ Highgate, then ⛡ 134
Largely organic, this place has been a real
hit with locals, who come here in droves.
It's all you could hope for in a local café –
seasonal menus, all-day breakfast, good
coffee, light lunches, afternoon tea, relatively adventurous evening meals, newspapers and a welcoming atmosphere.

STOKE NEWINGTON

BLUE LÉGUME Map p64 · Vegetarian £-££

☎ 7923 1303; 101 Stoke Newington Church St N16;
mains £5.95-16.95; ⛡ Stoke Newington, ⛡ 73
This lively but laid-back local has mosaic
tables and slightly kooky décor with a little
conservatory at the back, though there's
nothing odd about the big, late breakfasts. Throughout the day there are light
vegetarian snacks and trays of delicate,
delicious pastries. Try its signature 'blue
vegetable' dish: roasted aubergine with
goat's cheese.

MANGAL OCAKBASI Map p156 · Turkish £

☎ 7275 8981; www.mangal1.com; 10 Arcola St E8;
mains £6.50-8.50; ⛡ Dalston Kingsland
Mangal is the quintessential Turkish
ocakbasi (open hooded grill) restaurant:
cramped and smoky and serving superb
meze, grilled lamb chops, quail and *lah-
macun* (Turkish 'pizza' topped with minced
meat, onions and peppers). It's been here
for almost 20 years and is London's worst-
kept secret.

RASA Map p64 · Vegetarian, Indian £

☎ 7249 0344; www.rasarestaurants.com; 55
Stoke Newington Church St N16; mains £3.70-5.95;
⛡ lunch Sat & Sun, dinner daily; ⛡ Stoke Newington, then ⛡ 73
Flagship restaurant of the Rasa chain, this
superb South Indian vegetarian eatery can't
be missed – not with its signature shock-
ing-pink façade! Friendly service, a calm
atmosphere, jovial prices and outstanding
food from the Indian state of Kerala are
its distinctive features. If in doubt, don't
bother with the menu and order the mul-
ticourse Keralan Feast (£16). Rasa Travancore
(Map p64; ☎ 7249 1340; 56 Stoke Newington Church
St N16) just across the road is more of the
same, but with fish and meat.

WEST LONDON

The sheer variety on offer in multicultural West
London means rich pickings for those seeking
truly excellent restaurants. Notting Hill is the
epicentre of this zone and offers a superb range
of eateries whatever the size of your belly or
purse, from venerated chippers to fashionable
fusion. Shepherd's Bush is constantly abuzz
with new openings and revamps of old favourites, while Earl's Court offers a good range
of cheaper options and some great people-
watching. Hammersmith makes up for its lack
of sights with some unique eateries, which are
well worth travelling for. Both St John's Wood
and Maida Vale have some interesting offerings
that are well worth the trek out here.

ST JOHN'S WOOD &
MAIDA VALE

JASON'S Map p175 · Mediterranean ££

☎ 7286 6752; wwww.jasons.co.uk; Jason's Wharf,
opposite 60 Blomfield Rd W9; mains £12.50-18.50;
⊖ Warwick Ave
Jason's has cosy outside tables and a main
dining room in a high wooden-ceilinged
boathouse that feels almost alfresco. After a
total overhaul and refit it has moved away
from serving predominantly fish and seafood dishes and has headed south to the
Mediterranean. Weekend brunch (10.30am
to 3pm Saturday, to 4.30pm Sunday) is a
treat here – especially in fine weather.

GREEN OLIVE Map p175 · Italian ££

☎ 7289 2469; 5 Warwick Pl W9; mains £13-18;
⛡ closed lunch Sat & all day Sun; ⊖ Warwick Ave
The Maida Vale cognoscenti hold this
neighbourhood Italian place in high esteem.
Dishes, although creative and very tasty, are
rather daintily portioned. The plain brickwork, wood floors and art on the walls give
the place an upmarket rustic kind of feel.

MANDALAY Map p175 · Burmese £

☎ 7258 3696; www.mandalayway.com; 444
Edgware Rd W2; mains £4.40-6.50; ⛡ closed Sun;
⊖ Edgware Rd
Despite looking not unlike a greasy spoon
and being located on this grim part of
Edgware Rd, Mandalay is actually one of the
capital's most wonderful secrets, not to mention its only Burmese restaurant. Burmese
cuisine is never going to win any awards
on the world culinary stage but the crispy *a*

kyaw fritters of vegetables and shrimps and the spicy bottle gourd soup with noodles make great starters, while the twice-cooked fish curry with tamarind and lime is delicious.

PADDINGTON & BAYSWATER

MANDARIN KITCHEN Map p175 Chinese £-£££
☎ 7727 9468; 14-16 Queensway W2; mains £5.95-24.50; ⊖ Queensway
This popular Cantonese restaurant with the naff décor prepares some of the best seafood in town so be prepared to wait for a table at the busiest times (eg Sunday lunch) if you haven't booked. Lobster, prawns, whole steamed grouper – all is excellent and it has a particular way with what must be house-made XO sauce, a newfangled condiment made from crushed dried scallops, chilli, garlic and oil.

LEVANTINE Map p175 Lebanese £-££
☎ 7262 1111; www.levant.co.uk; 26 London St W2; mains £9.50-19, set lunch £4.95-9.95, set dinner £19.50-27.50; ⊖ Paddington
Levantine is an atmospheric *Thousand and One Nights*–themed restaurant (lots of red velvet cushions and brassy stuff) where the set menus (including a vegetarian one) are the best value. The fare is well prepared and delicious, including wonderful renditions of Lebanese staples such as tahini, hummus and *muhammarah* (mixed nuts crushed with red pepper) as well as more complex grills. The inevitable belly dancer makes an appearance at weekends.

COUSCOUS CAFÉ Map p175 Moroccan £-££
☎ 7727 6597; 7 Porchester Gardens W2; mains £9.95-15.95; ⊖ Bayswater
This cosy and vividly decorated place does a faultless line in familiar favourites from all over North Africa but really excels with Moroccan-style couscous and *tajines, pastillas* (filled savoury pastries) and slightly exaggerated service. Alcohol is served but you can BYO (no corkage fee).

NOTTING HILL & PORTOBELLO

ELECTRIC BRASSERIE
Map p175 Brasserie £-£££
☎ 7908 9696; www.electricbrasserie.com; 191 Portobello Rd W11; mains £9-28; ⊖ Ladbroke Grove
The name comes from the adjoining Art Deco cinema, but it's possible to believe that it's a comment on the atmosphere here too, as this place never seems to stop buzzing. Whether it's for brunch over the weekend, a hearty lunch or a full dinner, the Electric certainly draws a trendy and wealthy Notting Hill crowd with its British–modern European menu, which includes treats such as crumbed pollock, beetroot and goat's cheese salad and – a personal favourite – lobster and chips (£28).

KENSINGTON PLACE
Map p175 Modern European ££-£££
☎ 7727 3184; www.egami.co.uk; 201-209 Kensington Church St W8; mains £16.50-21.50, 3-course set lunches/dinners £19.50/24.50 (£39.50 with wine); ⊖ Notting Hill Gate
This restaurant has an impressive glass frontage, a design-driven interior and consistently good food, but seating seems cramped and the acoustics are bad. The attached Fish Shop and its mounds of fresh seafood should help you to make up your mind when ordering.

HARLEM Map p175 American £-£££
☎ 7985 0900; www.harlemsoulfood.com; 78 Westbourne Grove W2; mains £9.95-21; ⊖ Bayswater or Royal Oak
The funky feel, chunky chandeliers and smiling staff are just the first things that might impress you about this excellent restaurant serving black American cuisine. The menu is just as noteworthy, including such exotica as buttermilk fried chicken, fried catfish and chicken and shrimp gumbo. It's a great place for a meal, and breakfast is served until 6pm every day.

GEALES Map p175 Fish & Chips £-££
☎ 7727 7528; 2 Farmer St W8; fish & chips £8-12.50; ⊙ closed lunch Sun; ⊖ Notting Hill Gate
Gregarious Geales, established in 1939 and recently overhauled (both premises and menu), has become a popular fixture with locals and tourists alike. The menu now includes fish pie and even sirloin steak. Geales is, of course, more expensive than your everyday chipper, but it's arguably the best there is in London. There's outside seating.

NYONYA Map p175 Malaysian, Chinese £
☎ 7243 1800; www.nyonya.co.uk; 2a Kensington Park Rd W11; mains £6.50-8.50; ⊖ Notting Hill Gate
One day in the not-too-distant future the world will discover *nyonya* (or peranakan)

cuisine as prepared and enjoyed by the so-called Straits Chinese of Malaysia and it will be bigger than Thai and sushi combined. Neither Malay nor Chinese but both, *nyonya* highlights include *laksa* (soup noodles with seafood), Penang *char kway teow* noodles, bean sprouts with salt fish and fiery sambal dipping sauce. The *kuih* desserts are the luridly coloured coconut and jelly concoctions.

COSTA'S FISH RESTAURANT
Map p175   Fish & Chips £

☎ 7229 3794; 12-14 Hillgate St W8; mains £4.70-6.30; ✆ Notting Hill Gate
This fondly regarded local puts a Cypriot spin on the traditional chippy and has a huge array of fresher-than-fresh fish dishes at market prices, which many prefer to the more upmarket Geales (p267) nearby. Not to be confused with Costa's Grill at No 18 of the same street.

CHURCHILL THAI KITCHEN
Map p177   Thai £

☎ 7792; 1246; 119 Kensington Church St W8; mains £6; ✆ Notting Hill Gate
This leafy little restaurant in a conservatory behind a traditional English pub renowned for its Sir Winston memorabilia (and, bizarrely, chamber pots suspended from a great height) serves some of the most authentic (and reasonably priced) Thai food in West London. All dishes are a uniform £6.

TAQUERIA Map p175   Tex-Mex £

☎ 7229 4734; www.coolchiletaqueria.co.uk; 139-143 Westbourne Grove; tacos £3.50-5.50; ✆ closed Sun; ✆ Bayswater or Notting Hill Gate
You won't find fresher, crispier tacos anywhere in London and that's *seguro* (definite) because the 'Tacory' (for lack of a better translation) makes it own fresh corn tortillas next door as you'll see through the window. It's a small casual place serving the American version of Mexican food as enjoyed in Texas and California.

Also recommended:

Churrería Española (Map p175; ☎ 7727 3444; 177-179 Queensway W2; mains £5.50-8.50; ✆ Bayswater) This unlikely café serves a variety of cheap dishes, from English breakfasts to a range of Spanish staples, including paella.

Arancina (Map p175; ☎ 7221 7776; www.arancina .co.uk; 19 Pembridge Rd, W11; mains £3-5; ✆ 9am-10pm; ✆ Notting Hill Gate) A fantastic place to indulge in Sicilian snacks, try the *arancini* (fried balls of rice with fillings), the excellent pizza, and get hooked on the creamy desserts known as *cannoli*.

EARL'S COURT
LOU PESCADOU Map p177   Fish ££

☎ 7370 1057; 241 Old Brompton Rd SW5; mains £13.80-18, 3-course set lunches £10.90; ✆ Earl's Court or West Brompton
Simplicity and elegance meet at this wonderful seafood restaurant, an Earl's Court favourite among the many ordinary eateries on Old Brompton Rd. Should you have trouble understanding the mostly French menu, the staff are happy to help. The wine list is almost all French.

MR WING Map p177   Chinese, Thai £-££

☎ 7370 4450; www.mrwing.com; 242-244 Old Brompton Rd SW5; mains £8-14; ✆ Earl's Court or West Brompton
The oddly named Mr Wing is a very smart Asian-fusion place offering the full spectrum of Chinese cuisine with some Thai cooking thrown in. To recommend it are a plush, dark interior filled with greenery and tropical aquariums, helpful staff and a basement where live jazz sessions are held regularly.

Also recommended:
Krungtap (Map p177; ☎ 7259 2314; 227-229 Old Brompton Rd SW10; mains £7.25-12.95; ✆ Earl's Court or West Brompton) 'Bangkok' (in Thai) is a friendly café-style undertaking serving very good-value and authentic Thai food.

Tendido Cero (Map p177; ☎ 7370 3685; www.cambio detercio.co.uk; 174 Old Brompton Rd SW5; tapas 4.75-8; ✆ Gloucester Rd) Traditional tapas in Chelsea in just about the trendiest Spanish restaurant you've been in outside the Iberian Peninsula.

SHEPHERD'S BUSH & HAMMERSMITH
RIVER CAFÉ Map p177   Italian £££

☎ 7386 4200; www.rivercafe.co.uk; Thames Wharf, Rainville Rd W6; mains £28-32; ✆ closed dinner Sun; ✆ Hammersmith
The restaurant that spawned the world-famous eponymous cookery books is a serious treat off Fulham Palace Rd, overlooking

Barnes across the river. The simple, precise cooking showcases seasonal ingredients sourced with fanatical expertise. Booking is essential, as it's still a hot favourite of the Fulham set.

BUSH BAR Map p177   Modern European £-£££
☎ 8746 2111; www.bushbar.co.uk; 45a Goldhawk Rd W12; mains £8.95-16.50, 2-/3-course set meals £22.50/27.50; ☽ closed dinner Sun; ⊖ Goldhawk Rd
You have to keep an eye out for this bar-restaurant, housed in a converted warehouse and with its entrance down an alleyway off Goldhawk Rd. It's light and breezy with a wonderful tented terrace, and the decent restaurant and bar attract a trendy media crowd after work with its great cocktails and food. The menu is familiar and comforting – London Particular, salt beef with braised cabbage, smoked haddock fishcakes – rather than inventive.

GATE Map p177   Vegetarian £-££
☎ 8748 6932; www.thegate.tv; 51 Queen Caroline St W6; mains £8.50-13.50; ☽ lunch Mon-Fri, dinner Mon-Sat; ⊖ Hammersmith
Widely considered the best vegetarian restaurant in town, Gate has a horrible location surrounded by wasteland and flyovers. But the inventive dishes (Cajun aubergine, shitake wonton and pumpkin laksa), friendly and welcoming staff and the relaxed atmosphere make the trek here all worthwhile. Surprisingly enough, it's the white chocolate and amaretto cheesecake that gets recurring rave reviews, as do the simple but inspired starters and the fine wine list.

BLAH BLAH BLAH Map p177   Vegetarian £
☎ 8746 1337; www.gonumber.com/2524; 78 Goldhawk Rd W12; mains £9.95; ☽ closed Sun; ⊖ Goldhawk Rd
This vegetarian institution has been packing them in for years with imaginative, well-realised food and informal (and recently renovated) surrounds. Dishes lean towards the Mediterranean, though not exclusively, and you can bring your own bottle. Crayons are supplied for doodling on the paper-covered tables while you await your order.

ESARN KHEAW Map p177   Thai £
☎ 8743 8930; www.esarnkheaw.com; 314 Uxbridge Rd W12; mains £5.95-8.90; ☽ lunch Mon-Fri, dinner daily; ⊖ Shepherd's Bush
Welcoming you back into the 1970s is the very green interior of this superb restaurant

serving food from the Esarn (or Issan), the northeast of Thailand where people munch on chillies like chewing gum. The house-made Esarn sausage and green papaya salad are sublime. If you can handle it the 'Tiger's Cry' of grilled strips of ox liver served with a fiery chilli sauce is as authentic a northeast dish as you'll find west of Nakhorn Ratchasima.

Also recommended:
Patio (Map p177; ☎ 8743 5194; 5 Goldhawk Rd W12; mains £8.50-14.90, set meal with glass of vodka £15.99; ☽ lunch Mon-Fri, dinner daily; ⊖ Shepherd's Bush or Goldhawk Rd) Polish restaurant cluttered with curios and antiques and presided over by a kindly matriarch who sees all.

GREENWICH & SOUTHEAST LONDON

It's not that we've been lazy in compiling the following very brief section. It's just that Southeast London's culinary reputation is only starting to emerge, if at all. Even locals despair about where to eat in Greenwich; you'll pass plenty of eateries along the main street, but few places are really any good. Blackheath has a couple of notable eateries and Dulwich – especially Dulwich Village – is starting to support a gastropub culture, but nothing that's really noteworthy has arrived yet. We can only advise you to come back in a few years.

GREENWICH & BLACKHEATH

SE10 RESTAURANT & BAR
Map p180   Modern European ££
☎ 8858 9764; www.se10restaurant.co.uk; 62 Thames St SE10; mains £12.50-17.95, 2-/3-course set lunch £12.50/14.95; ☽ closed dinner Sun & Mon; DLR Cutty Sark
This outwardly scruffy restaurant and wine bar west of the Cutty Sark DLR station hides a light, airy and very warm interior of yellow and gold hues. There's a good concentration of fish dishes – though you'd hardly even know the Thames was at the back door – and traditional British dishes (though with only one mean vegetarian option). The desserts are pure comfort food, especially the sticky-toffee pudding. Sundays host both a breakfast (£3.95 to £4.75) and lunch (two/three courses for £14.50/17.50).

INSIDE Map p180 — Modern European ££
☎ 8265 5060; www.insiderestaurant.co.uk; 19a Greenwich South St SE10; mains £10.95-16.95, 2-/3-course set lunches £11.95/15.95 & early dinners £15.95/19.95; ⏰ closed dinner Sun & all day Mon; DLR/🚊 Greenwich

With white and panelled wooden walls, modern art and linen tablecloths, inside looks quite stuffy, but staff won't bat an eyelid if you turn up in jeans. The crisp food typically includes fresh pea and mint soup, smoked haddock and chives with risotto cake, and desserts such as rhubarb crumble. This is acknowledged to be Greenwich's best restaurant.

ROYAL TEAS Map p180 — Café £
☎ 8691 7240; 76 Royal Hill SE10; dishes £2.25-5.95; ⏰ 9.30am-5.30pm Mon-Fri, 10am-6pm Sat, 10.30am-6pm Sun; DLR/🚊 Greenwich

Royal Teas is not exactly vegetarian – you can get smoked salmon as part of a cream tea (£5.95) at lunchtime – but dishes are mostly comforting meatless things such as baked beans with melted cheese and Spanish-style eggs, and lots of baguettes and soups. We come for the ginger cake served with cream or ice cream.

Also recommended:

Spread Eagle (Map p180; ☎ 8853 2333; 1-2 Stockwell St SE10; 2-/3-course set meals £27/31; DLR Cutty Sark) Smart, French-inspired restaurant opposite the Greenwich Theatre in what was once the terminus for the coach service to/from London.

Everest Inn (off Map p180; ☎ 8852 7872; www.everestinn.co.uk; 39 Tranquil Vale SE3; mains £5.95-10.95, 2-/3-course set meals £11.95/13.95) Reliable Nepali and Indian dishes in the heart of trendy Blackheath Village.

Dog & Bell (Map p180; ☎ 8692 5664; www.thedogand bell.com; 116 Prince St SE8; mains £5.50-9.50; ⏰ noon-11pm Mon-Sat, noon-10.30 Sun; 🚊 Deptford) You probably wouldn't travel any (great) distance for the food at this pub in deepest, darkest Deptford but the choice of beers is a magnet. Despite the plates on the walls with caricatures of famous chefs, the food on offer is hearty pub grub not lean cuisine.

SOUTH LONDON

Most 'northerners' refuse to believe that there's anything of importance down here, but how ignorant they are when it comes to the dope on dining. The choice of restaurants in South London may not be as extensive as it is across the Thames, but the places that do exist

are often stellar. You'd actually travel here just to visit some of the restaurants in Battersea, Wandsworth and Clapham, while Brixton lays out a reasonably priced multicultural spread. Surprisingly, Kennington has one of the best Chinese restaurants in London.

BRIXTON

LOUNGE CAFÉ Map p200 — Café £-££
☎ 7733; 56-58 Atlantic Rd SW9; mains £5.50-13.50; ⏰ closed dinner Sun; ⏣ Brixton

As much a bar as a place to eat, this self-styled 'original urban retreat' has breakfast, day and evening menus with everything from vegetarian fry-ups and burgers to meze platters. It's an excellent place for a cocktail and a nosh, and there's live music.

FUJIYAMA Map p200 — Japanese £-££
☎ 7737 6583; 5-7 Vining St SW9; mains £5.40-10.75; ⏣ Brixton

This deceptively small Japanese place behind Dogstar (p293), with its welcoming dark-red interior and communal benches, has a large choice of bento (meal) boxes, noodles, tempura, miso soups and sushi and sashimi on its lengthy menu.

BAMBOULA Map p200 — Caribbean £
☎ 7737 6633; 12 Acre Lane SW9; mains £7.50-8.50; ⏣ Brixton

Decorated in the red, gold and green of the Jamaican flag, this takeaway and restaurant is cheap and cheerful, serving jerk chicken, oxtail, curried goat, ackee and saltfish, rice and peas, plantain and other Caribbean classics. Bread pudding laced with rum brings up the rear very nicely.

ASMARA Map p200 — Eritrean £
☎ 7737 4144; 386 Coldharbour Lane SW9; mains £4-7.50, 6-/7-course set meals £25/27; ⏰ dinner daily; ⏣ Brixton

A rare Eritrean restaurant, Asmara serves spicy chicken, lamb and beef stews and vegetable dishes that you scoop up with injera, the flat, slightly spongy sourdough bread that is a national dish. Staff provide colour in their traditional costumes, while there's a nod to the former colonial power, Italy, with four pasta dishes (£4 to £4.59) on the menu.

Also recommended:

Gallery (☎ 8671 8311; 256a Brixton Hill SW2; mains £6.95-13.95; dinner Thu-Sun; ⏣ Brixton) This convivial restaurant behind a takeaway shop in Brixton has Portuguese food every bit as authentic as you'll find in nearby Stockwell's Little Lisbon.

Satay Bar (Map p200; ☎ 7326 5001; 447 Coldharbour Lane SW9; mains £4.95-7.95; ❷ Brixton) This local fixture in Brixton just a notch above a fast-food house does acceptable Malay and Indonesian dishes.

BATTERSEA & WANDSWORTH

CHEZ BRUCE Map p64   French £££
☎ 8672 0114; www.chezbruce.co.uk; 2 Bellevue Rd SW17; 3-course set lunches £25.50-32.50, 3-/4-course set dinners £37.50/47.50; ❷ Wandsworth Common
This eatery, though Michelin-starred, actually feels more like a quality local than a flash restaurant. The restaurant's rustic façade, beside leafy Wandsworth Common, belies a modern interior. The fixed-price-only set-up means that there's fortunately no need to scrimp on desserts.

BUTCHER & GRILL Map p200   British £-£££
☎ 7924 3999; www.thebutcherandgrill.com; 39-41 Parkgate Rd SW11; mains £8.50-25; ☯ closed dinner Sun; ❷ Sloane Sq, then ☒ 19 or 319
This combination grill and butcher shop has made quite a slap south of the river, winning awards as fast as it sizzles T-bones. But while not everyone likes the idea of seeing their meat *au naturel* on entry, the quality of the ingredients, the wide choice of sauces and the views from the main dining room (all brickwork and exposed ducts) are more than compensation.

RANSOME'S DOCK
Map p200   Modern British ££-£££
☎ 7223 1611; www.ransomesdock.co.uk; 35-37 Parkgate Rd SW11; mains £10.50-21.50; ☯ closed dinner Sun; ❷ Sloane Sq, then ☒ 19 or 319
Diners flock to this restaurant not because it's trendy or on the dock of a bay (rather a narrow inlet of the Thames) but for fresh and very thoughtfully prepared food: smoked Lincolnshire eel fillets with buckwheat pancakes and crème fraîche, duck breast with apple sauce, red cabbage organic lamb noisettes with roast root vegetables. Weekday two-course lunch is £14.75.

SANTA MARIA DEL BUEN AYRE
Map p200   Argentine Steakhouse £-££
☎ 7622 2088; www.buenayre.co.uk; 129 Queenstown Rd SW8; mains £7-19.80; ☯ lunch Sat & Sun,

dinner daily; ☒ Queenstown Rd Battersea, ☒ 77, 137 or 345
This new branch of the much beloved Argentine steakhouse in Hackney (Map p156; ☎ 7275 9900; Broadway Market E8; ❷ Bethnal Green, ☒ Cambridge Heath) caters to carnivores south of the river with grilled meats and sausages. The brave will go for one of the *parrilladas* (braziers; £13.50 to £19.80) to share.

CLAPHAM

GRAFTON HOUSE
Map p200   Modern International ££
☎ 7498 5559; www.graftonhouseuk.com; 13-19 Old Town SW4; mains £12.50-15.50, 2-/3-course set meals £22/27; ❷ Clapham Common
The A-list of Clapham rub shoulders in this very stylish bar-restaurant with marble floors, tropical hardwood tables and curved leather sofas. The menu is modern international – simple but with that extra caress (pumpkin risotto, venison and plum burger, lobster, crab and salmon fishcake) – and brunch is a big deal here, served daily from noon to 4pm. There's live jazz on Sunday evenings.

VERSO Map p200   Italian £-££
☎ 7720 1515; 84 Clapham Park Rd SW4; mains £7.80-14.90; ☯ lunch Sat, dinner Wed-Mon; ❷ Clapham Common
This unpretentious neighbourhood restaurant serves consistently excellent pizza (£5.70 to £8.50), including such unfamiliar varieties as rocket, grilled prawn and courgette pizza *bianca* (without tomato paste). Pasta (£7.80 to £10.90) is also excellent, as are the seafood dishes and terrific homemade desserts.

CINNAMON CAY
Map p200   Modern International ££
☎ 7801 0932; www.cinnamoncay.co.uk; 87 Lavender Hill SW11; mains £10.75-14.50, 2-course set lunches Mon & Tue £12; ☯ lunch & dinner Mon-Sat; ☒ Clapham Junction, then ☒ 77A or 137
This neighbourhood restaurant offers a lively atmosphere, small open kitchen and Southeast Asian–influenced fusion. The Thai fish cake with mango salad and the sesame-crusted seared tuna with piperade are favourites and vegetarians are well catered for with such tasty exotica as Penang laksa with pumpkin, tofu and okra. Service is efficient and friendly.

KENNINGTON, OVAL & STOCKWELL

LOBSTER POT Map p198   Fish ££
☎ 7582 5556; www.lobsterpotrestaurant.co.uk; 3 Kennington Lane SE11; mains £14.50-18.50; 2-/3-course lunches £11.50/14.50, 3-course dinner £21.50; ☺ closed Mon; ⊖ Kennington or Elephant & Castle

This charming French-owned restaurant hidden in the wastelands south of Elephant & Castle turns out excellently prepared fish and seafood dishes *à la française* (think lots of butter and garlic) to an appreciative local cognoscenti. An eight-course tasting menu is £39.50.

DRAGON CASTLE Map p198   Chinese £-££
☎ 7277 3388; 100 Walworth Rd SE17; mains £7-18.50; ⊖ Elephant & Castle

It's hard to imagine that what just might be the best nonchain Chinese restaurant in London is hidden within one of the brutalist buildings of deepest, darkest Kennington. But it's true and even the incomparable food critic Fay Maschler of the *Evening Standard* concurs. The duck, pork and seafood (deep fried crispy oysters, crab with black bean) are renowned but come instead for the dim sum (£1.90 to £3) especially at weekend lunch.

Also recommended:

Kennington Tandoori (Map p198; 7735 9247; www.kenningtontandoori.com; 313 Kennington Rd SE11; mains £5.95-9.95; ⊖ Kennington) This local curry house is a favourite of MPs from across the river, including former Prime Minister John Major.

SOUTHWEST LONDON

Although not universally known for its cuisine, this area of London can lay claim to a number of decent gastronomic outposts, some of which are well worth crossing town for. If you're in Fulham, wander down Fulham Rd, up New King's Rd and along Wandsworth Bridge Rd for a good choice. In Putney, head down the High Street or the roads heading off it. In keeping with its high standard of living along the gentrified banks of the river, restaurants in places such as Richmond and Kew are usually exquisitely presented, featuring superlative food and wine lists.

FULHAM

BLUE ELEPHANT Map p205   Thai ££-£££
☎ 7385 6595; www.blueelephant.com; 4-6 Fulham Broadway SW6; mains £10.60-28; ☺ lunch & dinner Sun-Fri, dinner Sat; ⊖ Fulham Broadway

The sumptuous surroundings, attentive staff and excellent food of this Fulham institution with branches around the globe make dining at the Blue Elephant a memorable (if expensive) experience. The atmosphere is romantic, with candlelit tables, fountains and lush 'jungle' foliage though the 'gift shop' at the front is a bit naff. The best time to come is for the fab Sunday brunch (£22).

LOTS ROAD PUB & DINING ROOM
Map p205   Gastropub £-££
☎ 7352 6645; www.lotsroadpub.com; 114 Lots Rd SW10; mains £7-14; ⊖ Fulham Broadway

No one has a bad thing to say about this tucked-away gastropub, aside from the minor affectation of listing prices in hundreds of pence. Light floods through the windows into the high-ceilinged, wood-lined curved dining area and onto the black and chrome bar, where choice wines are sold by the glass. The regularly changing menu reads as pretty standard fare – roast pork, salmon, lamb – but it's all delicious and dependable. For dessert, try the sticky-toffee pudding or the honey-roasted figs.

BLUE KANGAROO Map p205   Brasserie £-££
☎ 7371 7622; www.thebluekangaroo.co.uk; 555 King's Rd SW6; mains adult £6.95-13.80, child £5.45; ☺ 9.30am-7pm; ⊖ Fulham Broadway

This very family-oriented restaurant allows you to enjoy a meal while watching, via CCTV, your under-eights run wild in the downstairs playroom (£3 to £4.50). Adult nerves are soothed with grilled goat's cheese, Thai king prawns and mushroom tagliatelle. The children's menu has home-made fish fingers, nuggets and pizza. There are different activities scheduled each day.

PUTNEY & BARNES

CHAKALAKA Map p205   South African ££
☎ 8789 5696; www.chakalakarestaurant.co.uk; 136 Upper Richmond Rd SW15; mains £13.95-19.95; ☺ lunch Sat & Sun, dinner daily; ⊖ East Putney

This South African restaurant done up in brash tiger patterns and colours serves springbok and kudu (both types of antelope), ostrich, zebra and other creatures that are usually seen grazing – not being grazed on – and is probably best visited on a dare. It also has *bobotie* (£9.95), a very South African dish of spiced minced meat baked with a bread custard topping, on the menu. Good selection of South African wines.

CHOSAN Map p205 — Japanese £-££
☎ 8788 9626; 292 Upper Richmond Rd SW15; mains £3.80-15.90; ⓨ closed Mon; ⊖ Putney Bridge, ⓡ Putney

This little Japanese restaurant whose name means Korea in Korean (go figure) doesn't look like much from the outside – or the inside for that matter – but it does turn out excellent sushi and sashimi as well as tempura and *kushiage* (more deeply fried than tempura) dishes.

ENOTECA TURI Map p205 — Italian ££
☎ 8785 4449; www.enotecaturi.com; 28 Putney High St SW15; mains £10.50-14.50, 2-/3-course set lunches £14.50/17.50; ⓨ closed Sun; ⊖ Putney Bridge, ⓡ Putney

The atmosphere at this stylish place is serene, the service charming. Enoteca Turi devotes equal attention to the grape as to the food, which means that each dish, be it a shellfish *tagliolini* or saddle of new season lamb, comes recommended with a particular glass of wine (or you can pick from the enormous wine list if you have ideas of your own).

MA GOA Map p205 — Indian £-££
☎ 8780 1767; www.ma-goa.com; 242-244 Upper Richmond Rd SW15; mains £7.85-10.50; ⓨ dinner Tue-Sun; ⊖ Putney Bridge, ⓡ Putney

The speciality here is the subtle cuisine of Portugal's erstwhile colony on the west coast of India. Dishes include the homemade chorizo topped with a spicy onion sauce; and fish *caldin*, a sour-sweet coconut-based concoction.

RICHMOND

FISHWORKS Map p208 — Fish £-£££
☎ 8948 5965; www.fishworks.co.uk; 13-19 The Square, Old Market TW9; mains £9.50-25; ⓨ closed dinner Sun; ⊖ Richmond

Spawning at a rate that can only discourage confidence, this Bath-based chain now counts 10 outlets in London alone, including an Islington branch (Map p168; ☎ 7353 1279; 134 Upper St N1; ⊖ Angel). But as FishWorks was London's first truly French *poissonnerie* (fishmonger) with a restaurant attached, its entranceway counters piled high with shaved ice, crustaceans and fish, we return regularly, especially for the sublime Dartmouth crab eaten cold and the incomparable *zuppa del pescatore* (fisherman's soup; £19.90), a symphony of delights from the deep.

PETERSHAM NURSERIES CAFÉ
Map p208 — Modern European ££-£££
☎ 8605 3627; www.petershamnurseries.com; Church Lane, off Petersham Rd TW10; mains £16-24; ⓨ lunch Tue-Sun; ⊖ / ⓡ Richmond, then ⓑ 65

In a greenhouse at the back of the gorgeously situated Petersham Nurseries is this award-winning café straight out of the pages of *The Secret Garden*. Well-heeled locals tuck into confidently executed food that often began life in the nursery gardens – organic vegetable dishes, such as artichokes braised with preserved lemon sage and black olives, feature alongside seasonal plates of, say, roasted quail with walnut sauce or white polenta with squid and sherry butter. There's a teahouse (ⓨ 10am-4.30pm Tue-Sat, from 11am Sun) should you have failed to book at the café (and well in advance).

CHEZ LINDSAY Map p208 — French ££
☎ 8948 7473; www.chezlindsay.co.uk; 11 Hill Rise TW10; mains £12.85-16.75, 2-/3-course set lunches £14.50/17.50 & dinners £16.50/19.50; ⊖ Richmond, ⓡ Richmond

Offering a slice of Brittany at the bottom of Richmond Hill, Chez Lindsay's simply furnished dining room draws visitors with its wholesome Breton cuisine, comfortable ambience and river views. The house specialities include galettes (£3.30 to £9.25) with a myriad of tasty fillings, washed down with a variety of hearty (and very dry) Breton ciders.

DON FERNANDO'S Map p208 — Spanish £-££
☎ 8948 6447; www.donfernando.co.uk; 27f The Quadrant TW9; mains £7.95-11.75; ⊖ / ⓡ Richmond

The Izquierdo family have been serving superb cuisine from their native Andalucía for nigh on 20 years now, and their enthusiasm shows no signs of waning. With

THE LONDON CHAIN GANG

While, of course, the usual bleak offerings of chain restaurants are to be found all over the capital, London also boasts some excellent chains of inventive and interesting restaurants, which locals patronise frequently. Here are some of our favourites; check their websites for a full list of outlets.

Carluccio's

Inventive and authentic, these Italian restaurants (www.carluccios.com) in London have a great ambience, helped along by the open space created by the deli-counter at each of the 20-odd outlets, including the Fitzrovia branch (Map p68; ☎ 7636 2228; 8 Market Pl W1; ✚ Oxford Circus).

Giraffe

There's a kind of sunny Californian feel to family-friendly Giraffe (www.giraffe.net), where the likes of coarse-cut chips, burritos, vegetarian salad wraps and burgers are on the menu, and friendly service is a given. There are 20 outlets, including an Islington branch (Map p168; ☎ 7359 5999; 29-31 Essex Rd N1; ✚ Angel)

Gourmet Burger Kitchen

The burgers at Gourmet (www.gbkinfo.co.uk) are the real deal, made from prime Scottish beef and enlivened by specially created sauces and superb chips (vegetarian versions available). Of the 17 outlets, the Bayswater branch (Map p175; ☎ 7243 4344; 50 Westbourne Grove W2; ✚ Royal Oak) is probably the most useful.

Hamburger Union

Highly recommended, Hamburger Union (www.hamburgerunion.com) delivers gourmet, calorific fast-food favourites to you in six smart and perennially packed central London locations, including a Soho branch (Map p68; ☎ 7437 6004; 22-25 Dean St W1; ✚ Tottenham Court Rd). All meat is additive free and free range, while vegetarians are guaranteed a minimum choice of two main meals each day.

Nando's

Among the better fast-food options in London Nando's (www.nandos.co.uk) offers chicken *a la portuguesa* by way of Africa and Brazil from dozens of high-street outlets in London, including a Camden branch (Map p166; ☎ 7424

an exhaustive list of tapas (£3.50 to £7), Spanish beers, wines and culinary specialities, including (unusually) some vegetarian options along with cheerful service, this makes a great place for a good lunch or a slow supper.

KEW

GLASSHOUSE Map p64   Modern European ££
☎ 8940 6777; www.glasshouserestaurant.co.uk; 14 Station Pde TW9; mains £16.50-19.95; ✚ / ☒ Kew Gardens

A meal at this splendid restaurant is a great way to cap off a day spent at the botanical gardens in Kew. Its glass-fronted exterior reveals a delicately lit, low-key interior, whose unassuming décor ensures that the focus remains on the divinely cooked food. Punters choose from such mains as a rump of veal with caramelised calf's tongue

and sweetbreads and roast fillet of cod with creamed white polenta that combine traditional English mainstays with modern European innovation. The Glasshouse is sister restaurant to Chez Bruce (p271) in Wandsworth.

NEWENS MAIDS OF HONOUR
Map p64   Traditional British £
☎ 8940 2752; 288 Kew Rd W9; set tea £6.50; ☒ 9.30am-1pm Mon, to 6pm Tue-Sat; ✚ / ☒ Kew Gardens

The name of this quirky Kew tearoom a short distance from the main entrance to Kew Gardens comes from its famed dessert, supposedly created by Anne Boleyn, Henry VIII's ill-fated second wife. It is made of puff pastry, lemon, almonds and curd cheese, and anyone visiting should try it at least once (£2.25).

9040; 57-58 Chalk Farm Rd NW1; ⊖ Camden Town). The décor is colourful and upbeat, the ambience laid-back and the signature *peri-peri* (chilli) sauce fiery.

Real Greek

This ever-expanding chain of Greek restaurants (www.therealgreek.com) serving souvlaki (Greek kebab) and meze now counts a half-dozen outlets, including the original Hoxton branch (Map p150; ☎ 7739 8212; 15 Hoxton Market N1; ⊖ Old St), which is a work of art in itself. There's a meze sharer and a few salads for vegetarians.

Strada

A cut (and a slice) above when it come to chain pizzerias Strada (www.strada.co.uk) serves only what comes out of its wood-burning ovens at some two dozen outlets, including a Clerkenwell branch (Map p150; ☎ 7278 0800; 8-10 Exmouth Market EC1; ⊖ Farringdon). The pasta is also recommended.

Tas

This is a chain of goof Turkish restaurants (www.tasrestaurant.com) with a roll call of stews and grills that never disappoint. There are seven outlets spread all over London, including a Waterloo branch (Map p126; ☎ 7928 1444; 33 The Cut SE1; ⊖ Waterloo), but our favourite is Tas Pide (Map p126; ☎ 7928 3300; 20-22 New Globe Walk SE1; ⊖ London Bridge), which specialises in *pide* (Turkish 'pizza' for lack of a better word), well placed opposite Shakespeare's Globe in Bankside.

Wagamama

There's nothing new or exciting about this chain of noodle bars (www.wagamama.com) with two-dozen London outlets, including a Marylebone branch (Map p100; ☎ 7409 0111; 101a Wigmore St W1; ⊖ Bond St); it's 'slurp, bam, thank you m'am' and you're out. But the food's reliable and cheap (for London) and the bench seating excellent for solo travellers.

Yo! Sushi

Smart makeovers and modernisations in the past few years have made London's original conveyer-belt sushi chain (www.yosushi.com) a fun place to come again. The original Soho branch (Map p68; ☎ 7287 0443; 52 Poland St W1; ⊖ Tottenham Court Rd) is among the 18 outlets spread across London.

Also recommended:

Olé (Map p205; ☎ 8788 8009; www.olerestaurants .com; 240 Upper Richmond Rd SW15; tapas £1.75-6.95, mains £9.50-15.50; ⊖ Putney Bridge, ⊠ Putney) Very unSpanishlike restaurant in Putney with lots of light and blond-wood furniture serves excellent tapas.

Kew Greenhouse (Map p64; ☎ 8940 0183; 1 Station Pde TW9; mains £6.50-8.75; ⊠ 8.30am-6.30pm daily; ⊖ Kew Gardens, ⊠ Kew Gardens) When in Kew it's worth paying a visit to this delightful botanically themed café will help set the mood for a visit to nearby Kew Gardens.

BLUELIST[1] (blu,list) *v.*
to recommend a travel experience.
What's your recommendation? www.lonelyplanet.com/bluelist

DRINKING

top picks

- George Inn (p283)
- Prospect of Whitby (p288)
- Ye Olde Cheshire Cheese (p282)
- At Proud (p288)
- Bistrotheque (p287)
- Jerusalem Tavern (p285)
- Foundry (p285)
- George & Dragon (p286)
- Lamb & Flag (p279)
- Hollybush (p289)

DRINKING

Things have changed for London's drinkers so much in the past decade that the city has gone from being the pub and ale capital to becoming what the *Independent* calls 'the cocktail capital of the world'. And what with the smoking ban coming into effect in July 2007, the Big Smoke has lost its puff, leaving the air in pubs and bars surreally clear.

London's drinking culture has been changing rapidly in recent decades (alongside many other facets of London life), making way for a huge choice of sensational venues for all sorts of imbibing. There are cocktail bars, DJ bars, old pubs, wine bars – and many are a night out in their own right, rather than just a preclub warm-up venue.

Pubs are the heart of London's social existence and the great social leveller. Their history is often written on the walls and etched in the bloodshot faces of the regulars who prop the bars. Virtually every Londoner has a 'local' and looking for your own and sampling a range of boozers is one of the highlights of any visit to the capital.

Unfortunately, an increasing number of London's traditional boozers, known for their particular atmosphere of sticky carpets, prawn cocktails, crisps and juke-box music, have been converted into a range of different venues, from soulless bars to supermarkets and car parks. Avoid High-Street chain pubs and head to one of the bars recommended following.

Aside from the bars we recommend, it's a great idea to check out a few drinking strips yourself, such as Islington's Upper St or Essex Rd; Shoreditch's Old or High Sts; Soho's Dean St or Greek St; West London's Portobello Rd; the Cut on the South Bank; Clapham High St and Borough High St in South London; or Parkway and Camden High St in Camden Town.

We've provided information on many of *our* favourite drinking dens here, although there's no substitute for individual research – your liver's the only limit.

Opening Hours

November 2005 saw new licensing laws granting pubs and bars, at the discretion of local authorities, to stay open past the traditional 11pm closing time gong. The new laws, which we warmly welcomed as long overdue, have made it somewhat easier to get a late drink in central areas, though closing times vary from place to place. Unless otherwise stated, all pubs and bars reviewed here close at 11pm from Monday to Saturday and at 10.30pm on Sunday.

THE WEST END

You have to do a bit of planning before you head out in the West End: most Londoners find it difficult to beat the crowds, get a table without a struggle and drink in bars that aren't mobbed by weekend visitors. The truth is that the West End, though the first port of call for most visitors, is no longer a prime drinking area for discerning Londoners. Yet Soho is still a wonderful place for a night out – Friday and Saturday nights are buzzing with excitement and decadence, and there are people, booze and rickshaws in the streets till the early hours.

SOHO & CHINATOWN

FRENCH HOUSE Map p68   Bar
☎ 7437 2799; 49 Dean St W1; ⊖ Leicester Sq
French House is Soho's legendary boho boozer (with a good restaurant downstairs) with a history to match: this was the meeting place of the Free French Forces during WWII, and De Gaulle is said to have drunk here often, while Dylan Thomas, Peter O'Toole and Francis Bacon all frequently ended up on the wooden floors. Come here to sip on Ricard, French wine or Kronenbourg and check out the quirky locals.

GARLIC & SHOTS Map p68   Bar
☎ 7734 9505; 14 Frith St W1; ☽ to midnight Mon-Wed, to 1am Thu-Sat, to 11.30pm Sun; ⊖ Tottenham Court Rd
A fantastic place if you like your make-up pale, your hair raven black and your drinks laced with garlic, though it's equally fun for anyone who wants to have a drink while checking out London's Goth crowd. It's never too crowded here and you can get a seat at the cosy back garden on summer days or head down to the slightly scary bar where monster masks watch as you order.

TWO FLOORS Map p68   Bar

☎ 7439 1007; 3 Kingly St W1; ☽ to midnight Fri & Sat, closed Sun; ⊖ Oxford Circus or Piccadilly Circus
It's amazing that Two Floors has managed to keep its relaxed atmosphere when so many bars in Soho have been mobbed by drunken weekenders, but it might have to do with the fact that it's hard to notice from the outside, and this low profile has helped maintain its cool personality. The punters are young, cool and bohemian, the bar staff equally so, and the music is usually über-now. The distressed décor is leather sofas and country-diner tables and chairs.

MILK & HONEY Map p68   Cocktail Bar

☎ 7292 9949, 0700 655 469; www.mlkhny.com; 61 Poland St W1; ⊖ Leicester Sq or Tottenham Court Rd
Milk & Honey's number one 'House Rule' reads: 'No name-dropping, no star fucking', so prepare for a tight-lipped, but glamorous clientele at London's most renowned cocktail bar. It's a members' club that lets nonmembers in on week nights (though it's preferred if the plebeians stick to the beginning of the week), and you have to phone in advance to reserve your own private booth for a two-hour slot. Once you're there, you have to ring the bell and whisper your name into the buzzer, the speakeasy way. This practice is heavenly if you like privacy and great drinks, and hellish if you prefer a more down-to-earth atmosphere. It's worth sampling the vast and exquisite cocktail list.

PLAYER Map p68   Cocktail Bar

☎ 7494 9125; www.thplyr.com; 8 Broadwick St W1; ☽ to midnight Mon-Wed, to 1am Thu-Sat, closed Sun; ⊖ Oxford Circus
Player was one of London's top cocktail bars during the 1990s, when Dick Bradsell, the Lenin of London's cocktail revolution, started mixing his substantial and stylish drinks behind the basement bar. He has since moved on, and although the bar still serves great drinks, the clientele is a lot less suave than when the bar was at its best. A cooler Soho crowd heads down after 9pm, when you too should descend and sample the cocktail list. Unfortunately, only members are admitted after 11pm.

COACH & HORSES Map p68   Pub

☎ 7437 5920; 29 Greek St W1; ⊖ Leicester Sq
Famous as the place where *Spectator* columnist Jeffrey Bernard drank himself

to death, this small, busy and thankfully unreconstructed boozer retains an old Soho bohemian atmosphere with a regular clientele of soaks, writers, hacks, tourists and those too pissed to lift their heads off the counter. Pretension will be prosecuted.

SUN & 13 CANTONS Map p68   Pub

☎ 7734 0934; 21 Great Pulteney St W1; ⊖ Oxford Circus or Piccadilly Circus
Certainly Soho's oddest-named pub, the Sun is a music-industry mainstay and a great place for young hopefuls to network. Everyone from the Chemical Brothers (first London gig) to Underworld (global smash hit written here) to this place, and there are still regular DJ nights downstairs. A far better reason to visit is the historic décor and relaxed drinking vibe upstairs.

COVENT GARDEN & LEICESTER SQUARE

FREUD Map pp72–3   Bar, Café

☎ 7240 9933; 198 Shaftesbury Ave WC2; ☽ to 1am Thu, to 2am Fri, to 1am Sat; ⊖ Covent Garden
Make this the first stop on your crawl because there's no way you'll make it down the stairs (not much more than a ladder) after a few bevvies. It's a small basement bar-café-gallery with the sort of beige walls that could look just plain dirty, but there are purposefully arty pictures to head off scrutiny. The décor and punters are suitably scruffy and arty, and the cocktails are fat and fancy, but beer is sadly only by the bottle.

CROSS KEYS Map pp72–3   Pub

☎ 7836 5185; 31 Endell St WC2; ⊖ Covent Garden
Covered in ivy and frequented by loyal locals who come here for pints of Young's and spicy fry-ups, the Cross Keys is Covent Garden's tourist-free, local pub. Eccentric landlord Brian shows off his pop purchases as bar decorations (such as his £500 Elvis Presley napkin); brass pots, kettles and diving gear hang off the ceiling; and the punters range from bar props and fruit machine devotees to Covent Garden professionals, all of whom spill onto the pavement and outside tables on summer days.

LAMB & FLAG Map pp72–3   Pub

☎ 7497 9504; 33 Rose St WC2; ⊖ Covent Garden
Good pubs can be hard to come by in over-touristy Covent Garden, but the Lamb &

Flag makes up for any character or soul lost in the area – the interior is more than 350 years old, with creaky wooden floors and winding stairs, there's live jazz on Sunday afternoons and come sunshine or summer evenings, it's a miracle if you can approach the bar for all the people crowding outside. Its setting is equally charming: the main entrance is on top of a tiny cobbled street, but you can also reach it from the back-street donkey path that'll make you think of Victorian England.

SALISBURY Map pp72–3   Pub
☎ 7836 5863; 90 St Martin's Lane WC2; ☽ to midnight Fri & Sat; ⊖ Leicester Sq
Facing off the superchic St Martin's Lane Hotel, the Salisbury offers everything its opposite number doesn't: warmth, centuries of history, and a glorious, traditionally British pub interior. The Salisbury is packed in the evenings by pre- and post-theatre drinkers, and while it can be a little touristy, it's still a true London gem.

HOLBORN & THE STRAND

GORDON'S WINE BAR Map pp72–3   Bar
☎ 7930 1408; www.gordonswinebar.com; 47 Villiers St WC2; ⊖ Embankment or Charing Cross
We shouldn't really include Gordon's here – it's already too crowded as soon as the office hours are over – but it's simply too good to leave out. It's cavernous and dark, and the French and New World wines are heady and reasonably priced; there's also bread, cheese and olives to pick on.

POLSKI BAR Map pp72–3   Bar
☎ 7831 9679; 11 Little Turnstile WC1; ☽ closed Sun; ⊖ Holborn
Formerly known as Na Zdorowie ('cheers' in Polish), Polski Bar changed its name probably as a result of no-one being able to pronounce it before or after many-a-flavoured vodka shot, but the spirit (no pun intended) has remained: around 60 different types of vodka, from coffee to fruity to wheat flavoured, there's even kosher vodka, or simple old Polish *slivowica* (liquor). There's great Polish food here, too.

AKA Map pp72–3   DJ Bar
☎ 7836 0110; www.akalondon.com; 18 West Central St W1; ☽ to 3am Tue-Fri, to 7am Sat, to 4am Sun; ⊖ Tottenham Court Rd

Sitting on a dark backstreet like all good secrets, the AKA bar is one of the West End's best DJ bars. A great sound system is exercised by many of London's up-and-coming and already established DJs, and the young, good-looking clientele is propelled by precision-made cocktails late into the night.

PRINCESS LOUISE Map pp72–3   Pub
☎ 7405 8816; 208 High Holborn WC1; ⊖ Holborn
We might have used the word gem before, but we take all of the other instances back. This late-19th-century Victorian pub is spectacularly decorated with a riot of fine tiles, etched mirrors, plasterwork and a stunning central horseshoe bar. It was closed for refurbishment at the time of writing, but was expected to reopen in December 2007.

SEVEN STARS Map pp72–3   Pub
☎ 7242 8521; 53-54 Carey St WC2; ⊖ Holborn or Temple
Even though it's packed with lawyers in the after-office booze rush hour, the tiny Seven Stars is still a relative secret to many Londoners. Sitting behind the Royal Courts of Justice and originally a sailors' hangout, this is a place overflowing with character, great food, beer and wine. The eccentric landlady and chef, Roxy Beaujolais, a former TV chef and raconteur, lets her cat, Tom Paine, roam around the pub and snooze on the window sills; the bar staff are friendly and the game dishes ravishing.

BLOOMSBURY

KING'S BAR Map pp92–3   Bar
☎ 7837 6470; Hotel Russell, Russell Sq WC1; ⊖ Russell Sq
Nestled behind the awesome Victorian Gothic façade of the Hotel Russell, the King's Bar is an oasis of booze in a neighbourhood sorely lacking in decent bars. The grand Edwardian décor, huge leather armchairs and table service make the prices worthwhile. There's a great selection of cocktails and wines, and you're always guaranteed a seat.

LAMB Map pp92–3   Pub
☎ 7405 0713; 94 Lamb's Conduit St WC1; ☽ to midnight Mon-Sat, to 10.30pm Sun; ⊖ Russell Sq

The Lamb's central mahogany bar with beautiful Victorian dividers has been its *pièce de résistance* since 1729, when the screens used to hide the music stars from the punters' curious gaze. Just like three centuries ago, the pub is still wildly popular, so come early to bag a booth. There's a decent selection of Young's bitters and a genial atmosphere perfect for unwinding.

LORD JOHN RUSSELL Map pp92–3   Pub
☎ 7388 0500; 91 Marchmont St WC1; ✆ Russell Sq
If you're pining for your student days or just want a cheap pint, head down to the Lord John Russell. Here you can blend in with the under- and postgrads who are escaping the local halls of residence. It's a traditional one-room bar where chatting is the norm, and the relaxed atmosphere is perfect for getting away from noisy Central London bars.

MUSEUM TAVERN Map pp92–3   Pub
☎ 7242 8987; 49 Great Russell St WC1;
✆ Tottenham Court Rd
This is where Karl Marx used to retire for a well-earned pint after a hard day's inventing communism in the British Museum Reading Room, and where George Orwell boozed after his literary musings. A lovely traditional pub set around a long bar, it has friendly staff and is popular with academics and students alike, and while tourists check-in for the atmosphere, the place retains its loyal regulars.

PERSEVERANCE Map pp92–3   Pub
☎ 7405 8278; 63 Lamb's Conduit St WC1;
✆ Holborn or Russell Sq
Perseverance is a charming Victorian boozer downstairs with a very pleasant upstairs dining room. It's always busy with office workers during the week, but it also does a brisk trade with locals over the weekend, when you can be guaranteed a seat.

QUEEN'S LARDER Map pp92–3   Pub
☎ 7837 5627; 1 Queen Sq WC1; ✆ Russell Sq
In a lovely square southeast of Russell Sq, this pub is so called because Queen Charlotte, wife of 'Mad' King George III, rented part of the pub's cellar to store special foods for him while he was being treated nearby. There are benches outside for fair-weather fans and a good dining room upstairs.

FITZROVIA

BRADLEY'S SPANISH BAR Map p68   Bar
☎ 7636 0359; 42-44 Hanway St W1; ✆ Tottenham Court Rd
Hanway St is home to several tapas-and-flamenco bars and speakeasy Spanish bars that open till dawn and serve beer from crates. Bradley's is vaguely Spanish in décor, though it's really Spanish in its choice of booze: San Miguel, Cruzcampo and some decent wines. The punters are squeezed under low ceilings in the nooks of the basement, while a vintage vinyl jukebox plays out rock tunes of your choice.

MAYFAIR

SALT WHISKY BAR Map p100   Bar
☎ 7402 1155; www.saltbar.com; 82 Seymour St W1; ⏲ to 1am Mon-Sat, to 12.30am Sun; ✆ Marble Arch
Two hundred whiskies and bourbons, lots of salt, and a sleek, dark wood interior make this friendly bar and comfortable lounge a fab place for drinking. Staff are knowledgeable and keen to share their tips with customers.

GUINEA Map p100   Pub
☎ 7409 1728; 30 Bruton Pl W1; ✆ Green Park or Bond St
Top-quality Young's beers, famous autographs on the toilet walls and the whiff of money define this quiet and out-of-the-way pub in London's most exclusive neighbourhood of Mayfair. There are very few places to sit, though, and it sometimes feels little more than a waiting room for the rear restaurant (renowned for its pies).

MARYLEBONE

MOOSE BAR Map p100   Bar, DJ Bar
☎ 7224 3452; 31 Duke St W1; ⏲ to 2am Mon-Thu, to 3am Fri & Sat; ✆ Bond St
We bet you never thought you'd find a Canadian Rockies sky lodge in the middle of the West End? Well, the Moose Bar is just that. It's a wood-lined space on two floors, with a simple ground-floor bar and a downstairs lounge/DJ 'n' dance space that has antlers for lampshades and cowhide on the seating. The cocktails are reasonable (£6.50 to £8.50), you can have a bite (of pies and nibbles) to eat and there's dancing until late on weekend nights.

THE CITY

So close and yet so far… While the famous 'Square Mile' is surrounded by neighbourhoods offering some of the hippest and most stylish drinking venues in London, for the most part the City does traditional pubs. And because they cater to bankers, dealers and other suits, it's usually a Monday to Friday after-work deal here and best avoided at the weekend. In fact, it can be difficult to find any boozer open here on Saturday and Sunday.

VERTIGO 42 Map p110   Cocktail Bar
☎ 7877 7842; www.vertigo42.co.uk; Tower 42, 25 Old Broad St EC2; 🕑 closed Sat & Sun; ⊖ Bank or Liverpool St
The stratospheric views from this 42nd-storey champagne bar are matched by the stratospheric prices – the cheapest bottle of champers is £44 – and for security reasons you must book ahead and go through airportlike security checks. Seats are arranged around the glass-walled circular space, where you quaff champagne while taking in an unforgettable 360-degree view; evenings are the better time to visit, when you can watch the lights come on across London. The crowd, not surprisingly, is as rarefied as the view.

BLACK FRIAR Map p110   Pub
☎ 7236 5474; 174 Queen Victoria St EC4; 🕑 to 11.30pm Thu & Fri; ⊖ Blackfriars
It may look like Friar Tuck just stepped out of this 'olde pubbe' just north of Blackfriars tube station, but the interior is actually an Arts and Crafts makeover dating back to 1905. Not surprisingly, the Black Friar is the preserve of City suits during the week, but they disappear at the weekend, leaving it to the rest of us. There's a good selection of ales and bitters here.

COUNTING HOUSE Map p110   Pub
☎ 7283 7123; 50 Cornhill EC3; 🕑 closed Sat & Sun; ⊖ Bank or Monument
They say that old banks – with their counters and basement vaults – make perfect homes for pubs and this award-winner certainly looks and feels most comfortable in the former headquarters of NatWest. Even though the central hall and island bar are mammoth, the Counting House can feel like Clapham Junction in the early evening.

JAMAICA WINE HOUSE Map p110   Pub
☎ 7929 6972; 12 St Michael's Alley EC3; 🕑 closed Sat & Sun; ⊖ Bank
Not a wine bar at all but a historic Victorian pub, the 'Jam Pot' stands on the site of what was the first coffee house in London (1652); such places were often just fronts for brothels. At the end of a narrow alley, this is a difficult place to find.

YE OLDE CHESHIRE CHEESE
Map p110   Pub
☎ 7353 6170; Wine Office Ct, 145 Fleet St EC4; 🕑 to 2.30pm Sun; ⊖ Blackfriars
The entrance to this historic pub is via a picturesque alley just down from Dr Johnson's House (p114; he drank here as did Thackeray, Dickens and the visiting Mark Twain). Cross the threshold and you'll find yourself in a wood-panelled interior (the oldest bit dates from just after the Great Fire of 1666) with sawdust on the floor; it's divided up into various bars and three restaurants.

EL VINO Map p110   Wine Bar
☎ 7353 6786; www.elvino.co.uk; 47 Fleet St EC4; 🕑 closed Sat & Sun; ⊖ Blackfriars or Temple
A venerable institution that plays host to barristers, solicitors and other legal types from the Royal Courts of Justice across the way, this wine bar (one of five in a small chain) has one of the better wine lists in the City and prices at the attached shops are reasonable. El Vino 'appeared' as the wine bar Pomeroys in the TV series *Rumpole of the Bailey*.

THE SOUTH BANK

The South Bank may have changed rather dramatically in the past few years, however, the majority of the drinking establishments in the South Bank are good, down-to-earth boozers, which just happen to have been here for hundreds of years and are now patronised by a younger, trendier set.

WATERLOO

BALTIC Map p126   Bar
☎ 7928 1111; www.balticrestaurant.co.uk; 74 Blackfriars Rd SE1; 🕑 from noon Mon-Sat; ⊖ Southwark
This very stylish bar at the front of an Eastern European restaurant specialises – not surprisingly – in vodkas; some four dozen of them are at hand for your perusal and

enjoyment. The airy, high-ceilinged dining room, with a glass roof and lovely amber wall, is just behind should you need some blotter.

LAUGHING GRAVY Map p126 Bar
☎ 7721 7055; www.thelaughinggravy.com; 154 Blackfriars Rd; ☽ noon-11pm Mon-Fri, 7-11pm Sat; ⊖ Southwark

This casual bar and restaurant has a delightfully shambolic, almost louche atmosphere. With vintage ad posters, paintings, potted plants and piano, it resembles a bohemian late-1940s living room. The small bar is well stocked with 'laughing gravy' (whisky).

KING'S ARMS Map p126 Pub
☎ 7207 0784; 25 Roupell St SE1; ☽ to midnight Thu & Fri; ⊖ Waterloo or Southwark

A well-kept secret on the corner of a terraced Waterloo backstreet, the award-winning King's Arms is a delightful boozer full of character. The large traditional bar area serving up a good selection of ales and bitters gives way to a fantastically odd conservatory bedecked with junk store eclectica of local interest. It's a relaxed and friendly place; you'll find few better south of the river.

BANKSIDE & SOUTHWARK

BAR BLUE Map p126 Cocktail Bar
☎ 7940 8333; www.vinopolis.com; 1 Bank End SE1; ☽ 9am-11pm; ⊖ London Bridge

This stylish bar attached to Vinopolis (p131) and close to the Thames has floor-to-ceiling windows and a colour scheme supposedly derived from a bottle of Bombay Sapphire Gin. The stools, the bar, the ceiling – everything but the nearby river – are bluer than blue. It's a great place for a cocktail before or after a performance at nearby Shakespeare's Globe.

ANCHOR BANKSIDE Map p126 Pub
☎ 7407 1577; 34 Park St SE1; ⊖ London Bridge

This riverside pub dating back to 1775 (but rebuilt after a fire destroyed it a century later) has superb views across the Thames from its terrace and is the most central (and most popular) riverside pub in London. Samuel Johnson (1709–84), whose brewer friend owned the joint, wrote part of his

dictionary here. Even better than the terrace is the small seating just off the 1st floor.

BOROUGH & BERMONDSEY

GEORGE INN Map p126 Pub
☎ 7407 2056; Talbot Yard, 77 Borough High St SE1; ☽ to midnight Fri & Sat; ⊖ Borough

The George is a rare bird indeed – a National Trust pub. It's London's last surviving galleried coaching inn, dates from 1677 and is mentioned in Dickens' *Little Dorrit*. It is on the site of the Tabard Inn (thus the Talbot Yard address), where the pilgrims in Chaucer's *Canterbury Tales* gathered before setting out (well lubricated, no doubt).

MARKET PORTER Map p126 Pub
☎ 7407 2495; 9 Stoney St SE1; ☽ 6.30-8.30am & 11am-11pm Mon-Fri, noon-11pm Sat, noon-10.30pm Sun; ⊖ London Bridge

This pub opens early on weekdays for the traders at Borough's wholesale market. It's good during normal opening hours, too, for its convivial atmosphere and excellent selection of real ales and bitters. This is the stuff of great pubs, and it's well worth making a detour or stopping by for a quick 'un while perusing the stalls of Borough Market at the weekend.

MAYFLOWER Map p180 Pub
☎ 7237 4088; 117 Rotherhithe St SE16; ⊖ Rotherhithe

East of Bermondsey in Rotherhithe, this 15th-century pub, originally called the Shippe, is named after the vessel that took the pilgrims to America in 1620. The ship set sail from Rotherhithe, and the captain supposedly charted out its course here while supping schooners. There's seating on a small back terrace, from which you can view the Thames.

ROYAL OAK Map p126 Pub
☎ 7357 7173; 44 Tabard St SE1; ☽ from 6pm Sat, noon-11pm Sun; ⊖ Borough

This authentic Victorian place owned by a small independent brewery in Sussex is tucked away down a side street and is a mecca for serious beer lovers. The literati might find their way here too; it's just a hop, skip and a handful of rice from the Church of St George the Martyr where Little Dorrit (aka Amy) got married in Dickens' eponymous novel.

SPICE ISLAND Map p180   Pub
☎ 7394 7108; 163 Rotherhithe St SE16; ☽ to midnight Fri & Sat; ⊖ Rotherhithe
What this enormous place lacks in history it surely makes up for with views. Just opposite the flagship YHA hostel (p360) in Rotherhithe, it has a large bar on the ground floor, a restaurant above and a large heated terrace overlooking the river.

WINE WHARF Map p126   Wine Bar
☎ 7940 8335; www.winewharf.co.uk; Stoney St SE1; ☽ closed Sun; ⊖ London Bridge
Located in a smart warehouse space close to the culinary joys of Borough Market, this wine bar's selection will delight oenophiles as well as people just coming along for a drink. The range is truly enormous, and the staff is more than happy to advise, offering you the chance to taste before buying.

HYDE PARK TO CHELSEA

This is where high style and traditional pubs meet and coexist in surprising harmony. You can choose between the sultry lights of expensive cocktail bars, frequented by the deep-pocketed Knightsbridge and Chelsea dwellers, or join the area's ale lovers in some of the most beautiful of London's old pubs.

WINDOWS OF THE WORLD BAR
Map pp138–9   Cocktail Bar, Bar
☎ 7493 8000; Hilton Hotel, 28th fl, Park Lane W1; ☽ to 2am Mon-Thu, to 3am Fri & Sat; ⊖ Hyde Park Corner
This swish bar is a popular place for observing London from a great height: the 28th floor of the Hilton Hotel. You might think it resembles something out of Miami Vice, with its '80s-style armchairs, suave and extortionately priced (£20) cocktails and live entertainer who pretends to be playing his guitar (he has a prerecorded track, really). The views of the city are breathtaking, particularly at dusk. Nonhotel guests arriving after 11pm will have to pay a £7.50 cover charge.

COOPERS ARMS Map pp138–9   Pub
☎ 7376 3120; 87 Flood St SW3; ⊖ Sloane Sq or South Kensington
A classic Chelsea pub just off King's Rd, stuffed with taxidermists' delights such as a moose head and a stuffed pig's face, among other stiff critters, and railway advertising cartoons. Newspapers abound near the bright and sunny bar, and the clientele is mixed and jolly.

NAG'S HEAD Map pp138–9   Pub
☎ 7235 1135; 53 Kinnerton St SW1; ⊖ Hyde Park Corner
Located in a serene mews not far from bustling Knightsbridge, this gorgeously genteel early-19th-century drinking den has eccentric décor, a sunken bar and no mobile phones. A dreamy delight; don't bother if you're not pure of pub heart.

STAR TAVERN Map pp138–9   Pub
☎ 7235 3019; 6 Belgrave Mews West SW1; ⊖ Knightsbridge or Sloane Sq
This cheery place is best known for West End glamour and East End skulduggery; it's where Christine Keeler and John Profumo rendezvoused for the scandalous Profumo affair and where the Great Train Robbers are said to have planned their audacious crime. These days it's just a lovely boozer with reliable Fuller's beers.

CLERKENWELL, SHOREDITCH & SPITALFIELDS

If you want hipness that hurts, this is where you'll find it. The streets of Hoxton and Shoreditch are swamped with groovers who live fashion and (usually) study art, sporting wild hairdos, tight jeans and plenty of attitude. Bars are either cool and tattered or glamorous and decadent, and you've got to keep your ear to the ground for what's on each week – there's always an exhibition opening you might crash or a music night showing new talent. In any case, walking up Old St on a weekend night is infectiously lively and a perfect chance to see cosmopolitan London. Though Clerkenwell is a little more down to earth and calm, it still has some excellent bars.

CLERKENWELL

CHARTERHOUSE BAR Map p150   DJ Bar
☎ 7608 0858; www.charterhousebar.co.uk; 38 Charterhouse St EC1; ☽ to midnight Wed & Sun, to 1am Thu, to 2am Fri & Sat; ⊖ Barbican or Farringdon

Charterhouse Bar is most people's pit stop before going on to Fabric (p300), so expect loud and relentless music on weekends, with a good preclub atmosphere. For those preferring something quieter, pop by for brunch – the food is great – and enjoy the wedge-shaped structure, a traditional Clerkenwell warehouse design. DJs are on every evening and entry is free at all times.

JERUSALEM TAVERN Map p150   Pub
☎ 7490 4281; 55 Britton St EC1; ⊖ Farringdon
This has to be London's most beautiful pub. Well, actually, it was one of the first London coffee houses (founded in 1703), with the 18th-century décor of occasional tile mosaics still visible. It's teeny, so come early and get a seat. There's good lunch food and, this being the only London outlet of St Peter's Brewery (based in North Suffolk), it has a brilliant range of drinks: organic bitters; cream stouts; wheat and; mmm, fruit beers, many of which are dispensed in green, apothecary-like bottles.

SLAUGHTERED LAMB Map p150   Pub
☎ 7253 1516; 34-35 Great Sutton St EC1; ☉ noon-midnight Mon-Thu, noon-1am Fri & Sat; ⊖ Farringdon
A great Clerkenwell local, which although it opened only in 2004, feels like an old favourite already. It is spacious, with flea-market furniture, large windows, wooden floors and loud wallpaper, and the bar is lit by granny-style lamps. The beer on offer is good and the food is old England (fish and chips, fish fingers, sausage and mash etc). The black wall-papered downstairs room hosts regular live music and open mic nights.

YE OLDE MITRE Map p150   Pub
☎ 7405 4751; 1 Ely Ct EC1; ⊖ Chancery Lane or Farringdon
A delightfully cosy historic pub, tucked away in a backstreet off Hatton Garden, Ye Olde Mitre was built for the servants of Ely Palace. There's still a memento of Elizabeth I – the stump of a cherry tree around which she once danced. There's no music, so the rooms only echo to the sound of amiable chitchat.

SHOREDITCH

BAR KICK Map p150   Bar
☎ 7739 8700; 127 Shoreditch High St E1; ⊖ Old St
A much larger sister venue to Clerkenwell's Café Kick, this place has a slightly edgier

Shoreditch vibe. This time, too, there's some floor space left over after four footy tables were installed, so there are leather sofas and simple tables and chairs.

FOUNDRY Map p150   Bar
☎ 7739 6900; www.foundry.tv; 84-86 Great Eastern St EC2; ⊖ Old St
Everything about the Foundry is truly bonkers. Let's start with the look: it's 'decorated' with genuinely shabby (not chic) furniture that clutters the space, the bar is made out of a plank of wood and propped by a yellowing old man, and the floor is icky. There's usually a nutter poet reading their verse on the makeshift stage, or a piano rendition of vintage David Bowie that'll stay with you for a long time, while downstairs is a live gig venue. It's so bonkers we love it. The Foundry rules.

BEDROOM BAR Map p150   DJ Bar
☎ 7613 5637; 62 Rivington St EC2; ☉ 7pm-midnight Mon-Thu, to 2am Fri & Sat; admission after 10.30pm Fri & Sat £3; ⊖ Old St
A great place for a cheap postpub night of dancing, Bedroom Bar has good cocktails, banquettes to lounge on, and enough floor space for dancing to the DJ's tunes.

CARGO Map p150   DJ Bar
☎ 7749 7840; www.cargo-london.com; 83 Rivington St EC2; ☉ to 1am Mon-Thu, to 3am Fri & Sat, to midnight Sun; ⊖ Old St or Liverpool St
Cargo is really one of a kind on London's club scene. It doesn't go for the obvious, but chooses international music, live bands and brilliant DJs, all of which you can enjoy while eating great 'street food' and sipping cocktails or massive bottles of beer. It's the sort of place where you can feel cosy or go crazy, and a club that comes closest to feeling like your 'local'. There are dishevelled sofas to chill out on, and a courtyard with a hammock, a Mexican canteen and a great dance floor. See also p300.

DRAGON BAR Map p150   DJ Bar
☎ 7490 7110; 5 Leonard St N1; ☉ to 11pm Sun & Mon, to midnight Tue & Wed, to 1am Thu, to 2am Fri & Sat; ⊖ Old St
Dragon's been supercool since it opened in the mid-1990s, and it's maintained its style thanks to the fact that it's easy to miss: the name is hardly visible and only embossed on an entrance stair. Inside it's all exposed

brick, Chinese lanterns, velvet curtains and one of those illuminated waterfall pictures you buy on Brick Lane – it's ironic, of course.

DREAMBAGSJAGUARSHOES
Map p150   DJ Bar

☎ 7729 5830; 34-36 Kingsland Rd E2; ☺ to midnight; ⊖ Old St
The bar's name is a lazy leftover from the names of the two shop spaces the bar now occupies, and this nonchalance is a typical example of the we-couldn't-care-less Shoreditch chic. Inside, the small space is filled with sofas and Formica-topped tables, the walls are covered in drawings and graffiti, a DJ plays in the corner, lads wear the nu rave look and the gals are sleek-looking.

GEORGE & DRAGON Map p150   DJ Bar, Pub
☎ 7012 1100; 2 Hackney Rd E2; ⊖ Old St
Once a scuzzy local pub, the George (as ye shall dub it if you value your Shoreditch High Street cred) was taken over and decorated with the owner's grandma's antiques (antlers, racoon tails, old clocks), cardboard cut-outs of Cher and fairy lights, turning this one-room pub into what has remained the epicentre of the Hoxton scene for a decade. It's one of the most exciting places to go out, though prepare to be sandwiched between jolly, dancing boys and girls when it gets busy. Some of the best DJ nights in London are on offer here, with cabaret performances taking place on window sills (Sunday cabaret is *trés* popular). It's total fun and mindless hedonism. Not a place for a quiet pint.

MOTHER BAR Map p150   DJ Bar
☎ 7739 5949; www.333mother.com; 333 Old St; ☺ to midnight Sun-Thu, to 2am Fri & Sat; ⊖ Old St
Where can you go dancing till late on a Sunday night, you may wonder? Come to Mother. Still one of the best bars in town, it's above Shoreditch's original hipster club, 333. Though it's mobbed at weekends, don't be put off – there's a lounge, a dance floor and a fun, up-for-it crowd.

OLD BLUE LAST Map p150   DJ Bar, Pub
☎ 7739 5793; 39 Great Eastern Rd, EC2; ⊖ Old St or Liverpool St
You walk into this inconspicuous pub and expect to find old geezers sitting at the bar, watching the snooker on the telly in the corner, but you find a massively trendy teenage-and-up crowd of Hoxtonites wearing hooded tops, fluorescent T-shirts and nylon caps. The seedy and trendy look is courtesy of *Vice* magazine – the hipster bible/global conglomerate and try-hard bad boy magazine – which owns the place. It hosts some of the best Shoreditch parties, has a rocking juke box and does a mean square pie to boot.

BRICKLAYERS ARMS Map p150   Pub
☎ 7739 5245; 63 Charlotte Rd EC2; ⊖ Old St
A determinedly down-to-earth stalwart of the Hoxton scene, the Bricklayers Arms attracts an unpretentious but cool-looking, generally mid-to-late-20s crowd. This essentially old-style pub is often seen as a solid place to start the evening, before heading off elsewhere.

SPITALFIELDS
LOUNGELOVER Map p150   Cocktail Bar
☎ 7012 1234; 1 Whitby St E1; ☺ to midnight Mon-Thu, to 1am Fri & Sat, closed Sun; ⊖ /rail Liverpool St
Evincing the junk-shop-rearranged-by-gay-stylist look, here chandeliers, antiques, street lanterns and comfy lounge chairs materialise just seconds away from the run-down streets outside. Coming here once is never enough, but prepare to cough up around £10 for a cocktail.

1001 Map p150   DJ Bar
☎ 7247 9679; www.cafe1001.co.uk; 91 Brick Lane E1; ☺ to midnight Fri & Sat; ⊖ Aldgate East or Liverpool St
'Laid-back' is an understatement here – 1001 is frequented by those who haven't yet been to bed after their night out or those who come here to snooze in the candlelit atmosphere at noon. Coffee and cocktails are prepared while DJs play excellent music, and seating is all comfy sofas and massive cushions. The crowded outside area dishes up burgers all day Sunday.

T BAR Map p150   DJ Bar
☎ 7729 2973; www.tbarlondon.com; 56 Shoreditch High St E1; ☺ to 2am Thu-Sun; ⊖ Liverpool St
A recent closure was a slap-on-the-wrist for wild and loose T Bar that tends to host all-day club events on Sunday and raucous

weekend nights. Now, with some bouncers brooding at the front door, it's still the same fun, with excellent DJs on Friday and Saturday. It's housed on the ground floor of the Tea Building, a creative hub for various hip companies cashing in on Shoreditch's aching coolness.

VIBE BAR Map p150   DJ Bar
☎ 7377 2899; Truman Brewery, 91-95 Brick Lane E1; ⊖ Old St or Aldgate East
Once the epicentre of the Hoxton scene, the Vibe is part bar, part club and still attracts a regular crowd, although it's safe to say that its time has long passed. On quieter nights drinkers can still enjoy themselves in the spacious bar, which has scuffed leather sofas, arcade games and computer terminals.

GOLDEN HART Map p150   Pub
☎ 7247 2158; 110 Commercial St E1; ⊖ Liverpool St
It's an unsurprisingly trendy Hoxton crowd that mixes in the surprisingly untrendy interior of this brilliant Spitalfields boozer. As it's famously a hangout for the YBAs (Young British Artists), you may well catch Tracey Emin giving it some to her interlocutor over a pint and chips, although most agree that the person to come and see here is the charming (and, yes, possibly bonkers) landlady, Sandra, who ensures that the bullshit never outstrips the fun. Smashing.

THE EAST END & DOCKLANDS

Once famous for gangster assassinations and Saturday night fights at drinking-up time, the pubs of the East End have come a long way in the past few years. There are still some fairly odious dives where only locals will feel comfortable, but the pubs listed following are just fine and welcome all. And some of the pubs in Hackney have become positively trendy.

WHITECHAPEL
BLIND BEGGAR Map p156   Pub
☎ 7247 6195; 337 Whitechapel Rd E1; ⊖ Whitechapel
Notorious as the place where Ronnie Kray shot George Cornell in 1966 in a gang war over control of the East End's organised

crime, the Blind Beggar has had a makeover in recent years and looks like just about any other boozer along this stretch of the East End's main thoroughfare. But its historical associations (not to mention garden with benches) continues to draw visitors and locals alike.

BETHNAL GREEN & HACKNEY

BISTROTHEQUE Map p156   Bar, DJ Bar
☎ 8983 7900; www.bistrotheque.com; 23-27 Wadeston St E2; ⊖ Bethnal Green
The lovely Bistrotheque offers three things: dining in its stylish white restaurant, where the food is very fine; partying and cabaret in the Cabaret Room; and drinking in the Napoleon Bar, a moody, slightly decadent room with dark walls and plush seating. The drinks are expertly mixed and the bar staff is always friendly. The whole building is a converted East End warehouse and the bar draws people from all over London to the depths of Bethnal Green, so good are its cocktails and parties. You might see the Puppini Sisters singing, the likes of Stephen Bayley giving talks and a bit of gay bingo (though not all on the same night).

CAT & MUTTON Map p156   Pub
☎ 7254 5599; www.catandmutton.co.uk; 76 Broadway Market E8; ⏱ from 6pm Mon, from noon Tue-Sun; ⓡ London Fields, ⛶ 26, 48, 55, 106 or 253
As if to seal the deal on East London's most up-and-coming eating and drinking strip, the once terrifyingly rowdy pub on the edge of London Fields (the 'Cat' is short for 'cattle' that grazed here before being slaughtered) has metamorphosed into an airy and well-run gastropub. It has mostly lagers on tap but offers a full wine list and modern European menu.

DOVE FREEHOUSE Map p156   Pub
☎ 7275 7617; www.belgianbars.com; 24 Broadway Market; ⏱ from noon Mon-Thu, noon-midnight Fri & Sat; ⓡ London Fields, ⛶ 26, 48, 55, 106 or 253
This pub attracts at any time with its rambling series of rooms and wide range of Belgian Trappist and wheat beers. But there's something about the dim back room, with its ethnic bohemian chic, that makes this pub a great place to hunker down against the chill. Of course, everyone feels the same so don't count on solitude.

MILE END & VICTORIA PARK

ROYAL INN ON THE PARK Map p156   Pub
☎ 8985 3321; 111 Lauriston Rd E9; ⓨ from noon Mon-Thu, noon-midnight Sat; ⊖ Mile End then ⊜ 277

Only a fool would divulge the name of their much loved local and – whoops! – we think we just have. On the western edge of Victoria Park this excellent place, once a poster pub for Transport for London, has a half-dozen real ales and Czech lagers on tap, outside seating to the front and an enclosed terrace in back. It's always lively and attracts a mixed boho/louche Hackney crowd.

ROYAL OAK Map p156   Pub
☎ 7729 2220; 73 Columbia Rd E2; ⓨ from 6pm Mon-Thu, noon-11pm Fri & Sun, noon-midnight Sat; ⊖ Bethnal Green, ⓡ Cambridge Heath, ⊜ 26, 48 or 55

This traditional boozer gone trendy gastro-pub has a good selection of bitter and a better-than-average wine list. It gets into its stride on Sunday when the Columbia Road Flower Market is on just outside the door.

DOCKLANDS

CAPTAIN KIDD Map p156   Pub
☎ 7480 5759; 108 Wapping High St E1; ⊖ Tower Hill then ⊜ 100

The Kidd, with its large windows, fine (but small) beer garden and mock scaffold recalling the hanging nearby of the eponymous pirate in 1701, is a favourite riverside pub in Wapping.

DICKENS INN Map p156   Pub
☎ 7488 2208; St Katharine's Way E1; ⊖ Tower Hill, DLR Tower Gateway

Popular with both City folk and tourists who have strayed too far east from the Tower, this flower-bedecked three-storey warehouse is always heaving. But what keeps us going back is the waterside location, the outside tables and the fact that the building dates from the 1790s and not the 1970s as everyone thinks (though it was moved here from elsewhere).

GRAPES Map p156   Pub
☎ 7987 4396; 76 Narrow St E14; DLR Westferry

One of Limehouse's renowned historic pubs – there's been a drinking house here since 1583 – the Grapes is cosy and very narrow. Actually, it's absolutely tiny, especially the riverside terrace, which can only really comfortably fit about a half-dozen close friends. But it continues to radiate olde-worlde charm.

PROSPECT OF WHITBY Map p156   Pub
☎ 7481 1095; 57 Wapping Wall E1; ⊖ Tower Hill then ⊜ 100

Once known as the Devil's Tavern, the Whitby in Wapping dates from 1520 and is one of London's oldest surviving drinking houses. It's firmly on the tourist trail now, but there's a terrace to the front and the side overlooking the Thames, a decent restaurant upstairs and open fires in winter. Check out the pewter bar – Samuel Pepys once sidled up to it.

NORTH LONDON

Camden Town is one of North London's favoured areas, with more bars and pubs pumping music than you can manage to crawl between. The hills of Hampstead are a real treat for old-pub aficionados, while Muswell Hill and Crouch End will give you incoherent celebrities and North Londoners at play. Gentrified Stoke Newington and Dalston have some excellent pubs and interesting new bars thanks to their slightly boho and organicoholic residents.

CAMDEN

AT PROUD Map p166   DJ Bar
☎ 7482 3867; www.atproud.net; The Gin House, Stables Market, Chalk Farm Rd NW1; ⓨ to 1am Sun-Thu, to 3am Fri & Sat; ⊖ Camden Town

Opened in 2006 as part of Proud Gallery's space, At Proud is the summer venue London's been in need of for decades. It's a bit tricky to find, hidden among the nooks of Camden's old Stables Market, but once you step onto the sunny roof terrace overlooking the industrial but attractive skyline, you'll be charmed into submission. It's really a summer venue, though it's open in winter too, with live bands playing most nights (when there's a cover charge of around £5), a crowd of socialites and beautiful people, and, most importantly, an excellent atmosphere.

BAR VINYL Map p168   DJ Bar
☎ 7681 7898; 6 Inverness St NW1; ⊖ Camden Town

Bar Vinyl is the epicentre for Camden's young and urban crowd, with cool kids behind the decks, a record shop downstairs and graffiti whirling along narrow walls. It's superfriendly at the same time, though, and everyone's here to relax, enjoy some music and gobble a pizza, rather than pose. Weekends are packed and buzzing, midweek nights are quieter, and the music is always good.

BARTOK Map p166 — DJ Bar
☎ 7916 0595; www.bartokbar.com; 78-79 Chalk Farm Rd NW1; ✆ to 3am Sun-Thu, to 4am Fri & Sat; ⊖ Chalk Farm or Camden Town
Here's a true oasis: an elegant classical-music lounge-bar in the midst of grungy Camden. And not only is it an original find in Camden, Bartok is pretty unusual in the whole of London. Named after the Hungarian composer and pianist, Bartok specialises in classical concertos, live jazz or brilliant DJ sets blending jazz, classical, electro and world music. There are fantastic cocktails (try the Espresso Martinis), low sofas and intimate lighting, with fun until the wee hours.

CROWN & GOOSE Map p168 — Pub
☎ 7485 8008; 100 Arlington Rd NW1; ✆ to 1am Mon-Thu & Sun, to 2am Fri & Sat; ⊖ Camden Town
One of our favourite London pubs, this square room has a central wooden bar between British-racing-green walls studded with gilt-framed mirrors and illuminated by big, shuttered windows. More importantly, it combines a good-looking crowd, easy conviviality, top tucker and good, inexpensive beer.

EDINBORO CASTLE Map p168 — Pub
☎ 7255 9651; 57 Mornington Tce NW1; ⊖ Camden Town
This beautifully attired, relaxed and welcoming pub has more of a Primrose Hill atmosphere than that of a Camden boozer. It boasts a full menu, gorgeous furniture designed for slumping, and a huge outdoor seating area that is perfect for summer evenings.

QUEEN'S Map p166 — Pub
☎ 7586 0408; 49 Regent's Park Rd NW1; ✆ to midnight Fri & Sat; ⊖ Camden Town or Chalk Farm
While the ghost of actress, royal 'friend' and former next-door neighbour Lillie Langtry is said to reside in the cellar of this spirited joint, the pub proper is haunted by contem-

porary beauties such as Jude Law and the other fashionistas of Primrose Hill. The food and drinks won't disappoint, and there's plenty to look at among the clientele.

KING'S CROSS

BIG CHILL HOUSE Map p150 — DJ Bar
☎ 7427 2540; www.bigchill.net; 257-259 Pentonville Rd N1; ⊖ King's Cross St Pancras
Want to celebrate the spirit of the Big Chill festival all year round? Well, head out to King's Cross and party at this huge bar, where the owners' idea is to give Londoners a place to feel free and festive by naming parts of the 'House' after the eponymous festival's different musical areas and hosting lots of live and exciting music nights. Sister to the popular Big Chill bar (☎ 7392 9180; Dray Walk E1; ⊖ Liverpool St) off Brick Lane.

RUBY LOUNGE Map p168 — DJ Bar
☎ 7837 9558; www.ruby.uk.com; 33 Caledonian Rd N1; ✆ to midnight Thu, to 2am Fri & Sat; ⊖ King's Cross St Pancras
King's Cross is being groomed slowly, so what was once an area frequented only by hardened clubbers (or prostitutes and junkies) is now turning into a three-Starbucks-per-square-metre neighbourhood. But Ruby Lounge was around when the going was tough and it's here to stay. It's a great place, with a warm interior, excellent DJs and an up-for-it preclubbing crowd.

HAMPSTEAD & HIGHGATE

BOOGALOO Map p166 — Bar
☎ 8340 2928; www.theboogaloo.org; 312 Archway Rd N6; ✆ to midnight Thu, to 1.30am Fri & Sat; ⊖ Highgate
'London's Number 1 Jukebox' is how Boogaloo flaunts itself and how it's been described in the local media, thanks to its celebrity-musician-fiddled-with jukebox playlists, featuring the favourite 10 songs of the likes of Nick Cave, Sinead O'Connor, Howie B and Bobbie Gillespie, to name but a random few. There's plenty to boogie to with the regular live music that's on every night of the week. If you're into music in a big way, it's worth going out to Archway.

HOLLYBUSH Map p166 — Pub
☎ 7435 2892; 22 Holly Mount NW3; ⊖ Hampstead
A beautiful pub that makes you envy the privileged residents of Hampstead,

Hollybush has an antique Victorian interior, a lovely secluded hilltop location, open fires in winter and a knack for making you stay longer than you had intended at any time of the year. Set above Heath St, it's reached via the Holly Bush Steps.

SPANIARD'S INN Map p166 Pub
☎ 8731 6571; Spaniards Rd NW3; ⊖ Hampstead then 🚌 21
This marvellous tavern dates from 1585 and has more character than a West End musical. Famously, it was highwayman Dick Turpin's hangout between his robbing escapades, but it's also served as a watering hole for more savoury characters, such as Dickens, Shelley, Keats and Byron. Perhaps we owe English language's greatest works of literature and poetry to this pub's ale? There's a big, blissful garden, and the food ain't half bad.

WRESTLERS Map p166 Pub
☎ 8340 4397; 98 North Hill Rd N6; ⊖ Highgate
Another great, great local where the ambience, beer, food and décor just combine to make you happy to be alive, although when the very friendly Irish governor gets chatting you can begin to have second thoughts.

ISLINGTON

ELBOW ROOM Map p168 Bar
☎ 7278 3244; 89-91 Chapel Market N1; ⊖ Angel
Don't be fooled by the row upon row of pool tables, this place is packed on the weekends with punters just as interested in the cocktails, beer, bar food and DJs. It's relaxed, unposey and reckoned by many to be a top place to meet members of the opposite sex. Entry on Saturday costs about £5.

SALMON & COMPASS Map p168 Bar
☎ 7837 3891; www.salmonandcompass.com; 58 Penton St N1; ⏰ to 2am Sun-Thu, to 4am Fri & Sat; ⊖ Highbury & Islington
It's all about music here, be it in DJ or live set form, with young and trendy Islingtonites crowding in over the weekend. There are large sofas for sitting, but it's mainly standing, drinking and dancing that take place, illuminated by fairy lights and a couple of sky lights during the day, when the bar serves Thai food. Monthly comedy nights are held here, too.

EMBASSY Map p168 DJ Bar
☎ 7359 7882; 119 Essex Rd N1; ⏰ to 1am Fri & Sat; ⊖ Angel
It's been around for years, but Embassy's reputation and appeal just keeps rising, so get there early on weekends and mingle with the cool music and media crowd and enjoy the good DJs. The darkened windows and black walls make it look secretive, but inside everyone's relaxing on the ubiquitous comfy sofas on the ground and basement floors. There's a cover charge (£3) on weekends.

MEDICINE BAR Map p168 DJ Bar
☎ 7704 9536; 181 Upper St N1; ⏰ to midnight Sun-Thu, to 2am Fri & Sat; ⊖ Highbury & Islington
Still one of the coolest bars along Upper St, the Medicine Bar attracts 30-something clubbers and drinkers, as well as a younger crowd. One reason you'd come to this converted dark-red pub, with low sofas and dim lighting, is its music, ranging from jazzy funk to hip-hop; another attraction is minor celebrity spotting – you might catch sight of your fave DJ, model or TV star (if you can see through the crowds, that is).

ELK IN THE WOODS Map p168 Pub
☎ 7226 3535; 39 Camden Passage N1; ⊖ Angel
A wonderful take on a stylish countryside hunters' pub, this is by far the coolest bar in Islington and equally notable for its food. With its large, rough oak-wood tables, old mirrors, stuffed deer head and wonderfully friendly staff, this is a spot to savour.

STOKE NEWINGTON

FOX REFORMED Bar
☎ 7254 5975; 176 Stoke Newington Church St N16; 🚉 Stoke Newington, 🚌 73
Stoke Newington's firm favourite for more than two decades, the Fox has all the qualities of a good local: a friendly landlord, loyal regulars, good food, wine and beer, and a cosy back garden. Its quiet atmosphere and chess and backgammon boards for entertainment on relaxing afternoons always bring new converts to its charms.

JAZZ BAR DALSTON Cocktail Bar
☎ 7254 9728; 4 Bradbury St N16; ⏰ to 1am Mon-Thu, to 2am Fri & Sat, to midnight Sun; 🚉 Dalston Kingsland
Jazz Bar is Dalston's most excellent and unexpected find, hidden just off the chaos of

Dalston Junction. Housed within glass walls, it's not really a jazz bar but a cocktail place where the neighbourhood's hip and friendly inhabitants congregate at the weekends to party on to hip-hop, R&B and reggae.

AULD SHILLELAGH   Pub
☎ 7249 5951; 105 Stoke Newington Church St N16; 🚌 73

The Auld Shillelagh is one of the best Irish pubs in London and full of old-style liver pounders. It's many things to many people: a theatre and a cosy room, centre stage and a sanctuary, a debating chamber and a place for silent contemplation. The staff are sharp, the Guinness is good, and the live entertainment is frequent and varied.

BIRDCAGE   Pub, DJ Bar
☎ 7249 5951; 58 Stamford Hill N16; 🚊 Stoke Newington

Once Stoke Newington's roughest and least inviting pub, the Birdcage has been refurbished with distressed sofas and gentle wall colours, inviting Stokey's more 'respectable' young population with a local gastropub-cum-DJ bar. Chairs no longer fly out of the windows at closing time – now the DJ sends out soothing tunes to a trendy and boozy audience most nights of the week, and there's DJ music even during Sunday lunch.

WEST LONDON

While Old St appeals to artists and fashionable youths, West London's Portobello Rd draws a very mixed crowd of rich kids (or 'trustafarians') and a keepin'-it-real crowd. There are illegal drinking dens right next to superexclusive cocktail bars, and if you stream along the side street, you'll discover more fun hangouts. The bars and pubs of the more down-to-earth areas of West London are restful, many with excellent river views. Shepherd's Bush is good, and Earl's Court attracts travellers, especially from Australia and South Africa. Maida Vale and St John's Wood have some London classics.

ST JOHN'S WOOD & MAIDA VALE
PRINCE ALFRED Map p175   Pub
☎ 7286 3287; 5a Formosa St W9; ⊖ Warwick Ave

Pubs don't really come much better than this charming place. Originally designed in

Victorian times to separate the classes and sexes, the semicircular bar is divided into five gorgeous booths, each with its own little door. Thankfully, nowadays everyone's allowed to sit where they please, and the pub is always busy with adoring locals. The Formosa Dining Room is an excellent place to eat, and the chef has an unbeatable reputation.

WARRINGTON HOTEL Map p175   Pub
☎ 7266 3134; 93 Warrington Cres W9; ⊖ Warwick Ave or Maida Vale

This former hotel and brothel is now an ornate Art Nouveau pub with heaps of character and an atmosphere that's so laid-back it's virtually horizontal. The huge saloon bar, dominated by a marble-topped hemispherical counter with a carved mahogany base, is a fabulous place to sample a range of real ales. There's outdoor seating and a good Thai restaurant upstairs.

NOTTING HILL & WESTBOURNE GROVE
CASTLE Map p175   Bar
☎ 7221 7103; 225 Portobello Rd W11; 🕒 to midnight daily; ⊖ Ladbroke Gve

The Castle gets lively on Saturday, when the market crowds pour in to rest their feet on the comfortable armchairs and sofas and enjoy the odd décor of industrial meets Moorish charm. There's Leffe and delicious strawberry beer, and the place is mainly populated by a crowd of local characters who keep the place buzzing all day long. There's a full menu and live jazz on Saturday and Sunday evenings.

TWELFTH HOUSE Map p175   Bar, Café
☎ 7727 9629; www.twelfth-house.co.uk; 35 Pembridge Rd W11; ⊖ Notting Hill Gate

This is a lovely Notting Hill coffee house with a kooky astrological edge. The bar is dominated by an amazing astrological clock and the owner, Priscilla, is an astrologer who comes in three times a week (phone to find out when) and works out your chart or reads your 'tarot card of the day' on request (for a £5 charge). If she's not in, the waitress can provide you with a card detailing the characteristics of your star sign.

LONSDALE Map p175 — Cocktail Bar

☎ 7727 4080; www.thelonsdale.co.uk; 48 Lonsdale Rd W11; ◷ to midnight Mon-Sat, to 11.30pm Sun; ⊖ Notting Hill Gate or Westbourne Park

The once superslick Lonsdale, with its bumpy space-age walls suffused in purple light, is looking a bit worn out nowadays and the crowd is not as groomed as it once was. The exceptional cocktails are what people come for, although there are also beers and wines.

EARL OF LONSDALE Map p175 — Pub

☎ 7727 6335; 277-281 Portobello Rd W11; ⊖ Notting Hill Gate or Westbourne Park

We love this place. Especially when we've been schlepping around the market all morning and we need a nice cold drink. Despite the fact that it's bang in the middle of the market, the Earl is peaceful during the day, with a mixture of old biddies and young hipsters who seem to cohabit happily as they munch the so-so fish and chips and burgers and sit in the private booths surrounding the bar. There are Samuel Smith ales, and a fantastic back saloon with huge leather armchairs to sink into.

WESTBOURNE Map p175 — Pub

☎ 7221 1332; 101 Westbourne Park Villas W2; ⊖ Royal Oak or Westbourne Park

The Westbourne has a largish outdoor area, although inside it's more cramped and there is a little more attitude. As you'd expect, the crowd is beautiful and trust-fund fuelled.

WINDSOR CASTLE Map p177 — Pub

☎ 7243 9551; 114 Campden Hill Rd W8; ⊖ Notting Hill Gate

A wonderful, relatively out-of-the-way tavern between Notting Hill and Kensington High St, this place has history, warmth and charm on tap. It's worth the search for the roaring winter fireplace, great beer garden, historic interior and friendly regulars.

EARL'S COURT

PRINCE OF TECK Map p177 — Pub

☎ 7373 3107; 161 Earl's Court Rd SW5; ◷ to midnight Fri & Sat; ⊖ Earl's Court

This Earl's Court mainstay is nearly always packed with travellers and is festooned with Australiana (well, stuffed kangaroos, anyway). It's large and comfortable, and has big screens on both floors. This is the default pub for young Aussies and Kiwis in the neighbourhood.

SHEPHERD'S BUSH & HAMMERSMITH

DOVE Map p205 — Pub

☎ 8748 5405; 19 Upper Mall W6; ⊖ Hammersmith or Ravenscourt Park

A 17th-century coffee house-cum-pub, the Dove has many claims to fame, namely that it was in the *Guinness Book of Records* in 1989 for having the smallest bar in England. It was Graham Greene's local and Hemingway drank here too; William Morris lived next door. There are good river views from the charming dark-wood interior, but if the sun is shining fight for a place on the terrace.

OLD SHIP Map p205 — Pub

☎ 8748 2593; 25 Upper Mall W6; ⊖ Hammersmith

This restful towpath pub is the prime stop-off for families and couples on their walks by the Thames. It looks south across the lazy bend of the river towards Putney, and it's popular during the rest of the week, especially on spring and summer days, thanks to its outdoor dining area, terrace and 1st-floor balcony.

GREENWICH & SOUTHEAST LONDON

If you're looking for pubs of the old school, this part of London can oblige – and will throw in some wonderful views to boot. We'd steer clear of the new bars in the area looking to accommodate recent arrivals – stick to traditional boozers and you can't go wrong. Though of course there are always one or two exceptions.

GREENWICH

NORTH POLE Map p180 — Bar

☎ 8853 3020; www.northpolegreenwich.com; 131 Greenwich High Rd SE10; ◷ noon-midnight Mon-Thu, noon-2am Fri & Sat, noon-11pm Sun; DLR, ◉ Greenwich

Still going strong after almost a decade, this quirky Greenwich bar-restaurant-club on three levels attracts a crowd with partying in mind. Upstairs is the Piano restaurant, downstairs a club called South Pole. On the ground level it's more relaxed, with the DJ playing R&B and low sofas for chatting etc.

CUTTY SARK TAVERN Map p180   Pub
☎ 8858 3146; 4-7 Ballast Quay SE10; DLR Cutty Sark, 🚇 Greenwich
Housed in a delightful Georgian building directly on the Thames, the Cutty Sark is one of the few independent pubs left in Greenwich. There are a half-dozen ales on tap and a wonderful sitting-out area along the river just opposite. Count on about a 15-minute walk from the DLR station.

TRAFALGAR TAVERN Map p180   Pub
☎ 8858 2437; 6 Park Row SE10; 🕐 noon-1pm Mon-Thu, noon-2am Fri & Sat, noon-midnight Sun; DLR Cutty Sark, 🚇 Greenwich
This cavernous pub with big windows looking onto the Thames and the O2 (the erstwhile Millennium Dome) is steeped in history and you can see some of it illustrated in the plethora of prints on the walls. Dickens apparently knocked back a few here – the Trafalgar is mentioned in *Our Mutual Friend* – and prime ministers Gladstone and Disraeli used to dine on the pub's celebrated whitebait when the start of the season here was so keenly anticipated that Parliament would suspend sitting for a day.

SOUTH LONDON

Brixton pub regulars turn up their noses at all the pretentious posing that goes on in many of London's neighbourhoods *du jour*, but nearby Battersea and Clapham have a stylish bar or two and there's even a decent riverside pub in Wandsworth. Brixton remains one of the most vibrant and exciting places to go out drinking in South London, though.

BRIXTON
BABALOU Map p200   Bar
☎ 7738 3366; www.babalou.net; St Matthew's Church, Brixton Hill SW2; 🕐 7pm-2am Wed & Thu, to 5am Fri & Sat; 🚇 Brixton
The Bug Bar in the crypt of a Methodist church has metamorphosed into a bar-lounge-club called Babalou with fabulous cocktails and parties. The neogothic architecture stays but there are now North African touches and discreet little 'snugs' (OK, booths) done up in red velvet.

DOGSTAR Map p200   Bar
☎ 7733 7515; 389 Coldharbour Lane SW9; 🕐 4pm-2am Mon-Fri, noon-4am Sat, 11am-2am Sun; 🚇 Brixton
Downstairs this long-running local institution has a cavernous DJ bar, always mobbed with a young South London crowd. The main bar is as casual as you'd expect from a converted pub – comfortable sofas, big wooden tables – so dressing to kill is not imperative.

PLAN B Map p200   Bar
☎ 7733 0926; www.plan-brixton.co.uk; 418 Brixton Rd SW9; 🕐 6pm-late Tue & Wed, 5pm-3am Thu, 5pm-5am Fri, 7pm-5am Sat, 7pm-3am Sun; 🚇 Brixton
It doesn't have to be plan B – it could be an evening's plan A if you're looking for a friendly, low-key DJ bar any night from Thursday to Sunday. Even on Tuesday and Wednesday nights the decent cocktails are enough to woo you to this large room, decorated in an urban minimalist style – all concrete, exposed brick and benches with frosted-glass side panels.

WHITE HORSE Map p200   Bar
☎ 8678 6666; www.whiethorsebrixton.com; 94 Brixton Hill SW2; 🕐 5pm-1am Mon-Thu, 2pm-3am Fri, noon-3am Sat, noon-1am Sun; 🚇 Brixton
This mixed bag of a pub-bar-club might appear to house some people for the entire weekend. It consists of just one big room decorated with modern art against the long bar, but it's lots of fun. We usually play pool here.

BRIXTON BAR & GRILL Map p200   Cocktail Bar
☎ 7737 6777; www.bbag.me.uk; 15 Atlantic Rd SW9; 🕐 4.30pm-midnight Tue & Wed, to 1am Thu, to 2am Fri & Sat, to 11pm Sun; 🚇 Brixton
This stylish bar under the railway arches is a superb choice for 'slinky' (their word) cocktails and listening to live music. It also has an interesting menu of small and large 'plates' as well as tapas.

BATTERSEA & WANDSWORTH
DUSK Map p200   Bar
☎ 7662 2112; www.duskbar.co.uk; 339 Battersea Park Rd SW11; 🕐 6pm-12.30am Mon-Wed, to 1.30am Thu-Sat; 🚇 Battersea Park
This rather remote stretch of Battersea Park Rd seems a truly unusual location for

BEER: THE NATIONAL TIPPLE

In a public house it is possible to order a glass of wine or even a simple cocktail. But the *raison d'être* of a 'pub' is first and foremost to serve beer – be it lager, ale or stout in a glass or a bottle. On draught it is served by the pint (570mL) or half-pint (285mL). The percentage of alcohol (minimum: 2%) can reach a lurching and staggering 8%.

Most beers are made from malted barley and flavoured with hops. The term lager refers to the amber-coloured bottom-fermented beverage found the world over. In general lagers are highly carbonated, of medium hop flavour and drunk cool or cold. In London, the best known home brews are Tennent's and Carling, but there's nothing special about either of them.

Ale is a top-fermented beer whose flavours can run the gamut from subtle to robust; proponents of 'real ale' (ie beer made according to traditional recipes and methods) use the language of oenologists to describe them. Ales can be very slightly gassy or completely still, have a strong hop flavour and are drunk at slightly above room temperature (seldom colder). Real ale is sometimes pulled from barrels. Among the multitude of ales on offer in London pubs, London Pride, Courage Best, Burton Ale, Adnam's, Theakston (in particular Old Peculiar) and Old Speckled Hen are among the best. If in doubt, just ask for 'a bitter' and you'll be served the house ale. Stout, the best known of which is Irish Guinness, is a slightly sweet, dark beer whose distinct flavour comes from malt that is roasted before fermentation.

this glamorous, recently refurbished (and award-winning) bar but it's worth the trek. Staff make killer cocktails and there's a DJ (and sometimes live music) at the weekend.

SHIP Map p198   Pub
☎ 8870 9667; www.theship.co.uk; 41 Jew's Row SW18; ⏰ to midnight daily; ⓧ Wandsworth Town
Though the Ship is right by the Thames, the views aren't really spectacular along this stretch of the river – unless you're partial to retail parks and workaday bridges (which the owners freely admit). Still, the outside area is large, the barbecues in fine weather a real treat and the conservatory bar fun in any weather.

CLAPHAM

SO.UK Map p200   Bar
☎ 7622 4004; www.soukclapham.co.uk; 165 Clapham High St SW4; ⏰ 5pm-2am Mon-Wed, to 3am Thu-Sat, to 1am Sun; ⊖ Clapham Common
So.uk is a stylish Moroccan-themed bar that's light and airy and serves unusual cocktails (Twisted Mojito, anyone?) and shooters. It's extremely popular, with the chance to spot a few well-known faces among the Clapham professionals on the pull.

WHITE HOUSE Map p200   Cocktail Bar
☎ 7498 3388; www.thewhitehouselondon .co.uk; 65 Clapham Park Rd SW4; ⏰ 5.30pm-5am Tue, Wed & Fri, 6.30pm-5am Sat, 5pm-2am Sun; ⊖ Clapham Common
Attracting Clapham's beautiful people with its stylish low-lit interior – all tan sofas, small square tables, expansive bar and pol-

ished wooden floors – this recently renovated chic bar on three floors also boasts a decent restaurant serving dim sum and a fantastic roof terrace in summer.

PRINCE OF WALES Map p200   Pub
☎ 7622 3530; 38 Old Town SW4; ⏰ 5-11pm Mon-Wed, 5pm-midnight Thu, 5pm-1am Fri, 1pm-1am Sat, 1-11pm Sun; ⊖ Clapham Common
While pubs that hang eclectic kitsch from their ceilings in a bid to seem quirky can be tedious, the Prince of Wales is still a very pleasant Clapham hangout, and its décor, unlike that of most pubs of the genre, is genuinely collected rather than supplied en masse. Real ales appear regularly.

TIM BOBBIN Map p200   Pub
☎ 7738 8953; 1-3 Lillieshall Rd SW4; ⏰ to midnight Thu-Sat; ⊖ Clapham Common
This charming boozer a short walk from Clapham Common is worth seeking out if you're trying to avoid Cla'am boys and girls on the piss. It's decorated with copies of its namesake caricaturist's rather rude 18th-century sketches, there are some decent ales on tap and there's a garden and brick conservatory with open kitchen in back.

SOUTHWEST LONDON

Going out in Fulham is mainly about cheesy nights with lots of drinking, dancing on tables and generally behaving badly. Don't head to this part of town if you want a classy evening. Putney, Chiswick and Richmond offer an altogether more sedate and neighbourhood experience – so unlike the anonymous pubs of central London, where the transience of both staff and punters is a major theme. Often centuries old, many of the best pubs in this area overlook the river and make a great place to stop for a drink at any time of day.

FULHAM

FIESTA HAVANA Map p205 — Bar
☎ 7381 5005; www.fiestahavana.com; 490 Fulham Rd SW6; ⏰ 5pm-2am Mon-Sat, from 6pm Sun; ⊖ Fulham Broadway
The epitome of a cheesy night out, you'll have to be up for it (in every sense) to enjoy yourself at Fiesta Havana, a neonlike turquoise-and-mustard 'little bit of Cuba' that you couldn't miss even if you did blink. The music (groovy Latin beats) is great, happens almost nightly and there are free dance classes at the beginning of the evening.

TROUBADOUR Map p177 — Bar, Café
☎ 7370 1434; www.troubadour.co.uk; 265 Old Brompton Rd SW5; ⏰ 9am-midnight; ⊖ Earl's Court or West Brompton
Bob Dylan and John Lennon have performed here and this friendly café-bar remains a wonderfully relaxed boho hangout decades later. There's still live music (folk, blues) most nights and a large, pleasant garden open in summer.

ATLAS Map p177 — Pub
☎ 7385 9129; www.theatlaspub.co.uk; 16 Seagrave Rd SW6; ⏰ from noon Mon-Sat; ⊖ West Brompton
This cosy Victorian-era pub attracts a younger local crowd with its real ales, excellent food and with a lovely side courtyard. The gastropub menu features essentially Mediterranean-inspired dishes.

MITRE Map p205 — Pub
☎ 7386 8877; www.fulhammitre.com; 81 Dawes Rd; ⊖ Fulham Broadway
A beautiful, light-filled and airy pub with a large semicircular bar and walled courtyard at the back, the award-winning Mitre gets very crowded in the evenings and at the weekends, especially at lunch.

WHITE HORSE Map p205 — Pub
☎ 7736 2115; 1-3 Parson's Green; ⏰ to midnight Mon-Sat, to 11pm Sun; ⊖ Parsons Green
Directly on Parsons Green, the White Horse is an inviting pub with a diverse clientele. Come here for the good hearty fare, barbe-

cues during summer, the warm and friendly atmosphere and – most important – the extensive range of beers (draught ales, Belgian Trappist beers). There's pleasant outside seating at the front.

PUTNEY & BARNES

COAT & BADGE Map p205 — Pub
☎ 8788 4900; www.geronimo-inns.co.uk; 8 Lacy Rd SW15; ⏰ to midnight Fri & Sat; ⊖ Putney Bridge, ▥ Putney
The Coat & Badge has gone for a tried and tested lounge-room approach (large sofas, second-hand books on shelves, standard lamps, sport on the telly), which seems to please the local clientele. It has a short but excellent menu and a fantastic large terrace out the front.

JOLLY GARDENERS Map p205 — Pub
☎ 8780 8921; 61-63 Lacy Rd SW15; ⊖ Putney Bridge/ ▥ Putney
Our favourite pub in Putney, the JG has been lovingly and eclectically kitted out; you'd never guess that Victorian oak cabinets went quite so well with Art Deco lamps. The pub plays host to amiable 30-somethings and boasts excellent wine and food menus. Its large terrace fronts a quiet road.

YE WHITE HART Map p64 — Pub
☎ 8876 5177; The Terrace SW13; ⏰ to midnight daily; ▥ Barnes Bridge
This riverside Young's pub in Barnes has a lovely terrace that is somewhat marred by the busy road outside. Housed in a one-time Masonic lodge, the place is huge but if you've been to a Young's pub before, you will know exactly what the interior looks like: swirly carpets, fruit machines and an old man supping a pint at the bar.

CHISWICK

BOLLO Map p64 — Pub
☎ 8994 6037; 13-15 Bollo Lane W4; ⏰ from noon daily; ⊖ Chiswick Park
Out of the way even by Chiswick's standards, this backstreet gastropub has been a huge success, run by local restaurateurs who redeveloped it from a simple local. It's best at the weekend when it is at its busiest, catering to a well-heeled, older crowd looking for a pub and dining room rolled into one.

CITY BARGE Map p64 — Pub
☎ 8994 2148; 27 Strand on the Green W4; ⊖ Gunnersbury
The Barge, perched dramatically close to – but not on – the Thames, has been operating as a pub since the Middle Ages (1484, to be exact). It is split into two bars (go for the downstairs one) and there is a small water-side terrace. Little known fact: a scene from the Beatles' film *Help!* was shot here.

RICHMOND
CRICKETERS Map p208 — Pub
☎ 8940 4372; The Green TW9; ⊗ from noon daily; ⊖ , ⊠ Richmond
Facing Richmond Green from its southern side (where its very own team bats and bowls), the Cricketers is a friendly and comfortable, themed (guess what) pub with a decent selection of ales and a mixed clientele.

DYSART ARMS Map p208 — Pub
☎ 8940 8005; www.thedysartarms.co.uk; 135 Petersham Rd TW10; ⊖ Richmond or ⊠ Richmond then ⊠ 65
This wonderful, almost churchlike place with stone walls and open fire is a great family pub facing Richmond Park's Peter-sham entrance. It succeeds on all fronts: families are made to feel welcome, the food is very good, and the large terrace is packed on a warm afternoon. Best of all there are musical evenings – jazz and classical – twice a week (usually Thursday and Saturday).

WHITE CROSS Map p208 — Pub
8940 6844; Water Lane TW9; ⊗ to midnight Mon-Sat; ⊖ Richmond
The riverside location, good food and fine ales make this pub on the site of a former monastery a winner. There are entrances for low and high tides, but when the river is at its highest, Cholmondeley Walk running along the Thames floods and the pub is out of bounds to those not willing to paddle (wade).

TWICKENHAM
BARMY ARMS Map p64 — Pub
☎ 8892 0863; The Embankment TW1; ⊠ Twickenham
This is a popular Twickenham pub that gets packed to capacity on international match days; it claims to welcome *all* rugby fans. It's just by Eel Pie Island, a once-funky hippy hangout that still attracts the alternative crowd, despite its heyday having long passed. There's also decent pub food and a charming beer garden to recommend it.

LONDON APPRENTICE Map p64 — Pub
☎ 8560 1915; 62 Church St TW7; ⊠ Isleworth
If you're really into sunning along the Thames, you may want to venture north of Twickenham to Isleworth and this riverside pub dating back to the early 17th century. Henry VIII is believed to have dallied with wife-to-be No 5, Catherine Howard, at an earlier tavern on the site.

WHITE SWAN Map p64 — Pub
☎ 8892 2166; Riverside TW1; ⊠ Twickenham
This traditional pub in Twickenham over-looks a quiet stretch of the Thames from what must be one of the most English-looking streets in London. It boasts a fan-tastic riverside location, a great selection of beer and a loyal crowd of locals. Even if you are not in Twickenham, the White Swan is worth a detour.

WIMBLEDON
FOX & GRAPES — Pub
☎ 8946 5599; 9 Camp Rd SW19; ⊗ to midnight Fri & Sat; ⊖ Wimbledon
This very countrylike Wimbledon inn started serving pints in 1787 and is one of the most popular locals. The low-ceilinged bar is intimate and cosy, while the bigger bar (converted from the stables) has high beams and is loaded with atmosphere. Though it's practically inside Wimbledon Common, there's no outside seating.

BLUELIST[1] (blu‚list) *v.*
to recommend a travel experience.
What's your recommendation? www.lonelyplanet.com/bluelist

NIGHTLIFE

top picks

You could live in London for a hundred years and still not be able to 'do' all the nightlife. It's no wonder, then, that Londoners can get a bit overwhelmed with all that's on offer: clubs, live music, comedy, cabaret, and within all of those, hundreds of subsections catering to all kinds of tastes and preferences.

You'll probably come here knowing what you want to experience (it might be big clubs such as Fabric, or sweaty shoebox clubs with the latest DJ talent), but the one thing you should definitely do is branch out from your usual tastes and try something new. There are clubs across town (though East London is the top area for cutting-edge clubs), with House, electro, glam, indie or rave nights. Nu rave is the latest club fad to have gripped the capital, with youngsters mashing old hits and nu rave at warehouse parties, and the last few years have seen people going bananas for burlesque queens, who wave their nipple tassels in decadent clubs.

If clubbing is not your thing, try out the stand-up comedy scene and see if you can heckle without being singled out for the next joke (dangerous if you go for front-row seating).

London's live-music scene is still rocking, jazzing, folking and booming, so you'll be able to hear as many established or up-and-coming artists as your ears desire. Prepare to cough up for the pleasure of seeing big bands live in mega venues, or revel in the pleasure of a tiny club in East London or Camden Town where you can witness a performance by the latest scandal-clad indie superstar.

CLUBBING

When it comes to clubbing, London's where it's at, and anyone who can get here on a Friday or Saturday night, be it from zone 2, the suburbs or a Ryanair flight, wants a night in London's clubs. Whether you're a lover of thumping techno, rock, nu rave, Latin, ska, pop, country, grime, minimal electro, hip-hop, or 1950s lindy hopping, there's something going on every night. Thursdays are loved by those who want to have their fun before the office workers mob the streets on Fridays; Saturdays are the busiest and best if you're a serious clubber, and Sundays often have surprisingly good events across town.

93 FEET EAST Map p150

☎ 7247 3293; www.93feeteast.co.uk; 150 Brick Lane E2; ⌚ 5-11pm Mon-Thu, 5pm-1am Fri, noon-1am Sat, noon-10.30pm Sun; ⊖ Liverpool St or Aldgate East

Brick Lane's hotspot is immediately evident by the long queue outside. This great venue has a courtyard, three big rooms, an outdoor terrace that gets crowded on sunny afternoons, and it's packed with a cool East London crowd. There are some excellent nights, such as the superpopular 'rave, bling and trash scene' from Styleslut and Wasteclub on Friday. Relaxed Sunday afternoon rock and roll sessions have short film screenings, with girls on roller skates selling popcorn. It's worth getting a ticket in advance through the website, to beat the queue.

333 Map p150

☎ 7739 5949; www.333mother.com; 333 Old St EC1; ⌚ 10pm-5am Fri, 10pm-4am Sat & Sun; ⊖ Old St

Hoxton's true old-timer, 333's stripped-down manner doesn't bow down to Shoreditch's silly cool and pretence. The club keeps hosting great nights, remaining a favourite London club for more than a decade. Just off Hoxton Sq, it's simultaneously scruffy and innovative – it's been a key player on the electro-glam and indie rave scene, with the riotous monthly Troubled Minds night that mashes up

SECRET TREASURES

You can find something happening in any part of town, but prepare to do a bit of research if you want to dig out really alternative nights. 'Hidden' warehouse parties are the new big thing, especially around the Dalston and Whitechapel areas. There, the return of rave, or the birth of the nu rave scene, is in full flow, with young things in tight jeans mixing grunge records with rave anthems and glo-sticks in abandoned warehouses. Want a clue for how to find a secret party? One word (or is it two?): MySpace.

TIPS FOR CLUBBERS

- Most Londoners start their nights in a bar before moving on to clubs and gig venues, gravitating from Soho towards Shoreditch and Hoxton – the location of the majority of London's cutting-edge bars and clubs. Notting Hill also has some excellent clubs, while Brixton is top for hip-hop, R&B, reggae and grime venues.
- Clubbing can be an expensive pastime, but not always. Midweek prices are reasonable, and there are plenty of student nights or those oriented to a budget crowd. Search through the listing magazines during your visit. If you want to go to big clubs such as Fabric or Pacha, on a Saturday night (*the* night for clubbing), expect to pay up to £20 for the pleasure.
- Exclusivity is not such an issue as it is in, say, New York or Moscow – very few people are turned away from London clubs, but queuing in the cold while the gorgeous and connected jump out of cabs and straight into the warmth of the club can be a humiliating experience.
- As ever, get there early and try to get advance (or 'queue-jump') tickets for bigger events if you can't bear being left in door-whore hell.
- Dress codes vary widely though you'll find that London's clubs are relaxed and you won't need to worry about being turned away from clubs for your appearance – it's more about whether you care to blend in with a particular venue's crowd. Generally, the 'posh' clubs will want a glam look – which can include trainers and jeans – and the more alternative venues will be full of skinny jeans worn hip-hop style (bums on display), mad haircuts and baggy shirts.
- Always check the weekly listings in *Time Out* or the *Evening Standard* – part of the charm of London's nightlife is that it's always changing and new venues and club nights sprout every week, so keep your eyes peeled!

grime, rave, dancehall, electro, indie, hip hop and hardcore.

AQUARIUM Map p150

☎ 7253 3558; www.clubaquarium.co.uk; 256-264 Old St EC1; ☉ 10pm-3am Sat, 10pm-4am Sun; ⊖ Old St

The Saturday night hitch-up between '70s disco evening Carwash and this converted gym seems like an excellent match: clubbers dressed in sexy, retro gear – compulsory, but disco wigs not allowed – now mingle around the huge pool or in the trendy bar. Absolutely Sunday focuses on old-school House, garage and R&B. Trainers are not welcome here.

BAR MUSIC HALL Map p150

☎ 0871 223 5736; www.hellshoreditch.com; 134-146 Curtain Rd EC2; ☉ 8pm-midnight Sun-Thu, 8pm-2am Fri & Sat; ⊖ Old St

This venue has had many incarnations, from a bar to club to cabaret spot, but Bar Music Hall seems to be making something that'll last. It's large and therefore rarely too crowded, and it hosts some of the hottest nights in Shoreditch. Wednesday's Slipped Disco is all underground acid and clipped electro, and Saturday night's Foreign is all the rage with drag queen DJ Jodie Harsh and fabulous Molaroid, art projections, techno, electro, rave, pop, ragga and anything in between. Oh, and it's free to get in.

BAR RUMBA Map p68

☎ 7287 2715; www.barrumba.co.uk; 36 Shaftesbury Ave W1; ☉ 10.30pm-3am Mon & Wed, 8.30pm-3am Tue, Thu & Fri, 9pm-5am Sat, 8pm-1.30am Sun; ⊖ Piccadilly Circus

A small club just off Piccadilly with a loyal following and fab DJs, specialising in hip-hop, Latin and drum and bass. Head down here on Thursday for Movement, a drum and bass night with a star studded DJ selection, or Get Down on Friday for a hip-hop party. There are also salsa and Latin urban dance parties on Tuesday.

BETHNAL GREEN WORKING MEN'S CLUB Map p156

☎ 7739 2727; www.workersplaytime.net; 42-44 Pollard Row E2; ☉ opening times vary; ⊖ Bethnal Green

This is a true rags-to-riches story: BGWMC was on the brink of bankruptcy, its working men about to become destitute and pintless, until a clever promoter spread the news of trashy burlesque nights taking place in the club's main hall – sticky carpets, shimmery stage set 'n' all – and (literally) overnight, half of London stormed the venue, making it one of the most successful and popular clubs in the capital. Whoopee, London's top burlesque bonanza people host regular nights, in addition to tassel-twirling contests, alternative Eurovision nights and many more sweet selections.

Check the website for what's on when you're around.

CARGO Map p150

☎ 7739 3440; www.cargo-london.com; 83 Rivington St EC2; ⏰ noon-1am Mon-Thu, noon-3am Fri, 6pm-3am Sat, noon-midnight Sun; ✦ Old St or Liverpool St

Cargo rules as one of London's most eclectic and excellent clubs. It has three different spaces – a dance-floor room, bar and lounge, and a little diner – under brick railway arches. The music policy is innovative, with plenty of Latin House, nu-jazz, funk, groove and soul, DJs, global bands, up-and-coming bands, demos and rare grooves. Some of its nights have included the dark burlesque Torture Gardens annual party, African music festival, Balkan brass bands and Cuban ska. There's also an excellent bar (see p285).

CHERRY JAM Map p175

☎ 7727 9950; 58 Porchester Rd W2; ⏰ 6pm-late Mon-Sat, 4-11pm Sun; ✦ Royal Oak

Once a must-experience club, part owned by Ben Watt of the Notting Hill Arts Club and Everything But the Girl (who still sometimes DJs on Saturdays), Cherry Jam has lost the edge it had some years ago. It's still worth a peek, though, especially for the music and good, reasonably priced cocktails (£6.50). Friday and Saturday nights have electro and House DJs and the atmosphere is always good. Might need a shake-up or a face-lift soon, though.

CROSS Map p168

☎ 7837 0828; www.the-cross.co.uk; Goods Way Depot, York Way N1; ⏰ 10.30pm-5am Fri & Sat, 10.30pm-4am Sun; ✦ King's Cross St Pancras

This is one of London's best venues, comprising several low brick rooms built under railway arches hidden in the wasteland off York Way. Sunday is run by Vertigo, a Continental-style clubbing operation, which brings over lots of Italian guest DJs. There's a great outdoor terrace for the summer months, too.

DOGSTAR Map p200

☎ 7733 7515; 389 Coldharbour Lane SW9; ⏰ 9pm-3am Fri & Sat; ✦ Brixton

You'll have to push your way through the huge downstairs bar (see p293) of this converted pub to get to the House-music club upstairs, but that's what all the Brixton clubbers do.

EGG Map p168

☎ 7428 7574; www.egglondon.net; 5-13 Vale Royal N1; ⏰ 10pm-4am Fri, 10pm-5am Sat; ✦ King's Cross St Pancras

Egg has the most superb layout with three exposed concrete rooms (across three floors), a garden and two gorgeous tropical roof terraces (relieving the edgy, exiled smokers). Some say it would fit perfectly in New York's meat-packing district thanks to its design, but it's ours and we're keeping it because it rocks. Located off York Way, the club hosts 'omnisexual' nights, with a mix of electro, minimal and House. At weekends, a free shuttle bus runs from outside American Carwash on York Way to the venue between 10pm and 2am every 30 minutes.

END Map pp72–3

☎ 7419 9199; www.endclub.com; 18 West Central St WC1; ⏰ 10pm-3am Mon & Wed, 10pm-4am Thu, 10pm-5am Fri, 9.30pm-6am Sat; ✦ Holborn

The End is a glam club with minimalist industrial décor and a reputation for some of the city's best all-nighters. It's situated in a West End backstreet, close to its sister-bar AKA (p280). Friday and Saturday are devoted to guest DJs, Wednesday's Swerve with Fabio is mega-popular, and the rest of the week includes Sunday's alternating electro tech House Superfreq and glam Clandestino. What was once one of London's best club nights, Monday's disco/glam/punk/ '80s electronica Trash, which featured live guests such as the Yeah, Yeah, Yeahs; Bloc Party; or Scissor Sisters in between DJ sets, has now mutated into Durrr, with Trash's Erol Alkan joined by Rory Phillips, The Lovely Jonjo and Matt Irvin behind the decks. They promise to keep those bands coming.

FABRIC Map p150

☎ 7336 8898, 7490 0444; www.fabriclondon.com; 77a Charterhouse St EC1; ⏰ 9.30pm-5am Fri & Sun, 10pm-7am Sat; ✦ Farringdon

This most impressive of superclubs is still the first stop on the London club scene for many international clubbers, as the lengthy queues attest (worst from about 9pm to 11pm). A smoky warren of three floors, three bars, many walkways and unisex toilets, it has a kidney-shaking 'sonic boom' dance floor. The crowd is hip and well dressed without overkill, and the music – mainly electro, house, drum and bass and breakbeat – is as superb as you'd expect from London's top-rated club. Superstar DJs often sell out Friday-night's Fabric Live when big names such as Goldie, DJ Diplo, Plump DJ or DJ Hype take over.

FAVELA CHIC Map p150
☎ 7613 5228; www.favelachic.com; 91 Great Eastern St E1; ☯ 6pm-late Tue-Sun; ⊖ Old St
Smaller sister of the original Paris club, this place profits from 'slum chic' just like the producers of Havaiana flip-flops did. It's a one-room bar-club with permanently long queues on Friday and Saturday and innovative music nights. The décor is very much about the vintage, distressed and flea-market pieces, though markedly self-consciously so, but if you can endure the long wait and get past the high'n'mighty door whores, you'll have a good night.

FORUM Map p166
☎ 7284 1001; 9-17 Highgate Rd NW5; ☯ 10pm-3am Sat; ⊖ Kentish Town
The supremely successful School Disco has moved north from its former Hammersmith Palais location and is now held every Saturday night, still attracting fetishists, cheeky schoolboys and girls, and the odd teacher. A uniform is compulsory or you'll be expelled – check the website (www.schooldisco.com) for details.

FRIDGE Map p200
☎ 7326 5100; www.fridgerocks.com; 1 Town Hall Pde SW2; ☯ 9pm-2.30am Mon-Thu & Sun, 10pm-6am Fri & Sat; ⊖ Brixton
Poor old Fridge has hit hard times after years of being one of London's best and longest-running venues, with closing-down threats and suspicions for drug offences (hence the heavy searching at the door). Despite its problems, the Fridge is pulling through. This is an excellent bar and club venue that has a wide variety of club nights and live music, from African gospel and Cuban salsa to reggae and punk.

HERBAL Map p150
☎ 7613 4462; 10-14 Kingsland Rd E2; ☯ 9pm-2am Wed, Thu & Sun, to 3am Fri, 10pm-3am Sat; ⊖ Old St

You'll recognise Herbal by all the plastic grass stapled to its front wall. Inside is a two-level bar-club. The laid-back, grown-up loft upstairs has a small dance floor, seating and a window overlooking Shoreditch. Downstairs is more minimalist and can get very sweaty. There's a mix of drum and bass, House, funk-house and hip hop, interspersed with live shows.

KOKO Map p168
☎ 0870 432 5527; www.koko.uk.com; 1a Camden High St NW1; ☯ 10pm-2.30am Tue, 10pm-6am Fri & Sat; ⊖ Mornington Cres
Once the legendary Camden Palace where Charlie Chaplin, the Goon Show, the Sex Pistols and Madonna all played gigs in the past, Koko is keeping its reputation as one of London's better gig venues – Madonna played a Confessions on a Dance Floor gig here in 2006 and Prince gave a surprise gig in 2007. The theatre has a dance floor and decadent balconies, and attracts an indie crowd with Club NME on Friday. There are live bands almost every night of the week.

MADAME JO JO'S Map p68
☎ 7734 2473; www.madamejojos.com; 8 Brewer St W1; ☯ 10.30pm-3am Wed-Fri, from 9.30pm Thu, cabaret 7-10pm & club 10pm-3am Sat; ⊖ Leicester Sq or Piccadilly Circus
The renowned subterranean cabaret bar and all its sleazy fun kitsch comes into its own with Lost & Found on Saturday, where R&B, ska, northern soul and rockabilly attract all sorts of dressed-up ladies and gents itching to party. Keb Darge's Deep Funk night on Friday is equally legendary, attracting a cool crew of breakers, jazz dancers and people just out to have a good time. Madame Jo Jo's loves burlesque nights too, so look out for weekly performances.

MASS Map p200
☎ 7737 1016; www.mass-club.com; St Matthew's Church SW2; ☯ 10pm-6am Fri & Sat; ⊖ Brixton
Mass is an appropriately named venue, situated in St Matthew's Church, with its vaulted ceilings, pews and frescoes. The most popular night here is Rodigan's Reggae, with legendary broadcaster David Rodigan and Papa Face joined by guest DJs every week. It's the hottest place to be in Brixton on a Wednesday night.

MEAN FIDDLER Map p68

☎ 7434 0403; www.meanfiddler.com; 165 Charing Cross Rd W1; ⊕ 10.30pm-4am Wed-Sat; ⊖ Tottenham Court Rd

The little sister to the Astoria (p307), the Mean Fiddler (still known to many as the LA2) is a great venue over two floors, one overlooking the other through thick glass. Downstairs there's a stage for live acts and dark nooks for all kind of rock-and-roll goings-on; traditional rock is played on Friday at Rock.

MINISTRY OF SOUND Map p198

☎ 7378 6528; www.ministryofsound.com; 103 Gaunt St SE1; ⊕ 10.30pm-6am Fri, midnight-9am Sat; ⊖ Elephant & Castle

This legendary club-cum–enormous global brand suffered from a loss of 'edge' among clubbers in the early naughties, but with the club pumping in top DJs, the Ministry is rejoining the top club ranks. Recommended Friday's Ministry Presents… is all drum and bass, garage, funky House, hip-hop and R&B, across the four areas – Box, Bar, Baby Box and Lounge – with top DJs and live acts performing, while Saturday Sessions gives the *crème de la crème* of House, electro and techno DJs.

NEIGHBOURHOOD Map p175

☎ 7524 7979; www.myspace.com/neighbourhoodclub; 2 Acklam Rd W10; ⊕ 6pm-late Thu-Sun; ⊖ Ladbroke Grove

Cherry Jam (p300) and Notting Hill Arts Club (below) supremo Ben Watt's (other) excellent venue, Neighbourhood has a capacity of 500 and a mixed programme from author readings to House, electro and R&B nights, and there's even an occasional burlesque bonanza; so check what's on when you're around.

NOTTING HILL ARTS CLUB Map p175

☎ 7460 4459; www.nottinghillartsclub.com; 21 Notting Hill Gate W11; ⊕ 6pm-1am Tue-Sat, 6pm-2am Fri & Sat, 4-11pm Sun; ⊖ Notting Hill Gate

London simply wouldn't be what it is without places like NHAC. There's a night for everyone in this small basement club, from knitting societies, to country folk, House nights and Eastern European punk. The famous Thursday night monthly Yo-Yo night, where singer Lily Allen and producer Mark Ronson met, is one of the best nights for R&B, '80s boogies, hip-hop, ragga and diverse live sets; the bimonthly Sunday Radio

Gagarin features 'experiments in Sunday Socialism', Monday has Dive Dive Dive with bass-driven electro and Wednesday is überpopular Death Disco – a rock-and-roll, indie and punk evening from Creation Records founder Alan McGee, which has attracted celeb DJs such as Courtney Love – is still going strong.

PACHA Map pp138–9

☎ 7833 3139; www.pachalondon.com; Terminus Pl SW1; ⊕ 10pm-6am Fri & Sat; ⊖ Victoria, ⊕ Victoria

The London outpost of the seminal 'Aybeefa' club is one of London's most sumptuous venues, eschewing the 'industrial' look that dominates London clubland for the oak-wood panelling, upholstered booths and stunning stained-glass ceiling of a 1920s gentlemen's club. Friday is filled with gorgeous people who come for Funky4Love's glam funky House, and Saturday nights alternate the very popular bimonthly Kinky Malinki, Defected and Gate 21. The crowd is glitzy and showy, so dress up sexy to fit in.

PLASTIC PEOPLE Map p150

☎ 7739 6471; www.plasticpeople.co.uk; 147-149 Curtain Rd EC2; ⊕ 10pm-2am Thu, 10pm-3am Fri & Sat; ⊖ Old St

This is a tiny club with just a dance floor and bar and a booming sound system that experts say easily kicks the butt of bigger clubs. It's also a venue that features the most progressive club nights, without fear of introducing new or controversial music. Head here on Friday for And Did We Mention Our Disco with Rory Phillips (of ex-Trash, current Durrr DJ), Saturday for Balance with a healthy mix of Latin, jazz, hip-hop, House and techno. Ben Watt hosts occasional Sunday nights at Buzzin' Fly, while once a month Thursday's Forward has filthy grime sounds ripping the dance floor. Highly recommended.

SCALA Map p150

☎ 7833 2022; 275 Pentonville Rd N1; ⊕ 10pm-5am Fri & Sat; ⊖ King's Cross

On Friday this multilevel former cinema hosts Popstarz, a laid-back gay/mixed potpourri of indie, alternative and kitsch. On Saturday it's UK garage night Cookies and Cream. The venue is expansive but excellent, with a glass bar at its centre overlooking the stage but insulated from the noise.

BURLESQUE-TASTIC!

After years of low-profile parties with high-glitter gowns, the burlesque scene burst onto the mainstream, showering London with nipple-tassels, top hats, sexy lingerie and some of the most excellent parties in town. Young Londoners caught the dressing-up bug with such a frenzy that many poor grandmas' wardrobes were looted for frocks. Subsequently, the 'alternative' burlesque scene became overwhelmingly mainstream, and club night organisers, passionate about their dedication to dress up and take fun seriously, raised prices in many of the venues in order to ward off those who wouldn't buck up and dress up. So prepare to pay an average of £25 for some (but not all) of the city's best burlesque nights, and make sure you look like a million dollars. Best burlesque venues are Bethnal Green Working Men's Club (p299), where you can find anything from male burlesque contests to girls on roller skates hosting tea parties, and Volupté (Map p110; ☎ 7831 1622; www.volupte-lounge.com; 9 Norwich St EC4; ✛ Chancery Lane), a tiny but elegant cabaret club with some excellent nights, such as Wednesday's Cabaret Salon and once-monthly Black Cotton Club.

Outstanding nights are: Whoopee (www.thewhoopeeclub.com), with nights that are always original (it's our favourite); Lost Vagueness (www.lostvagueness.com) which, apart from great parties, also hosts a summer festival; and Flash Monkey (www.theflashmonkey.biz), whose parties are always a sell-out. The long-running Lady Luck night (www.myspace.com/theladyluckclub) is the city's top for rockabilly and old jazz, while the old-timer, Rakehell's Revels, hosts 'secret' nights (just Google it) at various venues.

TURNMILLS Map p150
☎ 7250 3409; www.turnmills.co.uk; 63 Clerkenwell Rd EC1; ◷ 6pm-midnight Tue, 10.30pm-7.30am Fri, 9pm-5am Sat; ✛ Farringdon

This cavernous long-running institution gets rammed on weekends when minifestival Together kicks up a storm with its DJs, and all-weekend parties take over with big names and tonnes of good fun.

COMEDY

You might not think Londoners are a cheerful lot when they growl at you on the tube, but actually, they love a good chuckle. This is evident in the fact that despite the winter gloom and drizzly rain (or perhaps because of it), you can roll up at any one of the 20-plus major comedy clubs or countless other venues (including pubs) and warm your heart and exercise your lungs with laughter.

Most comedy acts gravitate around the Edinburgh Festival season, so spring and early summer see new acts being tried out on audiences, which means that this is the best time for comedy; August is the cruellest month for comedy in London, because everyone's shifted up north for the festival itself, and winter has the comedians doing the stuff that went down well at the festival. Check Edinburgh Festival's if.commedie awards for the new bright stars.

Some of the world's most famous comedians hail from, or made their names in, London. To whet your appetite a quick roll call from recent decades might include Peter Sellers, Peter Cook, Spike Milligan, Dudley Moore, Tommy Cooper, Dawn French, Jennifer Saunders, Ruby Wax, Lenny Henry, Ben Elton, Alexei Sayle, Harry Enfield, Victoria Wood, Julian Clary, Rowan Atkinson, Reeves & Mortimer, Eddie Izzard, Jo Brand, Sacha Baron Cohen (aka Ali G and Borat), Ricky Gervais, Matt Lucas and David Walliams.

Recent years have unearthed Russell Brand, one of the UK's most loved and prolific comedians, and rising stars such as young but sharp Josie Long, Paul Sinha, Tiernan Douieb and Russell Howard. It's hard to name all the excellent comedians on this jolly circuit, but do look out for the fantastic London-based American comedian Rich Hall; Geordie sonic-waffler Ross Noble; musician, poet and Luton-towner John Hegley; controversial and politically minded Mark Thomas; and dead-pan and dirty Jimmy Carr. Alan Carr, Omid Djalili, Gina Yashere, Lee Hurst, Simon Amstell, Jenny Eclair, Arthur Smith, Richard Herring, Bill Bailey, Daniel Kitson and Simon Munnery are all brilliant.

Many of London's established comedians get together to goof around at inventive comedian Robin Ince's legendary Book Club night (www.myspace.com/bookclublive) at Lowdown at the Albany (☎ 7387 5706; 240 Great Portland St W1; ✛ Regent's Park); Fat Tuesdays is another popular night, held every other Tuesday at the Salmon & Compass (p290) in Islington, specialising in the surprise element of having a famous comedian turn up unannounced to try out new material; Union Chapel (p310) hosts a monthly Live at the Chapel (http://liveatthechapel.co.uk) with big names and live music at this wonderful venue.

AMUSED MOOSE SOHO Map p68

☎ 7287 3727; www.amusedmoose.com; Moonlighting, 17 Greek St W1; ⊖ Tottenham Court Rd
One of the city's best clubs, Soho's Amused Moose is popular with audiences and comedians alike, perhaps helped along by the fact that heckling is 'unacceptable' and all of the acts are 'first date friendly' in that they're unlikely to humiliate the front row. At Camden's Enterprise pub (see the boxed text, p317) there's also Amused Moose Camden, with a similar crowd and policy. Check out its Absolute & Almost Beginners comedy course if you think you can cut it too.

CHUCKLE CLUB Map pp72–3

☎ 7476 1672; www.chuckleclub.com; Three Tuns Bar, London School of Economics, Houghton St; admission from £10; ⊙ Sat; ⊖ Holborn or Temple
The comedian's favourite, this club has a great atmosphere thanks to comedy stalwart, resident host and all-round lovely bloke Eugene Cheese, who begins every night with the Chuckle Club warm-up song.

COMEDY CAFÉ Map p150

☎ 7739 5706; www.comedycafe.co.uk; 66–68 Rivington St EC2; admission free Wed, up to £14 Sat; ⊙ Wed-Sat; ⊖ Old St or Liverpool St
A major venue, the Comedy Café is purpose-built for, well, comedy, hosting some good comedians. The meal-and-show deal will cost you around £20, though during summer months it offers a £5 ticket for the Friday show (no dinner). It can be a little too try-hard and wacky, but it's worth seeing the Wednesday-night try-out spots for some wincing entertainment.

COMEDY CAMP Map p68

☎ 7483 2960; www.comedycamp.co.uk; 3-4 Archer St W1; admission £8-10; ⊙ 8.30pm Tue; ⊖ Piccadilly Circus
This gay (but very straight-friendly) comedy club, hosted by Simon Happily, has become one of Soho's favourites. It's held in the basement area of one of Soho's more enjoyable gay bars, Barcode (p334). Comedy Camp features both up-and-coming queer comedy acts as well as more established gay and lesbian comics.

COMEDY STORE Map p68

☎ 7344 4444; www.thecomedystore.co.uk; Haymarket House, 1a Oxendon St SW1; admission from £13; ⊙ Tue-Sun; ⊖ Piccadilly Circus

This was one of the first (and is still one of the best) comedy clubs in London. It was established down the road in Soho in 1979, the year Margaret Thatcher came to power, which we're sure was no coincidence. Although it's a bit like conveyor-belt comedy, it gets some of the biggest names. Wednesday and Sunday night's Comedy Store Players is the most famous improv outfit in town with the wonderful Paul Merton and Josie Lawrence, and Thursday's, Friday's and Saturday's brilliant The Best in Stand Up features (you guessed it) the best on London's comedy circuit.

DOWNSTAIRS AT THE KING'S HEAD

☎ 8340 1028; www.downstairsatthekingshead .com; 2 Crouch End Hill N8; adult/concession £7/4; ⊙ Sat & Sun; ⊖ Finsbury Park then ☐ W7
A club that hails from the 1980s, with success stories of starting Eddie Izzard and Mark Lamarr's careers in its busy, smoky and intimate room. It hosts newbies and biggies in equal proportions.

HA BLOODY HA

☎ 8566 4067; www.headlinerscomedy.com; Ealing Studios, Ealing Green, St Mary's Rd W5; admission £10; ⊙ Fri & Sat; ⊖ Ealing Broadway
This club is worth going to just to see the old Ealing Studios, where so many of London's best comedies, Ealing Comedies, were filmed. But the stand up is great here too with big names hosting Friday and Saturday night shows.

HEADLINERS

☎ 8566 4067; www.headlinerscomedy.com; George IV, 185 Chiswick High Rd W4; admission £5-10; ⊙ Fri & Sat; ⊖ Turnham Green
The first purpose-built venue in West London, and younger sibling to Ha Bloody Ha (above), Headliners is comfortable and has a traditional shape in that the compere introduces the act and scarpers, try-outs open the night, and the best is saved until last.

JONGLEURS Map p168

☎ 0870 787 0707; www.jongleurs.com; Dingwalls, 11 East Yard, Camden Lock NW1; admission from £16; ⊙ Fri & Sat; ⊖ Camden Town
This is something like a Starbucks-size international chain, that serves comedy instead of coffee. There's eating, drinking and laughing (probably all at the same,

choke-risk time). Friday and Saturday nights normally feature one big-name comedian and a couple of guys on unicycles (or thereabouts) and the shows are so popular, you usually have to book in advance. There are other venues in Battersea (Map p200) and Bow (Map p156).

LEE HURST'S BACKYARD COMEDY CLUB Map p156

☎ 7739 3122; www.backyardcomedyclub .moonfruit.com; 231-237 Cambridge Heath Rd E2; admission £10-15, concession £2-5; ✆ Fri & Sat; ⊖ Bethnal Green

Reputed to be the place the comedians most love to play, you can expect excellent shows and a chuckling, chortling, guffawing and shrieking atmosphere. It's established and maintained by Lee Hurst, himself a successful comedian and dedicated promoter of the venue's name.

UP THE CREEK Map p180

☎ 8858 4581; www.up-the-creek.com; 302 Creek Rd SE10; admission £10-14; ✆ Fri & Sat; ⓡ Greenwich, DLR Cutty Sark

Bizarrely enough, the hecklers can be funnier than the acts at this great club. Up the Creek was established and is still living in the spirit of the sorely missed (and indeed legendary) Malcolm Hardee, who died in 2005. Hardee, who was the patron sinner of British comedy, famously stole Freddie

Mercury's 40th birthday cake and donated it to his local old folks home. Mischief, rowdiness and excellent comedy are the norm.

JAZZ CLUBS

London's jazz scene was always hot and smoky (though with the smoking ban, it's just hot now). Great jazz names play regularly on the circuit, and particularly good times of the year for jazz are: November, when the 10-day London Jazz Festival (www.serious.org.uk) takes place in venues across central London; July, with a week of Jazz on the Streets (www.jazzonthestreets.co.uk) mainly gravitating around Soho, while Ealing Jazz Festival (www.ealing.gov.uk) goes in Walpole Park over five evenings; and September's the month for Riverfront Jazz Festival (www.riverfrontjazz .co.uk) in Greenwich with gigs over the whole month.

100 CLUB Map p68

☎ 7636 0933; www.the100club.co.uk; 100 Oxford St W1; ⊖ Tottenham Court Rd or Oxford Circus

This legendary London venue has always concentrated on jazz, but it's spreading its wings also to swing and rock nowadays. It once showcased Chris Barber, BB King and the Stones and was at the centre of the punk revolution as well as the '90s indie scene. There are lunchtime jazz sessions from 11.30am to 2.30pm once a month (£5).

JAZZ JAMS Gabriel Gatehouse

London probably has the most vibrant jazz scene anywhere in the world outside the US, and if you want to hear it at its rawest and most spontaneous, head for one of the capital's many jam sessions, where up-and-coming young players cut their teeth and vie with the more established musicians. Obviously the quality of the playing varies from session to session, but while you may have to sit through a few dud numbers, you will almost certainly stumble across an unexpected gem or two and get a taste of where the new generation is heading. In addition, it's usually free.

Jams are where musicians go to show their peers what they can do, and the atmosphere, while friendly, can get quite competitive. If you're a rhythm-section player and want to sit in, you can usually turn up empty handed. If you're a horn player travelling without your instrument, your best bet is to bring your own mouthpiece, scan the crowd for a friendly face, and ask nicely.

Sunday is the most popular day for jams, but you can find somewhere to play any night of the week – if you know where to look; check the weekly Time Out listings. On Thursday nights, head to Charlie Wright's International Bar (Map p150; ☎ 7490 8345; 45 Pitfield St N1; ⊖ Old St) in Shoreditch – catch the gig which goes on until around 11pm, after which you can join in. Rising stars of the jazz scene go to saxophonist Tim Whitehead's jam at the 606 Club (p306) – usually on the third Thursday of each month but call the venue for dates – worth a visit even if you don't feel like sitting in. Finally, if you've got the energy, try Uncle Sam's Bar (Map p168; ☎ 7275 0105; 438 Kingsland Rd E8; ⊖ Liverpool St, then 🚌 243) on a Sunday night. London's jazz-playing hardcore head here, after they've finished their own gigs, to unwind with a few drinks and try out new ideas. Things don't get going until midnight and the playing carries on until at least 3am, sometimes later. Happy jamming!

606 CLUB Map p205

☎ 7352 5953; 90 Lots Rd SW10; ⊖ Fulham Broadway or Earl's Court

A lovely, but slightly out-of-the-way basement jazz club and restaurant that gives centre stage to contemporary British-based jazz musicians nightly. The club frequently opens until 2am, although you have to dine at weekends to gain admission (booking is advised). There is no admission charge, but you'll be charged a music fee at the end of the evening on top of your food/drink bill (£8 during the week and £12 on weekends).

BULL'S HEAD Off Map p205

☎ 8876 5241; www.thebullshead.com; 373 Lonsdale Rd SW13; ⑧ Barnes Bridge

This traditional pub dates from Tudor times and has hosted modern jazz concerts in its Jazz Room since 1959. It continues to offer some of the best British jazz nightly and at Sunday lunchtime.

JAZZ CAFÉ Map p168

☎ 7916 6060; www.meanfidler.com; 5 Parkway NW1; ⊖ Camden Town

Though its name would have you think that jazz is this club's main staple, its real speciality is the crossover of jazz into the mainstream. It's a trendy industrial-style restaurant with jazz gigs around once a week, while the rest of the month is filled with Afro, funk, hip-hop, R&B and soul

---

FOLK'N'ROLL

Folk music has become the new rock and roll over the past few years, swamping London with tonnes of new nights hosting anything from acid folk to old-school folk, alternative and psycho folk, and surprisingly, antifolk. If you're a fan of folk, you'll be licking your lips, with nights such as In the Pines (www.inthepines .org) and Tapestry (www.tapestryclub.co.uk) where unheard or forgotten '70s records are salvaged from oblivion; for real folk go to Cecil Sharp House (Map p166; ☎ 7485 2206; www.efdss.org; 2 Regent's Park Rd NW1; ⊖ Camden Town), the headquarters of the English Folk Dance & Song Society, and *the* venue for English folk music (an acquired taste, it must be said), with ceilidhs, barn dances and all sorts of rural-style fun. The antifolk crowd gather at the Blang nights at the legendary 12 Bar Club (Map pp72–3; ☎ 7240 2120; www.12barclub.com; 22-23 Denmark Pl WC2; ⊖ Tottenham Court Rd).

---

styles with big-name acts and a faithful bohemian Camden crowd.

PIZZA EXPRESS JAZZ CLUB Map p68

☎ 7439 8722; www.pizzaexpress.co.uk/jazz.htm; 10 Dean St W1; ⊖ Tottenham Court Rd

Believe it or not, this is one of the most consistently popular and excellent jazz venues in London. It's a bit of a strange arrangement, having a small basement venue beneath the main chain restaurant, but it seems to work well. Patrons listen attentively to modern jazz, and lots of big names perform here.

RONNIE SCOTT'S Map p68

☎ 7439 0747; www.ronniescotts.co.uk; 47 Frith St W1; ⊖ Leicester Sq

Ronnie Scott originally opened his jazz club on Gerrard St in 1959 under a Chinese gambling den. The club moved to its current location six years later and became widely known as Britain's best jazz club. It was the only place the British public could listen to modern jazz – luminaries such as Miles Davis, Charlie Parker, Thelonious Monk, plus Ella Fitzgerald, Count Basie and Sarah Vaughan. Even rock bands such as The Who played here. Over the years the club has survived a roller coaster of uncertainty over its existence, overcame the death of its saxophonist owner in 1996 and continues to build upon its formidable reputation by hosting a range of big names and new talent. The atmosphere is excellent, but talking during music is a big no-no. Door staff can be terribly rude and the service slow, but that's how it's always been. Gigs usually last until 2am daily.

VORTEX JAZZ CLUB Map p168

☎ 7254 4097; www.vortexjazz.co.uk; 11 Gillet St N16; ⊟ 73

This was Stoke Newington's (and London's) favourite jazz place before relocating to the Dalston Culture House in 2005. Many feared the Vortex would never reopen, but all are celebrating its return to the live jazz scene. While the venue still feels a little new, the programme is as good as ever, with musicians from the UK, US and Europe.

ROCK & POP

Everybody who likes pop knows Blur, Oasis, Suede, Pulp, Garbage, Elastica and Radiohead, and remembers the golden age of London's live music – the 1990s and Britpop – when the

LOCAL VOICES: CARLOS HERRERA *Interviewed by Steve Fallon*

Carlos Herrera (carlosherrera100@yahoo.co.uk) is a trained musician from the Canary Islands who entertains Underground commuters with his acoustic guitar music. He lives in Camden Town.

A trained musician? Why do you busk? Busking is a beautiful thing. You can play as loud as you want and can see people's immediate reactions. It's ideal because music is all about sharing. It gives a chance to play in free time and not in a band or some other structured situation.

Money for old rope? I can make £35 to £50 on weekdays at a good station. It's an eight-hour job for me. I busk for four and practise for four. I've been at it for four years, since London Underground introduced the licensing system.

Are things getting better down here? It doesn't always sound that way. There's been a big improvement in the quality of the musicians since they started the auditioning process and most of the buskers here now are real musicians. Before that anyone could come and play. It didn't make much difference how good you were as long as you could get onto a pitch.

Competitive, huh? Well, now there's a one-year wait for approval. And no criminal record. We're allowed to book two pitches a day, each for two hours. It's like this: there are 36 pitches in zone 1 and only one phone line so some people use three phones to call at once.

Is everyone going for the same spots? I go for Bank. Other great ones are Tottenham Court Rd, Leicester Sq, Euston and Angel. But the best is Piccadilly Circus, especially from 4pm to 8pm. Four escalators all coming down to the pitch and they're full of tourists.

Do Londoners dig deeply into their pockets? The English are very generous. So are the Indians and the Americans, but they want to chat a lot. Asians take a lot of pictures but don't give. Spaniards? Forget it! They think I'm begging.

You seem to do a lot of mornings. Why's that? It's the best time of day for my type of music, finger-picking acoustic in the style of Leo Kottke, Michael Hedges and Tommy Emmanuel. On the other hand singing is an evening thing. Singers can make up to £100 on a Friday night if they sing familiar songs.

To drunks, no doubt. Any problems with hecklers? I've had very few bad experiences. Occasionally someone shouts out 'Get a job!' I'm used to it. Buskers are the lowest of the low so you've got to be careful, be polite.

Perils of the job? You can easily lose your mind in music. It's easy to become obsessive, practise too much, smoke too much dope. I need to relax at the end of the day. I'm an indoor kind of guy so I hang out in some of the cafés in Whitechapel.

British capital produced more cutting-edge bands than you could keep up with and play on your stereo. The 21st century, however, found the scene all washed up and London not so hip any more, and the lull lasted until the sun shone on the capital's music scene once again and London's bands were jamming the iPods of pop lovers worldwide. Suddenly there was Coldplay, the (now no more) Libertines, Babyshambles, Bloc Party and Razorlight; female singers such as Amy Winehouse and Lily Allen have been hogging the limelight recently. Madonna and Franz Ferdinand still live here, and the fact that rock and pop royalty have chosen to make London their home must mean that London is still the place to be for live music.

All major artists continue to consider London an essential place to tour, so prepare to find the biggies (from Bob Dylan to Björk) to the up-and-coming. The new band scene is particularly blossoming, and with MySpace it's easier than ever to keep up with your favourite unsigned band and alternative venue.

Together, these artists and bands keep London's wide range of rock and pop venues – from the aircraft hangar–sized Earl's Court Exhibition Centre (p308), Wembley Arena (p310) and the O2 (p309) to the tiny Borderline (p308) or Barfly (p308) – humming and full.

ASTORIA Map p68

☎ 7434 9592; www.meanfiddler.com; 157 Charing Cross Rd WC2; ⊖ Tottenham Court Rd

An extremely popular though not particularly salubrious venue, the Astoria's future may be cut short by plans to knock down the building as part of a programme to rejuvenate the area of Charing Cross Rd, to the general displeasure of Astoria's many fans. Still, until the final decision is reached, the venue is busy most nights of the week with indie, pop and rock acts before becoming a club later on in the evening. The adjacent Mean Fiddler (p302), at No 165 – a far more intimate venue that doesn't get used as much – is facing the same bleak future.

BARFLY@THE MONARCH Map p166

☎ 7691 4244, 7691 4245; www.barflyclub.com; Monarch, 49 Chalk Farm Rd NW1; ⊖ Chalk Farm or Camden Town

Barfly, Charles Bukowski, lounge lizards – you get the picture. This typically grungy, indie-rock Camden venue is full of small-time artists looking for their big break. The focus is on rock from the US and UK, with alternative-music radio station Xfm hosting regular nights. There's a new sister venue, the Fly (36-38 New Oxford St WC1), with a similar set up.

BORDERLINE Map p68

☎ 7734 2095; www.borderline.co.uk; Orange Yard W1; ⊖ Tottenham Court Rd

Through the Tex-Mex entrance off Orange Yard and down into the basement, you'll find a packed, 275-capacity venue that really punches above its weight. Read the writing on the walls (literally, there's a gig list): Crowded House, REM, Blur, Counting Crows, PJ Harvey, Lenny Kravitz, Debbie Harry, plus many anonymous indie outfits, have all played here. The crowd's equally diverse but full of music journos and talent-spotting record-company A&Rs.

BULL & GATE Map p166

☎ 7485 5358; www.bullandgate.co.uk; 389 Kentish Town Rd NW5; ⊖ Kentish Town

The best place to see unsigned-but-promising talent, the legendary Bull & Gate's old-school, smoky music venue still pulls in the punters eager to see guitar bands that might just turn out to be the next big thing.

CARGO Map p150

☎ 7739 3440; www.cargo-london.com; 83 Rivington St EC2; ⊖ Old St

Multitalented Cargo spices up its club nights (see p300) with performances from up-and-coming bands or visiting cult bands from overseas.

CARLING ACADEMY BRIXTON Map p200

☎ 7771 2000; www.brixton-academy.co.uk; 211 Stockwell Rd SW9; ⊖ Brixton

It's hard to have a bad night at the Brixton Academy, even if you leave with your soles sticky with beer, as this cavernous former theatre (holding 5000) always thrums with bonhomie. There's a properly sloping floor

for good views, as well as plenty of bars. You can catch international acts of the ilk of Madonna (once), but more likely artists are Amy Winehouse, Basement Jaxx or DJ Shadow.

CARLING ACADEMY ISLINGTON Map p168

☎ 7288 4400; www.islington-academy.co.uk; N1 Centre, 16 Parkfield St N1; ⊖ Angel

Many complain about Islington Academy's lack of atmosphere – it is, after all, set in a shopping centre – but all agree that the artists' line-up is pretty top class: Franz Ferdinand, Kings of Leon and even Tom Jones have played here. The acoustics are excellent and the discerning crowd is serious about their music. The adjacent Bar Academy hosts up-and-coming groups and can be a great place to see new talent.

DUBLIN CASTLE Map p168

☎ 7485 1773; 94 Parkway NW1; ⊖ Camden Town

A great place to catch indie bands trying their acts and hoping they'll make it as big as Madness (which launched its career here). It's also great for catching people like Blur and Amy Winehouse for an intimate gig.

EARL'S COURT EXHIBITION CENTRE Map pp177

☎ 7385 1200, 0870 903 9033; Warwick Rd SW5; ⊖ Earl's Court

The kind of large, soulless venue that gave stadium rock its bad name, Earl's Court was where Justin Timberlake was famously photographed pawing Kylie Minogue's bum and where most of the gigs you'll see will be by massively expensive, high-flying stars, whose faces will be a dot in the distance and whose songs will echo in the sky. You'll see artists such as Kaiser Chiefs and U2 here.

FORUM Map p166

☎ 0870 534 4444; www.meanfiddler.com; 9-17 Highgate Rd NW5; ⊖ Kentish Town

You can find your way to the Forum – once the famous Town & Country Club – by the ticket touts that line the way from Kentish Town tube. It's a really popular venue for seeing new big bands, and the medium-sized hall, with stalls and a mezzanine, is spacious enough and perfectly intimate.

GARAGE Map p168

☎ 8963 0940; www.meanfiddler.com; 20-22 Highbury Cnr N5; ✈ Highbury & Islington
This sweaty, indie-strong venue was closed for refurbishment at the time of research and should reopen by the time you read this – though the management was iffy when we inquired – so we don't know what wonders they will have installed to amp-up the space.

LUMINAIRE Map p64

☎ 7372 7123; www.theluminaire.co.uk; 311 High Rd NW6; ✈ Kilburn
The Luminaire has been getting nothing but the best of grades since it opened in 2005. *Time Out* named it Music Venue of the Year in 2006, and *Music Week* gave it its British Venue of the Year award in 2007. It deserves everything it gets – small but not crowded, with a big emphasis on friendly service and silence while music is playing – but what's really impressive is the list of people who've played here: Babyshambles, Bat For Lashes, Colleen, Editors, Dirty Pretty Things, Hanne Hukkelberg and Mark Eitzel of American Music Club are just a few. Check its website for latest listings.

O2 Map p180

☎ 0871 984 0002; www.theo2.co.uk; Peninsula Sq SE10; ✈ North Greenwich
Formerly the doomed Millennium Dome, this pricey fiasco has now reinvented itself as one of the city's major concert venues, hosting all the biggies – the Rolling Stones, Prince, Elton John, Scissor Sisters and many others, inside the 20,000-capacity stadium. Ticket prices start at £23 onwards.

RHYTHM FACTORY Map p156

☎ 7247 9386; www.rhythmfactory.co.uk; 16-18 Whitechapel Rd E1; ☾ to 3am Sun-Thu, to 5am Fri & Sat; ✈ Aldgate East
Perennially hip and popular, the Rhythm Factory is a relaxed and friendly coffee shop with a Thai lunch and dinner menu during the day, but come the evening it opens up the large back room, and tonnes of bands and DJs of all genres keep the up-for-it crowd happy until late.

ROYAL FESTIVAL HALL Map p126

☎ 7960 4242; www.southbankcentre.co.uk; Belvedere Rd SE1; admission £6-60; ✈ Waterloo
The Royal Festival Hall is one of the best places for catching world music artists. Some of its most popular programmes are the so-called 'Meltdowns' – basically a list of favourite music and musicians compiled by the likes of David Bowie and Jarvis Cocker. It reopened in Summer 2007 after two years of renovations. Allies and

---

CHURCH VENUES

Many churches host evening concerts or lunchtime recitals year-round or during the summer months. Sometimes they are free (with a suggested donation requested); at other times there is a charge. A few of the city's redundant churches now serve as concert halls.

St James's Piccadilly (Map p68; ☎ 7734 4511; 197 Piccadilly W1; admission £10-17; ✈ Piccadilly Circus) Concerts at 1.10pm on Monday, Wednesday and Friday; donation requested. Evening concerts at 7.30pm (days vary).

St John's, Smith Square (Map pp96–7; ☎ 7222 1061; Smith Sq SW1; admission £6; ✈ Westminster or St James's Park) Concerts at 1pm on Monday.

St Martin-in-the-Fields (Map pp72–3; ☎ 7839 8362; Trafalgar Sq WC2; lunchtime donation requested £3.50, evening tickets £7-18; ✈ Charing Cross) Concerts at 1.05pm on Monday, Tuesday and Friday. Evening concerts by candlelight from Thursday to Saturday at 7.30pm.

St Paul's Cathedral (Map p110; ☎ 7236 4128; New Change EC4; organ recitals £7; ✈ St Paul's) Organ recitals at 5pm on Sunday. Evensong at 5pm Monday to Saturday and at 3.15pm Sunday, special events permitting.

Southwark Cathedral (Map p126; ☎ 7367 6700; Montague Close SE1; ✈ London Bridge) Organ recitals at 1.10pm on Monday; other concerts at 1.10pm on Tuesday. Evensong at 5.30pm on Tuesday, Thursday and Friday, at 4pm on Saturday and at 3pm on Sunday.

Westminster Abbey (Map pp96–7; ☎ 7222 5152; www.westminster-abbey.org; Dean's Yard SW1; tickets usually £6-18; ✈ Westminster) Free organ recitals at 5.45pm every Sunday. Evensong on weekdays at 5pm (excluding Wednesday) and at 3pm on Saturday and Sunday. Ring or check the website for details of the spring/summer organ festival sometime between May and August.

Morrison architects worked on the £91 million renovations by using the existing 1950s materials – concrete, leather and wood – to excellent effects.

SHEPHERD'S BUSH EMPIRE Map pp177
☎ 7771 2000; www.shepherds-bush-empire.co.uk; Shepherd's Bush Green W12; ⊖ Shepherd's Bush
Excellent musicians perform in this lovely midsized venue, such as Björk, Coco Rosie or Antony and the Johnsons, and there's always something interesting going on. The floor doesn't slope, so if you're not so tall it's a little difficult to see from up the back in the stalls – it's worth paying for the balcony.

UNDERWORLD Map p168
☎ 7482 1932; www.theunderworldcamden.co.uk; 174 Camden High St NW1; ⊖ Camden Town
Hear all ye metal heads out there! The Underworld awaits! Metallica, Black Sabbath, Sepultura and other skull-clad screamers have made their appearance either live or as a DJ's choice in this underground warren beneath the World's End pub. It's got plenty of nooks and crannies for ritual head-banging, but it does also host some 'softer' musicians such as KT Tunstall and Radiohead.

UNION CHAPEL Map p168
☎ 7226 1686; www.unionchapel.org.uk; Compton Tce N1; ⊖ Highbury & Islington
One of London's most atmospheric and individual music venues, the Union Chapel is an old church that still holds services, and concerts – mainly acoustic – in between. It was here that Björk performed one of her most memorable concerts to a candlelit audience. The chapel hosts a monthly comedy night (see p303).

WEMBLEY ARENA Map p64
☎ 0870 060 0870; www.whatsonwembley.com; Empire Way, Wembley; ⊖ Wembley Park
Some years and £30 million later, the Wembley Arena has been vastly improved, though its size will never make you feel 'at one' with the artist. It's the place to come and see big names such as Gwen Stefani, vintage artists such as Lionel Richie, or dance and scream to Girls Aloud. Tickets can be massively overpriced (up to £100 for really big names).

BLUELIST[1] (blu,list) *v.*
to recommend a travel experience.
What's your recommendation? www.lonelyplanet.com/bluelist

THE ARTS

top picks

THE ARTS

There are no two ways about it: London's cultural life is fantastic. Its theatre is the most diverse and rich in the world, from Shakespeare's classics performed in the traditional manner, to innovative productions that involve Indian street dancers and acrobatics. There's a wealth of new writing and acting talent and, after many decades, politically provocative plays are making headlines again. Theatre in London is taken so seriously that many deem performing in the West End to be the only way to earn respect among their peers, so much so that even Hollywood stars abandon their glitzy lives for a season treading London's boards.

But it's not all drama and seriousness. In fact, one of the most popular forms of entertainment in the capital is the musical. The 1980s revival put *Dirty Dancing* into musical form, making it one of the most successful shows around, and sending hundreds of ladies into excitement-overdrive every night (ah, the power of Patrick Swayze); Monty Python's surreal sketches and silly songs were transferred into *Spamalot;* and even *The Lord of the Rings* hasn't escaped the clutches of the musical. And that's without mentioning the many classics that still have actors exercising their vocal cords. Dance is another loved form, with performances ranging from classical ballet to modern dance, many of which are held in wonderful venues such as the Royal Opera House, Laban and Sadler's Wells.

The Royal Opera House (p316) stages classical opera and ballet in the grandiose new building in the heart of Covent Garden, while the English National Opera (p316) delves into adventurous experiments that don't always pay off. Lovers of classical music won't know where to start, from high-profile BBC Proms to fantastic lunchtime concerts at the Wigmore Hall (opposite).

London's a fantastic place for catching up on independent film and cinema seasons that celebrate the independents and the classics, though if you like a blockbuster, fret not, as there are many (overpriced) cinemas offering Hollywood flicks. Huge multiplexes give you endless screens and mega-sound systems, and smaller, independent cinemas offer the delight of a sofa for two, with a glass of wine at your side. The refurbished and expanded British Film Institute (BFI; p314) is a temple to the love of film.

CLASSICAL MUSIC

London's four world-class symphony orchestras, two opera companies, various smaller ensembles, brilliant venues, reasonable prices and high standards of performance make it the world's most desirable place for classical music followers. You can see traditional crowd-pleasers, new music or 'difficult' composers any night of the year.

BARBICAN Map p110

☎ 7638 8891; www.barbican.org.uk; Silk St EC2; admission £6.50-30, student & over 60yr on day of performance £6.50-9; ⊖ Moorgate or Barbican
The Barbican is home to the wonderful London Symphony Orchestra, but scores of leading international musicians also perform here every year. The lesser-known BBC Symphony Orchestra, City of London Symphonia and English Chamber Orchestra are also regulars.

KENWOOD HOUSE Map p166

☎ 0870 154 4040; www.ticketmaster.co.uk; Hampstead Lane NW3; admission £16.50-24.50; ⊖ Archway or Golders Green then 🚌 210

Attending an outdoor concert in the grounds of Hampstead's Kenwood House for Proms on the Heath has been a highlight of any good summer in London. People picnicked on the grass or sat in deck chairs, with strawberries and chilled wine, and listened to classical music and opera (staying for the fireworks) on selected weekend evenings in July and August. The concert season was cancelled in summer 2007, but the English Heritage committee is trying to reinstate the lovely tradition for summer 2008.

ROYAL ALBERT HALL Map pp138-9

☎ 7589 8212; www.royalalberthall.com; Kensington Gore SW7; admission £5-150, Proms admission £4-75; ⊖ South Kensington
This splendid Victorian concert hall hosts many classical-music, rock and other performances, but it is most famous as the venue for the (BBC) Proms – one of the world's biggest classical-music festivals. Booking is possible, but from mid-July to mid-September Proms punters also queue for £4 standing (or 'promenading') tickets that go on sale one hour before curtain up.

Otherwise, the box office and prepaid ticket collection counter are both through door 12 on the south side of the hall.

ROYAL FESTIVAL HALL Map p126

☎ 7960 4242; www.southbankcentre.co.uk; Belvedere Rd SE1; admission £6-60; ⊖ Waterloo

The Royal Festival Hall (RFH) is London's premier concert venue. It reopened in mid-2007 after two years of renovations, revealing an improvement in space, layout, vision and sound. Allies and Morrison architects worked on the £91 million renovations by using the existing 1950s materials – concrete, leather and wood – to excellent effect. You can see music and dance performances at the RFH and more eclectic gigs at the smaller Queen Elizabeth Hall and Purcell Room.

WIGMORE HALL Map p100

☎ 7935 2141; www.wigmore-hall.org.uk; 36 Wigmore St W1; admission £6-35; ⊖ Bond St

This is one of the best concert venues in town, not only because of its fantastic acoustics, beautiful Art Nouveau hall and great variety of concerts and recitals, but also because of the sheer standard of the performances. Built in 1901 as the recital hall for Bechstein Pianos, it has remained one of the top places in the world for chamber music. The Sunday-morning coffee concerts (£10) and the lunchtime concerts at 1pm on Monday (adult/senior £8/6) are both excellent value.

DANCE

London is home to five major dance companies and a host of small, experimental ones. The Royal Ballet, the best classical-ballet company in the land, is based at the Covent Garden Royal Opera House (p316); the Coliseum (Map pp72–3; ☎ 0870 145 0200; www.eno.org; St Martin's Lane WC2; ⊖ Charing Cross) is another venue for ballet at Christmas and in summer.

The annual contemporary dance event in London is Dance Umbrella (see p194). For more information about dance in the capital, visit the London Dance Network's website at www.londondance.com.

BARBICAN Map p110

☎ 7638 8891; www.barbican.org.uk; Silk St EC2; admission £6.50-30, student & over 60yr on day of performance £6.50-9; ⊖ Moorgate or Barbican

The Barbican Centre stages dance performances within its eclectic programme. Its multidisciplinary BITE (Barbican International Theatre Events) festival, which runs year-round, has fun dance shows.

LABAN Map p180

☎ 8691 8600; www.laban.org; Creekside SE8; admission £1-15; ⊖ Deptford Bridge, DLR Greenwich

This is an independent dance training school, which also presents student performances, graduation shows and regular pieces by its resident troupe, Transitions, as well as other assorted dance, music and physical performances. Its stunning £22 million home was designed by Tate Modern's architects, Herzog & de Meuron.

PEACOCK THEATRE Map pp72–3

☎ 7863 8222; www.sadlers-wells.com; Portugal St WC2; admission £10-37; ⊖ Holborn

The Peacock Theatre is a small venue in the West End, part of the Sadler's Wells complex (see p314), hosting dance and music performances.

PLACE Map pp92–3

☎ 7387 0031; www.theplace.org.uk; 17 Duke's Rd WC1; admission £5-15; ⊖ Euston

One of the most exciting modern dance venues, the Place was the birthplace of modern British dance. It concentrates on challenging, contemporary and experimental choreography. Behind the late-Victorian façade you'll find a 300-seat theatre, an arty, creative café atmosphere and six training studios. The Place sponsors an annual dance award, 'Place Prize', which strives to seek out and award new and outstanding dance talent.

ROYAL BALLET Map pp72–3

☎ 7304 4000; www.royalballet.co.uk; Royal Opera House, Bow St WC2; admission £4-80; ⊖ Covent Garden

Although the Royal Ballet's programme has been fluffed up by modern influences, classical ballet is still its bread and butter. This is where to head if you want to see traditional performances such as *Giselle* or *Romeo & Juliet*, performed by stars such as Sylvie Guillem, Irek Mukhamedov and Tamara Rojo. Standing tickets cost £4 to £5. There are same-day tickets, one per customer, from 10am for £8 to £40, and half-price stand-by tickets.

SADLER'S WELLS Map p150

☎ 7863 8000; www.sadlers-wells.com; Rosebery Ave EC1; admission £10-40; ⊖ Angel
The theatre site dates from 1683 and is one of the most eclectic and modern dance venues in town. It stagesRambert's excellent productions, Pina Bausch is a regular on the programme, there are experimental dance shows, hip-hop conventions and an annual flamenco festival. Sylvie Guillem and Akram Khan were made associate artists to the theatre in 2006 and staged the acclaimed *Sacred Monsters*. The Lilian Baylis Theatre here stages smaller productions.

SOUTHBANK CENTRE Map p126

☎ 7960 4242; www.southbankcentre.co.uk; Belvedere Rd SE1; admission £6-60; ⊖ Waterloo
The Royal Festival Hall (p313), Queen Elizabeth Hall and Purcell Room are regular venues for the Dance Umbrella citywide festival, as well as hosting independent dance productions year-round.

FILM

Londoners love their cinemas and they adore their film. That's why the city has so many fabulous independent cinemas, where you can put your feet up (often literally), sip your drink and feel at home (but better). Aside from general releases, there are monthly seasons and premieres, plus directors and actors talking about their films. If you're in town in October or November, attend at least one screening at the Times London Film Festival (www.lff.org.uk), Europe's largest of its kind, with plenty of previews, debates, talks and film-star spotting.

Latest Hollywood blockbusters play at the various Warner Villages, Odeons or UGCs; be prepared to pay up to an astonishing £17 for a first-run film. Many major premieres are held in Leicester Sq, which, although a bit of an eyesore, is where most screenings for the Times London Film Festival are held, as well as major movie premieres (eg the latest Bond or Spiderman flick).

If your tastes are a little more eclectic, try one of the cinemas following. Most art-house or mainstream cinemas offer price discounts on Monday and for most weekday-afternoon screenings.

BARBICAN Map p110

☎ info 7382 7000, bookings 7638 8891; www.barbican.org.uk; Silk St EC2; ⊖ Moorgate or Barbican
The several screens at the Barbican pull the crowds with great programming, regular film seasons, and talks by directors and stars. It's a dream to watch a film here, with brilliant sloping seating that ensures full-screen view wherever you sit and legroom that 1st-class transatlantic flights would be proud of.

BFI SOUTH BANK Map p126

☎ 7928 3232; www.bfi.org.uk; South Bank SE1; ⊖ Waterloo or Embankment
Spring 2007 gave London's cinema lovers a wonderful pressie: the British Film Institute (BFI). The spruced-up and extended former National Film Theatre (NFT) means that now not only do we have both new releases and golden oldies dusted off for retrospectives, directors' exclusive talks and an unrivalled screening programme, we now have the Mediatheque (a room with 14 state-of-the-art viewing booths where visitors can browse for free the hundreds of hours of film and TV from the BFI archive), a gallery space with shows relating to film, a well-stocked film and bookshop, a restaurant and a gorgeous café with free wi-fi access and a stand-up piano.

CINÉ LUMIÈRE Map pp138–9

☎ 7073 1350; 17 Queensberry Pl SW7; ⊖ South Kensington
Ciné Lumière is attached to South Kensington's excellent French Institute, and its large screen-room was launched by Catherine Deneuve in 1998. It screens great international seasons and French films subtitled in English.

CLAPHAM PICTURE HOUSE Map p200

☎ info 7498 2242, bookings 7498 3323; www.picturehouse-cinemas.co.uk; 76 Venn St SW4; ⊖ Clapham Common
The Picture House is much loved by its locals for its four comfy theatres and café-bar. The programme has everything, from first-run blockbusters to art-house cinema. The Picture House is now a chain with branches in Greenwich and Stratford and has taken over Brixton's Ritzy (p316) and Notting Hill's Gate (opposite) cinemas.

CURZON MAYFAIR Map p100

☎ info 7495 0501, bookings 7495 0500; www.curzoncinemas.com; 38 Curzon St W1; ⊖ Hyde Park Corner or Green Park
This is the original Curzon cinema, which although a bit shabbier than its Soho sister

(see below), is a real avant-garde outpost that screens new independent and foreign films, shorts and Sunday screenings.

CURZON SOHO Map p68
☎ info 7439 4805, bookings 7734 2255; www .curzoncinemas.com; 93-107 Shaftesbury Ave W1; ⊖ Leicester Sq or Piccadilly Circus
Curzon Soho is London's best cinema. It has fantastic programming with the best of British, European, world and American indie films; regular Q&As with directors; shorts and minifestivals; a Konditor & Cook café upstairs with tea and cakes to die for, and an ultracomfortable bar that often doubles-up as a place for a drink for many Londoners. A haven in the midst of the chaotic West End.

ELECTRIC CINEMA Map p175
☎ 7908 9696, 7229 8688; www.electriccinema .co.uk; 191 Portobello Rd W1; ⊖ Ladbroke Grove or Notting Hill Gate
If you've got a date who's hard to impress, head here for certain success. This is the UK's oldest cinema, updated with luxurious leather armchairs, footstools, tables for food and drink in the auditorium, and an upmarket brasserie. Seeing a flick at this Edwardian building is, of course, slightly pricier than elsewhere; on full-price nights the seats are £12.50, or £30 for a two-seater sofa. One of the most lavish venues in town.

EVERYMAN HAMPSTEAD Map p166
☎ 0870 066 4777; www.everymancinema.com; 5 Holly Bush Vale NW3; ⊖ Hampstead
Ever dream of having your own private cinema? For the next best thing, go to the Everyman. The two auditoriums have comfy armchairs and sofas where you can sprawl out and watch a film with your cup of tea or glass of wine. The programme has a wide range of films, from current blockbusters to *Singing in the Rain* or *The Godfather*.

GATE Map p175
☎ 7727 4043; 87 Notting Hill Gate W1; ⊖ Notting Hill Gate
The Gate's single screen has one of London's most charming Art Deco cinema interiors – although the bar area is a little squished. It's the programming it prides itself on, however, introducing new arthouse and independent films.

INSTITUTE OF CONTEMPORARY ARTS Map pp96-7
☎ 7930 3647; www.ica.org.uk; Nash House, the Mall SW1; ⊖ Charing Cross or Piccadilly Circus
The Institute of Contemporary Arts (ICA) is a treasure for all lovers of indie cinema – its programme always has material no-one else is showing, such as the latest American independents, odd seasons, all-night screenings and rare documentaries. The two screens are quite small, but comfortable enough.

NOTTING HILL CORONET Map p175
☎ 7727 6705; 103 Notting Hill Gate W8; ⊖ Notting Hill Gate
This *fin-de-siècle* stunner is one of London's most atmospheric places to watch a film. Indeed, a lovesick Hugh Grant munches popcorn here while watching Julia Roberts on the big screen in *Notting Hill*. The wonderful Edwardian interior, including a gorgeous balcony and even boxes, recalls the glory days of cinema, when filling a 400-seat house for every showing was easy.

PRINCE CHARLES Map p68
☎ bookings 0870 811 2559; www.princecharlescin ema.com; Leicester Pl WC2; ⊖ Leicester Sq
You'd be right to think that ticket prices at Leicester Sq cinemas are daylight robbery, so wait until the first-runs have finished and moved to central London's cheapest cinema (tickets generally cost from £1 to £4, with the best deals on Monday Madness night). There are also minifestivals and Q&As with film directors. Famously, the cinema also transformed *The Sound of Music* into a phenomenal – and very camp – sing-a-long hit.

RENOIR Map pp92-3
☎ 7837 8402; Brunswick Centre, Brunswick Sq WC1; ⊖ Russell Sq
This art-house cinema, affiliated with Curzon cinemas, has got a new lease of life thanks to the renovated and shiny Brunswick Centre. Not that the Renoir was ever short of loyal devotees, thanks to its share of international film, from French drama to slow-paced Iranian stories and Taiwanese love tales. There's also a range of art-house DVDs on sale in the lower foyer, plus coffee and cake.

RIO CINEMA Map p168

☎ 7241 9410; www.riocinema.ndirect.co.uk; 107 Kingsland High St E8; ⓡ Dalston Kingsland

The Rio is Dalston's neighbourhood arthouse, classic and new-release cinema, and *the* venue for off-beat festivals, such as the Kurdish Film Festival and the Turkish Film Festival (in autumn and December respectively), the East End Film Festival (April), the Spanish Film Festival and the Gay & Lesbian Film Festival (for which some screenings are held in April and March respectively). Despite its major renovation in the late '90s, you can still see traces of the lovely Art Deco theatre in the auditorium.

RITZY Map p200

☎ 7733 2229; www.picturehouses.co.uk; Brixton Oval, Coldharbour Lane SW2; ⊖ Brixton

Despite fears that making the Ritzy a multiplex would kill its cool style and community feeling (four new screens were added to this 1911 building in the late '90s, making it London's biggest independent cinema), this is still one of London's favourites, screening a good mix of mainstream and indie films. The Ritzy is an off–West End screen during the Times London Film Festival, and alternative gigs are often held inside the large original auditorium. The funky bar-café upstairs is a gathering spot for arty locals.

RIVERSIDE STUDIOS Map p205

☎ 8237 1111; Crisp Rd W6; ⊖ Hammersmith

Once a film and TV studio itself, where classics such as *Dr Who* and *Hancock's Half-Hour* were shot, the cinema at the Riverside now shows classic art-house flicks and those you might have missed a few months back.

SCREEN ON THE GREEN Map p168

☎ 7226 3520; 83 Upper St N1; ⊖ Angel

At a bustling junction of Islington's busy nightlife, this film house has a single auditorium with one large screen, attracting an upmarket crowd with a taste for independent cinema (and good ice cream). Pity about the seats, though – bring a cushion and don't have long legs.

OPERA

It's not just the classics that get staged in London's opera houses. Apart from the traditional Verdi tragedies or Mozart's comedies, you'll also find innovative productions that bring modern-day events to the bellowing music form.

ENGLISH NATIONAL OPERA

Map pp72–3

☎ 7632 8300; www.eno.org; Coliseum, St Martin's Lane WC1; admission £8-85; ⊖ Leicester Sq or Charing Cross

The ENO's new music director, Edward Gardner, is promising better years ahead, and God knows it needs better years. Generally renowned for making opera modern and relevant, the ENO has been suffering a miserable few years of bad reviews, financial difficulties and media flak (not helped by *Gaddafi: The Opera* in 2006). The company's home is the impressive Coliseum building, built in 1904 and wonderfully restored in 2004. Five hundred £10-and-under tickets are available for all weekday performances. All opera at the ENO is sung in English.

OPERA HOLLAND PARK Map p177

☎ 0845 230 9769; www.operahollandpark.com; Holland Park W8; admission £25-40; ⊖ High St Kensington

This is England Jane Austen–style, with picnics on the grass, opera and frightfully posh surroundings. Sit under the 800-seat canopy, which is temporarily erected every summer for a nine-week season in the middle of Holland Park, and enjoy the fabulous setting and good performances. The programme mixes crowd pleasers such as *Tosca* and *Fidelio* with rare works such as *L'Arlesiana* and attracts a wide range of guests.

ROYAL OPERA HOUSE Map pp72–3

☎ 7304 4000; www.royaloperahouse.org; Royal Opera House, Bow St WC2; admission £6-150, midweek matinees £6.50-50; ⊖ Covent Garden

The Royal Opera House has been doing its best to ward off the stuffy, exclusive image it was accused of having some years ago, and is attracting a younger, wealthy audience. Its £210 million redevelopment in 2000 has given the classic a fantastic setting, and coming here for a night is a sumptuous prospect. The renovated Floral Hall is now open to the public during the day, with free lunchtime concerts at 1pm on Monday, exhibitions and daily tours. If you're a student, you can register your details on the ROH website, and join the Travelex discount scheme which offers discounted tickets (£15 Opera, £12 ballet), but only if the performance isn't selling very

SPOKEN WORD

Londoners treat their literati like glitterati. It's not just home-grown UK talent such as Monica Ali, Louis de Bernieres, Patrick Neate, Zadie Smith, Tony Parsons, Will Self or even occasionally JK Rowling you might find here, but international writers such as Bill Bryson, Douglas Coupland and Andrey Kurkov on promotional tours.

The best place to see both established and budding authors is the once-monthly Book Slam (www.bookslam.com) held at Neighbourhood (last Thursday of the month; p302) club, and hosted by Patrick Neate. It's had guests such as Dave Eggers, Jonathan Safran Foer and Nick Hornby, and hosts readings, slam poetry, live music and DJs, and the literary fun can go on until late at night. It's the best literary night in London.

A monthly writers' Express Excess session is held at Enterprise (Map p166; ☎ 7485 2659; www.expressexcess.co.uk; 2 Haverstock Hill NW3; ✚ Chalk Farm). From small beginnings in 1996, the Express Excess evening has since managed to attract top names in British writing. John Cooper Clarke, John Hegley, Will Self and Murray Lachlan Young have all appeared in the cosy room at the top of this typically grungy Camden pub.

The Institute of Contemporary Arts (p315) has excellent talks every month, with well-known writers from all spectrums, from the hip to the seriously academic. The best events are those in the wonderful, high-ceilinged Nash Room upstairs.

Covent Garden's Poetry Café (Map pp72–3; ☎ 7420 9888; 22 Betterton St WC2; ✚ Covent Garden) is a favourite for lovers of (serious) spoken word. It has performances by established poets and a regular poetry and jazz evening every Saturday, writing workshops and open-mic evenings.

Additionally, bookshops, particularly Waterstone's (p218) and Foyle's (p217), often have readings. Some major authors now appear at the South Bank Centre (p314). As they tend to rely on the author's availability, many of these readings are organised on an ad-hoc basis, so if you're interested it's best to keep an eye on the listings in *Time Out* or the *Evening Standard*'s *Metro Life* supplement on Thursday.

well. This, apparently, doesn't happen very often, but it might be worth trying.

THEATRE

Don't even think about leaving London without a night at the theatre. This is the epicentre of theatrical innovation, great new writing, and if that's not enough, London is officially the world's greatest city for drama. See a West End show, spend a night at the National or the Old Vic, or go for a good old-fashioned pub-theatre performance.

Patrick Swayze, Kevin Spacey, Christian Slater and Kathleen Turner have all swapped the easy life of Hollywood for theatrical roles in London's West End, continuing a tradition of earning Equity minimum in return for some artistic credibility started by Nicole Kidman (successful in her bid) and Madonna (not) a few years previously.

For a comprehensive look at what's being staged, pick up the free *Official London Theatre Guide* or visit www.officiallondontheatre.co.uk.

BARBICAN Map p110
☎ 7638 8891; www.barbican.org.uk; Silk St EC2; admission to theatre £7-50, to Pit £15; ✚ Moorgate or Barbican
The Barbican turned 25 in 2007, and it's looking – and feeling – as great as ever.

Barbican International Theatre Events (BITE) continues to find exciting overseas drama companies, alongside local fringe-theatre troupes; among its recent outstanding performances were the National Theatre of Iceland's *Peer Gynt,* and Chekhov's *Three Sisters,* staged in Russian by Cheek By Jowl. Stand-by tickets are available on the day of the performance to students, seniors and the unemployed for about £12.

NATIONAL THEATRE Map p126
☎ 7452 3000; www.nationaltheatre.org.uk; South Bank SE1; admission Olivier & Lyttleton £10-36, Cottesloe £10-28; ✚ Waterloo
England's flagship theatre showcases a mix of classic and contemporary plays performed by excellent casts. Its outstanding artistic director, Nicholas Hytner, is not only using exciting stagings and plays to attract new audiences but has also slashed ticket prices. Look forward to Ralph Fiennes in *Oedipus* in 2008 and a new play by David Hare, commissioned by the NT.

In the revolutionary Travelex season, tickets have been sold at £10 for the peak period over the last few years, and this is set to continue. Otherwise, stand-by tickets (usually £17) are sometimes available two hours before the performance. Students or the unemployed must wait until just 45 minutes before the curtain goes up to

TICKETS, PLEASE!

Competition for tickets to the best theatre, dance, opera, gigs and exclusive club events can be stiff, so make the most of online booking forums. If you can, it's best to buy direct from the venue to save yourself commission charges. Events in London sell out astonishingly quickly, and agencies tend to have tickets after the venue has sold out. Ticketmaster (☎ 0870 534 444; www.ticketmaster.co.uk), Stargreen (☎ 7734 8932; www.stargreen.co.uk), Ticketweb (☎ 7771 2000; www.ticketweb.co.uk) and Keith Prowse Ticketing (☎ 0870 906 3838, www.keithprowse.com) all have 24-hour telephone and online booking.

For theatre productions you may be able to buy a returned ticket on the day of the performance, although for something really popular you might need to start queuing before the returns actually go on sale. On the day of performance only, you can buy discounted tickets, sometimes up to 50% off, for West End productions from the Tkts Booth (Map pp72–3; ☼ 10am-7pm Mon-Sat, noon-3pm Sun; ✆ Leicester Sq) in the clock tower on the south side of Leicester Sq. It's run by the nonprofit Society of London Theatre (SOLT; ☎ 7836 0971) and wholly legitimate, although it levies a £2.50 service charge per ticket and has a limit of four tickets per customer. Payment is by cash or credit/debit card. Note that commercial ticket agencies nearby, particularly those along Cranbourn St, advertise half-price tickets without mentioning the large commission added to the price. Student stand-by tickets are sometimes available on production of identity cards one hour before the performance starts.

For all gigs, be wary of ticket touts outside the venue on the night. If you're happy with the mark-up it's usually fine, but be sure to check with the holder of a genuine ticket before buying, to avoid the possibility of buying a forgery.

purchase stand-by tickets at a concession price of around £9. Registered disabled visitors are eligible for discounts.

ROYAL COURT Map pp138–9

☎ 7565 5000; www.royalcourttheatre.com; Jerwood Theatre, Sloane Sq SW1; admission Tue-Sun 10p-£25, Mon £10; ✆ Sloane Sq
Equally excellent for staging new plays and old classics, the Royal Court is among London's most progressive theatres. Starting with its inaugural piece in 1956, John Osborne's *Look Back In Anger,* it has continued to discover major writing talent across the UK from Sarah Kane to Conor McPherson; without it, London's theatre scene wouldn't be the same. Recent major sell-outs were a star-studded performance of *The Seagull,* and Tom Stoppard's latest play, *Rock'n'Roll.*

All tickets on Monday are £10; students, under 21s, seniors and the unemployed pay £10; and 10p standing tickets for eight people are sold just before the performance in the Jerwood Theatre. Stand-by tickets are sold an hour before the performance, but at full price.

SHAKESPEARE'S GLOBE Map p126

☎ 7401 9919; www.shakespeares-globe.org; admission seated £13-29, standing £5; 21 New Globe Walk SE1; ✆ London Bridge
If you love Shakespeare and the theatre, the Globe will knock you off your feet. This is authentic Shakespearean theatre, and

a near-perfect replica of the building the Bard worked in from 1598 to 1611, that follows Elizabethan staging practices. The building is a wooden O without a roof over the central stage area, and although there are covered wooden bench seats in tiers around the stage, many people like to do as the 17th-century 'groundlings' did, and stand in front of the stage, shouting and heckling. Because the building is quite open to the elements, you may have to wrap up. No umbrellas are allowed, but cheap rain coats are on sale.

The theatre season runs from May to September and includes works by Shakespeare and his contemporaries such as Christopher Marlowe. The theatre's new artistic director, Dominic Dromgoole, has decided to introduce new writing and we can't help but think that old William would have liked it that way.

A warning: two pillars holding up the stage canopy (the 'Heavens') obscure much of the view in section D; you'd almost do better to stand. In winter plays are staged in the new indoor Inigo Jones Theatre, a replica Jacobean playhouse at the Globe.

OFF WEST END & FRINGE

This is where most of the really creative and innovative theatre happens in the capital, thanks to new writing that can be experimental, amazing or even downright ridiculous, held in smaller theatres. Some of the better venues are listed here.

ALMEIDA THEATRE Map p168

☎ 7359 4404; www.almeida.co.uk; Almeida St N1;
⊖ Angel

A plush venue that can be relied on to provide the city with an essential programme of imaginative theatre, the Almeida, under its creative artistic director, Michael Attenborough, attracts directors such as Richard Eyre and Rufus Norris, and stages plays such as *The Mercy Seat* and the acclaimed *Dying For It*. Check out the Conran restaurant opposite.

ARCOLA THEATRE Map p156

☎ 7503 1646; www.arcolatheatre.com; 27 Arcola St E8; ⊖ Liverpool St then 🚌 30

Arcola's East End location makes it a bit of a trek, but many still flock to this innovative theatre whose director Mehmet Ergen has been staging adventurous and eclectic programmes since 2000. A season focusing on Turkish writers and plays about Turkey was met with acclaim in 2007, so check the programme for more cutting-edge, international productions.

BATTERSEA ARTS CENTRE Map p200

☎ 7223 2223; www.bac.org.uk; Lavender Hill SW11; ⊖ Clapham Common, 🚇 Clapham Junction, 🚌 77, 77A or 345

This is a friendly, down-to-earth community theatre where staff chat to you and the actors mingle in the bar with the audience postshow. Playwrights see it as a valuable nurturer and crucible of new plays and talent. Artistic director David Jubb's infamous Scratch programme is an excellent exercise in learning about the writing process: a developing play is shown to increasing audiences until it's finished.

BUSH THEATRE Map p177

☎ 7610 4224; www.bushtheatre.co.uk; Shepherd's Bush Green W12; ⊖ Shepherd's Bush

For what is essentially a pub-theatre, the Bush is exceptionally good and encourages new writing. Its success is down to strong writing from the likes of Tina Brown, Jonathan Harvey, Conor McPherson and Stephen Poliakoff. It also attracts top actors.

DONMAR WAREHOUSE Map pp72–3

☎ 7369 1732; www.donmar-warehouse.com; 41 Earlham St WC2; ⊖ Covent Garden

The small Donmar Warehouse will always be known as the theatre in which Nicole Kidman administered 'theatrical Viagra' nightly by peeling off her clothes in Sam Mendes' production of *The Blue Room*. Although nothing quite as headline-grabbing as Kidman's extravaganza has been staged since, the director Michael Grandage consistently stages interesting and inventive productions.

HAMPSTEAD THEATRE Map p166

☎ 7722 9301; www.hampsteadtheatre.com; 98 Avenue Rd NW3; ⊖ Swiss Cottage

Not only is this Ewan McGregor's favourite London theatre, the Hampstead is famed for putting on new writing and taking on emerging directors. It staged Harold Pinter's new work way back in the 1960s, which shows it knows a good thing when it sees one. The theatre is in a modern building, with two auditoria. One seats 80, the other 325.

LYRIC HAMMERSMITH Map p177

☎ 0870 050 0511; www.lyric.co.uk; King St W6;
⊖ Hammersmith

The Lyric is a great venue that turns classics on their head, staging Greek tragedies through mixed-media, with film projection, dance and music. A modern glass entrance takes you to the historic, plush auditorium (seating 550), and a smaller (180-seat) studio. The studio is aimed at audiences under 20.

MENIER CHOCOLATE FACTORY

Map p126

☎ 7909 7060; www.menierchocolatefactory.com; 51-53 Southwark St SE1; ⊖ London Bridge

Theatre and chocolate, two of life's major passions, have never been as gloriously paired up as they have here – a theatre inside a gorgeous conversion of a 19th-century chocolate factory. To make matters better, the theatre's superb restaurant makes for great combination deals (£20 per person for a two-course dinner and a ticket).

OLD VIC Map p126

☎ 0870 060 6628; www.oldvictheatre.com; Waterloo Rd SE1; ⊖ Waterloo

Never has there been a London theatre with a more world-famous artistic director – Kevin Spacey looks after this glorious theatre's programme, which although not meeting with the best reviews all the time,

WEST END THEATRES

Every summer the West End theatres stage a new crop of plays and musicals, but some performances really do run and run. Examples of immortal musicals are *Mamma Mia*, *Chicago* and *The Phantom of the Opera*, though new shows such as *Spamalot*, *Dirty Dancing* and *Billy Elliot* are looking to become new classics. Addresses and box-office phone numbers of individual theatres are given below. Consult weekly London bible *Time Out* to see what's on.

Adelphi (Map pp72–3; ☎ 7344 0055; The Strand WC2; ✛ Charing Cross)

Albery (Map pp72–3; ☎ 7369 1740; 85 St Martin's Lane WC2; ✛ Leicester Sq)

Aldwych (Map pp72–3; ☎ 0870 400 0805; 49 Aldwych WC2; ✛ Holborn or Covent Garden)

Apollo (Map p68; ☎ 7494 5070; 39 Shaftesbury Ave W1; ✛ Piccadilly Circus)

Cambridge (Map pp72–3; ☎ 7494 5080; Earlham St WC2; ✛ Covent Garden)

Comedy (Map p68; ☎ 7369 1731; Panton St SW1; ✛ Piccadilly Circus)

Criterion (Map p68; ☎ 7413 1437; Piccadilly Circus W1; ✛ Piccadilly Circus)

Dominion (Map p68; ☎ 0870 607 7400; 268-269 Tottenham Court Rd W1; ✛ Tottenham Court Rd)

Duke of York's Theatre (Map pp72–3; ☎ 7836 4615; St Martin's Lane WC2; ✛ Leicester Sq)

Fortune (Map pp72–3; ☎ 7836 2238; Russell St WC2; ✛ Covent Garden)

Garrick (Map pp72–3; ☎ 7494 5085; 2 Charing Cross Rd WC2; ✛ Charing Cross)

Gielgud (Map p68; ☎ 7494 5065; 33 Shaftesbury Ave W1; ✛ Piccadilly Circus)

Her Majesty's Theatre (Map p68; ☎ 7494 5400; Haymarket SW1; ✛ Piccadilly Circus)

London Palladium (Map p68; ☎ 7494 5020; 8 Argyll St W1; ✛ Oxford Circus)

Lyceum (Map pp72–3; ☎ 7420 8100; 21 Wellington St WC2; ✛ Covent Garden)

Lyric (Map p68; ☎ 7494 5045; Shaftesbury Ave W1; ✛ Piccadilly Circus)

New Ambassadors (Map pp72–3; ☎ 7369 1761; West St WC2; ✛ Leicester Sq or Covent Garden)

New London (Map pp72–3; ☎ 7405 0072; Drury Lane WC2; ✛ Holborn or Covent Garden)

Palace (Map p68; ☎ 7434 0909; Shaftesbury Ave W1; ✛ Leicester Sq)

Phoenix (Map p68; ☎ 7369 1733; 110 Charing Cross Rd WC2; ✛ Tottenham Court Rd)

Piccadilly (Map p68; ☎ 7478 8800; Denman St W1; ✛ Piccadilly Circus)

Prince Edward (Map p68; ☎ 7447 5400; 30 Old Compton St W1; ✛ Leicester Sq)

Prince of Wales (Map p68; ☎ 7839 5987; 31 Coventry St W1; ✛ Piccadilly Circus)

Queen's Theatre (Map p68; ☎ 7494 5040; Shaftesbury Ave W1; ✛ Piccadilly Circus)

St Martin's (Map pp72–3; ☎ 7836 1443; West St WC2; ✛ Leicester Sq)

Savoy Theatre (Map pp72–3; ☎ 7836 8888; Savoy Ct, The Strand WC2; ✛ Charing Cross)

Shaftesbury (Map pp72–3; ☎ 7379 5399; 210 Shaftesbury Ave WC2; ✛ Tottenham Court Rd or Holborn)

Strand (Map pp72–3; ☎ 7836 4144; Aldwych WC2; ✛ Covent Garden)

Theatre Royal Drury Lane (Map pp72–3; ☎ 7494 5060; Catherine St WC2; ✛ Covent Garden)

Theatre Royal Haymarket (Map p68; ☎ 0870 901 3356; Haymarket SW1; ✛ Piccadilly Circus)

Whitehall Theatre (Map pp72–3; ☎ 7321 5400; 14 Whitehall SW1; ✛ Charing Cross)

Wyndham's (Map pp72–3; ☎ 7369 1736; Charing Cross Rd WC2; ✛ Leicester Sq)

bowled the public and the critics over with the Howard Davies 2006 production of Eugene O'Neill's *A Moon for the Misbegotten*, with Spacey as Jim Tyrone. The production moved to Broadway and left the Old Vic with a deserving confidence boost.

SOHO THEATRE Map p68

☎ 0870 429 6883; www.sohotheatre.com; 21 Dean St W1; ✛ Tottenham Court Rd

The Soho Theatre Company dedicates itself solely to the noble task of finding new writing talent, having put on hundreds of new plays since it started operating from its smart Dean St premises in 2000. It has innovative programmes to support and develop new writing, and also showcases comedy and gets kids penning drama. This is the place to see where London drama is heading.

TRICYCLE THEATRE Map p64
☎ 7328 1000; www.tricycle.co.uk; 269 Kilburn High Rd NW6; ⊖ Kilburn
If political theatre is your thing, the Tricycle delivers. The Tricycle has made a name for itself in the recent years as the theatre-world's conscience, with plays that draw on world events (conflicts in Iraq, Afghanistan,

and the Middle East) in intelligent and provocative ways. There's a nice cinema and bar on site, too.

YOUNG VIC Map p126
☎ 7928 6363; www.youngvic.org; 66 The Cut SE1; ⊖ Waterloo
One of the capital's funkiest and most re-spected theatre troupes – bold, brave and talented – the Young Vic reopened in early 2007 to great acclaim, grabbing audiences with arresting plays such as *Vernon God Little* (as adapted from DBC Pierre's novel) and the fantastic *The Big Brecht Fest* season. There's a gorgeous bar-restaurant with a little summer balcony upstairs.

SPORTS & ACTIVITIES

top picks

SPORTS & ACTIVITIES

London's a great place for sport lovers, be it those who love to play or just sit back and watch a game, and for a place that's traditionally associated with cold and bad weather, you'll be surprised at the number of outdoor-swimming options. Those of you who like to get sweaty and pump some 'aayron' (Arnie-style) will find gleaming state-of-the-art gyms and community sports centres to work out in, while the lazybones among you have tons of pampering spas to choose from.

Needless to say that lovers of football, rugby, horse racing, tennis or cricket have come to the right place to see great matches and tournaments. Just prepare to queue for those tickets.

HEALTH & FITNESS

London loves to sweat on the dance floor and on the treadmill. And if you too love a good workout, there are so many gyms and swimming pools in the city, you'll always be in the vicinity of a chance to burn those calories. Gyms are either local authority-run places at the bottom end of the market or private enterprises at the top, with the latter often coming in large chains. Like most other things in London, keeping fit in the capital can be expensive and riddled with snobbery – the gym you're a member of says a lot about you.

Opening hours vary hugely even within certain leisure centres, where some facilities open or close before others. As a rule, most gyms are open until at least 9pm. However, it's best to call ahead.

GYMS

CENTRAL YMCA Map p68
☎ 7343 1700; www.centralymca.org.uk; 112 Great Russell St WC1; membership per day/week £15/49; ⊖ Tottenham Court Rd
The gym at London's YMCA is popular and busy. Membership gives you the chance to use the pool. The YMCA compares favourably with many of the more expensive and elitist London gyms, and of course it's very friendly.

FITNESS FIRST
☎ 01202-845000; www.fitnessfirst.co.uk
The largest health club in the UK as well as the whole of Europe, this pan-London organisation has a reputation as a good middle-range gym chain. Handily, you can use any Fitness First club, no matter where you joined up. With branches all over the city, this chain is the very popular with short-term visitors to London.

GYMBOX
☎ 7395 0270; www.gymbox.co.uk
With two big gyms in the West End (one is inside an old cinema), Gymbox is presently the most popular newish gym chain in town. It's got an array of innovative classes and facilities, including an Olympic-size boxing ring and Latino hip-hop workout/ dance classes.

LA FITNESS
☎ 7366 8080; www.lafitness.co.uk
With more than 20 gyms in all areas of London, from Victoria to the City, LA Fitness is another big player on the scene. Its gyms are modern and well equipped, and the membership packages are extremely flexible.

QUEEN MOTHER SPORTS CENTRE
Map pp138–9
☎ 7630 5522; www.courtneys.co.uk; 223 Vauxhall Bridge Rd SW1; membership per month from £22; ⊖ Victoria
This place is another reliable, central London gym, named after the Queen's late mum. It features three pools and comprehensive sporting facilities.

SEYMOUR LEISURE CENTRE Map p100
☎ 7723 8019; www.courtneys.co.uk; Seymour Pl W1; membership per month from £22; pool visit £3; ⊖ Marble Arch or Edgware Rd
The Seymour is a bit of a shabby, but long-standing London leisure centre. Its main advantage is the central location and reasonable prices, which means it's always quite busy.

THIRD SPACE Map p68

☎ 7439 6333; www.thethirdspace.com; 13 Sherwood St W1; membership per month £118; ⊖ Piccadilly Circus

London's most chic gym provides everything necessary for busy Soho media execs to relax in or work up a sweat on, at a hefty price.

VIRGIN ACTIVE

☎ 0845 130 4747; www.virginactive.co.uk

Virgin Active is the biggest chain in the UK, and is the best of the top-end gym chains in terms of quality and services. It has masses of facilities (pools, classes etc) and offers for families and children.

SWIMMING

London has something of a love affair with its lovely 'lidos'. They are what most people simply call swimming pools, though the term historically denotes an open-air establishment. There are some lovely 1930s Art Deco lidos and most neighbourhoods have at least one.

BROCKWELL PARK LIDO Map p200

☎ 7274 3088; www.thelido.co.uk; Dulwich Rd SE24; admission £2-5; ⏱ 6.45am-7pm mid-Jun–Aug, weather dependent rest of year; ⊖ Brixton, ▥ Herne Hill

A beautifully designed 1930s lido, Brockwell is one of London's best, as witnessed by the multitudes that descend in the summer months.

HAMPSTEAD HEATH PONDS Map p166

Hampstead Heath, Gordon House Rd NW5; adult/concession £2/1; ▥ Gospel Oak or Hampstead Heath, ▣ 214, C2 or 24

Set in the midst of the gorgeous Heath, the three ponds offer a slightly chilly dip surrounded by wild shrubbery; the men's pond is a bit of a gay cruising area (but it's also a fantastic, beautiful place for a swim), the secluded women's pond less so. The mixed pond can sometimes get rather crowded and isn't so scenically located.

IRONMONGER BATHS Map p150

☎ 7253 4011; www.aquaterra.org; Ironmonger Row EC1; per swim £3.40; ⊖ Old St

The Ironmonger Baths is a local authority-run gym and pool complex which is popular but not too crowded, and has a great pool and friendly atmosphere. There are wonderful Turkish baths downstairs (£10 per day).

OASIS Map pp72–3

☎ 7831 1804; 32 Endell St WC2; adult/concession £3.50/1.50; ⊖ Tottenham Court Rd or Covent Garden

A brilliant heated open-air pool has to be the best thing to find right in the heart of London. At such bargain prices, it often gets very crowded. There's an indoor pool for fresher London days.

PARLIAMENT HILL LIDO Map p166

☎ 7485 3873; Hampstead Heath, Gordon House Rd NW5; adult/concession 7-9am £2/1, 10-6pm £4/2; ▥ Gospel Oak, ▣ 214 or C2

This classic lido on Hampstead Heath is a wonderful place to come for a bracing morning swim during the summer months. It attracts a friendly but dedicated bunch of locals and boasts a children's paddling pool and sunbathing area.

SAVING THE LOCAL LONDON LIDO

The London-based listings magazine, *Time Out*, started the worthy Save Our Pools campaign in 2006 which set out to do just what it says – save London's local pools from closing or falling into disrepair due to the lack of funds and general care. The campaign found that seven pools had closed in the last 12 years and 16 faced imminent closure or were decaying fast.

The magazine ran the campaign, and got such a massive response from Londoners that it became one of the (local) political hot potatoes. The magazine found that Londoners were only too happy to challenge their local councils on the state of their pools, and had been struggling to get their voices heard on the subject. It was particularly ironic that the coming of the 2012 Olympics meant that the city's money was being poured into building new facilities while local pools were being neglected.

The campaign was quite a success, and 2006 saw 'a renaissance for lidos' – several were re-opened after laying closed for years, and many had their funding secured, while others prevented their local baths' closure altogether. For more details on the campaign, go to *Time Out's* website (www.timeout.com).

PORCHESTER BATHS Map p175

☎ 7792 2919; Porchester Centre, Queensway W2; admission £4.70; ⊖ Bayswater or Royal Oak
The lovely Porchester Baths' pool has had its 1930s Art Deco beauty fully restored and is loved by those wishing to swim in atmospheric surroundings.

SERPENTINE LIDO Map pp138–9

☎ 7298 2100; Hyde Park W2; ⊖ Hyde Park Corner or Knightsbridge
Perhaps the ultimate London pool inside the Serpentine lake, this fabulous lido is usually open in July and August. Admission prices and opening times are always subject to change, so it's essential to call ahead.

TOOTING BEC LIDO Map p64

☎ 8871 7198; Tooting Bec Rd SW17; adult/under 5yr/concession £3.65/free/£2.50; ⊙ May-Sep; ⊖ Tooting Bec
The first-ever public lido in London, Tooting Bec was built in 1906 and remains one of the largest in Europe at 90m by 36m. There are Jacuzzis and saunas.

YOGA & PILATES

TRIYOGA

☎ 7483 3344; www.triyoga.co.uk
One of London's first yoga centres and still its most prestigious, Triyoga has three venues (Primrose Hill, Soho and Covent Garden), first-class teachers and classes of all types of yoga, as well as pilates. Classes cost £11, and courses start at £45.

ACTIVITIES

If you love spending a day being attacked with hot towels, heated pebbles and facials, and pummeled with hands covered in aromatic oils, and, at the end of such harsh treatment swimming in heated pools and lying in wonderfully relaxing spaces for hours on end, London's spas will provide you with many joyous hours.

SPAS

ELEMIS DAY SPA Map p100

☎ 8909 5060; www.elemis.com/dayspa.html; 2-3 Lancashire Ct; ⊖ Bond St
This incredible Mayfair spa is almost ridiculously elaborate and features themed suites: Balinese, Moroccan, the purple room and the emerald room. Upmarket and offering a huge range of services, this is one hell of a place to treat yourself. Book ahead.

K SPA Map p177

☎ 0870 027 4343; www.k-west.co.uk; Richmond Way W12; ⊖ Shepherd's Bush
The K Spa is an important part of the K West hotel (p360), and has a good range of facilities: a Jacuzzi, eucalyptus steam room, sauna and two gyms. Alternatively, you can choose from a range of exotic treatments, facials and massages. It's one of the best complexes in West London.

SANCTUARY Map pp72–3

☎ 0870 770 3350; www.thesanctuary.co.uk; 12 Floral St WC2; ⊖ Covent Garden
A women's-only spa, the Sanctuary lives up to its name. With heated and exercise pools, saunas, Jacuzzis, masses of treatments, quiet rooms for napping, a café and a relaxing and friendly atmosphere, it's a haven to get away to from the chaos of the West End.

SPECTATOR SPORTS

As capital of a sports-mad nation, you can expect London to be brimming over with sporting spectacles throughout the year. The entertainment weekly *Time Out* is the best source of information on fixtures, times, venues and ticket prices.

FOOTBALL

Wembley Stadium (Map p64; www.wembleystadium.com), in northwest London, has been the premier national stadium since it was built in 1923. It's where England traditionally plays its international matches and where the FA Cup final is contested in mid-May. Its greatest moment came when the victorious England captain, Bobby Moore, held the World Cup trophy aloft in 1966. Controversially, the great stadium and its two landmark towers were demolished in 2001, and even more controversially the new 90,000-capacity, state-of-the-art Norman Foster–designed complex, due to open in 2003, hosted its first game four years late: the FA Cup final in 2007. Even though it was abysmally late and cost twice the original budget (at £798 million, it's the most expensive stadium ever built), Wembley is one of the world's most significant football landmarks.

CLUBS IN THE CAPITAL

Football is at the very heart of English culture, and attending a game is one of the highlights of any visit to London. At the time of writing, Arsenal, Chelsea, Fulham, Tottenham Hotspur and West Ham were all in the Premiership. For more on football in London, see opposite.

Arsenal (Map p64; ☎ 7704 4040; www.arsenal.com; Avenell Rd N5; admission £25-45; ⊖ Arsenal)

Charlton Athletic (Map p64; ☎ 8333 4010; www.cafc.co.uk; the Valley, Floyd Rd SE7; admission £15-40; ⊛ Charlton)

Chelsea (Map p177; ☎ 0870 300 1212, 7915 2222, tickets 7915 2951; www.chelseafc.com; Stamford Bridge Stadium, Fulham Rd SW6; admission £11-40; ⊖ Fulham Broadway)

Crystal Palace (☎ 0871 200 0071; www.cpfc.co.uk; Selhurst Park, Whitehorse Lane SE25; admission £20-26; ⊛ Selhurst)

Fulham (Map p205; ☎ 0870 442 1234; www.fulhamfc.com; Craven Cottage, Stevenage Rd SW6; admission £25-40; ⊖ Putney Bridge)

Leyton Orient (Map p64; ☎ 8926 1111; www.leytonorient.com; Matchroom Stadium, Brisbane Rd E10; admission £12-16; ⊖ Leyton)

Millwall (Map p180; ☎ 7232 1222; www.millwallfc.co.uk; the Den, Zampa Rd SE16; admission £16-25; ⊛ South Bermondsey)

Queens Park Rangers (Map p64; ☎ 0870 112 1967; www.qpr.co.uk; Loftus Rd W12; admission £14-20; ⊖ White City)

Tottenham Hotspur (Map p64; ☎ 0870 420 5000; www.spurs.co.uk; White Hart Lane N17; admission £12-55; ⊛ White Hart Lane)

West Ham United (Map p64; ☎ 0870 112 2700; www.westhamunited.co.uk; Boleyn Ground, Green St E13; admission £22-39; ⊖ Upton Park)

Arsenal Emirates Stadium (www.arsenal.com), on the other hand, opened on time in July 2006, and although quite a bit smaller (60,400 capacity), it is still the third largest in London. It's located in Ashburton Grove, Highbury, and was named after the project's biggest sponsor, the airline Emirates. Many were sorry to see the old stadium go, with its old tea ladies and working-class atmosphere, and the stadium's construction was met with objections from the unhappy locals whose houses and businesses were cleared for the stadium. Most have learned to love it, however.

There are a dozen league teams in London, and usually around five or six play in the Premier League, meaning that on any weekend of the season – from August to mid-May – top-quality football is just a tube or train ride away. If you really want to see a match, you might consider dropping a division and going to see one of the first-division teams, for which you can normally just rock up on the day.

CRICKET

If you're hot and bothered from seeing the sights, you could do a lot worse than packing up a picnic and spending a day enjoying the thwack of leather on willow and savouring the atmosphere of this most English of sports. Although the game was invented here, the England team has struggled on the international stage, with the notable exception of winning the Ashes in 2005, only to lose them again in 2006, becoming the shortest ever champion's reign.

The English Cricket Board (☎ 0870 533 8833; www.ecb.co.uk) has full details of match schedules and tickets, which cost between £20 and £50 and can be difficult to get. Test matches are regularly played at the venerable Lord's and Oval grounds. Tickets (between £5 and £10) are a lot easier to come by for county games; county teams compete in four-day, one-day and 20-over matches between April and September.

LORD'S Map p175

☎ tours 7616 8585, switchboard 7616 8500; www.lords.org; St John's Wood Rd NW8; ⊖ St John's Wood
The 'home of cricket,' a trip to Lord's is often as much a pilgrimage as anything else. As well as being home to Middlesex County Cricket Club, the ground hosts test

matches, one-day internationals and domestic finals. For more on Lord's see p174.

BRIT OVAL Map p198

☎ 7582 7764; www.surreycricket.com; Kennington Oval SE11; ⊖ Oval

County side Surrey plays at the Oval, known for its distinctive gasholders. It's also famous as the place where cricket-lover John Major went immediately after losing the election to Blair in 1997. For more on the Brit Oval, see p202.

RUGBY UNION & RUGBY LEAGUE

Between January and March, England competes against Scotland, Wales, Ireland, France and Italy in the Six Nations Championship, and there are always three games at Twickenham Stadium.

Union fans should head to southwest London, where mighty teams including the Harlequins (☎ 8410 6000; www.quins.co.uk; Stoop Memorial Ground, Langhorn Dr, Twickenham TW2; admission £12-25; ⓡ Twickenham) and Wasps (☎ 8993 8298; www.wasps.co.uk; Adams Park, High Wycombe W3; admission £7-18; ⓡ High Wycombe) play from August to May. London Irish (☎ 01932-783034; www.london-irish.com; Bennet Rd, Reading; admission £7-16; ⓡ Reading) and Saracens (☎ 01923-475222; www.saracens.com; Vicarage Rd, Watford; admission £12-35; ⓡ Watford High St) are also in the Premiership. Most matches are played on Saturday and Sunday afternoons.

LONDON BRONCOS Map p64

☎ 8853 8001; www.londonbroncos.co.uk; the Valley, Floyd Rd SE7; ⓡ Charlton

The only place in southern England to see rugby league.

TWICKENHAM RUGBY STADIUM Map p64

☎ 8892 2000; www.rfu.com; Rugby Rd, Twickenham; ⊖ Hounslow East, then 🚌 281, ⓡ Twickenham

The home of English rugby union. For information about guided tours, see p210.

TENNIS

Tennis and Wimbledon, in southeast London, are almost synonymous, and SW19 suddenly becomes the centre of the sporting universe for a fortnight in June/July when the world-famous tennis tournament takes place.

WIMBLEDON

☎ 8944 1066, 8946 2244; www.wimbledon.org; Church Rd SW19; ⊖ Wimbledon, then 🚌 493

The All England Lawn Tennis Championships have been taking place here in late June/early July since 1877. Most tickets for the Centre and Number One courts are distributed by ballot, applications for which must be made the preceding year. Try your luck by sending a stamped self-addressed envelope to the All England Lawn Tennis Club (PO Box 98, Church Rd, Wimbledon SW19 5AE). Limited tickets go on sale on the day of play, though queues are painfully long. The nearer to the finals, the higher the prices. Prices for outside courts are under £10, reduced after 5pm. You might be better off going to the men's warm-up tournament at Queen's Club (Map p205; ☎ 7385 3421; www.queensclub.co.uk; Palliser Rd, Hammersmith W14; admission per day £12; ⊖ Barons Ct), which takes place a couple of weeks before Wimbledon.

ATHLETICS

England – and London in particular – has a rich history in athletics and continues to produce world champions. There are major international meets each summer at the grand old venue of Crystal Palace in southeast London, which has been the site of many magical moments in recent years and where every major international athlete has competed.

CRYSTAL PALACE NATIONAL SPORTS CENTRE

☎ 8778 0131; www.crystalpalace.co.uk; Ledrington Rd SE19; ⓡ Crystal Palace

Athletics and swimming meetings attracting major international and domestic stars take place here regularly throughout the summer.

HORSE RACING

There are several racecourses within striking distance of London for those wanting to have a flutter. The flat racing runs from April to September, while you can see the gee-gees scaling fences from October to April.

ASCOT

☎ 01344-622211; www.ascot.co.uk; Berkshire; admission from £6; ⓡ Ascot

Best known for the fashion circus of Royal Ascot in June.

EPSOM

☎ 01372-470047; www.epsomderby.co.uk; Epsom, Surrey; admission from £5; 🚇 Epsom Downs
With much more racing credibility than Ascot, this famous racetrack's star turn is Derby Day in June, but it has meets all year.

KEMPTON PARK

☎ 01932-782292; www.kemptonpark.co.uk; Staines Rd East, Sunbury-on-Thames, Middlesex; admission from £6; 🚇 Kempton Park
Of its all-year meetings, summer-evening events are best.

ROYAL WINDSOR RACECOURSE

☎ 01753-865234; www.windsor-racecourse.co.uk; Maidenhead Rd, Windsor, Berkshire; admission from £6; 🚇 Windsor
An idyllic spot beside the castle.

SANDOWN PARK

☎ 01372-463072; www.sandown.co.uk; Portsmouth Rd, Esher, Surrey; admission from £12; 🚇 Esher
Generally considered the southeast's finest racecourse.

GAY & LESBIAN LONDON

top picks

London is, let's face it, pretty damn gay. The city of Oscar Wilde, Quentin Crisp and Elton John does not disappoint today, being a queer world capital on par with New York and San Francisco, with vast gay and lesbian communities that fan out throughout the city. There's also a superb film festival, one of the world's largest annual gay pride events, a simmering activist movement and more bars and clubs than most entire countries can claim.

Things have improved immeasurably in the past decade for gay and lesbian rights and recognition thanks almost entirely to the Labour government. Protection from discrimination is now enshrined in law, and civil partnerships now allow gay couples the same rights as straight couples, even with respect to adoption. That's not to say homophobia doesn't exist – outside the bubble of Soho, abuse on the street at public displays of affection is still shockingly common and sadly it's always best to assess the area you're in before walking hand in hand down the street.

The long-established gay village of Soho, once so central to any gay experience of London, has somewhat lost its pre-eminence in a city where redevelopment and high rentals have pushed people out to cheaper neighbourhoods. Soho retains the largest number of gay bars and pubs, and walk down Old Compton St at any time and you'll notice omnipresent gay and lesbian life, but many of the city's better clubs and venues are to be found elsewhere. The alternative two focuses of the city's gay life are in Vauxhall, south of the river, and Shoreditch, north of the City. Vauxhall, once a bleak concrete jungle, is now home to London's muscle boys, who party from Thursday to Tuesday without break. Fashionable Shoreditch is home to London's more alternative gay scene, often very well mixed in with local straight people; here you'll find arty parties, great shopping and the hipper clubs, where the muscle boys fear to tread.

The lesbian scene in London is far less visible than the flamboyant gay one, and lesbian bars are surprisingly few and far between. The most famous of these by far, the Candy Bar, is the place to head for a first-time visitor, although certain areas of the capital are well known to have large, thriving lesbian communities and are worth a visit in their own right – particularly Stoke Newington and Hackney in northeast London. Check out the excellent lesbian London website www.gingerbeer.co.uk for the full lowdown on events, club nights and bars.

SHOPPING

GAY'S THE WORD Map pp92–3   Books
☎ 7278 7654; http://freespace.virgin.net/gays
.theword/; 66 Marchmont St WC1; ⏰ 10am-6.30pm
Mon-Sat, 2-6pm Sun; ⊖ Russell Sq

London's excellent and much-loved gay and lesbian bookshop is on a quiet Bloomsbury street where it gets relatively little walk-by custom. So much so that in 2007 it announced it was to close imminently unless it could raise emergency funds to pay for rising rents and to offset losses created by the internet. At the time of writing its 'sponsor a shelf' campaign had been successful and imminent closure ruled out, but this could change. There's a great range of gay and lesbian books and magazines as well as a real community spirit here – let's hope it survives.

PROWLER Map p68   Department Stores
☎ 7734 4031; www.prowler-stores.co.uk; 5-7
Brewer St W1; ⏰ 11am-10pm Mon-Fri, 10am-
10pm Sat, noon-8pm Sun; ⊖ Piccadilly Circus

Prowler's flagship Soho store is a gay shopping mecca selling books, magazines, clothes and 'lifestyle accessories'. There's also a discreet 'adult' section selling the usual array of DVDs and magazines, but the overall feel of the shop is one of a respectable gay department store.

DRINKING & NIGHTLIFE

The queer drinking scene in London is wonderfully varied: whether you fancy a quiet pint in a traditional boozer that just happens to be gay or want a place to wet your whistle before going out dancing, you'll be spoiled for choice. Following are our favourite bars although there are plenty more; check the gay press for comprehensive listings.

London has some of the most exciting and varied gay clubbing in the world, but it's a moveable feast, as the clubbing scene is about club nights rather than venues. Whether it's drug-addled muscle boys, fetish clubs or skinny punk-rock guys and girls you're after,

BEST GAY CLUB NIGHTS

Monday

- **Popcorn (Heaven, p335)** Still a great and cheap night out, Popcorn is an 'Ibiza-style club night' with a great selection of music on offer in several different rooms and refreshingly priced drinks offers.

Tuesday

- **Salon (Shadow Lounge, p334)** This former lap-dancing club in the heart of Soho now hosts this favourite evening for the capital's fashionistas presided over by the fantastic Minty and Talulah.

Wednesday

- **Nag Nag Nag (Ghetto, p335)** Still the favoured haunt of the alternative cognoscenti in Soho, Nag's disco, nu-wave, synth-core and dirty electro beats make for one of the best midweek parties in town. See www.nagnagnag.info for more.

Thursday

- **Rude Boyz (Fire, p336)** London's notorious gay chav club attracts a young, badly behaved crowd who seem to spend most of the evening in the 'cruise cave' when they're not competing in amateur stripping contests on stage. Great fun.

Friday

- **A:M (Fire, p336)** One of the fiercest and most popular gay nights in Vauxhall, A:M packs in a beautiful crowd of serious clubbers for an incredible 12-hour stretch. The music features some of the best techno and electro DJs on the London scene.
- **Popstarz (Scala, p302)** This grand dame of gay indie has been revitalised in the past few years and often features excellent live bookings. It's popular with a studenty, friendly, mixed crowd. There are four rooms of great music from indie to the 'rubbish room'. See www.popstarz.org for more info.
- **Trailertrash (Map p150; www.clubtrailertrash.com; On the Rocks, 25 Kingsland Rd, Shoreditch E2; 10.30pm-late)** Dirty electro disco brought to you by the Trailertrash crew served up every Friday in Shoreditch's sweatiest venue, but it's well worth braving the heat and grime with music this good and a crowd this friendly.

Saturday

- **Duckie (Vauxhall Tavern, p336)** Get here by 10.30pm to avoid a massive queue because Duckie, hosted by the marvellous Amy Lamé, is the perfect antidote to pretension on the gay scene. Great indie tunes and some of the most unusual cabaret in London await you here.
- **Foreign (Bar Music Hall, p299)** The Bar Music Hall is the place to be in Shoreditch, and this hyperfashionable gay night is most popular of all, hosted by Jodie Harsh and Scottee. This is the place to meet the glamorous Hoxton crowd on their own territory – lots of fun. Oh, and it's free…
- **G-A-Y (Astoria, p307)** Love it or hate it, G-A-Y is a centre of gravity for the gay scene and seemingly where half of Soho is headed on a Saturday night when it's one of the world's largest gay clubs, attracting megastar PAs from the likes of Kylie. Bring your tight T-shirt. See www.g-a-y.co.uk for more information.
- **Rebel Rebel (www.clubrebelrebel.co.uk)** Held in various venues, this indie monthly (first Saturday of each month) is one to make a beeline for. Clubbers of all stripes come together for a fantastic night of indie rock, punk and pop. As well as the monthly parties, it holds specials now and again that have taken in some great venues.
- **XXL (Map p126; www.xxl-london.com; 51/53 Southwark St, London Bridge SE1; 10pm-6am Sat)** The world's biggest club for bears (hairy, stocky gay men) and their admirers is a real event. A very friendly crowd is spread out over a wonderfully quirky space, with two dance floors and a 'recreational maze'.

Sunday

- **DTPM (Fabric, p300)** The name apparently stands for Drugs Taken Per Minute, and that has some resonance when you see the glam crowd that rolls up here – none of them appear to have slept since Thursday. However, the atmosphere is incredible, with superb music in a superb venue.

look no further – London has it all. The few exclusively gay clubs are listed here, while most big nights are held in straight clubs that put on a gay night or two each week. The gay press and the Gay & Lesbian section in weekly listings magazine *Time Out* are the best places to check for up-to-date club listings as things change weekly.

THE WEST END

BARCODE Map p68 Bar
☎ 7734 3342; www.bar-code.co.uk; 3-4 Archer St W1; ⏰ 4pm-1am Mon-Sat, to 11pm Sun; ⊖ Piccadilly Circus

Tucked away down a side street is this fun gay bar, full of a diverse range of people enjoying a pint or two and some evening cruising. There are frequent club nights in the downstairs area, including the very popular gay comedy night Comedy Camp every Tuesday (see opposite).

CANDY BAR Map p68 Bar
☎ 7494 4041; www.thecandybar.co.uk; 4 Carlisle St W1; ⏰ to 2am Fri & Sat, to 11.30pm Sun-Thu; ⊖ Tottenham Court Rd

This is the hottest lesbian bar in town, a great, friendly place, with a long bar on the ground floor and a miniclub in the basement where DJs play most nights. Look out for karaoke every Tuesday, which is a blast. Men are admitted as guests to women (one man allowed per woman).

EDGE Map p68 Bar
☎ 7439 1313; www.edge.uk.com; 11 Soho Sq W1; ⏰ to 1am Mon-Sat; ⊖ Tottenham Court Rd

Overlooking Soho Sq in all its four-storey glory, the Edge is London's largest gay bar and heaves from the early evening until the early hours with preclubbing revellers fuelling up for the night ahead. There's a heavy straight presence though, as it's so close to Oxford St, but it's still a fun place to start the evening.

FRIENDLY SOCIETY Map p68 Bar
☎ 7434 3805; 79 Wardour St W1; ⏰ 6-11pm Mon-Thu, to midnight Fri & Sat, to 10.30pm Sun; ⊖ Piccadilly Circus

Definitely one of Soho's hippest gay bars, and thankfully one of the few fashionable queer drinking establishments that hasn't initiated a dubious door policy or membership scheme to ensure that only the rich

and beautiful arrive. A fun and up-for-it crowd assemble in the early evening, drink beer under S&M Barbie and Ken, and chill out to live DJs all evening.

KU BAR Map pp72–3 Bar
☎ 7437 4303; www.ku-bar.co.uk; 30 Lisle St WC2; ⏰ 5pm-midnight Sun-Thu, to 3am Fri & Sat; ⊖ Leicester Sq

This is the London gay teen hangout of choice and at the weekends it seems as if every under-20-year-old in the southeast converges on the Ku for preclubbing drinks. Its location doesn't hurt either, where Chinatown, Soho and Covent Garden meet, and there's always something going on, from karaoke to cabaret.

SHADOW LOUNGE Map p68 Bar
www.theshadowlounge.co.uk; 5 Brewer St W1; ⏰ 10pm-3am Mon-Wed, 9pm-3am Thu-Sat; ⊖ Piccadilly Circus or Oxford Circus

This home from home for the Soho glitterati is a stylish basement bar with plenty of comfortable coves to hang out in as well as a dance floor complete with pole for dirty dancing. The door policy is a little erratic: at quiet times you're usually fine although there's generally a £5 to £10 entry charge; other times you'll need to be with a member or a Soho 'face' to make it past the gorillas on the door.

TRASH PALACE Map p68 Bar
☎ 7734 0522; www.trashpalace.co.uk; 11 Wardour St W1; ⏰ 5pm-midnight Sun-Thu, to 3am Fri & Sat; ⊖ Piccadilly Circus

This cool two-floor space from the people who revolutionised London's gay scene with indie club Popstarz in the 1990s has great staff and an alternative yet unpretentious feel. The lines outside can be big at the weekends, so get here early – as with most cool places in London, demand way outstrips supply. There's a small dance floor downstairs with a more relaxed lounge upstairs.

YARD Map p68 Bar
☎ 7437 2652; www.yardbar.co.uk; 57 Rupert St W1; ⏰ 1-11pm Mon-Sat, 1-10.30pm Sun; ⊖ Piccadilly Circus

This old Soho favourite attracts a great cross section of the great and the good. It's a pretty attitude-free place, perfect for preclub drinks or just an evening out. There are DJs upstairs most nights in the cool loft area as well as the eponymous courtyard downstairs.

GHETTO Map p68 — Club

☎ 7287 3726; www.ghetto-london.co.uk; 5-6 Falconberg Ct W1; ⏰ 10pm-3am Mon-Thu, 10.30pm-4.30am Fri & Sat; ⊖ Tottenham Court Rd

In a sweaty basement, this leading gay club has nevertheless established itself as the hippest Soho has to offer, with its 1950s American milk bar–style white seats and red walls. The most talked about night is Nag Nag Nag, where both Boy George and Yoko Ono have appeared, followed by Friday's in-yer-face The Cock. There's also Thursday's indie-music Mis-shapes and Saturday's trashy Wig Out.

HEAVEN Map pp72–3 — Club

☎ 7930 2020; www.heaven-london.com; Villiers St WC2; ⏰ 10.30pm-3am Mon & Wed, 10pm-3am Fri, 10pm-5am Sat; ⊖ Embankment or Charing Cross

This long-standing and perennially popular gay club, under the arches beneath Charing Cross station, has always been host to good club nights, but its big draws today are its three long-established nights: Saturday is still the flagship night for gay clubbers who like very commercial House music, while Monday is the cheap and cheerful student-oriented Popcorn, possibly gay London's best-value night out. Wednesday is cheeky midweeker Fruit Machine.

CLERKENWELL, SHOREDITCH & SPITALFIELDS

JOINERS ARMS Map p150 — Bar

☎ 7739 9854; 116 Hackney Rd E2; ⏰ 6pm-2am Fri & Sat; ⊖ Shoreditch or Old St

Determinedly run-down and cheesy, the Joiners is Hoxton's only totally gay pub-club (perhaps reflecting the degree to which such distinctions are blurred around E2). It's a crowded, funky old boozer where hip gay boys hang out at the bar, dance and watch people play pool all night.

LOCAL VOICES: SIMON HAPPILY *Interviewed by Tom Masters*

Simon Happily is the creator and host of popular gay comedy night Comedy Camp (www.comedycamp.co.uk), the 'straight friendly' Tuesday-evening show held downstairs at Barcode in Soho (see p304 and opposite).

Where did the idea for a gay comedy night come from? Before I set Comedy Camp up I'd been shocked at how many comedians still made homophobic jokes or remarks and consequently how few lesbians and gay men tended to be in the audience. So I set up Comedy Camp as a safe environment for people to watch comedy, knowing they wouldn't have to listen to homophobic jokes. It doesn't only feature gay acts – that would get boring, not to mention repetitive – but those comedians who work well with a majority lesbian and gay crowd.

So it's been a success? Within a few months we had queues stretching round the block and major comedians, including some household names, asking to perform here. I never expected Comedy Camp to get so big, let alone be so critically acclaimed by the comedy critics in the mainstream press.

So anyone can go? Comedy Camp was always designed to be a 'straight-friendly' lesbian, gay and bisexual environment. A straight comedy-club promoter told me I should call it 'gay-friendly' – I said 'no, it's "straight-friendly"' and so the tag was born. It may be semantics, but it neatly sums up what the club is about. Everyone's welcome at Comedy Camp, regardless of sexuality, so long as they know and respect what they're coming to and recognise it's primarily 'our' safe space.

Best and worst of gay London? The best thing is definitely the variety due to London's large lesbian and gay population so there are lots of different places to go for different things. The worst is the large number of nightclubs that all seem to play the same heavy clubby dance music. I know they're very popular, but aren't my thing! I'm also not a fan of some of the snobbier, overpriced, more attitude-filled venues – there are plenty that are down-to-earth and better value so I'm more likely to head there.

Did London improve for gay people under Blair? Yes, London – like the UK – became much more tolerant under Tony Blair, not just in terms of equality legislation, but also there's been a clear social change – arguably his greatest legacy. Having said that, there are sadly still bigots and thugs in the capital. Personally, I like to keep my element of risk small, so while public displays of affection are unlikely to cause problems in Soho, I wouldn't risk it in some parts of the city late at night!

What would be your first act as Mayor of London? Ban cars for all but the disabled, put segregated cycling lanes on every road and bring back more trams rather than those hideous lane-hogging bendy-buses!

THE EAST END & DOCKLANDS

WHITE SWAN Map p156 · Club

☎ 7780 9870; www.bjswhiteswan.com; 556 Commercial Rd E14; ◷ 9pm-2am Tue-Thu, 9pm-4am Fri & Sat, 6pm-midnight Sun; DLR Limehouse

The White Swan is a fun East End kind of place, with a large dance floor as well as a more relaxed pub area. Its legendary amateur strip night has sadly disappeared, but there's still plenty of flesh on stage on Saturday. Club classics and cheesy pop predominate.

NORTH LONDON

BLACK CAP Map p168 · Bar

☎ 7428 2721; www.theblackcap.com; 171 Camden High St NW1; ◷ noon-2am Mon-Thu, to 3am Fri & Sat, to 1am Sun; ⊖ Camden Town

This friendly, sprawling place is Camden's premier gay venue, and attracts people from all over North London for its great terrace and downstairs club, where you'll find plenty of hilarious camp cabaret as well as decent dance music.

SOUTH LONDON

TWO BREWERS Map p200 · Bar

☎ 7498 4971; www.the2brewers.com; 114 Clapham High St SW4; ◷ noon-2am Sun-Thu, noon-4am Fri & Sat; ⊖ Clapham Common or Clapham North

Clapham may have a rather suburban feel in general, and the High Street in particular, but the Two Brewers endures as one of the best London gay bars outside the gay villages. Here there's a friendly, laid-back, local crowd who come for a quiet drink during the week and some madcap cabaret and dancing at weekends.

AREA Map p198 · Club

www.areaclub.info; 67-68 Albert Embankment SE1; ◷ 10.30pm-6am Sat; ⊖ Vauxhall

Home from home for circuit party boys but still very welcoming to all, Area describes itself as 'polysexual' and hosts some of the most inventive nights in town, including monthly Queer Kandi and Saturday nighter Evolve.

CRASH Map p198 · Club

☎ 7820 1500; 66 Goding St SE11; ◷ 10.30pm-6am Sat; ⊖ Vauxhall

If Vauxhall in general is one of London's newest gay hangouts, then Crash, in particular, is its Muscle Mary heaven. There are two dance floors churning out hard beats, four bars and even a few go-go dancers.

FIRE Map p198 · Club

☎ 0790 503 5682; www.fireclub.co.uk; South Lambeth Rd SW8; ◷ 10pm-4am; ⊖ Vauxhall

Sealing Vauxhall's reputation as the new gay nightlife centre of London, Fire is another expansive, smart space under the railway arches, hosting the infamous Rude Boyz for gay chavs and their admirers on Thursday night, as well as centrepiece of the Vauxhall weekend A:M on Friday, and Sunday all-nighter Orange.

HOIST Map p198 · Club

☎ 7735 9972; www.thehoist.co.uk; Arches 47B & 47C, South Lambeth Rd SW8; ◷ 10pm-3am Thu, Fri & Sun, 10pm-4am Sat; ⊖ Vauxhall

One of Europe's most famous fetish clubs, the Hoist is a one-stop shop for guys into leather and uniforms. The dress code is very strict – everyone has to wear boots, and either rubber, leather or uniform. Check out the array of fetish nights on the website.

VAUXHALL TAVERN Map p198 · Club

☎ 7820 1222; www.theroyalvauxhalltavern.co.uk; 372 Kennington Lane SE11; ◷ 7pm-midnight Mon-Thu, 7pm-4am Fri, 7pm-2am Sat, 2pm-midnight Sun; ⊖ Vauxhall

Rough around the edges to say the least, the Vauxhall Tavern is the perfect antidote to the gleaming new wave of gay venues now crowding Vauxhall's gay village. Friday's Le Phreeque and Saturday's Duckie, a wonderful indie performance night hosted by Amy Lamé, are rightly considered to be two of the best club nights in London.

FURTHER RESOURCES

London has a lively free gay press documenting the ever-changing scene. You can pick up these free publications at any gay venue and it's always a good idea to do so as the listings are the most up-to-date and wide-ranging available. Many different magazines come and go each year, but the mainstays are the tabloids *Boyz* (www.boyz.co.uk) and *QX* (http://qxmagazine.com), and the more serious and newsy *Pink Paper* (www.pink paper.com). They all include weekly listings for clubs, bars and other events, and often contain flyers that grant discounted entry to various venues. Magazines on sale at most London newsagents include *Gay Times* (www .gay times.co.uk), *Diva* (www.divamag.co.uk), *Attitude* (www.attitude.co.uk) and *AXM* (www .axm-mag.com), although some less enlightened proprietors still place them on the top shelf next to the pornography.

Check out the following listings and personal websites:

Gay London (www.gaylondon.com)

Gaydar (www.gaydar.co.uk or gaydargirls.co.uk)

Ginger Beer (www.gingerbeer.co.uk)

Time Out (www.timeout.com/london/gay)

Visit London (www.visitlondon.com/people/gay)

London Lesbian & Gay Switchboard (☎ 78377324; www.llgs.org.uk) Provides free advice, counselling and other help to anyone who needs a sympathetic ear.

lonely planet Hotels & Hostels

Want more Sleeping recommendations than we could ever pack into this little ol' book? Craving more detail – including extended reviews and photographs? Want to read reviews by other travellers and be able to post your own? Just make your way over to **lonelyplanet.com/hotels** and check out our thorough list of independent reviews, then reserve your room simply and securely.

SLEEPING

top picks

- Soho Hotel (p342)
- Rookery (p354)
- Clink (p356)
- Sumner Hotel (p348)
- Petersham (p361)
- Blakes (p352)
- Hazlitt's (p343)
- Stylotel (p357)
- Luna Simone Hotel (p354)
- Hoxton Hotel (p355)

SLEEPING

Accommodation in London is among the most expensive on earth, and you can expect to spend a very large portion of your travel budget on it. At the same time, despite the increase in hotel rooms in recent years, demand still outstrips supply in this, the capital of Europe, so it's essential that you book at least part of your accommodation before arriving, especially during holiday periods and in summer.

Another problem here can be quality – even in the midrange. A large part of readers' letters sent to Lonely Planet about London and the *London* guide concern accommodation, many of them complaining about the quality and cleanliness of hostels, guesthouses and some hotels, 'fauna' in the rooms and the rudeness of staff. Hopefully the descriptions in this chapter will help you make your choice.

Of course it's not all bad news. A miniboom in hotel building continues apace, with thousands of new rooms expected before the Summer Olympics open here in 2012. A slew of upmarket boutique hotels have brought a real sense of style to the city's digs, and scores of midrange hotels and B&Bs are following suit. At the other end of the spectrum, some places have begun to fill a gap in the market by providing boringly functional but affordable rooms. A very exciting trend recently has been the convergence of these two extremes in a new crop of 'budget boutique' hotels, providing a bit of chic at reasonable prices.

ACCOMMODATION STYLES

London has a superb range of deluxe hotels (from £350 per double) and you'll be spoiled for choice with old classics that combine the best in traditional atmosphere and modern comforts. There's also good choice in the top-end category (anything from £180 to £350), which offers superior comforts without the prestige. Also in this bracket you'll find many of the boutique and style hotels that have sprung up in recent years. Below £180 there's a bit of a slide in quality and choice. Although there's an increasing number of terrific places to rest your head without haemorrhaging your budget, it's still not enough. And if you were expecting to spend less than £100 a night on a double room during the week, your lodgings probably won't provide the most cherished memories of your trip. (On the other hand, you will find some good weekend deals for that price.) In London, cheap means less than £80 per en suite double. After B&Bs,

the cheapest forms of accommodation are hostels, both the official Youth Hostel Association (YHA) ones, of which there are six in London, and the (usually) hipper, more party-orientated independent ones.

Hotel rooms in the UK are subject to a 17.5% 'value added tax' or VAT. Many hotels quote rates inclusive of VAT, while others do not so it always pays to ask if you are uncertain. Remember, though, that many hotels – especially deluxe ones – regularly offer promotional deals on the internet that are much lower than their published rates. Unless otherwise indicated, accommodation prices quoted in this book include breakfast.

The accommodation options in this guide are listed by area and then by price, from most to least expensive. See the boxed text, left, for more information on accommodation prices. The choice is enormous, but the lower end is consistently oversubscribed, so if your budget is limited it's a good idea to book well ahead. Good resources for finding and booking hotels include www.hotelsoflondon.co.uk, www.londonlodging.co.uk and www.frontdesk.co.uk.

LONGER-TERM RENTALS
Apartments & Serviced Apartments

If you are visiting London for a few weeks or several months, staying in a short-term or serviced apartment is the best way to get a sense of

---

PRICE GUIDE

The symbols below indicate the cost per night of a standard double room in high season.

£££	over £180
££	£80-180
£	under £80

living in the city. Many agencies in *Loot* (p396) or other small ads have pretty insalubrious properties; ask to see rooms first. Some better agencies and their daily rates are listed here.

UPTOWN RESERVATIONS

☎ 7937 2001; www.uptownres.co.uk; s/d/tr/q £72/95/125/135, apt per week from £550
Offers short-let apartments or B&B accommodation in stylish private homes, mostly the West End, the City, Kensington, Chelsea or Knightsbridge.

196 BISHOPSGATE

☎ 7621 8788; www.196bishopsgate.com; studio/1-bedroom apt from £180/217, cheaper after 6 nights
Luxury serviced apartments in the City opposite Liverpool St Station. Has longer-stay properties.

ASTON'S APARTMENTS

☎ 7590 6000; www.astons-apartments.com; s/d/tr/f from £68/94/131/173, weekly rates 5% less
The company has three Victorian town houses in South Kensington, divided into serviced apartments of varying sizes.

CITADINES APART'HOTEL

☎ 0800 376 3898; www.citadines.com; 2-person studio £105-149, cheaper after 6 nights
Ever popular French chain has four apartment blocks throughout the city, including a Holborn/Covent Garden branch (Map pp72–3; ☎ 7395 8800; 94-99 High Holborn WC1; ⊖ Holborn).

ACCOMMODATION LONDON

☎ 8459 6203; www.accommodationlondon.net; s/d from £52/70, cheaper after 6 nights
Has some 300 studio flats and rooms in shared houses for foreign-passport holders (only) in the Willesden Green area. Clean and well-equipped properties, decent prices, popular with younger travellers.

Rooms & Flats

Most newcomers to the city still find leasing expensive (note that almost all rented accommodation in London is furnished). At the very bottom end, bedsits (£300 to £600 per month) are single furnished rooms, usually with a shared bathroom and kitchen, and they are always pretty grim. A step up is a self-contained studio (from £600), which normally has a separate bathroom and kitchen. You'll rarely get a two-bedroom flat for less than £1000. Shared accommodation offers the best value, at £300 and upwards for a room in a flat or a house with several bedrooms. Most landlords demand a security deposit (normally one month's rent) plus a month's rent in advance.

To get abreast of current prices, consult the classifieds in publications such as *Loot, TNT, Time Out* and the *Evening Standard*'s Wednesday supplement *Homes & Property* (www.homesandproperty.co.uk). Some of the better websites are Gumtree (www.gumtree.com), Move Flat (www.moveflat.com) and the primarily gay Outlet (www.outlet4homes.com).

RESERVATIONS & BOOKINGS

The London tourist organisation Visit London (☎ 0870 156 6366; www.visitlondon.com) offers a free booking service with a wide range of accommodation options and always has special deals. There's also the British Hotel Reservation Centre (☎ 7340 1616; www.bhronline.com), which has kiosks at Gatwick Airport, Heathrow Airport and Paddington, Waterloo and Victoria stations. There's also a kiosk on the mezzanine level of the Britain Visitor Centre (p400). Another excellent source for hotel bookings and discounts is LondonTown (☎ 7437 4370; www.londontown.com).

You can book a hostel through the YHA central reservations system (☎ 0870 770 6113; www.yha.org.uk). If you want to stay in a B&B or private home, reservations can be made through the following agencies.

LONDON HOMESTEAD SERVICES

☎ 7286 5115; www.lhslondon.com; per person £16-40
Small family-run business offering B&B rooms in private homes across London.

AT HOME IN LONDON

☎ 8748 1943; www.athomeinlondon.co.uk; s/d/tr/f from £45/69/85/101
This is worth looking at if you're considering staying two to four weeks, as some properties have weekly rates and minimum stays. However, daily rentals are more common.

LONDON BED & BREAKFAST AGENCY

☎ 7586 2768; www.londonbb.com; per person £25-55
Offering spare rooms in London homes. You share with the homeowner, many of whom tend to be of a mature age. Properties are concentrated for the most part in central and North London.

AIRPORT HOTELS

London's airports have plenty of hotels to cater for passengers with early morning flights. If you're one of these, the best thing to do is to go to the relevant airport website (see p381) and click on 'Airport Information' where you'll find a link to hotels at or near the airport and the best rates currently available. Otherwise, these easy options are worth considering:

Hilton Gatwick (☎ 01293-518080; www.hilton.co.uk/gatwick; South Terminal, London Gatwick Airport; r from £159) Conveniently connected to the airport building via a short walkway, this hotel is notable for its very large rooms and triple glazing.

Radisson SAS Stansted (☎ 01279-661012; www.stansted.radissonsas.com; Waltham Close, London Stansted Airport; r from £149) A two- to three-minute walk from the main terminal building, this hotel has 500 rooms in three 'styles': Urban (mostly red), Ocean (mostly blue) and Chili (mostly yellow). We don't know, either.

Park Inn Heathrow (☎ 8759 6611; www.rezidorparkinn.com; Bath Rd, Heathrow; s/d from £127/145) With 880 rooms, the largest of the Heathrow hotels and one of the closest to the airport, this is much more luxurious than you'd expect for the money, but is sometimes overrun with guests. Take H2 Hoppa Bus (£4 per person).

WHERE TO STAY

Where you choose to stay in London will have an effect on the kind of time you have here and the image of London you'll take home, so geography should be as important a consideration as comfort, style and expense. Base yourself in the West End and you'll soon get into the throbbing rhythm of London at play. If your idea of the British capital is one of stately Georgian houses, Regency crescents and private parks in the centre of leafy squares, book a place in Chelsea or Mayfair. Hoxton, Clerkenwell and Shoreditch are where it's at right now, and there are a few good places to stay here at London's cutting edge. Culture vultures and/or those with literary aspirations should look to Kensington, Bloomsbury or even Fitzrovia. Want workaday London, with barrow boys shouting out their wares in Cockney accents alongside ethnic Pakistanis selling prayer rugs? Choose somewhere out in the East End. If you want to feel how most Londoners live, you might hang out in Camden or Stoke Newington. If you don't care how Londoners live, you might pause with the travelling circus in Earl's Court or Shepherd's Bush.

THE WEST END

You're really at the hub of London life in the West End, where you won't have to worry about running for the last tube home. The city's major theatres, as well some of its best dining and drinking, is right on your doorstep, as are many major attractions. Of course such a privilege doesn't come cheaply.

Moderately priced hotels in the centre are as scarce as hen's teeth. Having said that Bloomsbury is a haven of B&Bs and guesthouses, and tucked away in leafy Cartwright Gardens, north of Russell Sq and within easy walking distance of the West End, you'll find some of central London's best-value small hotels. At the other end of the accommodation spectrum Mayfair can boast hotels so grand that many of them are tourist attractions in their own right.

SOHO & CHINATOWN

COURTHOUSE HOTEL KEMPINSKI
Map p68   International Hotel £££

☎ 7297 5555; www.courthouse-hotel.com; 19-21 Great Marlborough St W1; r £270-390, ste from £550; ⊖ Oxford Circus; 🐱 ﹠
Oscar Wilde, John Lennon and Mick Jagger all made appearances at this former magistrate's court, now a 112-room luxury hotel just south of Oxford St. Special features include a spa and pool as well as a bar whose tables sit within original prison cells – authentic iron bars cordon off the lounge area.

SOHO HOTEL Map p68   Hotel £££
☎ 7559 3000; www.sohohotel.com; 4 Richmond Mews W1; s £255, d & tw £315, ste from £370; ⊖ Tottenham Court Rd; 🐱
One of London's hippest hotels, the Soho is in a reconverted car park just off Dean St. All the hallmarks of the eclectically chic hoteliers and designers Tim and Kit Kemp have been writ large over 91 individually

designed rooms, the colours lean towards the raspberries and puces and there's a stunning black cat Botero sculpture at the entrance.

HAZLITT'S Map p68   Hotel £££
☎ 7434 1771; www.hazlittshotel.com; 6 Frith St W1; s £175, d & tw £205-265, ste £300; ✆ Tottenham Court Rd; ⊠
Built in 1718 and comprising three original Georgian houses, this is the one-time home of essayist William Hazlitt (1778–1830), and all 23 rooms are named after former residents or visitors to the house. Bedrooms boast a wealth of seductive details, including mahogany four-poster beds, Victorian claw-foot tubs, sumptuous fabrics and genuine antiques. It's a listed building so there is no lift.

PICCADILLY BACKPACKERS
Map p68   Hostel £
☎ 7434 9009; www.piccadillyhotel.net; 12 Sherwood St W1; dm £12-19; s/d £38/56; ✆ Piccadilly Circus
The most centrally located budget accommodation in London, Piccadilly Backpackers has more than 700 beds spread over five floors, with dormitory rooms containing anything from four to 10 beds. Rooms are bright and clean and we especially like the new pod dorms with wooden bunk beds in their own little compartments.

YHA OXFORD ST Map p68   Hostel £
☎ 7734 1618; www.yha.org.uk; 3rd fl, 14 Noel St W1; dm £19-25; ✆ Oxford Circus or Tottenham Court Rd
The most central of London's six YHA hostels is basic, clean, loud and not particularly all that welcoming. Most of the 76 beds are in twin rooms though there are dormitories with three and four beds. There is a large kitchen but no meals are served apart from a packed breakfast.

COVENT GARDEN & LEICESTER SQUARE

ST MARTIN'S LANE Map pp72–3   Hotel £££
☎ 7300 5500; www.stmartinslane.com; 45 St Martin's Lane; standard s & d £220-270, garden r £310, ste from £600; ✆ Covent Garden or Leicester Sq; ⊠ ♿
A 'slice of New York urban chic' just a stone's throw from Covent Garden, this

Philippe Starck–designed hotel is so cool you'd hardly notice it was there. ('What, in that glass box?!?') Its 204 rooms have floor-to-ceiling windows with sweeping West End views, the public rooms are bustling meeting points, and everything (and everyone) is beautiful. The overwhelmingly yellow reception area plays havoc with some complexions.

HAYMARKET Map pp72–3   Boutique Hotel £££
☎ 7470 4000; www.haymarkethotel.com; 1 Suffolk Pl SW1; r from £245-310, ste from £385; ✆ Piccadilly Circus; ⊠
Named by *Condé Nast Traveller* as one of the world's finest hotels *before* it opened, the 50-room Haymarket in a John Nash building next to the Theatre Royal is further proof that London is becoming the epicentre of stylish boutique hotels. It's the progeny of Tim and Kit Kemp and it shows – from the hand-painted Gournay wallpaper to the 18m pool with funky drawing room.

COVENT GARDEN HOTEL
Map pp72–3   Boutique Hotel £££
☎ 7806 1000; www.coverntgardenhotel.co.uk; 10 Monmouth St WC2; s/d from £225/275, ste from £375; ✆ Covent Garden or Tottenham Court Rd; ⊠
As fresh as the morning but in a stylishly reserved British sort of way, this 58-room boutique hotel housed in an old French hospital and dispensary uses antiques (don't miss the beautiful marquetry desk in the drawing room), gorgeous fabrics and quirky bric-a-brac to stake out its individuality. There's an excellent bar-restaurant just off the lobby called Brasserie Max.

TRAFALGAR Map pp72–3   International Hotel £££
☎ 7870 2900; www.thetrafalgar.com; 2 Spring Gardens SW1; s & d from £200, ste from £375; ✆ Charing Cross or Embankment; ⊠ ♿
The demand for designer digs was so strong in London a few years back that even the Hilton got in on the act with this tastefully minimalist hotel on the south side of Trafalgar Sq. Now it's become the capital's 'first unbranded Hilton property' (meaning no logo) though the stylish 129 rooms, jaw-dropping roof terrace and the two-tier Rockwell bar, with the largest selection of bourbon outside the USA, are all still in place.

top picks

B&BS

- Aster House (p353)
- B+B Belgravia (p352)
- 66 Camden Square (p355)
- Gate Hotel (p358)
- St Alfeges (p360)

KINGSWAY HALL Map pp72–3   Hotel £££

☎ 7309 0909; www.kingswayhall.co.uk; Great Queen St WC2; s & d from £195, ste from £325, breakfast extra £15.25-26.95, weekend rate incl breakfast £165; ✈ Holborn; ⊠ ♿

Tipping its cap fairly determinedly at the professional traveller, Kingsway nonetheless manages to provide 170 smart, comfortable and very central rooms for anyone with less business and more play on their mind. The atmosphere is more relaxed on the weekend, when rates are considerably cheaper.

SEVEN DIALS HOTEL Map pp72–3   Hotel ££

☎ 7240 0823; hotels@orange.net; 7 Monmouth St WC2; s £65-85, d £75-95, tw/tr £100/115; ✈ Covent Garden or Tottenham Court Rd; ⊠

The Seven Dials is a clean and comfortable budget/midrange accommodation in a very central location. The 18 rooms come in a number of varieties – from single with shared facilities to triple with bathroom – and half face onto charming Monmouth St. Just don't expect the Ritz at this kind of money.

FIELDING HOTEL Map pp72–3   Hotel ££

☎ 7836 8305; www.the-fielding-hotel.co.uk; 4 Broad Ct, Bow St WC2; s/d from £85/105; ✈ Covent Garden

You can almost feel the pulse of the West End – and the odd high C from the Royal Opera House a block away – at this 24-room hotel, located in a pedestrianised court in the heart of Covent Garden. It's named after the novelist Henry Fielding (1707–54) who lived on the street. Space is at a premium but you can't beat the location at this price.

HOLBORN & THE STRAND

SAVOY Map pp72–3   Hotel £££

☎ 7836 4343; www.fairmont.com/savoy; Strand WC2; s/d from £389/409, ste from £589; ✈ Charing Cross; ⊠

No doubt the grand dame of the Strand will still be under wraps as she undergoes a £120 million face-lift when you read this, but the 260-odd room hotel remains a beacon in these parts. Built on the site of the old Savoy Palace in 1889, the Savoy has welcomed the high, the mighty and the not-untalented, including a certain Monsieur Monet who immortalised the views from the 'river rooms' on canvas. Fun fact: the Savoy's forecourt is the only street in the British Isles where motorists must drive on the right.

ONE ALDWYCH Map pp72–3   Hotel £££

☎ 7300 1000; www.onealdwych.co.uk; 1 Aldwych WC2; s/d from £340/360, ste from £575, weekend rate from £185; ✈ Covent Garden or Charing Cross; ⊠ ♿

Housed in what were once Art Nouveau newspaper offices (1907), One Aldwych is a merry and upbeat hotel with 105 rooms and modern art everywhere (we love the bronze of a rower in the lobby). The spacious and stylish rooms are replete with raw silk curtains, natural tones and bathtubs with room for two; the health club has an 18m-long swimming pool.

WALDORF HILTON
Map pp72–3   International Hotel £££

☎ 7836 2400; www.hilton.co.uk/waldorf; Aldwych WC2; r from £320, breakfast extra £22, weekend package from £289; ✈ Temple, Covent Garden or Charing Cross; ⊠

The glorious Edwardian splendour of this renovated old pile still lives on in the heritage-listed Palm Court, the splendid hall where a certain Lonely Planet author is known to have once taken his mother to the weekend tea dance. So thorough is the break from the past elsewhere, however, that the 299 rooms are now divided into either just 'contemporary' or 'design' (the latter is slightly trendier and more minimal).

BLOOMSBURY
GRANGE BLOOMS HOTEL
Map pp92–3   Hotel ££

☎ 7323 1717; www.grangehotels.com; 7 Montague St WC1; s/d from £145/159; ✈ Tottenham Court Rd or Russell Sq

This elegant and airy 18th-century town house has the feel of a country home, which belies its position in the heart of London (in what used to be the grounds of the British Museum). Think floral prints, classical music, portraits on the walls of the 36 guestrooms and a delightful terrace garden in back.

AMBASSADORS BLOOMSBURY

Map pp92–3　　　　　　　　　Hotel ££

☎ 7693 5400; www.ambassadors.co.uk; 12 Upper Woburn WC1; s/d from £145/155, weekend rate from £115/125; ⊖ Euston; ⓖ
This 100-room hotel in a gem of a *belle époque* building just south of Euston Rd has received a long-overdue face-lift and is now ready for action. The emphasis here is on comfort, the style is contemporary and the attached Number 12 bar a welcome addition to the area.

ACADEMY HOTEL

Map pp92–3　　　　　　　Boutique Hotel ££

☎ 7631 4115; www.theetoncollection.com; 21 Gower St WC1; s/d £115/145, breakfast extra £11-15, weekend rate r incl breakfast from £130; ⊖ Goodge St; ⓧ
This terribly English 49-room hotel is set across five Georgian town houses but has a slight Regency feel. Quality rooms are kitted out with fluffy duvets, plump cushions and bolster pillows. There's a conservatory overlooking a leafy back garden with fish pond, and a contemporary-looking bar in blue tones called the Library.

MORGAN HOTEL　Map pp92–3　　Hotel ££

☎ 7636 3735; wwwmorganhotel.co.uk; 24 Bloomsbury St WC1; s/d from £80/100, ste £120; ⊖ Tottenham Court Rd
In a row of 18th-century Georgian houses with 20 rooms alongside the British Museum, this is one of the best midpriced hotels in London, where the warmth and hospitality more than make up for the slightly cramped guestrooms. The larger suites are well worth the extra money.

HARLINGFORD HOTEL　Map pp92–3　Hotel ££

☎ 7387 1551; www.harlingfordhotel.com; 61-63 Cartwright Gardens WC1; s/d/tr/f £79/99/110/115; ⊖ Russell Sq
With its 'H' logo proudly sewn on your bedroom cushion, and a modern interior design with lots of lavender and mauve and green-tiled bathrooms, this stylish Georgian hotel with 43 rooms is arguably the best on the street. You'll recognise it from all the ivy in front.

ARRAN HOUSE HOTEL　Map pp92–3　Hotel ££

☎ 7636 2186; www.arranhotel-london. com; 77-79 Gower St WC1; dm £18.50- 23.50, s/d/tr/q £55/95/113/117, with shared bathroom £45/72/90/105; ⊖ Goodge St
This welcoming place in Bloomsbury provides excellent value for the location and even has a garden. The 28 rooms range from basic dormitory-style accommodation to bright well-furnished doubles with bathrooms. The lounge is pleasant, guests can cook for themselves and there are laundry facilities.

CRESCENT HOTEL　Map pp92–3　　Hotel ££

☎ 7387 1515; www.crescenthoteloflondon.com; 49-50 Cartwright Gardens WC1; s £54-79, d/tr/f £95/108/118, s with shared bathroom £49; ⊖ Russell Sq
In the middle of academic London, this friendly, family-owned hotel built in 1810 overlooks a private square flanked by student residences. While the 27 rooms range from pokey singles without facilities to relatively spacious doubles with bathrooms, all are comfortable and maintained at a very high standard.

HOTEL CAVENDISH　Map pp92–3　　Hotel ££

☎ 7636 9079; www.hotelcavendish.com; 75 Gower St WC1; s/d/tr/q £75/90/120/140, with shared bathroom s £45-55, d £55-75, tr £65-85; ⊖ Goodge St
Run by an amiable family, this hotel has 32 recently renovated rooms both en suite and with shared facilities, and a lovely walled garden. The rooms are small but comfortable and the welcome here's always warm.

JENKINS HOTEL　Map pp92–3　　Hotel ££

☎ 7387 2067; www.jenkinshotel.demon.co.uk; 45 Cartwright Gardens WC1; s £52-72, d/tr £85/105; ⊖ Russell Sq
Close to the British Museum, this hotel in business since the 1920s has 14 comfortable rooms and a friendly welcome. Enter from Burton Pl. Guests get to use the tennis courts in the gardens across the road.

JESMOND HOTEL　Map pp92–3　　B&B £

☎ 7636 3199; www.jesmondhotel.org.uk; 63 Gower St WC1; s/d/tr/q/f £50/75/95/110/120, with shared bathroom £40/60/80/100/110; ⊖ Goodge St
We've received more than a few letters from readers singing the praises of this

top picks

BOUTIQUE HOTELS

- Guesthouse West (p358)
- Mayflower (p359)
- Southwark Rose Hotel (p351)
- Rockwell (p358)
- Zetter (p355)

B&B in Bloomsbury. The 16 guestrooms – a dozen en suite – are basic but clean and cheerful and it's a good choice if you're travelling in a small group. There's laundry service.

AROSFA Map pp92–3 · Hotel £

☎ 7636 2115; www.arosfalondon.com; 83 Gower St WC1; s £50-55, d/tr/q £75/88/102; ❸ Euston or Goodge St

While the 15 rooms might be small and fea-ture refurbished but tiny bathrooms, Arosfa (that's Welsh for 'a place to stay') does offer excellent value for such a central location. Beware that some doubles are larger than others, and light sleepers should get a room at the back.

RIDGEMOUNT HOTEL Map pp92–3 · Hotel £

☎ 7636 1141; www.ridgemounthotel.co.uk; 65-67 Gower St WC1; s/d/tr/f £50/70/87/96, with shared bathroom £39/54/71/86; ❸ Goodge St

This old-fashioned hotel offers its guests a warmth and consideration that you don't come across very often in the city these days. About half of its 30 utilitarian rooms have bathrooms. It also has a laundry service.

GENERATOR Map pp92–3 · Hostel £

☎ 7388 7655; www.generatorhostels.com; Comp-ton Pl, opp 37 Tavistock Pl WC1; dm £10-25, s £35-50, tw £40-50, tr £54-80, q £54-100; ❸ Russell Sq

With its industrial décor, blue neon lights and throbbing techno the huge Genera-tor is one of the grooviest budget places in central London and not for the faint-hearted. The bar stays open until 2am and there are frequent drinking competitions. Along with 214 rooms, which have dorm rooms of between four and 14 beds, there are pool tables, safe-deposit boxes and a large eating area, but no kitchen.

FITZROVIA

SANDERSON Map p68 · Boutique Hotel £££

☎ 7300 1400; www.sandersonlondon.com; 50 Berners St W1; d from £220, loft ste £760; ❸ Oxford Circus

Don't be deterred by the white aluminium and grey-green glass façade of a 1960s-era corporate HQ: this über-designed 'urban spa' – recognise Philippe Starck's hand, by any chance? – comes with a lush bamboo-filled garden, artworks and installations, bed sheets with a 450-thread count and a jumble of personality furniture, including a Dalí 'lips' sofa and swan-shaped armchairs. It's a quirky, almost surreal place, with 150 rooms, and decadent enough to die for.

MYHOTEL BLOOMSBURY

Map p68 · Boutique Hotel £££

☎ 7667 6000; www.myhotels.com; 11-13 Bayley St WC1; s £205, d & tw £235-265, ste from £355, weekend rate r from £129; ❸ Tottenham Court Rd or Goodge St; ▨

Its less-than-inspired name notwith-standing, this stylish place was one of London's first boutique hotels and still bears the classic boutique combination of colours (blacks, greys and reds) in its 78 guestrooms. The library is a welcome retreat for chilling but we're not sure about the attached branch of Yo! Sushi (p275). The quirkier Myhotel Chelsea (Map pp138–9; ☎ 7225 7500; 35 Ixworth Pl SW3; ❸ South Kensington) has 45 rooms.

CHARLOTTE STREET HOTEL

Map p68 · Boutique Hotel £££

☎ 7806 2000; www.charlottestreethotel.com; 15-17 Charlotte St W1; s/d from £210/240, ste from £350; ❸ Tottenham Court Rd; ▨ ♿

This wonderful 52-room hotel, where Laura Ashley goes postmodern and comes up smelling of roses, is a favourite of visit-ing media types. The bar buzzes by night, while Oscar restaurant is a delightful spot any time of day, but particularly for after-noon tea.

GRANGE LANGHAM COURT HOTEL

Map p68 · Hotel ££

☎ 7436 6622; www.grangehotels.co.uk; 31-35 Langham St W1; s/d from £145/165, breakfast extra £5-13; ❸ Oxford Circus

This 60-room hotel has a lovely black-and-white tile exterior but rather ordinary guestrooms and public areas (who chose the tartan armchairs and that diamond-patterned carpet?). But it's in a great location just north of Oxford St and Soho.

ST JAMES'S

RITZ Map p68   Hotel £££

☎ 7493 8181; www.theritzlondon.com; 150 Piccadilly W1; s/d from £399.50/493.50, ste from £728.50; ⊖ Green Park; ☒
What can you say about a hotel that has lent its name to the English lexicon? Arguably London's most celebrated hotel, this ritzy 136-room caravanserai has a spectacular position overlooking Green Park and is supposedly the royal family's 'home away from home'. The Long Gallery and Palm Court restaurant have Louis XVI themes; book weeks ahead if you want to sample afternoon tea (£36). A planned extension on Arlington St just east will add 45 rooms.

METROPOLITAN Map pp96–7   Hotel £££

☎ 7647 1000; www.metropolitan.co.uk; 19 Old Park Lane W1; s & d from £325-405, ste from £475, breakfast extra £25; ⊖ Hyde Park Corner; ☒ ♿
In the same stable as the Halkin, the 155-room Metropolitan is another minimalist hotel – 'stripped of nonessentials' (as they say) and decorated in shades of cream and burlwood. It attracts a supertrendy, well-heeled crowd (more rock star than royal, really). The hotel's Japanese restaurant, Nobu (p245), is outstanding.

SANCTUARY HOUSE HOTEL
Map pp96–7   Hotel ££

☎ 7799 4044; www.fullershotel.com; 33 Tothill St SW1; s & d £160-195; ⊖ St James's Park; ♿
A cut above your average pub hotel, the 34-room Sanctuary lives up to its name, although it's just a few minutes' walk from Westminster Abbey and the Houses of Parliament. The style is very much cosy English country cottage and some of the refurbished superior rooms even contain four-poster beds. Rates don't include breakfast.

MAYFAIR

BROWN'S Map p68   Hotel £££

☎ 7493 6020; www.brownshotel.com; 30 Albemarle St W1; s & d from £310, ste from £800; ⊖ Green Park; ☒ ♿

A stunner of a five-star number, this 117-room hotel was created in 1837 from 11 houses joined together. Some traditional features retained from an earlier refurbishment of the public areas include stained-glass windows, Edwardian oak panelling, working fireplaces and gilt mirrors. The 117 updated rooms have soft colours and works by young English artists.

CLARIDGE'S Map p100   Hotel £££

☎ 7629 8860; www.claridges.co.uk; 55 Brook St W1; s/d from £460/495, ste from £740, breakfast extra £21-25; ⊖ Bond St; ☒
Claridge's, with 203 rooms, is one of the greatest of London's five-star hotels, a cherished reminder of a bygone era. Many of the Art Deco features of the public areas and suites were designed in the late 1920s, and some of the 1930s-vintage furniture once graced the staterooms of the decommissioned SS Normandie. Foul-mouthed celebrity chef Gordon Ramsay reigns over the kitchen (see p245).

DORCHESTER Map p100   Hotel £££

☎ 7629 8888; www.dorchesterhotel.com; Park Lane W1; s/d from £385/465, ste from £710, breakfast extra £25; ⊖ Hyde Park Corner; ☒ ♿
This opulent tour de force has been the hotel of choice for movie stars, fashionistas and those with a wallop of cash to spend and an image to cultivate since it opened for business in 1931. The lobby is possibly the most lavish in London and the enormous ballroom with its sparkling mirrored walls remains one of the most grand today. In the 250 guestrooms a mixture of antique and individual furniture, four-poster beds, chaise lounges and roaring fireplaces evoke an English country-house feel.

CHESTERFIELD Map p100   Hotel £££

☎ 7491 2622; www.redcarnationhotels.com; 35 Charles St W1; s £180-225, d & tw £205-305, ste from £325, breakfast extra £17.50-19.50; ⊖ Green Park; ☒
Just a block west of Berkeley Sq, the 110-room Chesterfield comprises five floors of refinement and lustre hidden behind a fairly plain Georgian town house. It has ceilings with mouldings, marble floors and period-style furnishings as you'd expect from one of the grand dames of London digs. We love the four themed suites (Music, Garden, Theatre and Study).

NUMBER 5 MADDOX STREET
Map p68   Hotel £££

☎ 7647 0200; www.5maddoxstreet.com; 5 Maddox St W1; ste £260-640; Victoria;
This all-suite hotel with a dozen units aims to provide a 'contemporary, urban sanctuary' and succeeds, making you feel more like you're 'super styling' in your own rented pad than staying in a hotel. On show are Eastern themes, natural tones and an exquisite eye for detail along with all the technical facilities the contemporary traveller could require. Reception is on the 1st floor.

MARYLEBONE

DORSET SQUARE HOTEL
Map p100   Hotel £££

☎ 7723 7874; www.dorsetsquare.co.uk; 39 Dorset Sq NW1; s £176, d from £258, ste from £411; Baker St
Two combined Regency town houses contain this enchanting 37-room hotel overlooking leafy Dorset Sq, where the very first cricket ground was laid in 1814 (which explains the cricket memorabilia in glass cases in the lobby). Guestrooms are small but almost dreamily decorated with a blend of antiques, sumptuous fabrics and crown-canopied or four-poster beds.

MANDEVILLE
Map p100   Hotel £££

☎ 7935 5599; www.mandeville.co.uk; Mandeville Pl W1; r from £250, ste from £400; Bond St;
This wonderful new deluxe hotel, within listening distance of the Wigmore Hall and within view of the Wallace Collection, has 142 luxuriously appointed guestrooms designed by Stephen Ryan. What we find unforgettable are the explosively coloured DeVigne Bar (another Ryan creation) and the view from the roof terrace of the Penthouse Suite (£650).

CUMBERLAND HOTEL
Map p100   Hotel ££

☎ 0870 333 9280; www.thecumberland.co.uk; Great Cumberland Pl W1; s £100-295, d £120-370; Marble Arch;
You'll be forgiven for thinking you've accidentally stumbled into a contemporary art gallery in the hangar-sized lobby with larger-than-life sculptures and backlit Perspex columns. Some of the more than 1000 guestrooms have views of nearby Hyde Park. Celebrity chef Gary Rhodes is in charge of the in-house brasserie-bar called Rhodes W1.

DURRANTS HOTEL
Map p100   Hotel £££

☎ 7935 8131; www.durrantshotel.co.uk; George St W1; s £115-135, d/f £185/199, ste £325, breakfast extra £11.5-14.50; Bond St;
This sprawling 92-room hotel, just behind the Wallace Collection and excellently placed for Oxford St shopping, was once a country inn and still retains something of the feel of a gentleman's club. The same family has owned it since 1921.

LEONARD HOTEL
Map p100   Hotel ££

☎ 7935 2010; www.theleonard.com; 15 Seymour St W1; s/d from £110/170; Marble Arch
Originally four separate town houses and later a hospital, the Leonard has 46 guestrooms that are somewhat conservative in appearance but elegant and very comfortable nonetheless. Eschew the standard rooms if you can; they're on the 5th floor and the lift finishes at the 4th.

HOTEL LA PLACE
Map p100   Hotel ££

☎ 7486 2323; www.hotellaplace.com; 11 Nottingham Pl W1; s £99-135, d £134-145, f £160, ste from £160; Baker St
The 18 rooms here are very much in the traditional mode, but impeccably cared for, and some have updated bathrooms. The friendly family management has installed a 24-hour wine bar downstairs, with comfy – and stylishly colourful – modern lounge chairs.

SUMNER HOTEL
Map p100   Hotel ££

☎ 7723 2244; www.thesumner.com; 54 Upper Berkeley St W1; s £125, d £140-160; Marble Arch;
This new town house hotel just north of Oxford St and west of Portman Sq offers incomparable value for such a central location. The 20 rooms are contemporary, comfortable and of a good size but the focal point of the hotel is the sitting room with an original fireplace and hardwood flooring.

EDWARD LEAR HOTEL
Map p100   Hotel £

☎ 7402 5401; www.edlear.com; 28-30 Seymour St W1; s £55-66, d & tw £67-99, tr £82-99, f £97-125, with shared bathroom s £42-53, d & tw £60-74, tr £65-90; Marble Arch
Once the home of a Victorian painter and poet (well, composer of limericks), the 31 rooms of this flower-bedecked terrace hotel offer basic accommodation at spectacular prices. Indeed, never undersold, the man-

STUDENT DIGS

During university holidays, many student dorms and halls of residence are made available to visitors. Accommodation might not be of a high standard, but it certainly will be cheap.

Try LSE Collections (☎ 7955 7575; www.lse.ac.uk/collections/vacations; s/d/tr £48/67/86, s/d with shared facilities £31/49) the agent for the London School of Economics, whose halls include the 800-bed Bankside House (Map p126; ☎ 7107 5750; 24 Sumner St SE1; ❸ Southwark) on the South Bank and the High Holborn Residence (Map pp72–3; ☎ 7107 5737; 178 High Holborn WC1; ❸ Holborn) with 495 beds near Covent Garden.

Halls administered by King's College Conference & Vacation Bureau (☎ 7248 1700; www.kcl.ac.uk/kcvb; s £27-39, d £53-58) include the Great Dover St Apartments (Map p126; ☎ 7407 0068; 165 Great Dover St SE1; ❸ Borough) with 750 rooms in Borough and the Stamford St Apartments (Map p126; 7633 2182; 127 Stamford St SE1; ❸ Waterloo) with 537 rooms near Waterloo.

Other options worth trying include the following:

International Students' House (Map p100; ☎ 7631 8300; www.ish.org.uk; 229 Great Portland St W1; dm £12-19, s/d/tr from £34/52/63; ❸ Great Portland St) Unusual for a hall of residence this 700-bed place near Regent's Park has rooms available all year.

Finsbury Residences (Map p150; ☎ 7040 8811; www.city.ac.uk/ems; 15 Bastwick St EC1; s with shared facilities £19-21; ❸ Barbican) These residences between Islington and the City comprise two modern halls with 320 rooms belonging to City University London.

---

agement claims that 'if you can find a hotel as close to Oxford St that quotes a lower price, we will match it'.

PARKWOOD HOTEL Map p100 Hotel ££

☎ 7402 2241; www.parkwoodhotel.com; 4 Stanhope Pl W2; s/d/tr/f £75/89/99/115, with shared bathroom s/d/tr £49.50/68.50/79; ❸ Marble Arch
You certainly get value for money at this small hotel. The 16 refurbished rooms are pretty in pink and yellow with candy-striped spreads, crown canopies and potted plants. All but four guestrooms are en suite, although the bathrooms could stand with some updating.

GLYNNE COURT HOTEL Map p100 Hotel ££

☎ 7258 1010; www.glynne-court-hotel.com; 41 Great Cumberland Pl W1; s/d/tr/f £45/85/90/95; ❸ Marble Arch
Fairly typical for this price range and location, the Glynne Court has 15 rooms housed in an historic listed building dating back to the late 18th century. The owners are eager to please and will be happy to tell you about the colourful history of 41 Cumberland Pl.

THE CITY

Staying in this area gives you the chance to see London from the other side and it's a relatively recent development; until just a few short years ago the City offered virtually

nothing in terms of accommodation. With the West End perpetually overrun by crowds, the City is refreshingly quiet at weekends, yet offers easy access to such attractions as the Tower of London and the restaurants and bars of Shoreditch and Hoxton.

THREADNEEDLES

Map p110 Boutique Hotel £££
☎ 7657 8080; www.theetoncollection.com; 5 Threadneedle St EC2; s & d £295-355, ste from £400; ❸ Bank; 🖭
Discreetly located in the heart of the City, Threadneedles is an elegant 70-room boutique hotel that has been converted from a 19th-century bank. The centrepiece is the grand circular lobby, which is furnished in a vaguely Art Deco style and covered with a hand-painted glass dome. Rooms are just as elegant, with arty photography livening up the sand-coloured walls.

GREAT EASTERN HOTEL Map p110 Hotel £££

☎ 7618 5010; www.great-eastern-hotel.co.uk; Liverpool St EC1; s from £305, d from £325; ❸ Liverpool St; 🖭 🖭
While the dark-wood lobby still has a masculine feel, this stylish 267-room hotel attached to Liverpool St station has been softening the décor in some of its rooms and public areas, including a red neon sign above reception reading 'You Make My Heart Go Boom Boom'. The hotel sits

on the site of what was the Bethlehem Royal Hospital (more commonly known as Bedlam) for more than 400 years from the middle of the 13th century.

GRANGE CITY HOTEL Map p110   Hotel £££
☎ 7863 3700; www.grangehotels.co.uk; 10 Coopers Row EC3; s & d £293-351, weekend rate from £80, breakfast extra £24; ✆ Tower Hill; 🖥️ ♿
Many of the 307 rooms in this classy, five-star city hotel have close-up views of Tower Bridge and the Tower of London, and it's popular with conference guests and tourists alike. Other pluses include a state-of-the-art spa with 25m pool and a wing catering solely to women.

YHA LONDON ST PAUL'S Map p110 Hostel £
☎ 7236 4965; www.yha.org.uk; 36 Carter Lane EC4; 11-bed dm £17.20, 5-8 bed £21-26.50, 3-4 bed £21-27.50, s £27.50-34, d £47-60; ✆ St Paul's
This excellent 193-bed hostel stands in the very shadow of St Paul's Cathedral and opposite the Tate Modern. Most rooms have

two, three or four beds though 19 rooms have five to 11 beds. There's a licensed cafeteria called Big Bitez but no kitchen.

CITY YMCA LONDON Map p150   Hostel £
☎ 7628 8832; www.cityymca.org; 8 Errol St EC1; s with shared bathroom £34.90, tw £59.50; ✆ Barbican
Much nicer than its nearby Barbican counterpart, this 112-room budget hotel on four floors has better bathrooms, bedrooms with TVs and phones for incoming calls. It's very handy for Shoreditch, but you should book about one month ahead. There are also weekly rates (singles/twins from £172.50/283).

THE SOUTH BANK

With this once-neglected riverbank now one of the city's most vibrant stretches, the South Bank has become an increasingly good and useful base. Restaurant and bar pickings are slimmer than in the West End, but ever on the up. And who wouldn't be tempted by the

---

CHAINS WITHOUT FRILLS

London counts several discount hotel chains that offer clean and modern – if not especially full of character – accommodation for reasonable rates.

EasyHotel (www.easyhotel.com) uses the same pricing model as its sister easyJet airline to get bods on beds. It's a functional hotel that offers the best deals to early birds, with rates from £35 to £60 per room. Each of the garishly orange plastic-moulded rooms contains a bed next to a sink and a shower and toilet unit. There are no phones in the rooms, TV is an optional extra (as is cleaning and fresh linen at £10 a pop) and some rooms have no windows. There are several branches in London, including easyHotel Earl's Court (Map p177; 14 Lexham Gardens SW5; ✆ Gloucester Rd) and easyHotel Victoria (Map pp138–9; 36-40 Belgrave Rd SW1; ✆ Victoria).

Express by Holiday Inn (☎ 0800 434 040; www.hiexpress.co.uk) is the most upmarket of the chains listed here, and is most notable for its clever locations. Of the 18 or so properties in greater London, for example, is the so-called London City branch (Map p150; ☎ 7300 4300; 275 Old St EC1; ✆ Old St) in the heart of the Shoreditch nightlife area and the Southwark branch (Map p126; ☎ 7401 2525; 103-109 Southwark St SE1; ✆ Southwark or London Bridge) just behind the Tate Modern. Rates vary wildly but start at about £115 for a double during the week and sink to as low as £70 at the weekend.

Premier Travel Inn (☎ 0870 242 8000; www.premiertravelinn.com) is London's original cheap chain, herding them in and out of mostly converted older buildings at 18 properties. Hotels are fairly bare-bones beds are soft, the second bed is a pull-out sofa and there are more rules here than in a Victorian grammar school, but at from £94 a night per room on weekdays (£82 at weekends), few guests complain. The original property is in County Hall (Map p126; ☎ 0870 238 3300; Belvedere Rd SE1; ✆ Waterloo) near the London Eye but it doesn't have river views. The Euston branch (Map p168; ☎ 0870 238 3301; 1 Duke's Rd WC1; ✆ Euston or King's Cross) is handy to the train stations but is on a very busy street.

Travelodge (☎ 0870 085 0950; www.travelodge.co.uk) charges roughly the same price as Premier Travel Inn. Here you get a nicer room, but few public facilities; there's usually no lounge, the reception areas are small and service can be rather brusque. Of the 16 properties in greater London, central ones include the Travelodge Liverpool Street (Map p110; ☎ 0870 191 1689; 1 Harrow Pl E1; ✆ Aldgate), which is just west of Petticoat Lane, and the Travel Lodge Covent Garden (Map pp72–3; ☎ 0870 191 1745; 10 Drury Lane WC2; ✆ Holborn or Covent Garden).

thought of staying near the Tate Modern, where you can wander among the wonderful epicurean delights of Borough Market when you pop out for a coffee break? Further westwards you'll find yourself near the London Eye and convenient to Waterloo train station.

WATERLOO

LONDON MARRIOTT COUNTY HALL
Map p126   Hotel £££

☎ 7928 5200, 0870 400 7200; www.marriott
.co.uk/lonch; Westminster Bridge Rd SE1; r from
£249, with river views from £279, breakfast extra
£19.95-21; ⊖ Westminster; ▨ ⚭
This elegant 200-room hotel is famed for its fabulous close-up views of the Thames and the Houses of Parliament. It was formerly the headquarters of the Greater London Council; the atmosphere in the traditional rooms remains somewhat stuffy. There's a 25m-long pool on the 6th floor.

BANKSIDE & SOUTHWARK

SOUTHWARK ROSE HOTEL
Map p126   Boutique Hotel ££

☎ 7015 1480; www.southwarkrosehotel.co.uk;
43-47 Southwark Bridge Rd SW1; d & tw £125-170,
breakfast extra £7-12, weekend rate incl breakfast
£90; ⊖ London Bridge; ▨
Billed as London's first 'budget boutique' hotel, this 84-room place just minutes from the Thames is very versatile. Service is good, prices are reasonable and while the rooms are compact, they're stylish in a vaguely minimalist way with plum-coloured headboards, white fluffy duvets and silver lampshades. There's a great lounge bar on the 6th floor.

MAD HATTER Map p126   Hotel ££
☎ 7401 9222; www.madhatterhotel.com;
3-7 Stamford St SE1; r £135, breakfast extra
£6.75-9.35, weekend rate incl breakfast £70-80;
⊖ Southwark; ▨ ⚭
Its 30 rooms across three floors are quite generic, but the Mad Hatter feels slightly homier than most chain hotels, thanks to its traditionally styled reception area and an adjacent pub bearing the same name.

BOROUGH & BERMONDSEY

ST CHRISTOPHER'S VILLAGE
Map p126   Hostel £

☎ 7407 1856; www.st-christophers.co.uk; 163
Borough High St SE1; dm £10-22.50, d & tw £46-56;
⊖ Borough or London Bridge

This 172-bed place is the flagship of a hostel chain with basic, but cheap and clean accommodation in five London properties. There's a roof garden with sauna, solarium, hot tub and excellent views of the Thames as well as Belushi's bar below for serious partying. Dorms have four to 12 beds. Its two nearby branches (same contact details) are St Christopher's Inn (Map p126; 121 Borough High St SE1), with 48 beds, another pub below, a small veranda and a chill-out room, and the Orient Espresso (Map p126; 59-61 Borough High St SE1), with 36 beds, a laundry, café, and dormitory for women only.

DOVER CASTLE HOSTEL Map p126   Hostel £
☎ 7403 7773; www.dovercastlehostel.co.uk; 6a
Great Dover St SE1; dm £13-17; ⊖ Borough
This 80-bed hostel in a four-storey Victorian terrace house has a newly refurbished bar below it as well as TV lounge, kitchen facilities, luggage storage and internet access. It's a somewhat frayed but friendly place to stay. Dorms have four to 12 beds.

HYDE PARK TO CHELSEA

Gracious Chelsea and Kensington present London at its elegant best, though count on little to nothing in the midrange or budget categories. The theme of many top-end hotels in this part of London seems to be antiques – particularly the Victorian variety. Accommodation is more modest in Victoria and Pimlico, but you are near major transport links. Victoria may not be the most attractive part of London, but you'll be very close to the action, and the budget hotels in this area are better value than those in Earl's Court. Pimlico is more residential though convenient for the Tate Britain at Millbank.

CHELSEA & BELGRAVIA

41 Map pp138–9   Hotel £££
☎ 7300 0041; www.41hotel.com; 41 Buckingham
Palace Rd SW1; s & d from £200, ste from £395;
⊖ Victoria; ▨ ⚭
This hotel situated in a lovely old town house opposite Buckingham Palace's Royal Mews almost feels like you're staying in a private club. It offers the services of two full-time butlers working around the clock as well as 28 classically designed black-and-white rooms.

top picks

GARDENS & COURTYARDS

- Academy Hotel (p345)
- Garden Court Hotel (p357)
- Hempel (p357)
- Number Sixteen (opposite)
- Sanderson (p346)

JUMEIRAH LOWNDES HOTEL

Map pp138–9   Boutique Hotel £££

☎ 7823 1234; www.jumeirahlowndeshotel.com; 21 Lowndes St SW1; r from £199, ste from £299; ⊖ Knightsbridge; ✆ ♿

'Elegant' and 'intimate' are two words constantly used to describe this well-located and recently renovated boutique hotel, which is pretty funny considering the proprietors also own the overblown Jumeirah Beach Hotel in Dubai. The 86 guestrooms at the Lowndes have beige and brown tones offset by multicoloured (though subtle) blankets and drapes.

B+B BELGRAVIA Map pp138–9   B&B ££

☎ 7730 8513; www.bb-belgravia.com; 64-66 Ebury St SW1; s/d/tw/tr/q £97/107/117/137/147; ⊖ Victoria; ♿

This B&B, stunningly remodelled in contemporary style, boasts a chic black-and-white lounge where you can relax before a fire or watch a DVD, and 17 earth-toned rooms that aren't enormous but have flat-screen TVs. To our mind, it's truly the direction mid-range accommodation should take in London. Guests get to use hotel bicycles for free.

KNIGHTSBRIDGE, KENSINGTON & HYDE PARK

BLAKES Map pp138–9   Hotel £££

☎ 7370 6701; www.blakeshotels.com; 33 Roland Gardens SW7; s £175, d £265-275, ste from £645, breakfast extra £25; ⊖ Gloucester Rd; ✆

For classic style (and incognito celebrity spotting), one of your first choices in London should be Blakes: five Victorian houses knocked into one and painted an authoritative, very serious dark green. Its 48 guestrooms are elegantly decked out with four-poster beds, rich fabrics and antiques set on bleached hardwood floors.

LANESBOROUGH Map pp138–9   Hotel £££

☎ 7259 5599; www.lanesborough.com; Hyde Park Corner; s £315-375, d £435-525, ste from £625; ⊖ Hyde Park Corner; ✆ ♿

This is where visiting divas doze and Regency opulence meets state-of-the-art technology. The 95 guestrooms are lavishly appointed, including the three-bedroom Royal Suite, at £6000 among the most expensive digs in town. The staff, as you might expect, are impeccably dressed and know it.

HALKIN Map pp138–9   Hotel £££

☎ 7333 1000; www.halkin.como.bz; 5 Halkin St SW1; r from £350, ste from £550, breakfast extra £20-25; ⊖ Hyde Park Corner; ✆

The chichi Halkin is for business travellers of a minimalist bent. Bedroom doors are hidden within curved wooden hallways, and the 41 rooms are filled with natural light, cream walls and wood panelling. Gratefully they are as stylishly uncluttered as the staff, who wear Armani-designed uniforms. Nahm (p253) on the ground floor is one of the best Thai restaurants in London.

CADOGAN HOTEL Map pp138–9   Hotel £££

☎ 7235 7141; 75 Sloane St SW1; s & d £260-355, ste from £395, breakfast extra £15-19.50; ⊖ Sloane Sq; ✆ ♿

This 65-room hotel is a wonderful hybrid, with two lower floors contemporary in style and the rest a wonderful vestige from Edwardian times, filled with reminders of a bygone era: polished oak panels, wing chairs, rich heavy fabrics and a refined drawing room for afternoon tea. Not surprisingly, the two rooms that are the most indulgent (and fun) are the room (No 118) where Oscar Wilde was arrested for 'indecent acts' in 1895 and the Lillie Langtry room – all rose wallpaper, feather boas and pink lace – where the eponymous actress (and mistress to Edward VII) once lived.

KNIGHTSBRIDGE HOTEL

Map pp138–9   Hotel £££

☎ 7584 6300; www.knightsbridgehotel.co.uk; 10 Beaufort Gardens SW3; s £160-175, d & tw £195-210, ste £330, breakfast extra £16.50; ⊖ Knightsbridge

The Knightsbridge occupies a 200-year-old house just around the corner from Harrods and has elegant and beautiful interiors done in a sumptuous, subtle and modern

English style. Some of the 44 rooms, although beautifully furnished, are very small for the rate asked though the bathrooms in granite and oak are lovely.

BAGLIONI Map pp138–9   Hotel £££
☎ 7368 5700; www.baglionihotellondon.com; 60 Hyde Park Gate W1; r from £300, ste from £320, breakfast extra £22; ⊖ Gloucester Rd or High St Kensington; 🖵 🕭
This luxury Italian hotel overlooking Kensington Gardens has raised an ostentatiously bejewelled finger to minimalism, with its baroque lobby (black glass chandeliers, a water feature in the lobby, gold reception desk) and opulent low-lit rooms. It's over the top, in a refreshing, fun way.

LEVIN Map pp138–9   Boutique Hotel £££
☎ 7589 6286; www.lhotel.co.uk; 28 Basil St SW3; r from £195, ste from £295; ⊖ Knightsbridge; 🕭
There seems to be nothing but praise for this new boutique hotel with a dozen rooms. Sister property to the Capital Hotel and its fabulous Capital (p252) restaurant with two Michelin stars, it doesn't need to shout about its comforts, amenities and great location round the corner from Harrods.

GORE Map pp138–9   Hotel £££
☎ 7584 6601; www.gorehotel.co.uk; 189-190 Queen's Gate SW7; s £130-170, d £190-210, breakfast extra £10-15; ⊖ Gloucester Rd or High St Kensington; 🖵
Charismatically kooky, this splendid 50-room hotel is a veritable palace of polished mahogany, Oriental carpets, antique-style bathrooms, potted aspidistras and portraits and prints (some 4500, in fact) covering every square centimetre of wall space. The attached Bistrot One Ninety is a fine place for brunch or a pre- or postconcert drink for the nearby Royal Albert Hall.

NUMBER SIXTEEN
Map pp138–9   Boutique Hotel ££
☎ 7589 5232; www.numbersixteenhotel.co.uk; 16 Sumner Pl SW7; s £110, d £150-250, breakfast extra £14.50-16.50; ⊖ South Kensington
With cool grey muted colours, tasteful clarity and choice art throughout, Number Sixteen is a stunning place to stay, with 42 individually designed rooms, a cosy drawing room and fully stocked library. And wait till you see the idyllic back garden set around a fish pond with a few cosy snugs or have breakfast in the conservatory.

ASTER HOUSE Map pp138–9   B&B ££
☎ 7581 5888; www.asterhouse.com; 3 Sumner Pl SW7; s £100-120, d & tw £165-220; ⊖ South Kensington; 🖵
What's made the Aster House the winner of Visit London's best B&B award not just once but three times? No doubt the quintessential English aura, the welcoming staff, the comfortable rooms with good-quality furnishings and sparkling bathrooms and the reasonable price all had something to do with it. Oh, and that's not to mention the lovely garden with its own little duck pond.

VICARAGE HOTEL Map p177   B&B ££
☎ 7229 4030; www.londonvicaragehotel.com; 10 Vicarage Gate W8; s/d/tr/q £85/110/140/155, with shared bathroom £50/85/105/112; ⊖ High St Kensington
Gilt mirrors, sconces, chandeliers and striped red-and-gold wallpaper greet guests as they enter this former Victorian home. The 19 rooms are less lavish, but atmospherically olde-worlde English all the same. The 3rd and 4th floorrooms have shared bathrooms.

HOTEL 167 Map pp138–9   Hotel ££
☎ 7373 0672, 7373 3221; www.hotel167.com; 167 Old Brompton Rd SW5; s £79-95, d & tw £99-110, tr £119-130; ⊖ Gloucester Rd
The mustard colour of the exterior sets the tone for this slightly quirky, slightly shabby 19-room hotel. Inside potted palms, a black-and-white tiled floor and ceiling fans lend a plantation-type feel to what was once a private Victorian residence.

YHA HOLLAND HOUSE HOSTEL
Map p177   Hostel £
☎ 7937 0748; www.yha.org.uk; Holland Walk W8; dm £19.50-22; ⊖ High St Kensington
This hostel has 201 beds and is built into the 17th-century Jacobean wing of Holland House, overlooking Holland Park. It's large, very busy and rather institutional, but the position is unbeatable. There's a café and kitchen, and breakfast is included.

VICTORIA & PIMLICO

CITY INN Map pp96–7   Hotel ££
☎ 7630 1000; www.cityinn.com; 30 John Islip St SW1; s & d £110-305, ste from £415; ⊖ Victoria/Pimlico; 🖵 🕭
The 460 rooms and suites at this large hotel just down from Lambeth Bridge are

uncomplicatedly modern, with big, fluffy white duvets and pillows, black armchairs and blond wood. Some rooms have stunning views of the Thames.

WINDERMERE HOTEL Map pp138–9 Hotel ££
☎ 7834 5163; www.windermere-hotel.co.uk; 142-144 Warwick Way SW1; s £89, d & tw £114-139, f £155; ⊖ Victoria

The award-winning Windermere has 20 small but individually designed and spotless rooms in a sparkling white mid-Victorian town house. There's a reliable and reasonably priced restaurant on site called the Pimlico Room.

MORGAN HOUSE Map pp138–9 Hotel ££
☎ 7730 2384; www.morganhouse.co.uk; 120 Ebury St SW1; d/tr/f £92/112/132, s/d/tr with shared bathroom £52/72/92; ⊖ Victoria

The Morgan House might be humble but it knows how to do pretty, with small bunches of fresh flowers placed in rooms using white or blue/mauve tones. The options range from a compact but livable single to a family room. The best rooms in the house are the two doubles in the back: No 2 with shared facilities and No 8 with en suite.

LUNA SIMONE HOTEL Map pp138–9 Hotel £
☎ 7834 5897; www.lunasimonehotel.com; 47-49 Belgrave Rd SW1; s £55-65, d £70-90, tr £90-110, q £100-130, s with shared bathroom £35-45; ⊖ Victoria

If all of London's budget hotels were like this central, spotlessly clean and comfortable 35-room place, we'd all be happy campers (or maybe that's what we *wouldn't* be). Modern art and some partially slate-tiled bathrooms provide some focal points, and there are free storage facilities if you want to leave bags while travelling.

VICTORIA HOSTEL Map pp138–9 Hostel £
☎ 7834 3077; www.astorhostels.com; 71 Belgrave Rd SW1; dm £17.50-20, s/d £35/60; ⊖ Pimlico

Part of the Astor group of hostels, this central place has 60 beds so it's busy without being too impersonal. It's staffed by travellers who are between trips and is conveniently located within easy walking distance of the Tate Britain and Westminster Abbey. Dorms have between four and eight beds.

WELLINGTON Map pp138–9 Hotel £
☎ 7834 4740; www.the-wellington.co.uk; 71 Vincent Sq SW1; s/d with shared bathroom from £35/45; ⊖ Victoria

This very sterile but clean former student residence on a large leafy square has 91 singles and doubles. It is easily reached on foot from the Victoria train and coach stations as well as the Tate Britain.

CLERKENWELL, SHOREDITCH & SPITALFIELDS

Clerkenwell, Spitalfields and especially Shoreditch, with its northern extension Hoxton, are very popular neighbourhoods, and there are a few good places to stay here. Accommodation choices are, for the most part, at the top end, but a midrange US-based chain of hotels has a branch here and the arrival of the no-frills Hoxton Hotel in the thick of things is changing the face of the neighbourhood by day and night.

HOTEL SAINT GREGORY Map p150 Hotel £££
☎ 7613 9800; www.saintgregoryhotel.co.uk; 100 Shoreditch High St EC1; s & d £229-329; ⊖ Liverpool St; ⊠ ⌖

A few minutes' bus ride from Liverpool St train station and close to the nightlife of Hoxton and the shopping of Spitalfields, the modern Hotel Saint Gregory has 198 pale rooms with attractive furnishings and very stylish bathrooms.

ROOKERY Map p150 Hotel £££
☎ 7336 0931; www.rookeryhotel.com; Peter's Lane, Cowcross St EC1; s £175, d & tw £205-265, weekend rate s/d from £119/149; ⊖ Farringdon; ⊠

This higgledy-piggledy warren of 33 rooms has been built within a row of 18th-century Georgian houses and fitted out with period furniture (including a museum-piece collection of Victorian baths, showers and toilets), original wood panelling shipped over from Ireland and open fires. Two highlights are the small city garden and the two-storey Rook's Nest suite (£495; £295 at the weekend).

MALMAISON Map p150 Hotel £££
☎ 7012 3700; Charterhouse Sq EC1; s & d £215-235, ste from £285, weekend rate from £120; ⊖ Farringdon; ⊠ ⌖

Facing a picture-postcard leafy square in Clerkenwell, this conservatively chic 97-room hotel is within easy walking distance of the City as well as the bars and restaurants around Smithfield Market. Public areas at the 'Mal' are moodily low-lit; rooms are colour-by-numbers hip.

ZETTER Map p150 — Boutique Hotel ££

☎ 7324 4444; www.thezetter.com; 86-88 Clerkenwell Rd; s & d £176-235, ste from £235, breakfast extra £9-16, weekend rate incl breakfast £150-200; ⊖ Farringdon; ▣

Mixing the homely comforts of knitted hot-water-bottle covers, blankets decorated with double-entendre Zzzzs and vintage Penguin books with hi-tech flat screens and air-conditioning (using water from the hotel's very own bore hole), this well-positioned establishment is miles more stylish and versatile than you'd expect from what was once a humble warehouse in Little Italy.

HOXTON HOTEL Map p150 — Hotel ££

☎ 7550 1000; www.hoxtonhotels.com; 81 Great Eastern St EC2; r £79-149; ⊖ Old St; ♿

This one-time car park takes the easyJet approach to selling its rooms – book long enough ahead and you might find yourself with a room for as little as £59 a night. The 205 guestrooms are simple but well designed – we like the way walls and carpets colour-coordinate – and are equipped with flat-screen TVs, work stations and fridges with complimentary bottled water and milk. And you couldn't get closer to the hip nightlife district of Shoreditch.

THE EAST END & DOCKLANDS

RCA CITY HOTEL Map p156 — Hotel ££

☎ 7247 3313; www.cityhotellondon.co.uk; 12 Osborn St E1; s/d/tr/f £140/150/160/190; ⊖ Aldgate East

This 87-room place is not exactly no-frills but has a long way to go before it features in *Wallpaper** magazine. Still it's at the southernmost extreme of Brick Lane so is well suited for those with business in the City or out on the town in Shoreditch. A planned addition of 25 rooms will be air-conditioned.

NORTH LONDON

North London is not particularly noted for its density of hotels. However, if you wish to base yourself away from the main tourist areas, it does possess a couple of decent options in several neighbourhoods, including King's Cross, Camden and even Hampstead, one of the city's leafiest and most sought-after residential areas. Here you're really living among Londoners, plus there's easy access to the wonderfully green expanse of Hampstead Heath. Camden makes a good base if you're into live music or the weekend market.

CAMDEN

66 CAMDEN SQUARE Map p168 — B&B ££

☎ 7485 4622; rodgerdavis@btinternet.com; 66 Camden Sq NW1; B&B per person £45-50; ⊖ Camden Town

This glass-and-teak B&B combines space, light and comfort in a quiet North London square not far from Camden Town and Regent's Park. The owners are fans of things Japanese and the whole house is attractively minimalist – apart from the occasionally noisy macaw.

ST CHRISTOPHER'S INN CAMDEN
Map p168 — Hostel £

☎ 7388 1012, 7407 1856; www.st-christophers.co.uk; 48-50 Camden High St NW1; dm £16-18, tw £50; ⊖ Camden Town

This 54-bed branch of the popular hostel chain is five minutes from Camden Town tube station along the High Street, atop the very busy Belushi's bar, which has a 2am licence. Staff are very friendly, there's no curfew and the lodgings are nice and clean, although some of the private rooms are very small. Dorms have between six and 10 beds.

KING'S CROSS & EUSTON

YHA ST PANCRAS INTERNATIONAL
Map p168 — Hostel £

☎ 7388 9998; www.yha.org.uk; 79-81 Euston Rd NW1; dm £21-26.50, tw £60-68; ⊖ King's Cross/St Pancras or Euston; ♿

The area isn't great, but this 152-bed hostel is modern, with kitchen, restaurant, lockers, bicycle storage and lounge, and it's in the hub of London's transport links. The more expensive rooms have private bathroom.

CLINK Map p168 — Hostel £

☎ 7659 1290; www.clinkhostel.com; 78 King's Cross Rd & 4 Great Percy St WC1; dm £15-26, s £58-70, tw £56-70, tr £75-87, with shared bathroom s £50-60, tw £48-60, tr £66-78; ⊖ King's Cross/St Pancras; ⑤

This fabulous 350-bed hostel brought to you by the same people who own nearby Ashlee House is housed in a 19th-century magistrates courthouse where Dickens once worked as a scribe and members of the Clash made an appearance in 1978; some parts of it, including seven cells converted to bedrooms and a pair of wood-panelled court rooms used as a café and an internet room, are listed. Inside the place is as new as the morning with pod beds (including storage space) in the coloured-coded dormitories (four to 16 beds) and about a third of the 128 rooms with their own bathroom en suite. There's a generous-sized kitchen and a bar in the basement.

ASHLEE HOUSE Map p168 — Hostel £

☎ 7833 9400; www.ashleehouse.co.uk; 261-265 Gray's Inn Rd WC1; dm £14-22, s £35-39, tw £46-54, tr £63-81; ⊖ King's Cross/St Pancras

This most welcoming, clean and well-maintained backpackers hostel has 170 beds on three floors, all conveniently close to charmless King's Cross station. The lobby, with a huge Underground map on the wall and shaggy-sheepskin sofa backs, looks interesting and although some dorms are pretty cramped (there are four to 16 beds to a room), they have cheerily striped duvet covers, washbasins and double glazing to keep out noise from the busy street. There is a TV lounge in the basement, plus a laundry, decent-sized kitchen, free left-luggage room and internet access.

HAMPSTEAD & HIGHGATE

LA GAFFE Map p166 — Hotel ££

☎ 7435 8965; www.lagaffe.co.uk; 107-111 Heath St NW3; s £70, d & tw £85-95, tr £125; ⊖ Hampstead

Perched above a popular Italian restaurant of the same name (see p264), La Gaffe is an eccentric but nonetheless comfortable and cheery 18-room hotel in a 200-year-old cottage in an affluent and very residential area.

HAMPSTEAD VILLAGE GUEST HOUSE Map p166 — Guesthouse ££

☎ 7435 8679; www.hampsteadguesthouse.com; 2 Kemplay Rd NW3; s/d £70/90, with shared bathroom s £50-60, d £75, studio apt s/d/tr/f £95/125/145/160, breakfast extra £7; ⊖ Hampstead

Only 20 minutes by tube from the centre of London, this is a lovely nine-room hostelry with a quirky character, rustic and antique décor and furnishings, comfy beds and a delightful back garden. There's also a studio apartment that can accommodate up to five people.

REGENT'S PARK

MELIA WHITE HOUSE Map p166 — Hotel ££

☎ 7391 3000; www.solmelia.com; Albany St NW1; r from £115; ⊖ Great Portland St; ⌧ ⑤

This enormous 545-room hotel in a white-tile Art Deco building might appear a bit 'standard issue' inside and too used to welcoming groups. But the location, just west of Regent's Park and within easy walking distance of Soho and three Underground stations, and the great price make it a winner.

WEST LONDON

From the style hotels of Notting Hill to the budget hostels of Earl's Court, this area has traditionally offered a broad range of accommodation options. Bayswater is an extremely convenient location, though some of the streets immediately to the west of Queensway can be run-down and depressing. Parts of Paddington are pretty seedy, too, especially right around the station, but there are lots of budget and midrange hotels and it's a good transit location; you can reach Heathrow in 15 minutes via the Heathrow Express. St John's Wood and Maida Vale are quiet, leafy neighbourhoods with a few attractive accommodation offerings.

ST JOHN'S WOOD & MAIDA VALE

COLONNADE Map p175 — Hotel ££

☎ 7286 1052; www.theetoncollection.com; 2 Warrington Cres W9; s £95-135, d £110-165, breakfast extra £10-15; ⊖ Warwick Ave; ⌧

A charmer in lovely Little Venice, the Colonnade is the handsome Victorian structure where Sigmund Freud sheltered after he fled Vienna. Apart from three in the basement, the 43 guestrooms are light, spacious and relaxing and just up from the Grand Union Canal.

PADDINGTON & BAYSWATER

HEMPEL Map p175   Boutique Hotel £££
☎ 7298 9000; www.the-hempel.co.uk; 31-35 Craven Hill Gardens W2; d from £295, ste from £480; ⊖ Lancaster Gate or Queensway; ⊠
This stunner of a boutique hotel, designer Anouska Hempel's minimalist symphony in white and natural tones where Kyoto meets *2001: A Space Odyssey*, still has the ability to wow us some 10 years on. The 42 rooms and studios are effortlessly beautiful, comfortable and unique (one room even contains a bed within a cage suspended over a living area) and the Japanese-style garden opposite is a restful oasis.

ROYAL PARK Map p175   Hotel £££
☎ 7479 6600; www.theroyalpark.com; 3 Westbourne Tce W2; s £170, d £195-225, ste from £265, weekend rate s/d from £130/150; ⊖ Lancaster Gate; ⊠
With tasteful Regency furniture throughout the lounge and immaculate bedrooms (plus discreetly placed plasma TVs etc), this 48-room hotel just north of Hyde Park is a classic example of a renovation gone right – indeed, even the sparkling bathrooms retain a semiperiod look and feel.

VANCOUVER STUDIOS Map p175   Hotel ££
☎ 7243 1270; www.vancouverstudios.co.uk; 30 Prince's Sq W2; s £79, d & tw £110-140, tr £155; ⊖ Bayswater
Everyone will feel at home in this broad church of 45 winning and very affordable studios. Rooms all contain kitchenettes but otherwise differ wildly – ranging from a tiny but well-equipped single to a generously sized family room with balcony and embracing all styles of decoration from faux-mink throws to Japanese to gingham. There's even a walled garden.

GARDEN COURT HOTEL Map p175   Hotel ££
☎ 7229 2553; www.gardencourthotel.co.uk; 30-31 Kensington Gardens Sq W2; s/d/tr/f £68/105/140/160, with shared bathroom £46/70/90/100; ⊖ Bayswater
Noteworthy for its Beefeater statue grasping a battle-axe, the spotless Garden Court is truly a cut above most classic English

properties in this price bracket. While the décor retains a few restrained traditional twirls, a recent overhaul has added a lift, modern bathrooms and some discreet designer touches in its 32 guestrooms. Guests have access both to the hotel garden and the leafy square across the street.

PAVILION HOTEL Map p175   Hotel ££
☎ 7262 0905; www.pavilionhoteluk.com; 34-36 Sussex Gardens W2; s £60-85, d & tw £100, tr £120; ⊖ Paddington
The quirky Pavilion boasts 30 individually themed rooms: Honky Tonky Afro has a 1970s and Casablanca a Moorish theme while Enter the Dragon conjures up Shanghai nights and Indian Summer is a tribute to Bollywood. They're meant to reflect the hotel's slogan – 'Fashion, Glam & Rock 'n' Roll' – and are a lot of good fun (and value).

CARDIFF HOTEL Map p175   Hotel ££
☎ 7723 9068; www.cardiff-hotel.com; 5-9 Norfolk Sq W2; s £49-55, d/tr/q £89/99/120; ⊖ Paddington
Run by the same family for half a century, the Cardiff overlooks lovely Norfolk Sq, a positive oasis in the warmer months. The 60 guestrooms are of standard size and level of décor but offer one of the best midrange deals around. The cheapest singles have shower but no toilet en suite.

STYLOTEL Map p175   Hotel ££
☎ 7723 1026; www.stylotel.com; 160-162 Sussex Gardens W2; s/d/tr/q £52/80/95/110; ⊖ Paddington
The industrial design – scored aluminium treads, opaque green glass, lots of stainless steel – of this 39-room hotel is as self-conscious as the name and you probably wouldn't want to tussle with the scary-looking angular-backed chairs in the basement breakfast room. But it's a real joy to get such a clean, sleek and contemporary look at these prices.

OXFORD LONDON HOTEL Map p175 Hotel £
☎ 7402 6860; www.oxfordhotellondon.co.uk; 13-14 Craven Tce W2; s/d/tr/f from £50/60/76/86; ⊖ Lancaster Gate
For a humble establishment, the 21-room Oxford sure tries hard with its sunny yellow walls and blue checked bedspreads, although the swirly carpets in the breakfast room and dodgy stairs are a reminder of how tired things used to be.

LEINSTER INN Map p175 Hostel £

☎ 7229 9641; www.astorhostels.com; 7-12 Leinster Sq W2; dm £13.50-18.50, s £28.50-41, d £46-60, tr £57-66; ⊖ Bayswater

In a large old house near Bayswater tube station and close to Portobello Market, this 372-bed hostel is the largest in the Astor stable and has a café, laundry and bar open till 4am. Dorms have between four and eight beds. Private rooms at the cheaper end have shared facilities.

NOTTING HILL & PORTOBELLO

PORTOBELLO HOTEL Map p175 Hotel £££

☎ 7727 2777; www.portobello-hotel.co.uk; 22 Stanley Gardens W11; s/d/tw £142/190/210, ste from £242; ⊖ Notting Hill Gate; 🎛

This beautifully appointed 24-room place is in a great location and has been a firm favourite with rock and rollers and movie stars down the years. Rooms and furnishings are eccentric in a funky, eclectic way and there's a 24-hour bar to fuel guests on their merry way.

MILLER'S RESIDENCE Map p175 B&B ££

☎ 7243 1024; www.millersuk.com; 111a Westbourne Grove W2; s & d £165-185, ste £230; ⊖ Bayswater or Notting Hill Gate

More a five-star B&B than a hotel, this '18th-century rooming house' is chock-a-block with curiosities and antique furnishings, and quite literally brimming with personality and *objets d'art*. The seven rooms come in all shapes, sizes and shades of antique opulence and are tailor-made for a romantic sojourn. Enter from Hereford Rd.

LENNOX Map p175 Hotel ££

☎ 0870 850 3317; www.thelennox.com; 34 Pembridge Gardens W2; s £100-125, d & tw £165-185, ste £220; ⊖ Notting Hill Gate

Behind an elegant neoclassical façade on a quiet and leafy street is this soothing contender for London's best small hotel. A bright and breezy welcome sets the tone, although you'll probably best remember the Victorian knick-knacks, zebra-patterned seat cushions and Bakelite bedside radio. The best of the 20 guestrooms are up the top.

GUESTHOUSE WEST Map p175 B&B ££

☎ 7792 9800; www.guesthousewest.com; 163-165 Westbourne Grove W11; s & d £155-185, Sun, Mon & Tue rate £140-170; ⊖ Westbourne Park or Royal Oak; 🎛

A fashionable take on the B&B concept, this lovely guesthouse in three town houses features 20 refreshingly bare and simple yet chic guestrooms with modern four-poster beds, flat-screen TVs, shiny kettles and cream mosaic-tiled bathrooms. The breezy terrace rooms on the ground floor have French doors leading onto a communal wooden terrace and modern artwork hangs in the communal lounge.

GATE HOTEL Map p175 B&B ££

☎ 7221 0707; www.gatehotel.co.uk; 6 Portobello Rd W11; s £55-70, d £75-100, tr £90-110; ⊖ Notting Hill Gate

The seven guestrooms in this old town house with classic frilly English décor and lovely hanging flower baskets all have private facilities. The management is very welcoming and helpful and you're as close as you're going to get to the action of Portobello Rd at this price.

PORTOBELLO GOLD Map p175 Guesthouse ££

☎ 7460 4910; www.portobellogold.com; 95 Portobello Rd W11; r from £70, apt £170; ⊖ Notting Hill Gate

This homely guesthouse above a pleasant restaurant has seven rooms of varying sizes and quality of furnishings. There are several small doubles and the so-called Large Modern Suite has antique furnishings, a four-poster bed and open-hearth fireplace. The Roof Terrace studio is more up to date and has a galley kitchen and exclusive access to the roof.

EARL'S COURT

ROCKWELL Map p177 Boutique Hotel ££

☎ 7244 2000; www.therockwellhotel.com; 181 Cromwell Rd SW5; s £120, d £150-180; ⊖ Earl's Court; 🎛

A very welcome addition to the greater Earl's Court neighbourhood, the 40-room Rockwell is a 'budget boutique' hotel *par excellence*. The décor puts a contemporary spin on English traditional and the rooms and restaurant overlooking the garden are a delight.

TWENTY NEVERN SQUARE

Map p177 Hotel ££

☎ 7565 9555; www.twentynevernsquare.co.uk; 20 Nevern Sq SW5; s £99-120, d £110-140; ⊖ Earl's Court

This 20-room sister establishment of the Mayflower (below) replicates the colonial style here, although with a little less black tile and a lot more carved wood that seems to whisper Batavia rather than Bombay. Several rooms come with four-poster beds but the focal point is the charming breakfast room–cum-bar in a conservatory in the rear of the building. A third property in the group, the New Linden Hotel (Map p175; ☎ 7221 4312; www.newlinden.co.uk; 58-60 Leinster Sq W2; ✛ Notting Hill Gate), is between Westbourne Grove and Notting Hill.

MAYFLOWER Map p177   Boutique Hotel ££
☎ 7370 0991; www.mayflowerhotel.co.uk; 26-28 Trebovir Rd SW5; s £69-75, d £89-105, tr/f £110/135; ✛ Earl's Court
One of London's cheaper boutique hotels, the 46-room Mayflower has chosen an updated colonial style, with wooden carvings from India, ceiling fans and black-tiled bathrooms. The deluxe doubles all have private balconies and individual furnishings such as a carved double bed.

BASE2STAY Map p177   Hotel ££
☎ 0845 262 8000; www.base2stay.com; 25 Courtfield Gardens SW5; s/d from £89/99; ✛ Earl's Court or Gloucester Rd; ▨
Base2stay has endeavoured to filter out all the 'unnecessary' extras most hotels offer and concentrate on the 'important' things like communications facilities, music systems and kitchenettes. The result is a pared-down but extremely comfortable 67-room hotel.

RUSHMORE Map p177   Hotel ££
☎ 7370 3839; www.rushmore-hotel.co.uk; 11 Trebovir Rd SW5; s £60-70, d £80-90, tr & q £110-130; ✛ Earl's Court
The soft pastel colours, draped fabrics and simple-yet-elegant designs of this modest hotel create a cheery, welcoming atmosphere. All 22 guestrooms, which have renovated bathrooms, are of a decent size and the triple on the 3rd floor is particularly spacious with French windows opening onto a private terrace.

PHILBEACH HOTEL Map p177   Hotel ££
☎ 7373 1244; www.philbeachhotel.co.uk; 30-31 Philbeach Gardens SW5; s/d/tr £58.50/81/95, with shared bathroom £49.50/63/81, student s/d £35/50; ✛ Earl's Court

This gay-run hotel has 38 rooms open to men and women and the interiors are simple yet stylish. One of the nicest rooms on offer is 8A, a double with bathroom en suite and a private balcony that overlooks the garden. The Philbeach has a lovely Thai restaurant called the Princess (open for dinner only) and Jimmy's Bar in the basement.

MERLYN COURT HOTEL Map p177   Hotel £
☎ 7370 1640; www.merlyncourthotel.com; 2 Barkston Gardens SW5; s/d/tr/f from £50/70/80/90, s/d with shared bathroom £40/60; ✛ Earl's Court
The Merlyn Court's 12 humble rooms are unremarkable, but the atmosphere is wonderful and it's very close to the Earl's Court tube station on a quiet street. The management is very friendly.

ACE HOTEL Map p177   Hostel ££
☎ 7602 6600; www.ace-hotel.co.uk; 16-22 Gunterstone Rd W14; dm £15-23, d £80-90, with shared bathroom £44-58; ✛ Barons Court; ♿
Squeaky clean and on a quiet residential street west of Earl's Court, this 157-bed place has a contemporary, upbeat feel to it and a fabulous back garden, complete with hot tub. Accommodation is in dorms with between three and eight bunk beds, and there is private accommodation in double rooms, some of them en suite.

YHA EARL'S COURT Map p177   Hostel £
☎ 7373 7083; www.yha.org.uk; 38 Bolton Gardens SW5; dm £17.20-24.50, tw £57; ✛ Earl's Court
The Earl's Court YHA hostel has had a remake in recent years but the great atmosphere remains. The whole place is cheerful but basic: most accommodation (186 beds) is in dormitories of between four and seven bunk beds. There's a good-sized kitchen and a garden out the back.

BARMY BADGER BACKPACKERS
Map p177   Hostel £
☎ 7370 5213; www.barmybadger.com; 17 Longridge Rd SW5; dm £16-17, d & tw £36; ✛ Earl's Court
Smack bang in the middle of a residential area, this Victorian town house turned backpackers haven is smaller than many other hostels in town, giving it a lovely homely feel. As a result, some guests settle in for the long haul, attracted no doubt by the lovely back garden and even more attractive weekly rates. There's a small

top picks

BEST POOLS

- Courthouse Hotel Kempinski (p342)
- Grange City Hotel (p350)
- Haymarket (p343)
- London Marriott County Hall (p351)
- One Aldwych (p344)

kitchen, laundry and 42 beds in 14 rooms. Dorms have four or six beds and there are five twins (three en suite).

SHEPHERD'S BUSH & HAMMERSMITH

K WEST Map p177   Hotel ££

☎ 7674 1000; www.k-west.co.uk; Richmond Way W14; s £99-119, d £129-165, breakfast extra £10.50-22; ⊖ Shepherd's Bush; 🐾 👍

K West is a hip and stylish 220-room place just off Shepherd's Bush Green. It doesn't look like much from the outside but inside dark wood and suede versus stainless steel and sandblasted glass run the bedroom gauntlet. Many people come to stay here to take advantage of the indulgent pampering at the K Spa.

ST CHRISTOPHER'S SHEPHERD'S BUSH Map p177   Hostel £

☎ 7407 1856; www.st-christophers.co.uk; 13-15 Shepherd's Bush Green; dm £18-21, tw £56; ⊖ Shepherd's Bush

St Christopher's Shepherd's Bush operation is right in the middle of the action with no curfew and the tube and a sprawling pub right on the doorstep. The accommodation is rather cramped, but special offers can often mean beds at £10 per night.

GREENWICH & SOUTHEAST LONDON

Somewhat insulated from the hustle and bustle across the Thames, Greenwich often feels more like a village than most other London neighbourhoods and no doubt you'll think you've moved to provincial England if you stay out here. It's ideal for those who fancy getting up early to go for a jog through Green-

wich Park, complete with great river views, or anyone going to a concert at the O2 (formerly Millennium Dome). Night revellers will find it less attractive as it's difficult to return to late at night.

GREENWICH

HARBOUR MASTER'S HOUSE
Map p180   Apartment ££

☎ 8293 9597; http://website.lineone.net/~harbourmaster; 20 Ballast Quay SE10; s & d £75-85, tr & q £85-95; 🚇 Greenwich, DLR Cutty Sark

This self-contained basement apartment is right on the river in a Grade II heritage-listed Georgian building. It combines mod cons such as TV, video, heated towel rails and full kitchen with the charm of vaulted white-brick ceilings and a vague maritime feel. As it's quite compact, it's likely to work best for couples.

ST ALFEGES Map p180   B&B £

☎ 8853 4337; www.st-alfeges.co.uk; 16 St Alfege's Passage SE10; s/d from £50/75; 🚇 Greenwich, DLR Cutty Sark

This gay-owned B&B situated in the centre of Greenwich has three rooms, individually decorated in shades of blue, green or yellow; the last two share a bathroom. The owners do their best to make everyone, gay or straight, feel at home, with chats and cups of tea. For such a central location, the immediate neighbourhood is quiet. Turn the corner into Roan St to find the main door. Discounts are offered for longer stays.

YHA LONDON THAMESIDE
Map p180   Hostel £

☎ 7232 2114; www.yha.org.uk; 20 Salter Rd SE16; dm £17.20-24, d & tw £53; ⊖ Canada Water; 👍

The facilities at this large flagship YHA hostel are very good, but the location is a bit remote. There's a bar, a restaurant, kitchen facilities and a laundry. Dormitory rooms have from four to 10 beds; the two dozen doubles and twins have bathrooms en suite.

ST CHRISTOPHER'S INN GREENWICH
Map p180   Hostel £

☎ 8858 3591; www.st-christophers.co.uk; 189 Greenwich High Rd SE10; dm £13-20, tw £45.50; ⊖ Greenwich, 🚇 Greenwich

The Greenwich branch of this successful chain of hostels has 55 beds and is quieter than some of its more centrally located sister properties (though it stands cheek-by-jowl to Greenwich train station). Dorms have four to 12 beds, there's just one twin room and there's a pub on site.

NEW CROSS INN Map p180   Hostel £
☎ 8691 7222; www.newcrossinn.co.uk; 323a New Cross Rd SE14; dm £10-16, d & tw £60-72; ⓧ New Cross Gate, New Cross
Sister property to the Dover Castle Hostel (p351) in Borough, this 80-bed hostel is in New Cross southwest of Greenwich. Rooms have basin and fridge, there's a big bar and two new kitchens. Reach here most easily by train from London Bridge station in about six minutes. Dorms have four to eight beds.

SOUTHWEST LONDON

Suburban Southwest London is not an obvious place to base yourself for a trip to London – it's quite a slog to the centre and more expensive than other parts of suburbia. However, anyone wanting to stay in a quieter, more-refined part of London will be right at home here – near greenery and within reach of the river.

PETERSHAM Map p208   Hotel ££
☎ 8940 0061; www.petershamhotel.co.uk; Nightingale Lane TW10; s £135-160, d £170-235, ste £300, weekend rate s £95-120, d £150; ⊖ Richmond or ⓧ Richmond then bus 65
Neatly perched on the slope down Richmond Hill leading across Petersham Meadows towards the Thames, the Petersham offers stunning, Arcadian views at every turn. And its restaurant, with its large windows gazing down to the river, has the very best of these. The 60 rooms are classically styled and offer a wonderful escape from the city – if that's what you're after.

RICHMOND PARK HOTEL Map p208 Hotel ££
☎ 8948 4666; www.therichmondparkhotel.com; 3 Petersham Rd TW10; s £84, d £95-110; ⊖ Richmond, ⓧ Richmond
This hotel at the bottom of Richmond Hill is a pleasant midrange place for anyone wanting to be in the centre of Richmond. All 22 rooms have private facilities and are comfortably furnished. While Continental breakfast is included, the owners will do a full calorific English slap-up for £5.

EXCURSIONS

EXCURSIONS

No matter how much you love, enjoy, live and breathe London, it's good to get out of the city every now and then. Many Londoners appreciate their city more once they've had a chance to relax from its relentless pace. For visitors, getting out of London is fantastic for understanding just how different the capital is from the rest of the country. You don't really know England (or indeed, Britain) until you leave the capital – it's wildly unrepresentative of the rest of the country. Forget ethnic and religious diversity, urban chaos and architectural variety (for the most part) – you're up for a whole different experience, a classic England that's about fish and chips, thatched roofs, cream teas, and pubs open until 11pm. That's not to say there isn't quality outside London – you'll find some fantastic places to eat (among them one that's run by Britain's best chef, Heston Blumenthal), and the alfresco culture that's taken over London is spreading to the provinces, too. If you're here in the summer and head for the coast, you may even get to have a swim in the sea.

There are plenty of options to choose from in London's surroundings: the classic towns of Oxford and Cambridge offer a serene but intellectual day out, while coastal towns will give you quaint streets, a sense of space and long, windy beaches. If you're a castle lover, some of Britain's best castles are within London's easy reach. But whatever you go for, we can bet you'll be glad when you come back to London, step out of the station and feel the big city's buzz.

CLASSIC TOWNS

If you want to immerse yourself in the historical and academic, Oxford (p366) and Cambridge (p369) are the obvious choices. Just over an hour away from London, both have quarters that have remained largely unchanged for eight centuries. Commanding Canterbury Cathedral (p376) may also take your fancy.

SEASIDE

'I do like to be beside the seaside' goes the 1920s song, and if you like the seaside and come from the Continent, prepare for something completely different. The weather may be unreliable, but that's part of the English experience. The sea here is not so much for enjoyment and swimming, but for gazing at while battling to save your chips from being blown away by gale-force winds. The coastal towns are usually more working-class, with charming fish-and-chip shops and seafood stands (selling lobster tails, jellied eels and so on), kitsch game halls and fantastic long beaches. But having said that, Brighton (p371) is only half like that – it's the most vivacious of the seaside places, its rapid gentrification having made it almost an extension of London, with cool bars, clubs and restaurants. During the summer you can even swim at its lovely pebbly beach. But the real charm is in the classic English seaside towns such as nostalgic Broadstairs, kitschy Margate or mussel- and oyster-rich Whitstable (for all three, see p374). Medieval Rye (p375) is a great combination of the seaside with a historic town. Romney Marsh and Dungeness (both p375) coastal areas bordering Rye are some of the weirdest you'll ever encounter – in an extremely beguiling way.

CASTLES

As if to prove the saying that an Englishman's home is his castle, successive kings, queens, princes, dukes and barons have outdone each

WHY NOT WALK?

Another way to get out of London for the day is to join an organised country walk. A good-value, quality and fun option is English Country Walks (www.englishcountrywalks.com; per person incl lunch, transportation & admission fees £30–68), which takes small groups rambling through farm fields, exploring castles such as Leeds (p379) in Kent or take you teetering on the edges of the seaside White Cliffs at Dover. You get the added delight of refreshing (with a beer, usually) at one of the traditional pubs along the way. The charming guide is full of informative and entertaining stories about local history, and walks start and finish at rural train stations that are easily accessible from London terminals.

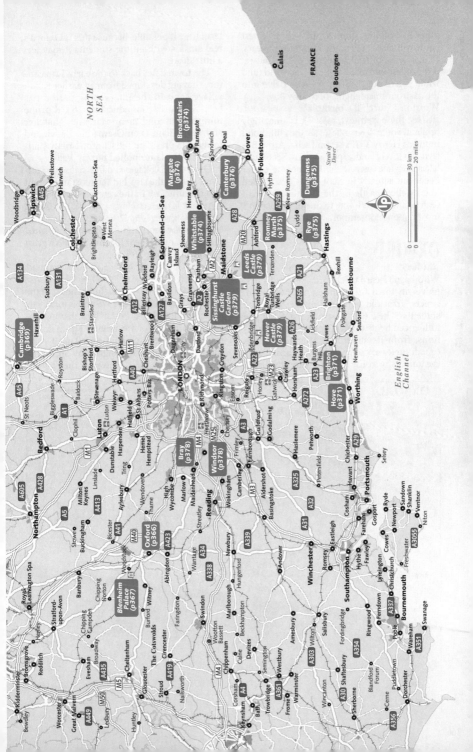

other by building some of the world's finest country houses over many hundreds of years. Windsor (p378), official residence of the Queen, is the oldest inhabited castle in the world (and while you're out this way you can delve into the gastronomic delights of nearby Bray, p378). Winston Churchill's birthplace, Blenheim Palace (see the boxed text, opposite), is amazingly opulent, while Hever Castle (p380), the childhood home of Henry VIII's second wife, Anne Boleyn, has lovely landscaped gardens. Set on two lakes, fairytale Leeds Castle (p380) – nowhere near Leeds but actually in Kent – has been called 'the loveliest castle in the world'. Sissinghurst Castle Garden (p380) is home to one of the planet's most famous contemporary gardens.

OXFORD

☎ 01865

Who hasn't heard of Oxford, England's first university town, full of spires, narrow ancient streets, great old pubs and masses of robed students? The city is so strongly defined and influenced by its university that most attractions, from its superb architecture, quads (quadrangles or courtyards) and gardens, are the university's property. It's better to visit in

term time if possible, because this is Oxford's real guise – without the students it may feel a little dead.

The town dates back to the early 12th century (having developed from an earlier Saxon village) and in the intervening period has been responsible for educating 26 UK prime ministers, among them Margaret Thatcher and Tony Blair. Even Osama bin Laden and former US president Bill Clinton briefly studied here (the latter puffed pot, as well).

Oxford's 35 colleges and five 'halls' are scattered around the city, but the most important and beautiful are in the centre. A good starting point is the Carfax Tower (☎ 792653; cnr Queen & Cornmarket Sts; adult/7-16yr £2/1; ❧ 9.30am-5pm Apr-Oct, 9.30am-3pm Nov-Mar), part of the now-demolished medieval Church of St Martin. There's a great view from the top (99 steps).

Christ Church College (☎ 276150; www.visitchristchurch .net; St Aldate's; adult/child £4.70/3.70; ❧ 9am-5pm Mon-Sat, 1-5pm Sun, last entry 4.30pm), the grandest of the colleges, was founded in 1525 and is massively popular with Harry Potter fans, having appeared in several of the movies. The main entrance to Christ Church is below Tom Tower, the top of which was designed by Sir Christopher Wren in 1682. However, the visitors'

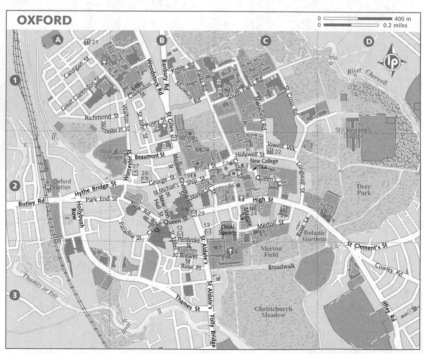

OXFORD

entrance is further down St Aldate's via the wrought-iron gates of the Memorial Gardens and Broadwalk. The college chapel, Christ Church Cathedral, is the smallest in the country.

Merton College (☎ 276310; www.merton.ox.ac.uk; Merton St; admission free; ☉ 2-4pm Mon-Fri, 10am-4pm Sat & Sun), founded in 1264, is on the brilliantly named Logic Lane, with the oldest medieval library still in use in the UK – the 14th-century Mob Quad. JRR Tolkien, author of *Lord of the Rings*, taught English at Merton from 1945 until his retirement in 1959.

The Church of St Mary the Virgin (☎ 279112; www .university-church.ox.ac.uk; tower admission adult/child £2.50/1.50; ☉ 9am-6pm Jul & Aug, 9am-5pm Sep-Jun) has a 14th-century tower that can be climbed for a fantastic view of the town's many spires. The stunning Magdalen College (☎ 276000; www .magd.ox.ac.uk; adult/child £3/2; ☉ noon-6pm mid-Jun–Sep, 1pm-dusk Oct–mid-Jun), on the River Cherwell (and pronounced maud-len), has huge grounds, including a deer park and Addison's Walk, which meanders through meadows to an island in the Cherwell. On 1 May it's traditional for students to leap off the Magdalen Bridge, al-

AROUND OXFORD

If you wish to extend your visit around Oxford, there are two obvious choices. First, Blenheim Palace (☎ 0870 060 2080; www.blenheimpalace .com; palace, park & gardens adult/child £14/8.50, park only £9/4.50; ☉ palace & gardens 10.30am-4.45pm mid-Feb–Oct, 10.30am-4.45pm Wed-Sun Nov–mid-Dec, park 9am-4.45pm year-round), near Woodstock, is the famously over-the-top Oxfordshire home of the Dukes of Marlborough and the birthplace of Winston Churchill. His bedroom is included on the interesting guided tour of the house, although the tapestries made for the first duke in the aftermath of his incredible military feats at Blenheim (in Germany) against the French are perhaps the highlight. You won't be alone in your journey, however, as the palace is hugely popular, especially in summer.

Oxford also acts as a secondary gateway to the rolling green hills of the Cotswolds (the primary gateway is Cheltenham). For information on sights and accommodation in the area, try www.oxford shirecotswolds.org, www.cotswolds.gov.uk/tourism or Lonely Planet's *England* guide.

though low water levels and recent injuries have left a question mark over this practice. The University Botanic Gardens are Britain's oldest, sitting by the River Cherwell since 1621.

Trinity College (☎ 279900; www.trinity.ox.ac.uk; Broad St; adult/child £1/0.50; ☉ 10.30am-noon & 2-4.30pm Mon-Fri, 2-4pm Sat & Sun) was founded in 1555, and next to it, at the corner with Magdalen St, is Balliol College (☎ 277777; www.balliol.ox.ac.uk). The wooden doors between the inner and outer quadrangles still bear scorch marks from when Protestant martyrs were burned at the stake here in the mid-16th century. A little further up St Giles, behind Trinity College, is St John's, whose previous students included Tony Blair.

The Palladian-style Radcliffe Camera (1749) is Oxford's most photographed building and functions as a reading room for the Bodleian Library (☎ 277000, tours 277224; www.bodley.ox.ac.uk; cnr Broad St & Parks Rd; tours £4; ☉ 9.30am-4.45pm Mon-Fri, 9.30am-12.30pm Sat, tours 10.30am, 11.30am, 2pm & 3pm Mon-Fri, 10.30am & 11.30am Sat Mar-Oct, 2pm & 3pm Mon-Fri, 10.30am & 11.30am Sat Nov-Feb), with Britain's third-largest dome. Check out the Bridge of Sighs, a 1914 copy of the famous Venice bridge, spanning New College Lane. Wren's first major work, the 1677 Sheldonian Theatre (☎ 798600; www .sheldon.ox.ac.uk; adult/child £2/1; ☉ 10am-12.30pm & 2-4.30pm Mon-Sat), is where graduations and

TRANSPORT: OXFORD

Distance from London 57 miles (92km)

Direction Northwest

Travel time 1½ hours by bus, one to 1½ hours by train

Bus Oxford Tube (☎ 01865-772250; www.oxfordtube.com) and Oxford Bus Company (☎ 01865-785400; www .oxfordbus.co.uk) run round-the-clock services from Victoria coach station (single £10, return £13). Megabus (☎ 01738-639095; www.megabus.com) has six departures per day from Victoria coach station and from Gloucester Green in Oxford (online returns from £2.50). Oxford Express (☎ 01865-772250; www.oxfordbus.com) also has frequent services (return £13).

Car The M40 provides access from London, but Oxford has a serious traffic problem and parking is a nightmare. We highly recommend that you don't drive. If you do, use the Park & Ride system – as you approach the city follow the signs for the four car parks.

Train There are two trains (☎ 0845 748 4950; www.nationalrail.co.uk) per hour from London's Paddington train station (adult same-day return £18.80).

other important ceremonies and occasional concerts take place.

Oxford has some excellent (free) museums, among them Oxford University Museum of Natural History (☎ 272950; www.oum.ox.ac.uk; Parks Rd; admission free; ☻ noon-5pm), famous for its dinosaur and dodo skeletons, and the eccentric Pitt Rivers Museum (☎ 270927; www.prm.ox.ac.uk; Parks Rd; admission free; ☻ noon-4.30pm), dark and crammed with crazy things such as voodoo dolls and shrunken heads from South America and the Pacific. Some days the museum hosts a children's exploration session, giving the kiddies torch lights and letting them open all the drawers. Brilliant stuff.

The Ashmolean Museum (☎ 278000; www.ashmol .ox.ac.uk; Beaumont St; admission free; ☻ 10am-5pm Tue-Sat, 2-5pm Sun) is Britain's oldest (opened in 1683), housing a stunning collection of European art from Rembrandts, Michelangelos and Pre-Raphaelite paintings to Turners and Picassos. Its antiquities area (2nd floor) was being renovated at the time of research, and is planned to open in 2009. The antiquities highlights are currently on the 1st floor. Check the fantastic Kandinsky landscape in the Sands room and the wonderful Moore and Hepworth sculptures.

Modern Art Oxford (☎ 722733; www.modernartox ford.org.uk; 30 Pembroke St; admission free; ☻ 10am-5pm Tue-Sat, noon-5pm Sun) is far removed from the musty and academic side of Oxford, having established itself as the best contemporary art museum outside London.

The Museum of Oxford (☎ 815559; www.oxford .gov.uk/museum; St Aldate's; admission free; ☻ 10am-4pm Tue-Fri, 10am-5pm Sat, noon-4pm Sun) offers an easy introduction to the city's long history, from prehistoric creatures to modern times.

A great way to soak up Oxford's atmosphere is to take to the Isis in a punt. These can be hired from Howard C & Sons (☎ 202643; www .oxfordpunting.com; Magdalen Bridge; punting per hr £10, on weekends £12, deposit £30, ID required, chauffeured boat max 5 people per 30 min £20; ☻ 10am-8pm Apr-Oct). If you want to pretend to be from 'round 'ere, note that in Oxford the tradition is to punt from the sloping end of the boat.

INFORMATION

The city centre is a 10-minute walk east from the train station and a few minutes' walk from the bus station at Gloucester Green.

Tourist office (☎ 726871; www.visitoxford.org; 15-16 Broad St; ☻ 9.30am-5pm Mon-Sat year-round, plus 10am-3.30pm Sun Apr-Sep) Staff can book accommodation; 1½-hour guided walking tours of the colleges (adult/ child £6.50/3) leave the tourist office at 11am and 2pm Sunday to Friday, and at 11am, 1pm and 2pm Saturday.

EATING & DRINKING

In addition to the following, there are plenty of ethnic eateries along Cowley Rd, off High St southeast of Magdalen College.

Quod (☎ 202505; 92-94 High St; mains £10-17) Perennially popular for its smart surroundings, as well as for its char-grills, fish and pasta; try its afternoon tea (£5.50; from 3.30pm to 5.30pm).

Branca (☎ 556111; 111 Walton St; mains £9-17) In the Jericho district a short walk northwest of the centre, this trendy brasserie serves modern Italian cuisine.

Grand Café (☎ 204463; 84 High St; snacks £6 12.50)
This museum-piece of a café is on the site of
England's first coffee house (1650), with great
cream teas in the afternoon.

Edamame (☎ 246916; 15 Holywell St; mains £6-8;
🕑 11.30am-2.30pm Tue & Wed, 11.30am-2.30pm & 5-8.30pm
Thu-Sat, noon-3.30pm & 5-8.30pm Sun) An excellent
little Japanese joint with massive queues that
move fast. One of Oxford's best.

Freud Arts Café (☎ 311171; 119 Walton St; mains £5-8) A
boho hangout in a restored church, with pews,
stained-glass windows and funky wire figures
hanging from the ceiling. It's popular with students, and serves sandwiches and pizzas.

Eagle & Child (☎ 302925; 49 St Giles; 🕑 noon-11pm
Mon-Sat, noon-10.20pm Sun) This fantastic old pub
is so atmospheric you'll easily conjure up JRR
Tolkien, CS Lewis and other literati sipping a
pint in one of the wooden booths.

CAMBRIDGE
☎ 01223

Even though Oxford students wouldn't like
to admit it, Cambridge beats Oxford as the
quintessential English university town. And
whereas Oxford has a solid record in educating
political grandees, Cambridge's reputation lies
more in the technological sphere. Past names to
have worked and studied here range from Isaac
Newton and Charles Darwin to the discover-
ers of DNA, James Watson and Francis Crick,
and renowned physicist Stephen Hawking. In
some senses it's the mother of English scientific
ideas. And even though you may think all those
medieval and neo-Gothic buildings look serious, Cambridge was where English humour
was nurtured, producing John Cleese, Michael
Palin and others of the Monty Python team.

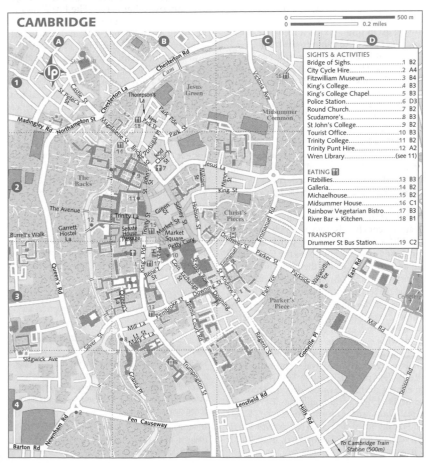

CAMBRIDGE

SIGHTS & ACTIVITIES
Bridge of Sighs..............................1 B2
City Cycle Hire..............................2 A4
Fitzwilliam Museum.....................3 B4
King's College...............................4 B3
King's College Chapel..................5 B3
Police Station................................6 D3
Round Church...............................7 B2
Scudamore's..................................8 B3
St John's College..........................9 B2
Tourist Office..............................10 B3
Trinity College............................11 B3
Trinity Punt Hire.........................12 A2
Wren Library...........................(see 11)

EATING 🍴
Fitzbillies....................................13 B3
Galleria.......................................14 B2
Michaelhouse.............................15 B2
Midsummer House......................16 C1
Rainbow Vegetarian Bistro........17 B3
River Bar + Kitchen....................18 B1

TRANSPORT
Drummer St Bus Station............19 C2

TRANSPORT: CAMBRIDGE

Distance from London 54 miles (87km)

Direction North

Travel time Two hours by bus, 55 minutes by train

Bus National Express (☎ 0870 580 8080; www .nationalexpress.com) runs hourly shuttle buses (day return £10).

Car The M11 connects the London Orbital Motorway (M25) to Cambridge. Take Exit 13 onto A1303 (Madingley Rd) and follow it towards the city centre.

Train There are trains (☎ 0845 748 4950; www .nationalrail.co.uk) every 30 minutes from King's Cross and Liverpool St stations (day return £17.90).

Founded in the 13th century, contemporary Cambridge is less touristy and more manageable than its competitor. However, note that during exam time – mid-April to late June – its colleges are often shut to the public.

The centre of town lies in a wide bend of the River Cam. The best-known section of riverbank is the mile-long Backs, which combines lush scenery with superb views of half a dozen colleges (the other 25 colleges are scattered throughout the city).

The Round Church (Church of the Holy Sepulchre; ☎ 311602; www.christianheritageuk.org.uk; cnr Round Church & Bridge Sts; adult/child £1/free; 10am-5pm Tue-Sat, 1-5pm Sun & Mon) was built in 1130 to commemorate its namesake in Jerusalem, and nearby is St John's College (☎ 338676; www.joh.cam .ac.uk; St John's St; adult/child £2.50/1.50; 10am-5pm), with a 16th-century gatehouse and three beautiful courtyards, two of which date from the 17th century. From the third court, the picturesque Bridge of Sighs spans the Cam. Stand in the centre and watch the punts float by.

Just south of St John's, Trinity College (☎ 332500; www.trin.cam.ac.uk; Trinity Lane; adult/concession £2.20/1.30, check website for free entry periods; 10am-5pm) is one of the largest, wealthiest and most attractive colleges. It was established in 1546 by Henry VIII, whose statue peers out from the top niche of the great gateway (he's holding a chair leg instead of the royal sceptre, the result of a student prank). The Great Court, the largest in either Cambridge or Oxford, incorporates some fine 15th-century buildings. Beyond the Great Court are the cloisters of Nevile's Court and the dignified Wren Library (noon-2pm Mon-Fri, plus 10.30am-12.30pm Sat full-term time), built by Sir Christopher in the 1680s.

Next come Gonville and Caius (pronounced keys) College and King's College (☎ 331212, 331100; www.kings.cam.ac.uk; King's Pde; adult/concession £4.50/3; 9.30am-3.30pm Mon-Fri, 9.30am-3.15pm Sat, 1.15-2.15pm & 5.30-6pm Sun term time, 9.30am-4.30pm Mon-Sat, 10am-5pm Sun out of term time), one of the most sublime buildings in Europe and Cambridge's foremost tourist attraction. The chapel was begun in 1446 by Henry VI and completed around 1516. Henry VI's successors, notably Henry VIII, added the intricate fan vaulting and elaborate wood-and-stone carvings of the interior. The chapel comes alive when the choir sings and there are services during term and in July (phone for performance times).

The Fitzwilliam Museum (☎ 332923; www.fitzmu seum.cam.ac.uk; Trumpington St; admission free, tours £3; 10am-5pm Tue-Sat, noon-5pm Sun, guided tours 2.45pm Sun), otherwise known as 'The Fitz', was one of the first art museums in the UK. It houses Egyptian sarcophagi, Greek and Roman art, Chinese ceramics and English glass in the lower galleries, while the upper galleries have paintings by Titian, Leonardo, Rubens, Rembrandt and Picasso, among others.

Taking a punt along the Backs is great fun, but can also be a wet and hectic experience. The secret to propelling these flat-bottomed boats is to push gently on the pole to get the punt moving and then to use the pole as a rudder to keep on course. In Cambridge, as opposed to Oxford, the tradition is to punt from the flat, decked end of the boat (for hire, see Information, below).

INFORMATION

City Cycle Hire (☎ 365629; www.citycyclehire.com; 61 Newnham Rd; bikes per hr/half-day/day/week from £3/5/8/15; 9am-6pm Apr-Sep, 9am-5.30pm Mon-Sat Oct-Mar)

Scudamore's (☎ 359750; www.scudamores.com; Granta Pl; per hr £12, chauffeured rides £40) Has punts for hire and chauffeured rides.

Tourist office (☎ 322640; www.visitcambridge.org; Old Library, Wheeler St; 10am-5pm Mon-Sat, 11am-4pm Sun Apr-Sep, 10am-5.30pm Mon-Sat Oct-Mar) Just south of Market Sq. Staff can arrange accommodation and two-hour walking tours (adult/child including entry to King's College £9/7), leaving at 1.30pm year-round, with more during summer.

Trinity Punt Hire (☎ 338 4800; www.trin.cam.ac.uk; Trinity St, Trinity College; punts per hour £6) Has punts for hire and chauffeured rides.

EATING

In addition to the places listed below, cheap Indian and Chinese eateries can be found where Lensfield Rd meets Regent St towards the train station.

Midsummer House (☎ 568336; www.midsummerhouse .co.uk; Midsummer Common; set lunch £20, 3-course dinner £55; ✌ Mon-Sat) Two Michelin stars adorn this fantastic modern French-cuisine restaurant, which has one of the best lunch offers around. It's a formal affair, with the restaurant's two floors sitting on the corner of the common, near the river. Book ahead.

River Bar + Kitchen (☎ 307030; www.riverbarkitchen .co.uk; Quayside; mains £9-13) Conran-designed, light and modern, this is a two-storey riverside brasserie that attracts a smart young crowd with its modern Mediterranean cuisine.

Galleria (☎ 362054; www.galleriacambridge.co.uk; 33 Bridge St; mains £7-10, 2-course set lunch £6.50) If you didn't manage the punting, watch others try from this Continental-style café overlooking the Cam that serves good French and Mediterranean cuisine.

Rainbow Vegetarian Bistro (☎ 321551; 9a King's Pde; mains £7-9) Massively popular and loved by herbivores, there's experimental vegetarian and vegan food, such as Latvian potato bake and spicy Indian veggie curries.

Michaelhouse (☎ 309167; Trinity St; mains £3.50-6; ✌ 9.30am-5.30pm Mon-Fri) A beautifully converted church, this stylish café has fair-trade coffee and sandwiches, eaten in a pew amid impressive medieval arches. A top choice.

Fitzbillies (☎ 352500; www.fitzbillies.co.uk; 52 Trumpington St) Cambridge's much-loved, oldest bakery is famous for its super sticky Chelsea buns and cakes, but it serves as a restaurant in the evenings.

BRIGHTON & HOVE
☎ 01273

Brighton is a bit like London on the sea, but with its own, distinct personality. If you want a cosmopolitan vibe, good food, atmospheric cafés, great clubbing and a long beach, this is your place. Despite its rapid gentrification (and rising house prices), Brighton hasn't lost its working-class soul, with the tacky but charming Brighton Pier and beach seafood huts still extant. The Victorian West Pier was sadly torched some years ago – the darkened skeleton of its former beauty still stands midwater, like a ghost.

Brighton has a young student population because of its university and language schools, a happening nightlife, as well as a decent cultural life. The Kemp Town (dubbed Camp Town) area, east of Brighton Pier, is home to one of the country's most vibrant gay scenes.

Brighton first became popular when the dissolute Prince Regent (later King George IV) built his outrageous summer palace, the Royal Pavilion, here in the 18th century as a venue for lavish parties. And that charmingly seedy, 'great-place-for-a-dirty-weekend' vibe lasted throughout the gang-ridden 1930s of Graham Greene's novel *Brighton Rock* and the mods-versus-rockers rivalry of the 1960s – think *Quadrophenia*. Julie Burchill, Nick Cave, Zöe Ball, Norman Cook (aka Fatboy Slim) and other media folk all live here (well, in Hove, actually, to the west).

Any visit to Brighton is essentially about life's simple pleasures – pottering about and shopping in the trendy boutiques in the narrow streets called 'The Lanes' or in the separate 'North Laine'; and eating, hanging out and buying a stick of hard 'Brighton rock' candy among the tacky stalls and amusement rides on Brighton Pier (Palace Pier; www.brightonpier .co.uk; Madeira Dr; admission free).

The Royal Pavilion (☎ 290900; www.royalpavillion .org.uk; Pavilion Pde; adult/child/student £7.70/5.10/5.90; ✌ 9.30am-5.45pm Apr-Sep, 10am-5.15pm Oct-Mar) should be your first port of call on any visit to the town. Originally a farmhouse and converted to a neoclassical villa in 1787, it only began to take its current shape when John Nash, one of London's prime architects (responsible also for Piccadilly Circus, Regent St and many of London's parks), got his hands on it between 1815 and 1822. As all things Asian were then the rage, he added onion domes and minarets to produce the final Mogul-inspired design. The interior features giant bamboo staircases and carved wooden palm trees. Don't miss the Music Room, with its nine lotus-shaped chandeliers and Chinese murals in vermilion and gold, nor the Banqueting Room, with its domed and painted ceiling.

Across from the Pavilion Gardens you'll find the redeveloped Brighton Museum & Art Gallery (☎ 290900; www.brighton.virtualmuseum.info; Church St; admission free; ✌ 10am-7pm Tue, 10am-5pm Wed-Sat & public holidays, 2-5pm Sun). Three new galleries – Fashion & Style, Body, and World Art – now join its ceramics, costume and fine-arts collections from the 15th to 20th centuries.

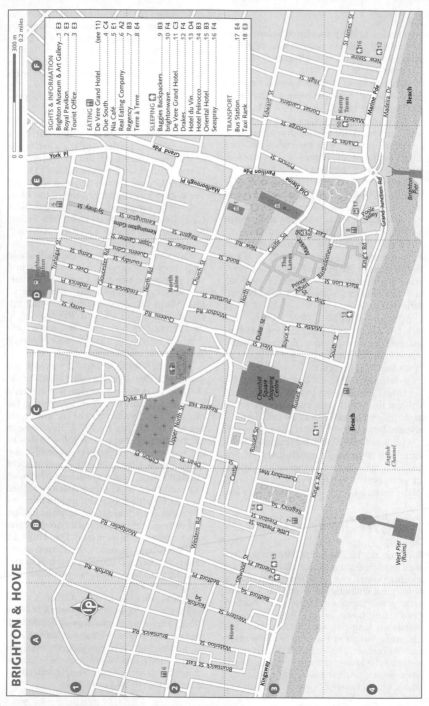

BRIGHTON & HOVE

SIGHTS & INFORMATION	
Brighton Museum & Art Gallery....1	E3
Royal Pavilion....................2	E3
Tourist Office....................3	E3

EATING 🍴	
De Vere Grand Hotel..........(see 11)	
Due South.......................4	C4
Nia Café........................5	E1
Real Eating Company.............6	A2
Regency.........................7	B3
Terre à Terre...................8	E4

SLEEPING 🛏	
Baggies Backpackers.............9	B3
brightonwave..................10	F4
De Vere Grand Hotel...........11	C3
Drakes........................12	F4
Hotel du Vin..................13	D4
Hotel Pelirocco...............14	B3
Oriental Hotel................15	B3
Seaspray......................16	F4

TRANSPORT	
Bus Station...................17	E4
Taxi Rank.....................18	E3

0 — 300 m
0 — 0.2 miles

The historic West Pier (www.westpier.co.uk) began to collapse into the sea in December 2002 and, having since caught fire twice, is a dark shadow on the water. It's still quite an arresting, beautiful sight and many visitors flock to see it. It's a shame that there are plans to replace it with a 360-degree observation mast – Brighton would lose one of its main landmarks.

INFORMATION

Tourist office (☎ 0906 711 2255; www.visitbrighton .com; 10 Bartholomew Sq; ☑ 9am-5.30pm Mon-Fri, 10am-5pm Sat, 10am-4pm Sun Mar-Oct, 9am-5pm Mon-Fri, 10am-5pm Sat Nov-Feb)

EATING

Brighton and Hove have more restaurants per head of population than anywhere in the UK, bar London. Pick up some fresh seafood in the little huts by the beach: lobster tails, jellied eel, mussels, oysters, king prawns and other delicacies start at £1.50. Perfect for eating on the beach while watching the sea.

Regency (☎ 325014; 131 King's Rd; mains £3-20) All things to everybody is how famed seafood chef Rick Stein has described this traditional seafood place, which is the equivalent of a greasy-spoon caf (though with good food), serving everything from fish soup to lobster, as well as pastas and steaks.

Terre à Terre (☎ 729051; 71 East St; mains £10-15) This gourmet vegetarian establishment proves that meatless food can be just as eventful as meat-based dishes. Though dishes sound overly complicated, the taste is simply delicious.

De Vere Grand Hotel (☎ 224300; King's Rd; afternoon tea £14; ☑ 3-6pm) You have to take afternoon tea at least once while you're in England, and if in Brighton, make it here. Piano music, sandwiches and tea inside the bright conservatory. Perfect.

Due South (☎ 821218; 139 King's Rd Arches; mains £11-14) On the seafront, with a wonderfully arched ceiling, this has been one of Brighton's top restaurants for years. The seasonally changing menu might include local wild rabbit kebabs with spicy peanut sauce or sirloin with garlic and onion butter confit, but always features lots of fish, mussels and oysters.

Nia Café (☎ 671371; 87-88 Trafalgar St; mains £9-14) Rustic chic, solid wood tables, large windows and a chalkboard menu make this one of the loveliest cafés in town. It's great for breakfast or lunch.

Real Eating Company (☎ 221444; 86-87 Western Rd, Hove; dishes £4-12.50; ☑ breakfast & lunch daily, dinner Wed & Sat) This hip deli-cum-café is about everyday eating and makes a top spot for breakfast (apparently it does 'the best eggs Benedict in town').

SLEEPING

Most places have a minimum two-night stay on weekends. You should book ahead for weekends in summer and during the Brighton Festival in May.

Hotel du Vin (☎ 718588; www.hotelduvin.com; Ship St; d/ste from £135/235) Located in a former wine merchant's Gothic home, this award-winning hotel has an ornate staircase, unusual gargoyles and elegant rooms.

De Vere Grand Hotel (☎ 224300; www.devere.co.uk; King's Rd; d from £140/220) Brighton's top hotel, this is a five-star affair with luxurious rooms, wrought-iron balconies and top-hat–wearing bellboys. A piece of lushness.

brightonwave (☎ 676794; www.brightonwave.com; 10 Madeira Pl; d £80-190) Combining the cool, muted design you'd expect from an expensive boutique hotel with the warm welcome of the small B&B it really is, brightonwave offers great value, service and style. Fantastic breakfasts, too.

Seaspray (☎ 680332; www.seaspraybrighton.co.uk; 25 New Steine; s £40-60, d £60-190) Themed rooms go from Venetian (suite) to New York (another suite), the Dalí room has the lobster phone

---

TRANSPORT: BRIGHTON & HOVE

Distance from London 51 miles (82km)

Direction South

Travel time One hour 50 minutes by bus, 50 minutes by fast train

Bus National Express (☎ 0870 580 8080; www.nationalexpress.com; return from £10, online funfares from £1) and Megabus (www.megabus.com; online fares from £1.50) run hourly services.

Car The M23/A23 runs straight into Brighton town centre.

Train There are about 40 fast trains (☎ 0845 748 4950; www.nationalrail.co.uk) each day from London's Victoria station (return £17.70), and slightly slower Thameslink trains from Blackfriars, London Bridge and King's Cross (return £16.40)

and the Warhol room's tables are soup cans. A fun choice in Kemp Town.

Oriental Hotel (☎ 205050; www.orientalhotel.co.uk; 9 Oriental Pl; s £35-40, d £60-125) Stylishly decorated in mint and rouge, this groovy boho hotel has fresh flowers, aromatherapy lights and organic breakfasts.

Drakes (☎ 696394; www.drakesofbrighton.com; 43-44 Marine Pde; s/d from £95/115) Classy atmosphere, fantastic sea views, obliging staff, and beautiful 'feature rooms' (£145 to £450) with clawfoot baths in front of curtained windows overlooking the sea. Need we say more?

Hotel Pelirocco (☎ 3327055; www.hotelpelirocco.co.uk; s/d from £50/80) Brighton's original punk'n'fashion hotel may not be at the cutting edge anymore, but its rooms are still brilliant – choose from Durex Play, Betty Page, Muhammad Ali, polka-dot room, Jamaican dub and more.

Baggies Backpackers (☎ 733740; 33 Oriental Pl; dm/d £13/35) Relaxed and central, this is the best hostel in town, with a good kitchen, and great music and a TV/video room.

BROADSTAIRS, MARGATE & WHITSTABLE

Each of these seaside towns has distinct character and bags of charm. Broadstairs is a nostalgic place with a patina of both Victorian and postwar history. Slightly dilapidated Margate is the archetypal kitsch English seaside resort, now forever associated with homegirl Tracey Emin, the Brit artist. Increasingly gentrified Whitstable is the best place for fresh, locally farmed oysters. It's been nicknamed 'Islington-on-Sea' since arty and wealthy Londoners began buying up the gorgeous fishermen's huts as second homes.

People mostly head to Broadstairs to soak up the atmosphere, swim (in good weather) and just hang around. Stroll along the Broadstairs Promenade, or take the cliffside walkway from Viking Bay to secluded Louisa Bay. The Dickens House Museum (☎ 01843-863453; www.dickenshouse .co.uk; 2 Victoria Pde, Broadstairs; adult/concession £2.30/1.20; 10am-4.30pm) commemorates the writer's love of, and association with, Broadstairs; there's also a Dickens festival in the middle of June.

Alternatively, you could visit Margate's unusual Shell Grotto (☎ 01843-220008; www.shellgrotto .co.uk; Grotto Hill, Margate; adult/child £2.50/1.50; 10am-5pm Apr-Oct, 11am-4pm Sat & Sun Nov-Apr), a mysterious underground temple dating from pagan times. It's off Northdown Rd. The 1000-year-old Margate Caves (☎ 01843-220139; 1 Northdown Rd, Cliftonville; adult/concession £3/1.50; 10am-5pm Apr-Oct, 10am-4pm Sat & Sun Nov-Apr) have a church, smugglers' refuge, dungeon, cave paintings and some witty (if not 100% proven) historical explanations.

Check out the summer huts on the beach in Whitstable, the traditional working-class summer weekend hangouts, painted in a rainbow of colours and given affectionate names. The annual Whitstable Oyster Festival (www.whitsta bleoysterfestival.co.uk) is held in the third week in July.

INFORMATION

Broadstairs tourist office (☎ 01843-583333; www .tourism.thanet.gov.uk; 6b High St; 9.15am-4.45pm Mon-Fri year-round, 10am-4pm Sat & Sun Apr-Sep, 10am-4.45pm Sat Oct-Mar)

Margate tourist office (☎ 01843-583333; www.tourism .thanet.gov.uk; 12-13 The Parade; 9.15am-4.45pm Mon-Fri year-round, 10am-4pm Sat & Sun Apr-Sep, 10am-4.45pm Sat Oct-Mar)

Whitstable tourist office (☎ 01227-275482; www .canterbury.co.uk; 7 Oxford St; 10am-5pm Mon-Sat Jul & Aug, 10am-4pm Mon-Sat Sep-Jun)

TRANSPORT: BROADSTAIRS, MARGATE & WHITSTABLE

Distance from London Whitstable 58 miles (93km), Margate 74 miles (118km), Broadstairs 78 miles (125km)

Direction East

Travel time 1¼ to 2¾ hours

Bus Five daily departures to Ramsgate stop at all three towns (outward 10.30am to 8.30pm, return 8.05am to 5.55pm). Same-day returns are £11 to Whitstable, £11.80 to Broadstairs or Margate.

Car Follow the M2; at the Margate/Ramsgate sign, follow the Thanet Way.

Train Trains (☎ 0845 748 4950; www.nationalrail.co.uk) from London's Victoria station to Ramsgate leave every 30 minutes (1¼ to two hours); a day return is £17 to Whitstable, £21.60 to Margate and £22.50 to Broadstairs.

EATING

Wheelers Oyster Bar (☎ 01227-273311; 8 High St, Whitstable; mains £6-18; ☺ Thu-Tue) This tiny place is a favourite with locals, with delicious fresh Whitstable oysters.

Whitstable Oyster Fishery Company (☎ 01227-276856; www.oysterfishery.co.uk; Royal Native Oyster Stores, Horsbridge, Whitstable; mains £13-25; ☺ lunch & dinner Tue-Sat, lunch Sun) Enjoy all kinds of seafood in the refurbished company HQ with great sea views. Have your oysters with champagne, of course.

RYE, ROMNEY MARSH & DUNGENESS

☎ 01797

The impossibly picturesque medieval town of Rye looks like it has been preserved in historical formaldehyde. Not even the most talented Hollywood set-designers could have come up with a better representation of a Ye Olde English Village: the half-timbered Tudor buildings, Georgian town houses, winding cobbled streets, abundant flowerpots and strong literary associations should be enough to temper even the most hard-bitten cynic's weariness of the made-for-tourism look. (All the same, such cynics should avoid crowded summer weekends.)

The town is easily covered on foot. Around the corner from the tourist office, in Strand Quay, are a number of antique shops selling all kinds of wonderful junk. From here walk up cobbled Mermaid St, with its timber-framed houses dating from the 15th century.

Turn right at the T-junction for the Georgian Lamb House (☎ 224982; www.nationaltrust.org.uk; West St, Rye; adult/child £3/1.50; ☺ 2-6pm Wed & Sat Apr-Oct), mostly dating from 1722. It was the home of American writer Henry James from 1898 to 1916 (he wrote *The Wings of the Dove* here). Continue around the dogleg until you come out at gorgeous Church Sq. The Church of St Mary the Virgin (tower views adult/child £2/1; ☺ 9am-4pm winter, 9am-6pm rest of the year) incorporates several styles. The turret clock (1561) is the oldest in England and still works with its original pendulum mechanism. There are great views from the church tower. Turn right at the square's east corner for Ypres Tower & Castle Museum (☎ 226728; 3 East Rye St, Rye; adult/child £2.90/1.50; ☺ 10.30am-1pm & 2-5pm Thu-Mon Apr-Oct, tower only 10.30am-3.30pm Nov-Mar), variously pronounced yeeps or wipers, part of Rye's former fortifications.

The town celebrates its medieval heritage with a two-day festival each August, and in September there is the two-week Festival of Music & the Arts.

East of Rye lie Romney Marsh and Dungeness, England's most otherworldly coast, pictured in Derek Jarman's film *The Garden*. The vast, flat Romney Marsh has a unique ecology, with unusual flora and fauna, and was once a favourite place for smuggling. Dotted across Romney Marsh is also a collection of tiny medieval churches – start with St Augustine's in Brookland. Desolate, barren Dungeness is the world's largest expanse of shingle and home to an unlikely combination of an old lighthouse (☎ 232 1300; tower views adult/child £3/2; ☺ 10.30am-5pm Jul–mid-Sep, 11am-5pm Sat & Sun mid-Sep–Jun), a nuclear power station and the Dungeness Royal Society for the Protection of Birds Nature Reserve (RSPB; ☎ 320588;

TRANSPORT: RYE, ROMNEY MARSH & DUNGENESS

Distance from London 54 miles (90km)

Direction Southeast

Travel time One to two hours

Bus To Dungeness, catch the hourly 711 from Rye train station to the Ship pub at New Romney, from where you can take the Romney, Hythe and Dymchurch Railway. Alternatively, get a bus to Romney and carry on down on the world's smallest railway, the Romney, Hyde and Dymchurch Railway (www.rhdr.org.uk; tickets from New Romney to Dungeness £6.50) which covers 13.5 miles from Hythe via Romney to Dungeness, on old-fashioned locomotives and cranky carriages. The service thins out at the end of the year, so check the timetable.

Car Follow the M2, M20 then A20.

Train Trains (☎ 0845 748 4950; www.nationalrail.co.uk) head to Rye from Charing Cross station via Ashford International or Hastings, where you will have to change. Two trains leave every hour, but both leave about the same time (day return £20.40).

www.rspb.org.uk/reserves/Dungeness; Dungeness Rd, Lydd; adult/child/concession £3/2/1; ⊗ reserve 9am-dusk, visitors centre 10am-5pm Apr-Oct, 10am-4pm Nov-Mar). Jarman's famous garden can still be seen on the road to the old lighthouse, although the new owner of the black cottage has a sign out asking you to respect their privacy, so please do.

INFORMATION

Hythe Visitors Centre (Red Lion Sq; ⊗ 9am-5pm Mon-Sat) Can book accommodation and offer information on Dungeness; open to personal callers only.

Romney Marsh Countryside Project (☎ 367974; www .rmcp.co.uk) This project has a useful website and organises all sorts of interesting guided walks across the marsh.

Rye Hire (☎ 223033; Cyprus Pl; bicycles per day £12) There is a cycle path to Lydd, followed by a road down to Dungeness.

Rye tourist office (☎ 226696; www.visitrye.co.uk; Strand Quay; ⊗ 10am-5pm Apr-Oct, 10am-4pm Mon-Sat Nov-Mar) Gives out a free guide to the town and offers audio tours (adult/concession/child £2.50/1.50/1). Can also help with basic information on Dungeness.

EATING

Fish Café (☎ 222226; www.thefishcafe.com; 17 Tower St, Rye; mains £7-12; ⊗ 10am-11pm) A new restaurant in a renovated antiques warehouse with simple and delicious, locally sourced seafood and fish dishes.

Mermaid Inn (☎ 223065; Mermaid St, rye) is typical of the olde-worlde half-timbered English pubs in Rye. There's also a casual restaurant. The similar Old Borough Arms (☎ 222128; The Strand, Rye) is a 300-year-old former smugglers' inn with a truly lovely guesthouse and an excellent café.

CANTERBURY

☎ 01227

Canterbury's greatest treasure is its majestic cathedral (☎ 762862; www.canterbury-cathedral.org; Sun St; adult/concession £5/4; ⊗ 9am-6pm Mon-Sat, 9am-2pm & 4.30-5.30pm Sun Apr-Oct, 9am-4.30pm Mon-Sat, 10am-2pm & 4.30-5.30pm Sun Nov-Mar, access may be restricted for services 9am-12.30pm Sun). Yet, despite the impressive 66m Bell Harry Tower lording it over the surrounding countryside, it's the assassination of archbishop Thomas Becket in 1170 inside that made the building famous, turning it into the site of one of Europe's most important medieval pilgrimages, as immortalised by Geoffrey Chaucer in *The Canterbury Tales*.

Becket clashed with Henry II over tax and then over the coronation of Henry's son. Hearing Henry mutter 'who will rid me of this turbulent priest?', four knights dispatched themselves to Canterbury, where they scalped the archbishop and amputated his limbs in the late afternoon of 29 December. The murder caused indignation throughout Europe, and Henry was forced to do penance at Becket's tomb, which was later said to be the site of many miracles.

The traditional approach to the cathedral, which dates from 1070, is along narrow Mercery Lane to Christ Church Gate. The main entrance is through the southwest porch, built in 1415 to commemorate the English victory at Agincourt. You'll pass a visitors centre before this, where you can pick up free leaflets, ask for information or book tours. One-hour guided tours (adult/concession £4/3) leave at 10.30am, noon and 2.30pm Monday to Saturday Easter to September, and noon and 2pm Monday to Saturday October to Easter. A 30-minute audioguide tour costs £2.95/1.95 per adult/child.

The perpendicular-style nave (1405) into which you enter is famous for its intricate ribbed vaulting, and there's more fabulous vaulting under the Bell Harry Tower. To your right (east) is the pulpitum screen that separates the nave from the quire.

Thomas Becket is believed to have been murdered in the northwest transept (before you reach the pulpitum); the modern Altar of the Sword's Point marks the spot. On the south side of the nave, you can descend into the Romanesque crypt, the main survivor of an earlier cathedral built by St Augustine in 597 to help convert the post-Roman English to Christianity.

Continuing eastwards through the pulpitum into the quire, you'll come to St Augustine's chair, the seat of the Archbishop of Canterbury. Behind this, in Trinity Chapel, a burning candle and a brass inscription mark the site of the former Tomb of St Thomas, which was destroyed on Henry VIII's orders during the Reformation. The chapel's stained glass is mostly 13th century, celebrating the life of St Thomas Becket.

Also in the chapel you'll find the magnificent Tomb of the Black Prince (Edward, Prince of Wales, 1330–76), with its famous effigy that includes the prince's shield, gauntlets and sword. The Corona once contained the slightly macabre relic of the part of Thomas' skull that was sliced off during his murder.

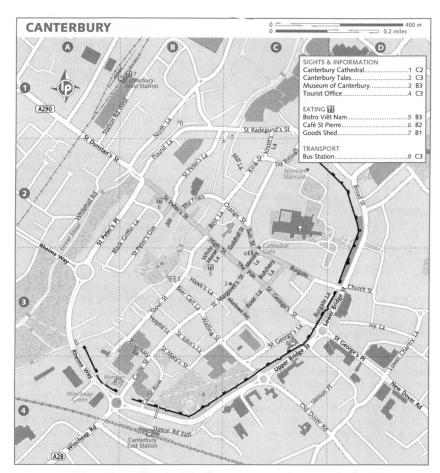

CANTERBURY

SIGHTS & INFORMATION	
Canterbury Cathedral.............................1	C2
Canterbury Tales...................................2	C3
Museum of Canterbury.........................3	B3
Tourist Office...4	C3
EATING 🍴	
Bistro Việt Nam....................................5	B3
Café St Pierre.......................................6	B2
Goods Shed..7	B1
TRANSPORT	
Bus Station...8	C3

Outside, walk around the eastern end of the cathedral and turn right into Green Court. In the northwestern corner (far left) is the much celebrated Norman Staircase (1151).

Canterbury's other attractions are very much epilogues to the main act.

The Museum of Canterbury (☎ 452747; www.canterbury-museums.co.uk; Stour St; adult/child/£3.30/2.20; ⏰ 10.30am-5pm Mon-Sat year-round, plus 1.30-5pm Sun Jun-Sep) has been given a thorough revamp, and is particularly aimed at children and families. New hands-on exhibits include a medieval discovery gallery (where you can look at medieval poo under the microscope) and a 'whodunnit' on the mysterious death of playwright Christopher Marlowe (originally a Canterbury lad). Children's cartoon characters Rupert Bear, Bagpuss and the Clangers also appear.

If you're really keen to acquaint or reacquaint yourself with Chaucer's famous stories, head to the Canterbury Tales (☎ 454888, 479227; www.canterburytales.org.uk; St Margaret's St; adult/child £7.25/5.25; ⏰ 9.30am-5.30pm Jul & Aug, 10am-5pm Mar-Jun, Sep & Oct, 10am-4.30pm Nov-Feb), where, armed with a storytelling audioguide, you pass puppets recreating various scenes. It might be better to just buy the book, though, to read on the train back to London.

INFORMATION

Tourist office (☎ 766567, 767744; www.canterbury.co.uk; 34 St Margaret's St; ⏰ 9.30am-5.30pm Mon-Sat, 10am-4pm Sun Apr-Oct, 9.30am-5pm Mon-Sat, 10am-4pm Sun Nov & Dec, 9.30am-5pm Mon-Sat Jan-Mar)

TRANSPORT: CANTERBURY

Distance from London 56 miles (90km)

Direction Southeast

Travel time One hour 50 minutes by bus, 1¾ hours by train

Bus National Express (☎ 0870 580 8080; www .nationalexpress.com) has 16 daily shuttle buses (day return £11.40).

Train Canterbury East train station is accessible from London's Victoria station, and Canterbury West from Charing Cross and Waterloo stations. Trains (☎ 0845 748 4950; www.nationalrail.co.uk) leave regularly (up to every 10 minutes); same day return is £18.70.

EATING

Goods Shed (☎ 459153; Station Rd West; mains £8-16; ☺ lunch & dinner Tue-Sat, lunch Sun) A fantastic place overlooking a farmers market, Good Shed is, unsurprisingly, in a converted railway shed, with high ceilings, huge windows and exposed brick. The changing French country menu uses fresh produce inventively.

Bistro Viêt Nam (☎ 760022; Old Linen Store, White Horse Lane; mains £5-11) The modern Southeast Asian menu here includes a range of Vietnamese tapas.

Café St Pierre (☎ 456791; 40 St Peter's St; pastries £2-3.50) The perfect place for breakfast or an after-noon break, with delicious pastries, pavement seats and a shady back garden.

WINDSOR & BRAY

☎ 01753

British monarchs have inhabited Windsor Castle (☎ 831118, 020-7766 7304; www.windsor.gov.uk; adult/5-16yr/senior/family £14.20/8/12.70/36.50, when State Apart-ments are closed £7.50/4.50/6.50/19.50; ☺ public areas 9.45am-5.15pm & last entry 4pm Mar-Oct, 9.45am-4.15pm & last entry 3pm Nov-Feb) for more than 900 years, but the Queen's weekend home hit the spotlight in 2005 when Prince Charles and Camilla Parker-Bowles were married in a civil cere-mony (shock, horror!) in Windsor's Guildhall in 2005 (a ceremony his mother, the Queen, did not attend).

Starting out as a wooden castle erected in 1070 by William the Conqueror, and rebuilt in stone in 1165, this is one of the world's greatest surviving medieval castles, and its longevity and easy accessibility from London guarantee

its popularity (indeed, it crawls with tourists all year round). However, it's not the only attrac-tion in the area. Across the River Thames lies Eton College, while the gastronomic hotspot of Bray is a short bus ride away.

The State Apartments – open to the public at certain times – reverberate with history. Any damage sustained during a fire in 1992 has long been erased by a £37 million restoration, completed in 1998.

After the Waterloo Chamber, created to com-memorate the Battle of Waterloo and still used for formal meals, and the Garter Throne Room, you move to the King's Rooms and Queen's Rooms. These are lessons in how the other half lives, with opulent furniture, tapestries and paintings by Canaletto, Dürer, Gainsborough, Van Dyck, Hogarth, Holbein, Rembrandt and Rubens.

Queues form in front of the impossibly intricate Queen Mary's Dolls' House, the work of architect Sir Edwin Lutyens. Built in 1923 on a 1:12 scale, it took 1500 craftsmen three years to finish and it's complete in every detail, right down to electric lights and flushing toilets.

One of Britain's finest examples of early English architecture, the castle's St George's Chapel (begun in 1475, but not completed until 1528) has a superb nave in perpendicular style, with gorgeous fan vaulting arching out from the pil-lars. The chapel contains royal tombs, including those of George V and Queen Mary, George VI, Edward IV and the Queen Mother.

Have a look at the central columns in Windsor's Guildhall (☎ 743900; High St; admission free; ☺ 10am-2pm Mon, except bank holidays) beside Castle Hill: the columns don't actually touch the ceil-ing. The council of the day, in 1686, insisted upon them, but Sir Christopher Wren was convinced they weren't necessary and left a few centimetres of clear space to prove his point.

Cross the River Thames by the pedestrian Windsor Bridge to reach Eton College (☎ 671177; www.etoncollege.com; Baldwins Shore; adult/child £4/3.25; ☺ 2-4.30pm term time, 10.30am-4.30pm Easter & summer holidays). This famous public (ie private) school has educated no fewer than 18 prime min-isters, and several buildings date from the mid-15th century. One-hour tours (£5/4.20 adult/child) are held at 2.15pm and 3.15pm.

The 1920-hectare Windsor Great Park (☎ 860222; admission free; ☺ 8am-dusk), where in 1999 Eliza-beth II's husband, Prince Philip, had an avenue of ancient trees beheaded because they got in the way of his horse and buggy, extends from behind the castle almost as far as Ascot.

The nearby village of Bray is home to some excellent restaurants (see opposite).

TRANSPORT: WINDSOR & BRAY

Distance from London 23 miles (37km)

Direction West

Travel time One hour by bus, 55 minutes by train

Bus Green line buses depart Victoria Central station to Windsor between eight and 12 times per day (day return £10); bus 6 operated by Courtney Coaches (☎ 01344-482200) leaves for Bray outside Barclays Bank on Windsor High St (return £4, 35 minutes, hourly 7am to 6pm).

Train Trains (☎ 0845 748 4950; www.nationalrail.co.uk) from Waterloo station go to Windsor Riverside station every 30 minutes, or hourly on Sunday (£8 day return). Trains from Paddington go via Slough to Eton and Central station (£8 day return). Alternatively, to go straight to Bray, catch a Maidenhead train (£8.20 day return) from Paddington station and take a taxi for the last five minutes of the journey.

INFORMATION

French Brothers (☎ 851900; www.boat-trips.co.uk; Clewer Court Rd; adult/child/concession/family £4.80/2.40/4.50/12) Runs a range of cruises, including 35-minute boat trips from Windsor to Boveney Lock (hourly 11am to 4pm mid-February to mid-March and Saturday and Sunday November to mid-December, half-hourly 10am to 5pm mid-March to October).

Tourist office (☎ 743900; www.windsor.gov.uk; 24 High St; ⏰ 10am-5pm Mon-Sat, 10am-4.30pm Sun Apr-Jun, Sep & Oct, 9.30am-6pm Jul & Aug, 10am-4pm Nov-Mar)

EATING

In Windsor, Peascod St and its extension, St Leonard's Rd, are full of restaurants, although most are pretty touristy. Bray is where to head for a once-in-a-lifetime gastronomic blow-out.

Fat Duck (☎ 01628-580333; www.fatduck.co.uk; 1 High St, Bray; 3 courses £80, tasting menu £115; ⏰ lunch Tue-Sun, dinner Tue-Sat) Fat Duck is the baby of self-taught chef, Heston Blumenthal, and it was named second-best restaurant in the world in 2007 in two consecutive years, so eating here is an experience to be cherished (once you get a reservation). Blumenthal's fascination with the science of taste means menus include incredible (and sometimes insane) combinations, experimenting with nitrogen (in nitro-green tea and lime mousse) and bizarre taste combinations such as sardine on toast sorbet, oysters and passionfruit, salmon poached with liquorice and smoked bacon and egg ice cream. It's all delicious and mind-boggling, and the atmosphere is refreshingly relaxed. You will need to book up to two months ahead.

Waterside Inn (☎ 01628-620691; www.waterside-inn.co.uk; Ferry Rd, Bray; mains £21-39; ⏰ Wed-Sun, plus dinner Tue in summer) Also voted among the world's top 50 restaurants, this Michel Roux establishment serves French haute cuisine in a rustic riverside environment.

Riverside Brasserie (☎ 01628-780553; Bray Marina, Monkey Island Lane; mains £13.25-15.95; ⏰ Tue-Sun) This is Blumenthal's pitch to the less adventurous diner, with a more conventionally British menu. Tuck into pork belly, its most famous dish, while overlooking the river.

KENT CASTLES

Castle buffs can enjoy a fabulous day in each of the three Kentish castles and stately homes. Perhaps the world's most romantic, Leeds Castle (☎ 01622-765400, 0870 600 8880; www.leeds-castle.com; Maidstone, Kent; castle & gardens adult/child/concession £13.50/8/11; ⏰ 10am-7pm & last entry 5pm Mar-Oct, 10am-5pm & last entry 3.30pm Nov-Feb) is spectacularly located on two small islands in the middle of a lake, provoking oohs and aahs from visitors. Surrounded by rolling wooded hills, it was colloquially known as 'Ladies Castle', being home to many queens over the centuries, including Catherine de Valois, Catherine of Aragon and even Elizabeth I, who was imprisoned here before she took the throne. The grounds are particularly striking, from the glorious moat to the gardens and a maze with an underground grotto. There is also an aviary, with more than 100 endangered bird species; a museum of dog collars; and interesting, avian-inspired wallpaper and other decorative features in the castle interior.

The gardens at the small but sweet Hever Castle (☎ 01732-865224; www.hevercastle.co.uk; Hever, Kent; castle & gardens adult/child £9.80/5.30, gardens only £7.80/5; ⏰ gardens 11am-6pm Mar-Oct, 11am-4pm Nov, castle opens 1hr later), the childhood home of Henry VIII's second wife, Anne Boleyn, are equally spectacular. They include roses, bluebells, rhododendrons, topiary, rockeries, Italian sculptures, fountains, lakes and a yew maze, and also combine several of the last two in a water maze, which is extremely popular with children. The castle is, however, a little tricky to get to (see transport details, below).

Sissinghurst Castle Garden (☎ 01580-7128500; www .nationaltrust.org.uk/sissinghurst; Sissinghurst, Cranbrook, Kent; adult/concession/family £7.80/3.50/18; ☻ 11am-6.30pm & last entry 5.30pm Mon, Tue & Fri, 10am-6.30pm & last entry 5.30pm Sat & Sun mid-Mar–Nov) is legendary among writers and the green-fingered – it's one of the most famous 20th-century gardens in the world.

The creation of poet Vita Sackville-West and her husband Harold Nicolson, it broke new ground by grouping similarly coloured plants to create 10 garden 'rooms' with distinct personalities. The famous White Garden, with its many shades of white, grey and green, was a particular source of inspiration for Sackville-West as she gazed upon it in moonlight from her study, which is also open to visitors.

INFORMATION

A useful source of information is the Visit Kent website (www.visitkent.co.uk).

TRANSPORT: KENT CASTLES

Hever Castle

Distance from London 33 miles (53km)

Direction Southeast

Travel time 40 minutes by car, 40 minutes (Monday to Friday) to 1½ hours (Saturday and Sunday) by train plus 10 minutes by taxi

Car Take the M25, turning off at Junction 5 or 6 and following the signs south to Edenbridge and the castle.

Train Catch a train from London Bridge to Edenbridge Town (£10 day return), then take a taxi (3 miles). Alternatively, the castle is a 1-mile walk from Hever station. On Sunday services terminate one stop down the line at East Grinstead; a taxi will cost £10.

Leeds Castle

Distance from London 44 miles (70km)

Direction Southeast

Travel time 1½ hours by car, 1½ hours by bus, one hour 10 minutes by train

Bus Both National Express (☎ 0870 580 8080; www.nationalexpress.com; adult/child combined ticket £18/13) and Green Line (☎ 0870 608 7261; www.greenline.co.uk; adult/child combined ticket £15/9) offer combined coach/admission tickets to Leeds Castle, with services leaving Victoria Central station in the morning and returning to Victoria around 5pm or 6pm, Monday to Friday.

Car Take the M20 southeast of London, turning off at Junction 8 and following the signs to the nearby castle.

Train Trains (☎ 0845 748 4950; www.nationalrail.co.uk) from London's Victoria station go to Bearsted station (day return £14), from where you can catch the connecting coach to Leeds Castle.

Sissinghurst Castle Garden

Distance from London 46 miles (74km)

Direction Southeast

Travel time 1½ hours by car, one hour by train plus 15 minutes by castle bus

Bus From Staplehurst train station, there's a special link to Sissinghurst Castle Garden on Tuesday and Sunday May to mid-September, leaving just after noon. Phone ☎ 01580-710700 for exact times.

Car Exit the M20 at Junction 5 or 6 and follow the A229 to the A262.

Train Head from Charing Cross station to Staplehurst station (day return £13) and catch the special castle bus (see Bus above) or a taxi (5½ miles).

TRANSPORT

Flights, tours and rail tickets can be booked online at www.lonelyplanet.com/travel _services.

AIR

Check www.cheapflights.co.uk, www.ebook ers.com, www.lastminute.com and www .opodo.co.uk for good deals on tickets.

Airlines

London is served by nearly every international airline, most with offices in the city.

Aer Lingus (☎ 0870 876 5000; www.aerlingus.com)

Aeroflot (☎ 7355 2233; www.aeroflot.co.uk)

Air Canada (☎ 0871 220 1111; www.aircanada.com)

Air France (☎ 0870 142 4343; www.airfrance.com/uk)

Air New Zealand (☎ 0800 028 4149; www.airnewzea land.co.uk)

Alitalia (☎ 0870 544 8259; www.alitalia.com)

American Airlines (☎ 0845 778 9789; www.aa.com)

BMI (☎ 0870 607 0555; www.flybmi.com)

British Airways (☎ 0870 850 9850; www.ba.com)

Brussels Airlines (☎ 0905 609 5609; www.brusselsair lines.com)

Cathay Pacific (☎ 8834 8888; www.cathaypacific.com)

Continental Airlines (☎ 0845 607 6760; www.conti nental.com)

Delta Air Lines (☎ 0845 600 0950; www.delta.com)

easyJet (☎ 0905 560 7777, per min £1; www.easyjet .com)

El Al (☎ 7121 1400; www.elal.com)

Emirates (☎ 0870 243 2222; www.emirates.com/uk)

Fly Be (British European; ☎ 0871 522 6100; www.flybe .com)

Iberia (☎ 0870 609 0500; www.iberia.com)

Icelandair (☎ 0845 758 1111; www.icelandair.net)

KLM (☎ 0870 243 0541; www.klm.com)

Lufthansa (☎ 0845 773 7747; www.lufthansa.co.uk)

Olympic Airways (☎ 0870 606 0460; www.olympicair ways.com)

Qantas Airlines (☎ 0845 774 7767; www.qantas.co.uk)

Ryanair (☎ 0871 246 0000; www.ryanair.com)

Scandinavian Airlines (SAS; ☎ 0870 6072 7727; www .scandinavian.net)

Singapore Airlines (☎ 0844 800 2380; www.singapore air.com)

South African Airways (☎ 0870 747 1111; www.flysaa .com)

TAP Air Portugal (☎ 0845 601 0932; www.tap-airpor tugal.co.uk)

Thai Airways International (☎ 7491 7953, 0870 606 0911; www.thaiair.com)

Turkish Airlines (☎ 7766 9333; www.thy.com)

United Airlines (☎ 0845 844 4777; www.ual.com)

Virgin Atlantic (☎ 0870 574 7747; www.virgin-atlantic .com)

Airports

London is served by five major airports: Heathrow (the largest), Gatwick, Stansted, London City and Luton.

HEATHROW AIRPORT

Fifteen miles west of central London, Heathrow (LHR; off Map p64; ☎ 0870 000 0123, www.heathrowairport .com) is the world's busiest international airport. It has four terminals, with a fifth under construction and due for completion in 2011. For information call the relevant terminal during the times listed below:

Terminal 1 (☎ 8745 5301; ⏰ 6am-11pm)

Terminal 2 (☎ 8745 4599; ⏰ 5am-11pm)

Terminal 3 (☎ 8759 3344; ⏰ 5am-10.30pm)

Terminal 4 (☎ 8745 7460; ⏰ 5am-11pm)

Each terminal has competitive currency-exchange facilities, information counters and accommodation desks. Two Piccadilly line tube stations serve the airport: one for Terminals 1, 2 and 3, the other for Terminal 4. There are also left-luggage facilities. The charge is £5.50 per item for 24 hours, up to a maximum of 90 days. All branches can forward baggage.

There are some 15 international hotels at or near Heathrow, should you be arriving or leaving particularly early or late. To reach them from Heathrow Terminals 1, 2 or 3,

CLIMATE CHANGE & TRAVEL

Climate change is a serious threat to the ecosystems that humans rely upon, and air travel is the fastest-growing contributor to the problem. Lonely Planet regards travel, overall, as a global benefit, but believes we all have a responsibility to limit our personal impact on global warming.

Flying & Climate Change

Pretty much every form of motor transport generates CO_2 (the main cause of human-induced climate change) but planes are far and away the worst offenders, not just because of the sheer distances they allow us to travel, but because they release greenhouse gases high into the atmosphere. The statistics are frightening: two people taking a return flight between Europe and the US will contribute as much to climate change as an average household's gas and electricity consumption over a whole year.

Carbon Offset Schemes

Climatecare.org and other websites use 'carbon calculators' that allow travellers to offset the greenhouse gases they are responsible for with contributions to energy-saving projects and other climate-friendly initiatives in the developing world – including projects in India, Honduras, Kazakhstan and Uganda.

Lonely Planet, together with Rough Guides and other concerned partners in the travel industry, supports the carbon offset scheme run by climatecare.org. Lonely Planet offsets all of its staff and author travel.

For more information check out our website: www.lonelyplanet.com.

take the Heathrow Hotel Hoppa bus, which departs every 15 minutes 5.30am to 9pm, then every 30 minutes until 11.30pm (£4). The bus does not serve Terminal 4.

Here are options for getting to/from Heathrow Airport:

Black cabs A metered trip to/from central London (Oxford St) will cost around £55.

Heathrow Connect (☎ 0845 678 6975; www.heathrow connect.com) Also travelling between Heathrow and Paddington station, this modern passenger service (one way/return £6.90/12.90, 28 minutes, every 30 minutes) makes several stops en route, in places such as Ealing and Southall. The first trains leave Heathrow at about 5.30am (6.15am Sunday) and the last service is around midnight. From Paddington, services leave between approximately 4.45am (6.15am Sunday) and 11pm.

Heathrow Express (☎ 0845 600 1515; www.heathrow express.com) This ultramodern train (one way/return £15.50/29, £1 off if booking online; 15 minutes, every 15 minutes) whisks passengers from Heathrow Central station (serving Terminals 1, 2 and 3) and Terminal 4 station to Paddington station. The Heathrow Central train runs approximately from 5.10am (in both directions) to between 11.30pm (from Paddington) and midnight (from the airport). To Terminal 4 takes an extra eight minutes.

National Express (☎ 0870 580 8080; www.national express.com) Buses 032, 035, 403, 412 and 501 (one way/return from £10/15, tickets valid three months; 45 minutes to 70 minutes, every 30 minutes to one hour) link Heathrow with Victoria coach station (☎ 7730 3466; 164 Buckingham Palace Rd SW1) about 50 times per day. The first bus leaves the Heathrow Central Bus station (at

Terminals 1, 2 and 3) at 5.35am with the last departure at 9.35pm. The first bus leaves Victoria at 7.15am, the last at 11.30pm.

Underground (☎ 7222 1234; www.tube.tfl.gov.uk) The tube (one way adult/child £4/2, from central London one hour, every five to nine minutes) is the cheapest way of getting to Heathrow. It runs from approximately 5am (5.50am Sunday) to 11.45pm (10.50pm Sunday). You can buy tickets from machines in the baggage reclaim areas of the Heathrow terminals or in the station.

GATWICK AIRPORT

Located some 30 miles south of central London, Gatwick (LGW; off Map p64; ☎ 0870 000 2468; www .gatwickairport.com) is smaller and better organised than Heathrow. The North and South Terminals are linked by an efficient monorail service, with the journey time about two minutes. For information call the relevant terminal during the times listed below:

North Terminal (☎ 01293-502013; ☾ 5am-9pm)

South Terminal (☎ 01293-502014; ☾ 24hr)

Gatwick also has left-luggage facilities. The charge is £5.50 per item for 24 hours or part thereof, up to a maximum of 90 days.

Here are options for getting to/from Gatwick Airport:

Black cabs A metered trip to/from central London costs about £85.

Gatwick Express (☎ 0845 850 1530; www.gatwick express.com) Trains (one way/return £14.90/26.80, 30 minutes, every 15 minutes) link the station near the South Terminal with Victoria station. From the airport, there are regular services between 5.50am and 12.35am. From Victoria, they leave between 5am and 11.45pm. In both directions, there are four less-regular overnight services.

National Express (☎ 0870 580 8080; www.nationalexpress.com) Bus 025 (one way/return £6.60/12.20, tickets valid three months; 65 minutes to 85 minutes) runs from Brighton to Victoria coach station via Gatwick nearly 20 times per day. Services leave Gatwick approximately hourly between 5.15am and 10.15pm and operate from Victoria between 7am and 11.30pm, with one very early service at 3.30am).

Southern Trains (☎ national rail enquiries 0845 748 4950; www.southernrailway.com) This service (one way/return £8.90/17.80, 45 minutes, every 15 to 30 minutes, every hour from midnight to 4am) runs from Victoria station to both terminals.

Thameslink service (☎ national rail enquiries 0845 748 4950; www.thameslink.co.uk) This service (one way/return £8.90/17, 70 minutes) runs through King's Cross, Farringdon and London Bridge train stations.

STANSTED AIRPORT

London's third-busiest international gateway, Stansted (STN; off Map p64; ☎ 0870 000 0303; www.stanstedairport.com) is 35 miles northeast of central London, heading towards Cambridge. It's become Europe's fastest-growing airport thanks to no-frills carriers Ryanair and easyJet, which use it as a hub. With many services to central and eastern Europe, it was also boosted by the expansion of the EU in 2004.

Here are options for getting to/from Stansted Airport:

Black cabs A metered trip to/from central London costs £105.

National Express (☎ 0870 580 8080; www.nationalexpress.com) Coaches run around the clock, offering some 120 services per day. The A6 runs to Victoria coach station (one way/return £10/17, one hour 45 minutes, every 15 to 20 minutes) via North London (£8/15, one hour). The A9 runs to Stratford (£8/15, 45 minutes, every 30 minutes), from where you can catch a Jubilee line tube (20 minutes) into central London. The A7 runs via Stratford to Victoria between approximately midnight and 5am.

Stansted Express (☎ 0845 850 0150; www.standstedexpress.com) This service (one way/return £15/25, 45 minutes, every 15 to 30 minutes) links the airport and Liverpool St station. From the airport the first train leaves at 5.30am (6am Saturday and Sunday), the last just before midnight. Trains depart Liverpool St station from 4.30am (5am Saturday and Sunday) to 11.30pm. If you need to connect with the tube, change at Tot-

tenham Hale for the Victoria line or stay on to Liverpool St station for the Central line. Some early services do not stop at Tottenham Hale. Stansted Express also operates a night coach service (one way/return £15/25, one hour, every 30 minutes) between the last train and the next morning's first service. Services depart Liverpool St between 2.30am and 4.30am. From the airport, they leave between midnight and 4am. They do not stop at Tottenham Hale.

LONDON CITY AIRPORT

Its proximity to central London, 6 miles to its west, and to the commercial district of the Docklands, means London City Airport (LCY; Map p64; ☎ 7646 0000; www.londoncityairport.com) is predominantly a business airport, although it does also serve holiday travellers with its 22 Continental European and eight national destinations.

Here are options for getting to/from London City Airport:

Black cabs A metered trip to/from central London costs about £25.

Docklands Light Railway (DLR; ☎ 7363 9700; www.tfl.gov.uk/dlr) The Docklands Light Railway stops at London City Airport (£4). The journey to Bank takes 20 minutes, and trains go every 10 minutes from 5.30am to 12.30am Monday to Saturday, and 7am to 11.30pm Sunday.

LUTON AIRPORT

A smallish airport some 35 miles north of London, Luton (LTN; off Map p64; ☎ 01582-405100; www.london-luton.co.uk) caters mainly for cheap charter flights, though the discount airline easyJet operates scheduled services from here.

Here are options for getting to/from Luton Airport:

Black cabs A metered trip to/from central London costs around £100.

Green Line bus 757 (Map pp138–9; ☎ 0870 608 7261; www.greenline.co.uk) Buses to Luton (one way/return £10.50/15, one hour) run from Buckingham Palace Rd south of Victoria station, leaving approximately every half-hour from 9.30am to 8pm, with hourly services between 8pm and midnight and one or two staggered services before 9.30am.

Thameslink (☎ national rail enquiries 0845 748 4950; www.thameslink.co.uk) Trains (off-peak one way/return £11.10/20.60, 30 to 40 minutes, every six to 15 minutes 7am to 10pm) run from King's Cross and other central London stations to Luton Airport Parkway station, from where an airport shuttle bus will take you to the airport in eight minutes.

BICYCLE

Cycling along London's canals or along the South Bank is delightful, but heading through the heavy traffic and fumes of central streets is pretty grim. So not only should you always wear a helmet and have lights on the front and back of your bike if cycling after dusk, you might also want to join the many Londoners who also wear facemasks to filter out pollution.

The London Cycling Campaign (LCC; ☎ 7928 7220; www.lcc.org.uk) is working towards improving conditions throughout the city, campaigning to establish a comprehensive London cycle network. Also, City Hall and the mayor are very procycling and its popularity has sky-rocketed since the 7 July bombings in 2005. In general things have never been better for cyclists in the city with massive increases in the numbers of cycle lanes.

In conjunction with the LCC, Transport for London publishes a series of free London Cycle Guides. These can be ordered via www.lcc.org .uk or www.tfl.gov.uk/tfl/roadusers/cycling/ cycleroutes/default.asp, or by calling ☎ 7222 1234. Online maps of cycle routes are also available at www.londoncyclenetwork.org.

Bicycles on Public Transport

Bicycles can be taken only on the District, Circle, Hammersmith & City and Metropolitan tube lines outside the rush hour, ie 10am to 4pm and after 7pm Monday to Friday. Folding bikes can be taken on any line, however. Bicycles can also travel on the above-ground sections of some tube lines and the Silverlink line, but not on the DLR.

Restrictions on taking a bike on suburban and mainline trains vary from company to company so you need to check before setting out. For details call ☎ 0845 748 4950.

Hire

London Bicycle Tour Company (Map p126; ☎ 7928 6838; www.londonbicycle.com; 1a Gabriel's Wharf, 56 Upper Ground SE1; ✆ Blackfriars) Rentals cost £3 per hour or £18 for the first day, £9 for days two and three, £6 for days four and five, £48 for the first week and £10 for second week. It also offers three-hour bike tours of London (2pm Saturday and Sunday) for £14.95 including the bike. (Those with their own bikes get a discount of about 20%.) Routes are on its website. You will need to provide credit card details as a deposit and must show ID.

On Your Bike (Map p126; ☎ 7378 6669; www.onyour bike.net; 52-54 Tooley St SE1; ✆ London Bridge) Rentals cost £12.50 for the first day, £8 for subsequent days, £35 per week. Prices include hire of a helmet. A deposit of £150 (via credit card) is necessary and you will be required to show ID.

Pedicabs

Three-wheeled cycle rickshaws, seating two or three passengers, have been a regular, if much-cursed, part of the Soho scene since the late 1990s. They're less a mode of transport than a nice gimmick for tourists and other pleasure-trippers. Prices start at £3 for a quick trip across Soho.

BOAT

With the drive to make use of London's often overlooked 'liquid artery', companies running boats on the river have been sprouting up in recent years. Only the Thames Clippers (☎ 0870 781 5049; www.thamesclippers.com) really offers commuter services, however. Running from 6.20am to 8pm, the services (adult single/ return £4/8, child half-price, roughly every 20 to 40 minutes) give you access to lots of the river sights. Boats run from Savoy Pier at Embankment to Masthouse Tce in Docklands, passing Tower Bridge, Tate Modern, Shakespeare's Globe and Canary Wharf. For sightseeing tours, see p386.

BUS

London's iconic double-decker Routemaster was phased out a couple of years ago, only to be brought back (by popular demand) to serve the more scenic routes (bus routes 9 and 15). Even getting on the modern double-deckers and single-decker 'bendy' buses, you see more of the city than while underground on the tube. Just beware that the going can be slow, thanks to traffic jams and the nearly four million commuters that get on and off the buses every day.

Fares

Any single-journey adult bus ticket within London costs £2; children under 16 travel free, and so do under-18s in full-time education. It now costs 90p to travel on buses with an Oyster card. Travelcards (p389) are valid on all buses, including night buses.

TRAVEL PASSES & DISCOUNT FARES

A Saver ticket (£6) is a book of six bus tickets valid on all buses, including those in central

London and night buses. They are transferable but valid for one journey only.

If you plan to use only buses during your stay in London, you can buy a one-day bus pass valid throughout London for £3/1 (adult/child). Unlike Travelcards, these are valid before 9.30am. Weekly or monthly bus passes cost £11/4 (adult/child) or £42.30/15.40.

You should definitely get an Oyster card (see p390) even if you're here only for a weekend, because you'll be paying double without it.

Information

Maps are available from most transport travel information centres, via the Transport for London Order Line (☎ 7371 0247) or from www.tfl.gov .uk/buses. For general information on London buses call ☎ 7222 1234 (24 hours).

Night Buses

More than 60 night bus routes (which are pre-fixed with the letter 'N') run from midnight to 4.30am, when the tube shuts down and the daytime buses return to the barn. Oxford Circus, Tottenham Court Rd and Trafalgar Sq are the main hubs, but check bus-stop information boards to familiarise yourself with routes. Night buses can be infrequent and stop only on request, meaning you must signal clearly to the driver to stop.

Many buses are also '24-hour buses', which means that they are different from night buses because they are the same bus you'd take during the day, though their frequency thins out during the night. Check the bus timetable for frequency details.

Within the UK & to Europe

National Express (☎ 0870 580 8080; www.nationalexpress .com) and low-cost Megabus (☎ 0900 160 0900, per min 60p; www.megabus.com) are the main national operators. Megabus operates a no-frills airline style of seat pricing, where some tickets go for as little as £1. National Express has dropped its fares to compete. Smaller competitors on main UK routes include Green Line (☎ 0870 608 7261; www.greenline.co.uk).

Eurolines (☎ 0870 514 3219; www.eurolines.com; 52 Grosvenor Gardens SW1) has buses to Continental Europe, operated via National Express and leaving from Victoria coach station (Map pp138–9; ☎ 7730 3466; 164 Buckingham Palace Rd SW1).

CAR & MOTORCYCLE

To drive in London is to learn the true meaning of road rage: traffic jams are common, parking space is at a premium and the congestion charge (below) adds to the general expense, including the high price of petrol. Traffic wardens and wheel clampers operate with extreme efficiency and if your vehicle is clamped it will cost you at least £215 to have it released. If this happens call the number on the ticket; this varies across different London boroughs. If the car has been removed, ring the 24-hour Tracing Section (☎ 7747 4747). It will cost you at least £200 to get your vehicle back.

Driving
ROAD RULES

We don't recommend driving in London. However, if you insist, you should first obtain the *Highway Code,* which is available at Automobile association (AA) and Royal Automobile Club (RAC) outlets as well as some bookshops and tourist offices. A foreign driving licence is valid in Britain for up to 12 months from the time of your last entry into the country. If you bring a car from Europe make sure you're adequately insured. All drivers and passengers must wear seatbelts and motorcyclists must wear a helmet.

THE CONGESTION CHARGE

London was the world's first major city to introduce a congestion charge to reduce the flow of traffic into its centre from Monday to Friday. While the traffic entering the 'congestion zone' has fallen as a result, driving in London can still be very slow work.

The original congestion charge zone (Euston Rd, Pentonville Rd, Tower Bridge, Elephant & Castle, Vauxhall Bridge Rd, Park Lane and Marylebone Rd) has been extended to encompass Bayswater, Notting Hill, High St Kensington, north and South

Kensington, Knightsbridge, Chelsea, Belgravia and Pimlico.

As you enter the zone, you will see a large letter 'C' in a red circle. If you enter the zone between 7am and 6pm Monday to Friday (excluding public holidays), you must pay the £8 charge before 10pm the same day (or £10 between 10pm and midnight the same day) to avoid receiving a £100 fine. You can pay online, at newsagents, petrol stations or any shop displaying the 'C' sign, by telephone on ☎ 0845 900 1234 and even by text message once you've registered online. There is now a pay later scheme, too, whereby you can pay before midnight on the day of travel for no extra charge, or by midnight the following day for an extra charge of £10. For full details log on to www.cclondon.com.

Hire

Although driving in London is expensive and often slow, there is no shortage of rental agencies. Competition is fierce, with easycar.com having significantly undersold many of the other more traditional companies over the past few years, forcing down prices. Compare prices, models and agency locations at one of the following websites: www.easycar.com; www.hertz.com; www.avis.com. You should always book in advance as early as possible as cars are often in short supply, especially at weekends.

ORGANISED TOURS

Although they're not particularly cool, it is true that organised tours can provide a decent means of seeing the main sights while allowing you to return to certain areas for more in-depth exploration under your own steam. Similarly, for anyone with very limited time, it is (just about) possible to see the major landmarks of the British capital in one day. A huge variety of companies offer countless wacky options, and with the very good 'jump-on, jump-off' services that allow you to combine group tours with individual exploration, you shouldn't necessarily run a mile at the suggestion, although do proceed with caution.

Air

Adventure Balloons (☎ 01252-844222; www.adventureballoons.co.uk; Winchfield Park, Hartley Wintney, Hampshire) Weather permitting, there are flights every weekday morning shortly after dawn from May to August. London flyovers cost £175. The flight lasts around one hour, but allow four hours including take-off, landing and recovery.

Aeromega Helicopters (☎ 01708-688361; www.aeromega.com; ✈ Debden, then taxi to Stapleford Aerodrome, Essex) Thirty-minute flights over London two Sundays every month for £120 per person. Hire an entire four-seater helicopter for £420.

Cabair Helicopters (☎ 8953 4411; www.cabair.com; Elstree Aerodrome, Borehamwood, Hertfordshire) Offers the same service as Aeromega at £149 twice a month on Saturday or Sunday.

Boat

Travelcard holders (see p389) get one-third off all boating fares listed here.

Circular Cruises (☎ 7936 2033; www.crownriver.com; adult/5-15yr/student & senior/family £7/3.50/6/21; ☼ tours every 30-40min 11am-7pm Apr-Sep, 11am, 12.20pm, 1.40pm & 3pm Oct-Mar) Vessels travel east from Westminster Pier to St Katharine's Pier near the Tower of

---

LONDON ON FOOT

The best way to get around the city is by walking – Dickens famously got to know the city he wrote about so well simply by walking around its streets, getting lost and finding new and surprising things around every (well, almost every) corner. You can just get a map and go walking, or if you're feeling really adventurous, leave the map and dive into the maze of London's streets. If you prefer having your walk planned, go online to www.walkit.com, where the quickest route from A to B is mapped out for you, and you're even given the walk's duration and how many calories you'll burn getting there! If you prefer guided walks, go for London Walks (www.walks.com) and be taken around Shakespeare's or Dickens' routes; one of the company's most popular walks is the Jack the Ripper walk that takes you through the dark streets of East London, giving you the gory details of the murders. It runs more than 100 walks and has something on every day. Also check out Time Out London magazine's weekly Walks listings for new and often amusing strolls through town. Another fantastic way to see the Big Smoke is through Photo Walks London (www.photowalkslondon.blogspot.com), founded by an art project coordinator and a landscape photographer, who take you around the city's main sights and icons – your camera in hand – telling you about history and local characters, while pointing out the most creative angle from which to photograph whatever you're looking at, so you walk away with some excellent cityscape photography.

London, calling at London Bridge and Embankment Piers, plus, on weekends in summer, at Festival and Bankside Piers. Fares are cheaper between just two stages (eg Westminster to/from London Bridge costs £6/3/5/17).

London Waterbus Company (☎ information 7482 2660, bookings 7482 2550; www.londonwaterbus.com; 2 Middle Yard, Camden Lock NW1; adult/child one way £6/4.30, return £8.40/5.40; ☺ hourly 10am-5pm Apr-Oct, every 2hr 10am-3pm or 4pm Sat & Sun Nov-Mar; ✆ Camden Town) Runs 90-minute trips on Regent's Canal in an enclosed barge between Camden Lock and Little Venice, passing through Regent's Park and London Zoo.

RIB London Voyages (☎ 7928 2350; www.london ribvoyages.com; London Eye, Waterloo Millennium Pier, Westminster Bridge Rd SE1; adult/child £26/16; ☺ tours hourly 11.15am-4.15pm year-round) Feel like James Bond on this high-speed inflatable boat that pelts down the Thames at 30 to 35 knots.

Tate-to-Tate Boat (www.tate.org.uk; adult/5-16yr/ student/family £4.30/2.15/2.85/10.80; ☺ tours every 40min 10am-5.30pm) The boat not only visits both Tate museums, but stops at the London Eye, plus Blackfriars and Savoy Piers during the week. Discounts are available for Travelcard holders, seniors, students and children.

Thames River Services (☎ 7930 4097; www.west minsterpier.co.uk; adult/child/senior/family one way £7.20/3.60/6/21, return £9.40/4.70/8/26; ☺ tours every 30min 10am-4pm or 5pm Apr-Oct) These cruise boats leave Westminster Pier for Greenwich, stopping at the Tower of London. Every second service continues on from Greenwich to the Thames Barrier. The last boats return from Greenwich about 5pm (6pm in summer).

Westminster Passenger Services Association (☎ 7930 2062; www.wpsa.co.uk; Kew adult/child/ senior/family one way £10.50/5.25/7/26.25, return £16.50/8.25/11/41.25, Hampton Court adult/child/ senior/family one way £13.50/6.75/9/33.75, return £19.50/9.75/13/48.75; ☺ 4 tours daily 10.30am-2pm Apr-Oct) These boats go upriver from Westminster Pier to the Royal Botanic Gardens at Kew (1½ hours) and on to Hampton Court Palace (another 1½ hours). It's possible to get off the boats at Richmond in July and August. While an enjoyable excursion, there's less to see en route compared with the trip east.

Bus

The following companies offer commentary and the chance to get off at each sight and rejoin the tour on a later bus. Tickets are valid for 24 hours.

Big Bus Tours (☎ 7233 9533; www.bigbus.co.uk; adult/child £20/10)

London Pride (☎ 0170 863 1122; www.londonpride .co.uk; adult/child/family £19/12/72)

Specialist

Black Taxi Tours of London (☎ 7935 9363; www.black taxitours.co.uk; 2hr for up to 5 passengers £90) Hire your own black cab with a trained tour guide at the wheel (although you are likely to hear equally amusing tales from any other cabbie in the city).

London Duck Tours (☎ 7928 3132; www.londonduck tours.co.uk; adult/child/concession/family £18/12/14/55; ✆ Westminster) Amphibious craft based on D-Day landing vehicles depart from outside County Hall and cruise the streets of central London before making a dramatic descent into the Thames at Vauxhall.

London Open House (☎ 7267 7644; www.londonopen house.org; 39-51 Highgate Rd NW5) Besides the annual weekend event, sometime in September, when more than 500 buildings are open to the public, there are architectural and school-group tours.

Walking

Association of Professional Tourist Guides (APTG; ☎ 7403 2962; www.aptg.org.uk) Hire a prestigious blue-badge guide: these guides have studied for two years and passed written exams to do their job.

London Walks (☎ 7624 3978; www.walks.com; adult/ concession £5.50/4.50) A huge array of walks, including Jack the Ripper tours at 7.30pm daily and 3pm Saturday, and Sherlock Holmes Tours at 1.30pm Tuesday and 2.30pm Thursday.

Mystery Tours (☎ 0795 738 8280; www.tourguides.org .uk; adult/concession £6/5) Tour Jack the Ripper's old haunts at 7pm on Wednesday, Friday and Sunday, and visit Haunted London at 7pm on Tuesday. Meet outside Aldgate tube station.

TAXI
Black Cabs

The black London taxicab (www.london blackcabs.co.uk) is as much a feature of the cityscape as the red bus. Licensed black-cab drivers have 'the knowledge' – ie they undergo rigorous training and exams, and are supposed to know every central London street.

Cabs are available for hire when the yellow sign above the windscreen is lit; just stick your arm out to signal one. Fares are metered, with a minimum charge of £2.20 (covering the first 336m during a weekday), rising by increments of 20p for each subsequent 168m. Fares are more expensive in the evenings and overnight. You can tip taxi drivers up to 10% but most people round up to the nearest pound.

Do not expect to hail a taxi in popular nightlife areas of London such as Soho late at night (and especially after pub closing time at 11pm). If you do find yourself in any of those areas, signal all taxis – even those with their lights off – and try to look sober. Many drivers are very choosy about their fares at this time of night. To order a cab by phone try Computer Cabs (☎ 7908 0207); it charges a £2 booking fee, plus what it costs to get to you, as well as your actual fare. You can only prebook using a credit card; if you're paying cash you must ring when you need the cab. (For cash prebookings, see Minicabs, below.)

Zingo Taxi (☎ 0870 070 0700) uses GPS to connect your mobile phone to that of the nearest free black-cab driver – after which you can explain to the cabbie exactly where you are. This service costs only £1.60, which is included in the final price of the taxi. It's a good idea late at night, when it's notoriously difficult to find a free cab. The service has only 1000 vehicles and it will find you a (more expensive) Computer Cab if none of these are available.

Minicabs

Minicabs, some of which are now licensed, are cheaper freelance competitors of black cabs. However, minicab drivers are often untrained and less sure of the way than black-cab drivers and may not be properly insured. Minicabs cannot legally be hailed on the street; they must be hired by phone or directly from one of the minicab offices (every High Street has at least one). Minicab drivers seeking fares might approach you; it's best to decline their offer, as there have been allegations of rape made against some unlicensed cab drivers.

The cabs don't have meters, so it's essential to fix a price before you start (it's therefore not usual to tip minicab drivers). Most drivers start higher than the fare they're prepared to accept.

Ask a local for the name of a reputable minicab company, or phone a large 24-hour operator (☎ 7387 8888, 7272 2222, 7272 3322, 8888 4444). Women travelling alone at night can choose Ladycabs (☎ 7272 3300), which has women drivers. Liberty Cars (☎ 7734 1313) caters for the gay and lesbian market and is used widely by straight Londoners too, although gay couples are extremely unlikely to experience open homophobia from drivers of black cabs.

TRAIN
Docklands Light Railway

Looking a bit like an urban ski train, the driverless Docklands Light Railway (DLR; ☎ 7363 9700; www.tfl.gov.uk/dlr) is basically an adjunct to the Underground. It links the City at Bank and Tower Hill with Beckton and Stratford to the east and northeast and the Docklands (as far as Island Gardens at the southern end of the Isle of Dogs), Greenwich and Lewisham to the south. The DLR runs from 5.30am to 12.30am Monday to Saturday and from 7am to 11.30pm Sunday. Fares are the same as those on the tube, although there are some group discounts and a Rail & River Rover ticket unique to the DLR.

For news of how services are running, call ☎ 7222 1234.

Suburban Trains

Several rail companies operate passenger trains in London, including the Silverlink (☎ 0845 601 4867; www.silverlink-trains.com) line and the crowded Thameslink (☎ 0845 748 4950; www.thameslink.co.uk). Silverlink links Richmond in the southwest with North Woolwich in the southeast via Kew, West Hampstead, Camden Rd, Highbury & Islington and Stratford stations. Thameslink goes from Elephant & Castle and London Bridge in the south through the City to King's Cross and as far north as Luton. Most lines connect with the Underground system, and Travelcards can be used on them. Note, however, that Oyster prepay cannot yet be used at all train stations.

If you're staying long term in Southeast London, where suburban trains are usually much more useful than the tube, it's worth buying a one-year Network Railcard. This card offers one-third off most rail fares in southeast England and on one-day Travelcards for all six zones. Travel is permitted only after 10am Monday to Friday and at any time on Saturday and Sunday. The card costs £20 and is available at most stations.

Most of the large mainline London stations have left-luggage facilities available, although due to the perceived terrorist threat, baggage lockers no longer exist. Excess Baggage (☎ 0800 783 1085; www.excessbaggage.co.uk) has services costing £6 per bag per 24 hours or part thereof. These services operate from Paddington, Euston, Waterloo, King's Cross, Liverpool St and Charing Cross stations.

Within the UK & to Europe

Main national rail routes are served by InterCity trains, which can travel up to 225km/h. However, with the privatised service known for its inefficiency, don't be surprised by delays. Same-day returns and one-week advance purchase are the cheapest tickets for those without rail passes (which are available from mainline train stations). National Rail Enquiries (☎ 0845 748 4950; www.nationalrail.co.uk) has timetables and fares.

The high-speed passenger rail service Eurostar (☎ 0870 518 6186; www.eurostar.com) moved to St Pancras International at the end of 2007, linking this central London station with Paris' Gare du Nord and making the formerly three-hour journey between last two hours and 15 minutes (up to 25 per day); a trip to Brussels is reduced to one hour 53 minutes (up to 12 per day). Some trains also stop at Lille and Calais in France. Fares vary enormously. To Paris/Brussels, for example, costs between £59 for a cheap APEX return (booked at least 21 days in advance, staying a Saturday night) and £300.

Le Shuttle (☎ 0870 535 3535; www.eurotunnel.com) transports motor vehicles and bicycles between Folkestone in England and Coquelles (near Calais) in France. Services run up to every 15 minutes (hourly 1am to 6am). Booking online is cheapest, where a two- to five-day excursion fare costs from £105, day/overnight fares cost from £40 and same day returns (travelling out and back on the same day you book) cost from £100. All prices include a car and passengers. At the time of writing, the company Eurotunnel was suffering dire financial difficulties, so if the listed number doesn't work, you can always ask for information at St Pancras International station.

For other European train enquiries contact Rail Europe (☎ 0870 584 8848; www.raileurope.co.uk).

TRAM

A small London tram network, Tramlink, exists in South London. There are three routes, one running from Wimbledon through Croydon to Elmers End, one running from Croydon to Beckenham and one running from Croydon to New Addington. Single tickets cost £1.20/40p per adult/child. Oyster cards and bus passes are also valid on trams. See www.tfl.gov.uk/trams for more details.

UNDERGROUND

Despite the much-needed renovations and the frequent threat of strikes, the London Underground, or 'the tube', is overall the quickest and easiest way of getting around the city. It is expensive, however: compare the cheapest one-way fare in central London (Oyster/no Oyster £2/4) with those charged on the Paris metro and New York subway and Londoners clearly pay over the odds.

Fares

The Underground divides London into six concentric zones. Fares for the more central zones are more expensive than for those zones further out. Oyster/non-Oyster adult and child fares, at the end of 2007, are listed here:

Zone 1 Adult £1.50/4; child 50p/£2.

Zones 1 & 2 adult £2/4; child 50p/£2.

All other combinations adult £2/4; child 50p/£2.

If you're caught on the Underground without a valid ticket (and that includes crossing into a zone that your ticket doesn't cover) you're liable for an on-the-spot fine of £20.

TRAVEL PASSES & DISCOUNT FARES

If you're travelling only by tube, bus, tram or DLR, Oyster is your best bet and cheaper than a Day Travelcard. But if you're using the National Rail, your Oyster will not be smiled at or accepted, so go for the Day Travelcard (peak/off peak zones 1 and 2 £6.20/5.10; zones 1 to 6 £12.40/6.70).

The three-day Travelcard is good for those over for a short break, and worth it only for the off-peak hours – after 9.30am (off peak zones 1 and 2 £16.10; zones 1 to 6 £20.10).

The longer the validity of the Travelcard, the proportionally cheaper it usually is, so if you're here for a longer period and are using the tube every day, get either a weekly (adult/child zones 1 and 2 £23.20/11.60) or monthly (£89.10/44.60) Travelcard.

Information

Underground travel information centres sell tickets and provide free maps. There are centres at all Heathrow terminals and at Euston, King's Cross St Pancras, Liverpool St, Oxford Circus, Piccadilly Circus, St James's Park and Victoria tube and mainline train stations. There is also an information office at Hammersmith bus station. For general information on the tube, buses, the DLR or trains within London ring ☎ 7222 1234 or visit www.tfl.gov.uk.

OYSTER CARD

The credit-card style Oyster card is the London commuter's new best friend, and tannoy reminders to 'touch in and touch out' have become as common as the warning to 'mind the gap' at stations. You pay a £3 refundable deposit for the card, which soon pays for itself handsomely.

The Oyster card is a smart card, on which you can store either credit towards so-called 'prepay' fares, a Travelcard or both. When entering the tube or boarding a bus, you need to touch your card on a reader (which have a yellow circle with the image of an Oyster card on them) at the tube gates or near the driver to register your journey. The system will then deduct the appropriate amount of credit from your card as necessary. The benefit lies in the fact that fares for Oyster-users are lower than the norm (see Fares, p389). If you are making many journeys during the day, you will never pay more than the appropriate Travelcard (peak or off peak).

When leaving tube stations, you must also touch the card on a reader, so the system knows your journey was only, say, a zone 1 and 2 journey. Regular commuters can also store weekly or monthly Travelcards on their Oyster card.

Network

Greater London is served by 12 tube lines, along with the independent (though linked) and privately owned DLR and an interconnected rail network. The first tube train operates around 5.30am Monday to Saturday and 7am Sunday; the last train leaves between 11.30pm and 12.30am depending on the day, the station and the line. Plans are underway to run services an hour later on Friday and Saturday nights, starting an hour later on Saturday and Sunday mornings.

Tube lines vary in their reliability, and the Circle Line, which links most of the mainline stations and is therefore much used by tourists, has one of the worst track records. However, when it works, this line is very fast. Other lines low in the league tables are the Northern line (though improving) and the Hammersmith & City (often referred to as the 'Hammersmith & Shitty') line. The Piccadilly line to/from Heathrow is usually pretty good, as are the Victoria line, linking the station with Oxford Circus and King's Cross, and the Jubilee line, linking London Bridge, Southwark and Waterloo with Baker St.

Remember that, although a design icon, the London Underground map is a graphical representation of the actual tunnels. Some stations, most famously Leicester Sq and Covent Garden, are much closer in real life than they appear on the map. Often, as between those two stations, it's quicker to walk the distance.

DIRECTORY

BUSINESS HOURS

London is a world business hub, and doing business here (not including the media and new technology industries) is as formal as you would expect from the English. Looking smart at all times is still seen as a key indicator of professionalism, along with punctuality and politeness. Business cards are commonplace.

While the City of London continues to work a very traditional Monday to Friday 9am to 5pm routine (the Square Mile is deserted at weekends), business hours elsewhere in the city are extremely flexible. Larger shops and chain stores are usually open until 7pm Monday to Friday, as well as until at least 5pm Saturday and Sunday. Thursday, or sometimes Wednesday and more often Friday, there's late-night shopping (for more details, see p216).

Banks in central London are open until 5pm, although counter transactions after 3.30pm are usually not processed until the next working day. Post offices vary in their opening times, but most are open from 9am to 5.30pm Monday to Saturday.

Traditionally, pubs and bars have been open from 11am until 11pm. The licensing laws were changed in 2005 to allow pubs and bars to apply for licences to stay open 24 hours, which means that some pubs are now open until midnight or later on weeknights and until 1am or 2am on weekends.

Restaurants are usually open for lunch from noon until 2.30pm or 3pm, and dinner from 6pm or 7pm until 10pm.

CHILDREN

London offers a wealth of sights and museums that appeal to children. It's a city with many green spaces, often including safe areas for children to play, and swings and slides.

There is nearly always a special child's entry rate to paying attractions, although ages of eligibility may vary. Children also travel more cheaply on public transport (and bus travel is free for under-16s, and under-18s in full-time education).

The only places where children are traditionally not accepted are pubs, although many now have a family area, a garden or a restaurant where kids are welcome. For more information on life on the road with the little ones, see Lonely Planet's *Travel with Children*.

Baby-sitting

All the top-range hotels offer in-house baby-sitting services. Prices vary enormously from hotel to hotel, so enquire with the concierges. You might also like to try Sitters (☎ bookings 0800 389 0038; www.sitters.co.uk). A quarterly registration fee costs £12.75 and prices vary between £5.50 and £7 per hour. Two other recommended baby-sitting services are Top Notch Nannies (☎ 7244 6053; www.topnotchnannies.com; baby-sitters & nannies per hr £8) and, in West London only, Nick's Babysitting (☎ 0798 652 1955; www.nicksbabysittingservice.co.uk; child care from per hr £10).

CLIMATE

Many who live in London would swear that global warming has added a twist to the city's unpredictable climatic conditions. While locals used to complain about the frequent, but still somehow always unforeseen, arrival of rain, now they find themselves faced with sudden outbreaks of sunshine and heat instead. Recent summers have seen record temperatures, approaching 40°C. As the tube turns into the Black Hole of Calcutta and traffic fumes become choking, London is particularly ill-equipped to cope with such heat.

However, meteorologists point out that recent statistics don't represent anything terribly out of the ordinary yet for such a naturally variable climate. The average maximum temperature for July, the hottest month, is still only about 23°C. In spring and autumn

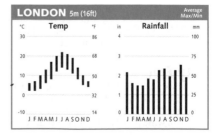

temperatures drop to between 13°C and 17°C. In winter the average daily maximum is 8°C, the overnight minimum 2°C. Despite the appearance of snow in the past few years, it still rarely freezes in London.

What weather forecasters do predict in the long term, as a result of climate change in London, is drier summers, wetter and stormier winters and more flash floods. Meanwhile, for more immediately useful reports on actual and imminent conditions in Greater London, ring Weathercall (☎ 0906 654 3268, per min 60p) or visit www.bbc.london.co.uk/weather for a five-day forecast.

See also p189 to help you decide on the best time to go.

COURSES

London is a centre of learning, and boasts countless colleges, universities and other educational institutions. The jewel in its crown is the University of London, whose world-renowned colleges include King's, University and Imperial Colleges as well as the London School of Economics.

Many people come to London to study English as a foreign language – walk down Oxford St and you're likely to be handed a flyer on the subject. The British Council (Map pp72–3; ☎ 7930 8466; www.britishcouncil.org; 10 Spring Gardens SW1; ◐ Charing Cross) publishes a free list of accredited colleges whose facilities and teaching reach the required standards. It can also advise foreign students on educational opportunities in the UK.

Thousands of London courses, from needlework to Nietzsche, photography to politics, are listed in the annual *Floodlight* (www .floodlight.co.uk) and the quarterly *Hotcourses* (www.hotcourses.com), both available from larger newsagents and bookshops. For more vocational courses, try the free Learndirect (☎ 0800 100 900; www.learndirect-advice.co.uk).

CUSTOMS REGULATIONS

Like other nations belonging to the EU, the UK has a two-tier customs system: one for goods bought duty-free and one for goods bought in another EU country where taxes and duties have already been paid.

Duty-Free

For goods purchased at airports or on ferries outside the EU, you are allowed to import 200 cigarettes, 50 cigars or 250g of tobacco; 2L of still wine plus 1L of spirits over 22% or another 2L of wine (sparkling or otherwise); 50g of perfume and 250cc of toilet water; and other duty-free goods to the value of £145.

Tax & Duty Paid

Although you can no longer bring in duty-free goods from another EU country, you can bring in duty-paid goods that cost less than you'd pay for the same items in your destination country. The items are supposed to be for individual consumption but a thriving business has developed, with many Londoners making day trips to France to load up their cars with cheap grog and smokes.

If you purchase from a normal retail outlet on the Continent, customs uses the following maximum quantities as a guide to distinguish personal imports from those on a commercial scale: 800 cigarettes, 200 cigars, 1kg of tobacco, 10L of spirits, 20L of fortified wine, 90L of wine (of which not more than 60L is sparkling) and 110L of beer.

DISCOUNT CARDS

Students studying full time in London are eligible for discounted travel on all London public transport. However, it takes some time to receive your discount card, as it needs to be sent by post for processing; ask for a form to fill out at any tube station.

For details on Travelcards offering discounts on public transport, see p389.

Possibly of most interest to visitors who want to take in lots of sights and attractions is London Pass (www.londonpass.com). Passes start at £12 per day (for six days), although they can be altered to include use of the Underground and buses. They offer free entry and queue-jumping to all major attractions; check the website for details.

ELECTRICITY

The standard voltage throughout the UK is 230/240V AC, 50Hz. Plugs have three square pins and can look rather curious to non-Brits. Adapters for European, Australasian and American electrical items are available at any electrical store. Check www.kropla.com for useful info on electricity and adaptors.

EMBASSIES

It's important to realise what your own embassy can and cannot do to help you if you get into trouble. Generally, it won't be much help if the trouble you're in is remotely your own fault. Remember that while in London you are bound by British law.

In genuine emergencies you might get some assistance, but only if other channels have been exhausted. The embassy will expect you to have insurance for any unpredictable costs. If you have all your money and documents stolen, it might assist with getting a new passport but a loan for onward travel is almost always out of the question.

The following is a list of selected foreign representative offices in London. Embassies are designed to help their own nationals but they often also contain a consulate section where visas are issued to other nationals wishing to visit this country. Where consulates have a separate address, these are listed. For a more complete list check under 'Embassies & Consulates' in the central London Yellow Pages (www.yell.co.uk).

Australia (Map pp72–3; ☎ 7379 4334; www.australia.org.uk; Australia House, the Strand WC2; ✆ Holborn or Temple)

Belgium Visa Application Centre (☎ visa information 020 7811 3979; www.vfs-be-uk.com; 5 Lower Belgrave St SW1; ✆ Victoria) Embassy (Map pp138–9; ☎ 7470 3700; www.diplobel.org/uk; 17 Grosvenor Cres SW1; ✆ Victoria)

Canada High Commission (Map p100; ☎ /258 6600; www.canada.org.uk; 38 Grosvenor Sq W1; ✆ Bond St) Embassy (Map pp72–3; ☎ 7258 6600; www.canada.org.uk; Canada House, Trafalgar Sq SW1; ✆ Charing Cross);

France (Map pp138–9; ☎ 7073 1000, for visas 0906 554 0700, per min £1; www.ambafrance-uk.org; 58 Knightsbridge SW1; ✆ South Kensington)

Germany (Map pp138–9; ☎ 7824 1300, for visa appointments 0906 554 0740, per min £1; www.london.diplo.de; 23 Belgrave Sq SW1; ✆ Hyde Park Corner) Appointments are necessary to obtain a visa.

Ireland Embassy (Map pp138–9; ☎ 0870 005 6725; http://ireland.embassyhomepage.com; 17 Grosvenor Pl SW1; ✆ Hyde Park Corner); Consulate (☎ 0870 005 6725, 7255 7700; Montpelier House, 106 Brompton Rd SW3; ✆ South Kensington)

Netherlands (Map pp138–9; ☎ 7590 3200; www.netherlands-embassy.org.uk; 38 Hyde Park Gate SW7; ✆ High St Kensington)

New Zealand (Map p68; ☎ 7930 8422; www.nzembassy.com; New Zealand House, 80 Haymarket SW1; ✆ Piccadilly Circus)

South Africa (Map pp72–3; ☎ 7451 7299; www.southafricahouse.com; South Africa House, Trafalgar Sq WC2; ✆ Charing Cross)

Spain Consulate (Map pp138–9; ☎ 7589 8989; 20 Draycott Pl SW3; ✆ South Kensington); Embassy (Map pp138–9; ☎ 7235 5555; http://spain.embassyhomepage.com; 39 Chesham Pl SW1; ✆ Hyde Park Corner)

USA (Map p100; ☎ 7499 9000, 0906 820 0290 per min £1.20; www.usembassy.org.uk; 5 Upper Grosvenor St W1; ✆ Bond St)

EMERGENCY

Dial ☎ 999 to call the police, fire brigade or ambulance in an emergency. For hospitals with 24-hour accident and emergency departments see p395.

HOLIDAYS

With typically four to five weeks' annual leave, Britons get fewer holidays than their European compatriots, but more than their American friends.

Public Holidays

Most attractions and businesses close for a couple of days over Christmas, and those places that normally shut on Sunday will probably also do so on Bank Holiday Mondays.

New Year's Day 1 January

Good Friday/Easter Monday Late March/April

May Day Holiday First Monday in May

Spring Bank Holiday Last Monday in May

Summer Bank Holiday Last Monday in August

Christmas Day 25 December

Boxing Day 26 December

For details of the many festivals London hosts throughout the year, see p189.

School Holidays

These change from year to year and often from school to school. Moreover, public (ie private) school holidays tend to differ from those of state schools. As a general rule, however:

Spring half term One week in mid-February

Easter holidays Two weeks either side of Easter Sunday

Summer half term One week end of May/early June

Summer holiday Late July to early September

Autumn half term Last week of October

Christmas holidays Roughly 20 December to 6 January

INTERNET ACCESS

Logging onto the internet shouldn't be a problem: if you have your own laptop you can go online with ease from your hotel room, and if you don't you can drop into any internet café or library throughout the capital. For internet café locations, visit www.cybercafes.com. The most popular internet service providers (ISPs) are: AOL (www.aol.com), BT (www.bt.com), Orange (www.orange.co.uk), Sky (www.sky.com) and Virgin (www.virgin.com). Zen Internet (www.zen.co.uk) was voted UK's best customer satisfaction ISP by *Which* magazine. The most readily available internet café chain in London is easyEverything (Map pp138–9; ☎ 7938 1841; www.easyeverything.com; Head office 12-14 Wilton Rd SW1; ☒ 24hr; ☻ Victoria), with 17 branches, including the following:

Baker Street (Map p100; 122 Baker St; ☻ Baker St) Inside McDonald's.

Kensington (Map p177; 160-166 Kensington High St W8; ☻ Kensington High St)

King's Road (Map pp138–9; Unit G1, King's Walk, 120 King's Rd; ☻ Sloane Sq)

Oxford Street (Map p100; 358 Oxford St W1; ☻ Oxford Circus)

Piccadilly Circus (Map p68; 46 Regent St; ☻ Piccadilly Circus) Inside Burger King.

Tottenham Court Rd (Map p68; 9-16 Tottenham Court Rd W1; ☻ Tottenham Court Rd)

Trafalgar Square (Map pp72–3; 7 the Strand WC2; ☻ Charing Cross)

Wireless access is improving. The City of London is now the biggest wi-fi zone in the world (see www.thecloud.net), which is free for the first month you use it and then you have to pay; Islington's Upper St is a 'technology mile' of free wi-fi access, and Leicester Sq has free wi-fi access (that you can even get inside

Starbucks!). Most major train stations and airport terminals, as well as Starbucks, have wi-fi access, but it can be quite pricey. Many cafés and public spaces offer wi-fi, although you usually have to ask for the password and sometimes pay. For more info on wi-fi spots go to www.wi-fihotspotlist.com.

LEGAL MATTERS

Should you face any legal difficulties while in London, visit any one of the Citizens Advice Bureaux (www.citizensadvice.org.uk) listed under 'Counselling & Advice' in the Yellow Pages, or contact the Community Legal Services Directory (☎ 0845 345 4345; www.clsdirect.org.uk).

Driving Offences

The laws against drink-driving are very strict and are treated seriously. Currently the limit is 80mg of alcohol in 100mL of blood. The safest approach is not to drink anything at all if you're planning to drive.

Drugs

Illegal drugs of every type are widely available in London, especially in clubs. Nonetheless, all the usual drug warnings apply. Cannabis was reclassified as a Class C drug in 2004, removing the risk of arrest for the possession of small quantities. New studies have prompted a government rethink, however, so the drug might be reclassified as Class B, warranting stiff penalties. Possession of harder drugs, including heroin and cocaine, is always treated seriously.

Fines

In general you rarely have to cough up on the spot for an offence. The exceptions are trains, the tube and buses, where people who can't produce a valid ticket for the journey when asked to by an inspector can be fined £20 there and then. No excuses are accepted.

Britain has introduced new 'Anti-Social Behaviour Orders' (ASBOs), allowing police to issue fixed penalty notices for antisocial behaviour. These run from £50 for minors attempting to buy alcohol to £80 for being drunk and disorderly, making false ☎ 999 calls or wasting police time.

MAPS

The *London A–Z* series produces a range of excellent maps and hand-held street atlases. All areas of London mapped on this system

top picks

FREE WI-FI ACCESS SPOTS

- Apple Store (p218)
- British Film Institute Southbank café (p314)
- Cargo café (p300)
- Ray's Jazz Shop café (p225)
- Two Floors (p279)

can be accessed at www.streetmap.co.uk, one of London's most invaluable websites.

Lonely Planet also publishes a *London City Map*.

Bookshops with a wide selection of maps include Stanford's, Foyles, Waterstone's and Daunt Books.

MEDICAL SERVICES

Reciprocal arrangements with the UK allow Australian residents, New Zealand nationals, and residents and nationals of several other countries to receive free emergency medical treatment and subsidised dental care through the National Health Service (NHS; ☎ 0845 4647; www .nhsdirect.nhs.uk). They can use hospital emergency departments, GPs and dentists (check the Yellow Pages). Visitors staying 12 months or longer, with the proper documentation, will receive care under the NHS by registering with a specific practice near their residence.

EU nationals can obtain free emergency treatment on presentation of a European Health Insurance card.

Travel insurance, however, is advisable as it offers greater flexibility over where and how you're treated and covers expenses for an ambulance and repatriation that won't be picked up by the NHS.

Dental Services

For emergency dental care, call into Eastman Dental Hospital (Map p150; ☎ 7915 1000; 256 Gray's Inn Rd WC1; ✪ King's Cross).

Hospitals

The following hospitals have 24-hour accident and emergency departments:

Charing Cross Hospital (Map p177; ☎ 8846 1234; Fulham Palace Rd W6; ✪ Hammersmith)

Chelsea & Westminster Hospital (Map p205; ☎ 8746 8000; 369 Fulham Rd SW10; ✪ South Kensington, then 🚍 14 or 211)

Guy's Hospital (Map p126; ☎ 7955 5000; St Thomas St SE1; ✪ London Bridge)

Homerton Hospital (Map p156; ☎ 8919 5555; Homerton Row E9; 🚈 Homerton)

Royal Free Hospital (Map p166; ☎ 7794 0500; Pond St NW3; ✪ Belsize Park)

Royal London Hospital (Map p156; ☎ 7377 7000; Whitechapel Rd E1; ✪ Whitechapel)

University College Hospital (Map pp92–3; ☎ 7380 9300; 253 Euston Rd NW1; ✪ Euston Sq)

Pharmacies

There's always one neighbourhood chemist that's open 24 hours; check the Yellow Pages for one near you.

Most people will be instantly struck by the almost total monopoly enjoyed by Boots the Chemist, which has a store at Piccadilly Circus (Map p68; ☎ 7734 6126; 44-46 Regent St; ☽ 9am-8pm Mon-Sat, noon-6pm Sun; ✪ Piccadilly Circus). The Superdrug chain is the only potential rival. Both chains are extremely well supplied.

METRIC SYSTEM

People in London use both the metric and imperial systems interchangeably. Some older people will not readily comprehend metric measurements and, similarly, some younger people will not readily understand imperial. See the inside front cover for conversions.

MONEY

Despite being a member of the EU, the UK has not signed up to the euro and has retained the pound sterling as its unit of currency. One pound sterling is made up of 100 pence (called 'pee', colloquially). Notes come in denominations of £5, £10, £20 and £50, while coins are 1p, 2p, 5p, 10p, 20p, 50p, £1 and £2. Unless otherwise noted, all prices in this book are in pounds sterling. See p16 for an idea of the cost of living in London.

ATMs

ATMs are a way of life in London, as the huge queues by them on Saturday nights in the West End attest. There is no area in London unserved by them, and they accept cards from any bank in the world that is tied into the Visa, MasterCard, Cirrus or Maestro systems, as well as some other more obscure ones. After a national campaign, most banks now allow their cardholders to withdraw money from other banks' ATMs without charge. However, those without UK High-Street bank cards should be warned that there is nearly always a transaction surcharge for cash withdrawals. You should contact your bank to find out how much this is before using ATMs too freely. There are nonbank-run ATMs that charge £1.50 to £2 per transaction. These are normally found inside shops and are particularly expensive for foreign bank card holders. The ATM does warn you before you take money out that it'll charge you so you don't get any surprises on your bank statement.

Also, always beware of suspicious-looking devices attached to ATMs. Many London ATMs have now been made tamperproof, but certain fraudsters' devices are capable of sucking your card into the machine, allowing the fraudsters to release it when you have given up and left.

Changing Money

The best place to change money is in any local post office branch, where no commission is charged. You can also change money in most High-Street banks and some travel-agent chains, as well as at the numerous bureaux de change throughout the city. Compare rates and watch for the commission that is not always mentioned. The trick is to ask how many pounds you'll receive in all before committing – you'll lose nothing by shopping around.

Credit & Debit Cards

Credit and debit cards are accepted almost universally in London, from restaurants and bars to shops and even some taxis. American Express and Diner's Club are less widely used than Visa and MasterCard, while most Londoners simply live off their Switch debit cards, which can also be used to get 'cash back' from supermarkets, saving a trip to an ATM if you are low on cash.

NEWSPAPERS & MAGAZINES
Newspapers

For a good selection of foreign-language newspapers, try the newsstands in the Victoria Pl shopping centre at Victoria train station, along Charing Cross Rd, in Old Compton St and along Queensway. See p336 for details of gay and lesbian publications.

DAILY PAPERS

Daily Express Midlevel tabloid.

Daily Mail This is often called the voice of middle England – the rabid voice of middle England, we reckon, given its regular anti-immigration campaigns.

Daily Star Tabloid with wacky tales that often beggar belief.

Daily Telegraph Dubbed the 'Torygraph', this is the unofficial Conservative party paper.

Evening Standard London's main daily paper has introduced a free London Lite to compete with the giveaways Metro

and thelondonpaper. Most useful on Thursday for its listings magazine Metro Life.

Financial Times Heavyweight business paper with a great travel section in its weekend edition.

Guardian Liberal and middle-class, the Guardian has good reporting, though it's sometimes a tad tendentious. An entertainment supplement, the Guide, comes with Saturday's paper.

Independent Not aligned with any political party the Independent is a left-leaning serious-minded tabloid with barking opinion columns and a good culture supplement.

London Lite A free paper launched in autumn 2006 by the Evening Standard as competition to thelondonpaper, Lite really is the right word when it comes to the substance and quality of this celebrity-fad-obsessed trashy publication.

Metro This free morning paper from the Daily Mail stable litters tube stations and seats, giving you an extra excuse to ignore your fellow passengers. It's as lightweight as it is thin.

Mirror Tony Blair briefly rediscovered this working-class tabloid bastion of Old Labour support during the 2005 election, when his front-page handwritten letter to readers explained why they should vote for him.

Sun The UK's bestseller, this gossip-loving tabloid is owner Rupert Murdoch's entrée to power here. Legendary for its clever (and sometimes offensive) headlines, it supported the Tories during their 1980s glory years, before switching to New Labour.

thelondonpaper A subsidiary of News International (who also publish the Sun and the Times), this is as empty of real news or any substance, and as full of celebrity life as its competitor, London Lite. Also free.

Times The first to follow the Independent in downsizing to a smaller format, this stalwart of the British press is now published in tabloid format, too. It's part of the Murdoch stable.

SUNDAY PAPERS

News of the World Sister to the Sun, this is the ultimate scandal mag, with an enormous readership. It has a passion for kiss-and-tell stories and rabid campaigns.

Observer Sunday-only paper similar in tone and style to the Guardian, which owns it, with a great Sunday arts supplement (the Review).

Sunday Telegraph As serious as its weekly sister.

Sunday Times Full of scandal and fashion. Probably destroys at least one rainforest per issue, but most of it can be arguably tossed in the recycling bin upon purchase.

Magazines

Dazed & Confused The heady days when Rankin made his name as a photographer are long gone, but Jefferson Hack (father of Kate Moss' daughter) has managed to keep his style magazine going many years.

Economist In-depth global news stories come with an unsurprising but unobtrusive financial bent in this quietly successful weekly magazine (or, as the proprietors insist, 'newspaper'). It's the one people say they read to create an aura of substance.

Heat This phenomenally successful celebrity mag created a whole new genre, as rivals raced to imitate its weekly dose of iconoclasm and sycophancy.

i-D This ubercool London fashion/music gospel is possibly too hip for its own good, but it's still turning out its trademark winking covers every month.

Loaded The original lads mag (as opposed to a men's magazine such as the market-leading *FHM*), *Loaded* reinvented itself as a 'new lads' mag, throwing some investigative journalism, real-life stories and an 'arty' black-and-white centrefold section into the mix.

London Review of Books Shunning the general trend for lifestyle journalism, this literary criticism magazine sticks to academic-style essays.

Loot (www.loot.com) This paper appears five times per week and is made up of classified ads placed free by sellers. You can find everything from kitchen sinks to cars, as well as an extensive selection of flat- and house-share ads.

New Statesman This left-wing intellectual news magazine was given a new lease of life in 2005 by editor John Kampfner after a difficult period, returning to its 'heritage of radical politics'.

Private Eye (see p52) This brilliant satirical weekly was established by comedian Peter Cook and is edited by Ian Hislop. Its twist on the news often borders on the surreal; check its always-hilarious front page.

Spectator Tory voters love this right-wing weekly, but its witty articles are often loved by left-wingers too. It claims to be Britain's oldest running magazine.

Time Out (www.timeout.com) The London going-out bible is published every Tuesday, providing a complete listing of what's on and where.

POST

The Royal Mail has suffered somewhat in its speed and accuracy since privatisation, though it's still generally very reliable. For general postal enquiries ring ☎ 0845 722 3344, or visit www.royalmail.co.uk.

Postal Rates

Domestic 1st-class mail is quicker (next working day) but more expensive (32/48p per letter, depending on the size of the envelope) than 2nd class (24/40p taking three working days). Postcards and letters up to 20g cost 42p to anywhere in Europe; to almost everywhere

else, including the Americas and Australasia, it's 54/78p up to 10/20g. Parcels up to 100/200g cost £1.19/1.83 to Europe and £1.58/2.69 to the Americas and Australasia. They must be taken to the post office for weighing.

Airmail letters to the USA or Canada generally take three to five days; to Australia or New Zealand, allow five days to a week.

Postcodes

The unusual London postal code system dates back to WWI. The whole city is divided up into districts denoted by a letter (or letters) and a number. For example, W1, the Mayfair and Soho postcode, stands for 'West London, district 1'. EC1, on the other hand, stands for 'East Central London, district 1'.

RADIO

For a taste of London on the airwaves, tune into the following stations:

BBC London Live (94.9 FM) Talk station focusing on London.

Capital FM (95.8 FM) The commercial equivalent of the BBC's national Radio 1 and the most popular pop station in the city.

Capital Gold (1548AM) Plays oldies from the '60s, '70s and '80s.

Choice FM (96.9 FM) Soul station.

Jazz FM (102.2 FM) Smooth jazz and cheesy tunes.

Kiss 100 (100 FM) Dance music.

LBC (1152AM) A talkback channel.

Magic FM (105.4 FM) Mainstream oldies.

News Direct (97.3 FM) An all-news station with full reports every 20 minutes.

Talk Sport (1089AM) Self-explanatory!

Virgin (105.8 FM) Pop station.

Xfm (104.9 FM) An alternative radio station playing indie music.

RELOCATING

If you're moving to London, make sure you have a valid residence and work visa; see p401 and p402. Those of you looking for accommodation, check the *Loot* newspaper or web page (www.loot.com), or see the brilliant www.gumtree.com, where you can look for flats and jobs.

If you're looking for areas to hang out with expats, try West London (Earl's Court,

UNDERGROUND ETIQUETTE

Given the vital role it plays in London life, it's natural that the tube should have its own code of customs. Not adhering to the code is how you can annoy Londoners most. Here's your guide on how to fit in.

Don't stop to get your bearings as soon as you get through the turnstiles. Absolutely under no circumstances should you stand still on the left-hand side of the escalator; it's reserved for people far busier than you and others keen to exercise and tone their bottoms. Do move along the platform and don't point at the little furry things running along the lines. When the train pulls in, stand aside until passengers have got off. Under pain of death, do *not* offer your seat to the elderly, disabled, pregnant or faint; instead, you should bury your head in a book and pretend you can't see them. It's fine, even courteous, to leave a newspaper behind in the morning but it's your bloody litter in the evening. Do mind the gap.

Fulham, Shepherd's Bush) for Aussie, US and Kiwi communities; there's a big concentration of South Africans in Putney. Poles are scattered over much of the city, but Balham and Hammersmith have Polish community centres and churches; Spanish are traditionally around the Portobello area, while the Portuguese are in Stockwell. Cypriot and Turkish communities are found in Dalston, Stoke Newington and along Green Lanes. Edgware Rd is a bustling Arab area; Dalston is known as the Caribbean core, together with Brixton.

Check the weekly freebies *TNT Magazine*, *Southern Cross* or *SA Times*, with Australasian and South African news and sports results. They are also useful for their entertainment listings, travel sections and classified ads for jobs, cheap tickets, shipping services and accommodation, and can be found outside most tube stations.

SAFETY

London's a fairly safe city considering its size, so exercising common sense should keep you safe.

If you're getting a cab after a night's clubbing, makes sure you go for a black cab or a licensed minicab firm. Many of the touts operating outside clubs and bars are unlicensed and can therefore be unsafe. The areas where you should try hard to avoid wandering around alone at night are King's Cross, Dalston and Peckham, though sticking to the main roads should guarantee a certain degree of safety. Pickpocketing does happen in London, so keep your handbag closed and any obvious pocket empty or buttoned up, especially in crowded areas, most particularly in the West End and within the Underground.

Annoyances are many in a big city. For correct Underground procedure, see the boxed text above.

TAXES & REFUNDS

Value-added tax (VAT) is a 17.5% sales tax levied on most goods and services except food, books and children's clothing. Restaurants must, by law, include VAT in their menu prices.

It's sometimes possible for visitors to claim a refund of VAT paid on goods, resulting in considerable savings. You're eligible if you have spent fewer than 365 days out of the two years prior to making the purchase living in the UK, and if you're leaving the EU within three months of making the purchase.

Not all shops participate in the VAT refund scheme, called the Retail Export Scheme or Tax-Free Shopping, and different shops will have different minimum purchase conditions (normally around £75 in any one shop). On request, participating shops will give you a special form (VAT 407). This must be presented with the goods and receipts to customs when you depart the country (VAT-free goods can't be posted or shipped home). After customs has certified the form, it should be returned to the shop for a refund (minus an administration or handling fee), which takes about eight to 10 weeks to come through.

TELEPHONE

British Telecom's (BT's) famous red phone boxes survive in conservation areas only (notably Westminster), and in the mobile-phone age the company is even lobbying to get rid of its more modern glass cubicles.

Some phones still accept coins, but most take phonecards or credit cards. BT's £3, £5, £10 and £20 phonecards are widely available from retailers including most post offices and newsagents. A digital display on the telephone indicates how much credit is left on the card.

The following are some important telephone numbers and codes (some numbers are charged calls):

Directory enquiries, international (☎ 118 661/118 505)

Directory enquiries, local & national (☎ 118 118/118 500)

International dialling code (☎ 00)

Operator, international (☎ 155)

Operator, local & national (☎ 100)

Reverse charge/collect calls (☎ 155)

Time (☎ 123)

Weathercall (☎ 0906 654 3268) Covers the Greater London area.

Following are some special phone codes worth knowing:

Local call rate applies (☎ 08457)

National call rate applies (☎ 0870/0871)

Premium rate applies (☎ 09) From 60p per minute.

Toll-free (☎ 0800)

Calling London

London's area code is ☎ 020, followed by an eight-digit number beginning with 7 or 8. You only need to dial the ☎ 020 when you are calling London from elsewhere in the UK.

To call London from abroad, dial your country's international access code, then 44 (the UK's country code), then 20 (dropping the initial 0) followed by the eight-digit phone number.

International Calls & Rates

International direct dialling (IDD) calls to almost anywhere can be made from nearly all public telephones. Direct dialling is cheaper than making a reverse-charge (collect) call through the international operator (☎ 155).

Some private firms offer cheaper international calls than British telecom (BT). In such shops you phone from a metered booth and then pay the bill. Some cybercafés and internet access shops also offer cheap rates for international calls.

It's also possible to undercut BT international call rates by buying a special card (usually denominated £5, £10 or £20) with a PIN that you use from any phone, even a home phone, by dialling a special access number. These cards are available at most corner shops.

Local & National Call Rates

Local calls are charged by time alone; regional and national calls are charged by both time and distance. Daytime rates apply from 6am to 6pm Monday to Friday; the cheap rate applies from 6pm to 6am Monday to Friday; and the cheap weekend rate applies from 6pm Friday to 6am Monday.

Mobile Phones

The UK uses the GSM 900 network, which covers Europe, Australia and New Zealand, but is not compatible with the North American GSM 1900 or the totally different system in Japan (though many North Americans have GSM 1900/900 phones that do work in the UK). If you have a GSM phone, check with your service provider about using it in the UK, and beware of calls being routed internationally. It's usually most convenient to buy a local SIM card from the nearest branch of the Link (☎ 0870 154 5540; www.thelink.co.uk) or Carphone Warehouse (☎ 0870 168 2002; www.carphonewarehouse.com). You can also rent phones, including possibilities including Mobell (☎ 0800 243 524; www.mobell.com) and Cellhire (☎ 0870 561 0610; www.cellhire.com).

TELEVISION

Five free-to-air analogue stations exist, along with digital channels that can be viewed through a Freeview box (free viewing after purchasing the box) or cable/satellite providers. The analogue channels and some of their leading programmes:

BBC1 *EastEnders, Strictly Come Dancing, Doctor Who, Panorama.*

BBC2 *University Challenge, Newsnight, The Apprentice.*

C4 *Hollyoaks, Channel 4 News, Big Brother, The Simpsons.*

C5 Mainly reruns of '80s B-movies but also has *CSI.*

ITV *Pop Idol; Who Wants to be a Millionaire; I'm a Celebrity, Get Me Out of Here!; Coronation Street; The Bill; Ant & Dec.*

TIME

Wherever you are in the world, the time on your watch is measured in relation to the time at Greenwich in London – Greenwich Mean Time (GMT). British Summer Time, the UK's form of daylight-saving time, muddies the water so that even London is ahead of GMT from late March to late October. To give you an idea, San Francisco is usually eight hours and New York five hours behind GMT, while Sydney is 10 hours ahead of GMT. Phone the international operator on ☎ 155 to find out the exact difference.

TIPPING

Many restaurants now add a 'discretionary' service charge to your bill, but in places that don't you are expected to leave a 10% to 15% tip unless the service was unsatisfactory. Waiting staff are often paid poorly. It's legal for restaurants to include a service charge in the bill but this should be clearly advertised. You needn't add a further tip. You never tip to have your pint pulled in a pub but staff at bars often return change in a little metal dish, expecting some of the coins to glue themselves to the bottom.

If you take a boat trip on the Thames you'll find some guides and/or drivers importuning for a tip in return for their commentary. Whether you pay is up to you. You can tip taxi drivers up to 10% but most people round up to the nearest pound.

TOILETS

Train stations, bus terminals and attractions generally have good have facilities, providing also for people with disabilities and those with young children. At train and bus stations you usually have to pay 20p to use the facilities.

It's an offence to urinate in the streets, although arrests are rare. However, with the streets of Soho so frequently stinking of urine, Westminster council has pioneered an excellent scheme whereby public urinals are set up on the streets at weekends for those who can't make it to the next bar without relieving themselves. These can be found on Soho Sq, Wardour St and the Strand, among other locations. The new street urinals are obviously only useable by men so women will need to cross their legs until they find somewhere they can go.

For information on toilets for the disabled, see opposite.

TOURIST INFORMATION

London is a major travel centre, so along with information on London, tourist offices can help with England, Scotland, Wales, Ireland and most countries worldwide.

Tourist Offices

Visit London (☎ 7234 5800, 0870 156 6366; www.visitlondon.com), formerly the London Tourist Board, can fill you in on everything from tourist attractions and events (such as the Changing of the Guard) to river trips and tours, accommodation, eating, theatre, shopping, children's London, and gay and lesbian venues. Its London Line (☎ 0906 866 3344, per min 60p) has recorded information.

London's main tourist office is the Britain Visitor Centre (Map p68; 1 Regent St SW1; ☯ 9.30am-6.30pm Mon, 9am-6.30pm Tue-Fri, 10am-4pm Sat & Sun, to 5pm Sat Jun-Sep; ⊖ Piccadilly Circus). It has comprehensive information in eight languages, not just on London, but on Wales, Scotland, Northern Ireland, the Irish Republic and Jersey too. It can arrange accommodation; tours; and train, air and car travel. It also has a theatre ticket agency, a bureau de change, international telephones and a few computer terminals for accessing tourist information on the web. The centre deals with walk-in enquiries only, so if you're not in the area, contact the British Tourist Authority (☎ 8846 9000; www.visitbritain.com).

Other useful tourist offices include the London Visitor Centre (Map p126; Arrivals Hall, Waterloo International Terminal; ☯ 8.30am-10.30pm), Heathrow Airport TIC (Terminal 1, 2 & 3 Underground station; ☯ 8am-6pm) and Liverpool Street tourist office (Map p110; Liverpool St Underground station; ☯ 8am-6pm). Hotel booking offices are also found in the halls of Paddington train station, Victoria train station (☯ 8am-8pm Mon-Sat, 8am-6pm Sun Apr-Oct, 8am-6pm Mon-Sat, 9am-4pm Sun Nov-Mar) and Victoria coach station. There are also accommodation booking services at other London airports.

A few London boroughs and neighbourhoods have their own tourist offices. These include the following:

City Information Centre (Map p110; ☎ 7332 1456; www.cityoflondon.gov.uk; St Paul's Churchyard EC4; ☯ 9.30am-5pm Apr-Sep, 9.30am-5pm Mon-Fri, 9.30am-12.30pm Sat Oct-Mar; ⊖ St Paul's) Opposite St Paul's Cathedral.

Greenwich (Map p180; ☎ 0870 608 2000; www.greenwich.gov.uk; Pepys House, 2 Cutty Sark Gardens SW10; ☯ 10am-5pm; DLR Cutty Sark)

Richmond (Map p64; ☎ 8940 9125; www.visitrichmond.co.uk; Old Town Hall, Whittaker Ave, Richmond, Surrey TW9 1TP; ☯ 10am-5pm Mon-Sat, plus 10.30am-1pm Sun May-Sep; ⊛ Richmond)

Southwark (Map p126; ☎ 7357 9168; www.southwark.gov.uk; Vinopolis, 1 Bank End SE1; ☯ 10am-6pm Tue-Sun; ⊖ London Bridge)

TRAVELLERS WITH DISABILITIES

For disabled travellers London is an odd mix of user-friendliness and downright disinterest. New hotels and modern tourist attractions are legally required to be accessible to people in wheelchairs, but many B&Bs and guesthouses are in older buildings, which are hard (if not impossible) to adapt. This means that travellers who have mobility problems may end up paying more for accommodation.

It's a similar story with public transport. Access to the tube is limited. However, some of the newer trains and buses have steps that lower for easier access, and there are two dedicated bus services with automatic ramps offering disabled access: the 205 and the 705. The 205 runs from Paddington to Whitechapel every 10 to 12 minutes. The 705 runs between Victoria, Waterloo and London Bridge half-hourly. Both services operate approximately from 6am to midnight.

Transport for London's Access & Mobility for Disabled Passengers (☎ 7222 1234, textphone 7918 3015; Windsor House, 42/50 Victoria St, London SW1 9TN) can give you detailed advice and it publishes *Access to the Underground*, which indicates which tube stations have ramps and lifts (all DLR stations do).

The Royal Association for Disability & Rehabilitation (Radar; ☎ 7250 3222; www.radar.org.uk; Unit 12, City Forum, 250 City Rd, London EC1V 8AF) is an umbrella organisation for voluntary groups for people with disabilities. Many disabled-user toilets can be opened only with a special key, which can be obtained from tourist offices or for £3.50 (plus a brief statement of your disability) via the Radar website. The organisation also has an accommodation website, www .radarsearch.org, listing hotels with appropriate facilities.

The Royal National Institute for the Blind (☎ 7388 1266; www.rnib.org.uk; 105 Judd St, London WC1) can also be contacted via its confidential helpline (☎ 0845 766 9999; ☺ 9am-5pm Mon-Fri) and is the best point of initial contact for sight-impaired visitors to London. The Royal National Institute for Deaf People (☎ freephone 0808 808 0123, freephone/textphone 0808 808 9000; www.rnid.org.uk; 19-23 Featherstone St, London EC1) is a similar organisation for the deaf and hard of hearing. Many ticket offices and banks are fitted with hearing loops to help the hearing-impaired; look for the ear symbol.

VISAS

Citizens of Australia, Canada, New Zealand, South Africa and the USA are given, at their point of arrival, 'leave to enter' the UK for up to six months but are prohibited from working without a work permit. If you're a citizen of the EU, you don't need a visa to enter the country and may live and work here freely for as long as you like.

Visa regulations are always subject to change, so check at www.ukvisas.gov.uk or with your local British embassy before leaving home.

Immigration authorities in the UK are tough: dress neatly and be able to prove that you have sufficient funds to support yourself. A credit card and/or an onward ticket will help.

Student Visas

Nationals of EU countries can enter the country to study without formalities. Otherwise you need to be enrolled in a full-time course of at least 15 hours per week of weekday, daytime study at a single educational institution to be allowed to remain as a student. For more details, consult the British embassy, high commission or consulate in your own country.

Visa Extensions

Tourist visas can only be extended in clear emergencies (eg an accident, death of a relative). Otherwise you'll have to leave the UK (perhaps going to Ireland or France) and apply for a fresh one, although this tactic will arouse suspicion after the second or third visa. To extend (or attempt to extend) your stay in the UK, ring the Visa & Passport Information Line (☎ 0870 606 7766, 8649 7878; the Home Office's Immigration & Nationality Directorate, Lunar House, 40 Wellesley Rd, Croydon CR9 2BY; ☺ 10am-noon & 2-4pm Mon-Fri; ⊕ East Croydon) before your current visa expires. The process takes a few days in France/Ireland. Trying to extend within the UK takes a lot longer.

WOMEN TRAVELLERS

In general, London is a fairly laid-back place, and you're unlikely to have too many problems provided you take the usual city precautions. Apart from the occasional wolf whistle and unwelcome body contact on the tube, women will find male Londoners reasonably enlightened. There's nothing to stop women going into pubs alone, though this is not necessarily a comfortable experience even in central London. Women travelling alone at night can choose Ladycabs (☎ 7272 3300), which has women drivers.

Information & Organisations

Marie Stopes International (Map pp92–3; ☎ 0845 300 8090; 108 Whitfield St W1; ☿ 9am-5pm Thu-Mon, to 8pm Tue & Wed; ⊖ Warren St) Provides contraception, sexual health checks and abortions.

Rape & Sexual Abuse Helpline (☎ 8239 1122; ☿ noon-2.30pm & 7-9.30pm Mon-Fri, 2.30-5pm Sat & Sun)

Safety Precautions

Solo women travellers should have few problems, although common-sense caution should be observed, especially at night. It's particularly unwise to get into an Underground carriage with no-one else in it or with just one or two men. If you feel unsafe, you should hang the expense and take a taxi.

WORK

Even if you're unskilled you'll almost certainly find work in London, but you will have to be prepared to work long hours at menial jobs for low pay. Without skills it's difficult to find a job that pays well enough to save money.

Traditionally, unskilled visitors have worked in pubs and restaurants and as nannies. A minimum wage (£5.52 per hour; £4.45 for those aged 18 to 21) exists, but if you're working illegally no-one's obliged to pay you even that.

Accountants, health professionals, journalists, computer programmers, lawyers, teachers, bankers and clerical workers with computer experience stand a better chance of finding well-paid work. Don't forget copies of your qualifications, references (which will probably be checked) and a CV (résumé).

Teachers should contact the individual London borough councils, which have separate education departments, although some schools recruit directly.

To work as a trained nurse or midwife you have to apply (£140) to the UK Nursing & Midwifery Council; the registration process that follows can take up to nine months and it will cost another £160 to register. Write to the Overseas Registration Department, UKNMC, 23 Portland Pl, London W1N 4JT, or phone ☎ 7333 9333. If you aren't registered then you can still work as an auxiliary nurse.

The free *TNT Magazine* is a good starting point for jobs and agencies aimed at travellers. For au pair and nanny work buy the quaintly titled *The Lady*. Also check the *Evening Standard,* the national newspapers and government-operated Jobcentres, which are scattered throughout London and listed under 'Employment Services' in the phone directory. It's worth registering with a few temporary agencies.

If you play a musical instrument or have other artistic talents, busking will make you some pocket money. However, to perform in Underground stations, you have to go through a rigorous process taking several months. After signing up at www.tfl.gov.uk, you will have to go through an audition and get police security clearance (£10) before being granted a licence to perform and then getting yourself on a rota of marked pitches. Buskers also need to have a permit to work at top tourist attractions and popular areas such as Covent Garden and Leicester Sq. Contact the local borough council for details.

Tax

As an official employee, you'll find income tax and National Insurance are automatically deducted from your weekly pay packet. However, the deductions will be calculated on the assumption that you're working for the entire financial year (which runs from 6 April to 5 April). If you don't work as long as that, you may be eligible for a refund. Visit the website of the Inland Revenue (www.inlandrevenue.org.uk) to locate your nearest tax office, or use one of the agencies that advertise in *TNT Magazine* (but check their fee or percentage charge first).

Work Permits

EU and Swiss nationals don't need a work permit to work in London but everyone else does.

If you're a citizen of a Commonwealth country and aged between 17 and 30, you may apply for a Working Holiday Entry Certificate, which allows you to spend up to two years in the UK and take 12 months' work 'incidental' to your holiday. You're not allowed to set up your own business or work as a professional sportsperson. You must apply to your country's British consulate or high commission before departure – Working Holiday Entry Certificates are not granted on arrival in Britain. It is not possible to switch from being a visitor to a working holidaymaker, nor can you claim back any time spent out of the UK during the two-year period. When you apply, you must satisfy the authorities that you have the means to pay for a return or onward journey and that you will be able to maintain yourself without recourse to public funds.

If you're a Commonwealth citizen and have a parent born in the UK, you may be eligible for a Certificate of Entitlement to the Right of Abode (or indeed a British passport), which means you can live and work in Britain free of immigration control.

If you're a Commonwealth citizen with a grandparent born in the UK, or if the grandparent was born before 31 March 1922 in what is now the Republic of Ireland, you may qualify for a UK Ancestry Employment Certificate, which means you can work in the UK full time for up to four years.

Students from the US who are at least 18 years old and studying full time at a college or university can get a Blue Card permit for US$250, allowing them to work in the UK for six months. It's available through the British Universities North America Club (Bunac; ☎ 203 264 0901; wib@bunacusa.com; PO Box 430, Southbury CT 06488). Once in the UK, Bunac can help Blue Card holders find jobs and accommodation; it also runs programmes for Australians, Canadians and New Zealanders but you must apply before leaving home. For more details visit www .bunac.org.

Most other travellers wishing to work and not fitting into any of the aforementioned categories will need a work permit and to be sponsored by a British company. See www .ukvisas.gov.uk for more details.

If you have any queries once you're in the UK, contact the Home Office (☎ 0870 000 1585).

BEHIND THE SCENES

THIS BOOK

This 6th edition of *London* was researched and written by Tom Masters, Steven Fallon and Vesna Maric. Sarah Johnstone and Tom Masters wrote the 5th edition. Martin Hughes, Sarah Johnstone and Tom Masters wrote the 4th edition. Steve Fallon wrote the 2nd and 3rd edition. Pat Yale wrote the 1st edition. The guide was commissioned in Lonely Planet's London office and produced by the following:

Commissioning Editor Clifton Wilkinson

Coordinating Editors Sasha Baskett, David Carroll, Louise Clarke

Coordinating Cartographer Diana Duggan

Coordinating Layout Designer Wibowo Rusli

Managing Editors Melanie Dankel, Bruce Evans, Geoff Howard

Managing Cartographer Mark Griffiths

Managing Layout Designer Adam McCrow

Assisting Editors Kate Evans, Anne Mulvaney, Charlotte Orr

Assisting Cartographers Anita Bahn, Anna Clarkson, Corey Hutchison, Kusnandar, Jolyon Philcox, Andrew Smith

Cover Designer Nic Lehman

Project Managers Bronwyn Hicks, Glenn van der Knijff

Thanks to Helen Christinis, Jennifer Garrett, John Mazzocchi, Wayne Murphy, Trent Paton, Paul Piaia, Celia Wood

Cover photographs Westminster and Big Ben at night, nagelestock.com, Alamy (top); Taxi cabs queuing, Lorcan Getty Images (bottom)

Internal photographs p6 (#2) Jon Arnold Images Ltd/Alamy; p6 (#3) VIEW Pictures Ltd/Alamy; p9 (#3) Aardvark/Alamy; p9 (#1 bottom) Neil Setchfield/Alamy; p10 (#2 top) Nick Hanna/Alamy; p10 (#2 bottom) David Pearson/Alamy; p11 (#3 bottom) Gavan Goulder/Alamy; p12 (#2 top) Kitt Cooper-Smith/Alamy; p12 (#3 top) TNT Magazine/Alamy; p190 Bettina Strenske/Alamy; p191 Paul Gapper/Alamy; p192 (#1) Dominic Burke/Alamy; p192 (#5) David Levenson/Alamy; p193 (#6) Homer Sykes/Alamy; p194 (#5) Lebrecht Music and Arts Photo Library/Alamy; p195 (#10) James Royall/Alamy; p196 (#6) Martin Norris/Alamy. All other photographs by Lonely Planet Images: p2 Tom Smallman; p3, 195 (#7) Adina Tovy Amsel; p6 (#1) Martin Moos; p7 (#4), p11 (#1, #2 top), p12 (#2 bottom), p82 (left) Juliet Coombe; p7 (#6), p79 (left), p80 Richard I'Anson; p7 (#5), 196 (#6) Wayne Walton; p8 (#1, #2), 9 (#2 bottom right), 10 (#1 top, #1, #3), 77, 79 (right), 84, 194 (#2) Neil Setchfield; p8 (#3) Barbara van Zanten; p9 (#2 top), p12 (#3 bottom), p82 (right), p83 Doug McKinlay; p9 (#1 top), p12 (#1 top) Elliot Daniel; p11 (#2 bottom) Charlotte Hindle; p11 (#1 bottom) Paul Bigland; p12 (#1 bottom) Guy Moberly; p78 Lee Foster; p189 Conor Caffrey; p192 (#8), p193 (#10) David Tomlinson; p196 (#7) Lawrence Worcester

All images are copyright of the photographer unless otherwise indicated. Many of the images in this guide are

THE LONELY PLANET STORY

Fresh from an epic journey across Europe, Asia and Australia in 1972, Tony and Maureen Wheeler sat at their kitchen table stapling together notes. The first Lonely Planet guidebook, Across Asia on the Cheap, was born.

Travellers snapped up the guides. Inspired by their success, the Wheelers began publishing books to Southeast Asia, India and beyond. Demand was prodigious, and the Wheelers expanded the business rapidly to keep up. Over the years, Lonely Planet extended its coverage to every country and into the virtual world via lonelyplanet.com and the Thorn Tree message board.

As Lonely Planet became a globally loved brand, Tony and Maureen received several offers for the company. But it wasn't until 2007 that they found a partner whom they trusted to remain true to the company's principles of travelling widely, treading lightly and giving sustainably. In October of that year, BBC Worldwide acquired a 75% share in the company, pledging to uphold Lonely Planet's commitment to independent travel, trustworthy advice and editorial independence.

Today, Lonely Planet has offices in Melbourne, London and Oakland, with over 500 staff members and 300 authors. Tony and Maureen are still actively involved with Lonely Planet. They're travelling more often than ever, and they're devoting their spare time to charitable projects. And the company is still driven by the philosophy of Across Asia on the Cheap: 'All you've got to do is decide to go and the hardest part is over. So go!'

available for licensing from Lonely Planet Images: www
.lonelyplanetimages.com.

THANKS
TOM MASTERS
First of all thanks to James Bridle for his enthusiasm,
company and love of all things London. A big thank you
to Steve and Vesna, my tireless coauthors, and for Cliff at
Lonely Planet for letting me get my hands on London for
the third time… I should also thank fellow Londoners and
friends who've been with me for various reviews, trips and
days out, including Leila Rejali, Gray Jordan, Zeeba Sadiq,
Stephen Billington, Edward Arthur, Gabriel Gatehouse and
Mike Christie.

STEVE FALLON
Thanks to my coauthors Tom Masters and Vesna Maric for the
exchange of ideas and general banter. As always, my share
of *London* is dedicated to my partner, Michael Rothschild,
with love and gratitude.

VESNA MARIC
Thanks to everyone who's gone out sightseeing, drinking,
shopping and day-tripping with me. Some particular names
are: Rafael Estefania, Gabriel Gatehouse, Josh Meggitt, Adele
Moon, Arijana Gurdon, Drazen Petkovic, Iain Stewart, and my
mum, as always. Thanks to Ben at MT's and Emma at London
Zoo for their time and kindness. Big thanks to my coauthors
Tom Masters (also coordinator) and Steve Fallon for being
easy and fun to work with – Tom, thanks for being there
when explanations and clarifications were needed. Thanks
to Clifton Wilkinson for commissioning me and putting up
with all the questions.

OUR READERS
Many thanks to the travellers who used the last edition and
wrote to us with helpful hints, useful advice and interesting
anecdotes:

Ana Anastasijevic, Kevin Anderson, Olaf G Apel, Alex Aristy,
Mary & Fred Attick, Tom Bartolomei, Riccardo Belletti, Kath
Blackler, Tammy Botsford, Lisa Britt, Dominic Bruton, Dina
Bullivant, Linda Cahill, Ben Casey, Bernard Chan, Ting-Hsu

SEND US YOUR FEEDBACK
We love to hear from travellers – your comments
keep us on our toes and help make our books better.
Our well-travelled team reads every word on what
you loved or loathed about this book. Although we
cannot reply individually to postal submissions, we
always guarantee that your feedback goes straight to
the appropriate authors, in time for the next edition.
Each person who sends us information is thanked in
the next edition – and the most useful submissions are
rewarded with a free book.

To send us your updates – and find out about Lonely
Planet events, newsletters and travel news – visit our
award-winning website: www.lonelyplanet.com/contact.

Note: we may edit, reproduce and incorporate your
comments in Lonely Planet products such as guidebooks, websites and digital products, so let us know
if you don't want your comments reproduced or your
name acknowledged. For a copy of our privacy policy
visit www.lonelyplanet.com/privacy.

Chen, Rachel Crossman, Christian Dahl, Dag Yngve Dahle,
Sally Davis, Caroline Elliker, Daniel Farrugia, Claire Fragonas,
Nicky Fullmoon, Rebecca Funk, Milind Gadgil, Christina Gel-
lura, Glenne Gilbert, Lynne Grabar, David Grumett, Miriam
Harris, Carol Heigh, Laurel Herold, Roz Jones, Judy Kenny,
Peter Kim, Bernard Lazarus, Kaung-Chiau Lew, John Mccaf-
ferty, DJ Mckinlay, Heather Monell, Phoebe Moore, Robert
Moore, David Mulhall, Edith Neele, David O'Shell, Gerald
Olsen, George Padova, Christophe Passuello, Torsten Peters,
Tom Plattenberger, David Rhodes, M Roach, Tom Rooke,
Marcin Sadurski, David Salter, Lynden Schofield, Howie
Schuman, Yvonne Sell, David Sojka, Joy Stephens, Melissa
Sullivan, Bronwyn Sutton, Wim Vandenbussche, Per Vinther,
Manuele Zunelli

ACKNOWLEDGMENTS
Many thanks to the following for the use of their content:
London Underground Map © Transport for London 2006;
The Central London Bus Map and Tourist Attractions Map ©
Transport for London 2006.

Notes

INDEX

A

accommodation 339-61, see also Sleeping index
Ackroyd, Peter 33
Adam, Robert 80
Admiralty Arch 85
air travel 381-3
Albert Memorial 144
Alexandra Park & Palace 172
ambulance 393
animals 47
antiques see Shopping index
apartments 340-1
Apsley House 142
architecture 78-84
arts 31-45, 311-22, see also Arts index
Ascot 328
athletics 328
ATMs 395-6

B

babysitters 391
Bacon, Francis 41
Bank 115-19
Bank of England Museum 118
Bankside 128-31
Banqueting House 105
Barbican 117
bars 277-96, see also Drinking index
bathrooms 400
Battersea 199-201, 200
Battersea Park 201
Battersea Power Station 201, 12

BBC 26, 52-3
Bedford Square 93
beer 294
Bermondsey 131-4
Bethnal Green 157-8
Bexleyheath 186
bicycle travel 384
Big Ben 102
birds 47
Black Death 20
Blackheath 183-4
Blair, Tony 29-30
Blitz 27
Bloomsbury 89-93
Bloomsbury Group 26
boat hire
  Hyde Park 146
  Richmond 209
body snatchers 25
Booker Prize 33
books 29, 35
Borough 131-4
Bourne, Matthew 45-55
Bow Street Runners 24
Bray 378-9
Brentford 209-10
Brighton 371-4, 372
Brick Lane 149-51
Brit Oval 202, 328
Britart 41-3
British Airways London Eye 125-7, 8
British Library 167-9, 83
British Museum 89-90, 6
Britpop 39
Brixton 199, 202-3, 200, 203
Broadstairs 374
Brown, Gordon 30-1
Buddhapadipa Temple 213
Burlington Arcade 70
business hours 216, 237, 278, 391, see also inside front cover
Bussell, Darcy 46

C

Cabinet War Rooms 104-5
Cable St riots 156-7
Cambridge 369-71, 369
Camden 165-7, 168, 10
Canary Wharf 161

Canterbury 376-8, 377
Carlos Herrera 307
cathedrals see Sights index
cell phones 399
Cenotaph 105
chain restaurants 274
Chamberlain, Neville 27
Changing of the Guard 95
Charles I 22
Charlton 184-5
Chelsea see Hyde Park to Chelsea
Chelsea Flower Show 193, 192
chemists 395
children, travel with 246, 391
Chinatown 67
Chiswick 206-7
church music venues 309
churches see Sights index
Churchill Museum 104-5
Churchill, Winston 27
cinema 43-4
cinemas see Arts index
City, the 109-24, 110, 124
  accommodation 349-50
  drinking 282
  food 248-9
Clapham 201-2, 200
Clapham Common 202
Clarence House 98
classical music see Arts index
Clerkenwell, Shoreditch & Spitalfields 148-54, 150
  accommodation 354-5
  drinking 284-7
  food 254-8
  shopping 227-9
climate 16, 391-2
Clink Prison Museum 131
clothing sizes 217
clubs 298-303, see also Nightlife index
Cockney rhyming slang 158
comedy 303-5
Constable, John 41
consulates 392-3
Corporation of London 49
costs 16-17, 237, 340, 392
courses 392
Covent Garden 71-86, 72-3

Covent Garden Piazza 85
credit cards 396
cricket 327-8
Crisp, Quentin 33
Cromwell, Oliver 22
Crouch End 172
Crystal Palace 327
customs regulations 392
Cutty Sark 183
cycling 384

D

dance 45-6, see also Arts index
Defoe, William 32
dental services 395
Deptford 183, 186-8, 187
Design Museum 132
development 47-8
Dickens, Charles 32
Dickens House Museum 90-1, 374-5
disabilities, travellers with 401
discount cards 392
Docklands 159-63, 160, 10 see also East End & Docklands
Dr Johnson's House 114
Doyle, Sir Arthur Conan 32
drug stores 395
Dulwich 185-6
Dulwich Picture Gallery 185
Dungeness 375-6

E

Earl's Court 174, 177
East End & Docklands 155-63, 156
  accommodation 355
  drinking 287-8
  food 258-61
  shopping 229
Edward V 20
Edward VII 26
Edward VIII 26
electricity 392
Eliot, TS 33
Elizabeth I 21
Elizabeth II 27
Eltham 186
Eltham Palace 186

INDEX

000 map pages
000 photographs

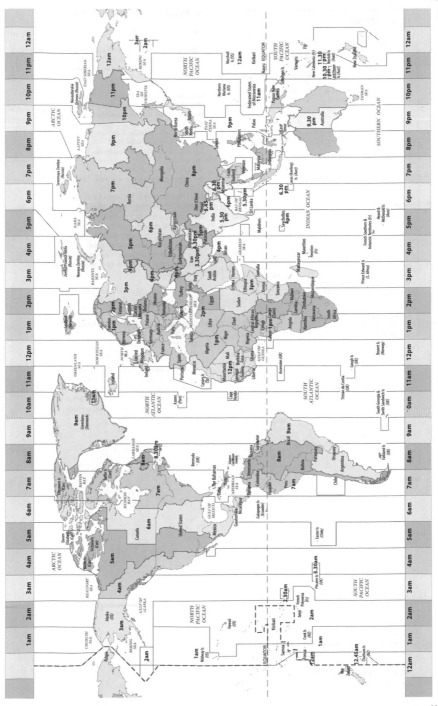

419

MAP LEGEND

ROUTES

	Tollway		Mall/Steps
	Freeway		Tunnel
	Primary		Pedestrian Overpass
	Secondary		Walking Tour
	Tertiary		Walking Tour Detour
	Lane		Walking Trail
	Under Construction		Walking Path
	Unsealed Road		Track
	One-Way Street		

TRANSPORT

	Bus Route		Rail
	Tube Station		Rail (Underground)

HYDROGRAPHY

	River, Creek		Canal
	Intermittent River		Water

AREA FEATURES

	Airport		Land
	Area of Interest		Mall
	Building		Market
	Campus		Park
	Cemetery, Christian		Rocks
	Cemetery, Other		Sports
	Forest		Urban

POPULATION

○	CAPITAL (NATIONAL)	◉	CAPITAL (STATE)
●	Large City	○	Medium City
●	Small City	○	Town, Village

SYMBOLS

Information
- Bank, ATM
- Embassy/Consulate
- Hospital, Medical
- Information
- Internet Facilities
- Police Station
- Post Office, GPO
- Telephone
- Toilets

Sights
- Castle, Fortress
- Christian
- Jewish
- Monument
- Museum, Gallery
- Point of Interest
- Ruin
- Zoo, Bird Sanctuary

Shopping
- Shopping

Eating
- Eating

Drinking
- Drinking
- Café

Nightlife
- Nightlife

Arts
- Arts

Sports & Activities
- Pool
- Trail Head

Sleeping
- Sleeping
- Camping

Transport
- Airport, Airfield
- Bus Station
- Cycling, Bicycle Path
- General Transport
- Parking Area
- Petrol Station
- Taxi Rank

Geographic
- Lighthouse
- Lookout
- Mountain
- National Park
- Picnic Area

Published by Lonely Planet Publications Pty Ltd
ABN 36 005 607 983

Australia Head Office, Locked Bag 1, Footscray, Victoria 3011, ☎ 03 8379 8000, fax 03 8379 8111, talk2us@lonelyplanet.com.au

USA 150 Linden St, Oakland, CA 94607, ☎ 510 893 8555, toll free 800 275 8555, fax 510 893 8572, info@lonelyplanet.com

UK 2nd Floor, 186 City Road, London, ECV1 2NT, ☎ 020 7106 2100, fax 020 7106 2101, go@lonelyplanet.co.uk